PELICAN BOOKS

BRITISH HISTORY IN THE NINETEENTH CENTURY AND AFTER

(1782–1919)

George Macaulay Trevelyan, O.M., C.B.E., F.B.A., born in 1876, was the third son of Sir George Otto Trevelyan and a great-nephew of Lord Macaulay. He was educated at Harrow and at Trinity College, Cambridge. In the First World War he was awarded the Silver Medal for Valour (Italy) and the Chevalier of the Order of St Maurice and St Lazarus (Italy).

He was an Hon. D.C.L., Oxford, and Hon. LL.D., St Andrews and Edinburgh, a Fellow of Trinity College, Cambridge, and an Honorary Fellow of Oriel College, Oxford. From 1927 to 1940 he was Regius Professor of Modern History at Cambridge and from 1940 to 1951 he was Master of Trinity. He was also a Trustee of the British Museum and the National Portrait Gallery. He was President of the Youth Hostels Association from 1930 to 1950, and was Chairman of the Estates Committee of the National Trust. He died in 1962.

Among his books on British history are: *Illustrated English Social History*, *England under the Stuarts* (both published in Penguins), *England in the Age of Wycliffe*, *The English Revolution 1668*, *England under Queen Anne*, and *History of England*. *Lord Grey of the Reform Bill*, *Lord Grey of Fallodon*, *The Life of Bright*, and the famous Garibaldi trilogy are his biographical works.

BRITISH HISTORY IN THE NINETEENTH CENTURY AND AFTER (1782-1919)

*

George Macaulay Trevelyan

PENGUIN BOOKS

Penguin Books Ltd, Harmondsworth, Middlesex, England
Penguin Books Australia Ltd, Ringwood, Victoria, Australia

—

First published by Longmans, Green and Co. Ltd, 1922 and 1937
Published in Pelican Books 1965
Reprinted 1968, 1971

—

Made and printed in Great Britain
by Cox & Wyman Ltd,
London, Reading and Fakenham
Set in Monotype Times

CONTENTS

MAPS

PREFACE

THE object of this book is to enable the student or general reader to obtain, in the compass of one volume, a picture of change and development during the hundred and twenty years when things certainly, and probably men and women with them, were undergoing a more rapid change of character than in any previous epoch of our annals. I have tried to give the sense of continuous growth, to show how economic led to social, and social to political change, how the political events reacted on the economic and social, and how new thoughts and new ideals accompanied or directed the whole complicated process.

For such a purpose, it would be a mistake to confuse the narrative with too much detail, but I have put into the story the main events which directed the course of the current, or were regarded as specially symbolic of each passing age. I cannot hold the epicurean doctrine, sometimes favoured nowadays, that because history increasingly deals with generalization it is safe for the student to neglect dates, which are the bones of historical anatomy. Still less is it safe, in pursuit of generalized truth, to overlook the personality and influence of great men, who are often in large measure the cause of some 'tendency' which only they rendered 'inevitable'.

Political writers, social philosophers, and founders of movements must take their place beside warriors and statesmen in any account of social and political changes in modern times. But religion, literature, and science are only mentioned here in connexion with social or political developments of which they were in some degree the cause or the symbol. I have made no attempt to appreciate their real significance in a century of British history famous for all three of these supreme efforts of the human spirit.

I have called the book 'British History', because, though it cannot claim to be a History of the Empire, it is more than a History of Britain. It is indeed, mainly, a history of Britain, but it treats of that island as the centre of a great association of peoples, enormously increasing in extent during the period under survey. The course of events in Canada, Australasia, Ireland, India, and British Africa have been indicated in broken outline. In particular, I have tried to show the relation of the various phases of our home affairs to each of those separate stories of Imperial development, and the effect of politics and persons at home on our relations with Europe and with the United States.

Where should a British History of the Nineteenth Century begin, and where break off? Clearly it should stop where the nominal century and the reign of Queen Victoria come to an end together. The finish of the Boer War leaves us on the threshold of our own times, which are still too near us to be seen in perspective.

Where to begin is perhaps less obvious. It would, I think, be absurd to begin exactly with the new century, with Addington and the Treaty of Amiens, at a moment's pause in the battle with revolutionary France, and in the most terrible years of the initial agony of our own Industrial Revolution. It is necessary first to describe the starting-point of this great era of change, to give a sketch of the quiet, old England of the eighteenth century before machines destroyed it, and the political scene before the French Revolution came to disturb it.

The fifty years that stretch from the loss of the American Colonies and the fall of George III's personal government down to Lord Grey's Reform Bill compose a single epoch in our political history; no true starting-point can be found between 1782 and 1832. I have chosen the former year, which among other advantages permits the inclusion of the whole career of the younger Pitt, who was, both in date and in spirit, the last great statesman of the eighteenth and the first of the nineteenth century.

Berkhamsted, January 1922.   G. M. TREVELYAN

NOTE TO THE REVISED AND
ENLARGED EDITION, 1937

I HAVE been asked to extend the narrative down to the end of the war. There are obvious disadvantages in this course, but the demand on grounds of educational utility is one that I find it hard to resist.

Cambridge, 1937

INTRODUCTION

DURING the last hundred and fifty years, the rate of progress in man's command over nature has been ten times as fast as in the period between Caesar and Napoleon, a hundred times as fast as in the slow prehistoric ages. Tens of thousands of years divided man's first use of fire from his first application of it to iron. Even in the civilized era, when literature, science, and philosophy were given us by Greece, the art of writing preceded the printing-press by tens of centuries. In those days each great invention was granted a lease of many ages in which to foster its own characteristic civilization, before it was submerged by the next. But in our day, inventions, each implying a revolution in the habits of man, follow each other thick as the falling leaves. Modern history, beginning from the England of 1780, is a series of dissolving views. In each generation a new economic life half obliterates a predecessor little older than itself.

One example will suffice, that of inland transport. In the reign of George III the civilization of the riding-horse and the pack-horse gave way to that of the coach, the waggon, and the barge, because the soft road was at length superseded by the hard road, flanked by the canal. But no time was given to develop a new civilization on that basis; Macadam had not yet taught Lord Eldon and the Duke of Wellington that they were living in a new world, before Stephenson's locomotive in its turn replaced the barge, the waggon, and the coach. And then, before the society based on steam has worked out its peculiar destiny, petrol in our own day gives a new life to the old roads, and opens out the pathways of the air.

The changes going on during the same period in sea-traffic, in manufacture, and in the transmission of messages, tell the same story of a series of economic civilizations rapidly superimposed one on another.

Under these conditions, new in the history of man, races set apart for aeons of time have been suddenly thrust together, not always in fraternal embrace. The vast, unvisited interior of Africa has been not only explored but overrun by Europe. The mysteries of Asia have been opened out. The conquest of America has been completed. Offshoots of our island civilization have overspread continents hidden in the bosom of the Southern Seas, and have ploughed up the Canadian wilderness. All the while, Europe herself has suffered convulsions at home, in the endeavour to adjust her political and social fabric to the rapidity of economic change.

The terrible pace at which the world now jolts and clanks along was set in our island, where, first, invention was harnessed to organized capital. For fifty years that great change was left uncontrolled by the community which it was transforming. So new was the experience that, for a while, the wisest were as much at fault as the most foolish. Burke for all his powers of prophecy, Pitt for all his study of Adam Smith, Fox for all his welcome to the new democracy, no more understood the English economic revolution, and no more dreamt of controlling it for the common good, than George III himself.

We are so like our ancestors of that period, and yet so unlike; so near them in time and in affection, so far removed from them in habits and in experience. There lie the paradox and romance of modern history. Our daily avocations, our modes of travel, our ways of life are as remote from theirs as were theirs from the Anglo-Saxon. Yet we should feel at home if we found ourselves among them. We speak their language, little changed. We think and feel much as they did, though things that we have to think and feel about are so different.

A British officer in Flanders in 1918, transplanted to a British messroom in the same country in 1793, would be more at home than in a foreign messroom of today. Though he would find the drinking too heavy for him, he would be surrounded by presumptions indefinably familiar. He would be critical of much, but he would understand from inside what he was criticizing. Most of us would be at home taking tea at Dr Johnson's, hearing the contact of civilized man with society discussed with British common sense and good nature, with British idiosyncrasy and prejudice. Only we should be aware that we had stepped back out of a scientific, romantic, and mobile era into an era literary, classical, and static. Dr Johnson and Burke had never heard of 'evolution' in our meaning of the word. They thought that the world would remain what they and their fathers had known it. With them, time moved so slowly that they thought it stayed still withal. A very different experience has taught us to perceive that the forms of our civilization are transient as the bubbles on a river.

In politics, a comparison between our age and theirs presents the same likeness in utter divergence. We are still involved in the outcome of what happened to Ireland in the days of Grattan and Pitt, to North America in the days of George III and Chatham. Our naval policy, and our interest in the independence of the

Netherlands, were the same in 1914 as in 1793. In spite of Tom Paine, we still have King, Lords, and Commons, and an established Church; the very mace still lies on the table as when Oliver ordered it away; half the customs of the House would be familiar to Fox, if he strolled in to a debate. But these forms sheltered, for our great-grandfathers, an aristocracy based on the tenure of land, with certain political rights reserved for the Crown and certain others for some of the common people. For us, the same forms enshrine a democratic system of representative government, extending over Imperial, national, and local affairs, in town and in country, for Motherland and Dominions – a democracy in which the women as well as the men of all classes, having in large part been educated at the public charge, are invited to take an equal part. There has been no solemn revision of the principles of our Constitution, only a constant amendment and extension of its details, and an entire though gradual change of view. There has been no revolution. Yet in 1794, Pitt's Attorney-General claimed that it was High Treason for any man to agitate for the establishment of 'representative government, the direct contrary of the government which is established here'.

Between that interpretation of the Constitution and our own there lie only 130 years. But into that brief space of time, which two human lives would outspan, has been crowded the long sequel of the French Revolution, now calculable by history; the European War and revolution of our own day, not yet calculable; and, more important than any series of political or military events, the Industrial Revolution, still in progress, that has forced and is still forcing politics and society to follow the suit of the inventors, the men who destroy and create classes, constitutions, countries, and modes of life and thought.

During the first half of the period surveyed in this book, these new forces work at their will, with no conscious aim but the production of wealth, to the cry of *laissez faire*; in the second half, attempts, increasingly systematic, are made to control them in the interest of the community that they are constantly re-shaping. In the first fifty years, ending with the Great Reform Bill of 1832, the Industrial Revolution is, in its social consequences, mainly destructive. It destroys, in town and country, the forms and pieties of the old English life, that could not be harnessed to the new machinery. The government, while it prohibited all legal and political change as 'Jacobinism', urged on the economic revolution. The result was that by 1832 there was scant provision for the political, municipal, educational, or sanitary needs of the population, most of whom were not even tolerably clothed or fed. The laws and institutions had been kept back in one place, while the men and women had been moved on to another, where they were living as it were outside society, under a guard of yeomanry and magistrates.

The second half of the period is the story of the building up of the new world, of a wholly new type of society, infinitely more complicated and interdependent in its parts, more full of potentialities for progress or disaster, than anything the world has before seen. It has been the work of all classes and of all parties, whether in cooperation or in conflict, over a space of eighty years of gradual but rapid and continuous reform. The contemporary experience of foreign lands, involved a little later than ourselves in the throes of the same industrial revolution, has more and more influenced us by example, as the distance between countries and their mutual ignorance has been reduced. But the work of reform has in our island been British, and most of its ideas and expedients have been of British origin.

The same fundamentals of British character and temperament that we observed in the quiet old eighteenth century – British common sense and good nature, British idiosyncrasy and prejudice – when brought face to face with this prolonged and terrible crisis in human affairs, have produced, after labours, errors, and victories innumerable, the strange world in which we live today.

CHAPTER 1

WHEN George III came to the throne in 1760, the old-world system of economic and social life had undergone little change. Prosperity and personal independence, though very far from universal, were widely diffused. Although few had any voice in the government, many had a stake in the country. The agriculturist or manufacturer in his cottage accepted his lot in life, whether easy or hard, as part of the order of things. It did not occur to him to question the framework of society, or to regard the oligarchy under which he lived as an oppression. He only raised his voice against the political and municipal corruption all around when it resulted in England being worsted by the French.

On one such occasion, the free spirit latent in our never wholly fraudulent Constitution enabled the people to raise up as their tribune William Pitt, afterwards Earl of Chatham, to give us victory in either hemisphere. After that, the reign of folly and corruption was resumed, this time under the King's favourites instead of the Whig oligarchs. But John Bull, though more suspicious and grumbling than before, had no means of exerting continuous control over government. At length, in 1782, he was again exasperated into action, by discovering that the corruptionists had lost him America. Then, after two years of confused counsels, he found for himself a second William Pitt.

When the French Revolution broke out, the political and legal institutions of the country were still unreformed. The second Pitt was doing all that an honest and able man could do as the administrator of a corrupt system. That system had become more than ever out of date, for by this time Great Britain was in process of rapid transformation. The Industrial Revolution had laid rude hands on the social fabric of old England.

At the time of George III's accession there had been no canals; few hard roads; practically no cotton industry; no factory system; few capitalist manufacturers; little smelting of iron by coal; and though there had been much enclosure of land, there had not yet been a wholesale sweeping of small farms into big. In these and many other respects, changes due to inventions and improved methods were in full progress soon after 1760. But it was only during the last ten years of the century that the pace of the movement became terrible. Then, too, it became disastrously involved in 'Jacobin' and 'anti-Jacobin' politics, and in the economic consequences of the war against the French Republic. Then first it began to attract the attention of statesmen. In that later period, the most characteristic developments of the Industrial Revolution will command our attention. But this and the following chapter are devoted to a sketch of the old England as it was in the early years of George III, already touched by the coming change, but not yet transformed.[1]

In the life of our day, the characteristic unit is the town, the factory, or the trade union. Then it was the country village. Village life embraced the chief daily concerns of the majority of Englishmen. It was the principal nursery of the national character. The village was not then a moribund society, as in the nineteenth century; nor was it, as in our own day, a society hoping to revive by the backwash of life returning to it from the town. It contained no inspected school imparting a town-made view of life to successive generations of young rustics, preparing for migration to other scenes. City civilization, with its newspapers and magazines, had not supplanted provincial speech and village tradition. At most a single news-sheet of four pages, with advertisements of the latest books, snippets of news from all countries, and attacks on the Ministry by 'Anti-Sejanus' and 'Patrioticus', went up twice a week to the Hall or the Rectory. After some days, a well-thumbed copy might find its way into the parlour of the inn.

The squire and the parson were usually resident. Even if they were absentees, their agents and the shadow of their greatness loomed large over everything. A few hardy Dissenters enjoyed a legalized exclusion from the religious domain of the parson. But against the landlord magistrate there was no group of men who could stand out, except his brother squires.

Among the villagers collectively subjected to this rule, there was

1. The reader must bear in mind that no single decade can be named for any one of the processes that together make up the Industrial Revolution. Even the most cataclysmic of the changes was not an event but a process. Dr Cunningham suggests that the Industrial Revolution begins about 1770, 'commencing with changes in the hardware trades'. The date will serve, if we remember that since 1720, if not before, there had been signs of the increase of capitalist industry and the decay of the apprentice system, that the improvement of roads had begun to be rapid about 1750, and that the movement for absorbing small farms into large farms was at least as old as that. Yet none of these movements was complete till well on in the nineteenth century. Brindley's Manchester–Worsley canal was opened in 1761; Brindley died in 1772; but only in 1790 were some of his greatest canals completed and opened. Which, then, is the decade of Brindley's canals? The same kind of problem arises in every case. See chapter 9, below, on the Industrial Revolution.

a considerable measure of equality and independence. Large tenant farmers, and agricultural labourers entirely dependent on their wages, did not then constitute the whole village society. It varied from place to place, but everywhere there were many classes, many sizes of holding, many forms of rights on land, and many occupations and means of livelihood.

In the first place, the village was less purely agricultural than it became in later times. Its craftsmen supplied its requirements locally in many articles now fetched from the towns. The wives and families of the yeoman and agricultural labourers, and the labourers themselves when field labour was slack, carried on various branches of manufacture in their own cottages. Spinning was the special task of women and children. But there were often in the villages professional weavers, men who never tilled the soil except of an evening in their own back gardens. This class was found thickly congregated in the stone-built villages around the infant Thames, or on the steep banks of Yorkshire dales. In Yorkshire, indeed, some of these rural communities were destined to change by imperceptible stages into urban districts.

The villages of England fed with the labour of their hands the great staple industries, like the woollen trade, by help of which our oversea commerce had already taken the lead of the world. Commerce had to be centred in the towns, but much of the manufacture that supplied it was put out to farm among the country cottages, and collected by the cloth merchants going round with their long trains of pack-horses – the constantly moving shuttles that wove together the threads of far-scattered British industry. So long as this system of manufacture continued, the rural population was much more numerous than the city population. A dozen of the southern counties retained more inhabitants to the square mile than any shire in the north, until the general adoption of machinery brought in the factory system.[1]

The work of women and children played as large a part in these cottage industries as in the factories that replaced them. We shall never know enough about the hours and conditions of their home work for any sure comparison with subsequent factory conditions. But it is safe to say that there was a greater variety of treatment, when the circumstances of each family, or the temperament of its most strong-minded member, dictated the habits of each household. The discipline of the home could seldom have been as severe,

1. Viz. Middlesex, Surrey, Wilts, Somerset, Gloucester, Oxford, Bucks, Hertford, Suffolk, Northants, Rutland, Warwick, Worcester. Yet by 1801 only Middlesex was in the category above Lancashire.

and never as artificial and dehumanized as in the mills of the worst period before the Factory Acts. On the other hand, the sanitary conditions in most of the cottages, and the long hours of labour in many, would not be tolerated by the factory code of the present day.

But the village was, first and foremost, an agricultural community, as indeed was England herself. Although our methods of tilling the soil were wasteful and antiquated, especially in the great corn-growing area of the Midlands, we were still able in 1765 to export corn abroad, after feeding the small population of seven millions in England and Wales. Afterwards, during the Napoleonic Wars, when the numbers rose to eleven millions, it became necessary to conduct agriculture on the principle of extracting from the soil the utmost possible quantity of corn. But in the early days of George III there was no such pressure of hungry population in the island, and the political economy of the village sought only to provide 'subsistence' for each family resident in the parish.

'Subsistence agriculture', as modern historians call it, was the theory and practice of our fathers from the earliest times until the Industrial Revolution. In the eyes of statesmen and economists, alike in the days of Alfred, Elizabeth, and George II, the duty of the village to the State was to breed and maintain not less than its traditional number of stalwart and contented men, rather than to accumulate wealth for taxation or to grow corn for the consumption of the towns.

'Subsistence agriculture' was still the rule[1] in the first years of George III, and it must needs have been so when the means of transport were so bad. Without canals, and with few roads capable of bearing wheeled traffic, the constant distribution of great quantities of foodstuffs was impossible. The first object in cottages on remote heaths and in hamlets at the end of miry lanes was that there should be enough food of all sorts produced in the immediate neighbourhood for the subsistence of all who dwelt there.

The object of the village was to supply itself not only with enough corn, but also with dairy produce, meat, pigs, and poultry, all of which a small peasant-holder and his wife could attend to better than a large farmer. The village produced also a part of its own purchases in cloth, basketwork, farm and household furniture, according as local conditions allowed. To grow corn on a large scale for distant markets was often but a secondary consideration.

1. The hugest of the exceptions to this rule was the feeding of London (see p. 28 below), a task that increased the labour and wealth of many country villages.

The subdivision of the land among so many of the inhabitants tended to the supply of these very various wants. The smallholding was indeed the true 'political economy', provided the population of the island remained stationary, and so long as England and the whole world with her desired to be stable and contented rather than progressive and rich.

Our ancestors did not think that the law of the Universe was progress, evolution, and perpetual change. There had indeed been great economic progress in the hundred years following the Restoration, but it had not been sufficiently rapid or symptomatic to colour the prevailing philosophy. Dr Johnson and his contemporaries would have scouted the modern notion that we must be for ever pressing restlessly forward on pain of falling back. The world as they found it in England was good enough for them, and their aim was to preserve, not to improve or to enlarge. This view of things – the static as opposed to the evolutionary – differentiated our ancestors from us, in agriculture and industry, as well as in politics and religion.

The typical village of the great corn-growing area of the East Midlands was a single long street of cottages, each standing in its garden, or a cluster of roofs huddled round the church, while the great 'open field' of the village, perhaps a mile long and half a mile broad, surrounded on all sides the group of houses where its cultivators lived together; in this type of parish scattered farms were few. Once outside the cottage gardens, there were no more hedges to be seen. Rupert and Cromwell used to charge their cavalry across the 'open field', as they could not have done over the chessboard landscape of modern English agriculture. This 'open field' was divided up by balks or furrows into several hundred oblong patches. The total effect to the eye was not unlike that of an allotment field of the present day, on a gigantic scale.

Many of the humbler villagers cultivated, each for himself, one, two, or three of these oblong strips; the larger farmers twenty, forty, or more. The plots of a well-to-do yeoman or farmer were scattered far and wide over the field, like the estates of a great abbey or feudal lord up and down medieval England. No one, great or small, could cultivate his strips as he thought fit, but only according to village rules of immemorial antiquity. The revolving three-year course of wheat, spring-corn, and fallow was usually enforced. On the 'open field' there was no room for experiment or improvement in agricultural methods. If, therefore, the idea of progress once got abroad, if 'improving landlords' came into fashion, if the population of the island increased and required more corn to feed

23

it, the 'open-field' system was certain to disappear. The only questions would then be, how would it disappear, on what terms for the bulk of the smaller cultivators, and what kind of social system would take its place?

All round the 'open field' the waste lands of moor and marsh, wood and coppice, stretched away to the confines of the parish. There were few of the hedges and plantations which are the chief beauty of the same land today, but the dingles were filled with the irregular beauty of self-sown wood, wreckage of the primeval English forest that had not yet been wholly swept away even in the most cultivated districts. These unreclaimed lands constituted the common, where many of the villagers, some by legal right and some by customary use, took fuel, and fed cows or sheep, pigs or geese. If 'subsistence' for so many independent families was to continue, the use of the common was an integral part of the system. Yet much good land was thus left uncultivated. From the point of view of the community at large, the old ideal of the village life began to appear retrograde and impossible.

The smaller yeomen had, since the beginning of the century, declined in numbers. Many of them had a hard struggle to live, and were glad to sell their land to the squires. There was a 'land-hunger' among the upper class of the day, eager to amass large consolidated estates, alike for reasons of profit, social prestige, and game-preserving. But in spite of this movement, small farming, labourers' allotments, pasturage on the common, and the independent system of society that these things favoured, were still the rule rather than the exception all over England. But the 'open-field' method of cultivation that we have described was an unnecessarily antiquated part of the system. It had already been abolished, at different epochs down the course of ages, in Kent, Devon, Cornwall, in most of Sussex, Suffolk, and Essex, in the greater part of the fruit-growing counties along the Welsh border, and in some parts of the North.[1]

In all these districts – perhaps in one half of England – the arable land had already assumed much of the appearance that it wears today. In 1782 a Prussian pastor, approaching our island for the first time by coasting up the Kentish shore past Gravesend, marvelled at 'those living hedges which in England, more than in any other country, form the boundaries of the green cornfields, and give to the whole distant country the appearance of a large and majestic garden'. When he wrote thus, the aspect which he describes was not characteristic of more than a moiety of the English

1. See Appendix, *Enclosures of Land* (*a*), at end of book.

shires, though it was already much more common than twenty years before. Kent, at which he was looking, had been famous for centuries for its enclosed fields and its good farming. So, too, had Devon.

These early enclosures of the 'open field', made under a former economic dispensation, had been consistent with the survival in Kent and the Western Shires of small farmers, yeomen, and labourers as independent as any in the island. But the later movement of enclosure by Act of Parliament, which between 1760 and 1840 abolished the remaining 'open fields' and most of the commons in England, was part of a general revolution in society, which introduced large farms as the almost universal rule. The revolutionary effect of the new enclosures was increased by the other industrial changes of the age, by roads and canals opening up new markets, by the cry of growing towns for more corn, and of landlords for more rent, above all by the removal of textile industry from the rural cottage to the urban factory. The various classes of small, independent agriculturists with industrial families, which had composed so important a part of the village community when George III ascended the throne, had almost completely disappeared when he died. In the course of those sixty years their place had been taken by the large farmer and by the landless and pauperized labourer whom he employed.[1]

Yet we must not idealize too much the old village society merely because it has passed away. No doubt the period of the first two Georges, with its good wages and moderate prices, compared favourably with the period of rural pauperism in the early nineteenth century. But there had been hard times before, in days when hard times meant famine. In the 'dear years' of William III, and often before, people had failed to 'subsist' on their 'subsistence agriculture'. The 'cottars' too, whose disappearance we deplore, had been classed with the 'paupers' by Gregory King, a publicist of William's reign. King's often-quoted analysis of English society at the time of the Revolution points to the existence of a rural proletariat more numerous than the yeomen and tenant farmers put together.

Much is guesswork in history before the age of statistics. But it is safe to say that, on the whole, there was more independence, variety, and joy in life under the old system than under the new system at its worst, and the worst of the new economic dispensation came when it was first introduced.[2]

1. See pp. 152–9, chapter 9, below.
2. See chapter 9, below.

The first unconscious step towards great economic and social change was taken between 1750 and 1770, when a perceptible improvement was made in the roads, with a resulting increase in the amount of wheeled traffic. So long as the products of agriculture and industry had generally to be carried along miry paths, slung across horses' backs, there could have been no very great expansion in the volume of external and internal trade, and 'subsistence agriculture' must have continued.

The old English road was not a metalled surface of definite limits, hedged off from the rest of the world, and maintained by an army of special functionaries paid from the public purse. It was an open track through the fields or over the common; its borders were metaphysical, for it was, in law, a right of way from one village to another, and if, as usually happened after bad weather, the customary track was 'foundrous', passengers had the right to take their beasts over the edge of the neighbouring field, even if it were under corn. Only in lands of enclosed agriculture like Kent or Devon was the road imprisoned by bank and hedge; in that case it was very often a winding lane, a few feet broad and many feet deep, across which, according to tradition, hounds and horsemen had been known to leap over the hood of a waggon. The roads had no prepared surface, though on some of the larger highways a narrow causeway of stones through the middle of the mud gave footing for the saddle- and pack-horses. In nine cases out of ten where we use a bridge, our ancestors splashed through a ford.

The duty of keeping the road open – that is, of removing obstacles and occasionally filling up the worst holes with a cartload of faggots or large stones – fell by law on each parish through which the highway passed. The unwilling farmers usually held in turns the office of Parish Surveyor, whose duty it was to direct the unpaid service of six days' annual work on the roads, obligatory on every parishioner, but largely evaded and nearly worthless. The villagers resented this *corvée*, on the ground that it was unjust to throw on them the whole upkeep of a highway constantly destroyed by the traffic of distant cities and shires. The users of the roads ought clearly to pay for their maintenance.

At the close of the Stuart epoch this situation was met in a few places by the Turnpike system. Local Trusts were formed and were empowered by Parliament to erect toll-bars, and there levy tolls from all passengers except pedestrians, in return for which the Trust kept up the few miles of road committed to its charge. But the Turnpikes only began to be really effective between 1748 and 1770, during which years the number of Trusts rose from 160

26

to 530, and the mileage under their control was quadrupled. An improvement in the roads of Britain was then noticed, perhaps for the first time since the Romans.

But even the Turnpike system had its faults. There was no co-ordination or general supervision. Many of the Trusts, like everything administrative in that epoch, became incompetent and corrupt. And the best of them had seldom the money or the power for up-to-date undertakings, for example, to divert the course of a road so as to avoid a steep bank, up which pack-horses could saunter, but which in slippery weather defied the new-fangled waggons and coaches. Northern fellsides even today show many bad examples of still undiverted 'pack-horse roads'. Worst of all, the Turnpike system was far from universal. A great part of the mileage was still maintained only by the Parish Surveyor and his unwilling gangs of conscript farmers. So it might happen that a main road would be good for twenty miles, indifferent for fifty more, and would suddenly become a quagmire for the next ten.

Such as they were, the roads in the early years of George III had hard usage, for canals were only beginning. The new era was represented on the larger roads by waggons and carts carrying goods, and by the first lumbering stage-coaches with the 'outsiders' clinging on precariously by handles to the unseated top. On the more improved roads, the new post-chaises, with their brisk and pert postillions, rattled along at ten miles an hour, the wonder of all beholders. But the bulk of the wayfarers were riders of all classes, on every kind of business and pleasure; trains of led pack-horses, bearing corn, hardware, and coal; and endless droves of cattle, sheep, and pigs, keeping the roads near great markets in a perpetual churn of filth.

The drovers, formidable in numbers if not in respectability, were opposed to the introduction of hard roads, as bad for the feet of their beasts. It was the users of wheeled vehicles who clamoured for improvement, and as they were usually the persons of most wealth or enterprise, and as they increased in number with every decade, their complaints received more and more attention. Yet as late as 1788 Gunning records that in North Herefordshire such was the state of the roads that

from autumn until the end of April all intercourse between the females of the neighbouring families was suspended, unless they would consent to ride on *pillions*, a mode of travelling at that time in general use. In the spring they levelled the roads by means of ploughs, drawn by eight or ten horses; and in this state they remained until the following autumn.

27

The roads converging on London were an epitome of the activities of the nation. The great city of some seven hundred thousand inhabitants, more than a dozen times as large as Bristol, the next largest in the island, had daily to be fed from the fat of the land. Night and day hundreds of horses in relays were coming up at trot and gallop, from the South Coast and even from the Berwick and Solway salmon fisheries, bringing fresh to Billingsgate the best fish of every port. A hundred thousand head of cattle and three-quarters of a million sheep yearly walked up to Smithfield for the slaughter, many of them from Scotland or from the borders of Wales. But strangest of all to the modern eye would be the droves of geese and turkeys, two or three thousand at a time, waddling slowly and loquaciously all along the roads to London for a hundred miles round, between August and October, feeding on the stubble of the fields through which they passed. On one road, from Ipswich to London, 150,000 turkeys walked over the Stour bridge each year.

Except Bristol, and possibly Manchester, no provincial town of Great Britain in 1760 had over 50,000 inhabitants.[1] Cities were still so small that even the town-dweller lived almost in the breath of the country, and could stroll out to enjoy it whenever he wished. This fact alone marks a vital difference in the mental environment of the leading part of the community in those days as compared to our own.

As in the village, so in the city, there was as yet no sharp division between the classes of employer and employed. The capitalist employer was still rare, though not nearly so rare as a hundred years before. England, indeed, already possessed the greatest quantity of easily realizable capital of any country in the world, at the disposal of government when it was waging a war of which 'the City' approved. Our great commercial companies, backed by the Royal Navy, were the masters of the ocean and the greatest traders on the face of the globe. But our moneyed men were usually bankers or merchants. The very word 'manufacturer' still signified, in accordance with its Latin derivation, a workman who makes goods with his hands. It had not acquired the modern sense of a capitalist who employs workmen to tend machines.

The clothier who supplied the cottage industrialists with wool, or who went round the villages to collect their finished cloth, was

1. In 1801, the first national census shows that Birmingham, Bristol, Glasgow, Leeds, Liverpool, and Manchester all had between fifty and a hundred thousand when the nineteenth century opened.

acting as a middleman. In the towns the normal establishment was either a solitary craftsman, or a master with a few hands working with him in the shop. The apprenticeship, through which the master and his journeyman[1] alike had had to pass in their youth, stamped them of the same class.

Apprenticeship, which had grown up locally under the medieval guild system, had been imposed on the whole country as the precondition of employment in any given trade by the Statute of Artificers of 1562, by which the Elizabethan statesmen strove with some success to make seven years' apprenticeship national and uniform. This system, at the beginning of the eighteenth century, still supplied a country sadly lacking in educational facilities with a vast machinery of personal training, discipline, and technical instruction, moulding the character of English boys and youths, whom it turned out as skilled workmen. Its method being the personal relation of master and apprentice, it would necessarily perish as soon as capitalism demanded a free labour market, and the right to expand each individual business indefinitely.

From about 1720 onwards apprenticeship had shown signs of decay, and the monopoly of employment for those who had been duly apprenticed was a rule ever less enforced by the authorities, national or local. But the guilds still struggled to maintain it. When George III came to the throne, apprenticeship was still the rule, and capitalist employment in an open labour market was still the exception.

The best-known song of apprentice life, Carey's 'Sally in our Alley', reproduces the real life and feeling of the people. Indeed, the popular songs of the eighteenth century, in England and in the land of Burns, when contrasted with those of our own day, remind us that the common life, though often narrow, ignorant, and rough, was more near to beauty and to poetry than it has since become in a world driven by machines, and vulgarized by hustle and advertisement.

Equally in the towns and among the craftsmen in the villages, many old-fashioned crafts, with their call on the artistic skill of the individual, gave to daily work a fascination, which has disappeared from many of the mechanical processes of modern manufacture with disastrous results to the interest and happiness of the working day.

There is indeed a reverse to any pleasant picture of town life in the eighteenth century, and Hogarth has painted it: behind his

1. The common term of the epoch for a hired workman, whether hired by the day or for a longer period.

jolly 'Beer Street' ran his foul 'Gin Lane'. In every town, besides the prosperous masters, journeymen, and apprentices, lived a mass of beings, physically and morally corrupt, for whose bodies no one, and for whose souls only the Methodists, had a thought to spare. With no police, save watchmen whose proceedings were a constant theme of mockery, with criminal laws that by their careless ferocity and irregular execution fostered crime, the mob of that period was a fearful thing. In the Gordon Riots of 1780 it went near to burning down London.

The degraded sediment at the bottom of English town life was not the result of the old social and economic system, which was sound and humane. It was the result, rather, of the antiquated and corrupt framework of government. Alike in central and local affairs there was no serious attempt made to supply education, sanitation, justice, police, prisons, or control of drink according to the needs of the community. Institutions that had passed muster in Tudor times were allowed to fester away without being brought up to date, or were even permitted, as in the case of much educational provision, to be alienated from the service of the general public.

The population had shifted in the course of centuries, but municipal areas were as fixed as the hills. The art of legislation, not unknown to the Tudors, had been lost.

Already, under the old economic system, these deficiencies in government were producing grave social evils. And when, after the Industrial Revolution had transformed everything else, the old fabric of government was still preserved as sacrosanct in its smallest detail, the new populations suffered a prolonged moral and physical catastrophe.

The Parliamentary inertia and the municipal stagnation which clogged the otherwise vigorous life of the country were closely connected. They both remained untouched till 1831–5, when they fell together. The chartered oligarchy which misgoverned the town sometimes enjoyed the further privilege of returning its two members to Parliament, at the dictation of a landed magnate, familiarly known as the 'borough-owner'. Elsewhere the 'borough-owner' returned the members not through the municipal oligarchy, but through a few other privileged individuals, the owners of certain favoured fields, houses, or in some cases pigstyes, to which was attached the right of voting for Parliament.

The House of Commons had, in effect, become a cooptive body, and was unwilling, by a Reform Bill, to make itself once more elective as it had been in former times. It could not therefore afford to reform the cooptive town oligarchies, which also sat in the seat once occupied by the democratic guilds and municipalities of the medieval boroughs. This great corruption had been wrought during centuries of time, by a thousand obscure exigencies of political and personal faction, by the migration of inhabitants, and latterly by the interference in the boroughs of the landed aristocracy.

The system was an abuse, but it had its historical meaning, and its relation to reality. For it must always be remembered that without the acquiescence of the landed aristocracy the powers formerly enjoyed by the Crown would not have been allowed to remain in the hands of the House of Commons. The failure of Cromwell's Commonwealth had proved that. The landlord class, in return for supporting the supremacy of the Lower House, obtained the right of nominating most of its members. That was an unwritten clause in the Settlement of 1689.

Now most of the members of the House of Commons were returned, not, as they should then have been, by the counties, but by the boroughs. These boroughs were some of them still important and populous, like Burke's Bristol; others were mere market-towns like Appleby, or villages like East and West Looe; or, like Old Sarum, had shrunk to deserted mounds since they were first represented in the Plantagenet Parliaments. In the days of their vigour, in the Middle Ages, these Parliamentary boroughs had not been able by their votes to control the King and the Barons, partly because the power of the Lower House was then very small, partly because decisions in the House did not go strictly by the counting of heads. In John of Gaunt's time, less than a hundred 'knights of the shire' had outweighed in influence the more numerous[1] representatives of the towns. But in the eighteenth century, when one vote in the House of Commons was as good as another, and when the majority of the House of Commons ruled the State, the borough members made and unmade governments. It was therefore in a sense natural that the most powerful social class, the landed aristocracy, should corruptly nominate most of the town representatives. The proper alternative to this corrupt system would have been a redistribution of seats, which would have made the county members more numerous than the representatives of the boroughs. Unfortunately, the idea of redistributing the Parliamentary seats had been buried in the grave of Cromwell.

The Parliamentary Revolution, in the final form that it took in

1. More numerous at least as regards members elected. But if Professor Pollard is right, only a small minority of the boroughs in the Middle Ages troubled to send up the members they had chosen.

1689, had effectively checkmated the attempt of the Crown to control the local authorities. This saved the political liberties of England, and prevented us from following the contemporary course of France, Spain, Italy, and Germany towards monarchical despotism. But it did not make for efficiency or reform in administration, and it was not accompanied by any attempt to revive or create a popular element in local government. Power was left in the hands of the landed aristocracy, with the municipal oligarchies as its congenial instrument.

So Municipal and Parliamentary corruption flourished together. Just so long as the old social and economic system survived, this scheme of government was tolerable, though it lost us America. Nor need it have lost us America, had not George III, taking advantage of the prevailing corruption, made a belated attempt to recover the lost powers of the Crown.

That unexpected assault of the young King on the rotten fabric of aristocratic Whiggism (1761–82) provoked a third party to join the strife – the democracy, vaguely reminiscent of its lost rights. Though at first under no more respectable leadership than that of Wilkes, it proved a formidable opponent both to Crown and aristocracy, because it found a *point d'appui* in London.

London was not part of the aristocratic system. Its municipality was no less independent and democratic than it had been in the Middle Ages. It had always been a third power in the State, alongside the King and Parliament, and it was so still. The fact that the Royal Court was held outside the city boundaries, usually in Westminster, had saved the capital of England from ever becoming identified with the Government. It had always been possible to close the gates of London on the King. The Crown had never been able to interfere with its municipal administration, save during the few years preceding the Revolution of 1688 – the exception that proved the rule of London's independence.

Even in the eighteenth century, the self-government of the City had not, like so much else, become a formality and a farce. No State official, and no landed magnate, could boast of exerting influence over London. Its Court of Common Council, which so often voiced the national feeling on foreign and domestic issues in the absence of any more representative institution, was a Parliament of small shopkeepers elected by their like. Even the more wealthy and dignified members of the Court of Aldermen, serving for life, were chosen by the ratepayers in their Ward elections.

The democratic municipality of London was indeed no more

efficient as a port and shipping authority, no more enlightened in providing education, public recreation, or sanitation than the oligarchies in less fortunate towns. As regards the management of prisons, John Wesley wrote to the papers, 'Of all the seats of woe on this side Hell, few, I suppose, exceed or even equal Newgate'; and Howard confirmed this condemnation of the City authorities. On the other hand, the streets of the capital were better paved, cleaned, and lighted than was usual in that era. Indeed, a German Prince, who came there one night, thought that the greatest city in the world had been illuminated in his honour!

The few other municipalities which were still based on popular election, such as Norwich, wasted the gift of liberty in Whig and Tory faction fights without a thought of the public welfare. The very idea of efficiency and reform in government seemed contrary to the spirit of that happy, careless old England; it was invented by the Benthamites for an age more serious and more grim.

But in the arena of national politics, the democratic London of Wilkes's day did a very real service to the country in defying a corrupted Parliament and a corrupting King. Between the accession of George III and the French Revolution, London and its environs became the scene of vigorous contests on political principles, which had been lacking in England since the days of Queen Anne. At the very gates of the capital, and within its political orbit, lay two constituencies most unlike the ordinary constituency of the day – the thickly populated County of Middlesex that insisted on electing Wilkes, and the City of Westminster, which enjoyed the rare privilege of an extremely democratic franchise.

The Westminster elections were of national importance, partly because of their exceptionally popular character in the age of rotten boroughs, partly because of their neighbourhood to the Court and Parliament, and partly because of the tie formed between the Westminster electors and Charles James Fox. The son of an old corruptionist who represented to the nation all that was most profligate in the political oligarchy, Fox became the first great democratic leader and orator of modern England. 'His inmost soul,' wrote Gibbon in horror, 'is deeply tinged with democracy.' Under the spell of this most aristocratic of democrats, whose life dramatized the paradox of English politics in that period, Westminster hustings became a notable scene. A subject of Frederick the Great of Prussia, who had strayed into the middle of a Westminster election in 1782, thus describes what he saw and felt there:

The election was held in Covent Garden. There was a scaffold erected just before the door of a very handsome church.[1] It was called the *hustings*, on which those who spoke to the people stood. In the area before the hustings, immense multitudes of people were assembled; of whom the greatest part seemed to be of the lowest order. To this tumultuous crowd, however, the speakers often bowed very low, and always addressed them by the title of *gentlemen*. When you see how in this happy country the lowest and meanest member of society testifies the interest he takes in everything of a public nature, when you see how high and low, rich and poor, all concur in declaring their feelings and their convictions, how a carter, a common tar, a scavenger, is still a man, nay, an Englishman – take my word for it you will feel yourself very differently affected from what you are when staring at our soldiers in their exercises at Berlin.

It is true that if the good man had witnessed an election at an average English borough, or had ascertained that Manchester and Birmingham were unrepresented, he might have felt less enraptured. Nevertheless, he had seen something great, which had then no parallel in France, Spain, Italy, or in his own country, something which, for all its absurdities, was of the heart of England.

CHAPTER 2

NOT only London, Westminster, and a few of the less rotten boroughs, but a fair number of the counties, were the scenes of genuine political contests. Whereas in the boroughs the franchise was as irregular as an extravagant and comic fancy could have made it, in the counties a uniform franchise had been fixed by an Act of Parliament, passed while our expeditionary force was fighting Joan of Arc. Ever since that distant day the county vote had been the proud privilege of all freeholders possessing land to the annual value of forty shillings.

The county voters, therefore, tended to be independent men. Their ranks contained all the landed gentry, the yeomen farming their own land, and many substantial citizens of unenfranchised cities and urban districts, who formed a specially numerous class in counties like Yorkshire and Lancashire. It is true that Rutland had two members, and the largest shire had no more.[2] It is true that the borough members outnumbered the county members by four

1. St Paul's in Covent Garden. This quotation, like that on p. 24, comes from the remarkable and fascinating work, *Travels through Several Parts of England in 1782*, by Charles P. Moritz, translated from the German, 1795.

2. In 1821 Yorkshire obtained four members. Otherwise no English county had more or less than two until the Reform Bill.

to one. But the county representation of England, unlike that of Scotland, at least gave some Parliamentary expression to a real section of popular feeling, even though in most counties it was mainly the feeling of the gentry. 'The voice of England,' it was said, 'spoke through her freeholders.'

The greatest Whig and the greatest Tory triumphs were both countersigned by the county members. In April 1780, when the House passed Dunning's famous Resolution that 'the influence of the Crown has increased, is increasing, and ought to be diminished', sixty-two members for English counties voted 'aye', and only eight 'no'. And when, four years after, Pitt defeated Fox and North at the polls, the fact that the counties went with the young man and that the Yorkshire freeholders chose Wilberforce, in spite of the great Whig families, gave assurance that not the borough-owners only but England herself had turned against the Coalition. Finally, in July 1831, the English county members voted by ten to one for the Reform Bill that abolished the rotten boroughs.

Yet it would be a mistake to suppose that the counties were wholly free from electoral dictation. In some shires, where two or three great families, together irresistible, had agreed to divide the spoils of battle, no contests took place at all. In 1794 we read of Cumberland: 'This County is completely aristocratic. An election contest, which is said to have cost £100,000, happened in 1768, between the interests of the Duke of Portland and those of the Earl of Lonsdale. To prevent expenses, these noblemen have agreed to send each one member.' And even in the most independent counties, though the contests were fought on political principles, the rival hosts were marshalled under the banners of great families who fought each other for the lead of the county, and who rode to the poll at the head of cavalcades of gentry and yeomen, their hats streaming with ribbons of yellow or blue.

This alliance between the spirit of aristocracy and the spirit of popular rights, each taking the other entirely for granted, was native of the soil of England. It was sanctified by custom, sport, and hospitality, deeply pledged in the punch-bowl, renewed in the hunting-field and at the race-meeting. It was the natural offspring of a healthy society based on widely diffused small properties and on the absence of very obvious economic oppression of class by class. The political spirit of the eighteenth century was based not on the equality but on the harmony of classes. It was far removed alike from the rebellious Radicalism and the reactionary Toryism which soon afterwards sprang up from the combined effect of the Industrial and the French Revolutions. Chatham's 'loyal Britons' had not yet become Burke's 'swinish multitude'. Poor and rich together took a patriotic pride in our 'free constitution', which they continually contrasted with the slavery of continental countries.

In such a society the members of the upper class were singularly fortunate in their lot. A position of such complete social and political supremacy as theirs, so little challenged, and so closely identified in history and in popular opinion with the liberties of their country, has never perhaps been seen in any other age or land. In the government of the country and the Empire there was much to blame as well as to praise, but no aristocracy has ever better fulfilled the functions for the performance of which aristocracy specially exists, but in which it too often fails – the intelligent patronage of art, philosophy, and literature, and the living of a many-sided and truly civilized life by means of wealth and leisure well applied. They look down on us, those fortunate beings, from the canvases of Gainsborough and Reynolds, with a self-satisfaction triumphantly justified.

Unlike the French nobles of that day, the English gentry were not a caste, refusing to intermarry with the bourgeoisie or to put their younger sons into commerce. Unlike the French nobles, they were so far from being unoccupied that they were overburdened with public affairs: they monopolized politics and administration, central and local, which in France was left to State officials. Unlike most French nobles, they rejoiced to live a country life on their estates: many of them, like Coke of Norfolk, became 'improving landlords', breeding sheep, sowing turnips, enclosing fields, moving among their farmers with patriarchal familiarity: and all of them, whatever else they did or failed to do, shot game or hunted the fox.

The smaller country houses contained all the year round the homelier squires, whose ideas of fashion and society were limited to an occasional visit with their family to the county capital or the nearest watering-place. The great country houses, which abroad would have been called palaces, received, for six months out of the twelve, the lords of London fashion and politics. From those centres of civilization, Stowe or Woburn, Holkham or Althorp, the latest novelties of the age were spread among the more bucolic squirearchy around. By the end of the peaceful century the rough and ignorant Osbaldistones and Squire Westerns had disappeared. The small provincial gentry of the West, as drawn by Miss Austen at the close of the century, are nice in their gentility almost to a fault, and are all either well-read or accustomed to pay a conventional homage to the Muses. It is significant of much that, although duelling was still practised under carefully enforced rules, gentlemen were ceasing to wear swords in the early years of George III, because 'iron of itself draws a man on'.

The improvement of the upper class as a whole, in education and manners, had been assisted by the disappearance of the small squires, not far removed by wealth and outlook from the yeoman; by the régime of 'Beau Nash' at Bath as a school of politeness in the first half of the century; by the institution of circulating libraries; by the increased habit of travel in search of antiquities and the picturesque abroad, and, with the advent of better roads, even in England. In September 1785 Gibbon was told that 40,000 English, counting masters and servants, were touring or resident on the Continent. Under Rousseau's influence, the dislike of mountains had so far diminished that every year more than one book on Swiss scenery was published in England, although Alpine climbing was still in the future. Already in 1788, according to Wilberforce, 'the banks of the Thames are scarcely more public than those of Windermere'. But few people except shepherds visited the mountain-tops that looked down upon the Lakes, and the day of Highland scenery had to wait for Walter Scott.

The English aristocracy were then the art patrons of the world. It was the custom of the great 'milords' and wealthier gentry to spend one or two years between college and the beginning of their Parliamentary careers in making the 'grand tour', living, not in English-speaking hotels, but in the polite *dilettante* society of French and Italian Courts. Here they formed artistic and antiquarian connexions that lasted them a lifetime. They bought up the old masters then in fashion, and subscribed more heavily than the native princes to French and Italian books of engraving and *éditions de luxe*. A pile of novels and magazines was not then held to be sufficient mental pabulum for a party of ladies and gentlemen at an English country-house. *Noblesse* obliged everyone who was proud of his country home to have a large library and to fill its shelves with the best authors, ancient and modern. Nor did the owner and his guests leave them wholly unread, as is proved by the copious fragments of Virgil and Horace, Shakespeare and Milton that they deftly threw at one another's heads in Parliament, in conversation and in their private correspondence. They used their monopoly of social power to compel the world to regard Shakespeare as the greatest of mankind, and to accept Hume, Gibbon, and Dr Johnson as among the first citizens of the State.

Fashion and sport were not then divorced from intellectual

culture. Fox-hunting, racing, and even the heavy gambling of the period by no means excused their devotees from a gentleman's duty to the Muses. Society, when Charles Fox was its leader, was as literary and as cultivated as it was fashionable, athletic, dissipated, and political. It made the most both of town and country, body and mind. It had faults, of which drunkenness and gambling were the worst, but it lived a life more completely and finely human than any perhaps that has been lived by a whole class since the days of the freemen of Athens.

Rural England, which was then three-fourths of England, was governed by the absolute patriarchal sway of the Justices of the Peace. Of county self-government there was none, till the establishment of County Councils in 1888. Of parish self-government there was little left, except in the organization of the partially communist agriculture of the 'open-field' system.[1]

The Justices of the Peace absorbed more and more judicial and administrative functions, thrust upon them by a Parliament composed of country gentlemen like themselves – justices gone up to the national Quarter Sessions at Westminster. Indeed, the magistrates in the eighteenth century were hardly in any way controlled or inspected by the central authorities. Though nominees of the Crown, they in fact coopted each other, for the Government accepted the recommendations of the Lord-Lieutenant, a local magnate primarily anxious to stand well with the squires of the county.

The office of Justice of the Peace had been established in Plantagenet times as a working compromise between the powers claimed by the Crown and the influence exercised by local landowners. Later on, the Tudor and Stuart monarchs had, for a period of two hundred years, tried to make these unpaid local magistrates subserve the purposes of a bureaucracy devoted to the partisan projects of the Crown. But this long experiment had broken down in the final crash of 1688. Thenceforward the Justices of the Peace may be said rather to have controlled the Central Government through the Houses of Parliament than to have been themselves under any supervision. Nominally State officials, they really represented feudal power tempered by civilization and public spirit.

1. This was often settled in the Manor Courts, which disappeared with the 'open fields'. The turbulent democracy of the rare *Open Vestry*, which became an organ of early Radicalism, seems to have asserted itself in towns and urban districts like Whitechapel, Leeds, and Manchester, rather than among the submissive rustics.

They were in fact responsible to no one, though they were subject to the bitter criticism of Fielding, Smollet, and other writers. And their powers and functions covered all sides of county life. They administered justice in Quarter or Petty Sessions, or in the private house of a single magistrate. They kept up the prisons and the bridges. They licensed the public-houses. They administered the Poor Law. They levied a county rate. These and a hundred other aspects of county business lay in their absolute control. But they had not, for the multifarious purposes of justice and administration, any proper staff in their pay. Prisons and workhouses, like everything else, were farmed out to contractors, with results disastrous to efficiency and humanity.

In Westminster and Middlesex – that is to say, in the greater London outside the jurisdiction of the City Magistrates – the amateur services of unpaid justices were inadequate to cope with so large and turbulent a population. The traditions of a more professional magistracy were started by the Fielding brothers in their office at Bow Street.[1] This led to the institution of Stipendiary Magistrates for Middlesex, at first out of secret service money, and in 1792 by Act of Parliament. But everywhere else, in town and country, the justices were unpaid.

At the time George III came to the throne, the justices who did most of the work in rural districts were substantial squires, too rich to be corrupt or mean, too proud to truckle to Government, anxious to stand well with their neighbours, but filled with all the prejudices as well as the merits of their class – fierce to the point of cruelty against poachers, and armed with such a combination of powers that the occasional tyrant among them became an irremovable curse to the countryside. On the whole, they rendered England great service. Nevertheless, it was a misfortune that when the Industrial Revolution began to set classes in bitter opposition to one another, justice, administration, and influence were entirely in the hands of one of the interested parties.

A characteristic feature of the eighteenth century was the number and prominence of clergy on the magisterial bench. Some of the most active, law-learned, and beneficent of the justices were clergymen, and it was only after the close of the century that the violent partisanship of the Church against the new Radicalism

1. Henry Fielding, the author of *Tom Jones*, was equally well known in his own day as Justice of the Peace for Westminster. The beginnings of an effective public service that he founded in that capacity were carried on, after his death in 1754, by his half-brother, the blind Sir John Fielding, who died in 1780.

brought the 'parson magistrate' into popular odium in the days of Peterloo.

The clergy were at this time more closely identified with the squirearchy than ever before or since. The clerical aspect of their office was little emphasized by the prevalent philosophy of religion. All 'enthusiasm' was condemned by well-bred persons and left to the Methodists. The fires of sectarian controversy that had blazed throughout the Stuart period and had flared up for the last time in Queen Anne's reign over the Sacheverell trial, had died down under the restraining influence of bishops appointed by Whig Ministers, whose motto in religious affairs was 'let sleeping dogs lie'. For a time the English clergy became the least clerical of priesthoods. The more public-spirited and ambitious among their number found an outlet for their energies on the magisterial bench, while many more hunted and shot and joined in the ordinary social life of the neighbouring squires.

In medieval and in Stuart times, when the economic position of the clergy was bad, their ranks had been recruited largely from a lower class. But with the rise of tithe and the value of the livings, their social status had gone up. It became more and more the custom, as the eighteenth century went on, for a rich landowner to add to the value of the family living, build on a few more rooms to the parsonage, and appoint one of his own sons. At length the gentry and the parsons became fused into a single type; in reading Miss Austen's novels, the most accurate of all miniatures of social life, it is often difficult to remember which of the young lovers is a clergyman and which a squire.

The Nonconformists, numerous only in the towns, even there enjoyed toleration but not equality. The sacramental test was designed to keep all save Church communicants out of municipal and magisterial office, and although the annual passage of an Indemnity Act allowed this law frequently to be evaded, the more conscientious Dissenters were in fact as well as law excluded. The close oligarchies that governed the towns were strongholds of Church and State, and seldom contained any but Churchmen. There were many other signs of religious inequality, most of which remained until the latter half of Queen Victoria's reign: the Dissenters were compelled to pay parish rates to maintain the Church fabric, though this was little objected to until the nineteenth century; legal marriages could only be celebrated by clergymen of the established Church; no service save that of the Prayer Book could be read over the dead; charitable and educational endowments were generally under the control of the clergy and used for Church people only; the Universities were a Church monopoly, from the advantages of which Dissenters and Roman Catholics were excluded.

The new fact of religious life in the eighteenth century was Methodism. The mission of John Wesley, by its astonishing success, goes far to upset all generalizations about the subdued and rational spirit of the eighteenth century, for the very essence of Wesley's movement was 'enthusiasm', and it swept the country. The upper classes, however, remained hostile to Methodism, and the established Church thrust it out to join its potent young force to that of the old Dissenting bodies. The ultimate consequence was that the Nonconformists rose from about a twentieth of the church-goers to something near a half. Wesley's Methodism became the religion of the neglected poor.

Eventually, too, Methodism reacted on the gentry in the polite and orthodox form of an evangelical movement inside the Church of England. But that movement, which under the leadership of Wilberforce had great effects both on society and on politics, was only beginning when the French Revolution broke out. In the earlier years of George III's reign, during the height of Wesley's missionary success, the upper class, and particularly the leaders of politics and fashion, were not distinguished by religious zeal or by strictness of life. The society of Gibbon, of Charles Fox, and of the Duchess of Devonshire, had the faults and virtues of people who make the most of this world, leaving the next one to take care of itself.

In that age, so vigorous in agriculture and commerce, in scientific inventions and geographical discoveries, and adorned in art, literature, and philosophy by the work of so many individual writers of genius, a creeping paralysis infected every established and endowed institution. This was mainly because the institutions had to fear no organized public opinion and no serious threat of change or reform. The resounding triumph of corporate rights and vested interests over the ill-advised attack of James II, though necessary to preserve our liberties in 1688, had for a long time afterwards the bad effect of freeing all privileged persons from any dread of inquiry or interference. As in the Parliamentary and Municipal system, so in the Church, sinecurism and absenteeism were rampant, and the better-paid posts were regarded, not as opportunities to do service to the community, but as provision made for the younger sons, the relations, and clients of the ruling

41

families. 'Parliamentary influence' was the centre of a vast ramification of personal 'graft', which decided the bestowal of all kinds of posts, civil and ecclesiastical, naval and military.

While all old-established institutions were more or less corrupted from their avowed purpose, it is not surprising that the University of Oxford should in this slumberous period have made very little pretence of fulfilling its functions. Early in the reign of George III a foreign visitor witnessed with amazement the Oxford examination as it was then conducted: 'The Presiding Examiner, the Candidate for a degree, and the three Opponents came into the Schools and amid profound silence passed the statutory time in the study of a novel or other entertaining work.' The election of Old Sarum was not more of a farce. Oxford's most famous children have confirmed the judgement of strangers. Newman declared, with a slight exaggeration, that Oxford 'gave no education at all to the youth committed to its keeping', prior to 1800, when a real examination for the degree was established. Gibbon, who had been there in the worst period, has left a terrible indictment. He ascribed the failure of the ancient Universities to the fact that their government 'still remained in the hands of the clergy', and he deplored the monopoly enjoyed by Oxford and Cambridge of all the University privileges in England, because, as he too truly remarked, 'the spirit of monopolists is narrow, lazy, and oppressive.'

'Cambridge,' added Gibbon, 'appears to have been less deeply infected than her sister with the vices of the Cloyster.' But if Cambridge shone at all, it was only in comparison with Oxford. Owing to the permanent influence of Newton, the Mathematical Tripos was a real test of knowledge, and had normally to be taken by candidates for degrees, though the number of entries was very small.[1] It had an enduring effect on the intellectual life and traditions of the University, and attracted to Cambridge clever, poor boys from the small schools of Northern England. But on the walls of the Cambridge Colleges there is a singular absence of portraits of great men of learning between the period of Bentley and the period of Porson.

The number of students at the two English Universities was disgracefully low, not much more than half what it had been in the time of Laud and Milton, and a bare tithe of what it is today in spite of the modern competition of numerous other Universities. The decay not only of Oxford and Cambridge but of the schools that fed them was indicated by this decline in numbers, which was most marked at Cambridge.

1. The Classical Tripos was only set up in 1824.

Although they were the only Universities in England and Wales, Protestant Dissenters and Roman Catholics were excluded from them by law.[1] Instead of being the national centres of learning and instruction, they were little more than comfortable monastic establishments for clerical sinecurists with a tinge of letters; while young men of family, between Eton and the Grand Tour, and a number of more ordinary individuals designed for the Church, spent their time there very pleasantly, some with a great deal of drinking and cheerful noise, and some with a little reading of books. The progress of reform in Oxford and Cambridge in the nineteenth century has been greater than the progress of reform in any other institution that we have inherited from the distant past. The history of the two senior Universities of England is the strongest case that can be quoted by the conservative reformer, who thinks that the most corrupt of ancient institutions are always capable of adaptation to the needs of a new age, without breaking the vital thread of a great historic tradition.

A nation that could see with indifference the prostitution of its University endowments was not very likely to set much store by secondary education. 'It has been estimated,' writes an eminent educational expert of our day,[2] 'that the condition of our "public" or higher schools was worse between 1750 and 1840 than at any time since King Alfred. The grammar schools were largely derelict, often scandalous. The endowments of the secondary schools were to a large extent embezzled by absentee masters, imitative of the example set them by the official class in other spheres of Church and State.'

But against this oft-told tale of the educational indifference of the Eighteenth Century, two important movements stand to the credit side – the Dissenting Academies and the Charity Schools. Excluded from Oxford and Cambridge, the Protestant Dissenters maintained numerous academies where their own people received higher and secondary education. They were real centres of science and intellect, conducted on more modern lines than the Oxford and Cambridge of that day, and they attracted many pupils who were not Dissenters. At the same time the needs of the poor for primary education and child discipline were to some extent met by the great Eighteenth Century movement for the founding and maintenance of Charity Schools, in which the Church of the land

1. Cambridge sometimes allowed Dissenters to matriculate and reside as undergraduates, but not to take degrees, emoluments, or offices. Oxford excluded them altogether from the sacred precincts.
2. Marvin, *Century of Hope*, p. 204.

took the leading part. And it must be remembered that, so long as the apprenticeship system was still vital, the training and discipline of boys and youths were not so completely neglected as the absence of schools would seem to us to imply.

Some, moreover, of the old endowed grammar schools were neither scandalous nor inefficient, for example the school at Hawkshead, where Wordsworth was so happily educated (1778–87) in the bosom of nature, and amid the healthy companionship of north-country yeomen's sons. The absence of organized athleticism,[1] examination, inspection, or competition, though it may have been bad for the public interest and for the average pupil, was good for genius, which flourished more when left to itself than it does under the constant pressure and excitement of our own day.

Only a small proportion of the people were properly educated, and most were not educated at all. There was no large half-educated class, and therefore the intellectual and literary standard of our ancestors was in some respects higher than our own. Though comparatively little was read, most of what was read was of value. The latter-day flood of newspapers, magazines, and indifferent novels had not yet come to submerge literature and provide substitutes for thought and taste. Bad books had not yet driven out good ones. The modern as well as the ancient classics held a much greater place in the national consciousness than today. Shakespeare and Milton were familiar to almost all who could read and write.[2] Common speech became interlarded with their phrases.

Dr Johnson, too, was already a national hero in his lifetime; Boswell only perpetuated his fame. It had been due in the first instance to his countrymen's reverence for literature, and to their interest in the problems of conduct, which he could discuss, as no one ever did so well in any other age or country, from the point of view of the plain man's thoughts and instincts. The nation, like Dr Johnson, was serious, ethical, and religious, without being either priest-led or puritanical. A very individualist form of Protestantism, based on Bible-reading, sermon-reading, and private prayer, was perfectly compatible with the best sort of worldliness. Such was the religion of the 'middle English'; above

1. Wordsworth, in his account of his school, does not mention cricket and football. The diversions, apparently, were skating, nutting, riding, scrambling, and rambling. So the poet in the child survived into the man.

2. 'The English national authors are in all hands,' writes the Prussian visitor of 1782. 'My landlady, who is a taylor's widow, reads her Milton; and tells me that her late husband first fell in love with her because she read Milton with such proper emphasis.'

floated a sceptical aristocracy; and below lay a neglected heathendom, to be redeemed by the Methodist mission.

The Inns of Court, on the road between the City and Westminster, were the seat of a learned trade union that linked up the general public with the political and governmental world. The lawyers were still, what the clergy had once been, the organization through which a clever son of the people had the best chance of rising to worldly greatness in an age of privileged aristocracy. The father of the remarkable man who became Lord Chancellor Eldon in 1801 had been apprentice to a coalfactor. The solicitors were in those days humbler folk than now, but their sons had certain obvious advantages over other people in starting on the more ambitious career of the Bar; several times in the eighteenth century the son of a poor solicitor became Lord Chancellor of the realm.

The much-admired British Constitution was explained to the world by the French philosopher Montesquieu, upon a theory that had some remarkable consequences on the framing of the Constitution of the United States. According to Montesquieu, British liberty was the result of the separation of the executive, legislative, and judicial functions of government, which could not be exercised by the same persons in any free State! But according to fact, the chief merit of the House of Commons was due to exactly the opposite cause, namely, that it controlled by its votes and largely contained within its walls the Executive and the Legislative together. So too, in spite of Montesquieu, the Judiciary who pronounced on the laws were in many cases, the same people who made and who executed them. The Justices of the Peace were at once judges, administrators, and local legislators. The Lord Chancellor was head of the Judiciary, a Cabinet Minister, and a leading politician, Barristers entered the House of Commons to increase their practice and eventually to become Judges.

The real protection afforded to the liberty of the subject in the law-courts was that, since the Revolution, the Judges could only be removed by the Crown with the concurrence of Parliament and for definite misbehaviour. This good law, and the milder spirit of politics since 1689, had transformed for the better the conduct of English trials. Whenever public opinion, as represented on the juries, was hostile, Government could make nothing of trials for sedition or attacks on the Press.[1]

1. Fox's Libel Act of 1792, the last year for many to come when so liberal a law could have been passed, finally decided a point in dispute all through the

This new relation of Government to justice in the cases where Government was most interested had reacted favourably on criminal trials of all kinds. Trials, whether political or not, were already conducted in a manner much more fair to the accused. In France the Judges still consider it their business to act in some sort as prosecutor on behalf of an outraged society. In England, since the Revolution of 1688, the Judges had adopted the attitude of impartial umpires in all criminal prosecutions. The national love of 'fair play' encouraged this development.

But our criminal law, though not unfairly administered, was in itself a 'sanguinary chaos'. The idea of reforming the law in accordance with humanity and common sense, or even on any consistent legal principle, was opposed to the mental habits of the age in England. Irrational reverence for the letter of the law as received from the fathers was common to nearly all the contemporaries of Blackstone,[1] partly because the institutions of which Englishmen so proudly boasted were the legacy of 1689, the most conservative and legal revolution in history. But though no change in the Constitution, or in chartered rights however obsolete, was likely to be mooted, nor any legal change proposed on broad and novel principles, yet additions were constantly being made in detail to the Draconian severity of our criminal code. During the reign of George II and the greater part of the reign of George III, capital offences were multiplied at a rate exceeding two a year. It was said that if a country gentleman could obtain nothing else from Government, he was sure to be accommodated with a new capital felony. The fact was that the dangers to property resulting from the want of efficient police in that golden age of footpads, highwaymen, and burglars, had driven a society uninstructed in the true psychology of crime into the grave error of threatening people with the gallows for every offence about which there was a temporary panic. And once passed, a new law became as sacrosanct as the rotten boroughs.

The haphazard list of two hundred crimes punishable by death had not even consistent severity to recommend it. It was death to steal from a boat on a navigable river, but not on a canal. To cut down trees in a garden was a capital offence, and also to slit a person's nose; but not so the most aggravated murderous assault which the victim managed to survive with nose intact. The unjust laws often resulted in a leniency as injurious to justice as the

1. Died 1870.

eighteenth century, laying it down that it was the function of the jury to decide not merely whether the libel had been published but whether it was a libel.

severity that had been decreed. Juries were unwilling to convict and witnesses to give evidence, in cases of theft that were capitally punishable. The burglar on his part was strongly tempted to escape the rope by murdering the householder who had witnessed his robbery. The chance of escaping capture for want of an efficient police, and in case of capture the uncertainty of what would happen in court, made a life of crime an agreeably exciting gamble.

Although only a small proportion of the death sentences pronounced were carried out, the number of men and women hanged in England every year was greater in proportion to population than on the Continent, where in the last half of the century several of the criminal codes underwent considerable revision, in accordance with the humane and scientific principles of Beccaria. But the good old English rule, inherited from earlier times, against inflicting death or extracting evidence by torture still gave us an advantage over not a few continental countries.

The state of the English prisons, brought to general notice by the philanthropist Howard, who died 1790, was far worse than the average on the Continent. The terrible 'gaol fever', the result of consistently insanitary conditions, was peculiarly scandalous in England. The prisoners, including forty thousand arrested every year for debt, most of whom were more unfortunate than criminal, were put under the absolute authority of gaolers who had taken the prisons on farm to make what they could out of the inmates. In some prisons nothing could be had for nothing, as not even a minimum allowance of food was supplied out of the public funds. The magistrates 'would not charge the county with the expense'. In other prisons the free food was filthy and inadequate. The debtor, the most innocent class of prisoner, was least able to purchase alleviation. Other men, who had been acquitted, or against whom no indictment had been brought, were frequently kept in prison for years because they could not pay the gaoler's fees.

The difference between England and Scotland was greater in the eighteenth century than it is today. But both countries, then as now, belonged to the same order of civilization, distinct from Ireland or the Continent. A great part of what has been here said about England is true, with local variations, of Scotland also.

The Union of 1707 had left the Scottish law and the Scottish Church untouched and permanently separate from the English. But it had united the trade and commercial privileges of North and South Britain, and it had merged the two Parliaments into one at Westminster. English and Scottish legislators sitting together

47

thenceforth made laws to apply either to Scotland or to England or to both.

The Scottish Parliamentary elections were more farcical than even the English. The Scottish burgh members were none of them elected by the inhabitants, but all by the municipal corporations; and there was scarcely a municipal corporation in Scotland that was not a cooptive oligarchy, like that so amusingly described in John Galt's *Provost*. The county franchise was on a much more restricted freehold qualification than in South Britain, and the elections were decided by small bodies of freeholders who might not even represent the landed wealth of the shire. The Government at Westminster, through the Lord-Advocate, was able to buy up almost every Scottish vote in Parliament.

The deadness of all political and municipal life, due to the want of representative institutions either central or local, resulted in Scotland's failure to take part in her own national drama of 1745. A few thousand savage and romantic tribesmen from the Highland mountains were allowed to occupy the capital and to march up and down the country at will with sword and target, while the civilized portion of Scotland took no vigorous steps either to further or to thwart their enterprise. It was English troops who suppressed the rebellion and broke up the tribal system in the Highlands. Scotland had been 'as one incapable of her own distress'.

It was a remarkable fact that Scotland, the most democratic and the best educated part of the British islands, had no representative institutions, either parliamentary or municipal, until 1832–3.[1] Scottish democracy had been matured in the national Church, but by the end of the eighteenth century, in a more secular age, that vessel was no longer able by itself to contain so strong a spirit.

The Presbyterian Church, at once so popular and so tyrannical, so jealous of free thought yet so eager to give education to all, had been reinstated by the Revolution of 1688, after being purified and hardened by the persecution of Claverhouse's 'killing times'. It inaugurated a period of severe and bigoted social discipline, which, combined with the poverty of the country and frequent famines, leaves the veil of gloom over the Scottish scene for fifty years after the accession of William. But as the eighteenth century goes on, the picture grows ever more cheerful. The laity threw off the stricter and more odious part of the Kirk discipline, and among the clergy themselves the moderate and latitudinarian party began

1. It is now regarded as certain that before 1469 the Municipal Councils of the Scottish burghs were chosen by popular election.

to triumph. At length the poet Burns came to harass the retreating rearguard of old-fashioned bigots with his lively satire. In his day young people were able to dance 'promisky'. Witches were fast disappearing, with the minds that bred them. David Hume, instead of being burnt as an infidel, held a great position in the intellectual society of Edinburgh. He and Adam Smith put Scotland among the foremost of the philosopher nations in a philosophic age.

The Universities flourished as they did not in England, being the real cornerstone of a real edifice of national education. Learning was fostered among the people by the Church itself, which was in much closer touch with all classes and their needs than in South Britain of that day. Every peasant with a clever son aspired, not without reasonable hope, to see him pass through the village school and the University into the sacred profession, which thus continued to be recruited from the people and to represent the best side of the national idealism.

If, in the English midlands before the enclosures, open-field agriculture was too little productive, the results of the system on the poorer lands of Scotland were yet more disastrous. Only in parts of the Lothians was wheat grown at all when the House of Hanover came to the throne. 'Oats,' wrote Dr Johnson in his dictionary, 'a grain which in England is generally given to horses, in Scotland supports the people.' In housing, in economic conditions, and in subjection to periodic famine, the Scot, when the century opened, resembled the Irish rather than the English peasant. Short leases discouraged agricultural improvement. The country, long ago well-forested, had become a treeless waste. The cattle were starvelings, often perishing for want of fodder. The small country gentry, known as 'pocket lairds', partook of the general poverty; in the shortage of money they were paid chiefly in kind.

The first steps on the path of progress were taken by certain of the nobles and richer lairds who introduced long leases, broke up the open fields, and enclosed the land within dykes and stone walls. In so doing they prepared the way for wheat, roots, and artificial fodder; for draining and manuring the poor soil; for scientific breeding of sheep and cattle, and the whole apparatus of modern agriculture. Long plantations of fir arose on the waste, tempering the bitter wind to man, beast, and crop. Before the Napoleonic wars, it had become apparent to all the world that the Scots were a peculiarly intelligent and highly educated people, capable of becoming not less but more progressive than the English farmers themselves. Early in the eighteenth century improving Scottish lairds had introduced English ploughmen and agriculturists to teach the new methods: in the nineteenth century the tide set the other way.

Wealth was flowing into the country from all sides, even before the Industrial Revolution. As soon as the Act of Union had opened the British Colonies to Scottish trade, Bailie Nicol Jarvie and his brother merchants of the great western port, previously with no handy outlet for their goods, made Glasgow flourish. Between 1700 and 1800 its inhabitants increased from about twelve to eighty thousand. Meanwhile the opening of free trade with England, and the turnpike movements in both countries, put markets at the door of Scottish agriculturists and manufacturing cottagers that enormously stimulated the general forward movement of the age. And finally, for evil and for good, there came the factories. In 1800 the revenue of Scotland was fifty times what it had been in 1700, while the population had only increased from about 1,100,000 to 1,600,000 souls.

All this progress was going forward while Scots were still generally despised and abused in England as proud and needy adventurers. The affair of 1745 had done little to remove this dislike and contempt, which formed a bond of union between Wilkes and Dr Johnson. It was only in the age of Sir Walter Scott that England discovered once and for all that she was linked with a partner not inferior to herself.

CHAPTER 3

THE machinery of politics and government, the nature of which has been touched upon in the previous chapters, had remained in the hands of the Whig aristocracy from the fall of the Tories at the death of Anne until the accession of George III. In the earlier part of their long supremacy, the great Whig families who had triumphed at the dynastic crisis were conscious that they bore rule as the interpreters of the national sentiment against the French and the Pretender, and as the champions of the free elements in our Constitution. Their political henchmen were the Dissenters, whom they had saved from renewed persecution by the High Church Tories; and the commercial classes, especially in London, who feared the 'little Englandism' and anti-commercial bias of the small Tory landowners. But the Whigs, as their fifty fat years rolled by, remembered less and less the rock whence they were hewn. They ceased to look to the people, and relied entirely on the manipulation of the machine of parliamentary corruption. Finally, in time of national danger, brought on by their incompetence, they were compelled, without loosening their grasp on the machine, to come to terms with the first Pitt, as popular tribune, because he alone was capable of wielding the might of England in time of war. The victorious conduct of the Seven Years' War seemed to foreshadow a new and more vigorous era of national and imperial unity. But the impulse ended with the danger that had called it forth.

The accession of George III closed the Jacobite question by affording a new object to the loyalty of believers in divine right, like Dr Johnson. The Tory king ceased to be 'over the water'; he appeared as a young Englishman, and the staunchest of Protestants. There was nothing French about 'Farmer George'. But unfortunately, though his habits of life were of the best and simplest English type, his political views were derived, through his mother, from petty German Courts. His fine strength of character and great political ability, unenlightened by large understanding or by generous sympathy with his people, degenerated into the low cunning of a wire-puller and the obstinacy that wrecks empires.

George could see no reason why Parliamentary 'influence' by which the country was governed should not be exercised by himself as King, instead of by certain great nobles, distributing the favours of the State in his name but contrary to his wishes. Why should not the taxpayers' money, with which the politicians were bought, be given away by the King himself instead of by the Duke of Newcastle? He might, indeed, have played the part of Bolingbroke's 'patriot king' to some purpose, if he had been content to give his confidence to the elder Pitt, and to put himself at the head of some, at least, of the popular elements of the Constitution. Against such a combination the 'great Whig families' would have struggled in vain. But George, while he shook off Pitt, who soon declined into the Earl of Chatham, sought out quarrels with the commercial classes and with the mob, with London and the Colonists. He purchased for himself a majority in the Commons by the distribution of the patronage of the Crown, which had been at the service of the Whig oligarchy in the reigns of his two predecessors. On these terms he was able to choose his own Ministers – Bute and North – and to dictate his own policy for the best part of twenty years.

At the end of those twenty years, the disastrous war against the American colonists was drawing to its close. It had extended itself into a maritime war against France and Spain, backed by the fleets of Holland, Russia, and the other powers of the 'armed neutrality of the North'. From the moment the first shot had been fired in America, it had been clear that the attempt to revive the personal rule of the King in England would fail or succeed with the issue of the rebellion over there. The surrender of Yorktown to General Washington was regarded as decisive, and a few months later Lord North's Ministry of 'King's Friends' fell from office. George III's system had at length collapsed, but for two more years of crisis and confusion it remained highly uncertain what men and methods would replace it.

The party that had overthrown Lord North and that succeeded him for three months in power was the Whig party under Lord Rockingham. The Whigs had been sobered and purified by misfortune, and educated by the genius of Edmund Burke and Charles Fox. Even the 'great families' had had time to reflect in the cold of opposition that the machinery of corruption was not by itself a safe and sufficient instrument for the government of an Empire. Under the benevolent and high-minded Lord Rockingham the party came back to office, determined to make a drastic reduction in the means by which their own party for half a century, and the King for the last twenty years, had corrupted the members of the House of Commons.

Burke's Economic Reform Bill is the one practical achievement that stands to the account of the most gorgeously eloquent of philosopher statesmen, the greatest publicist, with the possible exception of Cicero, of all ages and all lands. It remains also the one constructive feat for which England is indebted to the Rockingham Whigs, over and above the destruction of Lord North's Ministry. The Bill secured that the King's personal rule should never be revived; for the number of sinecures, and the amount of secret service money by which the House of Commons had been bribed, was drastically cut down; while at the same time Government contractors were prohibited from sitting in Parliament; and the Revenue Officers, who constituted more than a tenth of the electorate and were dependent on Government for their places, were one and all disfranchised.

After these reforms, the most degrading period of political corruption passed away, never to return. It was the first step in a hundred years' process of purifying English public life. But here the course of legislative reform was stayed, until in the year 1832 a new generation of Whigs passed the great Reform Bill. The Rockingham Whigs, though willing to disfranchise the revenue service, were divided on the expediency of disfranchising the rotten boroughs, many of which were their own property. Burke, too, the conscience of the party, was opposed on principle to Reform of Parliament. Himself a man of humble origin, he none the less believed that the 'Whig connexion' should remain 'aristocratic'. He wished to go back to 1689, not forward to any new thing. He still saw nothing in the vista of time to come save the members of a virtuous peerage combining to control the Crown, and indirectly to represent a grateful populace. It is strange that so large a mind desirous of honest and liberal-minded government of our whole Empire, which he beheld in the eye of his imagination stretching across the oceans and down the ages, should have thought that the main body of the Anglo-Saxon race, the outlying portion of which had just, with his full sympathy, rebelled against the shadow of control, would consent for all time to come to be ruled by an oligarchy posing as a representative government.

Fox, on the other hand, though born an aristocrat, was already a convinced supporter of Parliamentary Reform. But he could only carry with him half the Whigs on that question. Meanwhile, the Government broke up on another issue, which caused the utmost confusion of principles and parties, and paved the way for the astonishing career of the younger Pitt.

As so often happens in the history of parties, the rock on which the Whigs split was not a principle but a person. Lord Shelburne was a philosopher-statesman of less genius, but perhaps of greater insight, than Burke. The patron of Bentham, he was an advocate of Parliamentary Reform.[1] But in practice he was not a good Cabinet colleague; he was profoundly and perhaps unfairly distrusted, and nicknamed 'the Jesuit of Berkeley Square'. Politically, he inherited the traditions of Chatham, disliking the aristocratic 'Whig connexion', desiring the dissolution of all party ties and the formation of a patriot ministry on Liberal principles. Like Chatham and his son after him, Shelburne, while regarding the King's personal rule as a disastrous aberration, was not so jealous of the power of the Crown as were Burke and Fox, who vainly strove to reduce the Royal part in politics to such limits as were eventually set in the reign of Queen Victoria.

The King, on the look-out for a chance to intrigue against his own Ministers, saw his opportunity to divide the Rockingham Cabinet by ostentatiously granting his favour and confidence to Shelburne alone, to the exclusion of Fox and the nobles of the

1. Under his later title of Lord Lansdowne, he continued to be a Reformer even in anti-Jacobin times, and so became reconciled to Fox in old age.

stricter Whig connexion. Shelburne's peculiarities led him to accept and encourage this dangerous partiality. Fox was far too hot to put up with the revival of a Royal party in the bosom of a Whig Cabinet, or even to consider coolly what was the best way of meeting the situation. When Rockingham died and the King chose Shelburne as Prime Minister, Fox, Burke, and most of the Whig connexion refused to serve under him and left the Government.

If the seceding Whigs had been dealing, as they supposed, with George and Shelburne alone, they would soon have had things their own way. Their calculations were defeated by a boy of twenty-three. The King called in the young William Pitt, Chatham's second son, to be Chancellor of the Exchequer and Leader of the House of Commons. Pitt thus stepped suddenly to the front rank of statesmen in the character of frustrator of Fox and the Whigs, and saviour of George III. Yet at this time he agreed with Fox and the more Liberal Whigs on Parliamentary Reform and on almost everything else, except on the exact degree of opposition to be offered to the influence of the Crown. That, however, was the issue of the moment. The chances and personalities of these confused years, 1782–3, for ever prevented the cooperation of Fox and Pitt who, in talents and temper, were the complement one of the other, and who, if they had worked in union, might have passed a measure of Parliamentary Reform before the storm of the French Revolution broke over England, and have averted many disasters that fell on these islands. But Pitt, having taken office in alliance with the Tories and the King, was gradually moulded to their likeness, while Fox grew old and factious in opposition.

In the decisive struggle between the two men, Fox made one mistake after another, while Pitt displayed skill, patience, solitary courage, and Parliamentary ability such as no British statesman of mature years has ever shown before or since. Pitt, in a minority in the Commons, was in imminent danger of appearing as the tool and nominee of George III, while Fox's strength was to stand as the champion of the people against the Crown. Fox threw away these advantages by his disastrous coalition with North, the genial old man who had done the King's dirty work year after year till America was lost. With the help of North's votes in the Commons, the Whigs forced their way back to office, at the price of losing the people's confidence. They sold their birthright for a hasty spoonful of pottage, when the whole mess would have been theirs if they had waited.

George, trusting to the unpopularity of the Coalition, strained his prerogative and violated the spirit of the Constitution to get rid of the men whom he detested. He used his personal influence against his own Ministers to induce the Lords to throw out Fox's India Bill; and on the strength of the Lords' vote, which he himself had engineered, at once dismissed Fox and North and installed Pitt as Premier, in the face of a hostile majority of the Commons. After this outrage, Fox might have gained the upper hand once more, if he had, even now, thrown himself frankly on the people. But he strove to prevent the General Election which, above all things, he should have demanded. Pitt's magnificent courage and ability won the popular sympathy, which the Coalition did everything it could to alienate. At length, at the decisive General Election of April 1784, Pitt had the Liberal as well as the Royalist feeling on his side. The Yorkshire Reformers chose his friend Wilberforce for their great county, till then a preserve of the Whig families; it was to Pitt that they looked for Parliamentary Reform. But in the same General Election the government bought up many of the rotten boroughs with money supplied by the Treasury. Popularity and corruption worked together to secure the triumph of Pitt.

If ever there was a national party it was Pitt's in 1784. But the nation was ill-represented in Parliament. Owing to the electoral system, it was the Royalist and Tory borough-owners on whom he must mainly rely for his support in the House of Commons, and since he had quarrelled with Fox he had every year more and more to depend on these retrograde elements. In 1785, for the third time, his proposals for a mild Parliamentary Reform were rejected by the House of Commons. After that he made no further effort to improve the system by which he held power. Considering himself essential to the country as a Minister, he would not risk the loss of office for any cause. His good angel, Wilberforce, lamented that after 1785 he was content to govern by 'influence' instead of by 'principle'. He learnt only too well to maintain himself in power by the distribution of peerages and patronage among the owners of rotten boroughs. In the Army and Navy, in the Church and in the State, to be the relation or client of a borough-owner was the path to preferment. This was the system that became known to the Radicals of a later day as 'Old Corruption'. But though the brightness of Pitt's sun was gradually overcast, he continued until the French Revolution to give the country a sound and liberal-minded administration such as no one else could then have given it.

The net result of the complicated crisis of 1782–4 was the Pittite settlement of the Constitution, which remained as the unwritten law of the land for the next fifty years. The basis of power was

Ministers' 'influence' over Parliament, through the distribution of patronage, somewhat less corrupt than in the heyday of eighteenth-century public spoliation; but of real representation of the people there was no more than before. A new set of ruling Tory families, mostly risen by their wits from the professional and mercantile classes and from the smaller gentry – Rose, Dundas, Eldon, Liverpool, and Castlereagh, the Peels and Canning – took the place of the great Whig families, some of whom, however, came over to join the new régime.

As to the power of the Crown, there was a compromise. The King could no longer choose puppet Ministers like Bute and North; he could no longer dictate the policy of the Cabinet. On the other hand, the Crown retained, until after the death of George IV, the power of selecting the Prime Minister and thereby influencing the combination of the numerous groups into which the House of Commons was divided. Irrespective of party, the Government of the day could, as such, obtain the support of over a hundred members, so that when the Crown chose a man as Prime Minister it went far to supply him with a working majority. Thus all parties were agreed that if George III died, or was declared officially mad, the Prince of Wales could at once bring Fox and the Whigs into office, instead of Pitt and the Tories. The King also retained, as in the famous case of Catholic Emancipation, the power of forbidding the ministerial introduction of measures to which he had a strong objection. But for some years after 1784 George was still very much in the hands of Pitt.

Installed in power on these conditions, Pitt could not reform the internal polity of the British Islands, but he could re-establish their financial and diplomatic credit, while France, the apparent victor in the late war, went down through bankruptcy to revolution.

Our sea-power, though challenged by all the navies of the world, had not been overthrown. Our Empire had lost little beyond the one terrible mutilation which had divided in two the English-speaking race. In the darkest hour of danger and disgrace, great men had not been wanting to our need. Carleton had saved us Canada. Warren Hastings had saved us India. Rodney's sea victory over De Grasse (1782) and old Eliott's defence of the Gibraltar rock had, in the last years of the war, put a check that proved final to the long aspirations of the House of Bourbon after world supremacy.

The first Pitt had excelled as a War Minister; his son excelled as a Minister of peace and recovery. A self-acknowledged pupil of

Adam Smith, in an age when most Parliamentarians thought the art of Latin quotation more important than political economy, Pitt re-established our shaken finances and encouraged our trade and manufacture by a systematic reduction of the chaos of indirect taxes. He thereby threw out of work many smugglers and excisemen.

In pursuance of the policy of Free Trade and peace, Pitt consented to treat with the French Ministers when they proposed a Commercial Treaty. He secured from them arrangements decidedly more advantageous to the manufacturers of England than to those of France. Our staple industries obtained easy access to French markets, while French silks were still prohibited over here. Claret, however, at last shared the advantages which Whig foreign policy, since Anne's reign, had reserved for the heavy wines of our Portuguese ally, with such disastrous results to the gouty legs of our ancestors.

Pitt's French treaty, though approved by the commercial community, was attacked by the party of Fox and Burke. The arguments of the Opposition were directed, not so much against the economic principles involved, on which the Whigs who foregathered at Brooks's Club had the most hazy ideas, but against the political issue of improved relations with France. In so far as this criticism was more than factious, it was out of date. In the age of Voltaire, the French monarchy, already staggering to its doom, was very different from the formidable embodiment of autocratic insolence against which William III and Marlborough had made head in the era of the Dragonnades. The son of Chatham generously declared that 'to suppose that any nation can be unalterably the enemy of another is weak and childish. It has its foundation neither in the experience of nations, nor in the history of man'.[1]

But these just and liberal sentiments did not prevent him from standing up very effectively against both the French and the Spanish branch of the House of Bourbon, whenever he held that British interests were really endangered.

Then, as in the days of William III and George V, it was held to be vital to the safety of Britain that no power likely at any time to challenge our naval supremacy should gain a paramount influence

---

1. On the fall of the Bastille, July 1789, Fox declared that 'all my pre-possessions against French connexions for this country will be at an end, and most part of my European system of politics will be altered', viz. if France ceases to be an absolutist power. But the revolution that at once made Fox friendly to France ere long compelled Pitt to be hostile.

in any part of the Netherlands. The Dutch Republican party, aided by the diplomacy and gold of the French monarchy, was on the point of overthrowing the hereditary Stadtholderate of the House of Orange. If this revolution occurred, French influence would be supreme in Holland. Pitt joined with Prussia to prevent it, and the Prussian armies overawed the Republicans without France daring to intervene. A severe and public defeat was thereby inflicted on French influence in a part of the world where we could not afford to let it triumph.

So, too, when Spain attempted to exclude our settlers from Nootka Sound in Vancouver Island;[1] on the ground that the whole Pacific Coast was her own by right of discovery up to the borders of Alaska, Pitt instantly put a stop to these pretensions, at the risk of war with the House of Bourbon. Neither the United States nor Canada had yet become interested parties to disputes on the Pacific Coast; but their future development would have been imperilled by an admission of the Spanish claims.

With less good fortune, Pitt tried to take equally strong measures in the Black Sea. Side by side with his new ally, Prussia, he threatened the Empress Catherine with war if she annexed the district of Oczakoff from the Turks. The Opposition for once had the country on its side, when it protested against fighting about other people's boundaries in unknown and barbarous lands. Pitt had to give way, because this feeling was shared by members of his own Cabinet and of his own majority in Parliament.

The Oczakoff episode, the last independent action of the old diplomatic world before it was sucked into the maelstrom of French Revolution politics, presented the Eastern question in the form in which we were to know it throughout the nineteenth century, the apparent choice between supporting Turkish misrule or acquiescing in the ambitions of the Russian autocracy over its neighbours. Burke, in Gladstonian phrase, denounced Pitt's policy as 'an anti-Crusade for favouring barbarians and oppressing Christians'. The Foxite tradition, afterwards handed down through Grey and Lord Holland to the Whigs of the Byronic era, became definitely anti-Turk over the Oczakoff question, not without important consequences for Greece forty years later. The subsequent Crimean policy represented a veering round of the later Whigs to the policy initiated by Pitt.

Pitt's defence of his abortive proceedings in 1791 is not without some power of appeal to posterity. It was his object to confirm the alliance of England and Prussia, begun four years before over the

1. See map, p. 184, below.

Dutch affair, so as to use Prussia to protect Poland and Sweden, which then included Finland, from the encroachments of Russia. Only by the help of Prussia as well as of Austria could the Poles get enough protection from the hostility of Russia to enable them to consolidate their hopeful new Constitution, now taking the place of the oligarchic anarchy that had led to the First Partition of their country in 1772. Pitt's failure in 1791 to carry England with him in his stand against Russia over Oczakoff was good for the Christians oppressed by Turkey, but bad for the chances of Poland's survival. Prussia, seeing that she could not depend on British support, had the more reason for seeking friendship with Russia and taking her share in the Second and Third Partitions of Poland. When that policy was at length unashamedly revealed, British opinion was already so much preoccupied by the later aspects of the French Revolution, and by the Jacobin threat to the Netherlands, that we had no ears for the outcries of murdered Poland, which in that last hour appealed only to the Foxite Whigs.

Thanks in no small degree to the sober genius of Pitt, the decade between the American war and the war of the French Revolution saw the British Empire rise, in prosperity and prestige, from the degradation to which George III had reduced it. The wits of Brooks's Club jested at Pitt's youth, and celebrated in their *Rolliad* pasquinades –

> A sight to make surrounding nations stare,
> A Kingdom trusted to a schoolboy's care.

Yet, in fact, it was Fox who was always the schoolboy, and Pitt the schoolmaster. Pitt, as we all rejoice to know, was not incapable of pillow-fighting and having his face blacked in the strict privacy of a few familiar friends; but he never ventured, among colleagues and followers who, when he first took office, were all his seniors, to lay aside for an instant the armour of a haughty reserve before which he could make the greatest quail. By long use, the armour he had adopted as a defence to his youth became a part of his political nature in middle age. Prematurely old in spirit – cautious, dignified, formidable, experienced, laborious, wise – but with a mind that, after a splendid springtime, too soon became closed to generous enthusiasms and new ideas, he ceased to understand human nature save as it is known to a shrewd and cynical Government Whip. He cannot be said to have come too young to power, for he proved equal to the occasion of his call. But if the fates had allowed him, before it was too late, a few years in which to lay aside the awful burden of his country's cares, his nature might have shot

59

up once again, as marvellously as in his boyhood, till it had reached a true perfection, adaptable, comprehensive, and generous, as it was always prudent and strong.

But before the era of the Revolutionary wars, Pitt's limitations were still in the background, and his magnificent talents and virtues were apparent to all save a factious Opposition. And never was Opposition more factious than during the Regency debates. The one principle that united the whole Whig party, both the Whig Conservatives under Burke and Portland, and the Whig Reformers under Fox and Sheridan, was the strict limitation of the powers of the Crown. Yet when in the winter of 1788 George III's periodic madness first became so acute as to hold out to them the prospect of returning to power by the favour of the Prince of Wales as Regent, they were tempted and fell. They proclaimed a doctrine worthy of the Tories of a century before, that the Regency was vested in the Prince of Wales as of right, whatever Parliament might do. This mistake enabled Pitt, in his own phrase, to 'un-Whig' Fox, and to rally round himself, for the last time, Reformers like Wyvill and Cartwright. The Liberal, the Royalist, the Protestant, and the moral feelings of the nation were enlisted on the same side. Pity for the afflicted King and detestation for his dissolute son were enhanced by renewed rumours that the latter was secretly married to a Papist. And in spite of the Whig denials, the Prince's marriage with Mrs FitzHerbert was a fact.

The tone of the Opposition was as bad as its case. Burke's violence on behalf of the Prince was shocking, and already on both sides of the House men whispered that his noble mind was becoming unhinged. But such was then the practice of the Constitution that no one doubted that the Prince, if he became Regent, even on the terms of Pitt's Bill, could call in the Whigs and supply them with Government supporters enough to make up a Parliamentary majority against the will of the nation. Pitt, who had, contrary to all precedent except his own family traditions, scorned to enrich himself out of the public funds, was preparing to resume practice at the Bar, when, by an event resembling an act of retributive justice on the part of Providence, the King unexpectedly recovered, and the gates of Paradise were closed in the very faces of the expectant Whigs. These happenings, on the eve of the French Revolution, obliterated the recollection of George III's twenty years of misrule, prepared for the 'good old King' in his long decline a warm place in his people's heart, and renewed the popularity of the Tory party under the leadership of Pitt.

Perhaps the most successful and enduring part of the life's work of Pitt was his establishment and regulation of the British power in the East. No other man without leaving Europe ever had so great and good an influence on the destinies of India. At the beginning of his twenty years of power, Anglo-Indian affairs were in dire scandal and confusion; before he died, the rule of Britain in the East stood essentially where it remained until the period of change and crisis in our own day – itself due to the very success of what was then begun. The relations of the Anglo-Indian Government to the Indians and to the home country were then decided. The moral obligations implied by our presence in Bengal were recognized both in theory and in practice. And the methods by which the new system would perforce have to be extended over all India were so clearly marked out by Pitt's great Governor-General, Wellesley, that his successors had only to resume and carry through his political testament.

The Empire which had been founded by the military and political genius of Clive had been saved by the scarcely less extraordinary powers of Warren Hastings. During the gloomy period when we were losing an Empire in the West, when our prestige was shaken and our power challenged on the waters of every ocean, and along the shores of every continent, Hastings saved British power in the East. By his vigour as a War Minister he foiled the native States and the Maratha hordes who, with French help, sought to reverse the decision of Plassey. At the same time, he developed the 'subsidiary alliances' of the paramount power with protected native States, that Clive had begun and that Wellesley was destined to erect into a system for the whole peninsula.

By force of his solitary will, Hastings saved India, in the face of his own Council led by his bitter enemy, Philip Francis. Lord North's Regulating Act of 1773 had indeed set up a Governor-General at Calcutta, with authority over the East India Company's three Presidencies of Madras, Bombay, and Bengal, but had saddled him with a Council on the spot, empowered, if it wished, to thwart his action. Perhaps no other English statesman, except Cromwell, could have worked under the conditions over which Hastings triumphed. Hastings was hampered, not only by the veto of his own Council in India, but by the orders of his masters at home – the Directors of the Trading Company. They clamoured for dividends and did not stop to consider that the establishment and maintenance of a vast empire, so far from being, as they thought, a source of revenue, implied in periods of crisis a series of heavy war budgets. It was partly these clamours from the London merchants whom he served that led Hastings into extortionate courses at Benares and in Oudh. But, like Clive, he stood in his general policy for the defence of the Indian, and for the establishment of the great traditions of British justice, in place of the pitiless scramble of greedy, broken adventurers that had been the first result of our conquest of Bengal.

The more terrible of the accusations that were made against Hastings in the case of the Rohillas and Nuncomar have long ago been disproved. He was far from blameless, and there will always be a margin of dispute as to each of his several actions, but on the whole few men who have done so much good, have done so little wrong.

On his return home, his accusers combined in strange alliance the venomous personal malignancy of Francis and the generous prophetic fury of Burke. Burke's imaginative grasp of the moral obligations of Empire did a great work in instructing the statesmen and public at home that they had become, before God and man, the trustees of helpless millions. This new and vital idea, the basis of our Empire in Africa as well as in India, first made headway in public opinion during the era of Burke and Wilberforce. But the gift of prophecy in a hot Irish heart is liable to strange aberrations, and Burke allowed himself to be almost totally misled as to what Hastings stood for in the East. The awakening moral consciousness of England about India, which eventually saved our rule out there, and the more ephemeral social hatred of the 'Nabobs' as the returned Anglo-Indians were called, found, under Whig direction, a channel in exaggerated attacks on Hastings and led to his long but unsuccessful impeachment before the Peers. Pitt first acquiesced in the impeachment on some of the counts, but turned against it after a while. Fox, who had taken it up with all his rash ardour and eloquence, soon wished to have the proceedings against Hastings abandoned, but was held to the hopeless and ungrateful task by the inveterate zeal of Burke.

More important, though less dramatic than the trial of Warren Hastings in Westminster Hall, were the India Bills that took up these tangled matters which his administration had, for good and for evil, brought to the very forefront of English party politics. Serious statesmen were agreed that the government of our new Empire in the East could no longer be left to a Trading Company. During the brief Coalition Ministry of 1783, Fox's chief measure was his India Bill, which proposed boldly to transfer the whole political powers of the East India Company to the Crown, very much as was done after the Mutiny. The proposal was not so much wrong in itself, as impolitic in the extent of its defiance of vested interests, on the part of a Ministry that had as enemies, King, People, and Pitt, all watching for an opportunity of revenge. The proposed transference of all Indian patronage to a body of seven Commissioners, all of whom were certain to be Ministerialists, was denounced as a design to give the Coalition the means of corrupting Parliament. The consequent defeat of the Fox–North Ministry has already been described.[1]

So it fell to Pitt next year to solve the Indian problem. His India Bill was a compromise between Company and Crown, well suited to work quietly for the next seventy-four years, till times were ripe for the complete transference desired by Fox and Burke. Patronage, for all except the greatest posts, was nominally left to the Company. But in practice it was notorious that Henry Dundas, on behalf of Pitt's party interests, so manipulated Indian patronage as to purchase the Parliamentary support of Scotland for his friend, and at the same time to form that connexion between India and many able Scottish families which helped to mould the great Anglo-Indian traditions. The plain truth was that until English party government ceased to be carried on by the barter of seats and votes, and until the principle of competitive examination was introduced for the Indian Civil Service, neither Fox nor Pitt, nor anyone else, could have devised a method of governing India efficiently which would not have increased the governmental power of corrupting Parliament.

Under Pitt's Bill the commercial monopolies and functions of the Company were left intact. But its political authority was 'controlled' by a 'Board of Control' appointed by the Crown, and representing the British Cabinet of the day, with the power of supervising the correspondence between the Company and its servants in India. In effect, the members of the Board of Control, and more particularly Dundas, the Secretary of State, became all-powerful, and the Company a mere mouthpiece of their will – an antiquated cog in the new State machine. The cry against Fox's Bill had been very largely factious, for Pitt's methods indirectly obtained Fox's object.

The new arrangements in India itself were even better, because more thorough. It was Pitt's great merit to make the Governor-General despotic in the East where despotism was understood and needed, yet subordinate to the British Parliamentary Cabinet at home. By Pitt's Amending Act, the Governor-General was freed from the control of his Council, which became purely advisory.

1. p. 55, above.

No one would ever again be asked to govern India on the terms of Warren Hastings, subordinated to mercantile Directors at home, and thwarted by his own Council in Calcutta. Pitt tacked an efficient despotism in India on to a free constitution in England, without either suffering harm. He administered most skilfully the laws he had passed, and initiated the new era. He appointed first-rate men as Governors-General, and gave to each of them the attention, advice, and support for which Britain's servants overseas have a right to look from the home government. By the time that Cornwallis and Wellesley, backed by Pitt and Dundas, had completed their work, the modern Anglo-Indian system was a working part of the British Constitution, and a normal activity of the British race. The main outlines of our policy, internal and external, in the Indian peninsula had been securely laid.

The British Empire in Africa had not yet come into existence. The interior of the Dark Continent was still unmapped and unexplored.[1] Along the coast, the European forts and settlements were principally Portuguese and Dutch, though French and English disputed the ownership of the slave and gold depots of Guinea. The chief connexion of England with Africa was the slave trade, of which the largest share was naturally carried on by the most energetic of the seafaring peoples. Bristol and Liverpool were the centres of a vested interest that throve in supplying North and South America and the West Indies with slaves crimped along the African coast.

When the eighteenth century opened, the slave trade was looked on as perfectly respectable, and only a few stray voices were raised against it. The right of supplying Spanish South America with African slaves was one of the most valued prizes that our statesmen carried off from Utrecht, when the world was resettled after the Marlborough wars. But, during the middle part of the 'Century of Enlightenment', our poets, philosophers, and religious enthusiasts, including John Wesley himself, and the Quaker body as a whole, initiated the attack on the slave trade. Religion and humanitarianism began to renew a connexion that had not been obvious during the Middle Ages or the wars of religion. The initiation of the anti-slavery movement is the greatest debt that the world owes to the Society of Friends.

During the years of Pitt's peace-ministry began the formation of

1. Between 1795 and 1805, Mungo Park, a young Scottish surgeon, initiated the century's work of exploring and mapping, which Speke, Livingstone, and H. M. Stanley carried on.

Anti-Slave Trade Committees, not exclusively composed of Quakers, for the purpose of agitating the question politically among the British public. Granville Sharp and Clarkson founded the first of these Committees. The cause, at the same time, recruited William Wilberforce, as a result of his 'conversion' to Evangelicalism, while Pitt and Fox, without that incentive, both became strong adherents.

The success of this agitation, then unique in the character of its aims and methods, is one of the turning events in the history of the world. It led to the abolition first of the slave trade and then of slavery itself under the British flag, and thereby secured abolition by all those European nations who, in the course of the nineteenth century, divided between them the helpless bulk of Africa. It was only just in time. If slavery had not been abolished before the great commercial exploitation of the tropics began, Africa would have been turned by the world's capitalists into a slave-farm so enormous that it must have eventually corrupted and destroyed Europe herself, as surely as the world-conquest under the conditions of slavery destroyed the Roman Empire.

It is good to think that a movement of such immense and beneficent import to the whole world should have been begun and mainly carried through by the humanity and enlightenment of the British people as a whole, under the guidance of an entirely unselfish agitation, using new methods invented by Englishmen to suit English conditions. These methods of voluntary organization and open propaganda were directed first to persuade the public, and then to bring the pressure of public opinion to bear on the Government. The result proved that, in spite of the terrible corruption of our public institutions, the spirit of the British body politic was free and healthy as compared to any other then existing in the world. The systematic propaganda begun by Sharp and Wilberforce, just before the French Revolution, was stultified for some years by the anti-Jacobin reaction, but achieved its first great triumph early in the following century, long before other reforms could come to fruition. Its methods became the model for the conduct of hundreds and even thousands of other movements – political, humanitarian, social, educational – which have been and still are the chief arteries of the life-blood of modern Britain, where every man and woman with a little money, or a little public spirit, is constantly joining Leagues, Unions, or Committees formed to agitate some question, or to finance some object, local or national. In the eighteenth century this was not so. The habits engendered by the anti-slavery movement were a main cause of the change.

The life of William Wilberforce is, therefore, a fact of importance in the general history of the world, and in the social history of our island. He was not a man of genius, like Wesley; and his friends – Sharp, Clarkson, and Zachary Macaulay – bore, perhaps, most of the burden and heat of the movement which made his fame. But it was he who adapted it to its surroundings in the religious, political, and social England of that day. Having been, before his conversion, a man of the world and a favourite member of the best society, he retained his influence over the governing class, even after he had become its critic from the standpoint of an exacting religious code. In the strength of his personal charm, his virtues, and his very limitations, he seemed raised up to impress the Evangelical influence on English life during the half-century of his ceaseless and varied activities.

The French Revolution, as we shall see in the next chapter, inevitably caused among the well-to-do over here a horrified recoil from a considerable freedom of thought in religion and politics to the hard and narrow timidity of a class alarmed for its privileges and possessions. There was a concurrent change in manners from license or gaiety to hypocrisy or to virtue. Family prayers spread from the middle to the upper class. 'Sunday observance' was revived and enforced. 'It was a wonder to the lower orders,' wrote the Annual Register for 1798, 'throughout all parts of England, to see the avenues to the Churches filled with carriages. This novel appearance prompted the simple country people to inquire what was the matter?'

This mood of sudden sobriety, and the conservative call for more discipline, found satisfaction in the Evangelicalism of Wilberforce and his friends of the so-called 'Clapham Sect'. These men were striving to adapt the Church of England to a Puritanism of ordered and analysed emotions, closely allied to the Methodism that had recently been expelled from the established fold. Average Churchmen of the 'high-and-dry' school of that day were indeed strong Protestants; but they hated Dissenters, especially during the anti-Jacobin panic, and disliked the Evangelicals for showing friendship to Methodists and Quakers, and for their busy zeal about salvation, the slave trade, and a thousand other matters best left alone. Between these two schools of Churchmen the Tories who governed England for forty years were divided. This division is the key to much of the history of the period, for religious thought and observance then had a profound influence on all social and political action.

Pitt, who loved Wilberforce, but deplored his conversion and detested his Evangelical friends, became every year more and more the idol and the leader of the 'high-and-dry' in Church and State. Wilberforce, who believed that Christianity must be applied to politics, while he persecuted 'infidels and deists' with the zeal of an inquisitor, defended Dissenters and continued to desire Parliamentary Reform and to clamour for abolition of the slave trade; while Pitt, under the influence of Dundas, Bishop Tomline, and the anti-Jacobin reaction, was becoming indifferent or hostile to one after another of the movements which he had once led, and more and more the tool of vested interests of every kind.

Wilberforce found that the people who stood firm for the negro cause when others quailed were the Dissenters and the Democrats.[1] In 1800, Pitt had drawn up a Bill to permit the persecution of Dissenting ministers by Tory magistrates all over the country, in contravention of the Toleration Act of 1689. He was with difficulty persuaded by Wilberforce not to introduce it. 'That they should think of attacking the Dissenters and Methodists!' wrote the good man. 'Pitt has no trust in me on any religious subject. To see this design drawn out in a Bill! Never so much moved by any public measure.'

He was indeed stranded in a position between parties. But from that bank and shoal, he managed to exert – by his extraordinary tact, personal charm, and utter honesty of purpose – an ever-increasing influence on the changing world of the early nineteenth century. Directly Pitt died, he was able, with Fox's help, to get the slave trade abolished. Some of Pitt's successors, like Perceval, were members of the 'sect' of Evangelicals, and the bar against their ecclesiastical promotion was removed. But their strength, like that of the earlier Puritanism, was always among the laity. The strongest type of English gentleman in the new era, whether Whig or Tory, was often Evangelical. The army knew them with respect, and India with fear and gratitude. Their influence on Downing Street and in the permanent Civil Service, through families like the Stephens, gravely affected our Colonial policy on behalf of the natives of Africa and the tropics, sometimes with little wisdom, but oftenest and on the whole for the great good of mankind.

The hold of Wilberforce and the anti-slavery movement on the solid middle class in town and country was a thing entirely

1. 'I do not imagine that we could meet with 20 persons in Hull at present who would sign a petition [against the Slave Trade] that are not Republicans. People connect Democratical Principles with the Abolition of the Slave Trade and will not hear it mentioned,' writes Mr Clarkson to Wilberforce, 1793. In 1832 Wilberforce wrote that 'it cannot be denied that the Church clergy had been shamefully lukewarm in the cause of Slavery abolition'.

beautiful – English of the best, and something new in the world. For a whole generation, the anti-slavery champion was returned at every election for the great popular constituency of Yorkshire. He could, if he himself had consented, have sat for it during the rest of his life. In those days, all the free-holders had to come up to the cathedral city to vote. 'Boats are proceeding up the river [from Hull] heavily laden with voters,' says a letter in 1807, 'and hundreds are proceeding on foot.' 'Another large body, chiefly of the middle class, from Wensley Dale, was met on their road by one of the Committee. "For what parties, gentlemen, do you come?" "Wilberforce, to a man," was their leader's reply.' When on Sunday the vast floor of York Minster was packed with the free-holders of the three ridings, 'I was exactly reminded,' writes Wilberforce, 'of the great Jewish Passover in the Temple, in the reign of Josiah.'

It is right to praise highly the influence of Evangelicalism on our politics, in days when no other even partially enlightened doctrine could get a hearing. Evangelicalism brought rectitude, unselfishness, and humanity into high places, and into the appeal to public opinion. But there is one great defect in its political record under Wilberforce which it must share with the spirit of that iron time. Finely alive to the wrongs of the negroes and the corruption of the slave drivers, it was as callous as the 'high-and-dry', or the employers and landlords themselves, to the sufferings of the English poor under the changes wrought by the industrial revolution. Hannah More and her friends sincerely believed that the inequalities of fortune in this world did not matter, because they would be redressed in the next. They even persuaded themselves, and endeavoured to persuade the starving labourers, that it was a spiritual advantage for them to be abjectly poor, provided they were submissive to their superiors. Wilberforce urged upon the willing Pitt the duty of passing the Combination Laws which rendered Trade Unionism illegal. The attitude of early Evangelicalism to British poverty took the peculiarly nauseous form of charity as a vehicle for tracts and enforced religion. It was only in a late age that Evangelicalism produced Lord Shaftesbury, the Wilberforce of the whites.

During Pitt's peace-ministry, steps were taken which opened the path for the future development of Canada and Australasia as homes of the English-speaking races and as members of the British Empire.

Various parts of Australia (then called New Holland) and of

New Zealand had been discovered in the seventeenth century by the sailors of the Dutch East India Company centred at Java; but the wonderful voyages of Tasman had not been followed up. For more than another century, the Australasian seas and islands were outside the world's political and commercial orbit, and even beyond the range of its scientific curiosity. The charm was at length broken, not by the agents of commercial enterprise, but by Captain Cook, acting for the British Royal Navy in the interests of science and exploration. The fact that Cook claimed for the British Crown the coasts that he discovered in New Zealand and Australia was not really as important as the fact that he brought them to the notice and knowledge of our navigators and statesmen. The French discoverers were hard on the same track, and the prize was still for the country that should send the first or the most effective settlers.

The issue was decided by a grotesque event. Lord Sydney, the Home Secretary, persuaded Pitt that the felons whom it had so long been the custom to transport to the American colonies now lost, could be suitably disposed of at Botany Bay, about which Captain Cook had set people talking. There is no evidence that either Pitt or Sydney designed to build a new Britain in the Antipodes. If they had, they would scarcely have wished to lay the foundations in crime. But the colony of convicts, among whom order was kept by the King's troops and officers, afforded, at worst, a leaping-off ground for vast regions otherwise unapproachable, and proved, therefore, to have unexpected attractions to shipload after shipload of free immigrants, in the era of over-population which accompanied the Industrial Revolution in Great Britain. The real history of Australian development began, not with the felons, who were soon swamped, but with the capitalist 'squatters', who in the first decades of the nineteenth century introduced cattle and sheep farming on a large scale and opened out an attractive field of enterprise for adventurous spirits.

If Pitt helped to found Australia 'in a fit of absence of mind', his statesmanship was applied consciously and with good effect to the early problems of Canadian nationhood.

For twenty years after Chatham and Wolfe had wrested Canada from the French Crown, the only important element in the population had been the French *habitans*. They were reconciled to British allegiance by the respect paid to their alien laws and religion. Our policy in conquered Canada was in striking contrast to the folly and violence with which, in the same years, we alienated our brother-Englishmen of New England and Virginia. Canada was kept loyal during the great disruption by Sir Guy Carleton, Lord Dorchester, who governed it, with some intervals, from 1766 to 1796. Carleton was the originator of the spirit of liberal government which, formulated for a later age by Lord Durham, has held together the modern British Empire, and has never been neglected without disaster.

In the first part of his career, Carleton had reconciled the French priests and peasants to British rule. In the second half, he had to face, with the help of Pitt, the more complicated problem of fitting into the Canadian system an English-speaking element, as Protestant and progressive as the *habitans* were stationary and Catholic. He had to devise a policy for the Crown which would retain for it the common loyalty of two mutually antagonistic societies – the very problem in which England had so lamentably failed in her dealings with Ireland.

The first large English-speaking immigration into Canada was the direct result of the loss of the other North-American colonies. The American Loyalists, for the crime of having continued faithful to the government *de jure*, were driven as penniless exiles from their old homes by an act of democratic tyranny comparable to the worst acts of European despotism. They were men sifted out by a persecution and therefore, as in the case of the Pilgrim Fathers, or the Huguenots, made good immigrants. About forty thousand of them had been expelled from the United States. They poured in great numbers into Nova Scotia, created there the separate province of New Brunswick, and settled the neighbouring island of Cape Breton. Some ten thousand of them penetrated inland into Canada proper: of these, some stayed among the French, near Quebec, but more went further up the St Lawrence, into the primeval forests to the north of the Great Lakes. This district of Upper Canada or Ontario, then in the 'far West', was English-speaking from the moment of its settlement; the provinces on the Atlantic coast had also become mainly Anglo-Saxon. But in the centre, Lower Canada or Quebec remained chiefly French. In British North America, taken as a whole, the French still predominated in numbers, because Quebec was the most thickly inhabited district.

The newcomers, known as the United Empire Loyalists, were so far from being slaves and myrmidons of tyranny – as they were described by those who expelled them from their homes – that the first act of the pioneers on their arrival in the land of promise on the Upper St Lawrence was to agitate, after the manner of their race, for popular assemblies, which were a stumbling-block to the

THE
TWO CANADAS
AND THE
MARITIME PROVINCES
1791

English Miles
0   100   200   300   400   500

NEWFOUNDLAND

Cape Breton
Island

NOVA SCOTIA

NEW
BRUNS-
WICK

MAINE

LOWER CANADA
(QUEBEC)

St. Lawrence

Quebec

Montreal

R. Ottawa

HUDSON   BAY   COMPANY'S

H·U·D·E·S·O·N   B·A·Y

HUDSON
BAY
TERRITORY

Albany R.

UPPER CANADA
(ONTARIO)

L. Superior

L. Huron

L. Michigan

L. Ontario
Niagara
York
(Toronto)
L. Erie

Detroit
(U.S.)

French *habitans*. They wished also for the English land-law instead of the French feudal system, and, in fact, for a society on the Anglo-Saxon model.

It was the task of Carleton and Pitt to satisfy these demands without alienating the French. Pitt and his new Home Secretary, Grenville, decided, in opposition to Carleton who was wrong for once, that it was necessary to divide Upper and Lower Canada into two Provinces – the one to enjoy English, the other French law and customs. It was indeed the only way, at that time, in which the Anglo-Saxons, still a small minority, could enjoy free racial self-development, otherwise than by lording it over the French majority as the English settlers were allowed to lord it in Ireland: the division prescribed by Pitt for Canada was the means of concord, in contrast to his unhappy 'union' of opposites nearer home. Under the provision of the Canada Act of 1791, the English-speaking province which it created grew, in the half-century before the legislation based on Lord Durham's report, from 10,000 to over 400,000 inhabitants.

The institutions set up in the two Canadas by Pitt and Grenville were not those of 'responsible' government, for the executive could not be chosen or removed by the legislature. But representative assemblies were granted to advise the Governor, vote the taxes, and pass the laws, like our Parliaments in Tudor or early Stuart days. The French were thus gradually trained up in the use of electoral methods entirely strange to them, while the infant Anglo-Saxon community in the Upper Province was, for the time, satisfied with a degree of self-government adapted to its still primitive conditions of life in the clearings of the wilderness. During the ensuing period of transition, the French and English provinces both remained loyal in the main, and only gradually outgrew this provisional system of semi-popular government.

If Pitt has sometimes been overpraised for some aspects of his policy nearer home, he has never received the full meed of credit for his timely dealings with distant Canada. He was, fortunately, in a position to look across the Atlantic, with those wise eyes of his, over the heads of the vested interests that surrounded and dominated him in the affairs of Great Britain and Ireland.

Lord Grenville's proposal, adopted by Pitt, to give hereditary titles to the members of the Governor's Legislative Council, was never carried out in a land that had no feudal background. The clearings of the forests of Ontario were certainly very different, socially, from the English villages in the age of the enclosures and the 'Speenhamland Act'. It is difficult to exaggerate the advantage to the Empire and the race of the creation, at this particular juncture, of the pioneer province of Upper Canada, as a place ready made for the reception of the victims of the economic revolution then going on in Great Britain. The Canadian conditions, like those of Australia and New Zealand shortly afterwards, were almost ideal for rehabilitating the self-respect of the bullied and pauperized labourer of the English shires. 'In Canada,' wrote one of them, 'we can have our liberty, and need not be afraid of speaking of our rights.' 'We have no gamekeepers, and more privileges,' wrote another. The Scots, too, soon discovered the Canadian trail. The forests fell, the log huts rose, and the rich wilderness began its yield of crops and of men.

CHAPTER 4

THE Parliamentary government of England in the eighteenth century was, as we have seen, a form of aristocracy, tempered on the one hand by a remnant of monarchy that became more prominent under George III, and on the other hand by a certain deference to public opinion and by a very great respect for local and individual rights. It revered law and precedent much more than it aimed at effective administration or public utility. Its spirit had little in common either with the continental despotisms of that day or with the democratic Britain of our own. The idea of making Parliament the engine of a systematic democracy had indeed been advanced by the armed Radicals who attempted to recast the Commonwealth in the time of Cromwell, but their work had been uncongenial to the social structure and traditions of the land. When, after 1688, religious animosities had been damped down by a latitudinarian toleration, there was not left in England the stuff out of which revolutions or popular governments are made.

From the return of Charles II until the publication of Paine's *Rights of Man*, there was no movement to introduce democracy into our island. The speculative debates on popular rights and universal suffrage which the Army agitators had held with Cromwell and Ireton had left no impression on English political thought. And although the memory of the regicide Republic no doubt influenced the movements of the eighteenth century in France, America, and England, no continuous underground tradition, such as that which had passed on the fire from Wycliffe's Lollards to the men of the Tudor Reformation, connected John Lilburne and the Levellers with modern Radicalism and Socialism. The new movements had new origins.

Under the social and economic conditions of England in the eighteenth century, life had many pleasant aspects for the mass of the people both in town and country. Social differences and political inequalities were accepted cheerfully by all. High and low were 'freeborn Britons', satisfied with their lot, and despising the starved and frog-eating French. In spite of political corruption, it was in its social aspects the ideal age of a true conservatism.

Only when the Industrial Revolution had undermined the independence of large classes of society, had made their individual lives in field and factory intolerable, and had at the same time collected great masses of them together in the industrial districts, did democracy begin slowly to commend itself to the victims as a means of bettering their lot through politics. In the early years of the French Revolution this hope, first propounded to them by Tom Paine, was rejected by the great majority of working men. But the idea, though suppressed and persecuted, took root, and in the early decades of the nineteenth century made converts of many of the wage-earners, on account of their sufferings, and on account of the harsh interference of the State against any attempts on their part to secure a living wage from their employers. The enforcement of Pitt's laws against incipient Trade Unionism pointed the working classes to the need of political action through Parliamentary Reform.

Side by side with this new proletariat, the Industrial Revolution was creating, as the old century closed, a number of new middle classes, of varying wealth and importance, from humble clerks to those 'captains of industry' who began to rival the territorial magnates in wealth and in power over the lives of others. These new classes had no place allotted them in the political and municipal system of the old régime. The Toryism of the anti-Jacobin reaction, while in the economic field it gave them strenuous support against their working-class employees, would allow them no voice either in national or local government. They were encouraged by all means to make money for themselves and for the tax-gatherer, but otherwise they must learn that they had come into the world too late to be counted among the privileged orders. The new middle classes were patient of this feudal exclusiveness during one generation of anti-French Toryism, prompted in part by patriotic support of the great war. Then they too swung heavily round towards Radicalism, and ushered in the era of successful reform.

Although, as we shall see, the French Revolution was the immediate occasion of the democratic movement in England, and the occasion also of its initial defeat, our own Industrial Revolution was the more lasting and effective cause. It is fascinating to watch the complicated interplay of these two motive forces, the one external and the other internal, the one always in the limelight, and the other only gradually and partially forcing its greater importance upon the notice of Whig and Tory statesmen.

The first agitation for Parliamentary Reform, which had arisen among the old-fashioned Yorkshire freeholders and was supported by Pitt as well as by Fox, was not a democratic or even a modern movement. It had no relation to the Industrial Revolution. It proposed to abolish a few of the rotten boroughs and to increase the county representation. It advocated this degree of Parliamentary Reform, not on any theory of elevating the middle or lower class, or of enriching the poor, but merely to obtain good government for the nation as a whole. The agitation had been provoked by George III, and was intended to put an end to his personal rule exercised through the nominated and bribed majority of the House of Commons. It was as much a movement of occasion as of principle.

When, therefore, the rule of the 'King's Friends' came to an end after 1782, and when the disasters of the American war were being repaired by the healing policy of Pitt as peace Minister, the agitation lost so much of its force that Pitt threw it over, after the rejection of his Reform Bill in 1785. If this old-world proposal had been carried, it would at least have greatly eased the path of the new world, so painfully struggling on to the scene.

The second stage of the Reform movement, and the first that indicated the coming of a new era, occurred in the years immediately preceding and following the fall of the Bastille. The leadership lay with the philosophic Dissenters, Price and Priestley. Pitt not only dropped Parliamentary Reform, but in 1787 and again in 1789 opposed the abolition of the Test and Corporation Acts which debarred Dissenters and Roman Catholics from civil rights. Fox, on the other hand, warmly espoused the cause of religious equality and asserted the modern principle that 'religion is not a proper test for a political institution'.

The Dissenters, now hopeless of relief from Pitt or from the existing House of Commons, began to agitate for Parliamentary Reform as a step necessary to their own civil enfranchisement. Dissenters and Parliamentary Reformers alike were alienated from

Pitt and, in spite of the unsavoury memories of the Coalition with North and of the Regency debates, began with caution to draw towards Fox and the more liberal section of the Whigs. In this juncture of our affairs, the news from France began to affect the political imagination of Englishmen. France, not yet turned Jacobin, had replaced a despotism by a constitutional monarchy and was framing a code of laws which put men of every creed on the same platform of civil rights. The more progressive members of the Whig party, led by Fox, were at one with the philosophic Dissenters in acclaiming the dawn of world-wide political enfranchisement and religious equality, while Burke, who already heard the fall of civilization in the falling stones of the Bastille, flung himself against the Unitarian Reformers with all the heaviest weapons of his splendid armoury.

In magnificence of diction and loftiness of soul, Burke is the only English publicist who stands beside Milton. His *Reflections on the French Revolution* have enshrined in a perfect form the conservative principles which constitute one-half of our political and social happiness. But for recognition of the other half he was surpassed by many men far his inferior in genius. And, whatever he may have intended, he appealed to passions only less cruel than those which he so justly execrated in the French mob. It was not the first time in history that an angel's trumpet roused the fiends.

An unreasoned hatred of Dissenters, prevalent in the higher orders of society and locally in the slum population, was stirred to fury by the lead that Burke had given against Parliamentary Reformers and friends of the French Revolution. Priestley was a scientist of European reputation in an age when scientists were few. He was a man of blameless life and high public spirit. He was not a Republican, but he was a Dissenter – indeed a Unitarian – and he was now active in favour of Parliamentary Reform and repeal of the Test Acts, and in public approval of the general course of the French Revolution up to the summer of 1791. Therefore his house and scientific instruments were destroyed by the 'Church and State' mob of Birmingham, who had been incited against Nonconformists by sermons and pamphlets of the local clergy, and were personally encouraged on the night of riot by two Justices of the Peace. Dissenting chapels, and private houses of Dissenters, even if the owners had nothing to do with politics, were destroyed that night, with signs of connivance on the part of the magistrates. The riots took place more than a year before the September massacres, and a year and a half before the war between England and France, which was afterwards pleaded as a sufficient justification for the persecution of Liberal opinions.

The second phase of the Reform movement, as championed by the Dissenters in the palmy days of the fall of the Bastille, may be said to have been put down by popular violence before the end of 1791. Early in the following year a more significant agitation was begun among a class of men who had never yet acted in politics on their own behalf – the working men in the great towns.

The democratic movement in England – that is to say, the claim put forward by the common people themselves that they should choose their governors in order to improve their own conditions of life – owed its origin to the spectacle of the French Revolution and to the writings of Tom Paine. And the same causes that gave it birth proved in the first instance its undoing. The forcible suppression for so many years of the English movement was rendered possible by the course of the foreign revolution that aroused it, and by the impolitic and uncompromising logic of its first champion.

Paine was an English Quaker by origin. But he had early settled in America, where his pamphlet *Common Sense* had urged the colonists to cut the knot of their difficulties with the old country by declaring themselves an independent Republic. He may have been a good 'citizen of the world', but he was never a good Englishman. However, he was again in England, and as soon as he read Burke's *Reflections on the French Revolution*, he sat down to write a reply. The First Part of the *Rights of Man* appeared in February 1791.

In answer to Burke's ultra-conservative doctrine, which tended to bind up the English Constitution for ever by the pact of 1689, Paine stated the full democratic thesis: that government is derived from the people, can be altered at their will, and must be carried on for their benefit, through a system of popular representation. The pamphlet circulated by tens of thousands among classes who hitherto knew nothing of politics, save when at election time 'the quality' dispensed beer and money to make a mob for the hustings. The idea that politics was an affair of the common people as such, and a means by which they could alleviate their poverty, was new and strange. But the events in France had roused our ancestors to unwonted mental activity, and in 1791–2 Burke and Paine were read and discussed with a simple eagerness natural to men plunged for the first time into political speculation.

Government declined, in spite of much shrill advice, to prosecute the First Part of the *Rights of Man*, where the author had not clearly drawn out all the inferences of his representative theory of government. But in the Second Part, published in February 1792, Paine's logical sword came right out of the scabbard. He claimed that all the hereditary elements in the Constitution, both Monarchy and House of Lords, ought to be abolished, and the country governed by its representatives alone, sitting either in one or two Chambers. Government would then be carried on for the benefit of the mass of the people. Pensions on the taxes now granted to the rich would be diverted, and used, together with a graduated income-tax, to give education to the poor, old-age pensions, and maternity benefit.

Far the greater part of Paine's 'criminal propositions' are accomplished facts of the present day. The only part of the *Rights of Man* that could with any justice be stigmatized as 'seditious' lay in its republicanism. Yet that part inevitably attracted most attention, and in view of contemporary events in France aroused violent alarm. It is indeed true that Paine had not advised conspiracy or rebellion, and that the country could have sifted out for itself what it wanted in his doctrine, and rejected the rest – as indeed it has since done. But feeling was too hot and fear of the French Revolution too profound to allow of such nice considerations. The Government now prosecuted and suppressed the *Rights of Man*, and Paine, warned in time by his friend, the poet Blake, fled for his life to France, where he was as nearly as possible guillotined for denouncing the Terror and endeavouring to save the life of Louis XVI.[1] He was a man of undaunted courage and wholly devoted to the public interest as he saw it. But he was singularly deficient in patriotic feeling: in 1798, like any *émigré*, he was advising Bonaparte, as the champion of republicanism, how to invade England!

It was on the question of loyalty to the Crown that the Democratic and Liberal movements foundered. Paine committed the capital error of identifying the theory of representative government with a scheme of rigid republicanism. In advising the English

---

1. Cobbett, in his Tory days, sang of Paine:

> Tom Paine for the devil is surely a match;
> In hanging old England he cheated Jack Catch.
> In France (the first time such a thing had been seen)
> He cheated the watchful and sharp guillotine,
> And at last, to the sorrow of all the beholders,
> He marched out of life with his head on his shoulders.

In 1819 Cobbett, by a rather childish act of repentance, brought back Tom Paine's bones from America to England in his luggage!

to abolish the form of monarchy, he made a ruinous mistake. He was too much of an American, a theorist, a friend of the human race and altogether too little of an Englishman to see that his republican logic would not apply to our island. But the error was not as gratuitous as it would be today. Monarchy in the reign of George III was very different from monarchy in the reign of George V. George III had lost us America, and was destined to prevent the reconciliation of Ireland. He stood in the way of the abolition of the slave trade and of any chance of Parliamentary Reform.

The Whigs ultimately reduced the power of the Crown by passing the Reform Bill, and by instilling their doctrines into the youthful Queen Victoria. But in 1792 they had no remedy. Those of them who would not follow Burke into the Tory camp found it impossible to dissociate themselves in the public mind from Tom Paine, though they abjured and cordially detested him. For years he stuck to everything Liberal like a burr. Either you were for 'the good old King', or else you were set down as a rebel and a Paineite. The man in the street, as he gazed through the shop windows at Gillray's cartoons, began to think of the Foxite Whigs as people in red caps of liberty intent on beheading George III and setting up a ragged Republic.

At this stage in our affairs, in the early months of 1792, while the Second Part of the *Rights of Man* was appearing and men were choosing their sides at the dictation of the most extravagant hopes and fears about the new era, two societies sprang into being. Thomas Hardy, the shoemaker, founded the Corresponding Society, while Grey and his young Parliamentary allies founded the Friends of the People. Both societies aimed at Parliamentary Reform; both were shortlived, but one of them was the origin of the future Radical, and the other of the Whig-Liberal party. They stood for two principles of progress familiar in English history – the people helping themselves, and a section of the governing class helping the people.

Thomas Hardy's Corresponding Society was the first political and educational club of working-men. It supplied the natural leaders of that class with the opportunity to emerge and lead, with the means of study and debate, and with an embryo organization. There was then little Trade Union life and that little was of a purely economic character; there was no Co-operative Society life, and no higher education for the working class; and therefore the Corresponding Society, apart from its political aspect, had high educational and social value. If it had not been crushed by the authorities, it would have done a still greater work and would early have stimulated other movements in working-class life that began many years too late.

Yet in the actual circumstances of the time it was certain that the authorities would regard the Corresponding Society as seditious. Its political programme was Universal Suffrage and Annual Parliaments – that and nothing more. But its members did in fact circulate Paine's writings, and most of them were theoretically Republicans. And therefore, although it was for Parliamentary Reform that they worked as the practical object, their alarmed neighbours naturally supposed that Universal Suffrage was asked for as a step to the Republic.

Hardy and his friends were Londoners. London was then more radical than the North, perhaps because the Westminster and Middlesex elections, held on a democratic franchise and enlivened by Wilkes and by Fox, had accustomed the inhabitants of the capital to watch real political contests, unknown in most towns before the Reform Bill. At this time the working-men in Lancashire were still for 'Church and State'. The year after the Birmingham riots, the Manchester mob imitatively wrecked houses of Dissenters and bourgeois reformers. But the Tom Paine movement, working through the Corresponding Society and the somewhat more middle-class Society for Constitutional Information, acted from London, Sheffield, and Norwich on the rest of England, and sowed broadcast the ideas that re-emerged in the days of Peterloo as the Radical creed of the working-men in Lancashire and the Industrial North.

The action from which the Whig-Liberal party takes its origin was the founding of the 'Friends of the People' Society by young Charles Grey, forty years afterwards the Reform Bill Premier. It broke up the old Whig party on domestic issues, a year before the war with France. There had been no split in 1791 when Burke had renounced his friendship with Fox on the floor of the House, in a heated controversy on the merits of the French Revolution. At that time the majority of the Whig members, preferring Fox to Burke personally, regarded the views of both on the French question as extravagant, and refused to quarrel among themselves about the internal affairs of a foreign country. The incident had left Burke more angry and more isolated than before. That year he left Brooks's Club, to which all sections of the party belonged. The split in the party itself did not come till twelve months later. It was Grey's action in founding the Friends of the People Society to demand Parliamentary Reform, while repudiating Paine, which drove the anti-reform section under the Duke of Portland to concert measures with Pitt against their fellow-Whigs.

Fox was thereby compelled to choose whether in the future he would work only with the Reformers or only with the anti-Reformers of his party. He had hoped against hope to avoid making the choice, but he had no doubt how to choose, if choose he must. If he had declined to throw his shield over the Friends of the People, they and not the Portland Whigs would have had to go. For Fox was the Whig party, with whomsoever he chose to abide. In siding with Reform, he destroyed his own career and his good name in the world, but he prevented the Whigs from becoming bottle-holders to the anti-Jacobin Tories, and so enabled England, many years after his own death, to obtain reform without revolution.

In 1792 there seemed no immediate future for a party standing out for Parliamentary Reform. No politician who cared more for power and popularity than for the principles he held would ever have dreamed of joining so forlorn a hope. The storm of almost universal hatred that broke on the Foxites could only have been faced by a band of men thoroughly sincere at least on this issue. Their leader was a Titan, capable of bestriding the prostrate form of liberty, and giving back to angry Jove peal for peal of thunder. Those years, seemingly the most futile, were really the best and most useful in Fox's life. Pitt, Burke, and Fox were often in the wrong, but they were each of them great of heart. The times were tragic indeed, but the men were not mean who stood for the great principles now coming into conflict upon earth.

The very unanimity of the reactionary passion in the upper and middle class and among most even of the workmen made it the more desirable that there should be a Liberal Opposition in Parliament. The Foxites always remained a part of the privileged and borough-owning aristocracy, but they now drew aside from the rest of the political class, and handed on in their high circle the advocacy of Parliamentary Reform and the protest against political and religious persecution. The persistence of the Foxite tradition in one section of the governing class made it possible for Grey, at the end of his long career, to constitute a party in the unreformed Parliament, large enough, when backed from outside by the middle and lower classes, to pass the Bill that abolished the rotten boroughs. Nothing else could have ultimately averted civil war. It was certainly inevitable, and it may have been desirable, that a great Conservative reaction should emphasize our rejection of the French doctrines. But if the whole of the privileged class had joined Pitt's anti-Jacobin *bloc*, and had been brought up in the neo-Tory tradition, the constitution could not have been altered by legal means, and change could only have come in nineteenth-century Britain along the same violent and bloodstained path by which it has come in continental countries. It is 1832 that justifies the action taken by Fox forty years before. In detail he continued to make grave errors, but the main line that he took in 1792 was the service that he was best fitted to render to his country.

The war with the French Republic that was now fast approaching made it inevitable, in view of the limitations of human nature, that anti-Jacobinism of the most unreasoning kind should be regarded as synonymous with patriotism. For a generation to come, England, in the throes of industrial and agricultural rebirth, was completely in the hands of the anti-Jacobin Tories, whose fixed idea was that of the barons of old: 'we will not have the laws of England changed'. France was changing her laws too fast, so Britain should not change her laws at all – except, indeed, to abridge her ancient liberties and to silence all who advocated new things. The laws stood still, but social and industrial change rushed on.

In the early years of the war against France, the Government contracted the habit of suppressing freedom of speech and inflicting savage punishments on Reformers who ventured to utter their opinions anywhere outside the privileged walls of Parliament. This system of repression, which became highly dangerous after Waterloo when applied in an age too late against the working class as a whole, was in Pitt's time merely the persecution of an unpopular minority. The nation had already decided the issue against the Reformers and Paineites in the winter of 1792, before the outbreak of war with France. During the months that followed the news of the September massacres in Paris, which did for English Toryism what the massacre of St Bartholomew had done for English Protestantism, the Democrats were overwhelmed by hostile public opinion in every town and village of the country. After that it would appear that there was no sufficient reason from the point of view of public safety, even after the war had begun, for the Government persecution of unpopular doctrines. Yet the policy of repression, however much mistaken, was not unnatural to an upper class confronted for the first time with the full-blown doctrine of theoretical democracy at home, and the appalling proceedings in France just across the sea.

All through 1793 and 1794 the law-courts were filled with Government prosecutions of editors, Nonconformist preachers, and Radicals who had argued for Parliamentary Reform, or advocated in theoretical terms the establishment of 'representative government'. For crimes such as these, aggravated, indeed, in not a few cases by foolish and provocative phraseology borrowed from France, men were imprisoned and transported. The trials of the 'Reform-martyrs', Muir and Palmer, before Braxfield, the Scottish Judge Jeffreys, and their transportation to Botany Bay, are among the worst pages in our judicial and political annals, and the memory of them did much to foster the Radicalism of Scotland in the succeeding century.

Finally, in 1794 the Government tried to get Hardy, the founder of the Corresponding Society and of the political movement among the working classes, condemned to death as a traitor. But, thanks to Erskine's persuasive eloquence, the sense of fair play that has often distinguished our countrymen caused the twelve Tory jurymen to acquit Hardy and his fellow prisoners, and so to remind Pitt that the methods of Robespierre were not wanted over here. London, though strongly anti-Jacobin, broke into loud rejoicings at the acquittal.[1]

This timely check saved England from a course of bloodshed, and perhaps ultimately from a retributive revolution. The British Constitution, however imperfect, had vindicated its mild spirit through one of its most cherished forms, trial by jury. But short of bloodshed, the system of repression went on as before, in the main approved by public opinion for some years to come. Acts of Parliament were passed suppressing the Corresponding and other Societies, and so rendering illegal the first efforts of the working classes to interest themselves in politics, and to get together for education and discussion. The governing classes grew to believe that where two or three of the unprivileged were gathered together, there must be sedition be in the midst of them. All public meetings were prohibited that were not licensed by magistrates, and the magistrates were Tory partisans. *Habeas Corpus* was suspended, and in a few cases men against whom there was no evidence lingered in prison during the last years of the century. The Combination Acts, which rendered Trade Unions illegal, were inspired by political fear of all forms of combination among the

1. It was mainly about this trial that Wordsworth was thinking when, years later, he wrote in the Prelude:

> Our Shepherds, this say merely, at that time
> Acted, or seemed at least to act, like men
> Thirsting to make the guardian crook of law
> A tool of murder.

'labouring poor', no less than by the desire to keep down wages in accordance with the bourgeois political economy of the day.

The new working class that the Industrial Revolution was creating had thus early shown an instinct towards self-help along the two parallel lines of politics and Trade Unionism. This healthy double development, which wise rulers would have welcomed, controlled, and guided, was crushed out by the strong hand of Pitt's government and postponed for another generation. When it came up again in the era of Peterloo, it had again to fight its way, like an outlaw, against all the powers of the land. The mass of the people, hostile at last to the Tory system of government and impatient of the miseries of their own industrial servitude, found themselves confronted by the same persecuting habit of mind in the ruling classes which had grown up in the first instance during the repression of an unpopular minority a quarter of a century before. This partisanship of the Government against the poor and against all who pleaded their cause did much to distort and embitter the social processes of the Industrial Revolution.

Anti-Jacobin violence, when reduced to a system and prolonged for more than a generation, did grave injury to many sides of our national life. But, unfortunate as were its results, it was very natural. Its violence, which was in full blast many months before the war began, was due to the shock given to the English mind by the spectacle of French society falling into ruin. The panic has no analogy in our own experience, although we ourselves have witnessed the catastrophe of social order in foreign lands. For, to us, social revolutions are historical phenomena that we are accustomed to study, classify, and explain. The French Revolution was the first of its kind.

The philosophy of Dr Johnson's England was static, not evolutionary: the world was not expected to change. Civilization, it was thought, had 'arrived', after a number of barbarous ages, and was going to stay comfortably where it was. When in France it suddenly began to slide, and then exploded in smoke and flame that hid it from view, people on our side the Channel thought that the end of the world had come.

France, moreover, was held to represent civilization to a special degree. For a hundred and fifty years she had, somewhat unduly perhaps, been 'the glass of fashion and the mould of form' to civilized men. She filled a larger part in the mental horizon of our ancestors than that held at the present day by any single country, or any single continent. Our educated classes knew those of France as they knew no other foreigners. Atrocities as unjustifiable as those of the French Terror, when perpetrated in Poland by our allies, the Prussians and Russians, seemed to Englishmen but the distant feuds of savages with outlandish names, while the poor heads nodding on pikes in Paris had smiled in London drawing-rooms.

And yet for all our intimacy with the best society of France we knew nothing of her social structure, and had so little analysed our own that we were unable to perceive fundamental differences that prevented any danger of the French madness crossing the Channel. Burke, who undertook to explain the case, was peculiarly blind on this point; while the small and noisy minority that followed Tom Paine, by adopting some of the phraseology and aspirations of the new France, added greatly to the alarm. And when it became evident that large populations in Europe, who had indeed much to gain by the new French programme, welcomed the coming of the tricolour, it was excusable in our ancestors if they failed to perceive that England was a world by itself, with a social and political history entirely different from that of the Continent. It is possible at least to understand the earnestness that warmed Gibbon's cold eloquence to fire, when he wrote to his friend, Lord Sheffield:

Do not suffer yourselves to be deluded into a false security; remember the proud fabric of the French monarchy. Not four years ago it stood founded, as it might seem, on the rock of time, force, and opinion, supported by the triple Aristocracy of the Church, the Nobility, and the Parliaments. They are crumbled into dust; they are vanished from the earth. If this tremendous warning has no effect on the men of property in England; if it does not open every eye and raise every arm, you will deserve your fate.

Such was the origin of the anti-Jacobin state of mind. Its prolongation was due to the twenty years' war with France. These circumstances must affect our judgement of the action of Pitt and the Tories in abolishing the old rights of free speech and persecuting the advocates of Reform. We may regard it all as a tragedy rather than a crime, if we are no less charitable to the Whigs and Radicals for their lack of patriotism about the war. The tragedy was this, that England was forced to fight for her own security in alliance with the murderers of Poland and the worst reactionary forces in Europe, in an attempt to suppress the newborn hopes of mankind – hopes intolerably insolent indeed, and extremely French. Such a situation could not fail to turn British patriots into reactionaries, and those who disliked feudalism and obscurantism into lukewarm patriots. In such a confused medley of right and wrong, it was hardly possible for any statesman to act in a way that will now be wholly approved. Men alive must choose their parts and posterity be wiser if it can.

The *ancien régime* is a convenient term used for the type of polity that prevailed all over the Continent in the eighteenth century – decayed clericalism and feudalism in the social structure, surmounted by monarchical despotism as the organ of government. Under this system there was no recognition either of democracy or of nationality. The partitions of Poland were but the logical outcome of a system which regarded subjects as personal property and kingdoms as landed estates. Wars of aggression were not then inspired by the chauvinism of races but by the dynastic ambitions of sovereigns. In England alone was it possible to appeal successfully to the national spirit in war time, because in England alone, before the French Revolution, did the Government normally make appeal to public opinion. On the Continent, public opinion was the monopoly of the literary opposition, the 'philosophers' who were the first to exploit its untried powers.

The philosophy of the eighteenth century, which produced the French Revolution, planned in advance the destruction of the *ancien régime*, and conceived in thought the idea of democracy. The Masonic Lodges of the Continent had, many years before 1789, familiarized the *illuminés* with the fateful words that gave hope of new life to a dead society: '*Liberté, égalité, fraternité*'. Rousseau preached patriotism on the model of the ancient Republics, but not patriotism coextensive with the race. Democracy, as the philosophers conceived it, was to represent not the race or the nation, but the abstract multitude. The political man of their imagining was as bloodless and blameless, and unfortunately as non-existent, as the 'economic man' of another branch of science. They proclaimed the rights, not of Frenchmen, but of man. This cosmopolitan language – so different from the 'rights of Englishmen' and the 'privileges of Parliament' claimed by our own patriots in their struggle against the Stuart kings – made the new doctrine formidable as propaganda, able to glide, as swift as meditation, over all the frontiers of Europe. Its principles attracted, because they claimed to be universal.

How was it, then, that this cosmopolitan creed became in practice the great engine of nationalism, the creator of racial movements that did not exist in the soporific atmosphere of the *ancien régime*? If Voltaire and Rousseau had ever met a 'chauvinist',

Voltaire would have mocked and Rousseau denounced so strange a monster! Yet the doctrines of these two men, when put into practice after their deaths, let loose, along with the anti-clericalism and democracy which they had respectively taught, the forces of a racial chauvinism which they had never even envisaged. For when once an appeal was made, in consonance with the principles of the French Revolution, to the 'general will' of the population in any district of Europe, it appeared that the 'general will' was not purely rational and philanthropic as the philosophers had supposed, but racial, nationalist, potentially chauvinistic.

The first country in which this unexpected phenomenon occurred was France herself. The events of 1789–93 realized the dreams of the philosophers in tumbling down the old, moth-eaten system of feudal rights that had outlived feudal duties, and in arousing the general will to consciousness. But when it was aroused the 'general will' was found to take on the form of patriotic enthusiasm. 'La France', 'La Patrie', became the watchwords of the new liberty, when she was called upon to defend herself in bitter earnest. The result was an outburst of energy in every town and village of France, new in the Continent of that epoch. Thus inspired, France for a while became 'la grande nation', able to trample at pleasure over Europe, athwart all the feudal States still uninspired by the 'general will' or the patriotic idea. She was checked on the margin of the sea, because in England also there was a nation to be appealed to whenever the mastery of the waves was at stake. In the spirit of Nelson, his captains and his sailors, the spirit of the French Revolution for the first time encountered something that was a match for itself. But France was only conquered on land when her outrages had aroused a national spirit in the populations of Germany, Russia, and Spain.[1]

The events in the French Revolution which most nearly concern the history of our island are those which explain how this national spirit was aroused in France, unchained upon Europe, and enlisted as the enemy of England. It is from this point of view that we must briefly examine the course of events in France.

In the first stage of the Revolution, accomplished in 1789, the despotic monarchy which had held France together for good and evil, for so many centuries vanished in the night. The Legislative

---

1. Our experiences in the late world war, in matters of propaganda, 'defeatism', the 'will-to-victory', etc., throw back a flood of light on the French Revolutionary and Napoleonic wars. For a long time the French were the only people who, by our modern standards, really cared about winning – on land.

power was transferred to elective assemblies, tremulously afraid of the mob of Paris, from whom the members had no effective protection. As to the Executive power, no one could say where it resided. Louis XVI still chose his own Ministers, but they were 'transient and embarrassed phantoms,' their powers and functions uncertain, and their relations to assembly and to people all in the air. Since the weak, well-meaning king was under the influence of his reactionary Austrian wife, Marie Antoinette, it could safely be prophesied that, in case of war or public danger, a further revolution would take place to decide in whose hands lay the executive power by which alone the State could be saved.

The propaganda of the equalitarian gospel, and its swift translation into fact in 1789, had been organized mainly by the professional and bourgeois classes of the towns, working upon the land-hunger and class consciousness of the peasant. The French middle classes were in that epoch more open to 'general ideas' than the similar class in England, and much less conservative, because they were jealous of the exclusive and useless privileges of the do-nothing nobles. Although in the Bastille summer, alike in town and village, the sacking and murdering had been done by peasants and *ouvriers*, aided by the mutiny of the sympathetic and unpaid army, it was the bourgeoisie who, as a result of these unauthorized proceedings, first secured the revolutionary power. They restored order through their own National Guard, hoisted the new tricolour flag as the symbol uniting 'patriots' of all shades, and hoped to be able to make good against the increasing enmity of the dispossessed aristocracy on the one side and the unsatisfied town workmen on the other. In the approaching struggle of classes, it was clear that the balance would be decided by the peasants. And the peasants were certain to support whatever party offered the best security for the preservation of the agrarian revolution of 1789. It was hopeless for the dispossessed nobles to look for aid to those who had seized and divided their inheritance.

The agrarian revolution, involving the destruction of the economic and social privileges, and much of the other property of the nobles, had been the work of the peasants themselves, incited by the various types of agitators. The acts of the Legislature had followed tardily and with hesitating steps the headlong course of events in the countryside. But the bourgeoisie could hold power only by acquiescing in the agrarian revolution, for it was the determination to secure and maintain it that first roused the majority of French people to national consciousness and political passion. The peasant was neither Republican nor Jacobin at heart, but he was for any party that would enable him to keep what he had just won. Only in certain districts of the north-west the Vendéens and Chouans were hostile to the new order, chiefly on account of religion.

The revolutionary legislators attempted to solve the religious question by the Civil Constitution of the Clergy. This famous enactment, without touching doctrine, 'broke the bonds of Rome' as effectually as Henry VIII, turned the Church into a part of the civil service of the new democratic State, and ordered the bishops and priests to be elected by the people. The 'Civil Constitution' was largely the work of the Jansenist party in the Church, who had suffered so much persecution in the past that they could no longer think clearly about the present and the future. The proposed ecclesiastical revolution was based on a miscalculation of the forces which made up religious life in France, and it caused half the evils of the time that followed. Hitherto the 'lower clergy' had been not unfavourable to the course of an equalitarian revolution which destroyed the privileges of the nobly born, from which they themselves suffered in their professional prospects. But when the Civil Constitution was presented to them, two thirds of the priesthood felt conscientiously bound to reject it. Then the Legislature committed the irreparable error of depriving and ere long persecuting the recusants. So began the feud between the religious and the revolutionary parties, destined to devastate the Latin world for generations to come. The dispossessed nobles who were biding their time on the other side of the frontier as *émigrés* at last found a popular party in France ready to make common cause with them. But even so they were in a minority, for the bulk of the peasants were more concerned for their new-gotten lands and social indemnities than for their threatened religion.

Such was the state of things in France when the *émigrés* first began to conspire with feudal Europe against their own country-men. By our modern ways of thinking, their conduct in calling in the foreigner stands heavily condemned. But they had been bred up in a world almost without patriotic tradition, which regarded a Church and an Order as units commanding allegiance more strongly than a nation. Indeed, their 'nation' was the *noblesse* of Europe, not the French peasants and bourgeoisie. The horror that their conduct caused in France surprised them, for it was, in fact, something new. France, in becoming democratic, had doubled her sense of nationhood. The peasant had become not indeed a Jacobin, but a patriot, ready to shed his blood for '*la belle France*' who had given him his field and freedom. These traitors would bring the Teuton into our plains to rivet our chains once more! Let their blood stain our furrows! The terrible words of the Marseillaise perpetuate for posterity the cruel passions of that moment when modern France was born.

The quarrel between revolutionary France and feudal Europe was due to provocations on both sides. The feudal rights of foreign princes in French territory had been treated with undiplomatic contempt by the Revolutionary legislators. In 1791 Prussia and Austria began to menace the rebel nation. The 'flight to Varennes' was an unsuccessful attempt of the French Royal family to escape across the frontier into the arms of these alien enemies. Probably, after that, the immediate deposition of Louis would have been in the interest of public security and ultimately of public order, if only people could have agreed whom to put in his place. A nation cannot live with an executive which it distrusts so much that it dare not allow it to act. But the bourgeoisie, with an anxious eye on the ragged hosts behind them, were afraid to initiate further change, and permitted France to stagger on for another year practically without any sovereign executive power. By a policy of mere postponement, they made the crash much worse when it came.

The only justification of this feeble treatment of the monarchy after the flight to Varennes would have been an attitude of complaisance towards foreign powers, to maintain peace at any price. But the Girondin orators, then in the ascendant, took up the somewhat hesitating challenge of Austria and Prussia, in the hope that war would precipitate a further revolution at home. They knew so little of themselves as to suppose that they would be able to ride the whirlwind for which they whistled. The Jacobins at this time argued in favour of peace.

When, in the middle of 1792, war at last broke out with Austria and Prussia, the old French army was in dissolution, and the French executive was alike unpatriotic and powerless. A vigorous push by the enemy could hardly have failed to reach Paris. But Brunswick's invading forces were insufficient and his purpose was feeble, while the language of his manifesto, threatening death to all revolutionaries, did more than fifty new constitutions could have done to create the French nation. Nevertheless, the unarmed and headless State was for a few weeks in appalling danger. The Girondins proved helpless to master the crisis they had done so much to provoke, and made way for men more forcible and more wicked. The Jacobins, thrusting aside the embarrassed bourgeoisie, appealed to the peasants and workmen to save the country, which they identified with the common people. The mob of Paris stormed the Tuileries, massacred the King's Swiss Guard, and so over-threw the monarchy on 10 August 1792.

With Brunswick advancing on the city, there was no time for remaking the Constitution. The executive power was frankly usurped by a set of vigorous and bloody ruffians whose boast it was to rise 'to the height of the circumstances'. Dumouriez meanwhile held the remnant of the dissolving army together, and with the help of the weather checked the Austro-Prussian advance at Valmy. The September massacres of men and women in the Paris prisons signalized the beginning of the Terror, and were the prelude to the erection of a new portent – the guillotine. The tyranny of a faction reached the highest pitch of atrocity at the same moment that the pulse of a new-born patriotism roused the ardour of Frenchmen to defend their country against the invading hosts.

Hitherto Pitt had stood apart from the movement of feudal Europe to chastise rebel France. He had no ears for Burke's crusading outcries. As late as February 1792, he prophesied fifteen years of peace, and proved his sincerity by forthwith reducing our naval and military forces. Even the events of August and September did not make him less pacific, but they alienated all his sympathies from France. Brunswick's invasion and the resultant events in Paris divided Englishmen more bitterly than ever. The Government and the Portland Whigs looked eagerly to see France conquered and the Revolution put down by Brunswick; while Fox spoke of his advance as an 'invasion of barbarians', and rejoiced at Valmy as over the defeat of Xerxes. The September massacres seemed to most Englishmen to decide the merits of the dispute.

In the autumn and winter of 1792 things began to move rapidly towards war between France and England, partly on account of the mutual hatred of Tory and Jacobin, partly because of the French occupation of the Netherlands. The French armies made an offensive return into the territory of the late invaders, where large classes welcomed the tricolour. The Jacobins, finding that Danton's *audace* had saved them on the frontier, forgot their recent peace principles, appealed to the fast rising chauvinism of France, and proclaimed in general terms that they would help all peoples struggling to be free. The Alpine province of Savoy was annexed, and much of the Rhine country was overrun and revolutionized. The battle of Jemappes gave to the French armies the whole of the Austrian Netherlands, which corresponded to modern Belgium. Holland was threatened, and the navigation of the Scheldt through her territory declared open in accordance with the law of nature, all treaties notwithstanding. It was Jemappes rather than Valmy that began the new era for Europe, and by turning the heads of the Jacobins rendered war between England and France inevitable.

Pitt was determined to maintain, by force if necessary, the 'public law of Europe' against this new spirit of armed propaganda, that decreed its will and spurned negotiation. Nor can this determination be blamed. But it is perhaps unfortunate that, by refusing to recognize the French Republic and to treat with her officially, he gave the appearance at the critical moment of making no serious effort to obtain his ends without war, although it is scarcely possible that he could even so have succeeded.

The tragedy of the case was that in defence of the 'public law of Europe' he became the ally and paymaster of the powers who were engaged in overthrowing the 'public law' by the Second and Third Partitions of Poland. But whereas the fate of Poland did not threaten our maritime power, Pitt thought it his first duty to prevent the Netherland ports from falling under the control of the most powerful country in Europe. Such has been the policy of England in self-defence from the time of Elizabeth to our own. The French showed no serious desire to meet us on the question. Their excuse is that we refused to recognize their Republican government. To revolutionary France, in her moment of demoniac exaltation, all who were not with her were against her. And our Government was very clearly not with her. If, from 1789 on, we had adopted Fox's policy of warm though discriminating friendship to the French Revolution, if we had put our active veto on the first Prussian and Austrian attack on France, the excesses of Jacobinism might conceivably have been avoided, and England and France might conceivably have remained friends. But all that is the merest speculation. The existing structure of English society and the main stream of English opinion rendered any such alliance impossible. If Pitt had attempted to hold such a course, King, Parliament, and country would have thrown him over.

In January 1793 nothing could any longer have averted catastrophe, in the prevailing mood of the two peoples. The English were thirsting for the blood of the 'French cannibals', and the execution of Louis XVI was meant as a challenge to England and to all the non-revolutionary world. The French did not want peace. They preferred the stormy eloquence of Danton: 'The coalesced kings threaten us; we hurl at their feet, as gage of battle, the head of a King.'

CHAPTER 5

THE 'metaphysical war', as Lord Lansdowne called it, the war between the ideas of Rousseau and the ideas of Burke, had now drawn Great Britain into the field. Pitt, indeed, held the old-fashioned and official view that it was merely another of that long series of wars waged by his father before him, by Marlborough and by William III, to 'curb the ambition of France', and 'maintain the public law of Europe'. And since France this time was beginning in the state of bankruptcy which had usually marked the unsuccessful close of her wars, Pitt told his friends that the conflict would be over 'in one or two campaigns'.

England, however, was no longer fighting a Government, but a nation. 'The State' was no longer Louis XIV, but many millions of Frenchmen. Mere governments cannot wage war in a condition of bankruptcy, but nations sometimes can. It was a common saying among the ragged and unpaid troops of the Republic, that 'with bread and iron we can get to China.' And indeed, as Burke foresaw, if France were not quickly put down, her spirit would enable her to overrun all the mere governments of Europe. But no one foresaw that wherever her armies carried the new faith, the ideas that had made her a nation would in time make a nation out of every one of the buried races on the Continent – a process which we have seen nearly completed by the wars and revolutions of our own day. If the new France were given the run of Europe for a few years, she would plant the seeds of democracy and nationalism so widely that no subsequent return to the *ancien régime* would be either complete or permanent.

That is what actually happened. But it might all have taken a different turn at the beginning. France was in such chaos when the war began that, in August 1792 and again in August 1793, a spirited advance on Paris might have crushed those demonic energies before their latent power had been made known. In that case democracy and nationalism, neither of which had as yet any status in Europe, might have been suppressed for long years to come.

In 1815 it was too late to suppress them. By then, no capture of Paris, no restoration of the Bourbons, would overturn the new social order and the new administrative system in France. And by 1815, Italy and Germany, including the Prussia of Stein and Gneisenau, had undergone changes and experiences so profound that nationalism and democracy had both taken root as ideas in the European consciousness.

Pitt, as War Minister, had not the genius to compel a number of selfish, quarrelsome, and inefficient allies to capture Paris in 1793. But he had other qualities instead. He taught England to hold her head high when, contrary to his expectation, she became involved in terrible and protracted dangers. And he was capable of choosing the right men to organize those victories at sea which gave to our race and Empire the opportunity to expand in peace and safety for a hundred years.

The struggle with the French Republic from 1793 to 1801 was continuously maintained by Britain alone among the allies. It may be conveniently divided into four periods, each distinct in character.

Period I. *The First Coalition against France, 1793–5* (Britain, Prussia, Austria, Spain, Piedmont). In this period there were no great military or naval achievements on either side. Howe's victory of the First of June, easily rather than splendidly, vindicated the old superiority of England at sea. On land the selfishness or incapacity of every one of the allies gave France immunity while she was struggling out of chaos, and gave Carnot time to improvise her new armies in the autumn of 1793. They had still to wait for discipline and great leadership, but their numbers and their zeal sufficed to defend the Republic from the paltry and spasmodic efforts of the Duke of York and the German and Spanish generals. Pitt gave Prussia subsidies to fight France, which she used for the more agreeable purpose of slaughtering the Poles and dividing up their country with Russia. Meanwhile half the British Army was sent across the ocean to rot away from fever, fighting the Negroes of the West Indian Islands. In the spring of 1795 the First Coalition broke up, after its armies had been chased out of Flanders and Holland, and the Dutch fleet had been captured by the French Hussars riding over the ice. We recouped ourselves in the autumn by taking from the Dutch the Cape of Good Hope and Ceylon.

Prussia retired from the war for ten years to digest her portion of Poland. That great preoccupation in the East, which affected Russia even more, and Austria only a little less than Prussia, had saved the French Revolution from overthrow by the three despotisms. Spain also made peace with France in July 1795. Large parties in Holland, as well as Belgium, received the French as friends. England and Austria were left alone against France.

Period II. *Interval between the Coalitions, 1796–8*. Next comes an era of gigantic achievements, of Bonaparte in Italy and Nelson at the Nile, each giving to the national spirit the leadership of genius, and opening out new pathways in history. The French conquest of Italy and the first overthrow of the *ancien régime* throughout that peninsula was much more than a military episode. But its more restricted and immediate effect was to compel Austria to make peace, and to leave Britain alone in the struggle, while France was helped by the fleets of Spain and Holland. In 1797–8, with heavy taxation, distress, and discouragement in England, with the naval mutiny at the Nore, the rebellion in Ireland, the desertion of our allies, the enforced abandonment of the Mediterranean by our fleets, and the star of Bonaparte rising, the situation was gloomy enough to bring out Pitt's higher qualities of stubborn will and inflexible courage. He had his reward in the sudden flowering of Nelson's genius and the dawn of the heroic age of British sea warfare. Jervis and Nelson under him defeated the Spaniards at St Vincent, while Duncan destroyed the fighting power of the Dutch fleet at Camperdown. The battle of the Nile, which gave a new tradition to the Navy, re-established our hold on the waters and islands of the Mediterranean, locked up Bonaparte in Egypt, and encouraged the timid princes of Europe to form the Second Coalition.

Period III. *The Second Coalition, 1799–1800.* This new league, headed by England, Austria, and Russia, had rapid success owing to the absence of Bonaparte in Egypt. The Russian general, Suwarow, drove the French out of North Italy, Nelson aiding from the south with the counter-revolution at Naples. Suwarow's further advance was checked by Masséna in the Swiss Alps. Yet things did not look well for France, because she was being ruined internally by the Government of the Directorate, feebly violent and without any wider outlook than that of a political faction. But in the autumn Bonaparte slipped back through the British cruisers. He accomplished his *coup d'état* of Brumaire, was hailed as Dictator of France under the title of First Consul, revived the national energy, and next year reconquered Italy at Marengo. Russia had already deserted us. The Second Coalition of governments without peoples behind them broke up, leaving England once more alone.

Period IV. *The episode of the Armed Neutrality, December 1800– April 1801.* This short-lived League of Prussia, Sweden, Denmark, and Russia against the maritime supremacy of England was caused partly by the personal whim of the Tsar Paul, partly by two feelings then prevalent in the Courts of Europe, fear of France and jealousy of English naval power, which in those days was none too gently used. The Armed Neutrality was broken up by Nelson's capture of the Danish fleet under the guns of the Copenhagen forts, and by the assassination of the Tsar Paul by palace conspirators.

The Treaty of Amiens, that ended the war between France and England, left France supreme in Western Europe, and England on the oceans of the world.

The foregoing brief summary of the four phases or periods of the war with the French Republic will enable the reader to follow a more detailed account of some aspects of each of these periods in a decade of confused and ubiquitous warfare.

Period I. *Some aspects of the War of the First Coalition, 1793–5* (see p. 94, above).

In the summer of 1793 the French Army, in spite of its easy successes of the previous winter, was reeling to dissolution. Its old officers, nobles without exception, had nearly all disappeared, and discipline had been destroyed by Jacobin mismanagement, violence, and intrigue.[1] On the home front, the nation was in the grip of civil war and chaos. The Revolution was saved by the indecision of the allies, who pottered round fortresses when they should have made a combined march on Paris. Prussia preferred to conquer Poland with troops that might have been conquering France. And so, while Robespierre primly presided over the grotesque and bloody pageant of the Terror, Carnot, called to office as War Minister by the Terrorists who loved him not but needed him, had time to construct the modern French Army. He is known to his grateful countrymen as 'the organizer of victory'. 'The Terror,' says the great French historian Sorel, 'contributed nothing to his victories.'

Carnot's problem was to substitute for the old army based on the caste divisions of the *ancien régime* an army based on the equalitarian enthusiasm of the Revolution and the 'career open to talents'. Carnot's army was the rough sketch of the army of Napoleon, the army of Joffre and of Foch. He could not indeed, in the confused days of the Terror, do more than construct a very imperfect machine just able to conquer the inert Austrian and

1. The same spirit had wrought more irreparable havoc with the fine traditions of the French Navy. Equalitarianism on board ship is proverbially dangerous. A corps of trained gunners was dissolved because it was held to be contrary to equality that one set of men should have a monopoly of firing the guns of the Republic at sea! And the navy never got its Carnot, still less its Bonaparte.

British forces opposed to it. Its defect was want of drill, discipline, and science. Its merits were, first the energy of its new officers, inexperienced in war, but drawn from the best blood of the bourgeois and professional classes; before the Revolution they had been unable to obtain military commissions, but a marvellous career was now opening to them. Secondly, the numbers and zeal of the peasant soldiers, sworn to defend their new-won rights against the hated *émigrés*; they flocked to volunteer, or willingly submitted themselves to the Jacobin conscription. Of all the armies of Europe, the French alone embodied the national spirit, in spite of the horrible character of the Terrorist government and the blood feuds with which the body politic was torn.[1]

The French army, a zealous mob, officered by able civilians, could not be led to battle in the difficult formation of the long close-order line, in which the well-drilled professionals of the wars of Marlborough and Frederick the Great had manoeuvred. A new formation was improvised to suit raw material. The line was abandoned for the massed column, with the best men in the van and on the flanks, and the less trustworthy in the centre to make the weight of impact. The path of the column was prepared for it by the fire of batteries brought boldly to the front, and by a thick cloud of skirmishers (*francs-tireurs*), consisting of the most energetic officers and men, who occupied any farm or point of strategic vantage, shot down the enemy's gunners, and disordered his ranks. Last of all, the head of the column would appear through the smoke, the officers running in front with their cocked hats raised on their swords, officers and men together howling the Marseillaise like so many demons. At that psychological moment the 'myrmidons of the Princes', instead of coolly concentrating the fire of their long line on the head of the column, generally turned and ran away. That was how France conquered Europe.

The revival of the column, recalling the infantry formation of the seventeenth century, was technically retrograde, but it gained such prestige from the French victories that it soon supplanted the better formation of the line in all armies save the British. Our soldiers, who practically disappeared from the battlefields of Europe between 1795 and 1806, clung to the line tactics and the severe drill necessary for their successful employment; and so it came about that when we returned to the front at Maida and the

1. In 1793 the brief occupation of Toulon by the British fleet in league with French Royalists and Moderates only served to identify the Jacobin cause with that of the nation, and to elicit the genius of Bonaparte, the young captain of artillery.

Peninsula, the concentrated volley-firing of the 'thin red line' swept away the heads of the French columns.

But in 1793–4 the British line failed to establish its supremacy over its massed opponents, mainly from lack of leadership. The corruption and inefficiency which we have, in a previous chapter, noticed in all the official and institutional life of eighteenth-century England, were not wanting in the army, any more than in Parliament or the Municipalities, the Universities or the Church. Commands, high and low, went by favour and purchase, not by merit. True professional spirit and science were at their lowest ebb. In the Duke of York's army in Flanders, Colonel Wesley, a young man of twenty-five – afterwards better known as Arthur Wellesley, Duke of Wellington – saw with disgust his brother officers 'when wine was on the table, fling aside dispatches which arrived, to await such attention as they might be in a condition to give when they had finished the bottles'.[1]

A pair of monuments within a few hundred yards of each other at the very heart of the Empire, the Nelson and Duke of York columns, commemorate the greatness of our naval triumph and of our military failure under Pitt. Nelson up aloft keeps his watch for the enemy's fleet, over the roofs of the city whose prosperity he prolonged into new centuries, and whose influence he caused to extend over the uttermost parts of the earth. No fame more noble is anywhere in the world more fittingly symbolized. 'There is but one Nelson.' Yet, as his rival apparently, there stands on a neighbouring pillar the man whom the Jacobin armies drove headlong out of Flanders and Holland. No doubt the Duke of York got his tall monument because he was George III's son. What he really deserves is a bust in some gallery of the War Office because, when he was made Commander-in-Chief after his fiasco in the Netherlands, he helped Sir Ralph Abercromby, Sir John Moore, and others to reorganize a little and to improve a good deal, the army which he had led to defeat, and which Nelson's true rival was ere long to lead to victory.

In the summer of 1795, after our armies had been expelled from the Netherlands, a tragic mischance further dimmed our prestige

1. General Sir Robert Wilson in his Autobiography records that in this Flemish campaign cruel punishments for drunkenness were often ordered by officers who themselves had been guilty with impunity of the same offence, and had not even recovered from its effects. 'The halberds were regularly erected along the lines every morning,' for floggings, 'and the shrieks of the sufferers made a pandemonium from which the foreigner fled with terror and astonishment at the severity of our military rule.' In this particular form of cruelty our army held the bad eminence in Europe.

in Europe. The British fleet landed several thousand Frenchmen, many of them *émigrés* of noble family, on the Peninsula of Quiberon, with a view to encouraging a rebellion of Breton 'Chouans' against the Republic. The invaders were captured in sight of our ships, and 690 *émigrés* were subsequently massacred by order of the Paris authorities; the fall of Robespierre in 'Thermidor' the year before had been only the first step towards freeing France from methods of 'terror'.

Far the largest of our military operations in the war against the Republic was conducted in the West Indies. Although there were hardly any French troops in the islands, we lost in three years in that pestilential climate some 80,000 men, one-half dead and the rest unfitted for further service. A smaller loss spread over twice as many years afterwards sufficed us to wrench Spain and Portugal from the grasp of Napoleon.

The historian of the British Army who first brought to light the magnitude of this forgotten tragedy has severely blamed Pitt for the waste.[1] And certainly the best chance of obtaining an early conclusion of the war would have been to launch on Paris the troops we spent in the West Indies. But even this might have failed and the loss of the West Indies would in those days have been a fearful blow to our trade, and would have afforded the enemy bases for privateers to prey upon our commerce on the grand scale.

Pitt, for his part, never regarded England as a principal in the war on the Continent. He looked to our allies to carry on the invasion of France. He had taken for his model, not Marlborough, but his own father, Chatham, who had effectually succoured Frederick the Great with much money and a very few troops, while the British fleets and armies had harvested the French colonies in America. Indeed, they had left Chatham's son nothing but the gleanings. To our eyes, the West Indian islands for which he fought compare poorly to the Canada that his father won. But in 1793 imperial values were different from what they are now, and the sugar and coffee islands were then of the first order of commercial importance. Pitt, in proposing the income-tax of 1798, calculated that, of the incomes enjoyed in Great Britain, those derived from the West Indies very much surpassed those derived from Ireland and from the rest of the world outside the British Isles.

In the first two years of the war, before Spain and Holland by

---

1. 'They [the British Ministers] poured their troops into these pestilent islands, in the expectation that thereby they would destroy the power of France, only to discover, when it was too late, that they had practically destroyed the British army.' – Fortescue, iv. 385.

joining France made their colonies targets for our attack, there was nothing but the French West Indies for Pitt to take by way of war indemnity to the taxpayer. He was often thinking about that, while Burke was always thinking of putting down the French Revolution.

But, apart from all thought of gain, Pitt's attention was called to the West Indies by humanity and by the need of defending our existing interests. A social rising of Negro slaves in the French islands had been stirred up by the French Revolutionists' proclamation of freedom and race equality. The French planters repudiated their allegiance to the Negro-phil Republic at home, and applied to Great Britain to protect them from extirpation. The huge island of Haiti or San Domingo, part French, part Spanish, till then the wealthiest of the West Indian group, became the scene of unsurpassable horrors. Thence the revolt of the slaves spread to the other islands, French and English alike, not excluding Jamaica. The blacks, stirred up by the agents of the French Republic, threatened the whole white race in the Archipelago. It was not a situation that Pitt could have left entirely alone. We were indeed being punished for Parliament's refusal to stop the slave trade and mitigate the lot of the slaves in the British West Indies. If Wilberforce's advice had been taken earlier, the blacks would have been loyal to us instead of to the Jacobins. But whatever the cause of the fire, we had to put it out.

Want of medical provision and ignorance of tropical conditions caused our soldiers to die of fever by thousands, and when at last we were on the way to get the better of the situation, Spain in 1796 declared war against us and put her interest in San Domingo and other islands at the disposition of France. After many years, it all ended in the annexation by Britain of a few smaller French and Spanish islands, and the quelling of the servile revolt everywhere except in the largest area of dispute, Haiti, which remains a 'Black Republic' to this day.

Period II. *Some aspects of the War during the interval between the two Coalitions, 1796–8* (see pp. 94–5).

The governing condition of this period of the war is the desertion of Great Britain by her allies. Prussia, intent on Poland, slunk first out of the Western struggle which she had been the first to provoke. Then Spain made peace, and next year warlike alliance with France, in accordance with the fears and whims of Godoy, originally a handsome young gentleman serving in the ranks of the Royal Guards, who had become the Queen's paramour, and, therefore, the King's Minister. The Queen and he had at first adopted a policy of clericalism and reaction at home, coupled with war against the French Republic. But when the war with France proved unsuccessful and ere long became unpopular, they were not ashamed to change sides completely, and become allies of the infidel and revolutionary power. Such were the irresponsible creatures supplied by the *ancien régime* to rule States, and to defend them against the young vigour of the French Republic. Last of all, Austria, driven out of Italy and threatened through the passes of the Eastern Alps by Bonaparte, bought for herself peace and the territories of the murdered Venetian Republic, at the price of consent to the Rhine frontier for France. Meanwhile, the Swiss and the Dutch were in the French grip, not wholly against their own will, and not without some ultimate benefit to their own antiquated institutions.

In 1793 it had been France alone against Europe; in 1797 it was England.

How much was Pitt responsible for this diplomatic catastrophe? Its underlying cause was the moral collapse of the *ancien régime* all over the Continent, when brought into contact with the new France. But, when all is said, it argued diplomatic failure on the part of Britain's statesmen in relation to their allies. We had poured out gold like water for them in subsidies, with this result! Pitt's Foreign Minister was Lord Grenville, a man of unselfish patriotism, but without imagination, and devoid of sympathy with anyone outside the governing class of his own country. To foreigners, his manners and the style of his correspondence seemed repellent, and his ignorance of their affairs extreme. Indeed, neither Grenville nor Pitt had the qualities of a William III or a Marlborough, requisite to hold together a mob of decadent princes and selfish Courts, easily scared by the first shadow of defeat.

And so, when our armies had failed and our allies had deserted we came to the crisis of sea-power. What was it to be worth to us, with Western Europe united for our destruction under efficient leadership, and the rest of the world looking on as neutral? The limits of sea-power had been demonstrated in 1796, when Bonaparte had successfully invaded Italy from a base of supplies running along the Genoese Riviera under the guns of Nelson's ships.[1] Next year, as a result of the entry of Spain into the war against us, the Government decided to withdraw our fleet from the

1. It was the first time these two great men were in contact. Bonaparte erected a line of forts along the Riviera, which successfully defended his communications. Of course, most of our fleet in those parts had to attend to the French fleet in Toulon.

Mediterranean, which for nearly a year and a half remained a 'French lake'.

During this nadir of our fortunes and reputation occurred the naval mutinies at Spithead and the Nore. Spithead was a 'strike' of loyal men, who had no other means of getting their grievances redressed. It was successful, and it probably saved England from having to pay, at a later date, a higher price for her shameful neglect of the men on whom her safety depended. The mutiny at the Nore, on the other hand, which broke out after these concessions had been promised, was deeply resented by all loyal sailors and citizens. Such ill-conduct never recurred in the navy, after the reforms secured at Spithead had been put in force. The mutinies were a remarkable introduction to the heroic age of British seamanship. But officers and men, country and navy, having gone through it, understood each other better. Although there was thenceforth a marked improvement in the conditions of naval service, the treatment of the sailors remained throughout the war a disgrace to the humanity and to the gratitude of English public men.

While the mutinies were going on, Duncan, with two loyal ships kept the Dutch fleet in the Texel by a brilliant piece of bluff. When discipline had been restored, he captured nine out of the sixteen Dutchmen at Camperdown.

Pitt's courage never faltered throughout these terrible months, with the Mediterranean lost, Europe lost, and Ireland certain to be lost too, if a French army of any size could land on its shores.[1] He honestly tried to get peace with France in the negotiations of Lille, but when the war party, by the *coup d'état* of Fructidor, launched France decisively on the policy of endless war abroad, in order to maintain the despotism of an odious faction at home, he resolutely shouldered the burden he could no longer hope to lay down. His management of naval affairs is not open to the criticisms levelled at his military and diplomatic performance. He chose, as head of the Admiralty, Lord Spencer, who had come over to him with the Portland Whigs, and was as good for the Navy as Dundas, the Secretary of State for War, was bad for the Army. To Pitt and Spencer belongs the credit, shared with Nelson's professional chief, Admiral Jervis (Lord St Vincent), of choosing out one of the youngest flag-officers on the list for the epoch-making service of reconquering the Mediterranean Sea.

The decision to fly the flag there again, in the face of material odds, was peculiarly Pitt's own. Spencer and Lord St Vincent both

1. See next chapter.

had their doubts and no wonder. The Spanish fleet, though scotched at St Vincent, was still in being; the French fleet was in Toulon; and the ports of France, Spain, and most of Italy were closed against us. It was a bold stake, but desperate situations require hazardous remedies, as Marlborough knew when he marched on the Danube. That such a campaign was decreed and that Nelson was put in charge of it shows that in the crisis of our fate naval affairs were in strong hands.

When Nelson re-entered the Mediterranean in May 1798 Bonaparte was on the point of crossing the 'French Lake' to found a French Empire in the Levant and to dominate the East. He sailed for Egypt. Nelson, ignorant of his destination, hunted for him on the face of the hazy deep and missed him by a chance. He landed and conquered Lower Egypt. But his fleet was destroyed at the mouth of the Nile by that perfection of moral, intellectual, and professional qualities which we call the 'Nelson touch', a thing new in naval war. Bonaparte, locked up in Egypt was discredited. For want of sea communications, his attempt to conquer Turkey from Egypt failed, before no more serious opposition than Captain Sir Sidney Smith with a few British sailors and Turks on the top of the breach at Acre. The Princes of Europe who had been spellbound by the fascination of French success, dared to move again. The immediate consequence of the battle of the Nile was the Second Coalition, which, after a brief career of glory, soon went the way of the First, for it was made of the same stuff. The more lasting consequences of the Nile were British domination of the islands and waters of the Mediterranean and renewed influence along its shores, and, in the world as a whole, a superiority both material and moral over the enemy fleets which enabled us to survive the Napoleonic system in Europe, and to enjoy afterwards a hundred years of safety.

Period III. *Some aspects of the War of the Second Coalition, 1799–1800* (see p. 95, above).

The war had now fully acquired the character which it retained until 1812, of a series of spasmodic and ill-coordinated efforts to prevent the domination and exploitation of the European world by France. Ever since 1794 France could have had peace and safety if she had been content to remain within her own borders, but the temptation to embark upon wars of conquest was too strong. All along her eastern frontier, from the Netherlands to Italy, lay a series of small and un-warlike States, inhabited by populations discontented with their own political and social institutions, and looking towards France of the Revolution with fear and hope mingled in about equal proportions. The strong military States, less influenced by the revolutionary philosophers, lay far away in the East, and even they were incapable of sustained effort to protect conservative interests in the West. In the Second Coalition, Russia, after a brilliant beginning, showed herself as unreliable as Prussia in the First. England alone being in the true sense a nation, could alone be relied on.

Nor had even England the smallest intention of sending great armies to the Continent, or incurring any serious drain on her man-power. Her island position made it easy for her to keep out of the Continent for years together,[1] and yet remain in a state of war, perpetually offering alliance and money to any power who would try another fall with France. These conditions prolonged the struggle for twenty years, until the insatiable ambition of France had raised up 'nations' in Germany, Spain, and Russia, to suppress, not indeed the French Revolution, but the French war-party.

The French system of conquest was predatory and selfish in intention, but in effect it was often progressive and beneficent. The Governments between Robespierre and Napoleon refused to make peace, because they dared not disband their soldiers and face bankruptcy and unpopularity at home. They maintained the armies at free quarters on foreign soil, and levied systematic contributions on the wealthier classes of the conquered lands, in order to keep alive from month to month the sick finance of France, which Pitt perpetually expected to see expire. Such considerations largely dictated the foreign policy of the French Government in relation to Holland, the Rhine country, and, above all, Italy.

But there was another aspect to this system of predatory warfare on the part of the French. In the countries which they entered in order to rob, they presented themselves as enemies of the *ancien régime*, appealing to the forces of progress. They destroyed feudalism and clerical privilege and summoned the professional and middle class to take its proper share in the leadership of the community. Bonaparte, himself of Italian origin, formed Italian Republics, contrary to the original design of the French home authorities, who had intended to plunder Italy and barter her back to Austria in return for the Rhine frontier. Their masterful new

1. Between 1795 and 1806 (Maida), the only British military expeditions in Continental Europe were an unsuccessful landing under the Duke of York in Holland in 1799 and a landing in North Germany in 1805 that did nothing at all, as Prussia refused to cooperate.

servant developed a policy of his own, of which the effect was to evoke the spirit of the *risorgimento*, at once Liberal and National-ist, which in two generations placed a united Italy among the free nations.

In the course of these first political experiments of his in Italy, Bonaparte noticed that the common people were strongly averse to anything approaching that persecution of the priesthood which had become part of the stock-in-trade of the Revolution. He saw that the State could shake itself free of clericalism without there-fore oppressing the Catholic cult. On this and other points he con-ceived, from the lessons of his Italian experience, the idea of reconciling the great reforms of the Revolution with the permanent elements of the old life. This reconciliation was to prove the firmest basis of his future rule in France and in Europe.

The political aspect of French conquest condemned England, in her defence of Europe, to fight as the champion of the *ancien régime*, contrary to her main line of policy in the following century, and contrary even to her old position as the great anti-Papal power. The Pope and the leaders of the Catholic reaction became the clients abroad of the Protestant Toryism that would not allow Catholics to sit in the British Parliament. When Bonaparte was away in Egypt, the Russian general Suwarow's victories restored the *ancien régime* in Italy for a year, while Nelson, at Naples, under Lady Hamilton's influence, made England the abettor of some of the worst acts of those barbarous reactionary forces of which, in the days of Palmerston and Gladstone, she became the powerful enemy.

The Terror, under Robespierre, had killed off many of the most promising leaders of the French Republic, and had frightened generous youth from politics to the less dangerous trade of war. The domestic government of the Directorate was the incapable tyranny of a faction which offered its subjects no compensations, material or moral, for their servitude. Now that it had lost Italy, Frenchmen began to look out for a more attractive and able des-potism.

In the autumn of 1799, Bonaparte, leaving his army marooned in Egypt, stole back to France. She had learnt in his absence how much she had need of him. At the final revolutionary *journée* of Brumaire, the 'foggy month' of the Republican Calendar, itself now dated,[1] the Directorate fell at his touch like over-ripe fruit. He became nominally First Consul, really perpetual dictator,

1. At the end of 1805 the Emperor Napoleon restored the Gregorian Calendar.

acclaimed by the great majority of Frenchmen who now only desired to be protected in the quiet enjoyment of what the Revolution had won for them. They asked for order, security, and sound administration. For this they had applied to the right man, and, as they felt his master hand, they gave themselves to him in an ecstasy of self-surrender.

> To weld the nation in a name of dread,
> And scatter carrion-flies off wounds unhealed,
> The Necessitated came.

Italy was reconquered in a few weeks and the prestige of the new government established by the First Consul's sensational passage of the Alps over the Great St Bernard, and the brief campaign of Marengo. The Italian triumph, being followed by Moreau's victory of Hohenlinden in the snowy Bavarian forest, again drove Austria out of the war at the Treaty of Lunéville. Russia had already fallen off. The Second Coalition had collapsed. Western Europe was acknowledged as French, and Britain stood alone once more.

But for some years to come peace had for Bonaparte victories yet more renowned than war. During the five years between Hohenlinden and Austerlitz, France carried out no military operations of the first order. But in those years she received from her master new institutions, to replace those of the *ancien régime* which the Revolution had destroyed, but for which the Jacobins and the Directorate had found no better substitute than the lawless vigour of self-appointed Committees. The Revolution now crystallized into law and order. French life is based today on the highly centralized Napoleonic system of local administration, of education, and of justice, and on the laws of his great Code. Even the Napoleonic settlement of Church and State survived until the twentieth century. Governments and parties might change in the nineteenth century – Bourbons, Orleanists, Second Empires, Republics, might come or go – but they all moved and had their being inside the framework of French life that the First Consul shaped, securing in a permanent and solid form the social benefits of the Revolution.

Bonaparte and the able Civil Service that he chose and inspired worked in those five years more creatively perhaps than any set of administrators had ever worked before. They set up the machinery of the first modern State. On the example of France, the centralized States of modern Europe, particularly the German, were afterwards modelled. Even England, with her freer life, at once more local and more personal, has been influenced by that first great engine of State efficiency.

Bonaparte seemed only to be giving France what she craved. But in his own thought he was preparing her to be his weapon of conquest. When he took her in hand, she was already the one self-conscious 'nation' on the Continent. He gave her the only modern administration in the world. Thus doubly formidable, how could she fail, under the leadership of a genius as great as Caesar's, to conquer the antiquated incompetence of Europe? How indeed, until Europe caught from her something of her new spirit and borrowed from her something of her new machinery? Till then, England would have to hold out as best she could. But England also was strong for self-defence in the monopoly of two new things – a fleet like Nelson's and the Industrial system.

Period IV. *Some aspects of the Armed Neutrality, December 1800–April 1801* (see pp. 95–6 above).

When, owing to the Irish affair, Addington replaced Pitt in February 1801, the prospect was dark indeed. Bonaparte, with Western Europe united under him, with Austria retired from the contest, had drawn the powers of the North-East into a combination against England. Russia headed Denmark, Sweden, and Prussia in a League of 'Armed Neutrality'.

The Armed Neutrality was a revival of its predecessor of twenty years before. Its main object was to contest, by arms if necessary, the right of British ships to search neutrals for contraband. But there were further motives underlying the new combination. The half-crazy Tsar Paul was drawn into the scheme by his admiration for Bonaparte, his fury against his late allies, his excited visions of Muscovite armies invading India and striking down the power of England; Prussia by her designs on Hanover; Denmark by her fear of Russia; everyone by a fascinated dread of France and her young master.

The strangling of the Tsar Paul by the officers of his barbarian army, tired of holding their lives and properties at the mercy of a madman, might possibly have dissolved the League for a time, even without Nelson's help. But the destruction of the Danish fleet at Copenhagen, before the news of the outlandish murder had reached Denmark, produced a moral effect more profound and lasting than the death of any Tsar.

Technically and humanly, Copenhagen was the finest of Nelson's campaigns. On this occasion he had many unusual difficulties to overcome: the stubborn resistance of a northern and a seafaring race; an enemy fleet fed throughout the action from the capital, and aided by the guns of its forts; shoals which entrapped three of the attacking ships, and would have ensured disaster if retreat had been attempted. And all through he had to deal with Sir Hyde Parker as his Commanding Officer, sulky and secretive when the campaign opened, and always timid, except when under the direct personal magnetism of his famous subordinate. Over all these dangers Nelson triumphed by professional science and instinct, by courage that accepted great risks open-eyed, by temper and wisdom both in personal dealings with Parker and in diplomatic dealings with the Danes after the battle was won.

If Nelson had been in supreme command, he would have masked Copenhagen instead of attacking it, and would have gone straight up the Baltic to Reval to destroy the Russian ships there, and so strike at the political mainspring of the League. On the other hand, Parker, if left to himself, would have remained in the Kattegat and would never have entered the Baltic at all, in face of the fleets of Denmark, Russia, and Sweden. The decision to attack Copenhagen was a compromise between the two men, though Nelson planned and executed every detail. If the Tsar Paul had lived, the overruling of Nelson by Parker in the matter of Reval might have cost England dear.

When Nelson was dragging Parker into the Baltic 'to face the odds and brave the fates', he wrote to him on 24 March:

Here you are, with almost the safety, certainly with the honour of England more entrusted to you than ever yet fell to the lot of any British Officer. On your decision depends whether our country shall be degraded in the eyes of Europe, or whether she shall rear her head higher than ever.

Early that morning, all unknown to the two Admirals, the Tsar Paul had been murdered, and thereby perhaps the immediate safety of England had been secured. But Nelson's words remained true. It was owing not to the death of Paul, but to Nelson's spirit and to Nelson's action that, at the cost of nearly a thousand seamen killed and wounded, England 'reared her head higher than ever'. It was because England now 'reared her head high' at sea that she was able to survive the accumulated perils of the Napoleonic period. Copenhagen, indeed, together with the Nile and Trafalgar, gave a triple sanction to the international creed of British naval invincibility, which carried us through the nineteenth century with security unchallenged. When, in our own day, England was again in danger, these memories, sunk deep into the world's consciousness, did much to paralyse German naval initiative, and to foster, against the newer German *réclame*, the old belief that our hold on the sea could never be loosened. Nelson's victories have proved, both in space and in time, more far-reaching than those of Napoleon himself.[1]

Nearly a year passed after Copenhagen before Addington was able to bring to an end the negotiations for the highly unsatisfactory Treaty of Amiens, in which the First Consul scored most of the points. The only important event of that last year of war was the reduction of Bonaparte's old army, marooned in Egypt. The spirited operations on the shore near Alexandria cost us the fine old soldier, Sir Ralph Abercromby, killed in the hour of victory. The conduct of the British troops and their terrible volley-firing surprised the French. Such was the outcome of recent reforms and of a spirit in the Army that had not been noticeable in Flanders or the West Indies. Abercromby's last order, as he was being carried dying off the field, breathed that new spirit and is worthy to be remembered with Sir Philip Sidney's refusal of the cup of water: 'What is it you are placing under my head?' he asked. 'Only a soldier's blanket,' was the reply. 'Only a soldier's blanket! A soldier's blanket is of great consequence; you must send me the name of the soldier, that it may be returned to him.'

Having seen the French out of Egypt we had no wish to stay

1. The following is the first-hand evidence for the most famous of all Nelson stories. It is from the narrative of General Stewart, on board Nelson's flagship, the *Elephant*, at Copenhagen:

'When the signal No. 39 was made [by Sir Hyde Parker] the Signal Lieutenant reported it to Lord Nelson. He continued his walk and did not appear to take notice of it. The lieutenant meeting his lordship at the next turn asked "whether he should repeat it"? Lord Nelson answered "No, acknowledge it!" [viz. acknowledge it to Parker. To "repeat" it would be to hand it on as an order to the ships under Nelson's command]. On the officer returning to the poop, his lordship called after him: "Is No. 16 [for Close Action] still hoisted?" The lieutenant answering in the affirmative, Lord Nelson said: "Mind you keep it so." He now walked the deck considerably agitated, which was always known by his moving the stump of his right arm. After a turn or two, he said to me, in a quick manner: "Do you know what's shown on board the Commander-in-Chief? No. 39!" On asking him what that meant, he answered: "Why, to leave off action!" "Leave off action!" he repeated, and then added, with a shrug, "Now damn me if I do!" He also observed, I believe to Captain Foley, "You know, Foley, I have only one eye – I have a right to be blind sometimes." And then, with an archness peculiar to his character, putting the glass to his blind eye, he exclaimed: "I really do not see the signal."

'This remarkable signal was, therefore, only acknowledged on board the *Elephant*, not repeated.'

there ourselves. We had already one Eastern Empire in India, and the route to it in those days lay, not by the Suez Canal still undug, but by six months' sail round the Cape of Good Hope. The Cape, though given back to Holland at the Treaty of Amiens, was taken again for good in 1806, largely to secure the route to India from the attacks of France and her vassals.[1]

CHAPTER 6

THROUGHOUT the war with the French Republic, England had been hampered by her 'broken arm'.

Few countries of the *ancien régime* had been more actively misgoverned than Ireland. In the seventeenth century the natural leaders of the Catholic Celts had been destroyed as a class, and their lands given to a garrison of alien landlords. The priests had stepped into the vacant place prepared for them by Protestant statesmanship, as leaders of the oppressed and friendless peasantry. In the latter half of the eighteenth century the fiercer parts of the Penal Laws against Catholics, unsuited to the spirit of a latitudinarian age, became obsolete and were repealed. But Protestant ascendancy remained unimpaired. The gates of political power were still closed on the Catholic, and the peasant tilled the soil to pay tithes to an alien Church, and rent to an alien squirearchy.

In such circumstances, it might have been expected that the Churches of the Protestant Minority would have been closely united at heart with each other, and with Great Britain. But such was not the case. The Presbyterians, the strongest body in Protestant Ulster, were, until 1780, excluded by the Test Act from political power and from all the privileges of the governing oligarchy. Meanwhile the whole body of the inhabitants of Ireland were treated as economic helots by the British Parliament. Irish industries, mainly Protestant, were crushed out by laws dictated by English commercial jealousy. Many thousands of Ulster Protestants had sought refuge in North America, and found there revenge on the country that had so ill repaid their services.

1. It is an interesting fact that 2,000 Indian sepoys were sent to Egypt to help Abercromby to fight the French there. They arrived just too late for the battle of Alexandria. This occurred seventy-seven years before the immense excitement caused by Lord Beaconsfield bringing 7,000 Indian troops as far as Malta for a possible Russian war.

The Saxon re-conquest under William III broke the spirit of the native Irish for three generations. During the Marlborough wars and the British rebellions of 1715 and 1745 the enemies of England could make nothing out of Ireland's apathetic despair. Only in the last quarter of the century did she begin to feel 'fire in her ashes'.

The national revolt originated among Protestants. It was they who first called on Irishmen, irrespective of creed, to unite against English commercial tyranny and against the political and religious despotism of the clique in Dublin Castle who ruled in the name of England. This movement, though popular among the fierce Presbyterians of the North, found its leader in the temperate and enlightened genius of Grattan. If liberal statesmanship from Westminster had met him half-way, the Irish problem might have been started on the road to solution before the Catholics had become disloyal, before the Orange Lodges had been founded, and before the fires of fanaticism had been kindled on both sides. Irish history from 1782 to 1801 is the history of England's first failure to know her appointed hour.

During the war of the American Revolution, 'England's difficulty had been Ireland's opportunity'. The defence of Ireland against France had been undertaken by an army of Volunteers, at first entirely Protestants, but enthusiastically supported by the Catholics. Under the leadership of Grattan, the Volunteers exacted from England the abolition of Ireland's commercial disabilities, and the nominal independence of her Parliament from English control. She thus secured free markets for her goods, but she did not in fact secure free self-government. For the oligarchy in Dublin Castle, nominated from Westminster, continued to govern the island and to manipulate the Dublin Parliament through its rotten boroughs. The patriots saw that only a Reform Bill could secure the independence even of Protestant Ireland. And the Catholic majority was still excluded from voting or sitting in the national Parliament.

Any time in the decade following 1782, a Reform Bill, Catholic Emancipation, and the payment of the Catholic priests by the Government would have diverted the whole history of Ireland into happier channels. The attitude of eighteenth-century latitudinarianism still prevailed.[1] The control exercised by the Catholic priest over the laity was comparatively lax and he had not yet taken to politics. Politically, the two creeds were divided only by

1. Wesley had not had much success with his mission in Ireland. But the Catholics had come in crowds to listen to him!

111

the fragile barrier of Catholic disabilities. The island was not yet cleft in two by Orangeism and Catholic disloyalty. The popular movement was towards Grattan's reconciliation of creeds and races in a common Irish patriotism. It was against this reconciliation that Dublin Castle plotted successfully, and Pitt, though he more nearly agreed with Grattan, allowed the plot to succeed. It proved impossible for the head of the Tory and Royalist party in England to carry out a policy of reform and emancipation in Ireland.

In 1793 a step was taken in the right direction, when the Irish Parliament repealed another batch of the Penal Laws and gave the electoral vote to the Catholics, who were still however prevented from sitting in Parliament. The concession was too small, and came too late, for the French Revolution was on the point of evoking fiercer passions and wilder hopes.

Yet the first effect of the heightening of passion by the events in France was not to set creed against creed. The 'United Irishmen', as their name implied, sought to combine all creeds. The Republicanism of their first leaders was a blend of new American and French with old Puritan ideals. Their hatred of England tended at least to Irish unity, which concessions in the spirit of Grattan might still have guided back into the paths of loyalty and peace.

At this stage, when all hung in the balance, occurred the decisive episode of Lord Fitzwilliam. That nobleman, one of the Portland Whigs who had recently rallied to Pitt's Government, held strongly Liberal views about Ireland. He was sent there as Viceroy without a clear previous understanding as to the policy he should pursue. If Pitt had been negligent, Fitzwilliam was rash. He began to clear out the 'Castle gang' from the Government posts which they monopolized, and expressed himself in favour of immediate Catholic Emancipation. This policy, however right it may have been, was not that of the home government. Fitzwilliam was recalled, and his recall was held by the Catholics and the United Irishmen to signify that the constitutional channel to reform was closed. Submission or rebellion were the alternatives offered.

For the next three years the drift to rebellion was gradual, through anarchy and agrarian crime. And before rebellion came to a head, the breach between the two creeds had been reopened. In parts of Ulster, where Protestants and Catholics tilled their farms side by side, mutual outrages began, and, in the absence of any controlling force, degenerated into a state of local warfare of a peculiarly horrible kind. It was now that the Orange Lodges were founded to combat the Catholic 'Defenders'. England could not send the troops to keep order – they were dying of fever in the West Indies – so Government was fain to employ as umpires the Protestant Yeomanry and Orangemen, who were parties to the quarrel. This shocking necessity favoured the policy of the 'Castle' and of those whose object it was to foster the religious strife on the principle of *divide et impera*. The Viceroy, Lord Cornwallis, who held enlightened views, wrote, in September 1798, 'Religious animosities increase, and, I am sorry to say, are encouraged by the foolish violence of all the principal persons who have been in the habit of governing this island.'

The French greatly added to the trouble. Their fleet, carrying Hoche and 15,000 soldiers, appeared in Bantry Bay, but failed to land. If they had landed, there was no force sufficient to prevent their conquest of the island.[1] It was the French promises, and the apparent likelihood of their fulfilment, that wedded the leaders of the United Irishmen, Wolfe Tone and Lord Edward Fitzgerald, to the fatal policy of waging a Republican war on the British Empire. They hoped by that means to unite the creeds, but in fact they divided them afresh by a blood-feud that revived the fast fading traditions of Cromwell and the Boyne.

The danger to the ungarrisoned island from French invasion rallied to Government all Protestants who were not serious in their hatred of the British connexion. Fear of French conquest inspired the panic-stricken cruelties of the Protestant Yeomanry, to whom was entrusted the task of disarming the Catholic peasants. The search for arms was conducted by flogging, torture, murder, and loot. Sir Ralph Abercromby, commanding the British forces in Ireland, officially denounced their cruelty and indiscipline. In this way the passively disloyal districts of the South were goaded into the Rebellion of 1798.

The 'ninety-eight' was a local religious rising led by priests. This character, and the murders and atrocities that stained it, rallied the last Presbyterian farmers from the cause of United Ireland to the 'Orange' tradition. The sentimental feud that still divides Ireland had come into being as the result of these events arousing from sleep old memories and instincts. The storming of the rebel camp at Vinegar Hill was the decisive action of the brief and irregular war.

1. In August–September 1798, after the Rebellion had been put down, a small force of about a thousand French landed, routed an immensely superior force of militia at the 'Castlebar races', and were at length reduced by forces ten times their number.

The prostration that followed the 'ninety-eight' offered one last opportunity to peacemakers. Pitt now applied himself to the main problems of Ireland, which he had so long neglected. His great design was a Parliamentary union of the two islands, accompanied by Catholic Emancipation (that is, the admission of Catholics to sit in Parliament), the commutation of tithes, and the payment of the Irish priests. It could scarcely have been a permanent solution of the Irish question, but it might have been the best way to repair provisionally the terrible mischief of the last half-dozen years. But what he actually accomplished, the destruction of the Irish Parliament without the smallest concession to the Catholics, left matters worse than before.

The Union was carried, partly by buying the borough-owners of the Dublin Parliament, partly by securing the acquiescence of the Catholics with the promise of their emancipation to follow. It never occurred to Pitt to find out in advance whether he would be in a position to redeem this pledge which his agents were allowed to make. He never consulted George III beforehand, or seriously tried to overcome his resistance when he found, too late, that his master was violently opposed to Catholic Emancipation. Pitt salved his own conscience by resigning in favour of his anti-Catholic friend, Addington. But then, in a fit of generosity at other people's expense, he took the fatal step of promising the half-mad King that he would never move the Catholic question again so long as the King lived. The age of chivalry was not dead. George's wishes mattered more than the wishes of Ireland, and his health more than the health of the whole Empire.

The net result of these transactions was that the Catholic body in Ireland regarded themselves as the victims of a fraud. The position in which they were left by the Union was without hope, because the British Parliament and people were more obstinately opposed to Catholic Emancipation than the Irish had been. George III had taken what was, in England, the popular line. The Tories, in the generation after Pitt's death, found in 'No-Popery' the best antidote to their own increasing unpopularity, and a fine election cry against Whigs and Radicals. So the Union, instead of being the road to Emancipation, put it off till the Greek Calends. It might yet be extorted, but it would not be conceded.

Pitt had also designed another measure which, at that epoch, would have done as much as Catholic Emancipation itself to remove Irish disloyalty. He had intended to give a Government grant to the priests. The bishops in those days were ready to accept the arrangement, and it would have established a relation between the priesthood and the Government which might have gone far to alter the trend of Irish affairs. But Pitt abandoned this part also of his plan. The Irish Catholic world found itself once more as completely isolated as it had been in the middle of the eighteenth century. Presbyterian sympathy had curdled into Orange hatred. Government promises had been broken. Nothing more was to be hoped from Protestants or from Englishmen. At the Union the Catholics were barred out of the new Constitution to shift for themselves. These conditions nursed into active life that peculiar blend of Irish Catholicism and Irish democracy, profoundly antagonistic to England, which remained for the next hundred years the governing fact of Irish politics. Yet its two great leaders in the nineteenth century – O'Connell and Parnell – were both men of a certain moderation, prepared to come to terms with England inside the bounds of the British Empire. It was not until the German War of our own day engendered passions and policies as heated as those bred by the War of the French Revolution that the militant Republicanism of Wolfe Tone and the United Irishmen was revived on an extensive scale.

While the First Consul, at the glowing furnace of his brain, was forging the framework of modern France, a few hundred Englishmen, out of their practical experience, were more slowly doing the like for modern India. One, indeed, of these Englishmen, Richard, Marquis Wellesley, elder brother of Arthur Wellesley, Duke of Wellington, had in him a touch of the Napoleonic that considerably quickened the pace.

As a consequence of Pitt's Indian legislation,[1] his two great Governors-General, Lords Cornwallis and Wellesley, had many advantages over their predecessor, Warren Hastings. He had been hampered by the Council in Calcutta. They held absolute authority in the Company's territories. Hastings had been dependent on the timid commercialism of the Directors at home, and on the whims of a Parliament only half responsible for India and therefore more concerned to criticize than to help. Cornwallis and Wellesley were strengthened by the firm and intelligent support of Pitt and Dundas, representing Parliament and overruling the Directors.

Cornwallis completed the internal work of Hastings, bringing order out of chaos, and fixing the taxation and administration of Bengal as the example for all provinces subsequently acquired. Under Cornwallis and his successors there grew up in British territory a sense, novel in India, of security from outside attack and

1. See pp. 63–4, above.

115

from the grosser forms of domestic oppression. In the epoch when this was all that we had to give, it was enough to make our rule welcome to people to whom the yet more seductive idea of self-government was unknown either in theory or experience. Western education and Western ideas had not yet begun to penetrate.

The unforeseen and unintended union, in a permanent political relation, of two distant and dissimilar branches of the human family, was becoming an accomplished fact. It was initiated by men who, unlike the Anglo-Indians of later times, were divided by six months' voyage from their mother country, had few home ties, got little home news, and who in many cases had not European wives and saw but little European society. Their sports were in the jungle rather than on the polo ground and the tennis-court. For daily interests and for human intercourse they were forced into relation with the Indians, and in the political conditions of that epoch there were many with whom they had to deal as equals. One famous British Resident at a native Court married the niece of the ruler to whom he was accredited. Doubtless there were inferior men like Jos Sedley, but the better type of Anglo-Indian in the first decades of the century studied India closely and to good purpose, because he was fixed there in isolation from his own country, and with nothing else to do.

Although the extension of the Pax Britannica throughout all Hindoostan was a work only completed shortly before the Mutiny, the decisive steps in the process of expansion were taken in the last years of Pitt's life. The device, occasionally adopted by Clive and Warren Hastings, of 'subsidiary treaties' with protected native States was turned by Wellesley into a permanent and universally applicable policy for securing the British position in India.

During Wellesley's Governor-Generalship the system of 'subsidiary treaties' was developed on these lines: – a ruler whom the British Government guaranteed against attack by his neighbours would make a money payment, and the English in return would raise, train, and command an equivalent number of sepoys to defend him, while he kept the internal administration of the State in his own hands. The leading instance of this system was Hyderabad, which still remains a 'native State'. Hyderabad was being ground to pieces between its war-like neighbours. On the south was Mysore, governed by the fanatical Moslem Sultan, Tippoo, while to the north and west lay the Hindoo chiefs of the Maratha confederacy.[1] The defeat of these two common enemies of Hyderabad

1. See maps, pp. 304–5, below.

and of Britain was the great work of Marquis Wellesley, which left England the paramount power in the Peninsula.

After the death of England's bitterest foe, 'Tippoo Sahib', sabre in hand, at the storming of his capital Seringapatam, the remnant of Mysore, stripped of its outlying territories, was given back to the original Hindoo dynasty, and is a 'native State' today.

Both Tippoo and the Maratha chiefs were lured to destruction by hopes of French aid. The arrival of Bonaparte in Egypt, confessedly as a half-way house to India, excited in the more ambitious of the Moslem and Hindoo warriors the expectation of driving the English into the sea. French officers drilled their armies in the European fashion, and helped them to obtain an efficient artillery. The Marathas ceased to rely on their natural strength, the swarms of mounted spearmen, apt in guerilla warfare, who had ridden ravaging over all India between the banks of the Indus and the fortifications of Calcutta and Madras. In this later epoch they put their trust in an army on the European model. Whether this change did most to increase or diminish their ultimate power of resistance to the British is a question which it is hard to determine. The new force was more formidable for the conquest of other native States, and could put up a much stouter resistance before being defeated by General Sir Arthur Wellesley at battles like Assaye. But it was hampered in its movements by artillery and by the requirements of regular troops, and when it was once overthrown and dispersed, could not be replaced as easily as the 'Maratha hordes' of old.[1] In spite of the European fashion of their armies, the Marathas were conquered. The strife between the warrior chiefs of their confederacy, like Holkar and Sindia, helped the Wellesley brothers in the difficult task of bringing Central India under British control with small forces, operating over immense tracts of territory before the days of the railway.

The great Governor-General had the impatience and the autocratic temper that often accompanies real genius not quite of the first order – an impatience that combined with his 'cross-bench' views to disable him, after his return to Europe in 1806, from

1. Sir Alfred Lyall, in condemning the change in Maratha and Sikh military methods, points out that if the Boers and Afghans, in their wars with the British Empire, had abandoned their native tactics, and had attempted to meet us with armies trained on the European model, their resistance would have been less protracted and formidable. How far these analogies are applicable to the cases of the Marathas and Sikhs I have not sufficient knowledge to determine. Authorities differ in opinion.

rendering public services worthy of his Indian achievements.[1] When, during his Governor-Generalship, the Directors used to protest against Wellesley's policy and the fresh wars in which it involved the Company, he would write home in his letters to Ministers of the 'pack of narrow-minded old women' in 'the most loathsome den of the India House'.

Pitt had supported his friend's forward policy, though not wholly without misgiving. But after Wellesley's return to Europe, which coincided with Pitt's death, there was a period of retrogression. Again, as in the years preceding his arrival in India, an attempt was made to limit the area and obligations of the subsidiary treaties. But whenever the cautious policy of the Directors was given a trial, experience soon proved it to be impossible. In a country where, to use Wellington's phrase, 'no such thing as a frontier really existed', we could not, with the best will in the world, obtain peace and security even for our own territories until we had brought every State in the Peninsula into a fixed relation to our power, acknowledged as paramount.

CHAPTER 7

THE Napoleonic war (1803–15) that followed the brief interval of the Peace of Amiens was for us a war waged in self-defence, to prevent the systematic subordination of Europe to a vigorous military despotism sworn to our destruction. A few months at the Foreign Office in 1806 and an attempt to treat with our adversary for peace made this clear even to Fox, who had been till then singularly blind to the real character of Bonaparte. But the Whigs were only enthusiastic for the war by fits and starts. The honour of beating Napoleon fell as clearly to the Tories as the honour of beating Louis XIV had fallen to the Whigs.

From 1793 to 1830 the Whigs were almost as powerless in Opposition as the Tories had been under the first two kings of the House of Hanover. They were not only in a miserable minority in Parliament, but in the country they were no longer at the head of any powerful popular movement. During the last years of the eighteenth century Fox and Grey had continued to protest against Pitt's coercion bills and the suppression of press and platform, and

1. Wellesley's best work, after his return to Europe, was his impartial administration of Ireland as Viceroy, 1821–8. He died in 1842, after having held office in Grey's Reform Bill Ministry.

to introduce motions for Reform, culminating in Charles Grey's plan for household suffrage, for which unpopular proposal they mustered ninety-one votes in the House of Commons, while in the Lords the Foxites could be counted on the fingers of two hands. These hundred gentlemen, who foregathered at the most fashionable club in London, were able to profess democracy in the days of its darkest disrepute, just because they themselves were so unquestionably aristocrats. Neither their constituents, when they had any, nor the world of parsons and squires, still less the middle class, could exert over them political or social pressure, or counteract the influence of Brooks's. They continued to regard omnipotent Toryism as unfashionable, and Pitt's new peerage as slightly vulgar.[1]

After nailing the flag of Reform to the mast, the Whigs proceeded to desert the ship. Grey's Reform motion was followed by his 'secession' from Parliament, in which he induced Fox to join. The motive was mingled indolence and despair. The denizens of Brooks's Club retired to their country homes to forget the ills of the world in the best of company, living and dead – Charles Fox, the Greek and Latin writers, and the English and Italian poets. Conscious that they had little support in the country and that that little was silenced by Pitt's gagging bills, they regarded their work in Parliament as useless. They failed to consider that, if liberty of speech had been put down everywhere else, it was all the more incumbent on them to make the voice of liberty heard in the only place where she was allowed to speak. The full reporting of Parliamentary debates in the newspapers, which had recently been established as a most valuable part of constitutional custom, had been left untouched by the Anti-Jacobin repression. But during several important years the Opposition, by absenting themselves from Parliament, failed to turn to account this one remaining check on governmental tyranny. It was during the 'secession' of the Whigs that Englishmen were kept in prison for years without trial, on the principle of the old French *lettres de cachet*. During the same period Pitt would, but for Wilberforce's personal remonstrance on behalf of the Dissenters, have seriously modified the Act of Toleration.[2] No printer dared to publish even the most moderate Reform pamphlet. And these years of blackest eclipse

1. Pitt was said to have introduced into our Constitution the anti aristocratic principle that 'everyone who had ten thousand a year ought to be a Peer'! The possession of a couple of rotten boroughs established an equally good claim.
2. See p. 67, above.

of our domestic liberties in England were the years of the Irish tragedy.[1]

With the opening of the new century, the Foxites crept back one by one to their places in Parliament. On Pitt's resignation, personal issues broke up the anti-Jacobin phalanx into a number of conflicting factions. The value of the Foxites rose, as possible allies among a number of mutually hostile Tory groups. There was some relaxation in the persecution of liberal opinion in the country. Pitt's successor, Addington, was too weak in Parliament to keep people in prison without trial. And Reform pamphlets were again occasionally to be seen on the bookstalls.

Nevertheless, the Reform movement as a serious issue had been suppressed for years to come. England had reached what Fox called 'the euthanasia of politics', entire apathy on domestic questions and acquiescence in the existing régime. This was perpetuated by the concentration of the national thought on the Napoleonic struggle.

At the end of the war with the French Republic, such was the desire for peace that the Treaty of Amiens, though highly advantageous to France, was greeted with enthusiasm in England, before its implications were understood. When the first official representative of Bonaparte arrived in London, his carriage was drawn through the streets by a crowd cheering for peace. Not only Fox but many who had kindled to Burke's alarms now swarmed over to France in the Dover packet, stared in good-natured wonder at the military pomps of Paris, and waited round corners to catch a glimpse of the First Consul. There was no race hatred of the French. The crusading wrath of 1793 had died out. The 'French cannibals' had fought surprisingly fair, and the war had left us no bitter memories. The English were ready to accept the new form of French government on equal terms.

But the First Consul soon made it clear that he had not come into the world to live on equal terms with anyone. By his reading of the Treaty of Amiens we were to be excluded from all further interference on the Continent, while he was to be at liberty to push on annexation after annexation in Italy, Switzerland, Holland, and to parcel out the lands beyond the Rhine among his obsequious vassals, the German princes. We on the other hand regarded the Treaty of Amiens as fixing the utmost limits of his power at the

1. Even during their secession the Foxite Whigs came up to Parliament to protest against the maladministration that brought on the 'ninety-eight', and against the Act of Union.

dangerously large latitude of the Netherlands and the Rhine. We had agreed to a settlement of Europe which we thought it our business to see observed, while he held that we had retired beaten from high politics, to console ourselves with the pursuits of a nation of shopkeepers. When Addington protested, Napoleon was merely contemptuous, for Englishmen had set foreigners the example of despising their own Prime Minister. With Pitt in office, there would have been little chance of avoiding war; with Addington there was none.

After one year, the peace of Amiens came to an end. We were bound, even at the price of war, to resist the absorption of Europe by Napoleon. But it was a point of dispute whether we were wise to make our protest by refusing to give up Malta to a neutral in accordance with the treaty we had signed, since we could with our sea-power have easily controlled the fate of the island in case of war breaking out. The quarrel, on the main causes of which we were in the right, was brought to a head by the First Consul on the issue of Malta in the spring of 1803. A carefully staged scene of the kind he loved, when he angrily interpellated the British Ambassador, Lord Whitworth, at Josephine's evening party, announced to the world that a struggle to the death was coming on between the lord of the land and the lords of the sea.

For the first two years of the war, Napoleon had no enemy but Britain. His Grand Army was for the time 'the Army of England', camped on the cliffs of Boulogne, ready to be shipped across the Channel. There had been no such fear in our island since the Armada. In tardy obedience to the popular voice, Addington was replaced by Pitt. But the ideal wish for a coalition of national defence was frustrated by George III, whose refusal to admit Fox prevented the Whigs and Grenvillites from joining the administration, in spite of Fox's generous entreaties to his friends to go in without him. The whole awful burden was thrown back upon Pitt, already sinking to the grave. The King's motives for refusing Fox were personal and narrow, yet it may be doubted whether in fact Pitt would have shared real power with anyone, or whether Dictatorship in war-time is best exercised by two Consuls. Would Fox have agreed to the main feature of Pitt's policy, the negotiating of the Third Coalition which drew Russia and Austria into the field? Fox attacked it in Opposition, and always maintained that the outcome, which laid Eastern Europe at Napoleon's feet, fully justified his predictions. It is at least possible that he would have refused to agree to it if he had been in Office.

But before the Third Coalition came upon the scene the naval campaign had settled the practicability of the invasion of England. It is called in history the 'campaign of Trafalgar', but its strategic result had been reached three months before the battle.

The French had five-and-thirty ships of the line, divided between Brest, Toulon, and Rochefort, besides fifteen Spaniards in Ferrol and Cadiz after Spain had joined the war in March 1805. If several of these detachments could get out and unite they might hold the Channel long enough for a part at least of the Grand Army to cross, and do what damage it could in England. That their command of the sea would be more than local and temporary was most improbable.[1]

Close off each of the ports where the enemy ships lay a detachment of British men-of-war beat up and down in all weathers, performing, though under different conditions, the function that the Grand Fleet performed at Scapa Flow during our own war: they lay between the world and military conquest. The watch off Brest was the more easily kept because the home base was near at hand. The post of endurance and difficulty was the watch off Toulon, based merely on the roadsteads of Sardinia; that was Nelson's post for two years of unrelieved service. Finally, Villeneuve had his chance and slipped out from Toulon, leaving Nelson ignorant where he had gone. He had gone to the West Indies, picking up six Spanish ships on the way. In the West Indies, according to Napoleon's plan, Villeneuve was to meet the Brest fleet, destroy the British interests in the sugar islands, and return to hold the Channel for the passage of the Grand Army. But the Brest fleet remained locked up, and it was Nelson who crossed the Atlantic, not on certain information of Villeneuve's course, but on a bold calculation of probabilities.

The Nile and Trafalgar campaigns have the same general character, though the arena of the one was the Mediterranean, of the other the broad Atlantic. In both we have the first success of the enemy's fleet in getting away undetected, the pursuit and search so long baffled, the agonizing uncertainty made good by calculation, energy, and persistence, and the crowning victory at last. But whereas in 1798 the initial evasion enabled Bonaparte to land and conquer Egypt, in 1805 Nelson crossed the Atlantic so close on the heels of his enemy that Villeneuve had no time to capture our

1. The recent authoritative works of Corbett and Fortescue throw doubt, if not ridicule, on the actual preparations for transport and the chances of invasion on the grand scale.

colonies and destroy our shipping.[1] He escaped back to Europe only just ahead of his hunter, who missed the French by going to Gibraltar while they headed for North Spain. There Villeneuve fought an indecisive action with Calder's fleet watching off that coast, and ran to ground in the Spanish harbours.

Thus by the end of July the strategic campaign of the ocean was finished, and the scheme of invasion, for whatever it may have been worth, was dead. Yet the remainder of the year was to be occupied by a series of military and naval operations as famous as any in the history of war.

In August the world learnt of the existence of the Third Coalition against France. The armies of Russia and Austria, paid by Pitt at the annual rate of twelve pounds ten shillings a man, were moving against Napoleon, who had recently crowned himself Emperor of France. His answer to the new league came quick as the flash of a sword out of its scabbard. While the Russians and Austrians were dawdling up to their points of concentration, the Grand Army was hurried across Europe from Boulogne to the Danube, and on 20 October, the Austrian vanguard capitulated at Ulm. Next morning, off Cape Trafalgar, twenty-seven British ships of the line were bearing down in two columns on thirty-three French and Spaniards. Abandoning his usual policy of caution, the enemy had come out of Cadiz to give battle in a fit of desperation, which greatly lightened the burden of the next ten years' war to England. Ere sunset, eighteen great ships had struck their colours and the rest were in full flight – the British seamen were working with a will to save as many as possible of the enemy out of the sea and off the burning ships – and Nelson was lying dead in the cockpit of the *Victory*.

On Lord Mayor's Day, the Prime Minister was received in the Guildhall with the gratitude due to the man who had furnished Nelson with the means and the authority to save the British Empire. 'England,' said Pitt, 'has saved herself by her exertions, and will, as I trust, save Europe by her example.' This speech, the best and shortest ever made on an official occasion, acquired in a few weeks a deeper meaning. At Austerlitz, in distant Moravia, at the battle of the Three Emperors, Napoleon laid low the combined armies of Russia and Austria. Before Christmas the Third Coalition was no more, and Europe was at the feet of the conqueror.

1. The anxiety in the City at the presence of the French fleet and army in the West Indies on this occasion reminds us what a big part those islands were of British interests, and helps to explain why Pitt had sent half the army there in the previous war. See pp. 99–100, above.

When the news of the battle and of the armistice reached Pitt, his face took on the 'Austerlitz look'. He knew that, at the best, England was doomed to ten years' war against the Continent. His exhausted frame, no longer stimulated by immediate hope, ceased to struggle against the malady that wasted it. On 23 January he died. His last words and thoughts did not concern his own soul or his private affections: 'My country! How I leave my country!'

He left her in desperate straits, amid the ruins of those dynastic alliances by which he had three times striven in vain to make head against the French nation. He left her shorn of her ancient freedom of speech and thought, and that harmony of classes that had once distinguished 'merry England'. He left her with her foot on Ireland prostrate and chained. But he left her recovered from the dishonour and weakness of the state in which he had found her a quarter of a century before. He left her with Canada and India so established that they would not go the way of the lost Colonies. He left her able and willing to defy the conqueror of Europe when all others bowed beneath the yoke. He left her victor at sea, freshly crowned with laurels that have proved immortal. And if in the coming era Englishmen were divided class from class by new and bitter griefs, they had also a new bond of fraternity in the sound of Nelson's name.

The next year was marked by the fall of Prussia. For a whole decade she had kept out of the conflict, digesting Poland. In 1805, when her interference might have been decisive against French ambitions in Germany, Pitt had offered her every aid and inducement to join the Third Coalition. Only one thing he had refused to do, to barter away George III's beloved Hanover, the bait with which Napoleon dazzled the covetous imagination of the Court of Berlin. In the vain hope of deciding the hesitations and tergiversations of Prussia by a display of present aid, Pitt had landed a British army on the North German coast, but it had to be hastily withdrawn after Austerlitz.

At the beginning of the year 1806, Frederick William of Prussia, bribed by the offer of Hanover, turned towards alliance with Napoleon, and obediently excluded all British ships from the ports of his dominions. We were actually in a state of war with Prussia, when her king changed his mind once more and flung his country unaided into the struggle against France. He had been overborne by the movement against French domination of Germany, which Napoleon's execution of the patriotic bookseller,

124

Palm, had done much to arouse. So rapidly did events now move that the British envoy who hastened out to make peace with Prussia was met as he drove inland from the port of landing by the tide of fugitives from Jena! There was no question this time of Prussia having been pushed and paid by England to enter the war. Fox and Grenville, in their Ministry of All-the-Talents, had only too completely abandoned Pitt's policy of Coalitions and subsidies which had sent so many dynasties to their doom.

The efficiency of Frederick the Great's small and barbarous kingdom of serfs and junkers had depended on the energies and genius of the sovereign. When the King happened to be a fool as well as a knave, Prussia merely afforded another example of the effete *ancien régime*. From the eclipse that she underwent after Jena, she emerged in six years' time as a self-conscious national State with a modern army and a modern bureaucracy. She had been reformed by Stein, Scharnhorst, and Hardenberg, who sought, in an adoption of the new French institutions and principles, the means of combating the new France.

The Foxite Whigs, on returning to Parliament in 1801 at the end of their ill-advised 'secession', saw that domestic politics were dead and that it was useless to attempt to revive them. They kept silence on Reform, without renouncing it. The ranks of Pitt's former party being broken into a number of hostile factions by his retirement, the Foxites entered into alliance with the Tory group led by Lord Grenville, at first out of common contempt for Addington's Ministry, afterwards on the basis of common agreement in favour of Catholic Emancipation. For one year, and one year only, immediately after Pitt's death, the Whigs held office in the famous Ministry of All-the-Talents, in coalition with the Grenville group and with Addington and his followers. This brief and partial interlude in the long régime of anti-Jacobinism was of notable service to the Empire and to the world, because Fox and his friends insisted on the passage of the Bill abolishing the slave trade, about which Pitt had grown half-hearted in his later years. Abolition had sharply divided the Tory ranks, but when once it was on the Statute Book the anti-slavery men in the subsequent Tory Ministries, especially those of the evangelical 'sect', put down the slave trade by a vigorous use of the British navy; and, in the Treaties of Vienna and afterwards, pressed earnestly and with some measure of success to bring the Powers of the Holy Alliance into line with England on this question. The real abolition of the slave trade on the high seas, and the theoretical ban placed upon it in the as yet unpenetrated Dark Continent, prepared the way for the abolition of slavery itself, and saved the tropics, in the coming era of their commercial exploitation by Europe, from becoming a vast slave-farm.

But All-the-Talents added little to the fighting strength of the nation, especially after their loss of Fox who died in office, a late convert by experience to the impossibility of making peace with Napoleon. His last words were that he 'died happy'. And, in spite of all, he had lived happy, and spread happiness around him like a wind blowing from the hills. He had loved life too well to be a perfect statesman, but he had brought human life and love with him into the political world, and since he passed out of it, though it has been dignified by equal genius and higher virtue, it has never again been made Shakespearean by such a kind, grand, human creature.

The circumstances attending the fall of the Ministry of All-the-Talents, six months after the death of Fox, gave fresh proof of the power of the Crown. Though no longer able, as in the days of Bute and North, to form Cabinets and Parliamentary majorities out of his own creatures, George III could still exert authority as umpire between existing parties. He dismissed Lords Grenville and Grey because they had proposed to admit Roman Catholic officers into the British army, and because, when he had forced them to withdraw that Jacobinical measure, they had refused the promise he demanded of them, never again to moot Catholic relief in any form. A powerful Minister like Pitt, with a stable majority of his own in the House, could maintain himself against the Crown, though even Pitt had accepted the royal veto on the introduction of vital measures.[1] But the group-system to which parliamentary life had been reduced in the first years of the nineteenth century afforded to George III and his successor a field where they were able to choose their own Ministers from among the group-leaders of the day. The power of the Crown remained at this mean level until the great Reform Bill made the people of England and Scotland arbiters of their own destiny. That measure very soon placed the Crown in its present position in the Constitution. Burke and Fox had desired to reduce George III to the position afterwards

1. In this epoch the royal veto was not exercised openly against Bills that had passed both Houses, but privately to prevent beforehand the introduction of Ministerial measures. This practice became so much a custom of the Constitution under George III and IV that Grey himself in 1830–31 allowed that he could not introduce the Reform Bill till William IV had agreed to the whole of it.

held by Queen Victoria, but had failed because the alternative to the Crown was not then the people but only the aristocracy.

From 1807 to 1830 the Whigs were excluded from office, partly by the will of the Crown, partly by their own instinct against allying themselves with anti-Reformers. They steadily refused to join any Ministry except on the basis of Catholic Emancipation being made a Government measure. As the Catholic claims were extremely unpopular in our Protestant island, there was not much temptation to Tories like Canning and Castlereagh, who theoretically believed in Emancipation, to make serious efforts on its behalf. So it was left to Ireland eventually to extort for herself what England was never willing to grant.

Although the permanent exclusion of the Whigs and Grenvillites was a result arrived at on purely domestic grounds, it probably helped to a better directed prosecution of the war. All-the-Talents had had no more success abroad than Pitt, and its leading members afterwards went wrong in Opposition about Wellington and the Peninsula. On the other hand, their Tory successors, Perceval, Lord Liverpool, and Lord Castlereagh conducted the European war with great military and diplomatic success. It is indeed remarkable that the group of English statesmen who actually beat Napoleon were regarded by contemporaries and by posterity with something akin to contempt. They must have been giants indeed not to be dwarfed by the inevitable comparison with their great foreign antagonist and with their great predecessors, Fox and Pitt. They soon quarrelled with their most brilliant colleague, George Canning. And the reactionary and purely negative policy upon which they insisted at home even after Napoleon's fall, at a time when the underswell of the tide was veering round towards progress and liberty, exposed them to the angry ridicule of the younger generation, led by Brougham, Byron, and the Reverend Sydney Smith.

Castlereagh, unlike his principal colleagues, had the gifts of a brilliant man of action. So had Canning, with wit and eloquence added. They were looked on as the young disciples on whom Pitt's mantle had fallen. If the two had held together as colleagues in the long Tory Ministry it could scarcely have attained its reputation for dullness. Unfortunately the Dioscuri could not abide one another. A quarrel culminated in the scandal of a duel. The world sympathized with Castlereagh. Canning's brilliant and potentially liberal genius remained unemployed during the years when the fate of Europe was being decided. 'My political allegiance,' he told his constituents in 1812, 'is buried in the grave of

Pitt.' It was Castlereagh's fate to be associated in history and literature with Perceval, Liverpool, and Addington, now become Lord Sidmouth.

But Canning, before he left the Ministry, found time to perform one act of moral daring, which, whether right or wrong, bears the imprint of genius.

Napoleon, after the first check to the pace of his European conquests on the bloodstained snows of Eylau, had heavily defeated the Russian army at the battle of Friedland. East Prussia and Poland, up to the Russian border, were at his feet. The young Tsar Alexander, whose mutable fancies were one after another to play so great a part in history, now determined to give peace to Europe by entering into alliance with Napoleon at Tilsit. There, upon a raft on the Niemen, the Emperors of West and East agreed on the division of the world. Prussia was cut down to a small German principality. England was to be forced to accept the new settlement. If she remained obdurately at war, she must be reduced by the Continental System for cutting off her trade, which had been proclaimed the year before by Napoleon's Berlin Decree. Alexander undertook to enforce the prohibition of British trade in his vast dominions. And it was secretly agreed that the Scandinavian Powers and Portugal were, if necessary, to be compelled to close their ports, and to use their fleets against Britain.

Canning, as foreign secretary, got wind of the great conspiracy from secret agents, and what he did not know he shrewdly guessed. He sent an overwhelming military and naval force to demand of the Danes their alliance, and leave to hold their fleet in pawn. The Danes resisted, Copenhagen was bombarded from the land side, and their warships, which otherwise would have gone to Napoleon, were carried off to England.

It seemed hard to justify such a stroke against a Power that was not even in a state of 'armed neutrality' against us, as it had been at the time of Nelson's similar attack on Copenhagen six years before. Canning's action gave us a bad name in Europe, while the secret clauses of Tilsit were unknown, and while people were seeking an excuse to themselves for their submission to French tyranny. But Napoleon's proceedings in Portugal and Spain shortly turned the moral scales heavily against him, and did much to exonerate Canning retrospectively for seizing hold of a weapon before Napoleon's outstretched hand could be laid upon it.

After Tilsit, Napoleon was master of the whole Continent in the same sense that England in the following generation was master

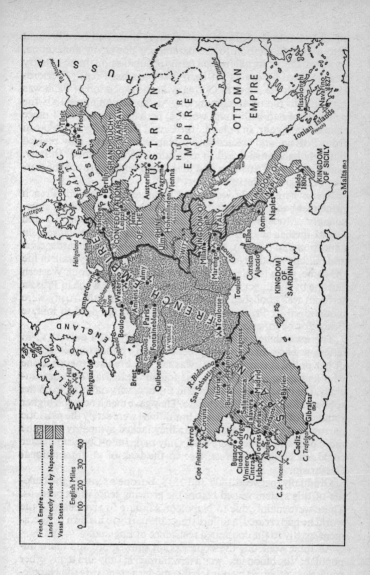

of all India. In the Europe of 1808 every State had been brought into a defined relation to the paramount power, by annexation, by vassalage, or by alliance on terms of submission. In no country had national feeling as yet been fused against French overlordship, though the anger in Germany at the execution of Palm was prologue to the omen coming on. At the beginning of 1808 the principle of nationality still worked, perhaps, less against France than in her favour. In Poland, 'the Grand Duchy of Warsaw', torn from Prussia, and erected into a Napoleonic State, fully revived but only half satisfied Polish aspirations to nationhood. In Italy, Napoleon's anti-Austrian and anti-Papal regime proved the nursery of Italian patriotism.

Everywhere the old world was being rejuvenated on 'French principles', identified with the dynamic force of Napoleon's personality. Modern bureaucracy in place of old municipal and feudal inefficiency; in law, the ideas of the *Code Napoléon*; in education and thought, the influence of scientific standards, civic and military, instead of clerical obscurantism; in every walk of life the career open to talents – these things were thrust upon Western Europe by the direct action of French governors, while in Prussia serfdom was abolished and the Universities and the Army were modernized by Prussian statesmen who saw the need to imitate France or be for ever fallen.

The ascendancy of France, since the days of Louis XIV, in letters, science, and life, had prepared men's minds for acceptance of her political supremacy. It was not the French generals alone who had conquered Europe. Napoleon created an able bureaucracy, the Proconsuls of France in Europe, very different from the robber ruffians of the Directorate. They gave men a new and higher standard of government. Their limitations were set by the patriotic narrowness of the French mind: they lacked sympathy with the races over whom they bore rule. Only their Italo-Corsican master could, in his own interest, rise to the idea of an international Caesarism.

Gradually, between 1808 and 1813, Europe's sense of the benefits of this system waned before the growing sense of its burdens. These were mainly due to Napoleon's failure to give peace to the world he had created, a failure traceable partly to his own temperament, partly to the continued resistance of England.

As time went on, the conscription grew more and more unpopular: 'the blood tax' was a new burden in Italy and many other countries, although by our terrible modern standards the Napoleonic demand on Europe's young manhood seems small indeed.

War taxation and the deprivation of trade, in accordance with his Continental System against England, pressed ever more heavily on the subject peoples of the Empire. Peace, permanence, and prosperity retreated further and further into the distance as the years went by. England's resistance unexpectedly continued and drew Napoleon on into more and more distant schemes of conquest in Spain and Russia, into ever stricter prohibitions against trade. It seemed that he must conquer and starve the whole world in order to starve and conquer the islanders. As he grew older the burden told on his nature and deepened its faults; he grew ever more harsh, exacting, sudden; he could not leave things alone; he must always be reshuffling the provinces of Europe, pulling up and redistributing his own political creations. The impression grew that his work was always in hot flux, that it would never set cold and solid. Permanence and rest seemed alien to his genius, and it was for permanence and rest that Europe sighed.

These discontents took the form of a new sense of nationhood, rendering French rule odious, in Holland, Germany, and Eastern Europe, and to some extent even in Italy. In France herself they became operative in the political parties of the new Liberalism and the old Reaction. But as yet opposition could find no means of public expression. Politics, journalism, literature had less freedom under the Empire than under the Bourbons of the recent past or of the near future. 'Napoleon's dominion,' said Ugo Foscolo, 'was like a July day in Egypt – all clear, brilliant, and blazing; but all silent – not a voice heard, the stillness of the grave.'

CHAPTER 8

NATIONAL sentiment, that destroyed Napoleon's cosmopolitan empire, was first brought to a head against him by his attempt to subject the Iberian Peninsula to his direct control. He believed it necessary, if England was to be starved out, to stop British trade with Portugal and its great dependency of Brazil, and to make more secure the enforcement of the Continental System along the coasts of Spain and the Spanish American colonies. He had begun in 1807 by sending Junot to conquer hostile Portugal. Next year, when his armies under this pretext had occupied friendly Spain, he committed the worst crime and error of his career: he compelled the Spanish Royal family to abdicate and proclaimed his brother Joseph King of Spain.

This act of vulgar ruffianism on a scale as gigantic as the Partitions of Poland would, if it had proved successful, have corrupted the West of Europe as surely as the Partitions corrupted the East. But the vengeance on Napoleon was direct and speedy. The Spanish people, whom the ex-Jacobin had left out of his calculations, rose on the French armies cantoned throughout the Peninsula and actually compelled one of them to surrender at Baylen. Baylen was the beginning of Napoleon's downfall. It began the long drain on his Grand Army for the irritating necessity of garrisoning every Spanish town and patrolling every Spanish road. And it was the first example to Europe of the national spirit rising against his power. The peoples were being goaded into self-conscious nationhood alike by French propaganda and by French tyranny. The ideas of 1789 had aroused throughout Europe a desire for self-determination which Napoleon outraged at every turn. It was the people who overthrew him, though it was the princes who reaped the benefit of his fall.

The world, just when it had begun to accept Napoleon as inevitable, was startled into a new train of thought by the success of the Spanish revolt, plainly resulting from its popular and national character. Deserted by their contemptible princes, grandees, and officials, the common people, in each several province and town, had fallen on the Frenchmen and the traitors. The improvised local Juntas, in which the strength of the movement lay, grouped themselves into a loose national organization under a central Junta; and in 1810 a Cortes or Parliament was elected. The Spanish rising had, in fact, two aspects, both of them popular. On the one hand the peasants were being urged on by the priests and monks against the infidel French; on the other hand the Cortes was the herald of liberal constitutionalism in despotic and reactionary Spain. It was only after the French had been expelled that these forces came into violent conflict.

In England the news of the rising was received with enthusiasm by all sections, and checked a growing agitation for peace. The Whigs called on the Government to send help to a people struggling to be free; the businessmen, whose warehouses were choked with goods which the new factory system enabled them to produce but which Napoleon forbade them to sell, found a new Eldorado in the markets of Spanish America[1]; while patriots, gloomily watch-

1. The Cortes soon afterwards tried to close South America again to foreign goods, thereby causing fresh distress in England, and sowing the seeds of much subsequent British enthusiasm for the cause of South American independence. See p. 212, below.

ing the fortunes of the war, saw that friendly hands had opened a gate in the hostile fortress of Europe through which not only our goods but our armies could enter at last.

Sir Arthur Wellesley, of Maratha fame, led the first small British force of 9,000 men to the Peninsula. His immediate object was to clear the French out of Portugal, an operation on which his victory at Vimiero put the seal. He was supplanted on the field of battle by superior Officers coming out from England with more troops. By the Convention of Cintra they permitted Junot to evacuate Portugal with his plunder. The British public was furious with the generals, including Wellesley, though he was not in fact responsible for the terms, and would probably have captured the whole of Junot's army if he had not been superseded.

During the winter, while Wellesley remained in England under a cloud, a British army of 30,000 men was operating in the Peninsula under Sir John Moore. Napoleon himself, at the head of 250,000 French, was engaged in putting down the Spanish rising. Moore's daring advance into the heart of the country to threaten Napoleon's flank and rear drew him off the Spaniards and saved Lisbon and Cadiz, and thereby perhaps the whole movement. By his retreat to Corunna through the winter mountains, Moore, at the cost of 5,000 stragglers, saved his main body from the eager pursuit of Napoleon, who, having failed in his *coup de théâtre* of capturing a British army, returned to Paris and never again crossed the Pyrenees. Soult came up with the English forces reconstituted at Corunna. The action fought there to cover their embarkation was brilliantly successful, but Sir John Moore was killed by a cannon-ball and buried on the foreign shore.

On the return home of Moore's force came the real crisis of the Peninsular War as far as England was concerned – a moral and political crisis. The discouragement was great. The British public, having expected from its new allies things beyond measure, was beyond measure disillusioned. The Spaniards had indeed failed for all purposes, military and political, except guerilla warfare, and it was not yet understood how much guerilla warfare might mean in Spain. Our own army, though victorious in battle, had been forced by overwhelming numbers to re-embark. Sir John Moore himself had written that it would no longer be possible to hold Lisbon. To pessimists, Napoleon again seemed invincible on land. Most of the Whigs changed their minds and clamoured for the abandonment of the Spanish adventure as hopeless. But the Government continued to supply the Juntas with arms and money, sent back a British force to Portugal, and placed Wellesley in command, in spite of his recent unpopularity. These decisions were not a little due to the personal influence which the young general had obtained over Castlereagh, and to a less extent over his rival Canning, who was still in the Cabinet. The policy of Wellington,[1] adhered to by successive Tory Governments through four dark and difficult years, proved the key to victory in the world contest. After the failure of the Walcheren expedition, designed to take Antwerp, but ending in the death of four thousand of our soldiers in the fever-laden swamps of the Dutch island, the Cabinet concentrated British military effort on the Peninsular War.

Wellington's campaigns of 1809–11 were actions to defend Portugal as his base, varied by raids into Spain that fostered the guerilla war in that country. Sometimes, as in the Talavera campaign of 1809, the chief event of the year was the raid into Spain, rendered possible by Austria's rebellion against Napoleon; while in 1810, after Austria had been suppressed at Wagram, Wellington's defence of Portugal was for a while confined to the famous lines of Torres Vedras which he constructed across the peninsula of Lisbon. But until in 1812 the quarrel with Russia seriously drained the French forces in Spain, Wellington could do no more than keep the war alive. The French in the Peninsula sometimes outnumbered the British by nearly ten to one, but out of some 300,000 men it was seldom that so many as 70,000 were available to crush the British and those Portuguese regiments that our officers had trained to stand fire as regular troops. The spearhead of the Napoleonic army of occupation was small in comparison with its shaft, because the Spanish guerillas saw to it that no city and no province could be left without a French garrison, on pain of an immediate revolt. Whatever their failings as regular troops, whatever their deficiency in political and military leadership, the Spaniards waged on the invader an unceasing partisan warfare such as Napoleon encountered in no other land.

The Peninsular War, indeed, had two very different aspects, the one immortalized in Napier's dignified and romantic history; the other in Goya's grim etchings of 'Los Desastres de la Guerra'. The British officer and the Spanish civilian each recorded the aspect that presented itself to his countrymen. As between French and English the war was a display of rival valour by two chivalrous nations. French and English prisoners were treated as

1. Sir Arthur Wellesley was made Lord Wellington for his services in 1809 (Douro and Talavera), Marquis for Salamanca in 1812, and Duke in 1814. Marlborough, who enjoyed more Court favour, had been made Duke in 1702, before his great victories.

the Black Prince and Du Guesclin treated the knights they captured; nor was the spirit of mutual admiration and courtesy confined to the officers of the two armies. Very different were the features of the war waged between the Spanish guerillas and the French invader – men sawed up alive and impaled on stakes; massacre, rape, and torture; all the most bestial passions let loose by hatred and by fear.

In the midst of such scenes as these it was fortunate that Wellington was at once a great humanitarian and a great disciplinarian. The first quality would have availed little without the second. Unlike Nelson he had no wish to be loved by his men. But he abominated the waste and cruelty of war, and kept it within its strictest limits. He revived and fixed the high traditions of the British Army in many things, and not least in respect for person and property. He once angrily defined 'booty' as 'what you can lay your bloody hand upon, and keep'. When he first took over the command there was much drunkenness, desertion, and looting, in a land flowing with wine; but by strenuous efforts he established a very different state of things, save on the few occasions when after the storm of cities like Badajos whole regiments ran amok for days together. When the other armies of Europe were a terror alike to friend and foe, he showed the world an army paying its way even on hostile territory, a protection rather than a burden to the astonished inhabitants.[1]

Wellington and the school of officers who served under him abroad, did as much as Nelson and his captains to raise the reputation of their country and their service. Only in one respect their system fell short. The common soldiers were, like the common sailors, treated too much like serfs, too little like citizens under arms. But in this the services only reflected the attitude towards the 'lower orders' then prevalent in civilian life. Nor must it be forgotten that the system of army recruitment filled the ranks with some of the roughest types. Wellington, with his naked sincerity of thought and speech, which gives a value to all his sayings, even to those which represent his prejudices, declared that his men were 'the scum of the earth, enlisted for drink'. It was not the view of some of his best officers, including the historian of the war who recorded the 'strength and majesty' with which the British soldier fought. Perhaps, too, the Duke never asked himself if the finest

1. In a remote valley of the Pyrenees, in 1905, I met a French peasant who was much interested on discovering I was an Englishman, because he said the English troops in passing down the valley in Napoleon's time had paid for a cow twice what it was worth! The sensation created in the valley had lived in oral tradition for close on a century.

spirits in the country would be drawn to enlist, when by so doing they rendered themselves liable, among other things, to the terrible and degrading torture of the military floggings. But he always maintained that without corporal punishment he could not have fashioned the rough customers of which his force was actually composed into the best disciplined and least criminal of all the armies who swarmed over France in 1814.

Whatever may have been the defects of its qualities, our army was the best fighting instrument in Europe, now that at last it had got efficient leadership. Owing to its superiority in discipline, fire-drill, and steadiness, the British could venture to oppose their thin line to the French column of attack.[1] Our volley-firing was excellent, and being delivered from a broad front could stop the phalanx of the Old Guard itself. Wellington, on the eve of sailing for the Peninsula in 1808, had foretold to Croker what would happen when the line was fairly pitted against the column. 'If what I hear of the French system of manoeuvres be true, I think it a false one as against steady troops. I suspect all the continental armies were more than half beaten before the battle was begun.' This had already been demonstrated on a small scale in the otherwise unimportant British victory at Maida in South Italy in 1806. The use of the line against the column proved the secret of our success in Spain, and finally at Waterloo. But the superiority of our fire would not have availed for the defeat of France without Wellington's genius; less original and daring than his rival, he was less prone to make mistakes, especially in tactics, than the Napoleon of later years.

In Wellington's campaigns the regimental traditions of the British Army attained that peculiar force and quality, which survived to pull us through the Crimea, although the staff and army organization grievously deteriorated during the long peace. And it was again the regimental traditions and the Peninsular memories that sent the British Army across the sea in 1914 with the inherited belief that it could not be beaten in the end.

Meanwhile the navy, which had no serious fighting to expect after Trafalgar, was busily employed in blockading the Continent. Napoleon had challenged us to a war of mutual starvation by the 'Continental System' which he devised against our commerce. It was embodied in a series of Decrees of which the most famous were issued from Berlin in 1806 and Milan in 1807. Neutrals and allies as well as subjects were forbidden by him to trade with

1. See pp. 97–8, above.

Britain or her colonies, and all ships and goods that had touched at our ports were rendered subject to confiscation. Our Government replied in a series of Orders in Council, of which the first was issued in January 1807 by the Ministry of All-the-Talents. But the full development of the policy became identified with the later Tory Cabinet of Spencer Perceval. The Orders in Council declared all the countries that enforced Napoleon's Decrees to be in a state of blockade, and instituted a rigorous search of neutral ships to prevent them from trading with our enemies.

Since we held the seas, our system was most acutely felt by the trans-oceanic neutrals. And since Napoleon held the land, his inveterate war on tea and coffee, sugar and cotton, was most resented in Russia, Scandinavia, and Germany, where men had to live without goods from oversea as the price of peace with France. It is therefore no wonder that by 1812 England was at war with the United States and Napoleon with Russia.

As the daily bread of men and women far from the scene of action became more and more affected by the war, the question of the 'home front', as we should now call it, grew acute, both for Napoleon as ruler of Europe, and for the British Cabinet. To Napoleon the catastrophe of the 'home front' came with the rebellion first of Russia, and then of Germany and Scandinavia, unwilling to bear the deprivations of his Continental System in the absence of any patriotic motives for endurance.

In England the sufferings of the working class during the Industrial Revolution were increased by the uncertainty of employment in supplying a world whose markets were perpetually opening and shutting according to the vagaries of diplomacy and war. Meanwhile the price of bread rose beyond the means of many of the wage-earners. The bulk of the population craved for peace. But discontent, though deep, was not formidable. Though there might be riots and machine-breaking, the men had in the end no choice but to work on the masters' terms or to starve outright. They were so little organized, so deeply trodden down into economic and political servitude, that their views could do little to help or hinder the conduct of the war. The Cabinet made no concessions to them of any kind during the Napoleonic struggle, a remarkable contrast to the domestic and industrial policy of 1914–18.

As to the class which the Government itself represented, the landlords and the clergy, they were patriotic enough and had, moreover, no great temptation to demand peace. For them the war meant the rise of taxation indeed, but also the rise of rents and tithes with the price of corn. And for them it meant very little else.

137

The blood tax was a light one on all classes; for many years there was no fighting on land, and even the seven years of the Peninsular War cost less than 40,000 British dead. At no period had the upper class been wealthier, or happier, or more engrossed in the life of its pleasant country houses. No young lady of Miss Austen's acquaintance, waiting eagerly for the forthcoming volume of Scott or Byron, seems ever to have asked what Mr Thorpe or Mr Tom Bertram was doing during the Great War!

If the war was a source of increasing revenue to the landlords and of prolonged calamity to the working-men, to the middling orders of society it was a gamble that made one man a profiteer and another a bankrupt. As a whole 'the nation of shopkeepers' longed for peace to bring security, to open the European markets once for all, and to reduce taxation. But they had no thought of surrender to Bonaparte. Many of the wealthier – the bankers, the merchants and the monied men – shared the Tory politics of 'the quality', to whose society they were occasionally admitted. But many a manufacturer of the new type, himself or his father sprung from the working class, more often than not a Dissenter, his thoughts engrossed by the factory he had built on the bank of some Pennine stream, hated the aristocracy and dumbly resented the war as something from the glory and interest of which he was excluded. Such men were making the new wealth of England, but they had no part or lot in her government, and were jealous of the haughty class that excluded them. They felt equally little sympathy with the real victims of the war, their own employees – as little almost as the landlords and farmers felt with the pauperized and starving peasants whose labour filled their pockets so full. It was a hard world of sharply divided interests, with no sense of national brotherhood, save occasionally in face of the foreign foe.

Since the businessmen wavered between approval and disapproval of the war, according as victory seemed to draw near, or ruin stared them in the face, it was in 1811 that Napoleon came nearest to starving England out and wearing down her resolution to conquer. But at that supreme crisis a sound instinct taught the middle class in its deep distress to agitate not for peace but for the withdrawal of the Orders in Council. The Orders were denounced by public opinion on the ground that they were involving us in a quarrel with the United States, the best of our few remaining customers. The movement, originating in the ports and manufacturing districts, was brought to bear on the House of Commons through the powerful energy of Henry Brougham, and it ended by imposing its will on the Government. When the accident of Perceval's assassination in the lobby by a lunatic removed the Prime Minister who was personally associated with the policy, the Orders in Council were allowed to drop. But the concession came too late to prevent the outbreak of war with the United States.[1] If Napoleon's Continental System had been still holding firm, the consequences might have been fatal to us. But Russia and Sweden had thrown off the yoke, and we had won the race of starvation by a neck.

It was not so much the Orders in Council which had beaten Napoleon's economic campaign, as the productiveness of the new machinery and the factory system, and the monopoly of trade which, thanks to the navy, we enjoyed with America and the tropics.

In the winter of 1811–12 Napoleon was preparing to invade Russia. His army in the Peninsula, so far from being recruited by fresh drafts, had to send away some of its best regiments, and the Poles were marched from Spain to Moscow on a campaign that was to decide the tragic fate of their country for a hundred years to come.

Wellington, therefore, was in a position to attempt something more than another raid; the time for the liberating conquest was at hand. Far surpassing the generals opposing him both as strategist and tactician, he prepared his way for a permanent advance out of Portugal into Spain by capturing, early in the year, the frontier fortresses of Ciudad Rodrigo and Badajos, before the French armies could manage to interfere. In the summer he destroyed Marmont's army at Salamanca. The position in the whole Peninsula was changed by this victory in the north-west; not only was Madrid liberated, but Soult was obliged to evacuate the South of Spain, whither the French were never again able to penetrate. At the price of the surrender of the South, Soult's vigour brought about such a concentration of French armies that Madrid was recaptured, and in the autumn Wellington, having failed at the siege of Burgos, had to fall back once more on Portugal, with the game only half won.

During the winter came the news of the retreat from Moscow. The year 1813 was to see Napoleon's struggle to retain hold of Central Europe, in face of the revolt of the German nation headed by Prussia and aided by the armies of Russia, Sweden, and after a while of Austria. The issue, that hung uncertain for many months, would have been very different if Napoleon had had with

1. See pp. 80–82, below, for the events of the war.

him in Germany the 200,000 veterans who were locked up in Spain for his sins of five years before.

Yet even these 200,000 did not suffice to hold their own against the British and Spaniards. King Joseph was hustled out of Northern Spain by a series of able manoeuvres, and routed at Vitoria with the loss of all his artillery, military stores, and chest. In forty days, starting from Portugal, Wellington had driven over the Pyrenees the enemies' main army and the whole paraphernalia of the usurper's government. It was a resounding catastrophe, and had its effect on hesitating nations and statesmen in the struggle for Central Europe, where the scales of war and diplomacy were still held even. In August Austria joined the allies. Napoleon alone still failed to read the signs of the times, and refused to make advantageous terms for himself and France while he still might. In October the issue was decided by the three days' Armageddon in the plains of Leipzig in Saxony. Central Europe was released, and the French fled back to the Rhine as rapidly as they had done a century before, after the battle of Blenheim.

On the Spanish frontier, the fortresses of Pampeluna and San Sebastian prevented the victors from penetrating into France in the summer of 1813 at the heels of King Joseph's stripped and demoralized army. The breathing-space afforded by the two sieges gave time for the reconstitution of the French forces under Soult, placed too late in supreme command. Then came the last trial of strength in the passes of the Pyrenees, between two veteran armies at the height of military efficiency, and each under splendid leadership. Soult nearly succeeded in relieving Pampeluna, through Roncesvalles, but was foiled by the quickness of Wellington and the stubbornness of his troops. At length, after the fall of the fortresses, the British advance began again, through mountain floods and snowstorms. One after another Soult's defences were forced on the precipitous heights between the Bidassoa and the Nivelle, and finally on the Nive, the gate of entrance to the plains of France. The art of war, as it was known at the end of that warlike age, touched its perfection in that last push over the Pyrenees,

> Followed up in valley and glen
> With blare of bugle, clamour of men,
> Roll of cannon and clash of arms,
> And England pouring on her foes.
> Such a war had such a close.

Meanwhile the battle of Leipzig had at one stroke secured the independence of Germany as far as the Rhine. But the fate of

Western Europe had yet to be decided. The results of Austerlitz and Jena had been cancelled, but the boundaries of the Treaty of Amiens were still possible. Great, even in eclipse, was the prestige of France and Napoleon. The allies had not thought out their war-aims in Western Europe and were bitterly quarrelling over the districts already recovered in the East. Their counsels were so confused that, a few weeks after Leipzig, the Austrian Metternich, with the hasty concurrence of the Tsar Alexander and of young Lord Aberdeen, the British representative on the spot, actually offered the Rhine frontier to Napoleon. The infatuated man hesitated to accept peace even on these terms, and the opportunity passed away.

Alarmed by this and other signs of allied vacillation and want of concerted policy, the British Cabinet, at the new year, sent its strong man, Lord Castlereagh, to the Continent to take charge of the whole situation. His first business was to hold together the alliance as a fighting machine, until the conditions indispensable to Britain's security had been won. These conditions, as laid down by the British Ministers, included the acceptance by the Powers of our definition of the rules of sea-warfare; the liberation of Holland and Belgium from French control; and if possible the reduction of France to her 'ancient limits' of 1789, instead of her 'natural frontier' of the Rhine. If security could thus be obtained, Great Britain was willing to be generous as regards the restitution of many of the colonies that she had taken from the French and their allies. Our Ministers hoped for the restoration of the Bourbons; but they were not yet at the beginning of 1814 prepared to carry on the war to obtain the dethronement of Napoleon, much as they desired that final security for a permanent peace.

Such was British policy in January 1814, when Castlereagh came to the Continent to give it effect. The whole programme was eventually realized, as the outcome of the storms and chances of the next two years, in which the military and diplomatic action of Wellington and Castlereagh were decisive factors.

In 1813 and 1814 Castlereagh played the part that William III and Marlborough had played more than a hundred years before, in holding together an alliance of jealous, selfish, weak-kneed States and princes, by a vigour of character and singleness of purpose that held Metternich, the Tsar, and the King of Prussia on the common track until the goal was reached. It is quite possible that, but for the lead taken by Castlereagh in the allied counsels, France would never have been reduced to her ancient limits, nor Napoleon dethroned.

The first great step towards a European settlement was the crossing of the Rhine by the allied armies, and the successful invasion of France, culminating in the capture of Paris and the abdication of Bonaparte. This outcome was uncertain till the very last moment. It was partly due to Castlereagh's reconstitution of the Alliance and his insistence on fighting until the 'ancient limits' were won, partly to Napoleon's unwillingness to accept a peace that would leave France any smaller than she had been when he first became responsible for her fortunes. His wonderful victories with inadequate means in defence of the invaded country confirmed him in this unyielding mood till it was too late to save either his capital or his throne. During these decisive weeks a large part of his available force was still engaged in the South, opposing Wellington's invasion. With rare sacrifice of personal ambition to humanity and policy, the Duke had saved the French population from outrage by sending home the Spanish army from the frontier. The battle of Toulouse was fought after Napoleon's fall, but before the news had reached either Wellington or Soult.

For nearly a year Elba contained Napoleon, while the Congress was sitting at Vienna. In theory, all the governments of Europe were parties to the Congress. Actually the 'big four', as we should now call them – England, Russia, Austria, Prussia – reserved all important decisions to themselves alone.

Meanwhile her 'ancient frontiers' had been assigned to conquered France, and the Bourbons had been restored, partly by the allies, partly by the French people. The policy of Louis XVIII was half constitutional, half reactionary, but wholly anti-militarist. The main social changes of the Revolution were tacitly accepted in the new France. The framework of administration and government that Bonaparte had constructed was taken over by his successors, but his system was improved upon by the novelties of a partially free press, and the beginnings of a parliamentary constitution.

French boundaries having been settled beforehand, it was intended to exclude France from sharing at Vienna in the more complicated task of dividing up the rest of Europe. But when Castlereagh, left to himself, failed to compose the quarrels of Russia, Prussia, and Austria, the astute Talleyrand, acting as the representative of Bourbon France, seized the occasion to assert his country's place with the 'big four' in these discussions. Castlereagh was fain to welcome him as fellow-moderator. The small countries and princes, on whose behalf Talleyrand had up till then claimed to speak, having served his turn, were now left without a champion, and their interests were mercilessly sacrificed whenever they did not coincide with those of the Great Powers.

The two questions which so nearly involved the allies in a fresh war among themselves were Saxony and Poland. Prussia wanted all Saxony, and Russia wanted all Poland. The Tsar Alexander, now in his 'liberal' phase, dreamed of a reunited and liberated Polish kingdom as a *dépendance* of the Russian crown, with a separate Polish constitution.[1] He was opposed by Prussia and Austria, who wanted a divided and enslaved Poland. Castlereagh, fearful of Russian power, preferred their scheme at any rate to the Tsar's. Eventually Alexander had to cede portions of the spoil to the two other claimants, but he managed to retain the lion's share of the Polish territory. As might have been foreseen by anyone but the visionary Alexander, the Polish constitution proved an impossible bedfellow for the Russian autocracy and ere long, disappeared.

Prussia's claims on the whole of Saxony were enforced in the most aggressive manner, till Castlereagh took the bold step of forming an alliance with France and Austria to resist these pretensions, if necessary, by war. Having thus brought Prussia to reason, he hastened to compensate her with two-fifths of Saxony itself, and with Cologne and other extensive territories on both sides of the Rhine. The aggression of France in Central Europe, ten years before and twenty years before, had been largely due to the absence of any nucleus of opposition along her eastern border. The small, weak States scattered along the course of the Rhine had neither national tradition nor military power. They had become a half-willing prey to the propagandist armies of the Republic, and had formed for Napoleon the obsequious Confederation of the Rhine. After this experience it was not unnatural that England should in 1815 assist Prussia to become the champion of the Fatherland in the 'Watch on the Rhine' against France. The gentler and more liberal civilization of Western Germany, having proved its own incompetence in self-defence, was subjected to the despotic and military ideals of Berlin. Under Napoleon the West of Europe had unwisely tried to conquer and hold down the East: the East was now rolling back upon the West, not altogether to the advantage of civilization.

Castlereagh also endeavoured to strengthen the guard of Europe along the French frontier at two other points, by uniting Belgium to Holland and Genoa to Piedmont. The first of these

1. Exactly a hundred years later this scheme was revived as the first programme of the allies against Germany.

policies broke down in 1830. But the aggrandizement of the Italian frontier State of Piedmont in the long run helped to make it the nucleus of a Liberal kingdom of all Italy. Castlereagh, who had no sympathy with the Italian Liberals of his day, did not foresee any such outcome to his policy, for Piedmont was then a reactionary State. But the later development of Victor Emmanuel's kingdom was all of a piece with Castlereagh's scheme of erecting barriers against French aggression in Italy, and justified, in result if not in intention, the annexation of the former territory of the oligarchical republic of Genoa to the Piedmontese monarchy. But in 1814 and for many years afterwards the treatment of Genoa was a stone of offence to all Liberal critics of the Treaties of Vienna. And it was to Austrian domination in Italy that Castlereagh mainly looked for security against the return of French armies into the plain of the Po.

On 1 March 1815 Napoleon returned from Elba and the 'Hundred Days' began. It will always be a point of controversy how far his lightning restoration was the act of the French nation, how far of the army alone. But the British Government had no time to institute nice inquiries. It had to decide at once. When Napoleon, speaking once more from the Tuileries, offered to become a constitutional monarch, and to live at peace with Europe on the terms of the treaties of 1814, there were risks in treating him as an outlaw. For if the French people were prepared to fight to the death to prevent his deposition, the Allies, who had a few weeks back so nearly come to blows among themselves, would certainly not hold together for another protracted struggle. Judging by past experience, England would soon find herself deserted, and be back again in the isolated position she had so often occupied in the course of the late war. If, on the other hand, the return from Elba was the work of the soldiers alone, a victory by Wellington would settle the affair.

The British Ministers declared themselves ready to wage war so long as Napoleon remained on the throne of France. This bold decision was attacked by the Whig leaders, but it was justified by the event. Probably the speed and completeness of the triumph at Waterloo had much to do with the acceptance by the French people of ordeal by a single battle. When the feelings are divided, it is the event that counts. France was not wholly for the Bourbons or wholly for Napoleon, but she was wholly for a settled government.

Wellington's victory was even more remarkable than it seemed. For Napoleon's army largely consisted of veterans brought back from their prisons in Eastern Europe, while the victors who bore the brunt of their attack were a relatively small number of British recruits, taking the place of our Peninsular regiments not yet returned from the wretched war in America.[1] Our raw troops stood the long and terrible ordeal because of their confidence in the Duke, and because he appeared again and again to take charge at the critical point and the critical moment, at great risk to himself and at the cost of nearly all his staff. Next day, in Brussels, he said to his gossip Creevey, 'It has been a damned nice thing – the nearest run thing you ever saw in your life. . . . By God, I don't think it would have done if I had not been there.'

The brilliant strategy with which Napoleon had opened the campaign nearly drove asunder the British and Prussian armies. His failure was due to his strategical errors of the last three days, his great inferiority to Wellington as a tactician on the field of battle, the mistakes of several of his subordinate commanders, the superiority of our line formation and volley-firing, and the determined energy with which old Blücher brought up his Prussians after Napoleon had written them off as in full retreat.

A political element should be added to the causes of French defeat – the indiscipline and self-distrust of the newly levied army of veterans. It had scarcely had time to be brigaded; men and officers did not know their immediate chiefs, or, if they did, distrusted their loyalty. The pure Napoleonic zeal was found only in the ranks. The higher the officers, the more strongly they felt the desire for peace, and the greater their misgivings as to the issue of a new war against Europe. Never did the French show greater courage than on that day, but it was ill directed. Officers dashed their troops forward at the wrong moment for fear of being suspected of treason. Finally, at the sunset hour, the panic cry of *nous sommes trahis* gave to the military defeat a completeness that was essentially political, but which for a hundred years deceived the world as to the power of endurance and resistance in the armies of France.

The reputation of England and Wellington was immensely enhanced by the campaign. The Peninsula had been the greatest of 'side-shows'. But Waterloo broke the neck of the war and dethroned Napoleon in a day.

1. At Waterloo Wellington had 27,000 British (of whom 7,000 were killed or wounded) and about 40,000 foreigners, some good, some worthless. Napoleon had on the field 74,000 French and a great superiority of guns. The arrival of Blücher turned the weight of numbers against the French, but not till the evening.

Prussia shared with England in the prestige of Waterloo. But she threw away the opportunities of her position by an uncouth desire for revenge on France, by military brutalities to the population, and by a policy of demanding the dismemberment of the French provinces, beginning with Alsace-Lorraine and the north-eastern frontier. British public opinion also was for the moment much inflamed against France after the Hundred Days, and our Cabinet was shaken in its generous policy. But the Tsar Alexander remained a friend of Bourbon France, while Castlereagh and Wellington, disgusted with the behaviour of the Prussian army of occupation, stood firm for the policy of 'security not revenge', which they finally succeeded in inducing the Cabinet to support. Their scorn of popular opinion and its moods, whether in the City or the clubs, was on this occasion most serviceable to Europe. Indeed, although the defects of the settlement of 1815 resulted from its being made by irresponsible monarchs and anti-popular statesmen, its merits in relation to the treatment of France were owing not a little to the absence of all democratic control in the critical treaty-making months that follow the end of a great war, while popular passions are still at blood-heat.

So the British soldier and the British statesman prevented the dismemberment of France, and handed back the French colonies, with the trifling exceptions of Mauritius, Tobago, and St Lucia. But while they scorned revenge, they insisted on security. They took a leading part in the formation of a new alliance pledged to prevent by arms the return of Napoleon. France had to pay a moderate indemnity, and while it was being paid a portion of her territory was occupied for three years by allied troops under the command of Wellington.

The European Alliance to prevent the return of Napoleon or any of his family to the throne was largely the work of Castlereagh. But he refused to let England be a party to another treaty, which the idealist Tsar induced his 'brothers' of Austria and Prussia to sign. By the Treaty of the Holy Alliance each of God's self-appointed viceregents solemnly undertook to regulate his home and foreign policy according to the principles of the Christian religion, 'namely, the precepts of justice, Christian charity, and peace', since 'the three allied Princes look on themselves as merely delegated by Providence to govern the three branches of one family, namely, Austria, Prussia, and Russia'. To Castlereagh, all this was 'a piece of sublime mysticism and nonsense'. Indeed, his objections to the Holy Alliance of 1815 were not those of a Liberal, but of an unsentimental Englishman. Nor, as Minister of a constitutional

State, had he any intention of allowing the Prince Regent to sign treaties on his personal account, as if it were he who directed the policy of Britain. At the time that Castlereagh first took objection to the treaty the principles of the Christian religion invoked in the document meant nothing in particular. It was only later that they came to be interpreted by the signatories to mean despotism and obscurantism, as Alexander passed out of his liberal phase and fell under the influence of Metternich.

A more practical 'Holy Alliance' which Castlereagh urged with partial success upon the Congress was world-wide cooperation to put down the slave trade. The English people, divided on so much else, were now united in a passionate enthusiasm for this particular use of our maritime powers. On this point the Evangelicals had at length captured the Tory party, where the slave trade had once found many friends.

The new Colonial Empire that was to replace the lost American colonies was slowly rising. It has already been shown how the war hastened the growth of our power in India. Canada and Australia were little affected by the Napoleonic struggle or by the treaties that ended it.[1] But we had to decide in 1815 how many of the colonies and ports of call all over the world, then in our hands as prizes of war, we intended permanently to retain. In that generation stations and ports of call were more highly valued by our statesmen than colonies. So Malta was kept; and Mauritius; and the Cape of Good Hope as the key of the route to India, though it turned out later to be a very large colony in disguise. Dutch Ceylon, too, was kept as an appendix to India; and Danish Heligoland, which had proved a most useful centre for smuggling goods into Germany during our fight with the Napoleonic embargo.

But on the whole we were generous in our restorations. France and Denmark got back their most valuable islands. Holland, to whom we had assigned the doubtful boon of Belgium, lost indeed the Cape and Ceylon, but we paid her three million sterling for what is now British Guiana, where before the war British planters had lived under the Dutch flag. Above all, we restored to Holland her wealthy empire in the East Indies: Java was given back to the Dutch in 1815, and shortly afterwards we ceded to them our ports and interests in Sumatra. It was the more remarkable because the brief period of our occupation had been signalized by the work of one of the greatest and best servants our Empire ever possessed, Sir Stamford Raffles. He was perhaps the first European who successfully brought modern humanitarian and scientific methods

1. See pp. 180–82, below, for Canada and the American war of 1812–14.

to bear on the improvement of the natives and their lot. Finally, in 1824, the trading station of Singapore was all that Britain chose to retain of Raffles's legacy in the Malay Archipelago – until in the following generation an equally remarkable man, 'Rajah' Brooke of Sarawak, without official aid, won northern Borneo by sheer force of personality and by the best British methods of treating native races.

The greatest gains with which Britain emerged from the war did not appear in the treaties. There were the unrivalled supremacy of our navy and of our mercantile marine; the reputation of having been the only Power that consistently withstood Napoleon; the possession of a Parliamentary system now more than ever the envy of 'less happier lands' since the relative failure of 'French principles' of liberty. With these advantages we faced the coming era.

The policy embodied in the treaties of 1815 was, in some of its chief aspects, generous and wise. It prevented a war of revenge by France, and it gave security to the British Empire for a hundred years; on both counts the policy of Castlereagh had been the decisive factor. The defect of the settlement, destined to imperil Britain once more when the wheel had come full circle, was its entire neglect of the craving of the European peoples for nationality and for freedom. While France secured the rudiments of constitutional government under the 'charter', of which Talleyrand and the strange Tsar Alexander had been the chief advocates, Germans, Italians, and Spaniards were thrust back under the crudest forms of reactionary despotism, and the populations of Poland, Belgium, Italy, and Germany were treated as mere assets and counters in bargains over the personal claims of alien sovereigns. It will always be open to controversy how far this was inevitable in view of the attitude of the Prussian, Austrian, and Russian governments; or how far England might have made a stand on the lines of Canning's policy a few years later if it had not been for the ultra-Tory doctrines of the Cabinet. It is certain that Castlereagh, not from negligence but on a consistent line of policy, in this respect did practically nothing. But it is more than doubtful whether he could have done anything if he had tried. Britain was not the lord of the land, but of the ocean, and, where Prussia, Russia, and Austria were agreed, they were in a position to impose their will on Central and most of Western Europe. That was the price that Europe paid for the overthrow of Napoleon.

Closely connected with this first defect in the settlement was another. The new distribution of territory fostered the undue growth in the European polity of the three Eastern despotisms, who would certainly be able to overpower German popular liberties and might some day be too strong for France and England combined. Not only were popular wishes absolutely ignored, but even the principle of 'legitimacy' – that is to say, the restoration of states and sovereigns as they had been before 1789 – was adhered to only where it suited Russia, Prussia, and Austria. Wherever the province in question was coveted by one of the Great Powers, historical claims were pleaded in vain. The kingdom of Poland, as it had existed in 1792, was not accounted 'legitimate' in 1814. Part of the kingdom of Saxony and the prince bishoprics of the Rhine were given to Prussia. The Republic of Venice and its Adriatic seaboard went to Austria. On the other hand, since the Temporal Power of the Pope over Central Italy suited Austria's game, it was restored, as if the eighteenth century had come back again. Protestant England set her seal to the arrangement, for the overthrow of which she was destined forty-five years later to hold the ring as an enthusiastic assistant.

The net result was that Russia, Prussia, and Austria were left with the chief power on the Continent, even if France and England for a while longer held the intellectual lead. This eastern and despotic predominance proved fatal to continental liberties in 1848–9, was recognized as the unwritten law of Europe after 1870, and caused the war of 1914 and its consequences. But again we may ask, how could Castlereagh have endeavoured, after Napoleon was conquered, to go back on the promises by which alone Russia, Austria, and Prussia had been induced to carry through the war of liberation? Indeed, by what possible means could he have resisted their will on the continent of Europe?

Thus the merits of the great settlement associated with the names of Wellington and Castlereagh gave Britain security which she used for a hundred years of progress in liberty and high civilization; while the defects of the same settlement, for which also they were in part though in small degree responsible, set a date to that happiness in the end.

CHAPTER 9

THE disciples of Burke and Eldon, with unconscious irony, daily proclaimed their aversion to change of every sort. They failed to understand that they themselves were living in the midst of a revolution more profound than that which drew all their thoughts across the Channel. Nor did they lift a finger to check its headlong course.

Since it was the destiny of the human race that the commonest methods of bread-winning and production were to undergo changes incomparably more rapid than those of any previous age there must in any case have been terrible suffering while the life of a whole people was being thus uprooted. But the misery in England, necessarily great, was increased by the political and intellectual atmosphere of the period in which the change began, just as it was greatly mitigated by the more humane politics and more liberal thought of the middle and later nineteenth century.

When George III ascended the throne on the eve of the Industrial Revolution the English labourer was in most cases a countryman. He enjoyed not a few of the amenities of the pleasant old-world life, and often some personal independence, and some opportunity of bettering his position. For a variety of reasons, real wages had been fairly good in the first part of the eighteenth century. The labourers and the small farmers had reason for the traditional pride that they felt as 'free-born Englishmen', and they appear to have looked up to the gentry, more often than not, without envy or resentment. This happy state of society did once in some sort exist, although at the time when anti-Jacobin writers invoked it as an ideal to rally Britons against the republican doctrines it was passing into the land of dreams, yielding place to the grim realities of Cobbett's England.

The 'labouring poor' in the eighteenth century had enjoyed many privileges, but they had lacked political power. This weakness proved their undoing alike in town and country, when the world of old custom, which had so long afforded them a partial shelter, was destroyed by the Industrial Revolution. When the common, the cow, the garden, the strips of corn land, the cottage industries, and the good wages of the early Georgian period disappeared together, the poor had no means of demanding analogous benefits under any new system. They had neither the influence nor the knowledge to plead so as to be heard, either before Parliament, or before their more immediate lords, the Justices of the Peace.

The wealthy classes then enjoyed, to a degree seldom paralleled in our history, a monopoly of every form of power. They had done more to earn and deserve it than any continental *noblesse*, but it was excessive. Because their position was unchallenged, they fell unconsciously and almost innocently into the habit of considering all national and economic problems in terms consonant with their own interest.

The effective political economy of this period that guided the action of Parliament, of the Justices of the Peace, of the new mill-owners, and of the enclosing landlords, was a selection and exaggeration of those parts of Adam Smith, Malthus, and Ricardo which suited the acquisition of wealth by the wealthy, and a quiet ignoring of the other doctrines of those eminent philosophers.[1] Such is the way in which any class, high or low, rich or poor, is sure to treat political economy, where it is not checked by the presence in the controversial arena of other classes in a position to make their side of the question heard.

In the days of Pitt and Castlereagh the average respectable man sincerely believed that Malthus had shown poverty to be inevitable for the majority of mankind on account of the natural increase of population; that the object of labour was not, as had formerly been thought, to supply a comfortable subsistence to the producers in the village community, but to turn out the greatest possible quantity of goods and so increase the nation's wealth; that this could best be achieved by freeing agriculture and industry from obsolete rights and customs; that common wastes and communal tillage must be abolished, together with apprenticeship and all forms of regulation of industry. It was held that the attempt of the State through the magistrates to settle wages fairly between employer and workman was an antiquated absurdity, because it was impossible to interfere with the inexorable economic laws which alone fixed what the wage must be; that for the same reason combinations of workmen to raise wages must be punished as crimes, more especially as they were politically dangerous and Jacobinical; that on the other hand the masters, who alone understood the needs of an industry, could properly consult together as to what wages it could bear; that it was impossible for the State to interfere in any respect with the bargains that a master made with a

1. Thus Adam Smith was opposed to protective duties and to State interference against labourers' combinations. Malthus favoured factory Acts and national education. He and Ricardo both favoured Parliamentary reform, and both took part in the movement for the repeal of Pitt's Combination Acts against Trade Unions. Neither of them really preached the dogmatic despair about the possibility of bettering the condition of the working classes, which was supposed to be their comfortable doctrine for the well-to-do. McCulloch, with his wages fund theory in the next generation, made their doctrines more rigid and inhuman; his was the 'dismal science' indeed. – (Adam Smith's *Wealth of Nations*, published 1776. Rev. T. R. Malthus's *Essay on Population*, 1798 (revised edition, 1803). Ricardo's *Principles of Political Economy and Taxation*, 1817. McCulloch's *Essay on the Rate of Wages*, 1826.)

workman, either as regards the hours, pay, or conditions of his own or his children's labour; and finally, that if the working classes obtained power they would use it to burn more ricks, smash more machinery, and destroy society like the French Jacobins.

Much of this creed was common ground between Whigs and Tories. The Foxite Whigs were indeed ready to enfranchise the middle classes, and to allow the poor to hold political meetings, but they failed to comprehend the economic and social realities below.[1] So, too, this same one-sided philosophy satisfied, during the Napoleonic war, both the unenfranchised millowners and the landlord governors of the Empire. The Corn Law of 1815 brought the first serious discord, for while the landlords were persuaded that corn must be kept artificially at eighty shillings a quarter or the State would perish, the master manufacturers thought that this was a gross interference with trade. So began the rift between upper and middle class, which gradually widened into such a chasm that labour from below was able to thrust through its head.

We have already indicated[2] the nature of the revolution in agriculture which between 1760 and 1840 transformed so much land from wastes and open fields to the chess-board of hedge and ditch that we know so well today. These changes were effected under the leadership of 'improving landlords'. Such a one was Coke of Norfolk, George III's enemy and, in Norfolk, one might say rival, with his Holkham sheepshearings, famous over two hemispheres. He reigned from the beginning of the American Revolution to the premiership of Peel, spent half a million on his estate, transformed it from something little better than a rabbit-warren into one of the most productive districts of England, and raised his rental from £2,200 to £20,000 a year. He was adored by all classes in the countryside, for he had made their fortunes. His life was a mixture of the patriarchal and the progressive – old English of the best.

During the half-century that followed the accession of George III our country led the world in the scientific progress of agriculture, largely because the grandees of that period, besides being men of high education and experience in great affairs, loved their

---

1. Lord Holland, indeed, opposed Pitt's Combination Laws against Trade Unions, and a dozen years later Byron and he in 1812 spoke up for the Luddites, when Byron told the House of Lords in his maiden speech: 'I have been in some of the most oppressed provinces of Turkey, but never under the most despotic of infidel governments did I behold such squalid wretchedness as I have seen since my return in the very heart of a Christian country.'

2. See p. 23–5, above.

country homes and the company of their rural neighbours, and depended on their estates for their vast incomes.

They invested much capital in the improvement of land, and were amply rewarded by rents that often rose during the Napoleonic wars to four or five times what they had been in the former generation.

The mouthpiece and inspirer of these men in the heyday of their agricultural zeal was Arthur Young, at once the practical and literary leader of English country life during the period of its revolution. His patriotic idealism drew him into a crusade against the waste lands; he saw that, if properly enclosed and cultivated, they would yield far more than the gains made by the poor of the neighbourhood whose cattle wandered by right over these commons. He was no less zealous against the great open field of the midland village with its hundreds of tiny strips[1]; he desired to see it hedged round into a score of fair-sized fields under farmers with enterprise and capital. Communal tillage was an anachronism, monstrously perpetuating into the age of enlightenment the methods by which Piers the Ploughman had toiled on the manors of John of Gaunt.

Young saw his dreams realized. In whole districts the very landscape was changed according to his desire. The break-up of the old cautious peasant life helped the population to increase at a pace unknown during the long centuries of 'subsistence agriculture'. The enclosures helped England, by producing more corn and wealth, to survive the economic struggle with Napoleon. But unfortunately they had also another effect, which their chief author in the latter part of his life had the humanity to recognize and the manhood to proclaim. In 1801, Arthur Young wrote to tell his fellow-countrymen that: 'By nineteen out of twenty Enclosure Bills the poor are injured and most grossly.'

Enclosure on a great scale was absolutely necessary in order to increase corn production and to keep pace with the changes in industry. But the method adopted from 1760 to 1840 was too uniform and paid too little regard to social consequences. Enclosure of open fields and common wastes, which meant the disappearance of innumerable small rights and properties, was during this period conducted by a long series of private Acts of Parliament, promoted by local landlords, and passed by two Houses composed almost entirely of that same class. The compensation given to the dispossessed commoner or small holder was often inadequate, usually taking the form of a little money; the

1. See p. 23, above.

recipient had seldom any chance of setting up again as a farmer under the new system, where considerable capital was required, if only for the necessary fencing.[1]

The legislators saw nothing but the good side of what they did. The new fashion of economic and political thought no longer judged things by the old criterion of rearing independent families, but by the aggregate national wealth. The doctrine not only attracted philosophers and patriots, but suited the game-preserving lords and squires, who rejoiced in the disappearance of the independent classes, the yeoman freeholder and the small cottar on the edge of the common, because the countryside was thus rid of rebels to feudal authority, and actual or potential poachers. Indeed, by the time the social consequences of the movement began to be plain, the anti-Jacobin feeling of the new age openly welcomed the enclosure of common land as a means of keeping the people in their place. The use of common land by labourers 'operates upon the mind as a sort of independence', we read in Mr Bishton's Report on Shropshire sent to the Board of Agriculture in 1794: but when the remaining commons are enclosed, then 'that subordination of the lower ranks of society, which in the present times is much wanted, would be hereby considerably secured'. The labourers, who are to be housed in cottages supplied by their employers, will then work every day instead of idling about on their own patches, and their children, who are now growing up wild, lazy, and vicious, will be 'taught to read and put out to labour early'. Mr Bishton and many others believed, from their own personal observation, that the economic as well as the moral condition of the squatter on the common would be improved if he was turned off it and given no choice but to work as a farm hand.

Not only the squatter on the common, but the small yeoman disappeared, even out of regions like Kent and Devon, where enclosure had taken place in former centuries in a manner compatible with small farming. Undoubtedly more corn had to be grown, and could be best grown on large farms. But the movement in that direction was too universal and uniform, even from the standpoint of production. While the large farm was best for corn, on the other hand poultry and livestock were best reared and sold by the small farmer and by his wife, who took the eggs, butter and pigs to market, or supplied geese and turkeys to the great towns. The big farmers would not be bothered with these things; they produced corn on the grand scale and thought of nothing else. Under the impetus of Napoleonic prices they took the plough

1. See p. 466, below, Appendix, *Enclosures of Land* (*b*).

over lands quite unsuitable for corn. When the fall in the price of corn came, they had too often no other string to their bow.

The enclosures had increased the food supply and the national wealth; but the increased wealth had gone chiefly in rent to the landlord, in tithe to the parson, and to the pocket of the more fortunate of the big farmers.[1] The lower middle class had become poor, and the poor had become paupers. Agricultural progress had been so handled as to bring disaster to the working agriculturist. This would have been avoided by leaving a larger number of small holders, and by enforcing the payment of a living wage by the farmer instead of throwing the farm hands as paupers upon the rates.

The pauperization of rural England, the long-drawn-out disaster with which the nineteenth century opened, can only in part be ascribed to the mistakes accompanying the necessary enclosure of the land. It was equally due to the decadence of the cottage industries.[2] As textile and other trades were year by year gathered round the new machinery and the new factories, the corresponding industries disappeared out of cottage after cottage and village after village, at the very time when efforts were being made in so many districts to convert common waste land and small holdings into large farms. The small yeoman or labourer, losing sometimes his own sources of income, sometimes those of his wife and children, and sometimes losing both together, was left in helpless dependence on the big farmer, who, just because the rural proletariat had nothing now to live on but the farm wage, was able to cut that wage down to the starvation rate.

At this crisis in the fortunes of the poor, prices rushed up; the harvests from 1792 to 1813 were exceptionally bad; the French wars interfered with the importation of corn; food was at famine prices. The population increased with a rapidity hitherto unknown. Many went off to the new factories and helped to lower

1. Cobbett thus describes the change of manners and style of living that accompanied the increased wealth of the tenant farmer: 'The English farmer has, of late years, become a totally different character. A fox-hunting horse; polished boots; a spanking trot to market; a "get out of the way or by G—d I'll ride over you" to every poor devil upon the road; wine at his dinner; a servant (and sometimes in *livery*) to wait at his table; a painted lady for a wife; sons aping the young squires and lords; a house crammed up with sofas, pianos, and all sorts of fooleries.' Of course much of this had its good as well as its bad side, though Cobbett could see nothing but the bad.

2. In some districts the disappearance of the cottage industries was the principal or only cause why the small yeomen sold their farms, because they could no longer make two ends meet (Wordsworth's *Description of the Lakes* ed. 1823, pp. 47, 85–6).

industrial wage rates. Some went to the New World, though the great tide of emigration only came in the second quarter of the nineteenth century. Enough of them remained on the countryside to prevent a rise of wages there, and even to create a danger that multitudes would perish of inanition.

The danger of wholesale death by famine, with which rural England was faced in 1795, was averted by a remedy that per-petrated and increased the evils of the time – the famous poor-rate in aid of wages. In May of that year the magistrates of Berkshire were summoned to meet at Speenhamland[1] for the expressed object of fixing and enforcing a living wage for the county in relation to the price of bread. It would no doubt have been hard to carry out during the period of violent price fluctuations between 1795 and 1815, but in principle this was the true remedy. If it had been adopted for Berkshire and for all England it might have diverted our modern social history at its source into happier channels. It was the course pointed out by ancient custom and existing law. Unfortunately the magistrates, who had come to Speenhamland for this good purpose, were there persuaded not to enforce the raising of wages, but to supplement wages instead out of the parish rates. They drew up and published a scale, by which every poor and industrious person should receive from the parish enough to make up the deficiency of his wages to 3s. a week for himself, and for every other member of his family 1s. 6d. a week, when the loaf cost a shilling. As the loaf rose higher the dole was to rise with it. This convenient scale, vulgarly known as the 'Speenhamland Act', was adopted by the magistrates in county after county, till, except in some of the northern shires, the labourers of all England were pauperized. 'Speenhamland' became a governing fact of English life until the Poor Law of 1834.

The result was that agricultural wages were kept unduly low. As the burden of maintaining the employee had been taken over by the parish and as labour was plentiful, the farmer had no motive to pay a higher wage. And the principle of supplementing wages out of rates, while it kept down wages, destroyed the self-respect of the labourer, by making pauperism the shameless rule instead of the shameful exception. The net result of the enclosures and of Speenhamland was that the labourer had small economic motive for industry, sobriety, independence, or thrift. The employee of the big farmer was often compelled to become a pauper; and to maintain him the small, independent man was crushed by the

1. Speenhamland seldom figures in modern maps; it is the northern part of Newbury.

exactions of the poor-rate. In every way it was made as hard as possible for the poor to be self-supporting. Enclosure had helped to put an end to the old methods of livelihood which once had been schools of modest virtue. Arthur Young, awakened to the evils that had accompanied the success of his own policy, thus summarizes the philosophy of the alehouse bench when the new century opened: 'If I am sober, shall I have land for a cow? If I am frugal, shall I have half an acre of potatoes? You offer no motives. Bring me another pot.'

The rapid increase of the population, so much deplored at this time by the disciples of Malthus, has been very generally ascribed first to the enclosures, and then to Speenhamland. In the days of 'subsistence agriculture' the English peasants had been 'small men', but each with a standard to maintain. The rustic lover had prudently waited before marrying till he could tell his bride of 'a pig put up in a stye', or some other basis for the family budget. And the small farmer, if he employed labour at all, preferred to hire young unmarried people who slept in the farm and shared his table. But under the new system all was changed. The big farmer put his labourers into hovels of their own, where now the Speenhamland Poor Law secured them eighteen pence a week for every child they brought into the world. Even the mother of a family of illegitimate children was offered, as such, a better income than the worker in the field.

These conditions, and the corresponding conditions of factory life with its child labour, have been held largely to account for the sudden increase in a population which, so far as we know, had grown only very gradually since the Norman Conquest. Yet, although the new social régime, as compared to the old, may have tended to encourage parents to bring children into the world, the fact remains that the great increase of population in the later years of George III was due not to a rising birth-rate but to a falling death-rate. In spite of all the acute miseries of the period, the average length of life was greater than in days before the industrial revolution. Vital statistics seem to indicate that the improvement in medical efficiency, resulting in the control of smallpox, scurvy, infant mortality, and common diseases of the poor, counterbalanced the accompanying evils of industrial change at least on the purely material side of life.[1]

When hope and self-respect had fled, crime made his seat on the hearth. In the era of Waterloo rick-burning was a common form

1. Griffith, *Population in the Age of Malthus*; Mrs George, *London Life in the Eighteenth Century*; *Economic History Review*, April 1935, p. 68.

of vengeance that often had the secret sympathy of the whole village, while highway robbery and thieving in barns were resorted to with dreadful frequency as a means of subsistence. But the particular crime most deeply resented and most severely punished by legislators and magistrates was regarded by the bulk of the population as no crime at all: to the man whom society had made a pauper *malgré lui* it must often have seemed that to snare hares and net partridges at risk to his personal safety was the most honourable part of the grim and sordid life in which he strove against fate to find food for wife and child. Poaching brought a gleam of romance and joyous living into the life of the disinherited peasant –

Oh, 'tis my delight, on a shining night, in the season of the year.

The game laws, severe when George III came to the throne, were still having fresh rigours added to them when he died. These later laws ascribed transportation for a long term of years even to the poacher carrying nothing more formidable than a net. Some indeed of the poachers were professional ruffians, coming armed from a distance and reckless of human life. The woods at midnight resounded with volleys when gentlemen and their servants, in parties of a dozen or twenty, were grappling with the banditti, man to man. It was in these years that the harsh spirit of the age introduced a new terror into the English woodland, the 'mantrap', with its crocodile teeth, and the yet deadlier 'spring-gun', lurking in the undergrowth and murdering not only the poacher, for whom they were meant, but the gamekeeper or the innocent neutral.

Partly because they slew and maimed at random, partly because legislators were beginning to think more humanely, these engines of refurbished feudalism were made illegal in 1827. But the poaching war still raged on, and in the next three years there were over 8,500 convictions under the game laws. Poaching diminished just in proportion as the game laws were softened down to the Victorian level of humanity and justice.

The agricultural revolution of George III's reign had been, for the labourer, a tragedy. But the part of villain need not be ascribed to the landlords.

In tragic life, God wot,
No villain need be

can apply as well to public as to private matters. It is true that the landlords' rents went up two- three- and fourfold during the Napoleonic wars. But that was largely because they had invested

158

their money in improving their estates. It was not the mere rack-rent of the unimproving Irish landlord of the same period. It was return on capital, well invested in an industry which enabled the island to increase its population in days when food could not be imported largely from abroad. Such was one aspect of the enclosures. And if the rents went up, so did war-taxation and the poor-rate. Speenhamland was a bad policy, but it was to a large extent a self-imposed levy on landlords to prevent the poor from dying of starvation.

The Corn Law of 1815, prohibiting the import of corn till the price of wheat stood above eighty shillings a quarter – a terrible price in the money values of that day – was indeed a great mistake, but Huskisson did not think so at the time. It was an almost inevitable outcome of the landowning monopoly of the legislature. Any other class with a like political monopoly would have been equally self-regarding. In the panic created by the sudden fall of corn prices after the war, farmers threw up their farms in multitudes, and became bankrupts and village paupers. The landlords themselves, who had unwisely launched out into expenses on the expectation of perpetual high prices, had often mortgaged their estates, and were now in great difficulties. Although rents were not reduced as much or as quickly as they should have been, they had fallen in 1816 it was believed by as much as nine millions. The collapse of prices in 1814–16 was more rapid and terrifying than the agricultural depression of 1875 and the following years. In spite of the great increase of rents during the Napoleonic war, landlords were probably nothing like so substantially prosperous as their grandchildren in 1875–80. And so, having the means, as they imagined, of saving themselves and the country with them, they passed the Corn Law of 1815 with the best intentions and the worst results.

Meanwhile, step by step with the rural revolution, advanced the urban revolution, similar in principle and in spirit, and at the outset similar in its social consequences. Just as the old theory of subsistence agriculture, associated with ancient rights, small properties, and communal tillage, was being replaced by a new habit of mind that looked for the greatest net productivity of the national soil, on a basis of unfettered individual farming on the large scale – so in the towns the old theory of a 'limited' and 'well-regulated' trade, based on the local monopoly of a chartered few, subjecting themselves to a common set of rules about trade and apprenticeship, was being gradually abandoned for the new

159

principle of open world-competition wherein all traders who could muster the capital and enterprise were invited to buy in the cheapest market and sell in the dearest, and to hire their labour wherever they liked and on what conditions each could secure. The change, in town as well as country, caused a wide cleavage of sympathy and of interest between classes which had previously shared, each in its degree, the common advantages of a fixed system of life and work; now that everyone scrambled for himself, the rich became richer and the poor poorer, and the law instead of attempting to redress the balance interfered heavily on the side of the employer. Such at least was the first phase of the new civilization in England.

A new civilization, not only for England but ultimately for all mankind, was implicit in the substitution of scientific machinery for handwork. The Greek scientists of the Alexandrine age, the contemporaries of Archimedes and of Euclid, had failed to apply their discoveries to industry on the big scale. Perhaps this failure was due to the contempt with which the high-souled philosophy of Hellas regarded the industrial arts conducted by slave labour; perhaps the great change was prevented by the disturbed and warlike state of the Mediterranean world during those three hundred years between Alexander and Augustus, when Greek science was in its most advanced state. In any case it was left to the peaceful, cultivated, but commercially minded England of the generation that followed Newton's death to harness philosophic thought and experiment to the commonest needs of daily life. The great English inventors negotiated the alliance of science and business.

The social and intellectual conditions of the England of that day would not have been enough to initiate the industrial revolution without the presence on the spot of coal and iron. Both had long been known and used, but they had not yet been used together. The British iron industry had flourished since primeval times in the weald of Surrey and Sussex, where lonely 'hammer ponds' still recall the vanished day. From times before the Phoenician traders came to Britain, down to the time of the elder Pitt, ironmasters had been feeding their furnaces from the local forests. So long as wood remained the only fuel, the output of iron or steel was necessarily small, and so long as it remained small there could be no age of machinery. But in the middle of the eighteenth century, just when the English woodland was giving out, and the iron industry was beginning to leave our shores for the Scandinavian and North American forests, methods were devised to apply coal to the smelting process. This discovery led, by a chain of closely interrelated developments, to the whole urban revolution.

Iron-smelting moved to the North and Midlands to be near the coal. As the demand for coal grew, steam-engines, invented by James Watt in the early years of George III, were used to pump water from the mines. More iron, the result of more coal, in turn made it possible to produce more steam-engines, and men looked round for other ways to employ them, whether in locomotion or manufacture. In Watt's own lifetime his steam-engines were applied to the cotton industry. Already the need for more coal had produced not only steam-engines but English canals, and many years later it produced the steam railways. Brindley's first canal and Stephenson's first locomotive were both made to carry coal from the pit's mouth.

It was characteristic of England, as opposed to the France of the *ancien régime*, that some of our nobility took an active part in these developments. The Duke of Bridgewater employed Brindley and invested his own capital in the first canals. There were great noblemen who were also great coalowners, working their own mines, and thereby becoming in due course still greater noblemen.

On the other hand, the changes in cotton and wool that followed hard on the changes in iron and coal were not patronized by the aristocracy, or even to any great extent by the merchant capitalists. The textile revolution was the work of a wholly new order of men, risen from the ranks by their energy in seizing the opportunities of the new industrial situation. A workman who had toiled at the hand-loom in his own cottage might borrow £100 to start as a small employer with the new machines. The more enterprising of the vanishing class of yeomen invested the price of their ancestral farms in a like venture. Such are the origins of not a few families who became honourably famous in the nineteenth century.

The first generation of these men had the defects as well as the merits of pioneers. A common type of 'millowner' in the days of the younger Pitt was a hard-bitten North-country working-man, of no education and great force of character, taking little stock of his social or political relations with the outer world, allowing neither leisure nor recreation to himself or to his hands, but managing somehow to convert the original £100 that he borrowed into a solvent 'mill', the prison-house of children, the hidden reef on which Napoleon's empire struck. As a rule, he bothered his head equally little about the children he employed and the foreign war in which he was to be a decisive factor – except in so far as they made or marred his own fortunes.

By the time the war came to an end, men and their manners were changing. A millowner of the second generation had been born and bred a bourgeois, but of a new and enterprising type. With more education and wider outlook than his grim old father, the young man looked about him for the uses, obligations, and privileges of wealth, as they were understood in that generation. He cast an eye on the world of gentry and clergy around him, with the result sometimes of alliance, more often of mutual repulsion. As likely as not he became a Unitarian, to express his intellectual and social independence, while his workmen sought simple salvation as Baptists or Wesleyans. As a young man, he believed in Mr Brougham, slavery abolition, and the 'march of mind', hated Church Rates, Orders in Council, Income Tax, and Corn Laws, and read the *Edinburgh Review*. His coming battle with the Tory borough-owners and landlords, delayed by the long struggle with Napoleon, was a thing as inevitable as the feud with his own workmen that he had inherited from his father. But his war on two fronts never degenerated into class-war pure and simple; with its constant regroupings, cross-currents, conversions, and compromises, it was the destined method of evolution for the political and intellectual life of the new Britain.

The cotton industry, though not absolutely created by the new machinery, derived thence almost its whole importance. Between the accession of George III and the passing of the Reform Bill its output increased a hundred-fold. Already by 1806 cotton was said to supply a third of the total British exports. The industry was concentrated in South and Central Lancashire, because the port of Liverpool was convenient to a trade depending on the import of raw cotton and the export of the manufactured article; because there it was near cheap coal; and because the climate of the damp Atlantic seaboard is peculiarly suitable to fine spinning.

The first mills, worked by water-power, were established on the upper reaches of the Pennine streams. But throughout the long war with France Watt's steam-engines were replacing water-power, and the industry was carried on by altogether more modern methods. This meant a change from small to large mills, real capitalist employers, great assemblies of working-people, and an increase in the proportion of skilled mechanics – circumstances all of which prepared the way for improved conditions of life in the future. The employees, now accumulated in one mill by hundreds instead of by scores, could not long fail to combine for economic and political action. The new type of large millowner had a secure financial position, more education, and sometimes more enlightenment. Individuals of this class introduced factory conditions which inspectors in a later time could enforce as standards. And when the age of Factory Acts came, it was easier to inspect properly one big mill than many small ones.

If the cotton industry showed England the way into some of the worst miseries of the industrial revolution, it also showed the way out, because it passed most rapidly through the period of semi capitalized and half-organized industry, with its mean cruelties, into full-blown capitalism where the workpeople, the masters, and the State could readily take stock of each other.

But before the age of Factory Acts, the condition of women and children in both small and big mills was as a rule very wretched. Mothers and children worked from twelve to fifteen hours a day under insanitary conditions, without either the amenities of life which had sweetened and relieved the tedium of family work in the cottage, or the conditions which make factory life attractive to many women today. The discipline of the early factories was like the discipline of a prison. Small children were often cruelly treated to keep them awake during the long hours, which shortened their lives or undermined their health.

The men were in little better case. Often out of employment, they were forced to sell their wives and children into the slavery of the mills, while they themselves degenerated in squalid idleness. The hand-loom weavers had flourished until the early years of the nineteenth century, weaving the increased product of the new spinning mills. But the coming of the power-loom destroyed their prosperity; their wages fell, they went on to the rates as paupers, and drank the dregs of misery, until after long years their old-world employment altogether disappeared.

The older branch of the textile industry, wool, was more widely spread over the island than its younger and half-foreign sister, cotton. But its chief centre remained in the dales of the West Riding of Yorkshire. Wool was subject to the same general conditions of employment as cotton, and underwent in the end the same kind of transformation. But the change came more slowly in wool. Although the spinning-jenny had in the last years of the eighteenth century gone far to destroy the spinning of wool by women and children in rural cottages, the power-loom was introduced for the weaving of worsted and wool several decades later than for cotton. In the early years of the century, therefore, the woollen weavers suffered little from the introduction of machinery, although the fluctuations of trade caused them much distress.

Coal-mining was an ancient industry, but its development in the age of 'iron and coal' was prodigious, and a large part of the population now worked underground. Women were used there as beasts of burden, and children worked in the dark, sometimes for fourteen hours.[1] The men laboured under conditions that showed but little regard for health or human life. In Durham and Northumberland it was not the custom before 1815 to hold inquests on the victims of the innumerable accidents. Payment was not on a cash basis, owing to the 'truck' system, and the oppression by the 'putties' or sub-contractors for labour. These things and the condition of the miners' cottages, which were generally owned by their employers, too often rendered the life of the miner of a hundred years ago 'brutish, nasty, and brief'.

If things were thus in the great textile and mining industries, they were no better in shops and smaller businesses where the new semicapitalized industry was breaking up the old apprentice system and the 'regulated' trade. Indeed in many small or less highly organized concerns, where Trade Unionism failed to take root, 'truck' payments and 'sweated' wages and hours continued till the end of the nineteenth century, though they were worse when it began.

The new urban proletariat was swelled in numbers and depressed in standard of life by constant arrivals of fresh swarms of impoverished rustics, driven by stress of famine from the English and the Irish countryside. Any attempt of workmen to combine for a living wage consonant with the rise of prices was illegal under Pitt's Combination Acts (1799). And though the law was frequently violated by the men it was frequently enforced by the Justices of the Peace. However little some of the magistrates who were squires might sympathize with the new class of millowner, they saw their duty in keeping down the 'Jacobinism' of the lower orders. But in fact they were thus preparing for 'Jacobinism' a powerful revival.

After the Tom Paine movement had been suppressed, the workmen in the early years of the nineteenth century had no political ambition. But they petitioned Parliament during the Napoleonic wars that a living wage should be enforced in accordance with existing statutes; such patriarchal protection by the authorities would seem the corollary of Pitt's laws that prevented the workmen from attempting to raise wages for themselves. But the answer of Parliament in 1813 was to repeal the assessment clauses

1. As late as 1842 the Royal Commission on Mines, that first threw light on the life of underground England, brought out such facts as these from a Lancashire woman: 'I have a belt round my waist and a chain passing between my legs, and I go on my hands and feet. The water comes up to my clog tops, and I have seen it over my thighs. I have drawn till I have the skin off me. The belt and chain is worse when we are in the family way.' It was also shown that children under five worked alone in the darkness.

of the Elizabethan Statutes for the enforcement of which the workmen were asking. Assessment of wages was condemned on the principle of non-interference proclaimed by the new political economy. *Laissez faire* was always invoked against the workman but never on his behalf, as was proved once more when in 1815 the price of bread was artificially raised by the Corn Law. It was this unfair political dealing at every turn that drove the masses of workmen now collected together in the great staple industries to renew their interest in politics.

The Tory panacea for unrest had been proclaimed in 1795 by Bishop Horsley when he said that 'the mass of the people had nothing to do with the laws but to obey them.' During the next twenty years the laws had almost invariably been used to make the mass of the people worse off. That was why the workmen, led by Cobbett and Hunt, began to demand the vote, before the middle classes had been stirred to a like demand. That was why Peterloo followed hard on Waterloo.

Before tracing the political history of the new era, it remains to notice some of the moral and intellectual influences to which men and women were subjected, when, uprooted from the pieties and associations of the old rural life, they drifted to the new factories to find work.

First they had to be housed, if only in the private and temporary interest of the employer. Consideration for the public and forethought for the future were absent from the planning of the new town. The man for the employer's purpose was the jerry-builder, who designed the outward aspect of the new civilization. Street after street sprang up, each more ugly, narrow, and insanitary than the last. They were barracks for cheap labour, not homes for citizens.

Citizens, indeed, the workmen were not. They had no word in the government of England, and no civic position in the local area which they had come to inhabit. If they happened to be lodged within a chartered town, they lived under a close corporation and its municipal magistrates. If they were outside such precincts, they were under the rural Justices of the Peace and the antiquarian relics of the Court Leet. Neither urban nor rural authorities were called upon to provide for health, lighting, decency, or education in a new factory quarter. They were content to quell riots and to arrest trade unionists, seditionists, deists, frame-breakers, and other criminals.

The municipal corruption of the eighteenth century had lost the civic traditions and the public spirit of medieval corporate life. The sudden growth of the new factory quarters hardly disturbed the complacency of the long inactive oligarchs, who were so well accustomed to neglect their old duties that they were not likely to attend to the new.

It is perhaps the greatest of our national misfortunes that the modern English town arose too rapidly and with too little regulation, either sanitary or aesthetic. The bodily and spiritual health of future generations was injured in advance. A type of city was allowed to grow up which it was fatally easy to imitate as the model for the whole industrial development of the new century, until the great majority of Englishmen were dwellers in mean streets, 'divorced from nature but unreclaimed by art'. When, indeed, in the course of the nineteenth century, local government was made to attend to its duties, by being subjected partly to democratic election and partly to an elaborate system of central control, large provision was made for health, convenience, and education. But ugliness remained a quality of the modern city, accepted by the public conscience in spite of Ruskin and his successors. It has yet to be dislodged.

Working-class life, a hundred years ago, divided between the gloom of these dreary quarters and the harsh discipline of the workshop, was uncheered by the many interests that now relieve the lot of the town dweller. Few of the workmen or their wives could read; the children had the factory and the slum, but not the school or the playground; holiday excursions and popular entertainments were rare, except some sporting events of a low type, such as setting on men, women, or animals to fight. In the vacant misery of such a life, two rival sources of consolation, drink and religion, strove for the souls of men. The annals of drink are much the same in all ages, though worst in ages of degradation. But the particular form that religion then took among the workmen influenced the course of political and social history.

The Established Church in that era scarcely paid more attention to the new slums than did the other constituted authorities. What Church expansion there was, took place chiefly at the expense of the taxpayer, who was compelled in 1818 to contribute a million pounds to build a hundred new churches. The beneficed clergy, many of whom were active magistrates, were suspect to the workmen as 'black dragoons' of the possessing classes. But many of the more self-respecting of the new proletariat found in the Baptist or Wesleyan chapel the opportunity for the development of talents and the gratification of instincts that were denied expression elsewhere. The close and enthusiastic study of the Bible educated the imagination more nobly than it is educated in our age of magazines, novelettes, and newspapers. And in the chapel life working-men first learnt to speak and to organize, to persuade, and to trust their fellows. Much effort that soon afterwards went into political, trade union, and co-operative activities, was then devoted to the chapel community. It was in Little Bethel that many of the working-class leaders were trained. In a world made almost intolerable by avarice and oppression, here was a refuge where men and things were taken up aloft and judged by spiritual and moral standards that forbade either revenge or despair.

The Wesleyans, unlike the Baptists, were originally conservative in their political associations, owing to the views of their founder, a Church of England clergyman. Wesley's religion could not indeed induce the workman of the new era to accept the conditions of his helotage, but it worked against violence and helped to develop many of the moral qualities and sober aspirations which have often distinguished the labour movement of England from that of the Continent.

The Radical 'infidelity' of the Peterloo era was a rival to Dissent, but like Dissent it nursed aspirations in the working class for better things. Before the French Revolution, unorthodox views had been common among the aristocracy of England, and indeed our free-thinking writers had given the original stimulus to the more formidable anti-clericalism of France. But in the days of Middleton, David Hume, Gibbon, and their upper-class patrons, the middle and working classes were orthodox Churchmen or Dissenters, or else were too ignorant to have any views on religion. With the publication of Tom Paine's *Age of Reason* (1794–6), a popularly written attack on miraculous religion from the point of view of ethical deism, the philosophic appeal to the people was fairly launched, and was associated with radicalism in politics owing to its author's burning reputation.

Partly on account of Paine's two-fronted attack against Church and State together, a strong religious reaction set in among the upper class under the combined influence of anti-Jacobinism and Evangelical religion. Only Fox, Lord Holland, and others of the high Whigs remained untouched by the movement, handing on in their party the tradition of a quiet and gentlemanly scepticism, half aristocratic, half liberal, wholly anti-ecclesiastical. Meanwhile the triumphant Tories were setting the law in motion against the propagators of Paine's doctrines, political and religious. *The Rights of Man* and *The Age of Reason*, after selling for a short while in thousands, were driven out of circulation before the century ended.

The two movements associated with Paine went on underground, and after Waterloo reappeared openly together among the northern factory hands. The leaders of the new radicalism, whose chief demand was universal suffrage, were nearly all either Deists or Dissenters. The Dissenting preachers were under the protection of Wilberforce and the Evangelical Churchmen, now powerful in the Tory party. But the blasphemy laws were refurbished, and a fresh war of prosecutions, fines, and imprisonments was waged against Radical publishers of deistic works, particularly the reprinters of Paine. The genuine horror felt by the respectable classes for a 'radical' was much increased by the supposition that he was also an 'infidel'.

In this connexion Richard Carlile suffered and achieved more for the liberty of the Press than any other Englishman of the nineteenth century. He and his like bore the brunt of this early struggle, which secured immunity for those who published unorthodox works. Thanks to these sturdy predecessors, the decorous and well-to-do philosophers of the Victorian era were able without fear of the law to write whatever they thought about the relation of science and literature to dogmatic belief.

If the real meaning of the Industrial Revolution and the breakup of the apprentice system had been understood, men would have seen that education was no longer a luxury for the few, but a necessity for all members of the new society. Generations were to pass before this idea was acted upon by the State, as a corollary of the working-class enfranchisement of 1867. The first effect of the Industrial Revolution, and the misery and unrest that it caused among the poor, was to render education suspect as 'Jacobinical'. This notion was still prevalent in Parliament in 1807; the House of Commons took the compulsory element out of the Bill by which Whitbread[1] proposed, somewhat on the Scottish model, to establish parish schools in England out of the rates. In the Lords the Bill, thus mutilated, was introduced by Lord Holland, but was rejected without a division, on the complaint of the Archbishop of Canterbury that it did not leave enough power to the clergy.[2]

1. Whitbread understood the social question better than the other Whig leaders. He moved to have a living wage enforced. He and Lord Holland were often peculiarly right about social questions.

2. In the Commons debate, Mr Giddy, afterwards President of the Royal Society under the name of Gilbert, said: 'However specious in theory the project might be of giving education to the labouring classes of the poor, it

But there was a counter-current setting towards a better future for education; and it gained ground as the French Revolution slowly receded into the background of men's consciousness. At the head of the new movement were the Quakers, ever ready with the purse; the more intelligent Whig leaders – Holland, Whitbread, Brougham; the Radical philosophers headed by Bentham; the few educated leaders of the workman, Owen and Place; and, in a separate group, the Evangelical Churchmen with their desire to promote among the humblest the personal study of the Bible. All these assisted to provide voluntary education since public funds were not available. More conservative educationalists, who dreaded lest a learned peasantry would turn Jacobin or desert agriculture for clerical professions, were appeased by the arrangement that only reading, and not writing, should be taught in the Sunday schools, now rapidly on the increase.

But, during the Peninsular War, the foundation of day-schools and the propagation of the dangerous art of writing received a fresh impulse. For some years past the Quaker Lancaster, partly helped by the ideas of the Churchman Bell, his future rival, had been working out a cheap education based on the 'monitorial system of instruction'. Lancaster's early efforts led to the formation of the 'British and Foreign School Society' under Dissenting and Whig patronage, on the basis of undenominational Bible-teaching; while the Churchmen, partly to counter Lancaster's early efforts, had founded the 'National Society for the Education of the Poor according to the Principles of the Church of England'.

The claim of the Church to control the spending of any public funds that might be devoted to education was in accordance with her privileged position in the law and theory of that time, but it was naturally resisted by many indignant laymen and Dissenters. The result was that all chance of public money going to education was put off to the Greek Calends. But religious rivalry, so disastrous in the legislative sphere, had a healthy effect on private benefaction,

---

would be prejudicial to their morals and happiness; it would teach them to despise their lot in life instead of making them good servants in agriculture or other laborious employments; instead of teaching them subordination it would render them fractious and refractory, as was evident in the manufacturing counties; it would enable them to read seditious pamphlets, vicious books, and publications against Christianity; it would render them insolent to their superiors; and in a few years the legislature would find it necessary to direct the strong arm of power towards them.'
This represented an attitude towards popular education very general among gentry and farmers.

'British' and 'National' schools multiplied, and the Church began to pull ahead, especially in rural districts. In 1818 as many as 600,000 children out of two million were attending schools of some sort. In the year of the Reform Bill, when Bell died, there were as many as 12,000 'National' schools.[1] But the 'monitorial system of instruction', though it made it easy to set up schools cheaply, gave very poor results. The master kept order while certain children whom he had instructed before school-hours imparted their newly acquired knowledge to the others by rote. This was at least better than nothing. But in the great factory districts, especially London and Lancashire, the employment of children in mills and workshops prevented them from receiving education of any kind, and made illiteracy common in parts of England where it should have been most rare.

The cause of Adult Education received its first stimulus from the Industrial Revolution in the desire of mechanics for general scientific knowledge, and the willingness of the more intelligent part of the middle class to help to supply their demand. It was a movement partly professional and utilitarian, partly intellectual and ideal. Disinterested scientific curiosity was strong among the better class of workmen in the North. From 1823 onwards Mechanics' Institutes, begun in Scotland by Dr Birkbeck, spread through industrial England. The flame was fanned by the bellows of Henry Brougham's organizing and advertising genius, in the period of his greatest public service, when he stood for the real 'Opposition' in Parliament and country, pointing to

The young time with the life ahead.

Self-satisfied classical scholars like Peacock might laugh at the 'learned friend' and his 'steam-intellect society', but the new world could not live wholly on classical scholarship carefully locked away from common use in the close ecclesiastical corporations of the Oxford and Cambridge of that day. Nor, in an age that needed first and foremost to be converted to see the need for

1. Cobbett, anxious to disprove that learning to read the Bible was a sufficient cure for the misery of the poor, wrote in 1816 with his usual terse exaggeration: 'It is notorious that where one person could read and write a hundred years ago, fifty persons can now read and write; it is notorious that, where one Bible was printed a hundred years ago, a hundred Bibles and perhaps a thousand Bibles are now printed; it is notorious that within the last twenty years schools of all sorts for the poor have increased a hundred-fold; it is notorious that where one man was hanged in England, fifty men are now hanged; it is notorious that where one person was a pauper when Pitt became minister, there are now more than twenty persons paupers.' – *Political Register*, 7 Sept. 1816.

education, was there so much harm in a 'semi-Solomon' from Scotland, irrepressible in zeal as a propagandist and not afraid of making a fool of himself before the learned if he could help the ignorant to learn.

The success of these democratic Mechanics' Institutes, with an annual subscription of a guinea, reminds us that there was one section of the working men, the engineers and mechanics who had already gained more than they lost by the Industrial Revolution.[1]

Of that Revolution, the men who made and mended the machines were indeed the bodyguard. They were usually better paid than their fellow-workmen, they were on the average more intelligent, and they often took the lead in educational and political movements. They were less looked down upon by the employers, who had to consult them and to bow to their technical knowledge. They were in the forefront of progress and invention, and rejoiced in the sense of leading the new age. Such workmen were the Stephensons of Tyneside; there was nothing 'middle class' about the origins of the man who invented the locomotive, after having taught himself to read at the age of seventeen.

It is indeed easier to reconstruct the early history of the coal-miners and textile hands than that of the mechanics and engineers, because the latter were scattered up and down the country. But any picture of the earliest and worst stage of the Industrial Revolution is too black if it omits the life of the mechanics. The motto of the coming age was 'self-help', a doctrine that left behind many of the weaker and less fortunate; but at least there were from the first other classes besides employers and middlemen who reaped a large share of its benefits, and who grew to a larger manhood under the moral and intellectual stimulus of the individualist doctrine.

CHAPTER 10

IT has been pointed out in an early chapter[2] that the way for the Industrial Revolution had been prepared by an improvement in roads. About 1750, private Turnpike Companies with Parliamentary powers began on a large scale to perform the neglected duties of the parish authorities, who had from time immemorial been

1. In March 1824 Place describes his joy at seeing 'from 800 to 900 clean, respectable-looking mechanics paying most marked attention' to a lecture on chemistry. That year the *Mechanics' Magazine* sold 16,000 copies and 1,500 workmen subscribed a guinea to the London Institute.
2. pp. 26–7, above.

charged in vain with the maintenance of the highways. The Turnpikes did so well that wheeled traffic began to oust the pack-horse, and distant markets were opened up, rendering possible a new economic régime. Half a century later, business men were becoming increasingly impatient of the continued badness of many of the roads. Transport was the life-blood of the new agriculture and of the new industry, and, although heavy goods could on certain routes go part of their journey by the new canals, there were as yet no railways.

John Loudon Macadam was a public-spirited Scottish gentleman, living in the west of England, who devoted his energies to the improvement of English roads during the first thirty years of the nineteenth century. He invented and applied a method of solidifying the road with hard, small stone, in which the hopeful part of the public saw the secret of new markets, wider activities, and unbounded wealth. 'Macadamizing' was not only, in its literal sense, a practical work of great public utility; it became the symbol of all progress, and was metaphorically used in common parlance for any aspects of the new age where improved and uniform scientific methods were in demand. The fact that the word suggested Scotland made it specially appropriate in the days of Brougham and the Edinburgh philosophers.

The Board of Agriculture, anxious to bring the produce of the new farming to the new urban markets, supported Macadam in his endeavours to combine and reform the innumerable and largely inefficient Turnpike Trusts of the day. Backed by public opinion, this policy had a great measure of success. It is remarkable that local government was not, at this period, chosen as the machinery of road reform: the Parish had failed because it was too small an area for the purpose – and the time for effective and popular County administration was still far distant.

The Post Office rivalled the Board of Agriculture in its zeal for the improvement of roads. It was indeed a change, prophetic of much in the new century, that two public departments should take the initiative in schemes for the public welfare. The Post Office employed the engineer, Thomas Telford, a Scottish shepherd's son, to construct the road to Holyhead. The *pontifex maximus*, as Telford was called, to the wonder of the world threw an iron suspension bridge across the Menai Straits to Anglesey. It was the crowning performance of a new movement in bridge-building which made use of the abundant iron produced by the coal furnaces. Telford, besides making canals and aqueducts in England, had made many roads in his native land, which proved even more useful than his most famous achievement, the Caledonian Canal. The combined result of Telford's roads and Scott's romances was that tourists and sportsmen poured every summer into the Highlands.

When Macadam and Telford had covered the island with a network of hard, smooth roads, trimly-built stage-coaches galloped where their heavy predecessors had crawled. The coach had its brief day of glory and perfection – from those proud summer mornings when, hung with laurels, it left behind the news of fresh victories in Spain, as it careered without a halt through cheering villages, to the time when its daily message on the fortunes of the Reform Bill was no less eagerly awaited by assembled multitudes, staring down the road for its coming. When Sir Walter Scott was a young man, the coaches still crawled; when he died, they were on the point of being eclipsed, at the height of their speed and glory, by the steam-engine. But during that one generation, the inn-yard whence they started was the microcosm of the national life. And the 'coaching days', from Waterloo to *Pickwick*, still stand in popular imagination for the last era of 'old England', jovial, self-reliant, matter-of-fact, but still as full of romance, colour, character, and incident as the world of Chaucer's pilgrims who rode so slowly along the green tracks so many centuries before.

Until the coming of the railway, the macadamized roads made the horse more than ever the cynosure of English eyes. To ride him had been the chief delight for centuries; to drive him was now no less desired. The aspiration of youth was to sit beside the mail-coachman on the box, or to keep a gig and bowl along the highroad among the post-chaises.[1] The breed of horses was improved to meet the new opportunities for speed that Macadam had created.

On the hunting-field, as on the road, the breed of horses had altered with the pace. Though hunting has survived coaching, we still look back on that period as the great days when the red coat, not of the soldier, ruled in the island that Wellington had saved. During the eighteenth century, fox-hunting had expelled stag-hunting, and had itself gradually expanded from a sedate watching of the hounds from horse-back on the village common and inside a gentleman's own estate to a break-neck gallop across the country, which, having been largely cleared of its bogs and woodlands, presented the hedges and channelled watercourses of the new enclosures under the cheerful aspect of innumerable 'jumps'. The Pytchley under Lord Althorp set the standard of Shire hunting;

1. Thomas Carlyle devised the word 'gigmanity' for 'respectability', because at Thurtell's trial one of the witnesses said 'he was a very respectable man: he kept a gig.'

many country gentlemen in the Midlands shut up their own houses for the season and came with their families to live at Pytchley.

Shooting had, during the preceding century, entirely replaced hawking. The change induced an insatiate demand for more birds and hares, and ever stricter preservation of wild animals in a famishing countryside. Artificial pheasant-breeding and battues were only beginning to come in, and it was not yet common to drive the birds. To shoot pheasants, partridges, or grouse over dogs was the ordinary day's business, involving hard exercise, field-craft, and Spartan habits. It was a fine sport, and helped to inspire the class that then set the mode in everything from poetry to pugilism, with an intimate love and knowledge of woodland, hedgerow, and moor, and a strong preference for country over town life which is too seldom found in the leaders of fashion in any age or land.

Indirectly, therefore, the passion for shooting game did much for what was best in our civilization. But it was unfortunately connected, as fox-hunting was not, with the poaching war and all manner of unneighbourliness. The legislation affecting 'game' was exclusive and selfish, not only towards the poor but towards everyone except an aristocratic few. It was illegal for anyone to buy or sell game – with the result that prices obtainable by poachers were much increased; and it was illegal for anyone who was not a squire or a squire's eldest son to kill game even at the invitation of the owner.[1] This inconvenient law was indeed sometimes evaded by a process known as 'deputation'. And it was abolished by the Whig legislators of 1831, in spite of the opposition of the Duke of Wellington, who was convinced that these extraordinary restrictions were the only means of keeping game in the countryside. The event proved that he was too pessimistic.

It was characteristic of the early years of the century that, although savage punishments were meted out to poachers if they were poor men, 'gentlemen poachers' used to shoot with impunity over other people's estates in the open day, deceiving the gamekeepers by elaborate artifices or barefaced lying, and in some cases by threats of violence.

1. In 1822 a farmer coursed a hare on his own farm by leave of his landlord. The gamekeepers of the neighbouring landlord, the Duke of Buckingham, had him up before their master as magistrate, who in his own house and on his own keepers' evidence, convicted him. Such churlish separation of the interests of neighbour sportsmen was unknown in the traditions of the fox-hunting community. For this reason, perhaps, there are many hunting-songs, and songs of fishing, cricket, and football, but I have never heard of an English shooting-song. The 'Lincolnshire Poacher's' song suggests that game-preserving is alien to the muse!

174

In all sports save those connected with 'game', the upper class appeared as the patrons of the popular enthusiasm, pleased to share a common emotion which did much to unite a deeply divided society, and to keep its hereditary leaders popular as sportsmen, if they were ceasing always to please as politicians. Coaching, horse-racing, fox-hunting, boxing, cock-fighting, furnished the hourly thoughts of multitudes. The prize-ring in its 'most high and palmy state' was thus described by that soul of chivalry and honour, Lord Althorp, speaking in his old age to a friend:

He said his conviction of the advantages of boxing was so strong that he had been seriously considering whether it was not a duty he owed to the public to go and attend every prize-fight which took place. In his opinion cases of stabbing arose from the manly habit of boxing having been discouraged. He gave us an account of prize-fights he had attended, how he had seen Mendoza knocked down for the first five or six rounds by Humphreys, and seeming almost beat, till the Jews got their money on; when, a hint being given him, he began in earnest and soon turned the tables. He described a fight between Gully and the Chicken. How he rode down to Brickhill – how he was loitering about the inn-door, when a barouche-and-four drove up with Lord Byron and a party, and Jackson the trainer – how they all dined together, and how pleasant it had been. Then the fight next day; the men stripping, the intense excitement, the sparring; then the first round, the attitude of the men – it was really worthy of Homer.

The professional prize-ring, as Althorp here indicates, had two aspects. Some of the champions whom it bred were as fine English-men as ever stepped, but it was no more a school of virtue than the race-course, and indeed it eventually lost patronage because it was so dishonestly conducted.

Outside the prize-ring, men and boys were in the habit of settling their differences with their fists. It was a national custom of which everyone was proud, and it united and equalized all classes. The coachman could challenge his fare, if he 'handled his fives well'. The more aristocratic and bloody custom of the duel, disapproved as impious by Evangelicals, and as foolish and wrong by the rising middle class, was gradually dying out among gentlemen, who had long ceased to wear swords, and many of whom had not even learnt to fence. Duelling by pistol had none of the artistic interest and antique romance of the foils, 'the immortal passado! the punto reverso! the hay!' To pit human life on the vagaries of a bullet offended the common-sense spirit of the age, although there was a curiously large number of such encounters between eminent states-men – Pitt against Tierney, Canning against Castlereagh, and Wellington against Lord Winchilsea as late as 1829.

Boxing helped the duel to die out by substituting another field of honour, suited to a more democratic age. Keats as a schoolboy was more devoted to pugilism than to poetry, and when he grew to manhood attacked and defeated a butcher whom he found ill-treating an animal. In 1825 the Hon. F. A. Cooper, a brother of the future philanthropist Lord Shaftesbury, was killed at the age of fourteen in a two hours' fight of sixty rounds with another Eton boy, a nephew of the Marquis of Londonderry, a large part of the school looking on. Young swells about town would figure as popular heroes by knocking down at fisticuffs the last generation of old-fashioned watchmen, and carrying off their rattles and staves as trophies – before the advent of Sir Robert Peel's 'police' made such pranks unsafe. Strong self-will and eccentricity were the qualities admired in that age of individualism. The leaders of sporting and fashionable circles sought to be eccentric and were not afraid to be literary – from Lord Byron and Lord Barrymore down to Thurtell, the murderer, who talked and acted as if he were always on the stage.

Thurtell's murder of Weir was the event that created most popular interest between the Queen's trial and the Reform Bill. Because he was a 'sporting character', of strong personality, well known in boxing and theatrical circles, Thurtell's vogue with a large public survived the proof that he had committed a peculiarly horrid murder of a man he suspected of having cheated him at cards. After his execution, children were known to write as their copy-book exercises the amazing sentiment: 'Thurtell was a murdered man.' Sir Walter Scott, who had too much sense to take this view, collected the popular literature of the trial as assiduously as the minstrelsy of the Border.[1]

While interest in 'sporting events and characters' was almost universal, organized games and athletics did not play what we should now consider a large part in the life of the ordinary Englishman, or even of the English schoolboy. Cricket had been for the last hundred years slowly rising to its local fame on the village green. Football, though a far older game in various primitive forms, had not yet obtained its modern rules or its modern popularity. The upper-class public schools, whence the passion for organized athletics afterwards spread to the adult democracy, were not yet dominated by cricket and football, nor were the exuberant energies of boyhood channelled off into athletic routine.

1. The best account of Thurtell, outside the records of the trial, is at the end of Chapter xxiv of Borrow's *Lavengro*, a book that breathes the spirit of that period of strong and eccentric characters.

In the ill-regulated boarding-houses to which a certain number of the upper class were bold enough to entrust their sons, some boys used their ample leisure, which was larger then than now, for scholarship, promiscuous reading, and poetic or botanic rambles in the country; but among the normal features of public school life were fighting, bullying, poaching, rough practical joking, drunkenness, gambling, and disorder of every sort, with no monitorial system to keep them within bounds. The masters lived apart from the boys, whom they regarded as their 'natural enemies', and generally treated as such in the matter of flogging. Public school 'rebellions' had on more than one occasion to be suppressed by the military forces of the Crown!

The beginning of reform in upper class boarding-schools was at Rugby, during the headmastership of Dr Thomas Arnold. The example which Rugby set to other such schools led to improved discipline and humaner life, secured partly on a closer relation of the masters to their pupils, and partly on self-government among the boys through selected monitors or prefects. But it would not be accurate to ascribe to Arnold's own wishes the undue predominance of athletics, which by the end of the century had become the bane of the reformed public school, as well as the means of spreading the athletic gospel to other grades of society, and to humbler schools where a modicum of organized athletics has been of untold value. Arnold did nothing directly for athletics at Rugby. He only put a stop to certain other ways in which boys spent their time decidedly less well. For the rest he occasionally 'stood on the touchline and looked pleased'. Compulsory athletics and the glorified athlete were not in his scheme of things. But the spread of Rugby football, which dates from his era, and of Public School and University athletics in all their subsequent extent and influence, came as a natural development, as soon as boys and men turned away in boredom and disapproval from pugilism, rowdyism, dog and cock fighting, and other 'sporting events' in which their fathers had delighted in the age of Byron.

The public schools of the Waterloo era had either to be reformed or to give place to some entirely new system that could pass muster with a more humane and critical age. The improvements effected by Dr Arnold met the case. And if reform had stopped where its originator intended, it might all have been pure gain. But in later years the leisure and initiative of the individual boy were increasingly sacrificed to meet the demands of the athletic time-table, with the organized mass-opinion of the boys and often of the masters to enforce obedience to a stereotyped ideal of games and 'good form'.

It may well be that this was one among many causes why after two generations of 'steady progress', although the average perhaps rose, genius and strong individual characters were less common at the end of the nineteenth century than they had been in pre-reform days. An examination of the facts will show that the great men of letters, science, and politics who made the fame and fortune of the early and middle Victorian age had been brought up with more variety and freedom, either at home, or at day schools, or in small academies or grammar schools, or else in the unreformed public schools, where the wheat and tares were for better and worse allowed to grow up, each in their own way, until the harvest.

One thing that boisterous old England decisively was not – it was not militarist. The race that had conquered on the fields of the Peninsula and Waterloo had martial instincts but not military ideals. Foreign observers, coming over at the peace from a Continent that had just exchanged the rule of French for the rule of German officers, were struck with the absence of military display in the victor island, and the absence of military habits of thought even among the dominant aristocracy. That aristocracy consisted of rural squires, some of them with a turn for books, and nearly all of them with a turn for sport, administration, and politics. Their younger sons supplied the Church, the Army, and the Navy.[1] The English gentry had on these terms proved far better able to stand up for their order than the French *noblesse*, who had lost all during the very years when the English squires were gaining more land, and more power over the land, at the expense of the peasantry. But the English squires established their power not, like the Prussian Junkers, by identifying their class with the Army and the Army with the State, but by taking the lead in politics, justice, administration, agriculture, sport, and in the patronage of art and letters, as well as by fighting their country's battles on land and sea.

The tradition of the Tory squires was anti-militarist, beginning with the reaction against Cromwell and continuing through the Whig wars against Louis XIV. The original Tories had made a favourite of the Navy as against the Army. And so in these later wars, which were preeminently Tory wars, all classes and parties

1. At the peace a considerable number of officers passed straight into the Church, very few into business. The salaried Civil Service was then a small affair.

were agreed in regarding the Army not as the master of the State, but as one of its servants.

It was a fact of historic importance that England's greatest soldier was the least militaristic of men. His example was effective in perpetuating the custom of getting into mufti at the earliest possible moment off duty, a practice which has fostered the peculiarly English idea that an army officer is only a gentleman engaged on a special public service. After Waterloo, Wellington covered the operation of disarmament with the shield of his unrivalled authority.[1] When the Duke of York died in 1827, he could not be given a military funeral, because, as Wellington reported, there were not enough troops in England to bury a field-marshal! The Tories at home, like the Holy Alliance abroad, stood for 'peace and order'. 'Order' was sometimes a euphemism for oppression, but 'peace' really meant 'peace'. And the Tory peace was used to reduce armaments and so to get rid of a large portion of the taxes, with the unpopularity and distress that they implied. Before the creation of an effective police, the military force maintained was barely enough to secure public tranquillity in time of riot. The general belief that it would be incapable of putting down a determined rising of the middle and lower classes did much towards the peaceable solution of the crisis of 1832.

Wellington was a typical Tory. He wished England to be governed by her gentlemen, not by her generals. This attitude on his part did much to secure the peaceful development of our institutions in a new age with which he was in many respects out of sympathy.

The plantation of Upper Canada by loyalist refugees from the revolted Colonies had led Pitt to divide this new English-speaking province from Lower Canada with its French-Catholic civilization, and at the same time to establish in both provinces the rudiments of Parliamentary institutions, though not yet responsible self-government.[2]

It was the best arrangement for both parts of Canada at that stage of their development. But it implied a difficult period of transition, with friction between an executive still nominated by the Crown and a legislative with as little power as an early Stuart

1. Towards the end of his life he constantly complained to Ministers, and not without reason, of the smallness of the Army. But he himself had done much to let it become small in an epoch when heavy military expenditure would have been more dangerous than unpreparedness, since there was little against which to prepare.

2. See pp. 69–73, above, and map there.

Parliament. The official class, sent out by the inefficient Colonial Office of the day as a result of party jobs or personal favour, was justly unpopular in all the Colonies, which were made the dumping ground for worn-out general officers and cousins of peers with boroughs. Canada was no exception to this bad rule. The French Canadians complained that they had no representatives among the officials, who, whether English or Canadian born, spent their time in trying to turn the Governor against the French majority. The English-speaking Canadians found the same officials corrupt and snobbish, a pinchbeck aristocracy, keeping itself loftily apart from a democratic community of backwoodsmen which thoroughly despised them in return. The governors themselves had too often lost the 'Carleton touch' of confidence in the people.

But in spite of all this, Carleton and the two Pitts had built on the rock, and when the flood came in 1812 the house stood firm.

The war between Great Britain and the United States was the result of a dispute over two questions arising out of our conduct of the war with Napoleon: the enforcement of the Orders in Council restricting neutral commerce with the Continent, and the search of American vessels for deserters from the British Navy. On both counts there was much to be said for and against both sides. It was a case for compromise, and war or peace really depended on the mutual goodwill of the disputants. Unfortunately neither Government deserved well of posterity. The Tory Cabinet shared the aristocratic contempt felt by their party for the federation of rebel States, which had arisen by defying George III, and which was expected speedily to demonstrate by its dissolution the impracticable nature of democracy. On the other side, President Madison catered for an equally unintelligent anti-British tradition, against which President Washington had striven with success when faced by a similar crisis in 1793. But it was of good augury for the future that the British middle classes, led by Brougham, made their first appearance in nineteenth-century politics by compelling the Government to withdraw the Orders in Council, so as to avoid war with America.[1] Unfortunately the concession came just too late, for that week America had declared war. It was equally of good omen that the war was unpopular in New England. In 1814 the Northern States began to talk of secession if peace were not made. Although it was the merchants and sailors of New England who suffered from the grievances on the high seas that were the pretext of the war, yet it

1. See pp. 138–9, above.

was New England that protested against the war policy of the Southern democrats.[1]

The pacificism of New York and Massachusetts, the states that could have made the earliest and most formidable attack on Canada if they had been so minded, saved us from a desperate strait. When war broke out there were only 4,500 regular troops in the whole of Canada. The French Canadians, though they had no wish to be swallowed up in the United States, disliked British rule. And in Upper Canada itself, alongside of the United Empire Loyalists, there was a large recent immigration of men from over the border whose emotional allegiance was uncertain. Never before or since has the independence of Canada been in greater danger than in the summer of 1812.

Fortunately there was a man capable of meeting the crisis. Isaac Brock, the very best type of British soldier, then acting both as Governor and General in Upper Canada, determined to take the offensive as the likeliest means to rouse a national spirit. He captured Detroit with a force inferior in numbers to the enemy. Though he was killed in battle two months later, his bold policy and the ability and success with which he had carried it through had put both Anglo-Saxons and French on their mettle, and encouraged them to hold out in the following year when the Americans pushed into Canada in much greater force. This middle period of the war included a series of naval actions on the Great Lakes, in which the superior numbers of the American ships gave them the upper hand. But the conquest of Canada failed. After the first fall of Napoleon, the Peninsular troops were hurried across the Atlantic and all danger passed away.

Meanwhile, on the open sea, the frigates of the small American Navy had unexpected successes in single combats with British ships of their own size. The lords of the ocean were so seriously annoyed by these reverses that, when the tide turned and the *Chesapeake* was defeated in June 1813 by H.M.S. *Shannon* outside Boston harbour, the event won a place in song and history out of all proportion to its importance. The net result of the naval war was that the American mercantile marine suffered very severely, but a tradition of mutual respect was established between the two English-speaking navies that in later years developed into friendship.

1. In congress, Josiah Quincy spoke of the invasion of Canada as 'a cruel, wanton, senseless, and wicked attack upon an unoffending people, bound to us by ties of blood and good neighbourhood, undertaken for the punishment over their shoulders of another people, 3,000 miles away, by young politicians to whom reason, justice, pity were nothing, revenge everything.'

The last stage of the war had better have been omitted. Various points of the American seaboard were attacked by our regular forces from Europe, including the flower of the Peninsular Army. In one of these raids, up Chesapeake Bay, the public buildings of Washington were burned, in reprisals for the burning the year before of Toronto, then called York. The unsuccessful British attack on Fort McHenry, on the same expedition, inspired the words of 'The Star-Spangled Banner'. The last and biggest battle of the war was fought two weeks after peace, unknown to the combatants, had been signed in Europe. This action was the defence of New Orleans against another British raid from the sea, when 6,000 Americans, chiefly backwoodsmen of Tennessee and Kentucky, under Andrew Jackson, held a line of strong entrenchments against 6,000 British infantry, and killed and wounded a third of their number.

The self-defence of the two Canadas against invasion, and the historical traditions that the infant nation thus acquired, were an important result of the war. Otherwise it had been fought in vain. It solved none of the disputed questions out of which it arose. The treaty signed at Ghent on Christmas Eve 1814 very wisely did not even attempt to decide the embittered controversies on blockade and right of search. But one of the causes of war, the belief of the Southern democrats that Canada could easily be annexed, received its quietus. On the other hand anti-British tradition had obtained a fresh lease of life in the United States, whose orators now had the theme of a second war against Britain as the second romantic period of their national history.

The Tory Cabinet cannot be praised for the management of affairs that led to this breach of the peace. But Castlereagh's dealings with the United States after the war was over were a model of pacific statesmanship, reciprocated by the Government of Washington and its representatives over here, John Quincy Adams and Rush. Before Castlereagh's career as Foreign Secretary ended, the fortunes of Anglo-American peace had been established on the sound basis of disarmament along the Canadian border, enabling future generations to weather many fierce storms, and to settle a frontier problem that no other two Great Powers would have been able to decide without war.

The problem before Great Britain and Canada on one side and the United States on the other was nothing less than to fix a frontier of four thousand miles, which, except in the region of the Lakes, was not indicated by any natural boundary. It was perhaps the greatest operation that has ever been achieved in the interest of peace, and it took many years and many statesmen to accomplish and perfect it. But the most important stage of the whole proceeding came in 1817, when, after a sharp struggle inside the British Cabinet, the British and American Governments agreed to abolish their navies on the Great Lakes, and forthwith dismantled, sold, or sank the warships on Erie and Ontario. Those fleets have never been reconstructed. From that moment forward 'the long, invisible, unguarded line' that divides Canada from her neighbour has been successfully defended by the sole garrison of trust and good will, even during the frequently recurring periods of acrimonious dispute as to its whereabouts. If there had been armaments, there would some time have been war. And if the nations concerned had not spoken the same language and felt a half-conscious sympathy underlying their traditional feuds, disarmament would not have been adhered to for long. It helped greatly that the Americans and Canadians both disliked standing armies and navies and had no place or provision for them in their scheme of things, and that for some time after Waterloo the Tories at home had a strong and consistent policy of retrenchment based on disarmament and peace.

In 1818, the year after the scrapping of the navies on the Great Lakes, the first step was taken by Castlereagh towards the determination of the boundary westward. It was agreed that from the Lake of the Woods to the summit of the Rockies the frontier should follow the forty-ninth degree of latitude. With equal wisdom it was agreed to postpone negotiations as to the Pacific Coast. Beyond the Rockies lay the region then called 'Oregon', a name at that time covering the vast territory between latitude 42° and 54° 40′, which subsequently became British Columbia and the States of Washington, Oregon, and Idaho. The whole of this wilderness, joining what was then Russian Alaska to what was then Mexican California, had been saved from Spain by Pitt in the Nootka Sound dispute,[1] and in Castlereagh's time was claimed both by Great Britain and the United States. But though British and American fur traders had stations along the coast, neither side could as yet make any decisive show of occupation or settlement. The days of the immigrants and the 'Oregon trail' across the great prairies were yet to come. The arrangement made in 1818 for the 'joint occupation of Oregon' postponed a dangerous dispute, not yet ripe for adjudication. A generation later, Sir Robert Peel was able to settle it by compromise, in the same pacific spirit that Castlereagh had introduced into our dealings with the New World.

1. See p. 58, above.

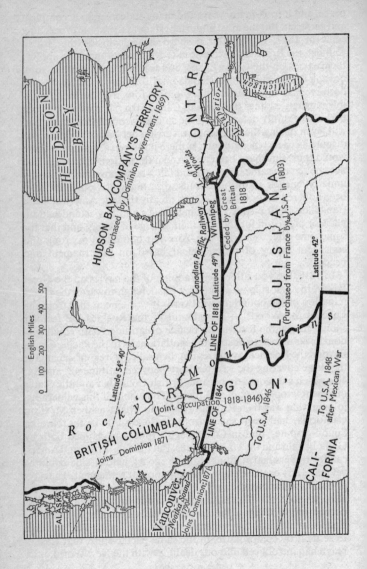

HUDSON BAY COMPANY'S TERRITORY
(Purchased by Dominion Government 1869)

HUDSON BAY

ONTARIO

L. Superior

L. Michigan

L. of the Woods

Winnipeg

Canadian Pacific Railway

LINE OF 1818 (Latitude 49°)

Ceded by Great Britain 1818

LOUISIANA
(Purchased from France by U.S.A. in 1803)

Latitude 42°

Rocky Mountains

O R E G O N
(Joint occupation 1818-1846)
LINE OF 1846

Latitude 54° 40'

BRITISH COLUMBIA
Joins Dominion 1871

To U.S.A. 1846

To U.S.A. 1848
after Mexican War

CALIFORNIA

Vancouver I.
Nootka Sound 1790
Joins Dominion 1871

ALASKA

English Miles
0   100   200   300   400   500

CHAPTER 11

DURING the last half-dozen years of the war, the official Whig leaders went politically to sleep in their country seats, muttering pessimistic prophecies of the impossibility of conquering Napoleon. But the social and political revolt beginning in the new middle class against the Tory aristocracy found more vigorous expression in the self-assertive and ubiquitous energy of Henry Brougham, the very type of *novus homo*, with his square, plebeian nose, restless movements, and hard yet lively features.

It was Brougham who had organized the agitation against the Orders in Council.[1] As soon as the war was over, he compelled Government by a similar agitation to drop the Income Tax, which the middle classes, before Peel taught them to think more wisely, regarded as an inquisitorial interference with liberty and property, not to be borne save in war-time. The unpopular tax, which is one of the chief claims of Pitt to the gratitude of posterity, was bringing in fifteen millions in 1815. Its removal, due to Brougham's agitation, was one of the main reasons of the slow progress of fiscal reform and trade recovery prior to the time of Peel.

With the revival of the spirit of opposition after the war, Brougham gave voice to the growing indignation of all classes with the sinecures and pensions. To abolish them would have done much less to relieve the economic misery of the land than he and Cobbett made people believe, but it was a peculiarly gross insult to starving millions to make rich parasites richer out of taxes. Brougham also put his universal energies at the disposal of the champions of the negro, who were already preparing against slavery the same sort of campaign that had proved fatal to the slave trade. And, true to his Scottish upbringing, he gave, as we have seen, his own vigour to the movement for popular education in England.

Though north-English by birth, Brougham belonged to the group of lawyers and University men at the Scottish capital who had founded the *Edinburgh Review*. They included the Rev. Sydney Smith, also of England, and the Scot, Francis Jeffrey. At first these young partisans had only their wits to protect them in a time and country in which, as one of them said retrospectively, 'it was almost safer to be a felon than a Reformer'. But their caution and ability gained a hearing for the new school of liberal ideas in

1. See pp. 138–9, above.

fashionable and learned society throughout Great Britain. In days when the means of diffusing knowledge and opinion were scanty, the Edinburgh Reviewers played an indispensable part in preparing the mind of the coming age. But their want of firmness over the Peninsular War incited Sir Walter Scott and other Tories to found the rival *Quarterly*. Judged by Victorian standards of criticism and science the early numbers of the *Edinburgh* and *Quarterly* seem very thin; but they were in their day a great advance.

The close connexion of poetry and literature with political faction, illustrated by the history of these two famous Reviews and by the lives of Scott and Byron, Wordsworth and Coleridge, Shelley and Keats, though it had its regrettable side, was due to the high importance attached to poetry and to the Muses by the active world of that era as distinguished from our own. The lives of many of our greatest poets and painters also remind us how little the Napoleonic wars interrupted the daily work of civilization in our island, when it was reaching a higher point of literary achievement than it had ever touched since the age of Shakespeare.

It would be difficult to find a better instance of that favourite maxim of our grandfathers that 'the pen is mightier than the sword' than the effect upon British institutions of the uneventful life of Jeremy Bentham, a shy recluse of unimpressive speech and appearance, who was so little of a politician that even in 1817 he was not prosecuted for publishing his highly 'seditious' *Reform Catechism* in favour of household suffrage. Born in 1748, and dying in 1832 just when his principles were beginning to invade the seats of power, he was never the man of the moment, but his influence was a force in history during more than a hundred years. As early as 1776 – that seminal year when the Declaration of Independence, Adam Smith's *Wealth of Nations*, and the first volume of Gibbon's History were given to the world – young Bentham's *Fragment on Government* also appeared. It challenged the legal doctrine of the age, sanctioned by Blackstone himself, that law was a fixed and authoritative science and the British Constitution perfect. Bentham, on the other hand, proclaimed both law and politics to be perpetual experiments in the means of promoting 'utility' or happiness.

For the rest of his long life Bentham's propaganda among the higher intellect of the country was never intermitted, though the French Revolution and the anti-Jacobin reaction, both of which he disliked, delayed the acceptance of his doctrine. In his old age, and after his death, his ideas inspired the slow but sure reform of British institutions, as the ideas of Rousseau had inspired the cataclysm of old France.

Bentham impressed upon his countrymen the notion that existing institutions were not to be taken for granted, but to be judged by their results, and perpetually readjusted so as to produce 'the greatest happiness of the greatest number'. He did not invent that useful formula, which he had taken from Priestley, but he drove it into men's minds, and, by reiterating it for half a century with a thousand different applications, he undermined the easy acceptance of chartered inefficiency and corruption, characteristic of the eighteenth century. Parliamentary, municipal, scholastic, ecclesiastical, economic reform all sprang from the spirit of Bentham's perpetual inquiry, 'what is the use of it?' – his universal shibboleth, that proved in the end the real English antidote to Jacobinism. The weakness of his system, even in the realm of politics, was the mechanical nature of its psychology, which misrepresented the multiform workings of the human mind.

Although the principles of his 'utilitarian' philosophy were applied in the end to all spheres of government, his most direct and measureable success was the application that he himself made of the 'utility' test in the realm of law. Brougham said of him that 'he was the first legal philosopher that had appeared in the world', and Dicey in our own day has quoted this judgement with approval. As law reformer, Bentham was fertile in practical invention as he was broad in principle. To him is owing the first suggestion of almost every one of the long series of law reforms which, beginning about 1820, in forty years swept away the sanguinary and unintelligent code which Eldon loved, that hanged men for theft and struck about in blind panic with the sword of justice. In the dry tree of Parliament from 1808 to 1818, Sir Samuel Romilly preached Bentham's doctrine of law reform to unwilling ears; after Romilly's tragic suicide, Sir James Mackintosh took up the work in the green tree of a more hopeful era.[1]

Bentham's utilitarianism[2] was most directly connected with the creed of the 'philosophic Radicals' like James Mill and Francis

1. See pp. 46–7, above, and p. 202, below.
2. This famous word was first applied to the Benthamite doctrine by John Stuart Mill, who adopted it in 1822 from John Galt's recently published *Annals of the Parish*, in which the old Scottish minister warns his parishioners not to 'secede from Christianity and become utilitarians'. When, as a moral philosopher, Bentham attempted to use the juridical and political test of 'utility' as the basis of ethical motive, and to 'grind out virtue from the husks of pleasure,' he was going off his ground, as Carlyle, Macaulay, and John Mill, each after his fashion, pointed out. Bentham's influence helped to transform our language from a thing of beauty to something more useful and scientific. We owe to him such words as 'minimize', 'codify', 'international'. When told by the doctor that he was dying, he replied: 'Then minimize pain.'

Place, and with the sweeping away of abuses and privileges to clear the path for democratic individualism and *laissez faire*. But it also inspired the movement towards Socialism, co-operation, and State interference, which grew up side by side with 'classical' economics and radical politics, though not at first with such rapid growth. All were in debt to Bentham, even common-sense Whigs like Macaulay, though he was provoked to write *Edinburgh* articles against the pedantry of the Utilitarian sect.

Robert Owen was the first to find the Socialistic application of the doctrines of 'utility'. He was the father of the factory laws and of the co-operative movement.

Never was there such a combination as in Robert Owen of business ability with moral simplicity and earnestness, and visionary insight, occasionally running to the absurd. Brought up in a Welsh country town in the days of Wesley, his destiny lay in wider realms of thought and space, but his mind and character never lost the mark of an upbringing among poor people and among people aspiring earnestly towards an ideal outlook on everyday things. After a homely schooling at Newtown he went off into the great world and worked his way unaided up the ladder of the new industrialism, to become, before he was thirty, part owner and sole manager of the cotton mills of New Lanark in Scotland. In early life he was a magnificent example of 'self-help'.

While Napoleon was winning and losing Europe, Owen was quietly working out his social experiment. The Scottish factory, when he took it over, was not much better than other factories of the time. In fifteen years he had made it a model of humane and intelligent provision for mind and body, with moderate hours, good pay, healthy conditions both in the factory and the village, and good education, including the first infant school in the island. The outcome was a high morale among the hands. It was, he imagined, his great discovery that 'the character of man is formed *for* him, and not *by* him', or, as we should now say, that 'environment makes character'. To prove it, he had by environment made the characters of the New Lanark employees; and at the same time he had made the fortune of the New Lanark Mills!

Owen's double success proved that, if the social aspects of the Industrial Revolution had been attended to, its worst evils could have been avoided without a lowering of production, and that even in that age the big factory might have been used as a new and powerful engine of social amelioration. The world of that day admitted the facts; thousands of visitors drove all the way from the Thames to the Clyde, and the monarchs of Europe sent embassies to see the miracle of a happy factory-town. Men could not deny, yet would not believe, the living proof that Owen had set before their eyes.

In the year of Waterloo, Owen, having failed to persuade his brother manufacturers of the things that pertained to their peace, went up to London to persuade the Government itself. He was not by temperament and theory a democrat. He had been the patriarch of New Lanark, gently forming his men's characters 'for them'. He now wanted the Tory Cabinet to be equally paternal in its protection of all the factory hands in the island. With the simplicity of Parsifal, he came up to town expecting to make a convert of Castlereagh and a pupil of Parliament. His failure did not sour him, but it turned him back to the working-men themselves, whom he now regarded as the only possible agents of his vision of a new society.

His failure, though fundamental, had not been complete. Cabinet Ministers treated him with politeness, but gave no help. His plans were, however, taken up in Parliament by Sir Robert Peel, father of the great Sir Robert, a Lancashire millowner, originally of no good reputation as such, who had the family honesty to own that he had changed his mind on the need for factory legislation.

During Napoleon's Hundred Days, Owen and Peel drew up the first real Factory Bill.[1] It applied not merely to cotton, but to all factories; it forbade the employment of any child under ten years old, or after that for more than ten and a half hours a day; paid inspectors were to enforce its provisions. But the other manufacturers hastened up to London to protest against the insanity of these two eccentric members of their order. They established before a Committee the point that Owen was an infidel, and argued the more doubtful thesis that the children were well and happy in the mills. After four years' delay, a useless shadow of Peel's Bill was passed, for cotton only, with no important provision except the prohibition of child labour under nine. As there were to be no inspectors, the Act was ignored whenever employers and parents joined to break it.

1. Peel's Act of 1802, sometimes called the First Factory Act, was really a new provision of the Poor Law. It was an endeavour to protect pauper apprentices, with whom public authorities in the last quarter of the eighteenth century used to feed the small water-worked mills which were the first and worst stage of the cotton revolution. The larger steam factories that succeeded them used the 'free' labour of children living with their parents, who were fain to send them daily to the mill. It was these 'free' children who were in question in the Bill of 1815–19, and in all subsequent Factory Acts.

The first campaign was lost, but Owen had started on the right lines the hundred years' war for State control. Thanks to him and to his successor, Lord Shaftesbury, not only children but parents have since found protection in an area of legislation ever widening down to our own day.

Owen himself, meanwhile, despairing of the governors, turned to the governed. He abandoned politics for labour association. Parliament had failed him; he did not propose to get it reformed, but to set the labourers to work out their own salvation. He became in a certain sense a democrat, but not, like Place and Cobbett, a Radical. He put himself at the head of the economic as distinct from the political action of the working class. He devoted himself in the latter half of his life to starting the co-operative and extending the Trade Union movement. But that part of his life belongs to a later chapter of British history.

In spite of Owen's indifference to the cause, the movement for Parliamentary Reform, suppressed in the days of Pitt, revived first among the working-men, before it captured the middle classes. The reason is clear. While the middle classes were upon the whole prospering, except for severe fluctuations of trade, many of the workmen were suffering terribly, and their misery was much increased by the action of Parliament. While new laws were passed and enforced to prevent them from combining to keep up their wages, old laws which empowered the authorities to fix a fair wage were repealed, and finally, when peace promised a fall in the price of bread, a new Corn Law prohibited importation till wheat was 80s. a quarter. Parliament, in the interest now of employers, now of landlords, was always the enemy of working-men. They ate the rotten boroughs in their bread. Hence their hatred of the 'borough-mongers' was more intense than that of the middle class, and made emphatic entry on the political stage a dozen years before the 'respectable classes' under Whig patronage secured the first Reform Bill.

No doubt Owen understood the causes and some of the cures of working-class misery far better than Cobbett, whose economics were as wild as his history, and who disliked enclosures and factories too much to see any way out except an impossible return to the vanished 'yeoman' world of his boyhood. Yet William Cobbett was the man who diverted the working class from rick-burning and machine-breaking to agitate for Parliamentary Reform. His *Weekly Political Register* and the literature that sprang from it did much to convert the masses into thinking politicians, despite the

Government's anxiety to shut them out from all aspects of citizenship. Cobbett's extravagance of theory, recklessness of statement, and violence of diction obscured the fact that the whole tendency of his propaganda was to avert revolution and to guide the proletariat into the paths of constitutional action.

At the same time he made the wrongs and sufferings of the poor known to educated men. He angrily drew aside the curtain that hid their lives from public notice and sympathy. He proclaimed rich and poor to be one English nation, and demanded that the Constitution should include them both.

In spite of his gross unfairness and inaccuracy, Cobbett left his impress on all, even on those who hated him, because of his rare literary power, because of the fundamental sincerity and courage that underlay a good deal of posing, and because he was native of the soil. Paine, Bentham, Owen were citizens of the world. Burke, though he sang Britain's praises, had not our island note. But Cobbett, though he abused all that Burke praised, was John Bull incarnate.

The 'rights of men' were nothing to him in the abstract, and foreigners were antipathetic. Born of Surrey peasants of the old breed, his heart's desire was to restore their rights and liberties as he had known them in his boyhood, and as he imagined them to have existed in even greater degree in the idealized English history of his vision. In one sense he was the only consistent Tory, for he was averse to the economic and social revolution which the nominal Tories were hurrying on. He was neither a 'philosophic Radical' nor a Socialist. But he was the father of the unphilosophic Radicalism which played so great a part in English working-class opinion during the nineteenth century, because he saw that the only way to control economic change was to speed along political change till it had caught up with the furious pace of the Industrial Revolution.

Throughout the period of the Peninsular War, which he noisily and ignorantly opposed, Cobbett had been carrying on a Reform campaign in his *Political Register*, partly from prison where he lay two years to expiate his protest against the flogging of English militiamen at Ely by German soldiers. He invented a catchword – 'The Thing' – for the union of Ministers, boroughmongers, pensioners, squires, clergy, and manufacturers, by which he conceived England to be bound, bullied, and bled; giving thus to all those in power one head that he might break it. But the *Register* cost more than a shilling, and most of those who could afford a shilling a week dreaded Cobbett, or dreaded being seen to read him. The working-men clubbed to buy copies and read them aloud, a method particularly useful in those days of illiteracy, but gatherings held for this purpose were broken up and penalized. It was in 1816, when he boldly reduced the price to twopence, that he became the real leader of the masses in the manufacturing districts, among whom a fierce agitation had at length broken out.[1]

Peace had not brought Plenty. The demand for English goods among our allies, and our own monopoly of trade across the ocean, both ended with the war. The big war-orders stopped and peaceful Europe was better able to manufacture for her own needs. British firms broke by hundreds, and hands were thrown out of employment by scores of thousands. Farmers were going bankrupt and hanging themselves as the price of corn fell. It was now that Speenhamland had its full effect, and a vast proportion of the rural labourers became paupers. Meanwhile the landlords passed the Corn Law, in defiance both of middle-class anger and working-class agony.[2]

The Corn Law of 1815 was an object lesson in the need for Parliamentary Reform, but, because the working-classes led the way with a demand for 'radical' reform to enfranchise themselves, the middle classes and the Whigs took alarm and stood aloof, disapproving both of the Radical agitation and of the Government reprisals. Because the nation was rent not into two but into three, power to deal with the crisis rested in the hands of the Tory Government.

The Government misused its opportunity. No concessions were made politically, nor was any form of relief proposed for the distress of the poor. Repression was still the panacea for discontent. Riots of starving men addressed by the more violent of the Radicals and accompanied by spasmodic outrage were treated as levying war on the King. Men who deserved punishment as rioters were tried for treason, and were consequently acquitted by the juries. A war of prosecutions against the Radical Press resulted in some

1. Bamford, the Radical, tells us: 'At this time [1816] the writings of William Cobbett suddenly became of great authority. They were read on nearly every cottage hearth in the manufacturing districts of South Lancashire, in those of Leicester, Derby, and Nottingham; also in many of the Scottish manufacturing towns. Their influence was speedily visible. He directed his readers to the true cause of their sufferings, misgovernment, and to its proper corrective, Parliamentary Reform. Riots soon became scarce, and from that time they have never obtained their ancient vogue with the labourers of this country.'

2. See p. 159, above. The Whigs, though aspiring to lead the middle class, were divided on the Corn Law of 1815, their leaders being nearly all of the landlord class.

heavy sentences, and some triumphant acquittals as in the famous cases of Hone the Parodist and the *Black Dwarf* newspaper. Habeas Corpus Act was suspended, and Cobbett thereupon fled to America. His *Political Register* was still issued, but its principal work had been done. The Radical movement was launched.

Meanwhile public meetings, lectures, and debating societies were stopped by the hand of power, armed with the suspension of Habeas Corpus. Government spies, necessary before there was a proper detective or police force, were accused of stirring up starving operatives to sedition. But the notorious Oliver went too far in endeavouring to implicate some middle-class reformers in Lancashire, whereas the spy business, long carried on with impunity among the workmen, was promptly exposed in Parliament by the help of the Whigs. The class pride of the Lancashire manufacturers was aroused against the Government by this incident. In striking at the dreaded Radicals the Government had threatened the liberty of all.

In 1819, when another wave of economic distress followed after a brief interval, the Reform agitation flared up again. Since Habeas Corpus was no longer suspended, monster meetings of working-men were held in the industrial districts to demand universal suffrage. It would have been better if the authorities had prohibited such meetings altogether, according to their usual custom, rather than act as they acted in St Peter's Fields, Manchester, on 16 August. An orderly and unarmed crowd of about 60,000 men, women, and children was permitted to assemble; but then the magistrates, stricken with alarm at the sight of so great a multitude, sent in the yeomanry to arrest the speaker, the notorious Radical Hunt, after the meeting had fairly begun. When the horsemen, pushing their way through the throng on such an errand, were shouted at and hustled, the cavalry in reserve were ordered by the magistrates to charge. Their impact drove the dense mass of human beings, cursing and shrieking, off the field, while the yeomanry, who were Tory partisans, used their sabres with gusto. In the disturbances of that day some eleven persons, including two women, were killed or died of their injuries; over a hundred were wounded by sabres and several hundred more injured by horse-hoofs or crushed in the stampede. The women injured were over a hundred.[1]

1. In Prentice's *Manchester*, pp. 167–8, the particulars and names of the killed are given, while the particulars and names of the wounded and injured can still be read in the lists of the Committee that administered relief to the sufferers. The statement in the middle of an otherwise excellent chapter of the

Of the magistrates who had done this thing, one was a clergy-man; they can only be acquitted of inhumanity on the ground of panic induced by prejudice. The action of Government in sending them its thanks without waiting to make inquiry aroused an outburst of indignation among many respectable citizens who would never have dreamt of going to the Peterloo meeting. To the working-men themselves it seemed nothing less than a declaration of war upon them by their rulers. In spite of Whig and middle-class protests in and out of Parliament, the immediate victory lay with Government. The agitation was quelled that winter.

Nevertheless, Peterloo was the moral death-blow of the old Toryism. It might have passed unchallenged twenty years before, but, coming when it did, it was fatal. The long sterile reign of anti-Jacobinism had been compressed into one dramatic scene, revealing like a flash of lightning the real relations of rulers and ruled. Popular prints for a dozen years to come made all men familiar with the symbolic figure of a mounted yeoman in his shako, prancing over a heap of shrieking women and sabring them on the ground. British history had made it impossible for this island to be governed for long on such terms. The laurels of the victors of Waterloo hung tarnished, and young men began to look elsewhere for their heroes and deliverers.[1]

The change of feeling had its effect on some of the rising generation of Tory leaders. Men as sensitive as Canning, as central-minded as Peel, as much in touch with the merchant community as Huskisson could feel in their bones that the great wind which had been blowing for thirty years at length had shifted its quarter.

But for three more years the old spirit was still supreme in the counsels of government. Indeed, if Peterloo was not to be disowned, there was no course open but further coercion, for the

1. Feeling about Peterloo did much to bring round the new middle class to Reform, including the millowners who, though they had too little sympathy with their employees, had not asked to have them massacred. Young men of ability, who afterwards formed the *intelligentsia* of the Whigs in the days of their power, were shaken in the Tory faith of their fathers. One such, Macaulay, then an undergraduate, reported to his parents that Peterloo had caused great indignation among Cambridge students who had never before troubled about politics. The political faith of young Cambridge half a dozen years later has been well described by Carlyle in his *John Sterling*, at the end of Chapter iv.

Cambridge Modern History to the effect that only one man was killed and forty injured does not bear scrutiny. The most recent summary of the evidence on the number of casualties can be read on pp. 81–5 of *Three Accounts of Peterloo*, edited by F. A. Bruton (Manchester Univ. Press, 1921), and in an article by myself in *History* (Journal of the Historical Association), Oct. 1922.

working-men of the North were clamouring for revenge. The 'Six Acts', passed in the winter of 1819, were no more than an inevitable outcome of the policy previously adopted.

The Six Acts were not all of a piece. The Act that prohibited drilling was wise and has never been repealed. The Act to prevent large public meetings, at best a pitiable confession of the incompetence of the authorities, ran for five years and was not renewed. The most lasting injury to the community was done by the Act imposing a fourpenny stamp on all periodical publications, even though they were not newspapers. The object was to kill the Radical Press of the type of Cobbett's *Register* and the *Black Dwarf*, but incidentally it made it more difficult for the poor to get literature of any sort. The duty was reduced from fourpence to a penny in 1836 as a result of Radical pressure on the Whig Government of that later day, and the remaining 'taxes on knowledge' were repealed in the course of the fifties and sixties.

The year that followed Peterloo and the Six Acts, the first of George IV as king, was the year of the Cato Street conspiracy and of the Queen's trial.

In February, Arthur Thistlewood, head of a gang of 'physical force' Radicals prevented by the Six Acts from raising disturbance in other ways, plotted to murder the whole Cabinet as they dined together at Lord Harrowby's in Grosvenor Square. The conspirators, over twenty strong, met in a loft in Cato Street, off Edgware Road, where they were attacked by the Bow Street runners. Half of them fought their way out, but all were arrested within a few days. The reaction in favour of Government was naturally strong, but, considering the enormity of the fact, curiously evanescent. Thistlewood and four of his accomplices were executed on the first of May, and by the end of June Ministers were more universally unpopular than ever before, on account of Queen Caroline. Yet the Cato Street conspiracy was almost as bloody in its intention as the Gunpowder Plot, and more so than the assassination plots against Charles II and William III, which had ruined the parties in whose interest they had been designed. One of the intended victims was the Duke of Wellington, who had saved the country five years before, and lived to be the popular demigod of Victorian England. If, then, Cato Street caused no such prolonged reaction and left no such tradition as Gunpowder Plot, Rye House, and Turnham Green, it was partly because the Queen's trial supervened, and partly because the system of government for which the Duke and his colleagues stood was no longer so well rooted in any large section of popular opinion as the systems represented by James I, Charles II, or William III.

The Queen's affair, which swallowed up every other topic from June to November, was caused by the return from abroad of the new King's official wife, Caroline, unappeasably claiming her Royal rank. The King's reply was to induce his Ministers, in an evil hour for their good name, to set on foot divorce proceedings. The 'Queen's trial', for adultery, took the form of a Bill of Pains and Penalties introduced first into the House of Lords, and conducted there by the examination of evidence as in a Court of Justice. The chief witnesses were Italians of a low type, whom the British people believed to have been suborned. The principal one, Majocchi, broke down under Brougham's cross-examination, and blundered out again and again *Non mi ricordo* ('I don't remember') – a phrase that for a generation to come was current coin in England.

Non mi ricordo was fatal to the good repute of the 'existing establishment in Church and State'. The Radical cartoonists, strong in the rising genius of Cruikshank, battened on the shapeless figure of George IV, who was represented to his subjects in every abject guise that malice could suggest, now lolling on the couch as an Oriental voluptuary, now stammering out *Non mi ricordo* at the bar of public opinion. And though Caroline was in a sense the 'heroine', her low vulgarity was in itself an argument for republicans and levellers. As the Queen's trial dragged its foul length along week after week, an utter contempt for their rulers, Royal and other, sank deep into men's hearts, and prepared the way for change.

Whether Caroline was guilty or not no man can with certainty say. On the other hand, it is certain that her marriage had been a legalized bigamy, since her husband had previously been married in secret to Mrs Fitzherbert, who was still alive. It is also certain that George had cast off Caroline almost at once, before he had any ground against her, and that he had lived and was still living in open relations with a number of other women. Our ancestors passionately determined that a wife who had undergone such treatment, whether she were innocent or guilty, should not be divorced by such a man. The national instinct for fair play was too much for the loyalty of many Tories who had supported the Government on the Six Acts. The Cabinet found itself more nearly in collision with the whole nation than any Government since James II. Only the withdrawal of the Bill of Pains and Penalties saved the State from convulsion.

After Peterloo and Cato Street the Queen's trial comes like low comic relief in a too sombre tragedy. Indeed it did much to restore the good humour of the nation. All classes of a divided society had united in a common enthusiasm. And it helped the cause of reconciliation that the Cabinet had been disgraced and defeated; its working-class victims could laugh and feel themselves avenged. And so, with the help of a few years of better trade, the more liberal policy adopted by the Tory Cabinet after Castlereagh's death was launched on less troubled waters.

The history of the Queen's trial illustrates the law of political hydrostatics, that if the current of public opinion is denied course through constitutional channels, it will make its way out by the sewers. There had been other instances of such abnormal excitement, as when in 1809 the country had risen in fury to support the charges against the King's son, the Duke of York, then Commander-in-Chief, of selling military commissions through his mistress, Mrs Clarke.[1] These unsavoury controversies, and many others, now well forgotten, gave proof of a savage hatred of the Royal family, due in equal degrees to the bad private character of George III's sons and to the political position of George III and George IV after him as acknowledged chiefs of the extreme Tory party. The all-important change that afterwards took place in the popularity of the Royal family was due alike to its retirement from political leadership and to its changed private record.

But for the present the Crown still made and maintained Ministries. The Tory Cabinet survived the measureless shame and unpopularity of the Queen's trial, because George IV, much as he hated the Ministers for bungling the Bill of Pains and Penalties, hated the Whigs still more for voting against it, and for their association with his arch-enemy, Brougham, who had conducted the Queen's case in the Lords with astonishing eloquence and freedom.[2]

1. She had taken money, pretending to sell her influence with him, but the Duke of York appears to have known nothing about it.
2. He had quoted Milton to some purpose:
'My Lords, if I knew who the party is against whom I appear, *non constat* that I may not bring forward a mass of evidence furnished by himself. But who is the party? I know nothing about this shrouded, this mysterious being, this retiring phantom, this uncertain shape.

      If shape it might be called that shape hath none
      Distinguishable in member, joint or limb;
      Or substance may be called which shadow seems.
         What seems his head
      The likeness of a kingly crown has on.'
George is said to have remarked with bitterness: 'He might have left my *shape* alone.'

197

Now the choice of the Prime Minister effectually rested with the King. The Whigs only mustered some 170 votes in Opposition, and, largely owing to the rotten boroughs and the limited franchise, could not materially increase the number at election time. They would do nothing on the one hand to court the King for office and for the considerable number of votes in the House which was the perquisite of his Ministers as such. Nor on the other hand would they lead the Radicals in an agitation for a really extensive reform of Parliament. Ten years later, under another King, the Whigs did both these things at once, and only so managed to maintain themselves in office long enough to remodel the Constitution, heavily weighted in the interest of their rivals.

The Whigs had become for a while more lukewarm in the cause of Reform than in 1797, when they had voted 91 strong for household suffrage. The fact that they had held office even for a few months in 1806–7 on the basis of leaving the anti-Jacobin system of society and politics untouched had compromised the future of Reform inside their body, and increased the mutual suspicion between Whigs and Radicals. Many old Whig families who had left the party in the days of Burke and the French Revolution, but had never had the heart to leave Brooks's, came back to the party fold, and the alliance with the Tory Grenvilles continued until 1817. Such connexions rendered it difficult for the Whigs to adopt a popular programme. Indeed, if they had ever taken office again in a Coalition such as 1807, their connexions with Reform would have been snapped altogether, and the historic purpose for which fate was preserving them would have been frustrated.

Lord Grey, in 1819–20, refused to take the field in a campaign for Parliamentary Reform, because, as he wrote to his confidant, Lord Holland, the proposal of any large measure would split the Whig party. He declared indeed that he himself favoured the abolition of no less than a hundred of the rotten borough seats, and was sure that any smaller proposal would fail to arouse popular enthusiasm without which no Reform had the least chance of being carried. Partly because he knew that so large a proposal would break up the Parliamentary party that he led, partly because he shrank from open alliance with the disreputable Radicals, partly because he preferred domestic ease and studious leisure at Howick, the Whig chief put off the hour of action. In refusing to give the country any more positive lead than a denunciation of Peterloo and the Six Acts, Grey left the Tories another decade in which to make good, and, under Canning, Huskisson, and Peel, they did not let the opportunity slip.

198

The ground was cleared for change in the Tory counsels by the death of Castlereagh in 1822. The great British statesman, who had done more than any European diplomat to bring about Napoleon's fall and to establish peace in Europe, had identified himself in his last years with the anti-Jacobin domestic policy in its final stage of decay. He had beaten Napoleon and made a peace that gave us security for a hundred years – but he had introduced the Six Acts into the House of Commons. When he died, it was the less fortunate side of his career that was uppermost in men's minds, but to us at a century's remove it seems the less important, as it was certainly the less enduring. His death by his own hand was hailed by most of his poorer fellow-countrymen with revengeful glee, which found voice in the horrible cheers that greeted his coffin as it passed into Westminster Abbey.[1] Posterity can look more impartially at the whole career of a man who was sometimes right and sometimes wrong, but who had in the main wrought greatly and beneficently, and had always, according to the light that was in him, devoted powers of the first order to his country's service.[2]

CHAPTER 12

IF Castlereagh's mind had not given way that month, or if his attendants in removing his razors had not overlooked the fatal penknife, George Canning would have started on the long sailing voyage to Bengal as Governor-General, and the history of England and Europe would have taken some different course.

For a dozen years past Canning had been kept in the background of politics by his personal unpopularity first with his colleagues, and then with the King, whom he refused to assist in the prosecution of Queen Caroline. His brilliancy had been eclipsed by the solid services that Castlereagh had rendered to Europe. But now at last his chance had come. Instead of being exiled to India, he stepped into his dead rival's place as Foreign Secretary and leader of the Commons, and became, under the mild premiership of Lord Liverpool, the first man in the kingdom.

1. Byron's epitaphs, if more indecent, were not more brutal than Cobbett's message to an imprisoned Reformer: 'Castlereagh has met his own and is dead! Let that sound reach you in the depths of your dungeon, and let it carry consolation to your suffering soul.'

2. The foreign policy of Castlereagh after 1815 is treated of in relation to that of Canning in chapter 12, pp. 209–11, below.

About the time of his promotion a great change had come to maturity in his mind. In youth the chosen disciple of Pitt, he remembered in the closing years of life that his master had once been a reforming and liberal Minister, before the French Revolution raised an issue that had now receded. This was unpalatable doctrine to the men who still shouted Pitt's name as a war-cry against every measure of justice and common sense, and met in Pitt Clubs to drink 'Irish Protestant Ascendancy', and the health of the yeomanry of Peterloo. But the influence of Canning in his new position permeated Westminster and Whitehall.

Indeed, though the popular rejoicings over Castlereagh's suicide were brutal, and unjust to a great public servant, his death, coming when it did, was fortunate. Not only did our foreign policy, which had become neutral under Castlereagh, become liberal under Canning, but at home reforms followed in rapid succession. Popular belief in constitutional and political action, which Peterloo and the Six Acts had nearly killed, was revived by the proof of what could be done even in an unreformed House of Commons. In such an atmosphere, improved still further by good harvests and a revival in trade, the prospect of violence and class war retreated into the background.

The liberal[1] Tories were the men of the hour. After the death of Castlereagh the ablest statesmen in the Cabinet belonged to their section of the party. The Whigs had failed to give a lead to the country through their official chiefs, but were ready, under younger men like Brougham and Russell, to cooperate in debates and divisions with the more enlightened part of the Government forces. Under these conditions not only were many valuable measures passed, but the Tory party was disintegrated and forced to resolve itself into its true elements, so that when after Canning's death men were forced to choose between a reversion to anti-Jacobinism under Wellington and Eldon, and an advance to Parliamentary and Municipal Reform under the rejuvenated Whigs, the liberal Tories, with the great exception of Peel, felt themselves prepared by the experience of ten years to break with their old connexions and join the party of Parliamentary Reform.

The happy issue of affairs for Britain in the nineteenth century was largely determined by the character and personality of the men who came to the front in the twenties – Canning, Huskisson, and Peel, Althorp, Durham, and Russell, and the school of states-

---

1. In England the word 'liberal' did not yet designate a party, but was used as an adjective connoting the character of those ideas which were held in common by Canning and Grey, Huskisson and Brougham.

men that they inspired. In an age of transition, they united to an unusual degree the merits of aristocracy and democracy. The merit of aristocracy lies in the families and individuals who are brought up to serve the State; its demerit lies in a policy dictated by a small class whose experience and interest are not those of the community at large. In democracy, on the other hand, public opinion and the interest of the majority prevail as the motive force, but there is no provision for the training of a class of statesmen. In the epoch of English history that opened in the reign of George IV, the tradition of the old aristocracy, shared by the rising bourgeoisie, still supplied both parties in the State with a large number of families, whose ablest sons were devoted from boyhood to high politics, and were placed early in Parliament with the consciousness that the government was upon their shoulders. The difference from former times was that these specially trained leaders now felt responsibility to the great public rather than to their own class, whose prejudices and monopolies they were often prepared to sacrifice to the general welfare. The eighteenth-century aristocrats and the anti-Jacobin Tories had been the master of the public, and sometimes therefore its robbers and tyrants. Peel and his successors were its servants. But they were not demagogues, because they still felt themselves to belong to a high and austere sect, devoted to the science of government. Part of that science was to keep in touch with the changes of public opinion – but it was by no means all.

Peel's father, the first Sir Robert, of Lancashire fame, calico-printer and Tory member, stood like his son after him for the reconciliation of classes. We have seen him, during Napoleon's Hundred Days, working out the details of a Factory Bill with Owen himself.[1] The calico-printer, even before he had been made a baronet, determined, like the elder Pitt, that his son should be Prime Minister. He vowed him from the cradle, and trained him from the nursery, not for business but for Parliament. He sent him to Harrow, then populous with future Premiers and party leaders, where he shared with Lord Byron a sound classical education. His classics and his aristocratic connexions received the finishing touch at Christ Church, where he figured as a gentleman commoner. As soon as he came of age, his father bought him a seat for an Irish borough. Next year his own abilities and training, and his father's influence, obtained for him a subordinate office. By 1812 he was Chief Secretary for Ireland.

Thus, before he had had time to observe the political scene, and to think out opinions for himself, Peel was immersed in official

1. pp. 189–90, above.

routine of flattering importance. The Tory party in its heyday of power and popularity, and the Protestant Ascendancy in Ireland, both shone on the manufacturer's son in their brightest and most alluring colours. Almost from his boyhood, the squires and rectors of both islands hailed him as their favourite spokesman, for he at least was staunch against Catholic Emancipation. At the age of twenty-nine he won the blue ribbon of Toryism, that had been denied to Canning, the membership for the University of Oxford. In another aspect, he was the business agent of Tory officialdom: so long as he was at work for twelve hours a day in Whitehall, the squires could hunt and shoot with the security that all was right. They trusted him indeed too blindly, and found in the end a master where they had placed a servant.

These circumstances of his youth partly explain why Peel never learnt that he was not a Tory. Yet Palmerston, who had been pushed forward equally young by the same party, carried his much more real Toryism over into the Whig camp, while Peel continued all his life, from force of early association, to regard Toryism as synonymous with the government of the country rather than with a particular set of opinions, many of which he ceased to share.

In 1822 Peel entered the Cabinet as Home Secretary. He at once cleared out the mystery of iniquity at the Home Office. He abolished the system of maintaining Government spies and *agents provocateurs* among the working-men, which had done so much to embitter class feelings during the last dozen years. He discontinued the political and Press prosecutions, and on every side broke off the connexion of Tory rule with coercion in England. The change passed unnoticed, since no legislation was necessary, but it was a change of profound importance.

After the suicide of Romilly in 1818, the agitation for reform of the Criminal Code on the principles of Bentham was carried on by Sir James Mackintosh, who as an Opposition member won the first great Parliamentary triumph of the cause in the legislation in 1820. In 1823 Peel as Home Secretary took up the movement on behalf of Government, and in a few years obtained the repeal of the death penalty for a hundred different offences.

There was equal need for a reform of legal procedure, above all of the procrastinating Court of Chancery, loved for its very faults by its ancient and apparently irremovable chief, Lord Eldon. The world's attention was first turned to law reform as a whole by Brougham's famous six-hour speech in the Commons in 1828, surveying the labyrinth of anachronism and delay that caused misery and injustice not only in Chancery, but in the realm of common law, ecclesiastical law, and the petty local courts. Under the impulse given by Brougham's speech, followed up by Royal Commissions, a long series of law reforms were carried in the middle years of the century.

Peel crowned his work at the Home Office by establishing in 1829 the Metropolitan Police Force. Its success in London caused it to be adopted throughout the whole country in the course of the next thirty years. The frequency and immunity of crime had scared the legislators of the eighteenth century into the creation of fresh capital felonies every session – a remedy that proved worse than useless. It had never occurred to the 'age of common sense' to find a substitute for the fumbling old watchmen, who preserved unimpaired the traditions of Dogberry and Verges.

Peel's 'new police' secured the success of his reform of the criminal law. And they were no less essential to his policy of avoiding a serious collision between the armed forces of Government and the working-class agitators. It was universally agreed that if there had been 'Peelers' in Manchester in 1819, or in Bristol in 1831, there would have been no Peterloo, and no burning of Bristol. The lower type of Radical rioters cursed 'Peel's bloody gang' as a serious restraint on their activities, but Francis Place, who knew that liberty implied order, was strongly on the side of an efficient civilian force, of non-partisan character, and armed only with staves – a boon unknown to the subjects of continental despotisms. Some of Place's Radical friends might have been not too well pleased to know that in November 1830 he advised the inspector of the new police 'when he saw a mob prepared to make an attack, to lead his men on and thrash those who composed the mob with their staves as long as any of them remained together, but to take no one into custody; and that if this were done once or twice there would be no more mobs.' The event justified the advice. There had previously been no force capable of doing anything with a London mob, short of shooting and sabring, and for that reason Lord George Gordon had been able to begin the sack of the capital.[1]

One important reform cannot be placed to the credit of the Ministry. Pitt's Combination Laws, a relic of the days of anti-Jacobin panic, still rendered all Trade Union action illegal. Had

1. Highwaymen, who had been the plague of the roads throughout the eighteenth century, had now disappeared, partly owing to the enclosure of so many wild heaths and commons where they used to lurk; partly as the result of a campaign against them of mounted patrols, coupled with a policy of taking away licences from public-houses that harboured them.

they been left on the Statute Book, the recrudescence of working-class combination, already very general in industry, must perforce have become revolutionary in the new age. The national service of repealing these dangerous laws was rendered by two determined and unselfish citizens, unaided by any recognized party leader. Joseph Hume, a private member, notorious in the Commons as the persistent advocate of retrenchment, took his orders about the Combination Laws from Francis Place, who manipulated the whole affair from his library at Charing Cross.

Place, like many self-made men, had somewhat too high an opinion of himself as compared to others, but his management of a recalcitrant Parliament of employers, through the sole agency of one private member, was a masterpiece of the political art. In 1824 Place and Hume secured the passage of a very liberal Act settling the status of Trade Unions, before members were aware of what they were doing. Next year the two had the more difficult task of preventing a reversal of the policy at the instigation of Huskisson and Peel, after a wave of strikes had caused a panic in the employing class. The crisis was severe, but, owing to the mass of evidence from the industrial districts which Place marshalled before the House of Commons Committee, the Act of 1825 was not in the end a reversal of Hume's Act of the year before, though very stringent provisions were added against intimidation.

The wage-earners were set free to work out their own salvation, not only by the repeal of the Combination Laws, but by analogous legislation passed at various dates, which permitted artisans to emigrate, and legalized Friendly and Co-operative Societies. These laws were not the work of Owen and the Socialists, but of the individualist Radicals and political economists of the 'classical' school. The Act of 1824 is the first case of the impartial application of the doctrines of *laissez faire* even when they benefited the workmen as against the master.[1] It was significant that Place and Hume had had the support of an important minority of employers who believed that Pitt's Acts were unjust and a principal cause of industrial strife. Place himself believed that, when once the workmen had the right to use the weapon of collective bargaining as freely as their masters, it would not be necessary for them to do so, and that Trade Unions would die a natural death!

The working class was fortunate in having at this critical epoch three servants of such widely different talents and opinions as

1. See p. 151, above. Not only Malthus and Ricardo but McCulloch himself supported the repeal of the Combination Laws.

Owen, Cobbett, and Place. They seemed made to supply each other's deficiencies. Place prided himself on the scientific character of his Benthamite individualism, but in him Bentham's teaching was modified and enlarged, as it was not in the case of James Mill and others of the sect, by his experience as a journeyman tailor in early youth. He devoted the last half of his life to raising the status and organizing the political action of the class from which he had raised himself by his business abilities. He despised the other working-class leaders. He saw that if the still uneducated proletariat cut itself off politically from the liberal elements in the middle class it would achieve nothing. In spite of his profound contempt for the wisdom of Parliament as the abode of the 'stultified Tories' and 'gabbling Whigs', he none the less was the first to develop the modern arts of lobbying, and bringing to bear on members the weight of evidence and argument from outside. It was partly because his procedure in 1824–5 was so novel that it succeeded so well. The cloud of witnesses from the industrial north that he had wafted into the aristocratic precincts of Westminster to testify to the working of the Combination Laws were the heralds of a new era in politics. Honourable gentlemen might stare, but they would have to grow reconciled to such sights in the lobbies of the 'best club in Europe'.

Huskisson began the administrative and ministerial side of the Free Trade movement which Peel and Gladstone completed. He became President of the Board of Trade early in 1823, as the friend and *protégé* of Canning, whom at the same time he succeeded as member for Liverpool, becoming thereby the accredited representative of the mercantile interest.

The *laissez faire* economic doctrine, propounded in majestic completeness by Adam Smith as far back as 1776, had captivated the understanding of Pitt in his precocious boyhood. Before the question had become generally understood either inside or outside Parliament, the young Minister was carrying a rapid reduction and simplification of tariffs. But this process was reversed by the war of 1793–1815. War expenditure and the interest on war debt were defrayed by unscientific taxation of almost all articles in common use. A revenue tariff, not really protective in its object, taxed raw materials more heavily than manufactured articles. The unwise refusal of the middle classes at the end of the war to submit to a continuation of the income-tax in time of peace helped to perpetuate this incubus of ill-adjusted taxation.

And so, for thirty years after the outbreak of the war with

France, the doctrine of *laissez faire* was seldom quoted except to prove the impossibility of the State enforcing a living wage or interfering on behalf of the employee. At length, in the more liberal atmosphere of the twenties, the time had come for a revival of its Free Trade implications. The financial genius of Huskisson was able to operate with the full support of the economists at the height of their fame and influence, under the patronage of the port of Liverpool and the bulk of middle-class opinion, and behind the shield of Canning, the favourite of the nation and the despot of the Cabinet.

Under these favouring conditions Huskisson resumed Pitt's earlier role, substituted moderate tariffs for total prohibitions, abolished bounties, cut down high duties to a percentage that discouraged smuggling and encouraged competition, and admitted many raw materials at nominal tariffs. Timber he excluded from this category in order to benefit Canada.

Huskisson had more vision of the Empire than any other statesman of his own or of the following generation, except Lord Durham. He encouraged and subsidized emigration. He showed the Colonies that their interests were to be consulted no less than those of the mother country. Such a theory was new in the world. Seizing the opportunity of changes in the tariff, he established a working system of preferential duties for colonial goods. When Free Trade reached its full development in the forties and fifties, preference was no longer possible. But Huskisson's idea that the Colonies were not mere stalking-horses for British interests at home outlived his preferential tariffs.

Though Huskisson laid the foundation of British Free Trade policy, he himself did not contemplate a total abolition of duties. But in one respect he was compelled to outstrip Adam Smith himself. The philosopher had pronounced the Navigation Laws injurious to our national wealth, but necessary for our national security, as a means of maintaining the school of seamen. These laws, first enacted against our Dutch rivals in the time of the Commonwealth, had the effect of confining British trade almost entirely to ships owned and manned by British subjects. The system was brought to the ground, not by attacks of *laissez faire* economists, but by the action of America in passing a navigation law of her own, which imposed special duties on goods imported in British ships. European countries began to follow suit, and Huskisson in 1823 was fain to pass a Reciprocity Act enabling government to negotiate a treaty with any foreign State, so as to secure to the ships of each country the free use of the other's ports.

Our Colonies were at the same time permitted to trade direct with Europe.

It was not till 1849 and the following years that the Navigation Acts were completely abolished, but they had received their death-blow in 1823. The new spirit of enterprise in the open market that asked for no protection, and the invention of iron ships just when our forests were failing, enabled British shipbuilders to compete against foreign rivals with the same success as before.

Huskisson's Free Trade measures unshackled the limbs of a vigorous giant. British commerce, unlike British agriculture, was as a young man rejoicing in his strength and confident in his power to make his own way in the world. Brilliant prospects were every-where opening out to capital and enterprise. When the colonies of Spain threw off her yoke, the merchants of Cadiz were no longer able to forbid the rest of mankind to trade with South America. At the same time Europe's purchasing power abroad was recovering from the effects of the war and the peace. England was the clearing-house and port of call for the trade between the two hemispheres, and London was the financial centre for the colossal operations of the coming age.

Canning and Huskisson were alive to all this. The old and the new member for Liverpool understood that England's future lay in commerce rather than in agriculture, and that already less than a third of the population worked on the land. The economic and political outlook of these two Tory chiefs was very different from that of the squires and rural clergy who composed the nucleus of their party.

In the British political world 'Corn was King'. It was more dangerous to tamper with that one item of the Protectionist system than with all the rest put together. For whereas the manufacturers were meagrely represented in Parliament and were coming round to Free Trade – at least in such articles as each man did not himself produce – on the other hand, the landlords, who nominated or composed the immense majority of both Houses, had no doubts at all as to the necessity for the protection of corn. The Corn Laws were the ark of the Tory Covenant, and half the Whig gentlemen regarded them as no less sacred.[1] Parliamentary Reform would have to precede any serious reduction in the corn duty.

Yet the Act of 1815,[2] in which Huskisson himself had been a

1. Lord Grey's son and heir wanted free trade in corn as early as 1827, but his father wrote that his views, if carried into effect, would injure the country, and 'at once ruin him and me.'
2. See p. 159, above.

participator, was working such general havoc that some change in the form of protection had to be devised. By the Waterloo Corn Bill import was prohibited when wheat stood below 80s. a quarter.[1] The result was to hamper foreign trade, to keep the price of corn artificially high, and in years of scarcity to starve the labourer's family in town and country alike. The Corn Law had been fiercely denounced by the middle and working classes from the moment of its introduction. It increased the revolutionary feeling among town Radicals and village rick-burners, and caused grave discontent among the unrepresented captains of industry and their lieutenants. At inns and places of public resort loud disputes between commercial travellers and farmers on the subject of the Corn Laws marked a growing division among the 'respectable' classes that boded ill for the permanence of the existing régime.

Yet the 'agricultural interest', the landlords and big farmers, were themselves harassed by the working of their own law. It had been assumed that the measure would keep wheat above 80s. a quarter,[1] and on the strength of that assumption farmers continued to discard the production of meat, poultry, and vegetables, and to plough up bad lands that ought never to have grown corn at all. The result of this over-production of corn in Britain was that prices fell below 80s., not indeed low enough to give food to the people at a reasonable price, but low enough to break many farmers and to prevent many landlords from obtaining the high rents on which they had calculated. Some new form of corn protection was loudly called for by the agricultural interest itself. A slight modification of the law in 1822 had made no change in the situation.

Huskisson therefore proposed a sliding scale – that is to say a tariff to vary with the price. The principle was accepted, but the question of its rate and incidence divided the Tory party as fiercely as Foreign Policy and Catholic Emancipation. Huskisson and Canning stood for a lower rate, Wellington for a higher. Finally, after Canning's death, the Duke fixed a sliding scale to begin when wheat was under 73s. a quarter. It was hoped that it would prevent the fluctuation of prices, but it had no such effect. It remained as the Corn Law against which the thunders of Cobden's League were in later years directed.

The liberal trend of British statesmanship in the nineteenth century was set in these years by Peel for domestic administration, by Huskisson for commerce, and by Canning for foreign relations.

1. It must be remembered that 80s. then was worth many times what it is now; 80s. a quarter was a terribly high price in 1815.

In our dealings with Europe, a continuous if winding stream of policy joins our breach with the Holy Alliance to the war of 1914.

Canning's tenure of the Foreign Office marked the fact that England had changed sides. In order to release Europe from the overlordship of France, we had fought in alliance with the Eastern despotisms and with all the most reactionary forces in the West. Our victory had involved the re-enslavement of Poland, the restoration of the Temporal Power and the Austrians in Italy, of the Jesuits, the princes, the nobles, and the Junkers throughout the Continent – while the military predominance had passed from the Western Powers to Russia, Prussia, and Austria.

It was partly because they had foreseen such consequences in case of victory that the Whigs had been factious and lukewarm about the war while it was still waging. Now they found themselves in touch with the rising anger of the nation at large against the obscurantism and despotism of our late allies. England had felt a generous warmth in helping the Spanish and German peoples to free themselves from Napoleon. When, after the common victory, the princes and priests of the Continent re-enslaved those who had done the fighting, many Englishmen felt that they had been taken in. It was not to restore the Inquisition that they had fought in Spain. England and Europe listened with delight to the invective of the Whig poet, Lord Byron, against forces which no one on the Continent could criticize without seeing the inside of a dungeon. All this was very fine, but would not have been very effectual had not the Tory Foreign Secretary taken up the cause. In a few years Canning attracted to England and to himself the loyalty of Liberals in all countries.

Castlereagh, who conducted foreign affairs until 1822, had withdrawn from interference on the Continent to neutrality, but he would never have positively changed sides. He refused, indeed, to take part in the policing of Europe against constitutional revolts, but not because he sympathized with those revolts. He spoke strongly in favour of Austria's rule in Italy and Turkey's rule in Greece. He had pledged the country, as was reasonable, to resist by force a Napoleonic restoration in France, but he had also approved of a secret treaty whereby Austria bound Ferdinand IV of Naples to maintain a system of absolutism in his territories. That was indeed the extent of Castlereagh's commitments, and he would go no further, even to please Metternich.

Metternich meanwhile had completely converted the Tsar Alexander to absolutism. The Holy Alliance in 1815 had been a vague aspiration of the Tsar's pietism.[1] Three years later it had taken practical form as the clearing-house of obscurantist diplomacy, settling the internal affairs of countries great and small at a series of European congresses. In both its phases it had been suspect to Castlereagh. The British statesman, who was a 'good European' and friend of peace, wished indeed for periodic congresses to arrange international disputes and avoid causes of war, but he did not wish these meetings to be made the instrument of interference in the internal affairs of States. Canning went still further, because he was already more sensitive than Castlereagh ever became to British public opinion. In October 1818 he told his colleagues in the Cabinet –

Our true policy has always been not to interfere except in great emergencies and then with a commanding force. The people of this country may be taught to look with great jealousy for their liberties, if our Court is engaged in meetings of great despotic monarchs, deliberating upon what degree of revolutionary spirit may endanger the public security, and therefore require the interference of the Alliance.[2]

The despots of Europe, however, went on without us, and in 1821 commissioned Austria to suppress the newly won constitution of the Neapolitan kingdom. Castlereagh disliked the collective action of the Congress for this purpose, but had no objection to Austria acting in Naples on her own account. He regarded this first great episode of the Italian *risorgimento*, on behalf of which Byron was collecting arms and Shelley writing poems, as 'a sectarian conspiracy and military revolt against a mild and paternal Government'. The man who wrote thus, and who used equally hostile language about the Greek struggle with Turkey, would never, if he had lived, have played the part taken by Canning in Europe.[3]

The 'mild and paternal Government', when restored by Austria to its absolute power in Naples, proceeded to a barbarous persecution of virtue and intellect, such as the Holy Alliance was organizing, with local variations, all over Europe. The dragooning of the

1. p. 146, above.
2. See *Castlereagh's Correspondence and Despatches* (1853), xii, pp. 56–7, and Temperley's *Canning*, 134–5. Bathurst writes to Castlereagh, who was abroad: 'I do not subscribe to Canning's opinions, nor did any of the Cabinet who attended.'
3. It is good that justice is now done to Castlereagh's immense services in 1813–15, and that his policy from 1816–22 is set in its right light. But the extreme eulogists of Castlereagh, who would have it that he initiated all that was good in Canning's policy, are doing a great injustice to Canning, who also has his rights.

German Universities, the destruction of the Polish constitution, the police system which put men in prison for possessing a volume of Gibbon or Montesquieu, bade fair to put out the light of Europe's culture in the course of suppressing her liberties. When the country that had overthrown Napoleon spoke out against this system through the mouth first of her poets and then of her Foreign Minister, the moral effect was all the greater because no other voice but England's could then be heard on behalf of freedom.

When Castlereagh died and Canning took over the Foreign Office, another Holy Alliance Congress was about to meet at Verona to decide on the suppression of the constitutional rights which the Spaniards had extorted once more from their perjured and bigoted King, Ferdinand VII. France was chosen as the executioner. The French Royalists and Clericals rejoiced to lead an invasion of Spain on absolutist principles. It would be a cheap way of reviving the glories of Napoleon on behalf of their own party. With the help of the Church in Spain, French conquest was this time easy, and the persecution that followed was ferocious. Ferdinand, as his subjects had good cause to say, had 'the heart of a tiger and the head of a mule'.

These proceedings infuriated all sections of British opinion. Anti-French, anti-Catholic, and Liberal feeling between them covered most of the ground in politics, and all three were outraged. Another reigning passion, the desire for foreign markets, was no less shrewdly touched, for if the colonies that had revolted from Spain were recovered by the aid of French arms Central and Southern America would again be closed to our goods. The 'family compact' of the French and Spanish Bourbons, so much dreaded in the eighteenth century, would be renewed against British trade and power. The spirit of Chatham was aroused. The memories of the Peninsula were revived. Once more, as in 1808, the shop windows were filled with coloured cartoons, generously but naïvely representing 'Spanish patriots', in the ruffs and slashed clothes of their great ancestors, slaughtering masses of shrieking Frenchmen!

Canning, though he confessed to a friend that 'he had an itch for war with France', decided not to plunge the country into another great struggle, with half the Spanish people and all the governments of Europe supporting the French. Indeed, such a war would probably have had the disastrous result of identifying French military and nationalist feeling, which was at that time anti-Bourbon, with all the worst forms of reaction. Where Canning did not intend to fight, he was too wise to bluff or threaten. He contented himself with a strong protest against the invasion of Spain. But he gave the French to understand that, if they attempted to send troops across the Atlantic, they would have to deal with the British fleet. And he let the restored Spanish absolutism know that the reactionary system was not to be carried by foreign arms into Portugal. When, in disregard of this warning, the Spaniards began to interfere with our little ally, Canning was as good as his word, and sent four thousand redcoats to Lisbon, who soon disposed of the reactionary forces. France and Spain shrank from a contest over Portugal. The successful landing of British troops on the Continent to defend the constitutional cause, even on this small scale, made a great sensation throughout Europe.

Although the revolt of our American colonists in the eighteenth century proved ultimately decisive as an example to those of Spain, it had had no immediate effect upon them. The revolutionary and separatist movement came to South America, not from the countrymen or contemporaries of Washington, but through the agency of Spanish-Americans resident in Europe in the time of Napoleon. In the same era, the wars of Spain against England and against France revealed to her subjects beyond the ocean the feeble and useless character of their home government, and broke up the isolation, comparable to that of China, which had so long divided South America from the rest of mankind.

In 1806–7, Spain being then at war with England, a British force from South Africa, crossing the Atlantic without orders from home on the strangest of escapades, landed in the Plata River and seized Buenos Aires. When the news reached London, British merchants at home raised a shout of greedy joy, and the Cabinet had the weakness to accept and support the move thus forced upon them. The Spanish Royal Governor had fled in panic, incapable of attempting to organize resistance. But as the British made the mistake of demanding allegiance for King George instead of proclaiming independence, the populace acted with the guerilla energy of their race, and in twelve months compelled the invaders to sail away again under an ignominious armistice.

These events were the prelude to South American Independence. The exhibition of helpless folly on the part of the Spanish Royal authorities, the habits of successful self-defence engendered in the population thus deserted, the taste of the pleasures of anarchy enjoyed by the wilder *gauchos* of the great plain, and the seeds of knowledge and civilization planted by the English during their year's occupation, all made for revolution. When next year the government of old Spain betrayed the race and gave its possessions on both sides of the Atlantic to the French, its action was repudiated in South America, and the English were welcomed as friends and deliverers.

The confusion of authority that followed in Spain, between the patriotic Juntas and a Court become vassal to Napoleon, favoured the designs of the small group who were working for the independence of Spanish America. From that time forward their cause made rapid progress, though it went through many vicissitudes. The English merchants fostered the revolt, partly as a means of obtaining markets in defiance of the veto from Spain, and partly out of political sympathy. It was not, perhaps, easy to feel great enthusiasm for revolutions which never led to anything more constitutional than military dictatorship. Spanish America had been for more than two centuries locked away from the world's intrusion, to vegetate in peace; Spaniards and Indians had worked out a *modus vivendi*, and there had been no third party. Now at length the new freedom, or more precisely the new independence, came rudely to disturb the calm of that curious society. There followed several generations of petty warfare between rival parties and rival States. But there followed also European trade, inventions, ideas, and interpenetration by foreign businessmen, at first chiefly from Great Britain.

In those days the scattered communities of so vast a continent were as much separated from each other as they were from Spain. The British merchant ships helped to keep up communications and to give the struggle for independence a certain unity of action. In the group of equatorial colonies along the Spanish main, the leading figure was Bolivar the Liberator. He owed much to an army of six thousand British volunteers, largely disbanded Peninsular veterans, who left their bones in that fierce struggle with man and nature in the tropical mountains. Farther south, along the coasts of Chile and Peru, a small rebel fleet decided the contest by its brilliant feats under the command of Lord Cochrane, then the finest of British sailors, whose career in our service had been cut short after a brilliant beginning.

At the time when the French reactionaries restored Ferdinand to Madrid, Spanish-American independence, though not yet recognized by any European Power, was an accomplished fact. It was also a British vested interest of great commercial value. And grave as were the shortcomings of the half-civilized republics, 'freedom' might without undue poetic licence be invoked to prevent the reconquest of half a hemisphere by the monarchs of the

213

Holy Alliance, who had just trodden out the embers of liberty in Italy and Spain.

It was at this stage of affairs that the United States entered on the scene as the world-champion of a democracy more advanced than Canning's Liberal Toryism, and as the leading American Power. In neither capacity was her advent altogether welcome to Canning, who curiously enough was more under the influence of aristocratic prejudices against the United States than his more high-born and conservative predecessor.[1] It was fortunate that he had only to deal with the United States at a time when our common interests were to the fore and our numerous differences were slumbering. He had indeed invited American diplomatic support against the Holy Alliance, and he made full use of it, while the Press on both sides of the Atlantic preached the novel doctrine of English-speaking union against a world of despots.

The veto laid on French action by the British fleet decided the crisis. Canning indeed had secured the acquiescence of the French Government in the inevitable, even before President Monroe laid down the famous 'Monroe doctrine' in the message to Congress of December 1823. The President's warning to the powers of the Holy Alliance to keep their hands off the revolted colonies of Spain was made in unequivocal terms, on the high ground of the political sympathies of the United States, and her own special interests in the New World. There was also a significant sentence of general application:

The occasion has been judged proper for asserting as a principle in which the rights and interests of the United States are involved, that the American continents, by the free and independent condition which they have assumed and maintained, are henceforth not to be considered as subjects for future colonization by any European powers.

It is true that the 'occasion' for 'asserting this principle' was certain designs of Russia on the still unoccupied Pacific coast. It is also true that 'existing colonies or dependencies of any power' were excepted from this veto. None the less, Canning saw in the Monroe doctrine a warning to Great Britain about the future, as well as an immediate defiance of their common enemies of the Holy Alliance. And such indeed was the spirit of the message in the mind of those who framed it. It signified that the United States was coming into the field as a great world power with a policy and ethos of her own. Much would have been saved if her advent on these terms had been accepted by Canning, Palmerston, and the other

1. See pp. 182–3, above, on Castlereagh and the United States.

semi-aristocratic statesmen of Britain in transition, as frankly as it was accepted after the American Civil War and after the full democratization of the British Parliament.

The closing scene of the Spanish-American drama was the official recognition by Great Britain of Mexico, Buenos Aires, and Bolivar's Colombia as independent States. Canning's High Tory colleagues had fought against his policy in the Cabinet from first to last, and George IV had intrigued against him with Metternich and the Russians. But, strong in the support of the British people, Canning had defied his enemies at home and abroad. They liked it little when he boasted in the Commons:

Contemplating Spain as our ancestors had known her, I resolved that if France had Spain, it should not be Spain with the Indies. I called the New World into existence to redress the balance of the Old.

On the American question, Canning, backed by the peoples of America and by the British fleet, was geographically master of the situation, and had simply overridden the will of Russia, Austria, Prussia, and France. But in the case of the Greek rebellion against Turkey, he was only able to achieve Greek independence by dexterous use of the divisions of the Holy Alliance itself, and the sympathy felt by France and Russia with the insurgents. He is almost the only British statesman who, by the consent of all today, added to his laurels by his positive achievements in the Near East. Combining the best points of the later policies of Disraeli and Gladstone, he kept Russia's ambitions within bounds by placing England and France alongside of her as champions of liberation from the Turk.[1] Canning visited Paris and with great ability won over Charles X and his reactionary but Christian Ministers to cooperate in this policy, thereby splitting the Holy Alliance from top to bottom, and forcing Metternich to look on in impotent fury while the English, Russian, and French fleets under Admiral Codrington blew the Turkish fleet out of the water in Navarino bay.

Two months before that decisive event, Canning had died. But though Wellington's bungling reversal of his policy eventually left France and Russia to divide the honour of clearing the Turks out of the Morea, the policy devised by Canning had triumphed. A new State representing a race with European traditions had been set up, only nominally subject to Turkey, yet not dependent on Russia.

1. The difference between Castlereagh's and Canning's policy can be measured by the following words of Castlereagh's written in December 1821: 'Whatever may be the views of the Turkish power, it is at least exempt from the revolutionary danger. The cause of the Greeks is deeply and inevitably tainted with it.'

Britain had prepared a dyke against the tide of the Russian advance, not by bolstering up Turkish despotism, but by taking the lead against it herself, and appealing to the new principle of nationality.

This policy was abandoned at the Crimea, when the Whigs, throwing over the traditions of Fox and Grey, and the Tories those of Canning, reverted to Pitt's pro-Turkish methods of checkmating Russia.[1] The same purely negative policy served Disraeli's turn once more in the seventies.

During the fifty years between Canning's liberation of Greece and Gladstone's campaign on the Bulgarian atrocities, the English people ceased to sympathize with national struggles for liberty against the Turks. The cause had aroused their generous ardour when Byron died for Greece at Missolonghi. Before Canning's official intervention, British gold and British volunteers, collected by enthusiastic committees, had done as much to maintain the insurgent cause in Greece as in South America. But whereas the sympathy with South America had its roots in commerce, the sympathy with Greece had its roots in culture. The very name of Hellas, like that of Italy in the next generation, had a strange power to move our apparently unemotional grandfathers. But when once the heirs of Athens had been freed, Serb, Bulgar, and Armenian appealed in vain for British sympathy, though the cause was the same of delivering ancient races long submerged under the stagnant water of Turkish misrule. The classical and literary education that then moulded and inspired the English mind had power to make men sympathize with Greece and Italy, more even than Christianity had power to make them sympathize with the Balkan Christians. It is significant of much that in the seventeenth century members of Parliament quoted from the Bible; in the eighteenth and nineteenth centuries from the classics; in the twentieth century from nothing at all.

CHAPTER 13

FOR five years England had been guided by the genius of Canning, and seldom have so much brilliancy and so much wisdom combined to produce such happy results. The constitutional medium through which that genius worked was the loyal friendship of the Prime Minister, Lord Liverpool, one of those statesmen whose

1. pp. 58–9, above.

chief art is to hold together Cabinets of imperious and discordant colleagues. Formerly he had been under the influence of Castlereagh, but he had since passed under the spell of Canning, and had more than once been of service to him by persuading Lord Eldon and the Duke to remain in office, though they objected to the whole current of the government policy. But in February 1827 a paralytic stroke removed the Prime Minister from the political scene. The Tory party could no longer avoid choosing between Canning and Wellington, for neither could possibly serve under the other. Though George IV had lately intrigued to get rid of Canning, he now felt his mastery and had no resource but to call him to the head of affairs. Wellington, Eldon, and Peel left the Cabinet.

Canning was dying, and he knew it. But, like his master before him, he rallied his failing energies to serve his country in the crisis that was upon her. He formed a Cabinet of his own followers: Huskisson stood by him, and Palmerston, whose cynical common sense began to read failure in the programme of what he called 'the stupid old Tory party'. Canning also gave a few minor places to Whigs, since he would have to eke out a majority by the help of Whig votes in the Commons. The group system had replaced two-party politics, which only the Reform Bill was destined to revive. For the moment the Whigs were as much divided as the Tories. But whereas the Tories were divided on questions of policy which time would render more acute, the Whigs were split on a question of tactics which Canning's death was certain to resolve.

Lord Lansdowne and Lord Holland, Lord Durham and Henry Brougham, and the bulk of the Whigs, young and old, supported Canning out of gratitude for what he had done and to prevent a Wellingtonian reaction at home and abroad. But Lord Grey and his young lieutenant, Lord Althorp, the most popular man in the House of Commons, both refused to sanction the coalition. Grey was partly influenced by that distrust of Canning as an 'adventurer', which was traditional among the elder statesmen on either side, but which none of the younger men could understand. With more reason, Grey complained that Canning had received the support of the Whigs without making the smallest concession, even on those points where he agreed with them, like Catholic Emancipation. That great question was still to be left on the shelf, while the Government would actively oppose the abolition of the Test Act, still more any measure of Parliamentary Reform.

The instinct of Grey and Althorp against merging the Foxite tradition on these terms in the Canningite branch of Toryism was perhaps justified by the fact that three years later the Canningite

Tories came and merged themselves in the Whig party and so enabled the Reform Bill to be carried. Canning himself was to the very last as illogically in love with the rotten boroughs as the other great liberal Tory, Peel; and he had ten times Peel's popularity at that time. If, therefore, the Whigs had accepted Canning as Liberal leader, and if he had lived, there would have been no Reform Bill. His death, like the last wonderful five years of his life, takes its place in a series of strokes of destiny which cleared the way for the peaceful emergence of the new order.

Canning died on 8 August 1827 in the house at Chiswick where Fox had passed away. There had been no time for his Ministry to be tested in practice, but by the fact of its formation the Canningites had been marked off as a distinct group, opposed to the High Tory party. After a brief attempt by the incapable 'goody Goderich' to construct a Canningite Government without Canning, Wellington came back to form a Ministry, nominally of Tory reunion. But the time for reunion had gone by. Perpetual friction in the Cabinet was too much for the patience of the Duke, who was no Liverpool. He brusquely seized an opportunity to get rid of the Canningites when their leader Huskisson made an offer of resignation not seriously meaning to be taken at his word.

By this proceeding, more soldierly than politic, the Duke condemned himself to govern Great Britain and Ireland through the agency of the High Tories alone. He had not calculated what that might imply. As soon as he had purged his administration of nearly every man who believed in Catholic Emancipation, he found himself suddenly compelled to emancipate the Catholics.

The political history of this period is bewildering to the student, and rich in paradoxical happenings, because, while the old parties are breaking up, 'the spirit of the age', and the constant pressure of the unenfranchised from without, overwhelm from day to day the policies of the nominal holders of power. The scene has all the confused inconsequence of a great military retreat, when no one knows what anyone else is doing, and positions are taken up only to be abandoned. Whereas Canning, the year before, had thought it necessary to pledge his Cabinet to prevent the repeal of the Test Act and to leave Catholic Emancipation alone, fifteen months after the Duke took office both relieving Bills had become law under the aegis of an ultra-Tory Ministry.

Lord John Russell's Bill to repeal the Test and Corporation Acts, which prohibited Dissenters from holding National or Municipal Office, passed the Commons by so great a majority that Peel and Wellington thought it wise not to oppose it, and even negotiated its passage through the Upper House. The blow to the spirit of Church ascendancy was theoretic and moral, for in practice a yearly Indemnity Bill had been passed to pardon any Dissenters who had broken the law by taking office, and a wholesale reform of Parliamentary and Municipal representation would be needed before the Church monopoly could be seriously affected and Non-conformists obtain a share of power at all commensurate with their rapidly increasing numbers, wealth, and influence.

The Repeal of the Test Act had been accepted with a good grace, largely owing to the moderation which the bishops had shown at Peel's instance. But the admission of Roman Catholics to Parliament would be a far more serious blow to the feelings of 'the Protestant and High Church party', as the Tories were called in those days before the Oxford movement. 'No Popery' was the one thing that still gave them popularity with large sections of the public. Yet Peel and Wellington in 1829 not only abandoned the policy in the faith of which they had been bred, and in vindicating which they had risen to power against all rivals, but they outraged all the precedents and expectations of party loyalty by themselves as Ministers forcing Catholic Emancipation through Parliament. Right or wrong, it was a course which only two very strong and disinterested men would have taken. Nothing that could have happened inside this island could ever have induced them to adopt it. It was dictated to them by the belief that no one else could win the consent of the King and the Lords to Emancipation, and that only if Emancipation were actually passed could England avoid the shame and danger of a civil war in Ireland.

Pitt's policy, or rather the policy which George III and the Tories had forced upon Pitt's weakness, had done everything to exasperate and nothing to reconcile Irish opinion.[1] The Union, unaccompanied by Catholic Emancipation, extinguished the last hopes of Grattan, the great Protestant statesman who had shown England the way to solve the Irish question before it was too late. 'The Irish Demosthenes', as a broken-hearted exile, won a kind of posthumous reputation in the alien Parliament to which he had been led captive by the Act of Union. He lived till 1820, but during the last twenty years of his life he knew that his day was over. The forces through which he had sought the reconciliation of creeds and races were played out – the religious toleration and indifferent-ism of eighteen-century thought had been succeeded in Ireland by Orange and Catholic fanaticism, and in England by an Evangelical

1. pp. 113–15, above.

propaganda against the Popish danger, which had spread from the mob to the rulers of Church and State.

The man who in the early years of the new century stepped into Grattan's place as Irish leader was a very different man, appealing to very different forces. Grattan, a Protestant, had appealed to the patience of Irish Catholics, to the wisdom and generosity of Irish and English Protestants. O'Connell, a Catholic, appealed to his own people to close their ranks and to extort through fear what had been denied to justice.

The Irish peasant democracy had lain crushed and dormant during the eighteenth century, until in the last decade spasmodic local convulsions had shown that it was about to awake. O'Connell aroused and organized its religious and social passions. British statesmen, both Whig and Tory, complained of this as a crime, but nothing less formidable would have gained attention for Irish wrongs in the island to which Pitt had moved the Irish justice-seat.

Though compelled to adopt methods of agitation, O'Connell was a man of peace and order, desiring to reconcile England and Ireland within the bounds of the Empire and by constitutional means. But he knew that the terms of reconciliation would have to be extorted. He proposed to extort them, not by the spasmodic violence which was the usual resort of each village when left to itself, but by organizing the national will through a machinery which he himself devised. The Catholic Association, founded in 1823, became nothing less than a regimentation of Catholic Ireland, under the priests as officers, with O'Connell as Commander-in-Chief. Though everyone in secular authority was outside the movement and hostile to it, the unanimity of the people was terrible. Such unanimity is seldom found except where the national life is comprised in a single class of ill-educated peasants, in whom the instincts of herd morality have been fortified by centuries of oppression.

English policy had indeed removed all the intermediary classes which usually form a bridge between an unpopular government and its discontented subjects. The whole official class by law had to belong to an alien religion, and by tradition had alien sympathies in almost every respect. The landlords, the natural leaders of a rural community, were nearly all of them Protestants, mostly holding their possessions as a foreign garrison intruded in the place of the native owners by the sword of Cromwell and of William.

Nor did the position of the Irish landlord among his tenantry resemble that of the English landlord in economic any more than in religious and political matters. The typical Irish landlord had never been an 'improver'. He did nothing for his estate. He neither built nor repaired the cabins, sheds, or fences of his tenantry. He was simply a consumer of rack-rent. Except in certain districts of Ulster, the tenant had no customary 'right'. There was no class of big farmer growing up as in England to govern the rural proletariat in his own and the landlord's interest. On the contrary, the farms in Ireland were getting smaller, in the eighteenth century, by subdivision into potato patches of half an acre each. This encouraged the population to increase, without reference to the real productive power of the soil or the reliability of the potato crop. The result was periodic famine. Before the great famine of 1846 and the subsequent emigration to America, there were more than eight millions of people in Ireland, nearly twice as many as are now supported by much improved agricultural methods.

One of the arguments that had been advanced in favour of the Union of 1800 had been that British capital would be attracted to Ireland. This hope had not been fulfilled. And during the half-century between the Union and the famine era the British Parliament, which had undertaken the duties of its Dublin predecessor with so light a heart, entirely neglected the economic aspect of its new functions. The government was content to apply rigorously the English land laws to totally different economic and social conditions. It did nothing to develop the economic resources of the country, or to fight poverty and over-population by any expedient, other than that of supporting by military force the wholesale evictions ordained by landlords anxious to clear their estates.

Such was the state of affairs in Ireland during the period of O'Connell's influence. The evicted had not even the provision of the English poor law to save them from starvation. Meanwhile, as it were to emphasize the connexion of religion with these evils, the peasant had to pay a tithe of his produce to the minister of a religion that he regarded as heretical. Till O'Connell arose, agrarian crime was the only form of protest. It led to the 'proclaiming' of districts and the maintenance of order by an army larger than that which garrisoned India.

Yet even under such conditions a kind of feudal loyalty attached many of the Catholic peasants to those of their Protestant landlords who were not absentees, and who had acquired the careless good nature of old Irish society. At any rate no one had dreamt of tenants voting against their landlords at election time, until O'Connell determined to use the strength of the Catholic Association to show once for all that political control of the peasant had passed from the landlord to the priest. In 1828 Vesey-Fitzgerald

221

was seeking re-election for the county of Clare. He was one of the most popular landlords in Ireland and he had voted for Catholic Emancipation. But O'Connell stood against him, the peasants marched to the poll with the priests at their head and the day was carried against the whole landlord influence of the county. A peculiar and powerful blend of clericalism and democracy had destroyed feudalism in Ireland.

O'Connell's election was legal, but as he was a Catholic the law prevented him from taking his seat. That was the situation which convinced Peel and Wellington that Catholics must be admitted to Parliament. By passing Catholic Emancipation they averted the danger of civil war. But though for this limited purpose they had the moral courage to sacrifice their party's welfare and their own consistency, they were not magnanimous enough to do it with grace and so turn it into an act of reconciliation. They seemed determined to show that it had been extorted, which was exactly the impression they should have striven to remove. Insults were heaped upon O'Connell in the hour of his triumph. He was forced to seek re-election on the paltry ground that his election, though legal, had taken place before the passage of Catholic Emancipation. When the first Catholic barristers obtained silk under the new Act, O'Connell was passed over, possibly on the ground that 'the whale is left out from the fishes in a Natural History Museum'. The liberator was a generous and kindly man, but he felt his treatment bitterly; he said of Peel words that no one but an Irishman would have found, 'His smile was like the silver plate on a coffin.'

No Catholic was promoted to the Bench, and everything was done to show that the new law did not mean a change of system in Ireland, and that the national leaders were not in fact to be admitted to a share of power. But the new law enabled O'Connell to gather a number of followers in the House of Commons, who henceforth exerted a direct and disturbing influence on British politics. Ireland was no nearer than before to self-government, but she had obtained some real representation at Westminster.

By passing Catholic Emancipation the Duke had alienated from his person and government the very elements on which he could best have relied to hold the fort against the coming Liberal assault. Old Lord Eldon, the Oxford dons, the country parsons, and the more old-fashioned squires raged against the King's government and the victor of Waterloo with the fury of men betrayed. Not till they had pulled down Wellington and put Lord Grey into Downing Street did the High Tories feel that they had been avenged. The

222

Ministry of Tory reunion had taken just a year in breaking up the party into three mutually hostile sections of Canningites, Ministerialists, and Eldonians. The Duke, who had driven the Canningites into opposition in 1828, showed as much contempt in 1829 for the indignation of the squires and parsons as he showed in 1830 for the demand of the 'middle and industrious classes' for Reform. With his soldier's mind and his strictly administrative way of dealing with political problems and forces, he unwittingly cleared the ground for the revival of the Whigs and for the passage of a much larger measure of Reform than had seemed remotely possible at the time of Canning's last illness.

In September 1830 the Duke attended the opening of the Manchester and Liverpool Railway. He was little suited to grasp the significance of the occasion, for he disliked inventions; it was largely due to his lifelong conservatism in this respect that British troops went to the Crimea armed with weapons precisely similar to those which had been used at Waterloo. Huskisson was also present, as behoved the member for Liverpool who had warmly supported the line in Parliament. He stepped out of the train on to the rails, to shake hands with the Duke of whom he had seen but little since their quarrel two years before; not realizing in time the danger of his proceedings, he was knocked down by one of George Stephenson's engines. The dying statesman was taken up and carried away at the pace of thirty-six miles an hour, although, when Stephenson had given evidence before the House of Commons, members had thought him crazy for claiming that one-third of that pace would be possible.

The events of this day, so tragic in depriving the country of Huskisson's services,[1] proclaimed to all the world the advent through steam locomotion of a new economic era. Steamships were already beginning to ply the waters. But this day registered the conquest of the land. For thirty years past, inventors had been working at the idea of using steam for traction, as it had already been used for pumping mines and turning machinery. At first it had seemed that the 'steam coach' would use the macadamized highways of the country without need of rails. Several of these primeval motors made experimental journeys along English roads

1. Huskisson was in negotiation with the Whig chiefs, and would, if he had lived, almost certainly have joined Grey's Ministry. Like the other surviving followers of Canning, he had become a moderate reformer; whether he would, like them, have accepted the whole Reform Bill with a gulp, no one can say.

223

during the Napoleonic wars. But they went no faster than waggon-horses and could only draw a twentieth of their own weight. The issue was decided when the mining industry, already accustomed to the use of rails to enable horses to drag heavily weighted coal trucks, employed the genius of George Stephenson of Tyneside gradually to perfect a steam-engine that gave the supremacy to the rail over the road. In our own day the coming of petrol has renewed the rivalry of road with rail.

The connexion of this new development with politics was felt by contemporaries both on its material and its symbolic side. Archibald Prentice, a typical Manchester man of the time, active in all that caused his city to arrogate to itself the leadership of England, thus writes of the day of Huskisson's accident:

The opening of the Manchester and Liverpool Railway was one of the events of 1830, which was not without its influence, in future days, on the progress of public opinion. The anti-corn-law agitation was wonderfully forwarded by quick railway travelling and the penny postage. Even in 1830 the railway promoted the cause of Reform. It was an innovation on the old ways of travelling, and a successful one; and people thought that something like this achievement in constructive and mechanical science might be effected in political science. It brought, besides, a little proprietary borough, which nobody had ever seen before, into full view. I recollect when passing over it for the first time, I said to a friend – 'Parliamentary Reform must follow soon after the opening of this road. A million of persons will pass over it in the course of this year, and see that hitherto unseen village of Newton; and they must be convinced of the absurdity of its sending two members to Parliament, whilst Manchester sends none.'

It was certainly a strange coincidence that one out of the half-dozen rotten boroughs which was all that the northern half of England possessed should have lain plumb on the new line from Liverpool to Manchester. But with or without the sight of Newton to stir the indignation of the cotton-lords and their bagmen, a mere thirty miles of railway could at best be no more than an additional argument for reform. Stephenson may perhaps be said to have abolished the Corn Laws in forty-six, but in that case Watt and Macadam passed the Reform Bill of thirty-two.

A new institution, highly characteristic of the new age, and of Henry Brougham's multifarious activities as the informal leader of 'opposition' and progress in the country, was the foundation under his auspices of University College, London – the 'godless institution in Gower Street'. Nonconformists and secularists, excluded from Oxford and Cambridge, had drawn together to found an undenominational teaching centre on the basis of keeping theology out of the curriculum, and having no religious tests for teachers or taught. The tendency of the embryo university was towards modern studies, including science. An exclusively classical curriculum was identified in men's minds with the close educational establishments of the Church and State party. 'Utility' appealed more to the unprivileged city population. It was an educational event of the first importance, but at the time its real significance was lost in sectarian and partisan recrimination, and not a little good-humoured satire of Brougham and his 'Cockney College'.

Next year the Church followed suit, and founded in rivalry King's College in the Strand, as another non-residential college, teaching on modern lines. In 1836 the two rivals were formed into the federal University of London. In the last twenty years of the century, when new Universities were founded up and down the country in the great industrial centres, it was not Oxford and Cambridge that served as model, but London, with its non-residential colleges and degrees for women.[1]

CHAPTER 14

THE genius of the English people for politics was faced by new problems arising out of those which it had solved of old. The age of the Tudors had seen the destruction of the medieval privileges of Church and Baronage that had prevented the unity and progress of the nation; in their place the full sovereignty of the Crown in Parliament had been established. Under the Stuarts, Parliament had won the supremacy in its partnership with the Crown, while the principle of local government had been preserved against despotic encroachment. In the eighteenth century, Parliament had acquired executive efficiency through the Cabinet system. These institutions were England's unique and native heritage. But they were administered by a privileged group of borough-owners, magistrates, and members of close corporations, roughly identified in sympathy with the country gentlemen, but not coextensive even with that class. This group had by long possession come to regard their own monopoly as synonymous with the Constitution itself. To speak ill of the rotten boroughs and close corporations was to utter 'seditious' words against our 'matchless Constitution'. But in spite of Lord Eldon and those who thought with

1. In 1878 London admitted women to degrees on the same terms as men.

him, Parliament, Cabinet, and local government had been created by England's practical imagination in the past, and had now by a fresh creative process to be adapted to the needs of a new type of society born of the Industrial Revolution. The process of adaptation would be complicated, and would never reach 'finality', because this new type of society was by its nature predestined to undergo perpetual change. It further remained to be proved whether the old institutions, remodelled, could be used to cure the new economic miseries of the mass of the people, a task far more difficult than any that had been thrown on King, Parliament, or local magistracy in old days. And, lastly, England would have to extend the principles of her revised Constitution to Scotland, to the Colonies, and to Ireland – a scale of ascending difficulty.

The spirit of the new age in face of these new problems, formulated in theory by Bentham, was first manifested in Government action by the Liberal-Tories in Canning's day. But the monopoly of power had still been strictly preserved. To the Whigs between 1830 and 1835 belongs the credit of destroying the monopoly, reinterpreting the Constitution, and harnessing public opinion to the machine of government. Whatever some of the Whigs might say about the 'finality' of their Bill, this new principle, when once admitted, could brook no limitation until complete democracy had been realized under old English forms. On the other hand the belief of the anti-Reform Tories that the Reform Bill would lead at once to the overthrow of Crown and Lords, Church and property, was the exact reverse of the truth. It was due to the Bill that England was not involved in the vicious circle of continental revolution and reaction, and that our political life kept its Anglo-Saxon moorings.

Both the Liberal-Tories in Canning's day, and the Whig followers of Grey and Althorp, were acting under the direct inspiration of middle-class opinion, and under compelling fear of working-class revolt.

It has been pointed out above[1] that the movement of Parliamentary Reform was revived in the nineteenth century first of all by the working-men, because their economic misery was the most acute. The middle classes had been divided or indifferent during the radical agitation of the Peterloo time. The Whigs, meanwhile, to prevent division in their own ranks, waited on the middle-class lead, Lord Grey always abiding by his declaration of 1810 that he would again move for Reform when, but only when, the English people had taken it up 'seriously and affectionately'. In the year

1. See p. 90, above.

1830 he saw his condition fulfilled. The middle classes, in whom he read public opinion, took up Reform 'seriously and affectionately'; whereupon, greatly to the surprise of friends and foes, the old nobleman was as good as his word.

There were many reasons why the middle classes moved rapidly towards Parliamentary Reform in the three years following Canning's death. The removal of the statesman whom so many had begun to regard as the national leader threw them back into their former attitude of opposition to Government, and the reversal of his foreign policy by Wellington was a sharp reminder that only Parliamentary Reform could secure that national affairs should be continuously guided on popular lines.

Meanwhile any avenue of escape through 'bit by bit' reform was closed by the action of the Parliamentary Tories in 1828, when they refused to allow the seats of certain boroughs disfranchised for peculiarly gross corruption to be given to the unrepresented cities of Manchester and Birmingham. It was on that issue that Huskisson, Palmerston, and Melbourne had left Wellington's Ministry, and the event made a deep impression on public opinion.

In January 1830 Thomas Attwood founded the Birmingham Political Union, to agitate for a large but undefined measure of Parliamentary Reform. It was, professedly and actually, a union of middle and working classes; it was the first step towards their cooperation in Radical politics which marked the Victorian era. In other industrial centres, such as Manchester, it was more difficult for employers and workmen to cooperate, though both were now avowed enemies of the 'borough-mongers'.

Bad trade and hard times had returned. Common economic misery sharpened the sense of common political wrongs and predisposed the whole nation to unite in the demand for Reform. In 1830 Cobbett enjoyed a second period of great popular influence, which he used as he had used his popularity in 1817 to turn all streams of discontent into the one channel of Parliamentary Reform. But whereas in 1817 he had been the leader of the working class alone, he found in 1830 that even the farmers thronged to hear him speak, as he rode on his cob from one market-town to another. Radicalism had become for the moment almost a national creed.

There were differences of opinion as to the economic cure for the distress of the time. Some, like Attwood, saw it in currency reform; more, like Cobbett, in retrenchment; others in Free Trade; others in Factory Acts or in Socialism. But all were agreed that reform of

Parliament was the necessary first step before anything effective could be done.

The greatest danger to the cause of Reform arose from dissension as to what the new franchise ought to be. Some claimed household suffrage, others desired government by 'the solid and respectable part of the community'. But the rallying cry of 'Down with the rotten boroughs' served to harmonize these discords. Every class that was hoping to exert greater influence over Parliament was enraged that more than half the House of Commons owed their seats to individual peers or commoners. The borough-owners, who for generations back had pulled the strings of ministerial favour and lived on the fat of patronage – they and their kinsmen and their servants – suddenly found themselves objects of universal execration, and the 'borough property' which they had inherited or purchased denounced as having been stolen from the nation. The cry against the 'borough-mongers' rose on every side. Capitalists, clerks, shopkeepers, besides that great majority of the inhabitants who were comprised under the two categories of working-men and Dissenters, all were talking against 'Old Corruption'. The very ostlers and publicans entered into the spirit of the hour. Even country gentlemen who did not happen to have an 'interest' in a borough began to think that they would like to see a fairer proportion of county members in the House, honestly chosen by themselves and their farmers. The only class that remained solid for the old system was the Church clergy, who were so conscious of unpopularity that they believed Reform would lead to the destruction of the Establishment.

Into the midst of a society thus agitated came the news of the Paris revolution of 1830, the 'glorious days of July'. Charles X and his minister Polignac had provoked their own downfall by illegally suspending the Constitution. Although the fighting on the barricades had been done by the workmen, the movement was not permitted to turn 'red', but solidified round Lafayette, the National Guard, and the *bourgeois* King, Louis Philippe. The *noblesse* and the Clericals had fallen once more, but property was safe. These events could not, like the French Revolutions of 1792 and 1848, and the Commune of 1871, be used as a warning against change over here. The year 1830 still stands as the one occasion when the French set a political example that influenced us otherwise than by repulsion.

The first effect of the inspiring news from France was to increase the number of open seats carried by the Opposition in the General Election that August. A new Parliament had to be elected, on account of the death of George and the accession of William IV, the popular sailor king. It was the House of Commons chosen in these circumstances that turned out Wellington and carried the Reform Bill by one vote. Brougham, the interpreter between the official Whigs and the national movement for Reform, was sent up as a member for Yorkshire, amid the rejoicings of the whole country. He never again touched such a height of popular influence.

But the French Revolution of 1830 did more than affect the elections. It gave Englishmen the sense of living in a new era, when great changes could safely be made. To act boldly on behalf of the people, it was seen, did not produce anarchy as the Tories had argued ever since 1789. Rather, it was half-measures that were dangerous, and resistance to the people that was fatal. Our middle class saw the *bourgeoisie* governing France, and blushed that in England they themselves were still subject to an aristocracy. The working-men heard that the *ouvriers* had defeated the Army in fair fight, and the word went round that what Frenchmen had done Englishmen could do at need. Pamphlets on the technique of street-fighting had a suggestive popularity. The knowledge that Englishmen were so thinking, and that Frenchmen had so acted, gravely affected the politics of the propertied class as a whole, and not a few of the borough-owners themselves, persuading them to make concessions they would never have dreamt of two years before.

The French Revolution of July, over and above its effect on our own domestic crisis, created an international crisis in which our Reform Bill was the deciding factor, just as our revolution of 1688 had been the deciding factor in the European resistance to Louis XIV. The change in France broke up the Holy Alliance as a pan-European affair, and arrayed Western parliamentarianism against Eastern despotism. But would Canning's England turn reactionary at the very moment when Bourbon France turned Liberal? Wellington, who had already reversed Canning's policy in Greece, could not but regard the resurgent tricolour as the mischievous flag which it had been the great achievement of his life to haul down. If the Duke had not fallen in November 1830, and if the High Tory party had not been destroyed by the Reform Bill, it is possible that England would soon have been fighting by the side of her old allies against revolutionary France, to the indefinite postponement of constitutional reform in our island.

The danger was made acute by the Belgian revolution. After

Napoleon's fall, Belgium had been united to Holland by the Treaties of Vienna. The reunion of the ancient Netherlands could only have been rendered permanent by statesmanship worthy of the House of Orange in times long past. The present King, though well-meaning, was unwise. In August 1830, Brussels, in imitation of Paris, rose and drove out the Dutch garrison, and the other Belgian cities followed suit. By the cooperation of her clerical and liberal forces, Belgium asserted her right to separate national existence.

For the second time in two months the Holy Alliance had been defied, and, although Prussia, Russia, and Austria had shrunk from challenging the right of the French people to self-determination, they had no such scruples about Belgium. They were preparing to put down the Belgian revolution in accordance with alleged obligations under the Treaty of Vienna. It was equally clearly the intention of the new French Government to fight, if necessary, to protect Belgian independence, and how much of Belgian independence would be left when France had done fighting for it was a question which made even Grey and the English Liberals anxious.[1]

The action of Wellington and his Foreign Minister, Aberdeen, in face of this new crisis was correct, but their sympathies were not with the new Belgium or the new France. Yet nothing short of the cooperation of England with France to protect Belgium could prevent war between France and the Eastern Powers, which might have involved England. From this catastrophe Europe was saved by a change of government at Westminster.

All autumn the agitation in the country was deeper than political. Economic misery, pauperism, starvation, and class injustice had brought society to the verge of dissolution. Rick-burning, under the orders of 'Captain Swing', that dark abstraction of the vengeance of the ruined peasantry, kept the rural south in terror. In the industrial north the workmen were drilling and preparing for social war. The middle classes clamoured for Reform, equally to pacify the revolutionary spirit below, and to secure their own rights against an aristocracy they had ceased to trust.

In the first fortnight of November, when Wellington met the recently elected Parliament, came the most important political

1. French Clericals as well as French Liberals had helped to stir up the Belgian revolution. Polignac's emissaries had been at work there and Polignac had hoped to see Belgium joined to France. The belief of English Liberals that Wellington was hand in glove with Polignac was mistaken. Polignac, though a reactionary in home affairs, was a Chauvinist at heart, and had none of the Duke's respect for the treaties of 1815.

crisis of the century. Everyone was looking to the new House of Commons to save the country, yet no one knew what it would do even in making its choice between Wellington and Grey. The group system still prevailed, and many of the groups had no defined political allegiance. As late as November the First, there were three future Prime Ministers waiting to find out whether they were Whig or Tory; for the Canningites under Lords Melbourne and Palmerston, and the independent group led by Edward Stanley,[1] 'the Rupert of Debate', came up pledged to moderate Reform and looking to see whether Wellington or Grey would give them what they wanted. If the Duke had made a declaration promising a peaceful and liberal policy towards France and Belgium, and a small measure of Parliamentary Reform, he could have rallied these men round him and stayed in office. It is indeed unlikely that a Tory Reform Bill would have been large enough to pacify the country. But in any case the experiment was not destined to be tried.

The King's speech mentioned the Belgian revolution with ominous disapproval, and when Lord Grey called attention to the absence of any promise of Reform the Duke replied that 'the system of representation possessed the full and entire confidence of the country.'

The Duke had challenged the nation, and the nation took up the challenge. The excitement inside Parliament was a feeble reflection of the feeling outside; yet never were the lobbies and clubs more busy, or busy to better purpose. In a week the basis had been laid of the Whig–Liberal party that was to dominate the next generation. The Canningites and moderate reformers all enlisted under Grey's banner, and were prepared to join a Whig Government on the programme of 'Peace, Retrenchment, and Reform'. With the help of a few High Tories who were still so anxious to be revenged on the Duke for Catholic Emancipation that they cared not what happened afterwards, the Government was beaten in the Commons on the Civil List. Wellington resigned, and the King sent for Lord Grey.

In choosing his Ministry, Grey was constituting a new party. He was fusing the Canningites and reforming Tories with the Whigs. The heirs of Fox were about to put his political testament into execution, with the help of allies from the ranks of Pitt. The object that Grey had in view in constructing his Cabinet was to carry a Reform Bill extensive enough to give peace to the land. He enlarged the boundaries of his Ministry enough to obtain a

1. Afterwards fourteenth Earl of Derby and Conservative Prime Minister.

majority in the Commons and a large minority in the Lords, without which even the popular enthusiasm could not have carried the Bill under the existing forms of the Constitution.

It has often been charged against Grey's Ministry that it was too aristocratic. And certainly the proportion of peers and their near relations was larger than in Tory Cabinets before and after. But, with the material to hand, a more bourgeois Ministry would not have been an abler Ministry, and would have been much less likely to get the Bill through. It was Grey's task, partly indeed to frighten, but partly also to persuade and cajole King, Lords, and borough-owners into giving up their power. For this purpose a Cabinet of aristocratic reformers would be the most useful. And, fortunately, although the cause of Reform was then popular, if ever a cause has been popular in England, the balance of ability among the reforming statesmen lay among the aristocrats. While its ablest opponents were plebeians like Peel, Wetherell, and Croker, its ablest supporters were scions of great houses – Grey, Durham, Holland, in the Lords; Russell, Althorp, Stanley, and Palmerston in the Commons. Apart from O'Connell, whom Grey certainly treated badly, the only reforming members of Parliament on the same level of ability with these aristocrats were Jeffrey, who was set to rule Scotland as Lord Advocate; Brougham, who was made Lord Chancellor and as such caused great trouble, though he would have caused more if left out;[1] and young Tom Macaulay, who got office after he had proved his powers by his Reform Bill orations. The Cumberland baronet, Sir James Graham, afterwards Peel's friend and colleague, was taken into Grey's Cabinet, which for average ability could vie with any that came before or after.

The old aristocracy still produced very able men, and most of the able aristocrats were reformers. It is remarkable that the peers of old creation were about equally divided on the Reform Bill; and the dissentient majority of the Upper House was due to the bishops and to Pitt's lavish creations of Tory partisans and borough-owners. The Whig borough-owners, who in 1831 held about sixty rotten borough seats out of two hundred, were prepared to sacrifice these cherished possessions and so produce a majority in the Commons consonant with the national will.

The decisive and permanent effect of the crisis of November

1. He went up to the Lords with the title of 'Baron Brougham and Vaux'. The promotion of the great agitator to the Chancellorship caused an immense sensation. Some prophesied, not entirely wrongly, that he would be 'Vaux et praeterea nihil'. His best days proved to be over.

1830 on the course of British politics is illustrated by the career of Lord Palmerston. He had held office for twenty years as a Tory, and was now to hold office for almost thirty years as a Whig. He was a Whig in his attitude to the Church and to foreign affairs, but he retained much of his old Toryism on other questions. At heart he disliked the Reform Bill. He was the member of the Cabinet who most constantly pressed to have it modified. But as Foreign Minister he rendered yeoman's service to his colleagues by keeping the Continent at peace while they passed their Bill.

In this his first and best tenure of the Foreign Office, Palmerston had the advantage of the advice of Grey, who was deeply interested in foreign affairs, and would never have tolerated the dangerous bounce and bluff of later 'Palmerstonianism'. The settlement of the Belgian question by these two in daily intercourse with the veteran Talleyrand, the French Ambassador at London, was one of the most beneficent and difficult feats ever accomplished by our diplomacy. The question ran through a series of crises punctuating the successive crises of the Bill at home, again and again threatening a war that would have made short work of the programme of 'Peace, Retrenchment, and Reform'. Again and again Grey and Palmerston warded off disaster.

The first and greatest step was secured in December 1830, when Palmerston, by standing firm beside France, won the recognition of Belgian independence by Austria, Russia, and Prussia. The next crisis followed early in 1831, when the French candidate, a son of Louis Philippe, was rashly chosen as king by the Belgian Congress. The choice was the more ominous because many French politicians were working to make Belgium a part of France. But when the statesmen of Paris were made to understand that even a Whig government would oppose by arms a French King of Belgium, his candidature was withdrawn. Such a retreat was rendered possible, in face of the French chauvinist party, only by the fact that the Whig government was known to be the sincere friend of the new France. A more acceptable king was found in Prince Leopold of Saxe-Coburg, the happiest possible choice for Belgium and for Europe. Leopold had lived for a long time in England, on familiar terms with the leaders of the more liberal school of British constitutionalism. He was the favourite uncle and adviser of Princess Victoria.

But meanwhile the Dutch and Belgians were quarrelling about the terms of separation. In August and September 1831 the dangers caused by a Dutch invasion of Belgium, and a counter-invasion by the French, were skilfully averted without causing a quarrel between ourselves and France. A year later (October to December 1832) Britain and France actually cooperated by sea and land to coerce the Dutch into the surrender of the citadel of Antwerp. All these delicate operations were carried out under the watchful and hostile eyes of the French war-party on one side, and on the other of English Tories and of the despotic powers of the East. Russia, Austria, and Prussia, jealous of Belgian independence as a breach in the reactionary system of the treaties of Vienna, only waited for a misunderstanding between France and England to pounce down on the small rebel kingdom. Finally in 1839 Palmerston set the seal on his task in a treaty fixing the vexed question of Dutch–Belgian boundaries, and guaranteeing Belgium as 'an independent and perpetually neutral State'. The treaty was signed by Belgium, England, France, Russia, Austria – and Prussia.

In a letter to Lord Grey in 1832, King Leopold had thus summed up the Belgian settlement from the point of view of British interests:

It has been the policy of Great Britain for centuries never to permit Belgium to fall into the hands of a great Power. Everything is now favourable to the policy. The Belgians are warmly attached to their newly-acquired independency. They hate the Dutch, and they are jealous of the French. The new Kingdom is quieter and better settled than many old countries. An object on which Great Britain lavished so much blood and money has been attained without costing a farthing to that country, or being the cause of the slightest hurt to any Englishman.

Elsewhere, Grey and Palmerston revived the policy of Canning. The boundaries of Greece were extended northwards at the desire of the new British Cabinet.[1] In Spain and Portugal we again befriended the constitutional cause under the more favourable conditions created by the Liberal revolution in France. Throughout the thirties the first principle of our foreign policy was friendship with France. Wellington and Aberdeen attacked it openly and King William remonstrated against it in private. But the Reform Bill gave the Whigs security of tenure independent of the growing alienation of the sovereign, and enabled them to carry through the change in our foreign policy which saved the peace of Europe.

At home, the three months between the formation of Grey's Cabinet and the introduction of the Reform Bill did not go smoothly for the new Ministers. Their budget was a failure and had to be recast. Finance was from first to last a weakness of the Whigs in contrast to the party of Huskisson and Peel. In opposition

1. See map, p. 365, below.

they had countenanced the rather wild talk about 'retrenchment' with which the hopes of the public had been inflamed. Cobbett had, in his loose way, taught men to suppose that most of the taxes were eaten up by sinecurists and pensioners, and that everyone would be prosperous if the wages of 'Old Corruption' were docked. The Whigs made reductions of this kind, but could not make enough to satisfy the public demand. It was not understood that a progressive community, as yet grossly ill supplied with those services which must in the modern world be rendered by the central and local authorities, would obtain less benefit from reducing the public burdens than from adjusting them fairly and spending them to the general advantage. The Tories had already done their duty in cutting down army and navy after the war. Whig 'retrenchment' was therefore foredoomed to fiasco.

At the very moment of the change of Ministry, the labourers of the southern counties, driven by famine, were marching through the countryside demanding a living wage of half a crown a day. They were cruelly punished at the assizes, when 450 of the rioters were torn from their families and transported to Australia, besides three unjustly executed. The new Whig Ministers, in a panic lest the propertied classes should confound 'Reform' with 'Jacobinism and disorder', would not mitigate these sentences. In connexion with the same riots they prosecuted Richard Carlile and Cobbett for articles in the Press. Cobbett at his trial in the following July made the Whigs look as foolish before a British jury as the Tories of old. His acquittal effectually discouraged a revival of that spirit of coercion which Peel as Home Secretary had so wisely abandoned.

The Whigs had made a bad start. But when, on 1 March 1831, Lord John Russell introduced the Reform Bill into the Commons, and revealed the well-kept secret that all the 'nomination' boroughs were to be abolished, without compensation to the borough-owners, Ministers sprang to the summit of popularity at a single bound. The Tories were dumbfounded. They had confidently expected a weak measure, buying up a few of the rotten borough seats to give them to a few great cities; such a Bill would have left the nation cold and the reformers divided; lacking support from outside, it could pass the Houses only by agreement, after being further whittled down; finally the Whigs would be turned out as incompetent sciolists and power would revert to its long-tried possessors. But instead of lending themselves to this plan, Ministers had summoned the whole nation to their support, to overawe the recusants at Westminster. The bold appeal was not merely a winning move in the political game, but it established the fundamental principle of 'the new constitution', namely, that in the last resort the opinion of the nation was to count for more than the opinion of the legislators.

The anger and amazement of Opposition were shared in a less degree by many of the Government's supporters in the Commons, who relished their position as privileged senators of the modern Rome, and had no wish to become mere elected persons in a paradise of Benthamite utility. If, as soon as Russell had sat down, Peel had moved the rejection of the 'revolutionary measure' on first reading, it was believed that the Bill would have been lost. But the Opposition, having come to the House expecting something very different, had no plan ready, and Peel's genius did not lie in dramatic moves and lightning decisions. The opportunity was let slip. As the second reading debate dragged on night after night, many who had at first been doubtful or hostile were converted by the unmistakable evidences of the national will. Three weeks after its introduction the Bill passed its second reading by one vote, in the most exciting division since the Grand Remonstrance.

A defeat in Committee soon narrowed the issue to a choice between a new Ministry with a much modified Bill, or a General Election to save Bill and Ministry together. In such circumstances a modern Prime Minister could claim a dissolution of Parliament as of right. But under George III and his sons dissolution was, in custom as well as in law, a personal prerogative of the king. Would William dissolve at Grey's request? The decisive crisis in the fortunes of the Bill had come, and the choice lay with a retired admiral of no great brains or experience in affairs of State, but with an instinct of personal loyalty to his Ministers which sharply distinguished him from his father and brother before him.

In January 1831, while the draft Bill had been a secret between William and his confidential servants, Grey had persuaded his master to allow him to introduce it – a permission necessary under the custom of the Constitution as George III had defined it. Grey had persuaded the King that the Bill was an 'aristocratical' measure, designed to save the Constitution from more revolutionary changes. And so it was in Grey's mind. Its 'democratical' implications only began to be apparent to William after it had become public, when the joy of the Radicals of whom he lived in terror, and the rage of the Tories with whom he lived in intimacy, gradually made him realize what he had done. In April he had to decide whether he would accept Grey's resignation or his advice to dissolve. The straw that weighed down the balance in his mind was the fact that there had been a majority of one for the second reading. With many misgivings he granted Grey his dissolution.

The General Election was almost as onesided and enthusiastic, so far as popular opinion was concerned, as the elections for the Restoration Parliament. The Reformers carried almost all the open constituencies, including seventy-four English county seats out of eighty. But no amount of popular intimidation could shake the hold of the proprietors on the nomination seats. In their last Parliament the rotten-borough members voted two to one against the Bill, in much the same numbers as before the election.

But there was now a majority of 136 for the Bill. It passed through the Commons that summer under Lord Althorp's patient management in Committee, and went up to the Lords, where it was thrown out on second reading by a majority of forty-one votes.

Under the old system of government, the average Englishman had had so little to do with politics that he was taken by surprise at this perfectly inevitable event, which had been long anticipated in Parliamentary circles. The popular enthusiasm, suddenly brought up against an obstacle which it had not expected and could at first see no legal way to remove, exploded in outrages against bishops and peers who had voted against the Bill. A single false step by the Ministers might have precipitated anarchy. The Army, smaller than at any other period in our modern annals, was insufficient to keep order in England and Scotland, in addition to its usual task in Ireland. Peel's police as yet only existed in London. It was impossible to raise volunteer forces to put down Reform mobs. The workmen in the North were drilling and arming to fight the Lords. In the South the ricks were blazing night after night. Unemployment and starvation urged desperate deeds. The first visitation of cholera added to the gloom and terror of the winter of 1831–2.

Employers and City men clamoured more loudly every week for a creation of peers to pass the Bill and save social order. The working classes, if it came to blows, would fight, not for this Bill of the Ten Pound householders, but for a Bill that enfranchised their own class, and for much else besides. Civil strife, if it came, might easily degenerate into a war between 'haves' and 'have-nots'. The Bill seemed the sheet-anchor of society. Even the burning of the central part of Bristol by Radical ruffians failed to cause a serious reaction, each side drawing its own moral from the event.

Grey kept his head. He neither resigned nor, as the King urged, whittled down the Bill. On the other hand he refused, in spite of the remonstrance of the leading members of his Cabinet, to force

237

the King to a premature decision about peer-making, before the time came when circumstances would be too strong for William's reluctance.

Before Christmas a new Bill was introduced, modified in detail to meet some reasonable criticisms and so save the face of the 'waverers' among the peers, but not weakened as a democratic measure. It quickly passed the Commons, and was accepted by nine votes on the second reading in the Lords.

The final crisis, known as the 'Days of May', was provoked by an attempt of the Lords to take the Bill out of the hands of the Ministers in charge, and amend it in their own way. This was countered by the resignation of the Cabinet. Resignation in the previous autumn, when the Lords had thrown the Bill right out, would have produced anarchy. Now it secured and hastened the last stages of a journey of which the goal was already in sight. In October 1831 the country, taken by surprise by the Lords' action, was not properly organized, as the riots had shown. But in May 1832, the Political Unions had the situation in hand. Grey's resignation was not followed by violence or rioting, but by a silent and formidable preparation for ultimate resistance in case he did not speedily return. The English genius for local self-government, voluntary combination, and self-help, which had little or no expression in the close municipalities, found its outlet in these unofficial Political Unions of citizens determined alike on order and on freedom.[1] These organizations, improvised by the British people, constituted the strongest proof of its fitness to work self-governing institutions of a more official character. Abhorred by the King and Tories who clamoured for their suppression, the Unions were tolerated by the Whig Ministers on the condition of their ceasing to arm and drill.

Grey had resigned because the King refused to create peers. But William was now prepared to do anything short of that to get the Bill through intact. He appealed to Wellington to form a Tory Ministry for the purpose of carrying 'the Bill, the whole Bill, and nothing but the Bill' through the House of Lords – on the precedent of Catholic Emancipation three years before. The most fearless, if not always the wisest, of public servants accepted this extraordinary commission, the nature of which was not understood

1. They had been formed in most towns. The model of Attwood's Birmingham Union, presided over by middle-class leaders, but including all classes, prevailed in the midlands and west. In the industrial north there were 'low Political Unions' of working-men only. In some towns there were both kinds of Political Union formed side by side.

in the country, where people naturally supposed that the victor of Waterloo, who had pronounced against all Reform, was coming back to rule them by the sword. If Wellington had succeeded in forming a Ministry, the Political Unions would have led resistance, with what result it is impossible to say. But the actual cause of the Duke's abandoning the task was not his fear of popular resistance, but the refusal of Peel and the Tories in the House of Commons to take part in a scheme so absurd and dangerous, no longer with a hope of modifying the Bill, but solely to save the face of the Lords. The King was obliged to come to terms with Grey, and could only get him back by a written promise to create any number of peers necessary to carry the Bill. The threat when known in the Upper House sufficed, and the Reform Bill became law.

The main provisions of the English, Scottish, and Irish Reform Acts of 1832 were as follows. The substitution of the principle of popular election for that of nomination by individual borough-owners in the case of more than 200 seats. This revolution was achieved by two distinct processes: first, by taking away seats from the nomination boroughs – to the amount of 140 in England alone[1]; secondly, by 'opening' to all Ten Pound householders the franchise of those 'close' boroughs whose population justified their retaining one out of two members. The seats obtained by disfranchisement were redistributed, partly among large centres of population converted into new boroughs – partly by an increase in the county representation, which had previously been unfairly limited to two members for each English shire.[2] The right to vote in all boroughs, new and old, was fixed at the uniform Ten Pound rating franchise. The vote in the counties, hitherto confined in England to Forty Shilling freeholders, was extended to tenant farmers, by an amendment which the Ministry had been forced to accept at the hands of the Whig landlord members composing the bulk of the Reform party in the House.

No one could have criticized the enfranchisement of the tenant farmers if it had been accompanied by the protection of the ballot. But under the system of open voting this new class of voter had no independence, and their enfranchisement only added to their landlord's hold over the county seats, which were at the same time

1. The famous 'Schedule A' was the list of boroughs that lost both their members, 'Schedule B' those that lost one out of two.
2. Except Yorkshire, which had obtained four members in 1821; it obtained six under the Reform Bill. In Wales, Scotland, and Ireland the proportion of County to Borough seats required less change than in England.

increased in number. Since, also, the smaller boroughs, that had just managed to escape the melting-pot of the Bill, were much under the influence of neighbouring squires, the landlords as a class were still greatly over-represented even under the new scheme. If it had not been so, the Bill would not have got through Parliament.

It is incorrect to say that the Bill gave all power to the middle class. Power, which had previously resided in a privileged section of the landlords, was now divided between all the landlords on one side and a portion of the middle class on the other. The Ten Pound household franchise was not set up in the counties at all, and even in the boroughs it did not affect the poorer clerks. It was because half the middle class were still left without votes that they eventually joined with the working-men to demand a further extension of the franchise under Bright and Gladstone. If the First Reform Bill had given full representation to the middle class, the politics of the Victorian era would have taken on a more distinctively class character than they actually did.

The uniformity of the new borough franchise was the least democratic part of the Bill of 1832, if considered as a final settlement, for it excluded nearly all the working-men. Yet this uniformity may seem its most democratic point if it is regarded as the first of a number of steps – *le premier pas qui coûte*. Uniform Ten Pound suffrage in 1832 ensured uniform household suffrage in 1867. The very absurdity of defining the sovereign people for all time to come as the Ten Pound householders had persuaded Cobbett and Place to support the Bill, in the interest of future working-class enfranchisement, although the Bill abolished the working-class vote previously existing in a few boroughs like Westminster and Preston.

The motives of most of the Whigs for adopting the uniform Ten Pounds were more simple. They idealized the middle class as the 'solid and intelligent' part of the community, and became its party chiefs by a pact of mutual advantage. But the Whigs of 1831 also knew what their modern critics sometimes forget, that the Ten Pound franchise was the only thing that could then have been passed into law. An amendment in favour of household suffrage received only one vote in the House that carried the Reform Bill by a majority of 136. And a mixed or fancy franchise, differing from one borough to another, such as Peel seems to have vaguely contemplated, would never have been accepted by anyone, and would have set the various boroughs quarrelling over their different positions under the Bill. A limited but uniform franchise was necessary, because nothing else could then have passed, and it was democratic, because it cleared a smooth path for the gradual inclusion of all in the sovereign nation.

For a generation after the Reform Bill, the benches on both sides of the House were still occupied by country gentlemen, and people of the social standing of Cobbett, Cobden, and Bright were stared at as oddities. But many of the country gentlemen, especially on the Whig side, had been chosen by the votes of the Ten Pound citizens. The trial of strength between the Ten Pound householders and the landlord interest came in the forties over the issue of the Corn Laws. It was decided in favour of the middle class not more by the elections than by the popular support of the unenfranchised. After the experience of 1832 the landlords shrank from saying 'no' to the great majority of the nation.

For the Reform Bill, by the fact and by the manner of its passing, had done a great deal more than enfranchise one-half of the middle class. It had asserted the power of the whole nation, enfranchised and unenfranchised, because it had been carried by the popular will against the strenuous resistance of the old order entrenched in the House of Lords. It had been a fair fight and a straight decision. Forty years before, the people had been told by Bishop Horsley that 'they had nothing to do with laws but to obey them', and they had submitted to the decree. But now at length they had learned how to organize their power and to exact obedience from the law-makers. The 'sovereignty of the people' had been established in fact, if not in law. George III and Pitt had once cut Fox's name off the Privy Council for drinking that toast, but the wheel had come full circle now. The people did not become sovereign in Germany when Bismarck granted limited popular rights, because those rights had not been won by the action of the nation itself, as the First Reform Bill had been won. In England, 'the nation' was defined afresh by each of the Franchise Acts of 1867, 1884, and 1918, but the fact that the nation was master in its own house had been settled once for all in the days of May.

CHAPTER 15

FOR three years after the passing of the Reform Bill the Whigs continued to show, under Benthamite and Radical impulse, a legislative activity on the grand scale. Their failure in the sphere of finance, subsequently made good by Peel, and their gradual sterilization first under Melbourne and then under Palmerston, have associated the Whig name with the idea of a too placid enjoyment of power. Such a judgement, not wholly unjust, leaves out of reckoning the years 1831–5. The Government that in five years recast our municipal as well as our parliamentary institutions passed the new Poor Law and the first effective Factory Act, and abolished Negro slavery, made more lasting change in the British world than any other Cabinet has done since Stuart times.

Because law-making of a character so new and comprehensive required a closer examination of complex facts than busy Ministers could give, Lord Grey's Government made the appointment of Royal Commissions the customary prelude to legislation. The lines followed by the Municipal Reform Act, the Factory Act, and the new Poor Law were all traced out beforehand by Commissioners, who had been selected not on account of their official experience or political weight, but as vigorous and able men, usually of known Benthamite proclivities. Jeremy Bentham himself, over eighty but 'codifying like any dragon' till the last, had died the day before the Reform Bill became law. But his spirit was scouring the country, armed with the force of government and of public opinion, inquiring into every local authority or endowment, and pertly asking 'What is the use of it?'

If ever a country was saved by Act of Parliament from open rebellion, Scotland was so saved by her Reform Bill drawn on the same lines as the English Bill, and by her Burgh Act of the following year. Political self-government, central and local, was an English invention, imported into Scotland by the Grey Ministry, but intensely popular in spite of its foreign origin. Although in temper, creed, and outlook on life the Scottish people were less submissive than the English, the civil institutions of their country contained in 1830 no elements of popular election such as always existed here and there in the south of the island. There was no safety-valve for all that pent energy. The Reform Bill, in England an evolution, in Scotland was a revolution, veiled in form of law, and the passions aroused over it had been proportionately more fierce.[1] As soon as its enactment had given the Scots for the first time real representation at Westminster, their impatience to begin

1. See pp. 47–8, above. Mr Gladstone wrote, sixty-two years after the Reform Bill of 1832: 'That great Act was for England improvement and extension, for Scotland it was political birth, the beginning of a duty and a power, neither of which had attached to the Scottish nation in the preceding period.'

governing themselves at home was so great that the Scottish Burgh Act of 1833 preceded the English Municipal Reform Act by two years. For this reason the new municipal electorate in Scotland was identified with the new Parliamentary 'Ten Pounders', while England, by waiting two years longer, obtained the more democratic municipal franchise of all who paid rates.

The political horoscope of the year 1835, when borough government was revolutionized in England, was favourable to Radical legislation owing to the events of 1834. The retirement of Lord Grey, the secession of the Conservative-minded Stanley and Graham on Irish questions, and the growing hostility of the King, who tried in vain to bring in a Tory Cabinet on his own royal authority,[1] drove the Whig Ministry, reconstituted under Melbourne and Russell, to rely for a while on O'Connell and the Radicals. Russell had still the energies of an advanced Reformer. Hence the English Municipal Corporations Act is the high-water mark of Benthamite Radicalism acting through the Whig machine. After that, the waters of Reform abate in the force of their onset, as the middle class settles down to a period of enjoying the fruits of victory.

The system of close corporations for governing the towns had been bound up with that of the rotten boroughs for returning members to Parliament. Municipal Reform would have been impossible without Parliamentary Reform. And the first use which the 'Ten Pounders' had made of their newly acquired Parliamentary votes was to claim popular government in the daily life of their localities. The most constant grievance of the ordinary shopkeeper, publican, or manufacturer was to be governed in his own town by a cooptive municipality, usually a local ring of certain attorneys, doctors, retired officers, and minor gentry, in close connexion with the local Tory organization, 'a shabby mongrel aristocracy' as their envious neighbours called them. On most municipal bodies no Dissenter, Whig, or Radical had the smallest chance of serving at a time when those categories together covered the vast majority of the inhabitants. A few municipalities were nominated by Whig grandees. A few had a democratic franchise.

Such was the social and political aspect of the municipal system that perished in 1835. Its administrative aspect was incompetence that refused to undertake the new duties called for by new conditions of urban life. The areas of the boroughs were those of bygone ages, and had no respect to the recent shifting of population. To make good the worst deficiencies of the inert municipal

1. See pp. 261–2, below.

243

corporations, powers had often been given to other *ad hoc* bodies to deal with lighting, drainage, paving, water, or police. Confusion had thus been worse confounded, and local government throughout the island had become a welter of divided powers and local anomalies. There was need of the two Benthamite principles of uniformity and popular election. These the Bill of 1835 largely provided.

The English Municipal Corporations Act applied to all the principal towns except London, which already enjoyed a democratic though very anomalous and unsatisfactory government.[1] Elsewhere the larger corporations were abolished and disendowed, and their place was taken by municipal bodies elected by all ratepayers. The path of the Whig government in carrying this democratic revolution was smoothed for them by Sir Robert Peel. Peel had, the year before, in his famous 'Tamworth manifesto' to his constituents, called on the Tory party to accept the logic of the Reform Bill and reconstitute itself as a 'conservative' party, which under his leadership was often very liberal.

Peel in the Commons had accepted Russell's Municipal Reform Bill, but Lord Lyndhurst – saying: 'D—n Peel! What is Peel to me?'–led his brother peers to amend it out of all recognition. A crisis seemed at hand recalling that of '32, but Peel persuaded Wellington to order a retreat, and the Bill finally passed with modifications consonant with its purpose, some of which were improvements.

The new corporations were not trusted with the licensing of public-houses, or with any judicial powers. The separation of the benches of magistrates from the town corporations, on the ground that the latter had now become elective, and that justice is incompatible with party electioneering, was regretted by one section of Radical opinion of that day, but the principle of a non-elective judiciary has been ratified by the experience and conviction of succeeding generations of Britons all over the Empire.

The Act readjusted the administrative areas of the boroughs to some extent, though not enough. Each of the new municipalities was empowered to levy a local rate, and gradually to resume the various functions, sanitary and other, then exercised by *ad hoc* local bodies. In this way in every municipal area a powerful and popular focus of authority was set up, which has in the course of time absorbed almost every local public activity except licensing and justice. Few would have prophesied in 1835 that the education of the people would one day be carried on by these new bodies, or that they would become traders and employers of labour on a great scale. Nor was any provision made in the Act for the close

1. See pp. 32–3, above.

connexion that eventually grew up between the municipalities and the government departments at Whitehall, the latter at once aiding and controlling the local bodies in all their activities through the instrument of national grants in aid of local rates. These developments, on which so much of the health and happiness of our modern society depends, were not foreseen, but were rendered possible by the bold and uniform legislation of 1835.

While town government became democratic as a sequel to the parliamentary enfranchisement of the Ten Pound householder, the rural districts remained under the government of the squires for another half-century. It was only in 1888 that the establishment of County Councils following on the enfranchisement of the rural labourer in 1884 did for the country what had been done in 1835 for the town. For half a century longer the Justices of the Peace conducted not only rural justice but rural administration – and the element of election did not enter into county affairs. These differences in government reflected and increased the social and political divergence between town and country, characteristic of nineteenth-century England. The spirit of the old régime, extinguished in the towns, continued its reign in the rural districts. This was the inner meaning of the battle over the Corn Laws, when rural and urban society came into conflict for the possession of the central government at Westminster.

For the present any such conflict was postponed. Radical reform worked off its first enthusiasm on subjects such as town government, factory acts, negro slavery, wherein the interests or affections of the country gentlemen were not involved. The Corn Laws remained unaltered. The Church, which had prophesied her own fall if Reform passed, did not even lose her less defensible outworks. The Whig Cabinet broke up when it proposed to touch with mildest hand the extravagant endowments of the Protestant establishment in Ireland, in the hope of appeasing the 'tithe war' between the Catholic peasant and the minister of an alien religion. In England the Church retained till 1868 the right to levy a rate for ecclesiastical purposes from parishioners of all denominations, till 1871 the monopoly of Oxford and Cambridge, and till 1880 the power to read her burial service at the graveside of Dissenters. Yet these were all subjects on which the Nonconformists felt deeply. So little is it true to say that England was governed by the dissenting middle class between the first and second Reform Bills.[1]

1. For the reform of ecclesiastical revenues in England, 1836–40, see pp. 278–9, below.

In these circumstances the Dissenters knew that a system of national education could only take the form of a system of Church education, and for this reason never seriously agitated the question, till the Reform Bill of 1867 had again altered the distribution of power in their favour. Meanwhile the Church was content to increase the number of her National Schools,[1] which became by far the largest group in the educational field. Thus denominational rivalry was a spur to educational endowment and activity, but discouraged State intervention which alone could cover the whole ground. In 1833, however, the State made a grant of £20,000 towards the school buildings of the voluntary societies – the small beginning of the national system of education. The grant was renewed annually, and led in 1839 to the establishment of an Educational Committee of the Privy Council, with a permanent secretary and a system of inspection of the State-aided schools – the origin of the Board of Education.

In 1833 the Whig Government, under pressure from an almost revolutionary agitation among the working classes in the north, passed the first effective Factory Act, which fixed legal limits for the working hours of children and young persons respectively, and prohibited the employment of children under nine except in silk mills. The peculiar merit of Lord Althorp's Bill, though it met with little favour at the time among the northern agitators, was the institution of government inspectors to enforce the law, a device suggested by some of the better-disposed among the millowners themselves. It was not merely bad employers but bad parents, living on their children's labour, who required watching. Government inspection was the only way to make this class of law operative. It secured the success of the factory code for adults that was gradually elaborated in later years.

Factory legislation was never a party question. The movement, started in the Waterloo era by Robert Owen, the Socialist manufacturer, and by Peel's father, the Tory manufacturer, was taken up in the thirties and forties with passionate enthusiasm by the factory victims themselves, who were mostly Radicals, under the leadership of Oastler and Michael Sadler, who may be described as Tory democrats, while the parliamentary management fell to the Conservative Lord Shaftesbury, aided by many Whigs and Liberals.[2]

1. See pp. 169–70, above.
2. Shaftesbury, together with Buxton of anti-slavery fame, may be said to have succeeded Wilberforce, who died in 1833, in the leadership of the Evangelical philanthropists.

Against factory legislation were arrayed the majority, though not by any means all, of the millowners, and politicians drawn in fairly equal proportions from both parties. The doctrinaire political economists declared that only long hours could enable England to compete with the rising power of foreign manufacture. They ignored the physiological fact that overwork reduces output.

The umpire between these disputants was the Parliament of English country gentlemen, Liberal and Conservative, who had no personal interest involved. On the one hand they had been brought up to believe the prophecies of the political economists; but on the other hand, since the manufacturers were attacking the Corn Laws on the ground of humanity, the landlords were driven to counter-attack with inquiries as to the seamy side of factory life, asking questions that in a former generation their fathers would have scouted as 'Jacobinical'.

The second crisis of factory legislation, growing out of the children's charter of 1833, came in 1844–7, contemporaneously with the repeal of the Corn Laws and heated with the fires of that great dispute. The 'ten hours Bill' limited the daily work of women and youths in factories, and thereby in fact compelled the stoppage of all work after ten hours, as the grown men could not continue the processes alone. This had for years been the aspiration of the working classes and the storm-centre of a fierce controversy. In Parliament it produced curious cross-voting[1] and brought into the same lobby the most embittered political antagonists. It passed in 1847.

What the Reform Bill of 1832 was to all later Reform Bills, the Factory Acts of 1833 and 1847 are to the far-spreading system of statutory regulation which now governs the conditions of almost all branches of industry. The factory system, which at its first coming bade fair to destroy the health and happiness of the race, has been gradually converted into an instrument for levelling up the average lot of the city-dweller. Robert Owen's vision, that he had first embodied in the New Lanark mills, was in the course of a hundred years made a standard for the greater part of the industrial world. And the decisive first steps were taken during the period which it is usual to condemn as obsessed by the doctrines of *laissez faire*. It is difficult to obsess people with a mere doctrine if once their hearts or their interests are touched. The former generation, being in a mood to grind the faces of the poor, had chosen out those parts of *laissez faire* which suited that purpose and had neglected

1. Melbourne, Cobden, and Bright were against it. Russell, Palmerston, and Macaulay were for it. The Conservatives were no less divided.

the rest. Now the process was being reversed by the generation that repealed the Corn Laws and passed the Factory Acts. At no period was *laissez faire* in force in all its main doctrines at once.

The Whig Poor Law of 1834 was based on the famous report of the Royal Commission, inspired by Chadwick and Nassau Senior. The pauperization of the English working class, especially in the country districts, by the Speenhamland system of supplementing inadequate wages out of rates, had caused grave social evils.[1] The self-respect and self-help of the rural working class were systematically destroyed by magistrates who, while stern against agitation for higher wages and instinctively disliking real independence, were ready enough to assist the cringing poor out of the public funds. It had been made profitable and easy to become a pauper.[2]

Society was perishing of this disease and the new Poor Law applied the knife. It had the great merit of putting an end to the systematic abuse of outdoor relief. But, since the idea of fixing a statutory minimum wage was outside the economic vision of the time, the necessary change could only be effected with great hardship. The sudden withdrawal of outdoor relief from the wage-earner without any security for an immediate rise of wages, often caused acute misery before wages actually rose. Families which had hitherto enjoyed an allowance off the rates for every child were driven to send mother and children to field labour under the terrible conditions of the 'gang system' that became prevalent on English farms, just when the children in the factories were passing under the effective protection of the law. The rural tragedy had only taken a new form.

Too great local variation and too much parochial independence had been among the faults of the old Poor Law. Centralization and national uniformity was the principle of the new. A permanent Commission of three persons was empowered to carry out the new policy; the local 'Boards of Guardians' set up in the 'Unions' of parishes served merely to execute the orders of the three. The 'three tyrants' concentrated on their heads the hatred of the poor

---

1. 156–7, above.
2. In 1831 an observer wrote: 'An English agricultural labourer and an English pauper, these words are synonymous. He pilfers when occasion offers, and teaches his children to lie and steal. His abject and submissive demeanour towards his wealthy neighbours shows that they treat him roughly and with suspicion; hence he fears and hates them, but will never injure them by force. He is depraved through and through, too far gone to possess even the strength of despair.' No doubt this was exaggerated as the portrait of a whole class, but it was the exaggeration of a very terrible reality.

of England, and came in for the last lashes of old Cobbett's whip. The youthful author of *Oliver Twist* (1838), by describing what workhouses meant for those who had to inhabit them, appealed from the Benthamite abstractions in which the Commissioners dealt to the flesh and blood realities which interested the more sensitive public of the Victorian era.

The Commissioners strove, not with complete success, to collect into their 'Bastilles', as the workhouses were popularly called, all able-bodied persons who applied for public relief, and so to subject the genuineness of each application to the 'workhouse test'. With the dreadful results of Speenhamland before them, they were determined that the pauper should be distinctly worse off than the independent labourer. Unfortunately, as they could not improve the lot of the one, they had to depress the condition of the other. They made workhouse life miserable as a matter of policy. Absorbed in the pressing problem of the able-bodied pauper, they gave too little thought to the case of the women and children, the sick and aged, whether outside or inside the workhouse, and they had no idea of curative treatment.[1]

In 1847 the Commission was turned into a regular Government Department, the Poor Law Board. The national and centralized character which the first Commissioners had stamped on the Poor Law made it easier to carry out the many improvements suggested later on by a philanthropy that gradually became more humane as it became more experienced and more scientific. Imperfect and harsh as was the work of 1834, it had been intellectually honest within its limits, and together with the Factory Act of the year before formed the first big attempt of the legislature to deal with the evils incident to the Industrial Revolution.

Meanwhile the working classes were endeavouring to help themselves – not very successfully in the thirties. Socialistic Trade Unionism led by Owen (1833–4), and the Chartist movement to obtain the parliamentary franchise (1838–9) were both failures.

It was largely due to the personal influence which Owen's services had earned for him with the working-men that a wave of Socialist enthusiasm swept British Trade Unionism for two years out of the path that it pursued with such success during the remainder of the nineteenth century. Owen, having started the Factory Code and sowed the ideas that in later years gave rise to the Co-operative Wholesale Society, was in his old age fired with

1. But Chadwick, the famous secretary of the Commission, soon saw the connexion between public health and pauperism. See pp. 275–6, below.

a Socialist gospel, much of which sprang up again with characteristic modifications in the doctrines of St Simon in France and of Marx in Germany. Owen now taught that 'labour is the source of all wealth', and induced some half-million working men and women to join in a Grand National Trade Union, for the purpose, at any rate in his own mind, of carrying out a system of communistic production. 'All individual competition,' said Owen, 'is to cease. All trades shall form Associations of lodges to consist of a convenient number for carrying on the business. All individuals of the specific craft shall become members.' But the 'Grand National' soon melted away, having no proper organization or finance and no very distinct idea what it was to do.[1] The normal development of Trade Unionism was resumed, in local and sectional action, on questions of wages and hours.

Trade Unions were still on their trial. They had only become legal in 1824–5. Partly owing to their temporary connexion with Owenite Socialism, the feeling of employers and of government against the Unions was very strong in these years, and broke out in 1834 in the transportation of the 'Dorchester labourers' for attempting to form an agricultural labourers' Union in which oaths were administered. The rally of the working classes all over the country to the defence of these men, the one thing in which the 'Grand National' was able to be of practical service, secured the shortening of their sentences and probably prevented further attempts to nullify the liberating Acts of 1824–5. But the farmers had other ways than transportation of suppressing Trade Unionism in agriculture.

After the failure of Owen's non-parliamentary programme, the political side of the Labour movement was revived in the People's Charter, with its six points of manhood suffrage, ballot, equal electoral districts, payment of members of Parliament, abolition of their property qualification, and annual Parliaments. All points save the last are now the law of the land. But the Chartist movement could find no abler chiefs than Feargus O'Connor and Lovett, and collapsed in 1839 in rioting and 'physical force' among the South Welsh miners. Government imprisoned the leaders and so broke the organization of the movement. The Trade Unionists looked on with an indifference which they had not shown over the fate of the Dorset labourers, and middle-class radicalism was equally supine. Sympathy had been alienated from a movement of which the aim was political, but which was too 'class conscious' to be a political success. Chartism repudiated

1. One of its objects was to be a national strike for an eight-hours day.

the alliance of middle-class radicalism on principle, its adherents rejoicing to interrupt anti-Corn-Law meetings. Its failure was sealed in 1839, but it lingered on till its second and final catastrophe in 1848. The working-class demand for the franchise only became effective when it found a leader in John Bright, whose household suffrage movement united classes which Chartism had striven to divide.

The economic condition of the working class in the thirties was indeed so bad as to render impossible their steady cooperation with other classes in a purely political programme. As young Disraeli said, there were 'two nations' in England, between whom a gulf was fixed. The bread-and-butter character of the Corn Law question bridged the gulf to some extent in the forties, but it was only in the sixties, when conditions of life had very materially improved, that Bright's conciliatory policy of uniting all the unenfranchised to demand political rights in common had any chance of success. Though the spirit of the Chartists was too intransigent and their leadership second-rate, they had pointed the working class back to political action and a belief in Parliament, and this tradition was fortified in later and happier years by the memory of much heroism and self-sacrifice. When British democracy at length won the vote, many an 'old Chartist' took part in the final victory.

CHAPTER 16

THE Tory statesmen who overcame Napoleon had rendered possible the reconstruction of a British Empire across the sea. The Whig statesmen rendered it two services of vital moment. They abolished the slave trade and slavery, and they introduced the principle of responsible government for the white colonies. But whereas the principle of complete self-government for Canada was specifically the work of Lord Durham, who almost alone of the British statesmen of his day seriously studied colonial problems from an Imperial point of view, the abolition of slavery in 1833, like that of the slave trade in 1807, was the outcome of the intense feeling of the country as a whole, stimulated and organized by William Wilberforce and his fellow-workers.[1]

In the last stages of the long battle Wilberforce was too old a man to take an active part. In 1823 the anti-Slavery Association

1. See pp. 64–8, and p. 125, above.

was formed, and began a vigorous propaganda in and out of Parliament under the leadership of Fowell Buxton. It was a continuance or revival of the old anti-slave-trade campaign, under much the same leadership of Evangelical Churchmen and Dissenters; but in the new age the alliance of Radicals, deists, and democrats was an added strength, instead of being a cause of reproach as in the old anti-Jacobin days.[1] Brougham filled the sails of the abolitionist movement with the great winds of popular agitation, and in 1830 won his famous election for Wilberforce's Yorkshire almost as much on anti-slavery as on reform. Wilberforce next year accepted the Reform Bill as a change that would be 'for the benefit of our poor West Indian clients'.

Slavery abolition had of course to encounter the contempt and dislike of cynics, but it met no such active opposition in this island as the Bristol shipping interest had formerly put up in defence of its valuable traffic in slaves. On the other hand the Imperial aspect of the question was one of much greater difficulty, for the planters of the West Indies had far more reason to be attached to slavery than to the slave trade.

The abolition of the slave trade had been good for Africa, but had not materially altered conditions in the West Indies, where slaves were thenceforth bred instead of being imported. But the planters argued, not without a measure of truth, that their sugar and other business depended on the labour of slaves, and that Emancipation would undermine the prosperity of the West Indian Islands.[2] The relative importance of those islands to the whole Empire was greater then than now, though not so great in 1833 as it had been a generation before. Discreetly managed, the opposition of the planters would have been very formidable, but they showed the same violent spirit as the slave-owners of the United States, in the following generation, without the same power to threaten secession. Their refusal to compromise by any amendment of the system, their continued severity to Negroes and roughness to missionaries, whom they regarded as agents of abolition showed a defiance of the tribunal of opinion at home, and hopelessly ruined their cause.

In 1833 the Grey Ministry passed a Bill to abolish slavery. It was put through Parliament with all the vigour and eloquence of Edward Stanley, then Colonial Minister. Twenty millions sterling

1. See note, p. 67, above.
2. The injury done them by the abolition of slavery was greatly increased by the free-trade policy of the forties, which enabled the home consumer to buy cheaper sugar elsewhere.

were paid in compensation to the slave-owners, by a nation which, though eager for 'retrenchment', was willing to pay the price of justice and freedom.

On the First of August 1834 all slaves in the British Empire were to become free. On the last night of slavery, the Negroes in the West Indian Islands went up on to the hill-tops to watch for the sun to rise, bringing them freedom as its first rays struck the waters. But far away in the forests of Central Africa, in the heart of darkness yet unexplored, none understood or regarded the day. Yet it was that continent whose future was most deeply affected. Before its exploitation by Europe had well begun, it had been decided by the most powerful of its future masters that slavery should not be the relation of the black man to the white. To enforce that decision in spirit as well as letter would be a more difficult task than Wilberforce knew, a burden as well as an honour to his countrymen in many lands. He meanwhile had died, having seen all his tasks accomplished, and was buried in Westminster Abbey among the great statesmen to whom he had so long held up a higher light than that of political ambition.

There was one consolation in the retrospect for the breach with the American colonies: it had relieved the British Empire from dealing with the resistance of the Carolinas and Georgia to Negro emancipation. On that reef either the cause of abolition or the unity of the Empire would very probably have been wrecked. But in the West Indian Islands the white planters were so few that they could not attempt to resist an Act of the Imperial Parliament. In tropical colonies the treatment of Negroes and natives can be supervised through the agents of the central Imperial authority, without the complications arising where white self-government is a necessary part of the social fabric.[1]

In South Africa, therefore, the political aspect of the coloured problem was more serious. The South African veldt is a dry and salubrious tableland, raised high above the malaria of the coast. It is potentially a white man's country, but was occupied beforehand by African tribes. The whites are indeed in a minority, but they are

1. In 1833 the planters of Jamaica, few as they were, were proud of their ancient inheritance of an Assembly and self-governing institutions, and were the more indignant with an Emancipation Act thrust upon them by the British Parliament. But after the Governor Eyre troubles in 1865 they acquiesced in the substitution of Crown Colony Government, with a certain elective element; since then trouble between black and white has been very small in Jamaica, as compared, for instance, to the more democratic United States.

so numerous outside the native territories that South Africa, unlike the West Indies, is now a self-governing Dominion.

For more than twenty years after our first annexation of the Cape (1795), the Dutch farmers lived out their patriarchal lives neither more nor less contentedly under a British governor than under the rule of the Dutch trading company in the past. It was only in 1820 that five thousand British immigrants settled in the Cape Colony. Shortly afterwards, the substitution of the English for the Dutch language in the law-courts began to cause ill-feeling.

The Boers had lived in great isolation since their first coming to Africa in the seventeenth century, and retained much of their ancestors' habits of thought on religion, life, and the management of natives. They disliked the modern English missionary, to whose views on the native problem, wise and foolish alike, the British government was beginning to lend a credent ear. In 1828 the free native was given equal civic rights with the white man. In 1833 came slavery abolition, which the Boers showed themselves ready to accept, being assured of full money compensation.[1] But when it was discovered that they had been allotted only half the estimated value of their slave property, they considered that they had been defrauded. In 1835 a dangerous and destructive raid into the Colony by one of the Kaffir tribes always hanging round its border led to another of the long series of Kaffir wars. The British Governor D'Urban punished the offending tribe by annexing its territory and policing it for the greater safety of the Boer farmers. Lord Melbourne's Colonial Secretary, Lord Glenelg, overrode his action, and, contrary to the feeling of both British and Dutch in South Africa, cancelled the annexation. The Government was held to have failed in protecting the outlying Dutch farms from Kaffir raids, and was accused of indifference not only to the wishes but to the safety of its white subjects.

This proved the last straw. The Dutch thought the British Government was in league with the natives inside and outside the Colony. Several thousand Boers sold their farms and taking their families with them in their long-spanned ox waggons set out into the wilderness, like the children of Israel going up out of Egypt. Among them was a boy named Paul Kruger.

So in 1836 the Great Trek began. Emigration across the veldt was no new thing to the Boers, but emigration on so great a scale as took place in the following twenty years was altogether new, as also was the establishment of republics outside the sphere of the

1. Slavery on the South African farms was less important and more out of place than in the tropical sugar plantations. It was also less inhuman.

Cape government. It broke the natural development of South Africa by leaving the Cape Colony too thinly peopled, while it opened out prematurely grave native questions in the interior. Above all, it prevented the peaceful amalgamation of the Dutch and British races in one community. The Boers went forth in anger, hoping never again to see the face of British folk and British government. But in a world about to be linked up by the steamship and the steam-engine such a wish was vain. They founded one farmer republic on the Orange River, and another in Natal, where they met and fought the Zulus. But by 1843 the British had already followed them to Natal and annexed it.[1]

The Boers had been badly handled. Lord Glenelg's action had been largely shaped by the advice of some, though apparently a minority, of the South African missionaries, and by the influence on Downing Street of the 'Clapham Sect' of Evangelicals. This influence was wholesome in the main, and without it the abolition of slavery would never have been made a reality all over the Empire, any more than Africa could have been explored and the native races studied and cared for without the work of the missionaries in the age of Livingstone. But unfortunately in 1835 a section of the missionaries and their patrons were almost the only source of intelligent information that the Colonial Office of that day possessed. Men who knew nothing about the Dutch or about South Africa from any angle save the one, failed to see its problems as a whole and sowed the seeds of future disaster.

Fortunately, in these critical years when the British Empire was being rebuilt after the catastrophe of 1776, other influences were at work besides the apathy and ineptitude of Lord Glenelg and the staff of the Colonial Office. It was the era of Gibbon Wakefield and Lord Durham. The second quarter of the nineteenth century was the period in the settlement of Canada, Australia, and New Zealand which decided that those lands should be peopled mainly from Britain and should become parts of a free British Commonwealth of Nations.

The sudden overpeopling of Great Britain deplored by Malthus, and the sorry plight of the English peasantry at home, caused in these years the great rural exodus to the Colonies on which the modern Empire was rebuilt. The tide of emigration also ran strongly to the United States and might have run there almost to the exclusion of British territories but for the organized effort of emigration societies, and the occasional assistance of Government,

1. See map, p. 398, below.

inspired by the propaganda of Gibbon Wakefield. He preached to his countrymen that emigration was the true relief of their economic miseries, and that colonies need not in all cases be mere ports of call or places of trade, but might be new British nations. To him is largely due the systematized and aided emigration that founded modern Canada, Australia, and New Zealand.

It was Wakefield who first brought the public to believe that New Zealand might accommodate other races besides the Maori tribes. His New Zealand Association, founded in 1837, made the first British settlements there, only just in time to prevent the annexation of the southern island by France. In this, as in their Canadian work, Lord Durham and Gibbon Wakefield were closely associated.

The New Zealand settlements of the next twenty years were partly idealist and religious in origin. Dunedin was planted by the new-born Free Church of Scotland; and Christchurch, with its Port Lyttelton and the plains of Canterbury behind, was planted by the Church of England as the first-fruits of its reviving apostolic energy. During this formative period of New Zealand, the relations of the settlers to the Maoris and other problems were ably dealt with by the greatest of the Australasian governors, Sir George Grey.[1] Another great man, Bishop Selwyn, contemporaneously founded the Anglican Church in New Zealand, giving to it in its new and democratic home a new spirit, partly represented in synods of clergy and laity. His work had influence on the spirit of the Church in other Colonies, and eventually had reactions on the Church at home.

Meanwhile Australian immigration was growing fast, from purely economic causes. During the French wars, Captain Macarthur, one of the officers of the garrison, had perceived that the empty continent was fitted for sheep-farming on a large scale. He had helped his brother officers to introduce a fine breed of sheep from the Cape, and, returning home, had preached his doctrine to the British manufacturers, then looking round desperately for more wool to feed their new machines, just when the Napoleonic wars made it impossible to count on the usual supply from Europe. Macarthur persuaded some of them to embark capital in a strange country at the other end of the globe. The 'squatter aristocracy'

1. The aborigines of Australia and Tasmania were of much more primitive types than the Maoris of New Zealand. Early in the nineteenth century, in the days of the ex-convicts and the first bushrangers, they were often the victims of great cruelty and were nearly exterminated.

of big sheep-farmers, many of them of the 'service' and 'university' classes from the old country, were the originators of Australian prosperity and free colonization. Later in the century their descendants and successors had to fight a prolonged and losing battle with the democratic land-policy of the small farmer and his friends in the legislature.

In 1840 the new Australia of some 130,000 white inhabitants was large enough to prevail on the mother country to stop the dumping of convicts, though the bad practice was revived fitfully in subsequent years.

In 1851 the discovery of gold at Ballarat produced such a sudden increase in the tide of immigrants that, in the phrase of Gibbon Wakefield, 'the colony was precipitated into a nation'. All the gold seekers could not make their fortunes, and many stayed on as farmers and artisans. In the fifties, the Australian colonies that already enjoyed representative institutions each demanded and received complete responsible self-government. But for the origin of that solution of Imperial relationships we must look to the history of Canada.

In 1861 the self-governing colonies on the continent were: the mother colony of New South Wales; South Australia, over whose infancy Sir George Grey had presided; Victoria, sprung to sudden greatness through the gold diggings; and Queensland, the latest to separate from New South Wales. Each of the four democracies was quite independent of the other, with no legal bond of union but the Crown. Together they numbered, in the census of 1861, just over a million inhabitants, who have increased nearly fivefold, partly by immigration, in the two generations that have since elapsed. Van Diemen's Land, that had changed its name to Tasmania, had also obtained responsible government in the fifties. Western Australia, though a separate province since 1829, was still too thinly inhabited for popular government. During the whole nineteenth century the epic of the Australian explorer's struggle with the wilderness and the desert was going on. Having conquered the east, the explorers were now continuing their battle with the vast spaces of the north and west.

But the tide of emigration from England and Scotland was setting strongest of all to Canada. At the time of the great Reform Bill as many as 50,000 emigrants from Great Britain were floated up the St Lawrence in one year. Then, for a decade, the disturbed political state of the two Canadas discouraged immigration. In 1837 there were already a million inhabitants, and already the

English-speaking outnumbered the French. The wise policy of Pitt had divided Upper or English from Lower or French Canada, and had endowed both provinces with elected Assemblies, without giving to the Assemblies the power of nominating the executive.[1] These institutions had weathered the storm of invasion in 1812, but no longer met the need of communities arrived at political manhood. In Lower Canada a growing English minority, the progressive and trading part of the province, were always at loggerheads with the French Catholic majority, who were in turn aggrieved at a wholly English administration, which they thwarted in the Assembly in every possible way. Finally, in 1836, the French Assembly refused supplies and things rapidly moved to a crisis. Next year a rebellion broke out under Papineau, but it speedily collapsed.

Papineau's rising proved the signal for a rising in the upper province. The English-speaking rebels had indeed less than no sympathy with the French rebels, but in both provinces the revolt was directed against an unrepresentative and unsympathetic officialdom. In Upper Canada one of the chief grievances was the 'clergy reserves', a vast acreage of rich lands kept out of cultivation as future endowment for the Anglican Church, then in a small minority among Scots and Dissenters. This rebellion, like that in the French province, was a half-hearted affair and was easily crushed.

The two rebellions compelled the mother country to attend to the Canadian problem as a whole. Melbourne's Government suspended the constitution and sent out Lord Durham as temporary despot, to act in place of the usual authorities and to report on the real state of affairs, which was very little understood in England, even by Lord Durham himself when he started on his mission.

The selection of Durham saved Canada and the Empire. His temper and his health were bad. But he had both ability and vision. And he had two predispositions, essential to the discovery of what we now know to have been the right solution: a belief in democratic institutions, then rare among Whig and Conservative statesmen, and a belief in the future of the Empire and of the Imperial connexion then rare among Radicals, Whigs, and even among Conservatives. He took with him two men worthy of himself and of the occasion, Gibbon Wakefield and young Charles Buller, whose early death cut short a great career.

Acting in the spirit of his instructions, Durham exerted the plenary powers of his temporary despotism to banish certain

1. See pp. 69–73, above, and map there.

agitators, preferably to putting them in prison. His personal enemy, Lord Brougham, who had since his Lord-Chancellorship degenerated into the malicious harlequin familiar to posterity in the early volumes of *Punch*, attacked this action as illegal, and led to the chase the Tory peers who hated Durham for his radicalism. Such an attack in the Upper House would have been nothing if the Government had stood firm. But Lords Melbourne and Glenelg feebly and basely deserted the man whom they themselves had chosen as dictator in the hour of need.

It was a gloomy winter day for Canada when Durham left her shores in disgrace, but with the full sympathy of the English-speaking population. Everyone now expected the worst, and indeed his recall was prelude to another brief rebellion. But it was darkness before dawn. Lord John Russell spoke in the House of Commons in a sense adverse to the cowardly betrayal of Durham, and persuaded the Cabinet to accept his report.

The Durham Report of 1839, which took effect in Russell's Canada Union Act of 1840, advised that the time had come for full responsible government to be given to Canada – that is, that the executive should in future be chosen from the ranks of the majority in the elected Assembly. This principle of responsible government was applied first to Canada, then to the rest of British North America, next to Australasia, and finally to South Africa.[1] It is acknowledged to have proved the cement of Empire. In the days of its first adoption it appeared to some statesmen, both Liberal and Conservative, to be a step towards an inevitable friendly parting of colonies and mother country. But this error in opinion as to the future did not involve those who held it in mistaken action in the present. The indifference that allowed colonists to go their own way was much less fatal to Imperial unity than any attempt to hold them to the connexion by force. But Durham saw his own recommendations in their true light, as being the only possible path to the Imperial unity that he desired.

The other principle of the Durham Report and of the legislation based on it was local and temporary in application. The two Canadas were thrown together in one, so that the English-speaking majority of a United Canada could outvote the French. If this had not been done, responsible government might have been unworkable in Lower Canada, where the large and progressive English minority were in no mood to have their interests left completely in

---

1. Responsible government was granted to New Brunswick and Nova Scotia in 1847, Prince Edward's Island 1851, Cape Colony 1872, Natal 1893. For Australia, see p. 257, above.

the control of inimical French peasants. The French were exceedingly angry at the Union, and by no means regarded Durham as a liberator. But the policy was justified by its success. The Union of the two provinces in 1840, by making responsible government possible, led to their re-division in 1867, as part of a Federation of British North America, among whose provinces the two Canadas stood as the chief among peers.[1]

Before that consummation could be reached, a difficult and dangerous period had to be passed through. The pilot who weathered the storm was Lord Elgin, Governor of Canada from 1847 to 1854.[2] Elgin carried out the political testament of his father-in-law, Lord Durham. He was, indeed, no slavish imitator; he made it his task to appease the deep animosity of the French, whose racial feelings Durham had, rightly or wrongly, felt himself obliged to disregard. Elgin's insistence that the late rebels should not be penalized lost him much popularity among the British loyalists. At the same time he helped the progressive part of both the French and English-speaking communities to work together and to establish the tradition of parliamentary self-government. He persuaded the Whigs at home to abandon the 'clergy reserves' to the Canadian Parliament. Canadian parties, to some extent cutting across racial divisions, now began to develop a healthy rivalry. The Liberal–Conservative party, under the leadership of John Macdonald, hastened the coming of a new and more hopeful age.

The question whether Canada would drift off from the Empire into political connexion with the United States was gravely affected, though never entirely dominated, by economic and commercial considerations. In 1846 the adoption of free trade inborn by the mother country was a severe blow to Canadian interests. Fortunately this was counterbalanced by the new principle of complete economic self-government for Canada, even to the extent of permitting her to abolish preferences for the mother country.

1. One of the tales put about by Brougham was to the effect that Buller wrote the Report and that Durham stole the credit. This story, which is about as just as to attribute the victory of Trafalgar exclusively to Collingwood and Nelson's captains, has unfortunately found its way, I hope not for ever, into the *Dictionary of National Biography*, where the very inadequate article on Durham was written before the appearance of Reid's *Life of Durham*. Buller, so far from claiming the credit himself, attributed the Report to Durham. Like many other such documents, the Report was the work of a chief with the help of his confidential secretaries. In this case both chief and secretaries were far above the average of public men. See Egerton's *Canada* (Lucas Series) pp. 150–51.

2. For the Oregon settlement of 1846 with the United States, deeply affecting the future western development of Canada, see pp. 286–7, below.

And in 1849 the abolition of the Navigation Laws by the Whig Government opened Canada to the commerce of the world. In 1854 Lord Elgin with great difficulty succeeded in obtaining from the United States a Reciprocity Treaty for a large measure of free trade.

The treaty gave Canada ten years of internal development and content, tending to allay the annexation movement during a critical decade, and established good relations between all the countries of the English-speaking world. Unfortunately the American Civil War of 1861–5, and the attitude adopted towards it by too many British statesmen and journalists, put an end to this state of things, and in 1865 the United States, sore with all things British, refused to renew the Canadian Reciprocity Treaty. But by that time the economic development and patriotism of Canada were capable of standing the shock, and the action of the United States, instead of compelling a renewal of the movement for annexation, helped on the federation of British North America in 1867.

The work of Elgin and Macdonald, following on that of Durham, had been to associate in men's minds the idea of colonial self-government with the idea of the Imperial connexion, which statesmen of all parties on both sides the Atlantic had been too prone to regard as mutually opposed. 'These wretched Colonies,' wrote Disraeli in 1852, 'will all be independent in a few years, and are a millstone round our necks.'

Lord Elgin thus summed up his own work:

I have been possessed (I use the word advisedly, for I find that most persons in England consider it a case of *possession*) with the idea that it is possible to maintain on this soil of North America, and in the face of Republican America, British connexion and British institutions, if you give the latter freely and trustingly. Faith, when it is sincere, is always catching; and I have imparted this faith more or less thoroughly to all Canadian statesmen with whom I have been in official relationship since 1848, and to all intelligent Englishmen with whom I have come into contact since 1850.

CHAPTER 17

DURING the reigns of George III and George IV the position of the Crown had been very strong in dealing with Parliamentary Ministers who represented the borough-owners rather than the nation. George III retained, on the threshold of the madhouse, enough power to prevent Pitt from emancipating the Catholics, and to dismiss the Ministry of All-the-Talents. Without the accident of the death of their enemy George IV, the Whigs could not have taken office or introduced their Reform Bill.

That Bill, by identifying the House of Commons more closely with the nation, indirectly reduced the power of the Crown as well as the power of the peerage. William IV's attempt to dismiss the Whigs and bring in the Tories on his own account was felt to be an anachronism. At his request Wellington and Peel held office for their 'Hundred Days', but could do nothing more than advertise the liberal character of Peel's new Conservative programme, and then retire. Although the unity and prestige of the Whigs had suffered many serious shocks in 1834, and although they were declining in popular favour, the result of William's attempted *coup de grâce* was to give them a majority at the next General Election, and a lease of office for another half-dozen years. They used their restored power to pass the radical Municipal Reform Act, and then sank into their long lethargy – employing their time mainly in a useful reform of the Church revenues.[1]

The gradual retirement of the sovereign from the arena of party politics, coinciding with the accession to the throne of a virtuous and attractive young lady, obliterated the memory of George IV and a generation of princes most of whom had won disapproval either for private vice and meanness, or for public espousal of antipopular causes, or on both counts at once. The Crown, on the head of Queen Victoria, associated itself in the public mind with a new set of ideas. Contrary to expectation, Republicanism waned as popular power grew.

For some years after her accession Queen Victoria was a heroine with the Liberals, and in much disfavour with the Conservatives.[2] In rows about Church rates, Dissenters would indignantly accuse the rector of disloyal expressions about the beautiful young Queen! This inversion of parts was accentuated by the curious episode that goes by the name of 'the bedchamber question'.

1. See pp. 278–9, below.
2. The following passage from a letter to the Queen on her accession, from her uncle, the King of the Belgians, who had an intimate knowledge of English politics, shows that the idea of the sovereign's right to choose which party should be in office was only dying, not dead, in 1837: 'The fact is that the present Ministers [the Whigs] are those who will serve you personally with the greatest sincerity. For them, as well as for the Liberals at large, you are the only sovereign that offers them *des chances d'existence et de durée*. Your immediate successor with the moustaches [Duke of Cumberland] is enough to frighten them into the most violent attachment for you.'

Melbourne, the Whig Premier, if he did little else as a statesman, indoctrinated his royal pupil in sound constitutional precepts adapted to the new age, which carried her successfully through her long reign. She liked the good-natured, fatherly old gentleman, and he exerted the charm and wit that had made him famous under the Regency to captivate the mind of a girl fresh from the schoolroom. Her personal friendships were in Whig circles. When therefore in 1839 the Whigs were at last sufficiently aware of their own incompetence to resign after a bad division, the Queen looked forward with apprehension to changing her old friends for the solemn Peel. He indeed, being in a small minority in the Commons, was not at all anxious to take office. A difficulty soon arose between these two unwilling parties to a transaction forced on them by Melbourne's resignation. Peel demanded and the Queen refused the dismissal of two Whig ladies of her household. Peel might perhaps have been wiser to indulge a mistress whose favour he had yet to win. But, justly fearful of Melbourne's backstairs influence, he preferred to stand out for what he regarded as his constitutional rights. The young Queen grew excited and unexpectedly obstinate. Melbourne and the outgoing Cabinet, moved by the distress of so kind a mistress, consented to resume office for two more uneasy years. The public, with human weakness, tended to sympathize with the Queen on the 'bedchamber question', but even so could not much longer endure the dregs of Whig rule. In 1841 a General Election brought Peel unequivocally into power, and Queen Victoria was not long in discovering how fortunate she was in such a servant.

The electors of 1841, in showing that they were weary of the Whigs, did but reflect the opinion of the unenfranchised masses. For five years past the Whigs had done nothing but produce an annual deficit, and confess that they knew no help either for the deficit or for the stagnation of trade which was its cause.[1] What Carlyle called 'the condition of the people problem' was chronic and acute, and the Whigs had exhausted their list of remedies. It really lay with them, as the representatives of Liberalism in Parliament, to repeal the Corn Laws. But although they were not like the Conservatives returned by the squires and farmers to protect those laws, the Whig personnel was too closely connected with landlord ideas and interests. A man like Palmerston was essentially opposed

1. An example of Peel's humour, that formed a real side of his character not often in evidence, was his description of the Whig Chancellor of the Exchequer 'seated on an empty chest by the side of bottomless deficiencies, fishing for a budget'.

to Free Trade in corn. For fear of breaking up their party the Whigs refused to touch the question, as they had refused to touch Parliamentary Reform twenty years before. And so the popular lead once more passed over to the Radicals and the Liberal–Conservatives, in the days of Peel no less than in the days of Canning.

Peel, who had skilfully built up his party's fortunes from their first abject condition after the Reform Bill, was now supported in office by Stanley's vigour in debate and Sir James Graham's high talents as Minister – these two having seven years before crossed over from the Whigs in defence of Irish Church interests. William Ewart Gladstone had only two years before been labelled in Macaulay's essay on his book as 'the rising hope of those stern and unbending Tories' who disapproved of Peel's liberalism. But by 1841 he was already a Peelite. He brought his genius to the common stock of the great administration, and learnt to his own astonishment, in the apprenticeship which Peel made him serve in the Board of Trade, that finance and commerce would absorb him no less than poetry and religion.[1]

The country, which these men were in a fortunate hour called upon to govern, was sunk very low. Bad trade in a rapidly increasing population meant multitudes 'sitting enchanted' in the workhouse, millions more starving – 'clemming' was the word of only too common usage in the industrial north – in horrible sanitary and housing conditions, presenting a sum total of wretchedness that rendered 'the hungry forties' a memory and a byword in years to come.

Peel's budgets from 1842–5 proved the first step out of the morass.[2] An unscientific revenue tariff still impeded trade by its duties on exported manufactures and on imported raw material. Huskisson had reduced it. Peel now swept away most of what was left. The loss to the treasury he made good by reviving the income-tax, Pitt's war measure which had been withdrawn at the peace,[3] owing to what Castlereagh more justly than wisely called people's 'ignorant impatience of taxation'. Peel, more clear-sighted on this point than the anti-Corn-Law manufacturers of the north, saw in the income-tax the key that would unlock the Free Trade cupboard. It is doubtful whether Peel would have been able to introduce it in time of peace if Pitt had not first introduced it in time of war.

The budgets of 1842–5 were great steps in the direction of Free

1. Gladstone, like Peel before him, had taken a 'double first' at Oxford, viz. in mathematics as well as in classics.
2. In 1842 exports of British produce had been forty-seven million pounds – lower than any of the four previous years. By 1846 they had risen to fifty-seven millions.
3. See p. 185, above.

Trade. But since they only very slightly reduced the Corn Duty they met with no serious opposition from the Protectionist party, of which Peel was head. For the Protection that the county members had been returned to support was not the protection of manufactures. For that matter the tariffs which Peel swept away were revenue tariffs that protected nothing at all. Out of twenty millions raised by Customs Duties in 1840, only one million had been raised on the plea of protection to industry. No one argued that any class in the urban community was benefited by the Protective system of the day. And the question of the Corn Laws was this – how far could the industry of the town population rightly be handicapped in order to keep land in cultivation and to maintain the 'agricultural interest'?

The battle between town and country would have been more equal and more prolonged if the peasantry had felt their interest to coincide with that of the landlords. But the rural changes of the last century had abolished the yeoman and the small farmer, who had had a direct interest in high prices. The poverty and starvation of the agricultural labourer inclined him to see his interest in cheap bread, and although he had no direct political weight his miserable condition was an effective argument *ad misericordiam* for the anti-Corn-Law champions, who pointed in triumphant pity to the hollow-cheeked serf of the fields, and produced him on platforms in his smock frock to say 'I be protected, and I be starving'.[1] In the last years of the controversy Cobden persuaded a large proportion even of the farmers that their advantage lay in Free Trade. The 'agricultural interest' was not solid. As a Protectionist party, it came dangerously near to being the 'interest' only of those who consumed rent and tithe. But it possessed the majority in both Houses of Parliament.

By his budgets of 1842–5 Peel had done all he could without attacking the principle of the Corn Laws. During those years he was gradually converted to Free Trade in corn, by his conscientious study of the facts, and by the economic arguments which Cobden poured at him across the floor of the House, in lucid streams of reasoning, until the day came when the Prime Minister crumpled up the notes he was taking and whispered to a colleague 'You must answer this, I cannot.'

1. The best thing that the bourgeois opponents of the Factory Acts (see pp. 246–7, above) had to say, not indeed for themselves but against their landlord and farmer critics, was that the serf of the village was at least as wretched as the serf of the factory. This process of mutual exposure by the two classes of employers, a great feature of politics in the forties, was very useful to the *tertius gaudens*, the employee in town and country.

But it was not by the economic facts and arguments alone that Cobden converted Peel. In the anti-Corn-Law League he had created a political force the mere existence of which was an argument to those Whig and Tory statesmen who had learnt the lesson of the Reform Bill and had adapted themselves to the spirit of the age. Among these Peel was the foremost. Though so long a Tory and never a Canningite, he was now in fact a Liberal–Conservative, instinctively the foe of corruption in any form, seeking to preserve British institutions by respect for public opinion and by careful thought for the general interest. He and his school of 'Peelite' statesmen, of whom Gladstone was the greatest, introduced into the public offices a more conscientious and more liberal tone, which was neither Tory nor Whig, and which still survives in Whitehall.

Peel, who had once denounced the Reform Bill as revolutionary, now saw that it had not gone far enough, that the Commons House was still too much a house of landlords. He began to be afraid that, if the Corn Laws were defended to the last moment possible under the existing forms of the Constitution, the Queen's Government would come into conflict with the nation. And after 1832 Peel had had enough of conflicts with the nation. When the French constitutional monarchy fell in 1848, his comment was 'This comes of trying to govern the country through a narrow representation in Parliament, without regarding the wishes of those outside. It is what this party behind me wanted to do in the matter of the Corn Laws, and I would not do it.'

This was perfectly true. Nevertheless, the reason why 'this party' had been 'behind' him at all was because he had undertaken to defend the Corn Laws. It is possible, while feeling gratitude to Peel, to understand the indignation of his followers at his *volte-face*, the more so as he refused to take the Conservative rank and file into his confidence, eschewed 'party meetings', and seemed, with his shy, secretive manner, to hold them all in more contempt than perhaps he did. As yet they could only murmur. But if ever they got a spokesman – ! There was fine combustible stuff among the squires on the back benches, if someone were to apply Promethean fire.

The wrath of the gentlemen of England was increased by the low and democratic character of the organization to which their chief was about to submit his judgement and their interests. The anti-Corn-Law League, though financed by 'leading firms', was teaching politics to the million. It gave a powerful organization to classes which had hitherto been left outside the national counsels, except during those months when the Political Unions had lined up behind the Reform Bill. But the Political Unions had been no more than a regimentation of the inhabitants of certain towns, ready to act together in a crisis. The League, on the other hand, undertook the education of each section of English society, in town and village, up to the point of uniting all in a common enthusiasm for a proposition in economics.

There had been Chartism, but Chartism had failed, and the League was not failing. It accomplished the miracle of uniting capital and labour. It combined argument and emotion, bringing both to perfection in meetings that began with Cobden and ended with Bright. It appealed equally to self-interest and to humanity. In an age when political literature was limited in quantity and inferior in quality, the League, in 1843 alone, distributed nine million carefully argued tracts by means of a staff of eight hundred persons. In an age when public meetings were rare, when finance and government were regarded as mysteries appertaining to the political families and to well-born civil servants, the League lecturers taught political economy, and criticized the year's budget, to vast audiences of merchants and clerks, artisans and navvies, farmers and agricultural labourers. The League not only invented modern methods of political education, but applied them to coerce both the official parties. The Whig with his proposal for a 'fixed duty' and the Conservative with his 'sliding scale' were both given notice to quit at the next General Election, and surrendered rather than try the event against the League candidates.[1]

No wonder the League was denounced as 'extra-constitutional' by parties in possession of the recognized organs of political life. Protectionists talked of putting it down by law. Half-hearted Free Traders, like the Whigs and *The Times* newspaper – the latest comer in the hierarchy of accepted political institutions – were jealous of it as a rival and ashamed of it as an ally. When in 1841 the League, characteristically enough, assembled seven hundred Nonconformist clergy to bear witness, from the evidence of their daily ministrations in the slums, to the material conditions unfavourable to the religious life of the mass of the population, *The Times* coupled this 'drollery' with 'The British Association for the Advancement of Science', and promised to 'put an extinguisher on humbugs' in both cases.

Nevertheless two years later *The Times* itself, while still denouncing 'gregarious congregations of cant and cotton men', wrote 'the League is a great fact'. That confession, appearing in the daily

1. The businessmen were at Cobden's orders buying land enough to qualify as county voters, and so threaten even the county seats.

bulletin of the ultra-respectable and official classes, caused rage and exultation now very barely imaginable. Perhaps the British Association also was another 'great fact', borne forward on the tide of time, in spite of an able editor's sense of the unfitting.

In the spring of 1845 Peel was at heart a convert to Free Trade in corn, as all the world knew. His plan was at the next General Election to announce his change of policy, and so put himself in a position gradually to abolish the Corn Laws without a betrayal of the election pledges of 1841. But his hand was forced by a combination of two accidents, which had no causal connexion with each other, the Irish potato blight and the English harvest weather. When it was first whispered that Ireland would soon be in the grip of famine, the Protectionists could still hope that a particularly good harvest in England would enable the British Islands to feed themselves. But a month of rain when the corn was in the ear 'rained away the corn laws'.

It was now clear that it would be physically impossible to feed the Irish from England, and it was morally impossible to allow them to perish wholesale with foreign corn waiting to enter. The ports of the United Kingdom must be opened for the emergency, and if once they were opened no statesman could ever hope to close them again in face of English and Scottish opinion. Peel's Free Trade budgets of 1842–5 and the accompanying revival of trade had considerably relieved the situation in Britain, but people who had tasted prosperity were not prepared to be thrown back into the depths from which they had escaped, by a sudden scarcity of bread. The demand for 'total and immediate' repeal rose as a cry of terror.

The League that winter entered on its last, irresistible campaign. The Whigs swung round to 'total and immediate', led by Lord John Russell, who had the strength of mind to write his famous 'Edinburgh letter' voicing the national demand, without consulting his more weak-kneed colleagues. They dared not challenge his *fait accompli*. It was now a choice between Peel and the Whigs, which of them would undertake to pass a necessary measure through a disorganized House of Commons and a hostile House of Lords.

Peel was prepared to abolish the Corn Laws, and *The Times* prematurely announced that he was to meet Parliament with this programme.[1] But Stanley refused to agree, and Peel, not being able

1. It was Peel's colleague, Aberdeen, who told *The Times* this secret that proved half untrue – not Mrs Norton, as Meredith supposed when he wrote *Diana of the Crossways*.

to carry his whole Cabinet, resigned. The task of abolishing the Corn Laws fell to the Whigs, to whom it properly belonged. Russell began the formation of a Ministry, and then suddenly threw it up, ostensibly on the ground that Grey, a son of the Reform Bill Premier, would not serve if Palmerston was allowed to go back to the Foreign Office to the danger of European peace. But Russell could perfectly well have formed his Ministry without Grey or without Palmerston. And Grey next year took office with Palmerston as Foreign Minister after all!

The real reason why the Whigs refused to form a Ministry was that they lacked nerve for the crisis. They shrank from the task of passing Repeal through the Lords. They had indeed Peel's promise of support, but, since Peel out of office might have little influence with the Protectionist peers, the Whigs might have to call in Crown and people to pass the Bill as in 1832. Now the Whigs were no longer inspired by the spirit of that time. Though pretending to be the popular party, they were afraid of the people. They had no wish to lead a democratic attack on the Lords, and hoped that Peel would be able to pass the Bill with the least possible disturbance.

The 'grand refusal' has gone far to discredit the later Whigs with posterity, but it gave them twenty years unchallenged possession of power. For it broke up the Conservative party.

When Lord John 'handed back with courtesy the poisoned chalice to Sir Robert', Peel did not know that it was poisoned. He came back cheerfully to the place behind the red box where he was so well fitted to stand. By the refusal of the Whigs to take office, his desire to repeal the Corn Laws himself had become a duty that he could no longer avoid.[1] Strong in the affection of the people, he saw before him many years of public service such as he alone could render.

Peel and Wellington remembered only that they were the servants of the Crown and country, and forgot that they had become so as representatives of agricultural Protection and the great county families. Wellington's loyalty to Peel and his belief that Peel alone was fit to govern are the more remarkable because the Duke was not himself convinced of the necessity of abolishing the Corn Laws. 'Rotten potatoes have done it,' he said; 'they put Peel in his d——d fright.' But it never occurred to him to desert his Queen

1. Disraeli indeed pointed out that Peel had wished to repeal the Corn Laws himself even before giving Russell the chance, and that only Stanley's refusal had caused his resignation in December 1845. That is the weakest point in Peel's conduct.

and his colleague in the interest of his party and his class. 'I did think,' he told the Lords, 'that the formation of a Government in which Her Majesty would have confidence was of greater importance than any opinion of any individual upon the Corn Law or any other law.' So he pulled his hat over his eyes, stretched out his legs, and reclined there silent and fortunately very deaf, while Noble Lords raved against the treachery of their chiefs. This attitude sufficed to secure the passage of the Corn Bill.

The Corn Laws were abolished in June; but contrary to what had been the general expectation when the session opened in January the Conservative party was blown in two by the explosion. The combustible squirearchy on the back benches of the Commons had been ignited by the hand of irresponsible genius. Disraeli's philippics broke Peel's prestige and destroyed his hold over the House. When he tried to answer, he was howled down by his former followers, maddened with the new wine of magnificent invective. With his ablest colleagues all save Stanley devoted to him, with the people in an ecstasy of affection and gratitude, Peel was an outcast in the House that had been elected to support him. The very evening that his Corn Bill passed the Lords, his Government was defeated in the Commons by a coalition between the Whigs seeking office and the Protectionists seeking revenge.

Disraeli had an unanswerable case against Peel from the point of view of the betrayed Protectionists, and it was easy for him to share with genuine passion the indignation of his party. He seems to have regarded agricultural Protection rather as the battle-flag of the great county families than as a policy in economics. He was on the side of the landed interest, and believed in England's 'territorial constitution'. He was a foreigner of genius forcing his way to the front as the champion of a proud and ancient aristocracy which he sincerely admired from the outside. Twenty-one years later, when he enfranchised the working-man, he acted as Peel was now acting on the great question of the day – only he carried the operation through without destroying his party, because he had not a young Disraeli to reckon with.

Owing to the intrusion into British politics of an alien element so potent and so incalculable as this man, the Conservative party was broken up in 1846 and kept out of office for twenty years. Owing to the same personal force it was compelled in 1867 to accept democracy and was launched on a new career of influence and power.

Peel lived until his riding accident in 1850, the most honoured figure in England after the Duke of Wellington, but he was never again in office. The feud between the Peelites and the rank and file of the party was too personal ever to be healed. The troops held that their officers had sold the fort; and the officers held that the troops, led by a Whitechapel drummer boy, had shot the colonel in the back. Graham, Aberdeen, Sidney Herbert, and Gladstone could never forgive the treatment to which Peel had been subjected, and had conceived on that ground the strongest aversion for Disraeli, who now, as Stanley's second in command, carried the fortunes of the Conservative party. Besides, the Peelites were Free-Traders, while Stanley and Disraeli continued to threaten the country with a return to agricultural Protection, until in 1852 they abandoned it during a brief attempt to hold office. By that time Peel was dead, Whigs and Peelites were no longer very easily distinguishable, and Gladstone had begun to travel by way of the Neapolitan prisons towards the Liberalism of his later years.

By the events of 1845–6 the Ten Pound voter had at length asserted his power, to the extent of insisting that the economic and financial policy of the State should no longer flout his interests. But the Cabinets still continued to be drawn exclusively from the landowning and higher professional classes. Cobden and Bright remained in perpetual opposition; there were few of their class and fewer of their opinions in the House.

The world indeed was changing, but not yet changed. The Universities were reformed by Parliament in 1854, but without their emoluments and offices being opened to Dissenters. The middle class, which is often said to have ruled Victorian England, never had a party or a policy of its own outside commercial questions, and even in that sphere its success was due to the peculiar genius of Cobden. The English bourgeoisie developed 'class-consciousness'. Many of the beneficiaries of Free Trade became Conservative, and intermarried with the landed wealth against which they had recently been tilting. Others, of more democratic tendency, worked with Bright to extend the franchise once more and to take the working-man into political partnership, rather on general Liberal principles than to carry out any special programme. To this invitation the working-man responded. There was indeed very little 'class war' in England for a generation after the repeal of the Corn Laws.

Agriculture had now to take the second place in the economic policy of the Empire. But the 'agricultural interest' of landlords and farmers was still as far as possible from being ruined. Those who had been most angry at Repeal found many compensations. For another generation the landlords still drew great rents, and could afford to entertain regiments of guests in their country houses. They were still piling up on an ever vaster scale structures which survive too often as an embarrassment to their descendants of today. It was still the golden age of hunting and shooting, in the cheery social atmosphere immortalized by Leech's pictures in *Punch* and Surtees's sporting novels. In county government there was still no element of popular election. The squires still administered the affairs of each neighbourhood in their capacity of Justices of the Peace. There were Radicals who murmured, but they came from and returned to the towns. Old England still survived in the rural parts.

British agriculture continued to flourish, and since it no longer depended on a monopoly it once more took to improved methods as in the eighteenth century. Corn was indeed being poured into the island from overseas, but prices and rents kept up very fairly, for there were more people than ever to feed, and as they were drawing better wages they were eating much more meat and corn per head.[1] It was no longer necessary for two millions in England to live on potatoes and other foodstuffs inferior to corn. So, during the rest of Cobden's lifetime, his agreeable prophecy that town and country would flourish side by side was amply fulfilled. Only in the late seventies, when a fuller development of America's resources had taken place, when cheap iron had cheapened sea and land transport for all the world, food came pouring into England in such quantities that Disraeli's ancient prophecies of agricultural distress took effect in his old age.[2]

When the Corn Laws had gone, all motive for further resistance to Free Trade had gone too, so far as England was concerned. No one troubled to fight for the relics of the Navigation Laws, for West Indian sugar, or for the remaining duties on raw material. The idea of Colonial Preference still lay buried in the grave of Huskisson. In the course of the next fifteen years, the Whigs and Gladstone completed the logical edifice of Free Trade, without meeting any serious opposition.

Partly on account of the free exchange encouraged by the abolition of the Corn Laws and the revenue tariff, partly on account

1. Another reason why the nominal price of corn only fell slightly as a result of Repeal was that in the fifties and sixties prices in general were rising owing to the gold discoveries in California and Australia, the Crimean War and other causes. The price of wheat would have risen immensely in England but for Repeal coming when it did. In the six years after 1846 a larger quantity of grain was imported than had entered the country in the thirty-one years between Waterloo and Repeal.

2. See pp. 368–9, below.

of more general world movements, a great development of trade and prosperity set in. Railways and ocean steamers created a world-market on a vast scale, of which England alone was prepared to take the first advantage. It is scarcely an exaggeration to say that in the middle of the century the five continents consisted of a number of countries, all chiefly and some entirely agricultural, grouped for commercial purposes round the manufacturing centre of England. The volume of our exports, which had risen from about forty millions a year in the first decade of the century to nearly sixty millions a year during Peel's Ministry, rose to two hundred millions a year by 1876. At home, the railway mania, though it led to overspeculation and the panic of 1846, left the island linked up with an effective railway system. The surplus population of town and country, recently crowding the workhouses, were drawn off not only as colonial emigrants, but as miners and navvies at home.[1]

Parallel with this expansion of trade and enterprise the conditions of life for the working class at length underwent rapid and general improvement. Real wages rose and employment became more regular. Conditions improved most of all in the great organized trades, where capitalism was replacing the pettifogging 'semi-capitalism' with its mean shifts and tyrannies, and where highly organized Trade Unionism was growing as the concomitant of big capital. In 1852 the Amalgamated Society of Engineers came to be regarded as the 'new model' for the aristocracy of labour. It was the union of a single craft, eminently practical in its aims and spirit, as opposed to the vague idealism of Owen's defunct 'Grand National' for all working-men. Various movements of self-help in the working class, such as Friendly Societies, were closely connected with 'new model' Trade Unionism, which combined the function and finance of a trade organization with those of an insurance and benefit Club. The Friendly benefits were administered by the local branches, and the strike pay and policy by the Central Executive. An expert salaried executive was one of the most important features of the 'new model'.

The Co-operative movement, which has done so much all over the world to stop the exploitation of the consumer by the retail dealer, and to train the working classes in self-government and

1. A 'navvy' originally meant an 'inland navigator', viz., a workman employed on digging canals; this class of labour, partly Irish, chiefly English agricultural in origin, was in the forties principally engaged in constructing the railways.

business management, originated from the enterprise of two dozen Chartist and Owenite workmen of Rochdale, who in 1844 opened in Toad (T'owd) Lane the store of the Rochdale Pioneers. It was a humble affair, and many larger attempts at co-operation had failed. But these men chanced to have hit on the right plan for realizing Owen's dream. Their rules were – the sale of goods at market prices, followed by division of surplus profit among members in proportion to their purchases. This secured democratic interest in the management of the business, while eliminating profit at the expense of the consumer. It was on these lines that the Co-operative movement reached such enormous development before the century closed.

The practical success of the movement was helped in the fifties by the zeal with which its idealist aspect was preached both by the Secularists led by Holyoake, the pupil of Owen, and by the Christian Socialists whom Maurice had inspired, especially Tom Hughes, the author of *Tom Brown's Schooldays*. The attempts of the shopkeepers to establish a boycott of the movement only increased its strength. In the seventies the Co-operative Societies added production on a considerable scale to their original activities.

The Co-operative movement was of more than financial importance. It gave many working people a sense that they also had 'a stake in the country'. It taught them business habits and mutual self-help, and drew them together in societies that encouraged the desire for education and self-improvement.

It is [writes one of its historians] in its intellectual and moral influence upon its members, even more than the financial savings that it effects and encourages, that the Co-operative movement has wrought a beneficent revolution among tens of thousands of working-class families, and has contributed so largely to the social transformation of Great Britain.

The movements by which the new Britain was striving to remedy the evils attendant on the Industrial Revolution – Co-operation, Factory Laws, Trade Unionism, Free Trade – were all, like the Industrial Revolution itself, British in conception and origin.[1]

The reformed legislature, and the reformed organs of adminis-

1. So too was Sir Rowland Hill's idea of a postal delivery prepaid by an adhesive stamp. His penny postage (1840), unlike some great British reforms, 'ran like wildfire throughout the civilized world,' increasing commerce, and enabling the poor, for the first time in the history of man, to communicate with the loved ones from whom they were separated.

tration which it had created, were helping on the general social improvement. The state no longer sat by with folded hands. Contemporaneously with the realization of Free Trade, a strong reaction against the wrong sort of *laissez faire* went forward, not only in the Factory Acts, but in Truck Acts, Mine Acts, and sanitary legislation.

Truck is payment of wages in goods, or cash payments subject to conditions as to the expenditure of the wages. It had been made illegal by Littleton's Act of 1831. But the Whigs, though they have the credit of laying down the principle, had not provided for its enforcement, as they provided for the enforcement of the Factory Act of 1833 by the appointment of inspectors. Truck payments had only been put on their defence by an Act too general in its scope. Many employers continued to swindle their men by paying them in the goods they produced, or by forcing them to purchase at the 'tommy-shop', where rotten goods were dealt out at extravagant prices. Truck was fought and beaten in a long struggle, chiefly by the Trade Unions; partly by the growth of larger capitalism that dispensed with middlemen and had no need to turn to such mean shifts for its profit; and partly by an elaborate code of anti-truck legislation for particular trades. Anti-truck clauses were inserted in the series of Acts that protected the life and health of the mining population, beginning with Shaftesbury's Mines Act of 1842.

The principle of State interference found another expression in the Sanitary Code which began in the forties as a result of the personal efforts of Chadwick of the Poor Law Commission.[1] His experience on that unpopular but conscientious tribunal had revealed to him the horrors of housing and sanitation, and the close connexion of bad health with the spread of pauperism. His energetic exposure of these evils compelled the Government to act.

The absence of sanitary control which had been characteristic of the nation's remoter past had been continued during the first seventy years of the Industrial Revolution, with appalling results, which have been by no means altogether removed in our own day. The jerry-builder and the thrifty manufacturer in a hurry had covered England with slums; trout streams had become sewers; rubbish-heaps festered unregarded till cholera or some milder epidemic threatened the well-to-do. The cottages of the rural labourer were no less disgraceful.

After ten years of agitation and collection of evidence, Chadwick secured the Public Health Act of 1848. This was the first compulsory measure of the kind imposed on the local authorities by the

1. See pp. 248–9, above.

central government. A General Board of Health was set up for the whole country. It had power to establish local Boards of Health wherever there was not a municipal body to carry out the provisions of the law.

The Public Health Act was the late beginning of a great series of sanitary reforms. It was also an important step towards control of Local Government by specialist departments at Whitehall, of which the Educational Committee of the Privy Council and the Poor Law Board were other early examples. A system of constant and delicate interaction between central and local authorities grew up after the middle years of the nineteenth century, in many cases through the characteristic English device of central 'grants in aid' of local rates. This system has never been proclaimed as a discovery in political science, but it became one of the most important elements of our State machinery. We thus managed to save from our own past what was good in the spirit of local initiative and independence, while compelling all to come up to a minimum standard insisted on by the State.

CHAPTER 18

THE original Oxford movement, as might be expected from the place and time of its birth, was scholastic and religious. In so far as it had any connexion with the social and political sides of life, the connexion is to be found in the hostile reaction of the minds of Keble and Newman against the liberal and utilitarian spirit of the early thirties, and the Whig proposals to secularize part of the property of the Irish Church. Nurtured in an Oxford then very remote from modern and secular influences, they conceived a new basis for religious and ecclesiastical conservatism in England. And the Anglo-Catholic movement, which they began, was allied, both in theory and practice, with a social and political conservatism which it has since very largely lost. The distance travelled by Mr Gladstone's mind in the course of a lifetime, though exceptional, is symptomatic.

In 1845 the conversion of Newman to Rome destroyed his influence as the dominant force in the University. As if a spell had been snapped, Oxford swung round to more secular interests and more liberal thought – so far as was consistent with Churchmanship, which was still a condition of residence at the University. What had been the Oxford movement went out into the world and became a pan-Anglican movement. It began to penetrate the general body of the clergy.

It had not, like the contemporary Free Church movement in Scotland, a hold on large masses of laity. It was not Cuddesdon but Exeter Hall that could raise the winds of popular agitation. Mid-Victorian lay religion, a very powerful and guiding force in all classes, was distinctively Protestant. The great Evangelicals, from the time of Wilberforce onwards, were laymen – Shaftesbury, the Buxtons, and many of the famous Anglo-Indian soldiers and civilians. But Evangelicalism had failed to breed great clerics, and was more interested in the religious life of the individual than in the Church. The Anglo-Catholic movement, on the other hand, found new motives and standards for the clergy as such. They became more distinctively professional. They ceased to hunt, to shoot, to sit on the magistrates' bench, and to behave, as they had for the last hundred years, as a rather more learned branch of the squirearchy. They no longer left 'enthusiasm' to Methodists.

With this new impulse the Church from the forties onwards began to make good the ground she had lost. She no longer regarded the Colonies and the industrial slums as outside her sphere because they had not been provided for by the parochial system of the seventeenth century. And as the clergy came in contact with this neglected outer world, it naturally did not appear to successive generations of High Churchmen exactly as the distant prospect of it from Oriel windows had looked at the time of the first Reform Bill.

But the process of change was gradual. In the thirties and forties the Church clergy of all sections regarded the Chartists with horror, and the Tractarians denounced all those who taught the people 'to rail against their rulers and superiors'. In the fifties a new movement of democratic sympathy was introduced into the Church by the Broad Churchmen, Frederick Denison Maurice and Charles Kingsley, whose 'Christian Socialism', though it was rather what we should now call 'Christian Radicalism', proclaimed the doctrine that Christianity was futile unless applied to economic and social relations. But for some time to come, the average clergyman, particularly in the rural parishes, can hardly be said to have had popular sympathies. In the seventies Joseph Arch found the rural clergy with some exceptions actively hostile to his movement for better agricultural wages. The penetration of the Church by the Anglo-Catholic movement, and the change of attitude of many adherents of that movement to society and politics, were both very gradual. But they began when Peel and Wellington were consuls.

The renewed activity of the national Church was one of the most important phenomena of the nineteenth century. The way for it had been prepared by the action of Parliament, which in 1836 had caused ecclesiastical revenues to be redistributed. Church revival was difficult so long as many of the bishops and other dignitaries enjoyed extravagant incomes and moved in an atmosphere of plurality, nepotism, and worldly self-interest. A bishopric was often regarded as an opportunity not only to serve Church and State, but to provide handsomely for family and clients. The unpopularity of the Church at the end of the old Tory régime was partly due to the political action of the Bishops in the House of Lords, and of the clergy on the magisterial bench; partly to the grievances of Dissenters; partly to the constant annoyance of farmers at paying tithes in kind; but very largely to the unequal distribution of Church revenues, an abuse in fact and exaggerated in common fame. The impression left on the vulgar mind by the Church at the time of the first Reform Bill was that prelates and pluralists drank port and hunted the fox, while poor curates worked and starved.

Like Parliament, Municipalities, Universities, endowed schools, and all other official establishments, the Church in the eighteenth century had come to be regarded too much as a lottery for the benefit of a few lucky individuals, and too little as an institution endowed for a great public purpose. At length a new age had come with new standards. The hour had struck not only for parliamentary and municipal, but for ecclesiastical and academic reform. Parliament, having succeeded in reforming itself, set about reforming the other institutions of the country.

Sir Robert Peel had in all things taken to heart the lesson of the Reform Bill. Loyal Churchman as he was, he saw that the Church must be helped by Parliament to set her house in order. It was no longer enough for her to cling to privilege. During his brief tenure of office in the winter of 1834–5, which he employed so usefully to adumbrate the Conservative policy of the future,[1] he appointed an Ecclesiastical Commission to inquire into Church revenues. His design was carried through by his Whig successors, with his constant support, and with the aid of the leading bishops, but in face of the opposition of Churchmen of the older school.

Under these conditions the Whig government, between 1836 and 1840, passed a series of Church reforms. A Tithe-commutation Bill put an end to the quarrel that had been renewed in the English village every year since the Conquest and beyond, over the par-

1. See p. 262, above.

son's tithe-pigs and sheaves. Tithes were commuted for a rent-charge made on all land, payable to the tithe-owners, whether clerical or lay. This was regarded as a convenience by all the parties concerned. It was not strictly speaking a subject of sectarian or political controversy, but it relieved the Church of a heavy load of unpopularity due to a system calculated to cause friction and dispute.

Another Act put an end to the worst abuses of plurality and non-residence. And, above all, a great internal redistribution of wealth relieved the Church of much odium, and equipped her for work in many districts hitherto neglected. The bishops, some of whom had their excessive incomes cut down, became stipendiaries instead of great landlords. A permanent Ecclesiastical Commission was established to administer revenues.

The work of the Ecclesiastical Commission was followed up by that of the Charity Commission, reconstituted with fresh powers by the Whig government in 1853, to deal with non-ecclesiastical Trusts. Endowed education and charity were in a state of corruption as bad as anything to be found in the Church. Brougham had long ago begun the exposure of the facts, as chairman of the original Charity Commission of 1818. The grammar schools were at length shaken out of the torpor of a century, and endowments left for education or charity were no longer permitted to be consumed as sinecures.[1]

Although the Church, with the help of her wiser friends and leaders, had been reformed by Act of Parliament in the matter of the distribution of her revenues, she maintained her privileges and monopolies almost intact between the first and second Reform Bills. It was largely for this reason that the 'dissidence of Dissent' was so marked a feature of the period. The Dissenters, who believed that they were almost as numerous as the Churchmen, and felt themselves to be daily growing in importance and power, were galled by the badges of inferiority which the spirit of Church ascendancy still insisted that they should wear.

Their exclusion from Oxford and Cambridge[2] tended to bar out their ablest men from the higher professional and political life of the age. This had the effect of supplying the Dissenting bodies with men of a very high type as preachers and leaders – able men

1. See p. 43, above. Readers of Trollope will remember with a smile the sad case of *The Warden* in these years of rigorous inquisition.
2. See p. 346, below. In 1834 a University Tests Bill to open degrees to British subjects, irrespective of religion, was passed by the reformed House of Commons by a large majority, and thrown out by the Lords by a majority of 102.

embittered by a sense of ill-usage and ostracism. It is only since Oxford and Cambridge have been thrown open to all creeds that men who would formerly have been the leaders of a militant Nonconformity have been absorbed in the general stream of national life. This change has contributed with other causes to the diminution of the Dissenting bodies both in self-consciousness and power.

The other chief grievance of the Dissenters, which affected a much greater number of persons, was the right of a majority of parishioners to levy a rate on all for the maintenance and repair of the Church fabric. At the beginning of the century this ancient usage had scarcely been felt as a grievance, but with the increase of the Nonconformists in numbers and importance it was resented as an injustice and a badge of inferiority. But even after the first Reform Bill they had not the political power to overcome the resistance of the House of Lords. In the middle years of the century the ill-feeling engendered by local contests over the Church-rate rendered it hard for Churchmen and Dissenters to live at peace. In some 1,500 parishes where the Dissenters could secure a majority of votes in the vestry, the rate was refused altogether, and after long disputes in the law-courts such refusal was held valid in law. But in parishes where the recusants were in a minority, they had to pay, and the goods of the more obstinate 'passive resisters' were sold up.

In some of these Church-rate contests in northern industrial districts in the early days of Victoria, political and religious enthusiasm were strangely blended, thousands of votes were polled on each side, amid scenes recalling the ardours and humours of the Eatanswill election. Rival bands paraded with music and party favours, liquor flowed, intimidation and bribery were general, and on some occasions the military were called out to keep the peace, as though in the streets of Belfast.

The Whig statesmen were not Dissenters, though they relied on the Dissenting vote. But they were for the most part not enthusiastic Churchmen, and some, like Russell and Palmerston, had inherited or acquired a decidedly secular point of view. They failed to legislate for the Dissenters as such, but they relieved the laity from ecclesiastical jurisdiction in testamentary and divorce cases, which had come down unbroken from the Middle Ages. In the face of strong opposition from Gladstone, divorce was made obtainable in Court by persons of moderate means, instead of being confined, as formerly, to people rich enough to pay for a private Act of Parliament.

The disruption of the Scottish Church was more closely connected with political history than was the Oxford movement. It was directly caused by the views on the relation of Church and State entertained by Sir Robert Peel and the British Parliament. But its ulterior causes and inner meaning lie far back in the depths of Scottish history and Scottish character.

It has been already pointed out that in the complete absence of popular institutions, prior to 1832, in a country so well educated and so democratic in spirit as Scotland, the Church had furnished the sole organ for the collective life of the people. It has also been pointed out that in the middle of the eighteenth century the Moderate or Latitudinarian party in the Church had established its position as against the Evangelicals who upheld the narrower and fiercer tradition of the Covenanters.[1] In the age of David Hume, Adam Smith, and Principal Robertson, the Moderates successfully protected the philosophers for whom the Scotland of the 'age of enlightenment' was justly famous. It was a victory of toleration of the first importance to Scotland and to mankind.

The victory of intellectual freedom had been won in part by the law of 'patronage', which enabled patrons to intrude Moderate ministers into the manses, against the will of the more fanatical democracy of the parish.[2] As a result of the 'intrusion controversy', small secessions from the Church had taken place, and the seceders had split up again into Burghers and anti-Burghers, Auld Lichts and New Lichts. But the secessions were not yet large enough to be dignified by the term Disruption.

In Scotland as in England, Erastianism had been used to fight fanaticism. And in Scotland as in England, the victorious Latitudinarian party, safe in possession of the loaves and fishes, lost its vigour and virtue before the eighteenth century closed. Like the contemporary English Church, the Scottish Church failed to take up the fresh opportunities and duties of the changing age. While their evangelizing spirit languished, the Moderates lost even their own peculiar virtue of tolerance, and under the influence of anti-Jacobinism became bigoted as well as official.

With the new century, the Evangelical party revived, but without the old fanaticism. The philosophers had done work that could not be undone, and with Walter Scott as the national mouthpiece it was impossible for the narrow spirit of earlier ages to return with the revival of their zeal. The Evangelical party found in Dr Thomas

1. See pp. 48–9, above.
2. Readers of Galt's *Annals of the Parish* will remember how in 1760 the minister is 'intruded' by the help of a guard of soldiers.

Chalmers a religious leader with all Knox's singleness of heart, some of his power, but none of his harsher spirit.[1] In the ensuing conflict between official Moderatism and the Evangelical party, 'patronage' was as formerly employed to intrude Moderates on unwilling parishes. Chalmers, though a strong Conservative in politics and believing in the principle of establishment, held that freedom of religion in Scotland meant the freedom of the parish democracy to choose its pastor, and in this cause he was ready in the last resort to sacrifice the establishment itself as of less importance.

For ten years after the Reform Bill Scotland was convulsed by the 'non-intrusion' controversy. Having just acquired political and municipal self-government, new in the history of their country, many Scots were more than ever determined to reassert what they believed to be their ancient national rights of self-government in religion. Various attempts at settlement were made, like the Veto Act which, while permitting appointments by patronage, left the people a veto on a minister whom they disliked. But the House of Lords in its judicial capacity ruled out all these compromises, and reasserted patronage and intrusion as the fundamental law of the land.

The Church Assembly, of which a majority was now Evangelical, had no alternative but to have recourse to Parliament for fresh legislation. Their demands were pitched very high, and seemed to Sir Robert Peel and to many Conservatives both in Scotland and England inconsistent with the principle of Church Establishment and the rights of the State. Modification of the existing law was refused. Then Chalmers proclaimed the Disruption. A third of the Scottish clergy followed him into the wilderness, giving up their manses, stipends, and prospects in life as their fathers had done before them in Stuart times. It was a great moral act and had a heightening effect on the life of Scotland, even among those who did not agree as to its necessity. The Free Church was set up in parish after parish in a zealous rivalry of evangelization with the Established Church.

In 1874 the Establishment itself obtained from Parliament the abolition of patronage, the original ground of the Disruption. In 1900 the various bodies outside the Establishment were amalgamated in the United Free Church of Scotland. And in 1929 the Established and Free Churches were happily reunited.

---

1. McCrie's *Life of Knox*, 1812, had a great part in promoting the Evangelical revival.

Catholic Emancipation and the coming of the Whigs to power had put O'Connell[1] into a position to drive bargains for Ireland at Westminster. Until the English and Irish Reform Bills had passed, he had the wisdom to support Grey's Ministry even when it prosecuted him. Grey would not meet his advances, and Edward Stanley as Irish Secretary seemed to have a personal quarrel with the Irish people, until he was removed to the Colonial Office in 1833. Althorp and Russell felt differently, and might have done something towards the conciliation of Ireland if they had been allowed to work heartily with O'Connell. But many of their own colleagues and supporters disagreed, and the House of Lords stood right across the path of conciliation.

Meanwhile the rent and tithe wars were raging in Ireland. In Queen's County alone sixty murders were committed in one year, and agrarian terrorism dominated the whole province of Leinster. It was a detestable spirit, but it was not unprovoked. For the British Army was being used to protect wholesale evictions by landlords 'clearing' estates which they had never improved, and to distrain for tithe on behalf of an 'alien Church',[2] largely composed of absentees and sinecurists. Twenty-two Protestant bishops drew £150,000 a year, and the rest of the Church £600,000 more, very largely from the Catholic peasants. In face of these conditions the Whig Cabinet was torn asunder between the policies of coercion and concession. The position was further complicated by the religious views of Graham and Stanley as to the sacredness of ecclesiastical property. They left the Cabinet and the party on that issue, when 'Johnnie Russell upset the coach' by an incautiously liberal pronouncement. Grey's retirement followed in a few months, after a Cabinet crisis about coercion.

From 1835 to 1840 the reprieved Whig Government under Melbourne was dependent on O'Connell's parliamentary support. They paid him in liberal administration, and as much liberal legislation as the House of Lords would swallow. The Under-Secretary, Thomas Drummond, governed Ireland justly, holding the balance between Orange and Catholic, discouraging informers, and introducing Catholics into the police force, which he thorough-ly reformed. But the good he could do in administration was

---

1. See pp. 220–22, above.

2. Disraeli invented this phrase in his penetrating analysis of Irish dis-content in 1847. But in 1868 he strove to defend the Church he had thus condemned, against its disestablishment by Gladstone, who in 1838 had written the high-flying volume on Church and State attacked by Macaulay. The virtue of Victorian statesmen did not lie in their consistency, which is perhaps no virtue in a long political career.

hampered by the repeated refusal of the Lords to pass remedial laws. With difficulty he kept the bloody tithe war within bounds, until in 1838 the Whigs at length prevailed on Parliament to commute the direct payment of tithes for a fixed rent charge. So too, after many attempts at Irish Municipal Reform, the Ministry at length induced the Lords to accept the shadow of such a measure. O'Connell was chosen Mayor of Dublin and Catholics began to appear on other local bodies. These concessions could not, at that date, go far to reconcile the races, as they might have done thirty years before. Something like Gladstone's Church and Land Legislation of 1868–81 was wanted in the thirties. But England was always a generation too late.

With the return to power of Peel and the Conservatives, from whom O'Connell had nothing to hope, he threw himself in good earnest into the agitation for Repeal of the Union, or, as we should now term it, Home Rule. This policy united against him all classes and parties in Great Britain. But he worked Catholic Ireland up to the same pitch of enthusiasm and unanimity for Repeal as formerly for Emancipation. Unfortunately he had not considered beforehand how the affair was to end. He was resolved, as always, to have no bloodshed, and this time Peel would not give way before mere agitation as in 1828. Peel called O'Connell's bluff. When Government forbade the monster meeting at Clontarf, to which all Ireland was looking forward as the long-expected crisis of the whole movement, O'Connell ordered submission. He was obeyed, but he lost in a day the confidence of his people.

The political influence of the Liberator had for some years been rivalled and now began to be outstripped by the more irreconcilable teaching of 'Young Ireland', led by Gavan Duffy. It was the spirit of nationalism, based on literature and history, like the contemporary racial movements of the Continent. It was in these respects the forerunner of the Gaelic League and Sinn Fein in our own day. But the appeal to physical force attempted in 1848 by Smith O'Brien and Meagher lacked the fierce efficacy of the agrarian terrorism of previous years, met with no popular response, and was suppressed with ludicrous ease by a few policemen.

The years of the famine were indeed no time to prepare rebellions among people who had only the strength to hold out their hands for food. For two consecutive seasons the potato crop failed, and in 1846 and 1847 the common task was to save eight millions of Irish alive. The peasants, abandoning their useless labour in the fields, squatted on the roadside, trying to break stones for relief work, and actually dying of hunger. Many of the resident landlords behaved well, but some of the absentee class continued in the midst of this frightful visitation to push forward the wholesale eviction of their starving tenants. The British Government bestirred itself, not only repealing the Corn Laws but carrying on food distribution, at first indeed under foolish restrictions, but later with increased efficiency. The people began to flee for their lives to the United States, seventeen out of every hundred dying on the voyage. As one of the emigrant ships was leaving Dublin harbour, it met the vessel that was carrying back O'Connell's body to burial in Ireland. A bitter cry arose, as the exiles bade farewell to the land they loved, and to the man who had been its only hope.

Over half a million died of famine and pestilence. And the steady toll of emigration to America, which now first became a habit of the race, reduced the population of Ireland from eight millions in 1841 to six and a half in 1851, and to less than four and a half in 1901. It is certain that without a considerable reduction in numbers there could never have been the improvement in Irish prosperity with which the century closed. Eight millions could only subsist on the verge of starvation. But the manner of their going was fatal. Between 1849 and 1856 as many as 50,000 families were evicted from their homes. They were not so much helped to emigrate as thrust forth from Ireland. The economic exodus, though it was to a large extent necessary, took place under political and social conditions which made the descendants of those who landed in America hereditary enemies of Great Britain.

In Peel's day the difficulties between the old country and the United States were still those of two branches of the same race and civilization, kept apart by historical, political, and social differences that were beginning to be less acute as England grew more democratic, and as increased trade and more rapid communication began to dispel mutual ignorance. A steady stream of British working-class immigrants had set in to the United States, forming a fresh link between the two nations and confirming the transatlantic belief that the people in Britain 'were a very decent body, shamefully oppressed by a haughty group of Peers and clergy', though less shamefully now than in former years. In spite of Castlereagh's great services to the cause of peace on the Canadian border, the old Tory view of America had as a rule been contemptuous, whereas the modern Whig was patronizing and the Radical friendly except about slavery. In spite of *Martin Chuzzlewit*, Dickens drew the ties closer, by revealing to Americans the existence of 'plain people' in England of a kind they could appreciate.

Peel's Ministry held power during the great crisis that settled whether the Pacific Coast should be divided up without a war between Britain and America. Several other causes of dispute were first cleared away. Aberdeen, almost immediately after taking over the Foreign Office, negotiated the Webster–Ashburton Treaty, which settled by compromise the long disputed north-east boundary between Maine and Canada. He then began, with less wisdom, to interfere in Texas and California, rebellious provinces of Mexico, with a view to preventing their annexation by the United States. That he attempted to promote slavery-abolition in Texas made him the more suspect in the eyes of the Southern slave-holding Democrats, then beginning to dominate American politics. They were also irritated by the activity of our fleet in suppressing the slave trade, and accused us to their Northern brethren of using anti-slave-trade sentiment as a stalking-horse for enforcing against American shipping our right-of-search claims, of ancient and unpopular memory.

On the top of these distinctively Southern questions, arose the issue of the future of the north Pacific Coast, then known as the 'Oregon question'.[1] The settlement of that problem could no longer be postponed, as the pioneers of both nations were coming into contact on the disputed ground. Here American claims had nothing to do with slavery, but they were excessive. The war-cry of the victorious Democratic party at the election of Polk to the Presidency in 1844, was 'Fifty-four forty or fight', meaning that they would at all costs annex the whole Pacific Coast up to the border of Russian Alaska at the latitude of 54° 40″. This would cut off Canada from the Western sea.

Between 1815 and 1847 the population of the United States had grown from eight to seventeen millions, but the vast immigration of non-English races was only just beginning. America's claims on Texas, California, and the north Pacific Coast were beyond her momentary needs and power of expansion, but not beyond her requirements in the near future. In the 'roaring forties', her aggressive democratic idealism, when it registered such vast territorial claims in advance, was inspired by a wise prophetic instinct. But Canada, too, had a destiny, and for that reason, if our claim in the southern part of Oregon was inadmissible, so was that of the United States on the northern part, Vancouver Island, and the future British Columbia.

Peel was one of the most wisely pacific Ministers that England

1. See pp. 183–4, above, and map there.

ever had. He understood that the social and economic situation in Great Britain and Ireland could not stand the strain of a war with our chief customer and the source of our cotton supply. He was no fratricide, and was appalled at the prospect of war with America. Nevertheless, he was prepared to fight rather than yield the whole Pacific Coast. Fortunately, the American people did not really wish for war with us. And perhaps, if the truth were known, the Polk administration, when once the election was won, was not so very anxious to fight in order to add more 'free' States to the Union, and so increase the strength of the anti-slavery party.

England refrained from further interference about Texas and California, which the United States annexed after the Mexican war. And at the very moment of his fall, Peel crowned his immense services to his countrymen and to the world by bringing into port not only the Repeal of the Corn Laws, but the Oregon Treaty, that settled the western frontier between the British territories and the United States. The boundary line following the forty-ninth degree of latitude, which Castlereagh's treaty had carried up to the Rockies, was continued to the coast. The compromise of 1846 can be seen on the map today, securing to Canada and to America respectively a just development on the Pacific, and securing to both nations the peace that has never been broken along four thousand miles of unguarded frontier.

CHAPTER 19

THE year 1848 was the turning-point at which modern history failed to turn. The military despotisms of Central Europe were nearly but not quite transformed by a timely and natural action of domestic forces. It was the appointed hour, but the despotisms just succeeded in surviving it, and modernized their methods without altering their essential character. The misfortunes of European civilization in our own day sprang in no small degree from those far-off events.

In 1848 nearly all the despotic Governments of the Continent were overthrown, but nearly all recovered power in the course of a year. The failure of the revolution to consolidate its success was due to want of experience and wisdom among its leaders; to the strife of constitutional monarchists with republicans and of middle-class liberals with socialists; and finally to the antagonism of races. In the wide dominions ruled from Vienna, racial animosity was the principal cause first of the success and then of the defeat of the revolutionary movements. Mazzini could persuade each of the peoples to demand its own freedom and nationality, but could not persuade them to make common cause, or to rise to the height of his idea that the nations were complements one of the other.

Europe after the fall of Napoleon was subject to an iron law, often overlooked, but always in the end proof against the high aspirations of the nineteenth century – the fact that Prussia, Russia, and Austria were more powerful on the Continent than France and England. It is true that the three Eastern despotisms acted together as seldom as the two Western powers. But they always stood together on the vital question of Poland, and they did not desert one another in the decisive political crisis of the century. In 1849 the King of Prussia refused the request of the Frankfort Parliament that he should take the lead of Liberal Germany, to the exclusion of Austria; while Russia aided the young Emperor Francis Joseph to re-establish military despotism throughout his Austro-Hungarian dominions.

The reduction of Austria's rebellious subjects was rendered possible by the aid of Russia, partly by the refusal of the Magyar Parliamentarians under Kossuth to treat the non-Magyar nationalities of Hungary as anything better than subject peoples. That refusal drove back Slavs and Roumanians into the arms of the despots of Vienna. Kossuth, in his subsequent exile, was regarded by his American and English sympathizers as a hero of liberty, which partly he was. But it may be doubted whether any man since Robespierre did so much injury to the Liberal cause. He deflected the Magyar national ideal from liberalism to chauvinism. The Magyar oligarchy, crushed in 1849, came to terms with their Austrian enemies after 1866 in a co-partnership of dual race ascendancy, and dragged Austro-Hungary to the final abyss.

In Germany the course of the revolution of 1848 was no more fortunate. The Germans indeed could more easily have been united on a basis of freedom. They had no race-divisions like Austria–Hungary. There was not, as in Italy, an Austrian army occupying the land, to suppress every native movement. But in 1848 Germany was anti-Liberal, if not in heart and mind, at least in energy and will. The Parliament of Frankfort, which was to have united her, lacked the powerful spirit of Pym or Franklin, of Mirabeau or of Cavour. If the King of Prussia would not, Germany could not. Her men of genius and her instincts for action were dedicated to other ideals. She was destined to be united, not in 1848 on a basis of freedom, but in 1866 and 1870 on a basis of military Kaiserdom.

The failure of 1848 permanently to overturn military despotism in the centre of the Continent was fatal to the healthy development of Europe as a whole. Austria and Germany, from their geographic position, radiate influence on all sides, and their bulk lies athwart the mutual intercourse of the States that surround them. Russia, as a result of 1849, was still left isolated from contact with freedom. If Germany had been liberalized, the Tsardom would ere long have been reformed.

Italy, on the other hand, was not cut off by physical causes from French and English influence. Italy's tragedy in 1848–9 was only the prelude to her deliverance of 1859–60. The Italians had the wisdom to learn the prudential lessons of their first failure, without abandoning the faith, common to Mazzini and Cavour, that freedom was essential to true nationhood.

In France the issues of 1848 were different. The French already enjoyed national unity, Parliamentary institutions, and popular self-expression, which were the objects of the revolutionaries in other lands. If King Louis Philippe's bourgeois government headed by Guizot – a great historian blind to the lessons of history – had had the sense to extend the franchise, there would have been no excuse for revolt in France. At it was, the Government had against it the two rising forces of Catholic reaction on the one side and working-class aspiration on the other. And since Louis Philippe, in spite of some rather gross intrigues in Spain, did not offer a spirited foreign policy to satisfy French pride, he was haunted by the ghost of Napoleon, the emotional rallying-point of all Frenchmen discontented with Government. The monarchy of the Citizen King fell in the uprising of Paris in February 1848, which gave the signal of revolution to the rest of Europe.[1]

When, in the weeks that followed, the barricades were rising in city after city, and the princes of Europe were flying from their palaces, or hastily signing new constitutions, while class was arming against class, and race against race in the wild confusion of universal overturn, the British people looked on at a spectacle that could not fail to interest, but scarcely seemed to concern them. The popular victory over the Corn Laws two years back and the far-

1. Actually the revolution of Sicily, January 1848, came first. It was the result largely of English influence and sympathy. The rebels against King Ferdinand ('Bomba') proclaimed for the island the constitution of 1812, which Lord William Bentinck had procured for them during the British occupation in the time of the First Napoleon.

spreading tide of new prosperity and well-being removed all fear of revolutionary contagion. The Chartist flame had been burning low for half a dozen years past, and its last flicker was the famous procession to Parliament in April 1848. So far from overawing Lords and Commons, the incident was more memorable for the alacrity with which the middle classes turned out as special constables than for any formidable display of working-class effervescence.

As between the foreign 'reds' and 'blacks' English sympathies were divided and lukewarm. It was difficult to understand what was going on across the Channel, but there was satisfaction in the thought that we were not as other nations. Our social and political troubles, it was held, lay behind us, wisely solved in advance – by Queen Elizabeth, William of Orange, Pitt, Lord Grey, Mr Cobden, or Sir Robert Peel, according to choice – and above all by the calm good sense of the British people. In the middle of the European revolutions the first part of Macaulay's history was published, and attained at once a popularity and influence analogous to that of Scott, Byron, or Dickens. There were many grounds for its success, but one was that it presented a reasoned eulogy of Britain and things British as that age understood them. Nor could the historian resist the temptation of inserting a passage proudly contrasting 1688 at home with 1848 abroad.

This same feeling of self-satisfaction, or pious thanksgiving, underlay the emotions of Englishmen three years later at Prince Albert's Great Exhibition, held under the glass pleasure-dome in Hyde Park. The unfortunate Europeans, having failed to master our secret of combining liberty with order, were invited, as a consolation prize, to come and admire the peace, progress, and prosperity of Britain. The Great Exhibition, the first of many such in all the capitals of Europe, began a new era of international trade advertisement.

Although in 1848 there had been English sympathizers with each of the opposing parties on the Continent, there had been no movement to wage war on behalf either of foreign princes or of foreign peoples. There was no Burke among the Conservatives of that day. And the more advanced Liberals were restrained from the crusading spirit by the peace doctrines of the Manchester school, then at the height of its influence during the years between its Corn Law triumph and its Crimean catastrophe. Mazzini, the noblest of the many exiles than sheltering in our island, altogether failed to persuade England that it was her interest as the leading Liberal power to fight for the victory of freedom in Europe. But on the Continent all men believed that the sympathy and moral weight of Great Britain was, if not friendly to the revolutionaries, at least hostile to the despots, and particularly to all things Austrian. This impression was mainly due to the personal policy of the Foreign Minister, Lord Palmerston.

Palmerston was very seldom out of office between 1808 and 1865, but he never lost his boyish enjoyment of life. The older he grew in the Foreign Office, the less was he restrained by its courtesies and traditions. The awful burden of public care had early marked Pitt and Peel as men set aside from their fellows. But Palmerston was untamed by fifty years of social responsibility and routine. This was part of the secret of his power. Between the abolition of the Corn Laws and the second Reform Bill serious political issues were at a discount, and people liked to watch 'Old Pam' performing with such obvious zest, nonchalance, and courage. Here plainly was a big man, yet one cast in the common mould, whose thoughts and motives everyone could understand, in contrast with the rival enigmas of Disraeli and Gladstone.

Palmerston became a national institution on his own account. Though in alliance with the Whigs since 1830, he was at heart neither Whig, Tory nor Peelite. In so far as he adhered to the doctrines of any party, he may be said to have remained a follower of Canning. Like his dead leader, he trusted the English people and rested his power on appeals to public opinion, while somewhat inconsistently opposing Parliamentary Reform. Throughout the period of his greatest influence, he kept the Whig–Liberal party bound to a domestic policy almost as negative as that of Walpole. Russell's spasmodic and half-hearted attempts to extend the franchise fell flat on the indifference of the public and the hostility of his most powerful colleague. Radicals like Bright, who were in real earnest about Parliamentary Reform, regarded Palmerston's commanding position in the counsels of the Liberal party as more fatal to progress than the official opposition of avowed Conservatives. They wished in vain that he would cross the floor of the House. They could only wait until he died, and he was an unconscionably long time about dying.

On the other hand, in foreign politics he was at once a Radical and a Jingo. Whenever there was a despot to be insulted, he joyfully insulted him, but always in the name of Britain's power and renown. He held it a disgrace that we should not speak our mind on Austrian atrocities, for of whom or of what should we be afraid ? If a British subject was ill-treated, were it only a Gibraltar Jew of doubtful honesty like Don Pacifico in Greece, he risked a breach with France to support the man's most extravagant claims, and appealed to the British public on the theme of protecting the 'Civis Romanus' all the world over. Such levity was quite as shocking to Peel and Aberdeen as to Cobden and Bright, and even Disraeli thought it misplaced. But Palmerston triumphed over them all.

He inherited from Canning the tendency of his policy, but not the practical wisdom of his measures. As Foreign Minister he achieved nothing tangible for the cause of liberty.[1] In 1848 his chief object was to prevent a European war. Although the year before he had sent Lord Minto on tour through Italy to encourage the Liberals there, when the crisis came he asked France and Charles Albert of Piedmont not to march to the help of the Milanese against the Austrians. If Charles Albert had taken that piece of advice, Italy would never have been united under his son. Again, in 1849 Palmerston approved the invasion of Hungary by Russia, much to the disgust of the Manchester men, who thought that he was violent when he should be moderate, and acquiescent when he should protest. But with all his faults, it was owing to him, to his generosity and to his open speech, that Britain's name was associated with the cause of freedom at a time when our public opinion was wavering, and when our Court and official influences were mainly on the side of reaction abroad.

In his conduct at the Foreign Office, Palmerston was under the fire not only of the regular Conservative Opposition and of the small Manchester group, but of his Whig and Peelite colleagues. Those of them who, like Russell, shared his liberal sympathies, dreaded his headlong methods, and all of them resented his attempt to withdraw the Foreign Office from Cabinet control, and to make himself alone answerable to the public for its policy. On one occasion the Cabinet held a special meeting to forbid him to receive the exile Kossuth in his house, but could not prevent him from openly demonstrating his sympathies, or from declaring that a less popular visitor to our land, the Austrian Field-Marshal Haynau, flogger of women, ought to have been 'tossed in a blanket'.

The statesman who was most of all opposed to him in temper and opinion was Lord Aberdeen. Trained in the school first of Wellington, and then of Peel, Aberdeen was now chiefly anxious to maintain the peace of Europe, which he believed could only be prolonged if existing boundaries were respected. An affection for the treaties

1. He was Prime Minister in 1859–60, but it was Russell as Foreign Secretary who helped Cavour through the crisis that made Italy.

of Vienna, however laudable from a Pacificist point of view, necessarily involved a friendly neutrality towards Austria and the despotic cause.[1]

Last but not least, Palmerston had to deal with the Court. The Queen had in 1840 married Prince Albert of Saxe-Coburg-Gotha. Her personal sympathies, which she could seldom distinguish from her political inclinations, were instinctively on the side of all German-speaking princes. In her mind, Milan, Venice, and Hungary were the possessions of the Austrian Emperor, and there was an end of the matter. Coached by Prince Albert, who had mastered European politics among so many other subjects, she tried to control Palmerston. She established the point that his dispatches must be submitted to her before they were sent off, and in this way she and her husband, who were not afraid of detail and hard work, were able to contest the foreign policy of the country inch by inch and day by day. But she had learned Melbourne's constitutional doctrine thoroughly, and never attempted to override her Ministers' policy if it proved to be the settled determination of the Cabinet as a whole.

Nevertheless, when the public began to find out that Albert was opposing Palmerston, there was a loud outcry against the interference of a German princeling in British policy, and questions were asked as to the constitutional position of the Queen's husband. It was a subject at once delicate and obscure. If Queen Elizabeth had ever married, or if Queen Anne's husband had been less negligible, there might have been a happier and more informing precedent than that afforded by Philip of Spain. In this case the problem was shelved rather than solved, first by the good sense of Prince Albert, and finally by his death in 1861. In home affairs his influence over the Queen was on the whole liberal; he greatly admired Peel, was a strong free-trader, and took more interest in scientific and commercial progress and less in sport and fashion than was at all popular in the best society.

Palmerston was the last man in the world to be browbeaten or cajoled by royalty. There was in him much of the aristocrat but nothing of the snob. Whiggish in his sympathies with continental Liberalism, he had developed a knack of appealing directly to British popular opinion that was too modern, too 'jingo', and

1. Aberdeen, as Wellington's lieutenant, 1830–33, had been very unpacific in his hostility to France and Louis Phillipe, while Palmerston, as Grey's colleague, had been pacific and pro-French. Later their parts were reversed. Aberdeen, as Peel's lieutenant, learnt to love peace and to tolerate Louis Philippe, with whom Palmerston, as Whig Foreign Minister in the forties, was always quarrelling.

too democratic to be pure Whig. After his fashion he stimulated a new popular interest in foreign questions, and put the Foreign Office more directly in touch with opinion outside the circles of the privileged. Strong in the people's support, he played on the whole a winning game for a dozen years against Court and colleagues. But he had several bad falls in the course of it; and these accidents occurred always when he had put himself for the moment out of touch with popular opinion by too great deference to Napoleon III.

His first great mistake was when, in December 1851, he was too hasty in expressing approval of Napoleon's *coup d'état*. He had not waited to observe that it was strongly condemned not only by Crown and Cabinet, whom he was accustomed to defy, but by the people of England who alone kept him in power. He had against him, for the moment, both the pro-Austrian and the Radical party. Russell seized the opportunity to dismiss from the Foreign Office a colleague who was attempting to become a dictator. But only two months afterwards Palmerston was boasting that he 'had his tit for tat with John Russell' by turning out the Whigs. After a brief interlude of Conservative government in 1852, Aberdeen's Whig–Peelite coalition received Palmerston back into the ministerial fold, in time for him to help to make the Crimean War.

By the *coup d'état*, Louis Napoleon, nephew of Napoleon I and President of the French Republic, usurped despotic authority, and shortly afterwards became Emperor with the title of Napoleon III. It is at least arguable that something analogous to the *coup d'état* was unavoidable. The reactionary Chamber which it overthrew was a danger to the State: it was clinging to power after it had lost popularity, like the Rump when dismissed by Oliver. And Napoleon in the early part of his reign as Emperor was a good deal more popular than Cromwell ever was as Protector. He had thrust himself in between the Reactionary and Republican parties, neither of whom really stood on a broad basis of public opinion, and both of whom acquiesced sulkily in his usurpation because they hated each other worse than either hated him. On the one side the new Emperor represented the Catholic and anti-socialist reaction that followed on the events of 1848, while on the other he gave security against the more extreme forms of reaction after which the Royalist parties hankered. He stood for the equality of all Frenchmen under government, which they valued more than freedom.

Nevertheless the *coup d'état*, accompanied as it was by a wholly unnecessary slaughter in the streets of Paris resulting from military mismanagement, destroyed Napoleon's pretensions to a moral position before the world. Now in some respects he aspired to a moral position, and he certainly needed one more than his uncle, who had had so many other resources. In his lifetime few gave credit to this 'cut-purse of the Empire' for the idealism and philanthropy that were blended with his inordinate personal ambition.

Like his uncle, Napoleon III appealed to the average Frenchman against the extreme parties in the State. And like his uncle he appealed to the professional feeling of the soldiers, and to the national desire for glory. A spirited foreign policy was essential to any Napoleonic régime. But was it to be conducted in the Liberal or the Catholic interest? He himself, a partisan by conviction of nationality and progress, preferred to fight in Liberal causes; but his wife and chief supporters wanted Catholic crusades. His two-fold interference in Italy, against Austria but on behalf of the Pope, was a self-contradiction ultimately fatal to France. Those who feel equally bound to fight on both sides of a quarrel would find it safer, from a selfish point of view, to stay at home.

But on one point he was determined. He would never quarrel with England. A great student of history, he had underlined for his own avoidance those of his uncle's mistakes which he was wise enough to detect. He read that hostility to England had lost France her colonies, and had in the end destroyed the Napoleonic power. Since he aspired to reconstruct a colonial empire in Africa and America, as well as to make France the leading country in Europe, he regarded it as a first condition that he should be friends with England. The weakness of the scheme, which became apparent in the last half of his reign, was that, in so far as he succeeded in his Colonial and European projects, England was sure to become jealous. Her hearty alliance could not be given to a Power that aspired to primacy.

Though there was often talk of war, England never came to blows with Napoleon. But the English would never believe that he honestly meant them well, though history has proved it in the retrospect. The very name of Napoleonic Empire frightened us. Even if we could have trusted him personally – and it was not easy to trust the author of the *coup d'état* – we could not see the Colonial and European power of France increasing year by year without grave misgivings about the future. Who could guarantee the attitude of the next emperor? Even those Englishmen who knew enough of Napoleon to trust him believed that France loved us little. The traditional feud with England had not yet been overlaid by a fiercer hatred of the Germans. Napoleon's life seemed our only security. So when Cobden and Bright preached confidence in French intentions, they did not always carry conviction.

But in the early fifties there was another Power whom we feared and distrusted even more than France. Since the interference of the Tsar Nicholas in Hungary in 1849, the shadow of Russia seemed to lie over Europe as well as over Asia. Napoleon, who was looking out for an adventure, was anxious to draw England along with him, for if not herself involved in any enterprise he might undertake she would certainly suspect and oppose it. He saw his opportunity in an anti-Russian alliance, which was the more attractive to him as he had a personal score to pay off against Nicholas.

So in 1853 we had to choose between our two bugbears – the Emperor Napoleon and the Tsar – both of whom sought our friendship. The Balance of Power, according to the British view of that decade, was threatened by France and by Russia severally. When Bright said that the Balance of Power was a fetish, he was wrong in theory if he held it to be a thing indifferent, but right in practice because the balance then actually existed if we had been content to leave well alone. Our difficulty in deciding whether France or Russia was the danger showed how nicely adjusted the balance really was.

It is impossible to seek the real causes of the Crimean War in its ostensible object, for the terms of settlement between Russia and Turkey, which we ourselves proposed in the 'Vienna note' of July 1853, were accepted by the Tsar and refused by the Sultan! Thus, without real object or occasion, we slid into war, contrary to the policy of the peace-loving Premier, Lord Aberdeen, but much to the satisfaction of his colleagues, Palmerston and Russell.

Although one result of our Crimean folly was to prolong Turkish rule over the Christian races of the Balkans,[1] the motive was not love of the Turks, to whom we were indifferent. The motives were, first a desire for military adventure that seized the English people after forty years of peace, a mood that involved a very dangerous doctrine of war for war's sake, clearly stated at the time in Tennyson's 'Maud'; the pacific ideals of the Great Exhibition of three years before were thrown to the winds, and it was said that what England wanted was not 'a good peace' but 'a good war'. The second motive was the theory of the Balance of Power,

1. In the first months of 1853, before the events leading to the war had shaped themselves, the Tsar Nicholas had talked to our Ambassador at St Petersburg about Turkey as 'the sick man', for whose certain death provision must be made. He proposed that England should take Egypt, and that Servia and Bulgaria should be independent principalities. The proposal was rejected as highly immoral.

and a belief that Europe and Asia were in danger of Russian aggression; Russell told the House of Commons that we were fighting 'to maintain the independence of Germany, and of all European nations'. The third motive, not entirely distinguishable from the second, was the Liberal hatred of the 'Cossack Tsar', his tyranny over the Poles and his reactionary influence in Europe, especially his suppression of Hungarian liberties. It is true that Palmerston had at the time condoned his interference in Hungary, and that our statesmen refused to hold out any hopes to Poland in connexion with the war. But the belief that we were fighting for liberty was genuine among the British people.

Nor can it be denied that the war helped in the long run to liberate Italy, for it drove Russia out of Central European politics and enhanced the influence of France. In this sense the blood shed in the Crimea was not shed in vain, though Balkan Christians might have had a different point of view. But the results so advantageous for Italy came about as much by chance as by design. For at the beginning of the war we made every endeavour to induce Austria to fight on our side, and, if Austria had consented, it would have been more difficult for France and England a few years later to take a leading part in depriving her of her Italian possessions. As it was, Austria's neutrality left her isolated during the next critical decade, for it alienated not only France and England, but Russia, who had also claimed the help of Francis Joseph in return for the Hungarian campaign of 1849.

When Austria refused to join us, Count Cavour, the ablest of European statesmen, already Prime Minister of young King Victor Emmanuel of Piedmont, stepped into Austria's place, and sent the Bersaglieri to fight by the side of the French and British Guards before Sebastopol. The one man besides Napoleon III who really knew what he was doing in the whole affair, the Minister of this little State with a population of five millions, secured to the Crimean War a Liberal character and Liberal consequences which it would certainly not have had if our statesmen had succeeded in their efforts to persuade Austria to take part.

The capture of Sebastopol, the great Crimean arsenal from which the Russian fleets dominated the Black Sea, was chosen as the allied objective. It was attained after a year's campaign and siege. This constituted practically all the war, except a futile naval expedition to the Baltic, and the gallant but finally unsuccessful defence of Kars in Armenia by the Turks under the Englishman Fenwick Williams.

Sebastopol would have been taken within a few days of the landing of the French and English in the Crimea if they had chosen to march into it at once from the north. But the French general, St Arnaud, who surpassed Lord Raglan in incompetence, insisted, even after the initial victory of the Alma, that the allies should march round the fortress to the south side and begin a siege in form. The enemy were given time to throw in reinforcements, and to prepare the defence works under the great engineer Todleben.

The besiegers were soon put on the defensive. They were unable to invest the town from more than one side, and were outnumbered by the arrival of fresh Russian field armies. The British, on the right, were most exposed to the attacks of these forces, and bore the brunt of the defensive battles of Balaclava and Inkerman. The first of these, celebrated for two gallant cavalry charges commemorated by Tennyson, and the second consisting of a desperate infantry action at close quarters in the mists of a November dawn, demonstrated that the British soldier could fight as well as ever. But he was without tents, huts, knapsacks, healthy food, or the most elementary medical provision. The little British army nearly disappeared in the 'Crimean winter', as a result of the breakdown of organized supply and transport. The French, and the Italians when

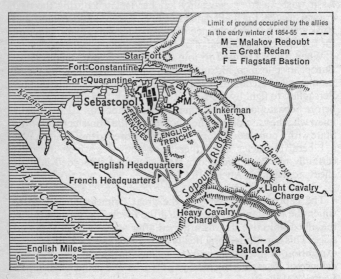

they subsequently arrived, were better off in these respects. The Russians, with whom official incompetence was a matter of course, were perishing by myriads on the long route marches to the Crimea.

That a nation leading the world in new methods of industrial organization should be unable to provide for twenty thousand soldiers half a dozen miles distant from her fleet in the port of Balaclava would be incredible without some knowledge of the army and the army chiefs of that time. The breath of reform, which was transmuting commerce, Parliament, Municipalities, Church, and education, had left the army untouched. The services which the army had rendered against Napoleon seemed to imply that it needed no reform. And the pacific atmosphere of the intervening age drew away public attention from things military. The Duke of Wellington, who died in 1852, had been Commander-in-Chief for many years, and had used his matchless authority to preserve the army in all things as like as possible to the great instrument with which he had conquered Napoleon. While the arts of peace were being revolutionized by ever new devices in machinery and organization, the Duke saw to it that the cannon, the muskets, the drill, the discipline, and the strategy of war remained unchanged. Even abuses, like the purchase of commissions and the overlapping of authorities were as dear to him as to the smaller men around him. The efficient staff and the good generals who had served him in the Peninsula had disappeared, and no effort had been made to train their successors. Fortunately the splendid regimental traditions which were the great bequest of Wellington's campaigns remained over to save us in the Crimea and to be transmitted with fresh honours – the names of Alma and Inkerman added on the flags to those of Vitoria and Waterloo – to keep alive in the records of the regiments the soul of an army not accustomed to yield.

The deficiencies in military preparation were due both to the obscurantist spirit of the Horse Guards and the War Office, and to the economic spirit of the Treasury and the public. One thing the Duke had been asking for during the last years of his life – a larger army. And Ministry after Ministry, in full accord with the general sentiment, had refused it. Nor did the Duke, who did not believe in democracy or in journalism, ever willingly head an agitation to educate public opinion.[1]

That age enjoyed a blessing of which ours has known too little –

1. The fact that the Duke was asking for an army increase only came out in 1847 because one of the Duke's letters was published, much to his indignation. There was a momentary panic, but the Ministry and public found in the fall of Louis Philippe a good excuse for abandoning an increased army budget.

freedom from competitive armaments. It could scarcely then expect military efficiency when war came at last. After all it did not very much matter if many of the regiments still used smooth-bore muskets, even though the value of rifles in war had been demonstrated over and over again for nearly a hundred years past. There was security in the fact that other powers were equally improvident. The philosopher may well regret that the nations did not agree to go on fighting with smooth-bores for yet another century!

It was not, however, necessary that our whole army should perish in the trenches before Sebastopol for want of shelter, clothes, food, and medicine. The remnants of the force were saved, reinforced, and supplied owing to two developments characteristic of the new age. One was the newspaper correspondent, a person unknown in Walcheren or the Peninsula. The other was a modern army hospital under Florence Nightingale.

William Russell of *The Times* exposed the state of things he saw before Sebastopol with a freedom which would not have been permitted either in earlier or later wars, and which in fact revealed much to the enemy. But the value of his work, in the circumstances, far outweighed any attendant disadvantage. Nothing but public exposure could have shaken the military authorities of that day out of their lethargy. *The Times* informed and roused the British people only just in time to save the army. One result of the agitation was the fall of Aberdeen, long unpopular as a pacifist, and the substitution of the more energetic Palmerston as Prime Minister.

But ere that, a still more important measure had been taken by Sidney Herbert, Aberdeen's Secretary at War. He had sent out Florence Nightingale in an official capacity. The fury of the British public over Russell's revelations caused all successive War Ministers to give her such a measure of support that she was able to put her foot on the dragon of official obscurantism at the front. The triumph of a woman at the seat of war over highly placed officers and hoary military traditions would be astounding in any age, and then seemed miraculous. But Miss Nightingale was a woman of administrative genius, and of more than masculine force of character, the stronger for the calm dignity of its outward manifestation. She saved the sick and wounded of the British army in spite of its medical chiefs by creating at Scutari a modern base hospital, the first of its kind, with trained women nurses and necessary material. She brought down the death rate at Scutari from forty-two per cent to twenty-two per thousand.

She emerged from the war with the only great reputation on our side. For the rest it was a 'soldiers' war', deadly to the good name of generals and of statesmen. Miss Nightingale used the position she had acquired in the hearts of her fellow-countrymen to make permanent changes in our national life. She saw to it that her work should not be a mere picturesque incident in the history of a single war, but that her methods should become an institutional part of normal civilized activities. Though she was now an invalid confined to her sofa, she ruled and legislated unseen. With the help of her friend, Sidney Herbert, again War Minister in the early sixties, she remodelled the Army Medical Service, and reformed barrack accommodation.

It was not only all future generations of British soldiers who were to bless her name. The Red Cross movement all over the world, starting from the Geneva Convention of 1864, was the outcome of her work and influence. So, too, were the great reforms in civilian hospital construction and management, and the establishment for the general public of nursing by trained women in place of the horrors of Mrs Gamp. Florence Nightingale's life gave a personal impulse, at once emotional and administrative, to the contemporary advance of science on its humanitarian side.

Whatever Italy or anyone else may have got out of the Crimean war, England's gain from it was the life work of this woman – an immense acquisition of moral territory, if all its secondary consequences and ramifications be followed out. Modern hospital work in peace and war owes to this Crimean episode the saving of many more lives than the 25,000 that Britain lost on the shores of the Euxine, of which Miss Nightingale ascribed 16,000 to bad administration. To her work was due a new conception of the potentiality and place of the trained and educated woman.[1] And this in turn led, in the sixties and seventies, to John Stuart Mill's movement for woman's suffrage, which Miss Nightingale supported, and to the founding of women's colleges, when at length some provision was made for the desperately neglected higher education of one-half of the Queen's subjects.

In September 1855 Sebastopol fell, after the Malakoff earthwork had been stormed by the French, and the British had failed before the Redan. The honours of the battles lay with England, of the siege with France. The French had been in the greater numbers, and their organization had never collapsed so miserably as ours.

1. Mr Cook quotes a letter from Lady Verney, dated April 1856: 'What Florence has done towards raising the standard of women's capabilities and work is most important. It is quite curious every day how questions arise regarding them which are answered quite differently from what they would have been eighteen months ago.'

France emerged from the war as the leading power in Europe, as Napoleon had planned. He had got what he wanted from the Crimea, but his very success made it doubtful if he could retain the friendship of England.

It was the ruler of France who, thus satisfied, forced the unwilling Palmerston to make peace. In March 1856 the Treaty of Paris ended the war. Turkey was set on her legs again, both in the Balkans and Armenia, with the formal recommendation to be kind to her Christian subjects. Russia was prohibited from keeping warships or arsenals in the Black Sea; in 1870 she treated this restriction on her sovereignty as a scrap of paper, England vainly protesting.

At the general Congress of Powers that followed the signature of peace, Cavour, with France and England as patrons, succeeded in having the sufferings of Italy discussed, to the rage of the Austrian representative, who saw the future that a discussion on such terms portended.

At the same congress an important step was taken in international law. The Declaration of Paris, to which England together with the other powers adhered, laid it down that privateering should be abolished, that a neutral flag should cover enemy goods if not contraband of war, and that blockades to be valid in theory must be effective in practice.

If British prestige had on the whole lost by the Crimea, the loss was speedily made good by the events of the Indian Mutiny, where all that is most competent in statesmanship and soldiering was represented by the men on whom fell the sudden burden of the crisis.

CHAPTER 20

THE struggle with Napoleon, which in the days of his expedition to Egypt had threatened the British rule in India,[1] in its later stages gave to Britain the monopoly of power and trade throughout the East. In India itself the allies of France had fallen one by one, when Lord Wellesley destroyed 'Tippoo Sahib', and curbed the Marathas. And in the next ten years the commercial war between England and Napoleonic Europe drove the French, Dutch, and other European merchantmen off the India and China seas. The

1. See p. 117, above.

Cape, Mauritius, and Ceylon fell permanently into our hands, and until the end of the war we held the Dutch Empire in the Eastern Archipelago.[2]

A new sense of the security of our rule in the East, together with the fulness of the Company's money chest, led to progressive improvement in the methods of the British Raj. The noble traditions of the Indian Civil Service were created by public servants like Sir Charles Metcalfe and the Scots sent out in such numbers by Dundas. Though still owing their original appointments to a system of personal favour and political patronage, they were already of a very different type from the parasites and adventurers through whom and against whom Clive and Warren Hastings so often had to work. In the first twenty years of the new century our administration already afforded, within its own area, security from the ravages of war, brigandage, and the worst forms of domestic oppression. Local police and local courts were instituted, and a standard of fair taxation and just government was set up, such as had not been known in Indian States. The British were entering into the third period of their relations with the East. A hundred and fifty years of quiet trading had been followed by fifty years of conquest not unaccompanied by plunder. The third period, of organized rule for the benefit of the Indians, had now fully set in.

The new era was marked by a readjustment of the privileges and powers of the East India Company. It was still preserved as the intermediary through which the British Cabinet Ministers preferred to govern, though its political power was a shadow. But the abolition in 1813 of its trading monopoly in India marked a big step in the direction of the new economic doctrine of open world competition, in place of the old conception of trade as a function of chartered and limited companies. Its trading monopoly in China was continued for another twenty years.

While inside the Company's territory reigned peace and justice novel to oriental States, beyond the border a dreadful anarchy had broken out through the whole of Central India. Though Lord Wellesley had curbed the Maratha power, it had not been finally broken, and his far-sighted plans for the permanent settlement of Central India by the system of 'subsidiary treaties' had not been carried through. In the supposed interests of peace and economy his successors had refused any longer to interest themselves in the disputes of princes outside British territory. This well-meant but retrograde policy of declining the responsibilities, after we had

2. See p. 147, above.

303

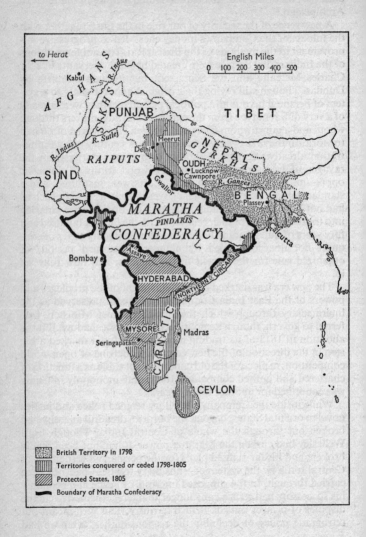

to Herat ←

AFGHANS

Kabul

R. Indus

SIKHS

PUNJAB

R. Indus

R. Sutlej

Delhi

RAJPUTS

SIND

Meerut

NEPAL

GURKHAS

TIBET

English Miles

0 100 200 300 400 500

OUDH

Lucknow

Cawnpore

R. Ganges

Gwalior

MARATHA

PINDARIS

CONFEDERACY

Bombay

Assaye

HYDERABAD

NORTHERN CIRCARS

MYSORE

CARNATIC

Seringapatam

Madras

BENGAL

Plassey

Calcutta

CEYLON

British Territory in 1798

Territories conquered or ceded 1798–1805

Protected States, 1805

Boundary of Maratha Confederacy

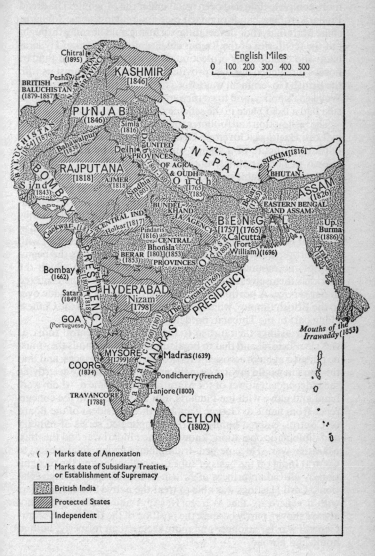

English Miles

0 100 200 300 400 500

Chitral (1895)

KASHMIR [1846]

Peshawar

BRITISH
BALUCHISTAN
(1879–1887)

NORTH WEST FRONTIER PROVINCE

PUNJAB (1846)

Simla (1816)

BALUCHISTAN (1854) (1876)

Bahawalpur (1838)

Delhi (1803)

DOAB

NEPAL

SIKKIM [1816]

UNITED PROVINCES OF AGRA (1803) (1801)

RAJPUTANA [1818]

AJMER 1818

Sindhia (1803)

& OUDH

BHUTAN

Oudh (1765) (1856)

ASSAM (1826)

BOMBAY

Sind (1843)

CENTRAL IND[IA AGENCY]

BUNDEL-
KHAND

Bahar (1765)

EASTERN BENGAL
AND ASSAM

Gaekwar (1817)

Holkar [1817]

Pindaris (1816)

BENGAL [1757] (1765)

Up. Burma (1886)

Bombay (1662)

PRESIDENCY

Peshwa (1802)

Satara (1849)

GOA (Portuguese)

CENTRAL
PROVINCES

BERAR (1853)

Bhonsla [1801] (1853)

ORISSA (1803)

Calcutta (Fort William) (1696)

Arakan

HYDERABAD

Nizam [1798]

Mouths of the
Irrawaddy (1853)

MYSORE [1799]

Madras (1639)

The Circars (1769)

PRESIDENCY

COORG (1834)

Karnatic (1801) (1801)

MADRAS

Pondicherry (French)

TRAVANCORE [1788]

Tanjore (1800)

CEYLON (1802)

( ) Marks date of Annexation

[ ] Marks date of Subsidiary Treaties,
or Establishment of Supremacy

British India

Protected States

Independent

T – B.H. – M

assumed the position of paramount power, resulted in anarchy more complete than had been usual under the Moghuls. The dread Pindaris, robber bands of mixed race and religion, some Afghans, some Marathas, rode devastating, torturing, and burning throughout the territories of the Rajput chiefs and the Nizam of Hyderabad, who claimed our protection as of right. Finally the Pindari hordes threatened our own province of Behar. Sore against its will, the British Government was forced to take up the broken thread of Wellesley's policy, and to go forward until every State in the peninsula had a fixed place in the scheme of the Pax Britannica.

The resumption and fulfilment of Wellesley's policy were effected by Lord Hastings, Governor-General from 1813 to 1823. With the tall athletic figure of a soldier and aristocrat, he had long been known in home politics, under the name of Lord Moira, as a rather unaccountable politician, the friend at once of the Prince of Wales and of the Irish people. He was to prove a great pro-consul. His initial task was to reduce the Gurkhas of Nepal, who had invaded our territory, to the state of friendly alliance in which they have remained ever since. It was the first campaign of the British in the great hill ranges bounding the peninsula, and our contact with the short-set warriors and mountaineers of Nepal was the beginning of the mountain craft of our Indian Army, in which the Gurkhas themselves afterwards took so great a part when enlisted in our service. A portion of their western territory was made over to the British Empire, which henceforth marched with the Chinese along part of the Thibetan border.

Lord Hastings then turned to the problem of Central India. It was clear beforehand that to break up the Pindari bands they must be pursued at large across the territories of many princes, and that this pursuit would involve us in the graver task of finally destroying the independent power of the Maratha chiefs, some of whom were hand and glove with the Pindaris. But Hastings, with the concurrence from home of George Canning, then President of the Board of Control, entered boldly on the complicated series of military and diplomatic operations known as the Pindari war and the third Maratha war. He emerged triumphant, giving final peace to Central India on the basis of subsidiary alliances and the recognition by all Indian princes of British overlordship in foreign relations. Lord Hastings was able to treat the native States and rulers with a generosity that Warren Hastings and Wellesley had not always shown, partly because the position of the British Governor-General was far stronger and more secure than formerly, both at home and abroad.

Between the departure of Lord Wellesley and the coming of Lord Hastings, we had given a fair trial to the system of a limited and local responsibility for what happened in India. It had broken down. Unwillingly and half unwittingly we shouldered the inevitable burden laid upon us by fate, no less a task than to give unity to the heterogeneous races of the sub-continent through the medium of the British rule and the English language.

The policy of accepting all responsibilities as paramount power in the Peninsula had involved us in the Maratha and Pindari wars and had achieved the settlement of Central India. The same principle involved us in the first Burmese war. The Burmese were in those days an aggressive military power that had never yet measured itself against an European army. They now occupied Assam, an outlying Indian State incapable of self-defence, and thence threatened and assailed British territory. Their reduction cost two years of difficult and expensive warfare that led to our protectorate over Assam and annexation of most of the sea-frontage of Burma. The rest of it was annexed by Lord Dalhousie after a second Burmese war in 1852, and Upper Burma, including Mandalay, in 1886.

In this way the guardianship of India led to the extension of our rule outside the Peninsula over a people of Thibeto-Chinese origin, differing from all the Indian races in habits and religion. This same guardianship over the external approaches to India was destined to involve us in relations with Persia, Afghanistan, and Thibet. But in none of those countries could the problem be solved by annexation, as in Burma, where the people proved singularly adaptable to the British methods of government, where access by sea and river was easy, and where no Great Power lay beyond.

After the first Burmese war there followed ten years of peace before the advance began again on the western frontier. This interlude takes character and unity from the policy of Lord William Bentinck, who represented in India at a propitious moment the liberal and humanitarian spirit of the new age in Europe. He made no change of policy, but he brought into fuller light a doctrine implicit in the theory and practice of his predecessors, namely, that the object of our Government in India was to promote the welfare of the Indians.

Bentinck successfully abolished Suttee – the burning of Hindoo widows – in despite of prophecies that this piece of interference with religious custom would endanger the State. He himself was anxious as to the result, but he was supported by reformers of

Indian birth, and the danger-point was safely passed. He also began the suppression of the Thugs, a caste of hereditary murderers who terrorized the roads. He promoted steam communications on the great rivers, and took many measures for the material prosperity of the millions committed to his care. He raised the status of officials of Indian birth, clearly perceiving that the British must train the Indians to the work of administration.

When in 1833–4 the monopoly of the China trade was abolished,[1] the East India Company ceased to be a trading concern, and retained merely the shadow of political power of which the substance had long ago passed to the Ministers of the Crown. The new charter embodied the tendency of Bentinck's policy in the words: 'No native of India, or any natural-born subject of His Majesty, shall be disabled from holding any place, office, or employment by reason of his religion, place of birth, descent, or colour.'

It was partly in relation to this question of preparing the Indians to help administer their own country that Bentinck approached the famous controversy which Macaulay's Education Minute decided. Macaulay was sent out in 1834 as the first Legal Member of Council under the new charter. He soon won the confidence and friendship of Bentinck. He drew up the Indian Penal Code, with lasting success. And he persuaded the Indian Government to adopt English instead of any oriental language as the medium of instruction in the scheme of State-aided higher education which Bentinck was pushing forward. The present position of India and the possibilities of its future have been deeply affected by this decision.

On the one hand the bringing up of orientals on an alien literature, largely devoted to the love of liberty in forms natural to an advanced Western democracy, has had many unhappy results. It has been said that 'we attempted to raise a race of administrators on the literature of revolt.' While another class of critic has pointed out that the contempt expressed in Macaulay's Minute for oriental learning was in large measure the result of ignorance and want of imaginative sympathy.

But it must be remembered on the other side that only the English language was capable of giving the races of India a common tongue for communication with each other and with the British. And it is arguable that, in spite of present dangers, the sense of Indian national unity which has resulted from this new *lingua franca* may in the end subserve the political and administrative welfare of the

1. See p. 303, above.

peninsula. The revival of Indian science, philosophy, and literature in our own day under such leaders as the Tagores is due in no small degree to their knowledge of the literature and science of Europe. The teaching of English has effected what we may, by historical analogy, call the 'renaissance' of Indian thought. And it is at least possible that, although the decision of 1835 has hastened the peculiar troubles of India as we now know them, it has prevented the growth of the worse trouble that must eventually have arisen from a deliberate policy of segregating the British and the Indians in water-tight compartments of thought and knowledge, so far as Government was able to do so, and endeavouring to prevent the spread of Western science and literature in a country governed by a progressive Western power. Such an attempt would largely have failed. Many natives were determined to obtain the educational key to Western learning, both for its own sake and because it was also necessarily the key to advancement in the Anglo-Indian world. Macaulay pointed out that already in 1835 'we are forced to pay our Arabic and Sanskrit students, while those who learn English are willing to pay us.' And Sir Charles Metcalfe in the same year, while foreseeing the unrest which Western learning would very likely cause in India, nevertheless declared 'It is our duty to extend knowledge whatever may be the result; and spread it would, even if we impeded it.'

Undoubtedly the new Anglo-Indian education partook too much of the literary as distinct from the practical, but in 1835 scientific education scarcely existed in England, and it could not therefore be improvised in India at that date. But the decision in favour of the English language rendered possible the subsequent development of scientific teaching and had been asked for on that express ground by the far-seeing Indian reformer, Raja Ram Mohan Roy. It may have been an evil that 'the literature of revolt' was put so lavishly into the hands of Indians, but, if the wrong text-books were chosen, that was a mistake in administration under Bentinck's successors, and was not implicit in the original decision that English should become the common language of educated India.

In 1838 the interlude of peace came to an end, and the north-westward expansion of British India was resumed, at first in circumstances disastrous and discreditable beyond any precedent in Anglo-Indian history. Lord Melbourne had, in an evil hour, appointed Lord Auckland as Bentinck's successor.

By this time the sense that Russia would ere long be a dangerous neighbour was beginning to be felt in India, while in England the Whig Ministers, from among whom Auckland came, had grown more and more hostile to Russia. Palmerston as Foreign Secretary regarded Tsar Nicholas, the oppressor of Poland, as the embodiment of encroaching military despotism, opposed both in principle and interest to the world-power of Britain. This Palmerstonian doctrine, which eventually led the Whigs round from the anti-Turkish sympathies of Fox and Grey to the policy of the Crimea, increased the growing uneasiness in India.

It would have been well indeed to provide against the ultimate arrival of Russia on the scene by preparing beforehand close and friendly relations with the warlike Afghan tribes, who, wisely handled, were capable of making their widespread labyrinth of mountains the most impassable of 'buffer' States between two great Empires. But Auckland determined to reduce Afghanistan to vassalage. He dethroned the able and popular Amir, Dost Mohammad, and attempted to rule the tribes through the agency of his rival, Shah Shuja. The policy at first met with apparent success, and for two years our troops occupied Kabul. Then the tribes rose on behalf of Dost Mohammad. The British forces, 15,000 strong including camp-followers, were destroyed in their retreat through the winter mountains. One survivor reached the fort at Jalalabad. This staggering defeat, followed as it necessarily was by the abandonment of the attempt to dethrone Dost Mohammad, shook our prestige and affected our relations with the Sikhs during the next half-dozen years, and with the Sepoys in the year of Mutiny.

The unsuccessful attack on Afghanistan was followed by the wars and annexations of Sinde and the Punjab, the two independent States of the river-plain then lying between the frontier of British India and the foot of the Afghan hills.

The Whig Ministers, the authors of the unfortunate attempt to dethrone Dost Mohammad, fell in 1841, and Peel's new Government sent out as Governor-General the able and headstrong Lord Ellenborough. After a campaign had taken place to rescue the prisoners and restore the honours of our arms, Ellenborough was fully prepared to withdraw from his predecessor's impossible undertakings in Afghanistan. But he himself carried through an equally aggressive though less impolitic interference with Sinde, which had come under British influence as a basis of recent operations against the Afghans. General Sir Charles Napier conquered the Amirs of Sinde at the battle of Meeanee, and then as administrator gave the advantages of British rule to their country. Its

310

annexation he described in his Diary as 'a very advantageous, useful, humane piece of rascality'.

The annexation of Sinde has often been stigmatized, with questionable justice, as the one case of unprovoked aggression in the expansion of British rule over India. No such bad eminence was attached to the conquest of the Punjab, which completed the subjugation of the river-lands of the north-west.

Sikh dominion over the Punjab rested on the military qualities of the dominant sect. The Sikhs, who had but one caste, were a democratic religious brotherhood of what may, by analogy, be called 'Protestant' Hindoos. They were embittered against Islam by an ancient history of revolt against the persecuting Moghuls of Delhi. For many years past the Sikhs had been guarding the gates of India, preventing the debouchment on to the plains of Mohammedan hill tribes or of invaders from Central Asia. For the last half-century the barbaric craft and valour of Ranjit Singh had given unity to the Sikh State. He had had the wisdom to keep friends with the British, and the strength to hold in awe his turbulent vassals and legionaries. He had even joined with us for objects of his own in the Afghan adventure. His death in 1839, like the death of Oliver Cromwell, let loose an anarchy of fanatical regimental officers, intriguing against each other in rival committees. The great military machine, that only Ranjit had had the power to keep idle, began –

> To eat into itself for lack
> Of somebody to hew and hack.

To save the tottering State, Ranjit's widow launched the army across the Sutlej to meet the British, and slay or else be slain.

The two Sikh wars that followed were characterized by more severe fighting than any that the British and sepoys had formerly had to face. The European arms and training that Ranjit Singh had given to his stubborn religionists enabled them to contend on nearly equal terms with the Queen's and the Company's regiments. But once General Gough had broken the army, the Punjab was subdued with ease.[1]

The Sikhs had begun the second war in revolt against a generous settlement granted them after their first reduction. They were punished by the annexation of the Punjab, decreed by Lord Dalhousie, who was just beginning his great period of office as Governor-General. The rule of the brothers Henry and John

1. The chief battles were – Moodkee, Firozshah, Sobraon, Dec. 1845 to Feb. 1846; and Chillianwallah and Goojerat in Jan. and Feb. 1849.

Lawrence in the Punjab prepared the loyalty of the Sikh nation against the unexpected trial of the Mutiny year, and created a tradition which went far to cancel any recent symptoms of weakness or violence in the British Raj.

The Governor-Generalship of Lord Dalhousie saw the completion of the internal and external framework of British India. The second Burmese war resulted in the annexation of Rangoon and the mouths of the Irrawady, where the new government became so popular that in the year of Mutiny it was safe to strip Burma of British troops.

Progress and Reform were the watchword of the hour in the British Eastern possessions. It was characteristic that in 1853 the Indian Government accepted wholesale Macaulay's proposals for the throwing open of the Indian Civil Service to free competition, thereby sacrificing the kind of patronage which British statesmen would not surrender as regards the Home Civil Service, save grudgingly and by stages during the next seventeen years.

Dalhousie, bold in his reforming zeal, disturbed the deep conservatism of the native mind. Railways and telegraphs, with which he covered India, were a terrible and suspected magic. But if they helped to cause the Mutiny they more certainly helped to quell it: the mutineers called the telegraph wire 'the string that strangled us'. Then again the evangelizing zeal of some of the best Englishmen in India, lay as well as clerical, helped to alienate the Brahmans. Western influence was making itself increasingly felt in many different ways, and could not fail to cause alarm and reaction.

In taking thought for the welfare of the subjects of Native States, Dalhousie favoured a policy of gradual annexation. He laid down the rule that, in the case of a prince dying without natural heirs, his sovereign rights should 'lapse' to the paramount power, so that the British Government could, for reasons of public policy, annex the State if it so wished, instead of allowing an adopted heir to succeed. In accordance with this 'doctrine of lapse', as it was called, several Native States were added to the Company's territories, while Oudh was annexed simply on account of gross maladministration. It followed that Oudh, in the Upper Ganges valley, became the centre of Indian discontent. The mutiny, when it came, was localized round that region and confined to the Bengal army. Dalhousie's policy, strong and just if somewhat over-eager, had ensured the respect and loyalty of the great Native States of the centre and south, as well as of the sepoy armies of Bombay and

Madras. And, thanks to Dalhousie and the Lawrences, the newly acquired North-Western frontier, where trouble might most naturally be expected from the lately conquered Sikhs and the lately victorious Afghans,[1] became in the hour of need the chief source of strength and safety.

Dost Mohammad, whom we had so foolishly and vainly tried to keep off the throne of Afghanistan, had not unnaturally been our enemy during the Sikh wars. But in 1855 Dalhousie and John Lawrence made a treaty of friendship with him, and next year Dalhousie's successor, Lord Canning, protected him from attack by the Persians, who had been stirred up by Russia to occupy Herat in Western Afghanistan. Canning sent an expedition to the Persian coast, captured Bushire, and caused the evacuation of Herat. Grateful for this relief, Dost Mohammad, during the Mutiny in the ensuing summer, kept Afghanistan friendly for Britain, a fact of supreme importance.

Meanwhile, the Sikhs of the Punjab received at the hands of John and Henry Lawrence the kind of government that speedily reconciled them to British rule. The brothers, differing on a question of policy, agreed to send in their resignations on the same day, for Dalhousie's decision. He decided to leave John as sole Commissioner for the Punjab, and removed Henry, who, when the Mutiny broke out, was found at the storm centre of Lucknow as Chief Commissioner for Oudh. His predecessor there had been tactless, but owing to his better management the local magnates of Oudh did not throw in their lot with the military mutiny at the outset, when such a junction might have had terrible results.

The Mutiny, as its historic name implies, was a rising of soldiers, not a revolt of civilians. Nevertheless, there were social, racial, and political causes for the soldiers' discontent. It was felt all over India that change and Westernization were being pushed on too fast, but the feeling was strongest in recently annexed Oudh. The Bengal army was largely recruited in that region from among high-caste Brahmans and Rajputs peculiarly sensitive to grievances, both general and personal.

In 1856 a new enactment that all sepoys who enlisted in future must be prepared to cross the sea if required had aroused among them fresh fears of outrage on caste. At the same time the belief that the cartridges for the new Enfield rifle were being greased with the fat of the sacred cow and the abhorred pig united Hindoo and Mohammedan sepoys against us. Since the rumour was based on fact, due to an unfortunate oversight, the situation was scarcely

1. pp. 310–12, above.

improved by Government denial, though made in good faith. All Eastern armies are liable to become overbearing in peace-time after a long course of conquest, and the Bengal army felt themselves to be the lords of India. Above all, in spite of Dalhousie's protests, the proportion of British to Indian troops in the peninsula was still as one to five, and most of the artillery was in the hands of sepoys.

The Mutiny of the Bengal army began at Meerut. Its immediate occasion was a display of unwise severity by incompetent officers, who did not know how to quell the storm they had raised. Some of the mutineers made straight for Delhi, where there was not a single British regiment. Delhi fell into the hands of the movement, Lucknow all except the Residency, and Cawnpore after three weeks of gallant defence. It was in this Upper Ganges region that the issue was fought out and won during the summer of 1857, by the little band of British then actually in India, and by the Indian troops faithful to their cause. Their boast that 'alone we did it' is substantially true, though there were many months of severe fighting after the arrival of reinforcements from England.

The old King of Delhi was dragged into the limelight and proclaimed Moghul Emperor by the mutineers, an act which gave a Mohammedan complexion to the movement in that region. It did not at once break up the union of Mussulman and Hindoo, on which the hopes of the Mutiny rested, but the news of it in the Punjab had the effect of throwing the wavering Sikhs heartily on to our side. They had no wish to see their old Mohammedan oppressors once more lording it over India, and were prepared to march to the storm of the Moghul capital.

Thenceforward the newly conquered Punjab instead of being a danger became the base whence Delhi was reconquered. Nothing was to be feared from the Afghans under Dost Mohammad, and John Lawrence found himself free to send the already almost mythical Nicholson and his column to aid the little army that was clinging to the Ridge outside Delhi. Again and again the defenders of the Ridge had beaten back the assault of overwhelming numbers of mutineers issuing from the city gates. The arrival of Nicholson's small reinforcements with siege guns emboldened them to attack and capture the city with its myriads of armed fanatics. This amazing adventure began on 14 September with the blowing in of the Kashmir gate, and after six days' street fighting, in the course of which Nicholson was killed, Delhi remained in the hands of the British. It was the decisive moment of the Mutiny.

At Lucknow early in July Sir Henry Lawrence had been killed by a shell, but his work and influence survived to inspire the defence of the Residency, which he had organized and begun. In September, a few days after the capture of Delhi, Havelock and Neill, who had already reconquered Cawnpore and had now been joined by Outram, effected the first relief or rather reinforcement of Lucknow, fighting their way through the town into the Residency.

As yet no soldier had landed from England, but in November the troops from England under Sir Colin Campbell again relieved the Lucknow Residency after desperate street fighting, and enabled the garrison to evacuate that glorious ruin in safety. In March 1858 the city of Lucknow was finally captured by Sir Colin. The end was now in sight, but an unfortunate proclamation by the Governor-General threatening to forfeit lands in Oudh threw the local magnates at length on to the side of rebellion, too late to affect the issue, but with the result of prolonging the strife.

Meanwhile, in the early months of 1858, Sir Hugh Rose, by his brilliant campaign crowned by the victory of Gwalior, stamped out the flame in Central India before it was able to spread to the South. If we had failed at Lucknow and Delhi it might have been different, but in fact Western, Eastern, and Southern India remained loyal – all Sinde, Punjab, and Assam; most of Bengal; all Madras and Bombay; Rajputana under the guidance of George, the third of the Lawrence brothers; the Native States of Mysore and Hyderabad, and the Maratha princes. Dalhousie's 'doctrine of lapse' was abandoned after the Mutiny, and the Native States were thenceforth regarded as essential buttresses of the structure of British India.

It had been a mutiny of part of the sepoy army, not a racial rebellion. This makes it the more regrettable that the struggle had been so ferocious as to leave bitter memories. It was difficult to restore the sense of 'glad confident morning again', in the relations of Englishmen and Indians. Nana Sahib, once the pet of London drawing-rooms, had, in circumstances of treachery almost as horrid as the cruelty itself, massacred the white women and children at Cawnpore. His crime had the effect he intended of giving to the conflict something of the nature of a war of colour. There were reprisals, though only against men. And a limit was set to revenge by the wisdom of 'clemency Canning'. Though heartily supported by John Lawrence, his humane policy lost the Governor-General much popularity with his enraged countrymen.

The Mutiny was followed by a long period of material improvement and quiet paternal government, with few wars or striking events of any sort. After this tranquillity has come our own era of change. The demand of Indians for self-government is the result in

315

general of the world forces which are stirring the somnolent East, and in particular of the unifying and educating work of the British in India. The difficulties of the present era of transition have been enhanced by that streak of blood, and of suspicion sprung from blood, long running underground, which can be tracked to its source in the year of the Mutiny.

Some formal changes were made in 1858. The old East India Company rule, long obsolete in fact, was abolished in name. The Governor-General became the Queen's Viceroy. But in spite of their proud new title, the successors of Wellesley and Dalhousie found the sphere of independent action reduced by the telegraph wire and the steamship. The government became more and more a dual consulship of the Indian Secretary in London and the Viceroy at Calcutta. Indeed improved communications have altered the conditions of life for all Anglo-Indians. They have been enabled to enjoy closer and more frequent connexions with the homeland, and to become more and more self-sufficient as a white society, a change that has meant both gain and loss.

John Lawrence, Viceroy from 1864–9, remodelled the Indian Army. The Queen's and the former Company's troops were amalgamated. In accordance with the lessons of the Mutiny the artillery were made wholly European, and the proportion of European to Indian troops was fixed at not less than one to two. In 1868 the new Indian Army was employed overseas in Africa in the almost bloodless occupation of the capital of Abyssinia by Lord Napier of Magdala, owing to our quarrel with King Theodore. We have never since had a serious dispute with the Abyssinian State, a fact of some importance after we became its neighbours in the Sudan.

In 1876 Disraeli's policy procured for the Queen the title of Empress of India.

CHAPTER 21

IN 1857 Palmerston as Prime Minister fought and won another battle against the collective wisdom of Parliament, in his old 'Don Pacifico' style of seven years before.[1] In dealing with China over the affair of the *Arrow* he abused the strength of Britain and brought on a war originating from an unworthy quarrel. So thought not only Cobden, but the Peelites, Lord John Russell, and

1. pp. 291–2, above.

Disraeli's Conservative party, who all combined to defeat him in the House. He appealed to the electorate, and came back victorious, having extinguished at the polls the weakest of the parties allied against him, the 'Manchester School'. The defeat of Cobden and Bright in the house of their friends, in those northern constituencies where they had for so many years been personally identified with the self-consciousness of the industrial community, was due as much to their former opposition to the Crimean War as to the Chinese question of the hour.

But their long battle with Palmerston, the most profound political antagonism of that easy-going period, resembled the alternate rise and fall of Punch and the Policeman, in rapid exchange of knock-out blows, each less fatal than appears at the moment to the applauding spectators. Hardly had the men of peace crept back at by-elections into the arena whence they had been expelled by Palmerston's 'Chinese' dissolution, before we find them again heading the alliance of his enemies, and again defeating his government, this time in a manner fatal to its continuance. The combination of parties – Tories, Peelites, Russellite Whigs, and Manchester schoolmen – was the same as that which had beaten Palmerston on Cobden's Chinese motion a year before. But this time he could not hope to appeal from the House to the nationalist passions of the electorate, because the motion of Bright and his friend Gibson charged Palmerston with neglect of his country's honour. The complaint was that his Foreign Secretary had left unanswered the rather insolent dispatch of Napoleon III's Minister on the subject of the Orsini bomb outrage which had been plotted by refugees in England. On this question Palmerston had the country against him, as on the occasion of his former complaisance to Napoleon over the *coup d'état*.

Another brief interlude of Conservative government under Derby and Disraeli ensued on Palmerston's fall. But after the General Election of 1859 the Conservatives found themselves still in a minority, and were replaced by a Cabinet of Whig–Liberal reunion under Palmerston, Russell, and Gladstone. The kaleidoscope of sections and parties remained fixed in this new formation for the next half-dozen years. The government of the 'Triumvirate', as it was called, after the three leaders whose cooperation was the condition of its survival, dealt with the Italian crisis on liberal principles, and with the American Civil War and the Danish question on no principles at all. In home affairs its motto was to let sleeping dogs lie.

Palmerston's last Ministry was in fact the final phase of the old

Whig–Liberalism which the first Reform Bill had brought into power, the alliance of the 'ten-pound voter' with the great Whig families. The reforms which that combination was capable of inspiring had been carried, and its motive force was spent. Palmerston, tamed by age and by repeated proof that he could not flout all his colleagues all the time, submitted with a good grace to share power with Russell as his Foreign Minister. The days of his dictatorship were over. But he yielded points less willingly to Gladstone, whom he felt to be his own antithesis both in policy and in character. Gladstone, now again Chancellor of the Exchequer, had, in middle age, become the rising hope of the younger Liberals and of the forces of the unenfranchised who, under John Bright, were already beginning to batter at the gates. But all those folk would have to wait till Palmerston died; after him the deluge would come, dreaded by fashionable Whig and Tory society under the name of 'American democracy'.

The question on which the Triumvirate worked most in harmony was the Italian. They took office in the middle of the summer campaign of Magenta and Solferino, when Napoleon, in alliance with the Piedmont of Victor Emmanuel and Cavour, was driving the Austrians out of the Milanese plain into the Venetian quadrilateral. The outgoing Derby government, inimical to the Italian cause as a disturber of peace, had felt no emotion to counteract the distrust that it shared with all Englishmen of Napoleon's bid for European supremacy. On the other hand, the incoming Liberal Cabinet was dominated by three men who were all of them enthusiasts for Italy, though each was in a different degree fearful of French aggression.

The change at Downing Street came at the very moment when English help could be most useful to the Italian cause, namely, at the moment when France and Italy were beginning to quarrel. In July 1859, a month after the new British Ministry had come into power, Napoleon made peace with the Austrians at Villafranca, giving liberated Milan to Piedmont, but ascribing the rest of Italy to its reactionary rulers, foreign and native. Napoleon himself would have liked to do better for Italy, but he dared not shed more French blood for a cause which his Clerical supporters at home detested, particularly as France was being threatened by the Prussian armies on the Rhine. Moreover, even if he could have had his own way, he would not have wished to see Italy united and strong, for then she would become independent of France. He aimed at a confederation of small, self-governing Italian States, presided over by a Liberal Pope and looking to France for protection. But there was no longer a Liberal Pope, the Italians had other aspirations, and the Napoleonic vision was not to be realized. Either Italy must be united, strong, and independent, or else remain the slave of Austria and of native reaction.

Just when the limitations of Napoleon's policy were becoming apparent, at the end of his half-successful Lombard campaign, the new British Government appeared on the scene, to run up the bidding for Italy, and eventually to compel France to acquiesce in the unity of the whole Peninsula.

Throughout 1860 every great Power on the Continent, including France, was hostile to Italian unity. But France was so far in favour of Italian freedom and Piedmont that she would not willingly see the work of her 1859 campaign undone by an Austrian re-conquest, diplomatically backed by Prussia and Russia. In this state of things, England, by her clear declaration that the Italians should be allowed to settle their own affairs, was able to keep the ring for Cavour and Garibaldi to work out at the chosen moment the unity as well as the freedom of Italy.

England's part in the creation of the Italian kingdom in 1859–60 was the most important and well-deserved success of British diplomacy between the Belgian settlement of Grey and Palmerston and the close of the Victorian era. In many of the other great questions that we touched – the American Civil War, Denmark, Turkey – our statesmen displayed a lamentable ignorance of the forces with which they were dealing, and produced no lasting settlement of which England has reason to be proud. Only our Italian policy of 1859–60 was based on a real understanding of the people and of the facts. Therefore it succeeded, and helped to raise up a new national power, which for more than half a century remained England's friend, partly from memory of the transactions of that crisis, partly from political affinity and common interests.

Of the Triumvirate, Palmerston knew least about the Italian question, though he hated Italy's despots. Gladstone, while still a Conservative, had in 1851 studied on the spot the Neapolitan prisons and 'Bomba's' judicial system, and had been converted to the Italian cause by what he had then seen. Russell had lived for years in domestic intimacy with the Italian exiles in England. Through these foreign friends, and through Sir James Hudson, our Minister at Turin, he was kept in close touch with the successive phases of Cavour's labyrinthine policy. Hudson, through his personal friendship with Russell, was able to make British policy in

Italy move fast enough to keep pace with the rapidity of events in a year of revolution.

First Hudson persuaded Lord John to accept the accomplished fact of the cession of Nice and Savoy to France, as being the necessary prepayment made by Cavour to Napoleon for permission to liberate any further portions of Italy. If Hudson had not made the real bearings of the question clear to Russell, the fury of Palmerston and of England in general at this transaction would very probably have involved us in a war with France, which would have been fatal to Italy and beneficial only to the Eastern despotisms.

In the summer, Garibaldi liberated Sicily by his adventure of the Thousand. The enthusiasm with which it was hailed in England was such as perhaps no other foreigner's enterprise has ever aroused in our island. Helped by the popular feeling for Garibaldi, Hudson persuaded Lord John, and through him the Cabinet, that the hour had struck for the complete unity of all Italians in one State – a solution to which Palmerston, Gladstone, Russell, and Hudson himself had been averse until Garibaldi took Palermo. That event made a willing convert of England. But France, as well as Russia, Prussia, and Austria, still continued hostile to Italian unity. In giving effect to this change of British policy, Hudson persuaded Russell not to become a party to Napoleon's design of sending the British and French fleets to Messina to stop Garibaldi from crossing from Sicily to the Neapolitan mainland. Such action to check Garibaldi's further progress would have been in accordance with the policy which Cavour was constrained by France and Austria to announce in public, but contrary to Cavour's secret wishes, as Hudson well knew. Any Minister but Russell, nay, Russell himself with different coaching, might have stopped Garibaldi at the Straits, and that might well have been fatal to Italian unity.

There went so many miracles to make Italy – the miraclemen, Mazzini, Garibaldi, Cavour, the right king on the right throne, the thousand wonderful chances of battle and debate – that we sometimes overlook a miracle in that age second to none, that in 1860 a British Foreign Minister thoroughly understood, by years of previous study and from the best sources of daily information, the main question with which he was called upon to deal.

Palmerston's admiration of the French Emperor did not survive the affair of Nice and Savoy, in which he saw the beginning of another era of Napoleonic aggrandisement. His formidable temper was at length stirred up against the man on whose behalf he had twice in years gone by suffered political ostracism. In the year 1859–60 the feeling against France ran high, led by *The Times* newspaper, and we came very near to war. If the Government had been a Palmerstonian dictatorship as in 1856 war would perhaps have broken out. Fortunately Russell was better versed in the realities of the situation, and Gladstone, the Chancellor of the Exchequer, came out as a belligerent champion of peace and economy, of a calibre to stand up even against Palmerston himself.

It ended in a victory for peace. Cobden, encouraged by Gladstone, went over to Paris on his own account, and with his marvellous persuasiveness began negotiations with Napoleon in person, which ended in a Commercial Treaty between France and England, the free-trade advantages of which bore down the clamour for war in our island. Beyond the Channel, where Protectionism was dominant, Napoleon's free-trade policy was a proof of his earnest desire to keep the peace with our country, even at the cost of unpopularity with his own subjects. At an ugly crisis peace had been preserved by what Mr Gladstone called 'a great European operation'. The credit was due in France to an 'enlightened despotism', in England to the more democratic elements of opinion led by Gladstone from the Treasury bench, in alliance with Cobden and Bright.

It was in the sweat and agony of that contest to avert war that Gladstone's friendship with Bright began, destined to bear notable fruit after Palmerston's death. The positive prizes they had secured in place of war – Cobden's Commercial Treaty and Gladstone's budgets of 1860–61, including the repeal of the Paper Duties[1] – are remembered as trophies of Palmerston's premiership, though certainly not of his policy.

A lasting benefit remained over to England from the war panic, in the shape of the Volunteer movement. This embodiment of the ideals and policy of Victorian England has grown in our own day into the Territorial Force, and has proved its value on the fields of France, though not, in the actual event, in conflict with Frenchmen. The song which Tennyson, as Poet Laureate, wrote for the original Volunteers of 1859, 'Form, form, Riflemen, form', is a denunciation of Napoleon III:

1. In 1860 the Lords had rejected Gladstone's repeal of the Paper Duty, aimed at giving people cheap books and journals, Palmerston secretly applauding the rejection. Gladstone next year put all his financial proposals together into one budget which the Lords could not amend and dared not reject. This action first marked him out as the future Radical leader. Much of the credit for the initiation of 'Cobden's Treaty' lies with Chevalier on the French side (see *Nineteenth Century*, 22 Nov., A. L. Dunham).

>True we have got – *such* a faithful ally
>That only the devil can tell what he means.

To us Englishmen he meant better than Tennyson knew.

In 1863 Palmerston consented to a most generous act of foreign policy. The Ionian islands off the coast of Greece, in our hands since the treaties of 1815, were given to Greece at the desire of their inhabitants. It was done on the advice of Gladstone, who had been sent to study the question as Commissioner a few years before. Hellenic sympathies and Liberal principles were the motives of an action which has few analogies in history.

Scarcely had we escaped the danger of a meaningless war with France when a yet darker fate threatened us, the danger of becoming involved in the American Civil War on the side of the Southern slave-owners. Our escape from that entanglement, and the final victory of the North, followed immediately by Palmerston's death, opened out the way for the enfranchisement of the working classes and the recognition of democracy as the governing force in Great Britain.

The issue in America arose from the demand of the Southern slave-owning States to dominate the politics of the whole Union, as the only means by which the ultimate extinction of slavery could be avoided. Slavery was indeed in no immediate danger of suppression. The abolitionist agitation had not converted the North, but it had maddened the slave-owners of the South, and driven them into a course of action which proved their undoing. For years they dictated to their fellow-citizens of the North, and bullied the whole Union. The Northerners, immersed in business, were more interested in developing the resources of the country than in conducting its politics, while the Southern gentlemen left the slave-driving to overseers, and interested themselves in affairs of State. But at last the apparently inexhaustible patience of the North gave out, and the choice of Lincoln as President-elect signified that a stand would be made.

It was no part of Lincoln's Presidential programme to abolish slavery in the existing slave States, but he would no longer permit them to control the policy of the Federal Government, or to force their 'peculiar institution' on new States forming in the West. Their answer was to secede from the Union under Jefferson Davis as President of a new Confederacy. The North, under firm guidance from the new President, denied their right to secede, and waged war to bring them back into the national fold.

Thus the origin of the quarrel was freedom against slavery, but its final form was Union against Secession. The two issues had become identified. Either the Union would emerge one of the most powerful States in the world, and a democracy in every sense; or else a new world-power would come into being based on slavery as an ideal, while democracy, not yet established in Europe, would have proved itself, on its own soil, incapable of preserving great political units from disruption.

In England the upper ranks of society sympathized generally with the South, and the lower with the North. Since, however, the Northern sympathizers had no votes, the Southern sympathizers were vocal and important out of proportion to their numbers. Journalists and statesmen were not then obliged to appeal to working-class opinion, and they made England appear more 'Southern' than she really was.

The reason of this social cleavage on the American question was twofold. In the first place the poorer classes had then many relations in the Northern United States who often wrote home to say what a fine land they had found; for a generation past there had been a great flood of emigrants in that direction as well as to our own Colonies. America was therefore better understood in the cottage than in the mansion. For the upper and political classes had not then contracted the habit of intermarriage with Americans, which has in more recent times helped to change their attitude to the Republic. So little was America known to the readers of *The Times* that, when the great newspaper declared pontifically that Yankees were cowards and that slavery was not an issue in the struggle, Belgravia and its dependencies believed what they read. Such ignorance about the affairs of a great English-speaking community was in striking contrast with the close knowledge of Italy displayed in the same quarters. If Mr Gladstone had watched a slave-auction in the South, as he had watched the Neapolitan political trials, he would not have said that Jeff Davis had 'made a nation'; and if Lord John had known Boston society as well as he knew the Italian exiles, he would have taken yet a little more trouble than he did to prevent the sailing of the *Alabama*.

The second reason for the cleavage of British opinion on the Civil War was that one section was dreading and the other eagerly expecting the advent of 'American democracy' in England by a further extension of the franchise. It is indeed remarkable that Gladstone, who was destined to be the chief beneficiary of the next Reform Bill, espoused the Southern cause. But in the main English Reformers sided with the industrial and democratic North, and the anti-Reformers, Whig and Tory, with the gentlemen of the Southern Confederacy.

John Bright put himself at the head of the democratic elements favouring the North. In these four years of the American Civil War, and the two years of the British Reform struggle that followed, the real battle of his life was fought and won. During the Corn Law controversy, he had only been Cobden's lieutenant. In opposing the Crimea he had only been one of two, though his eloquence, the reflection of deep moral qualities, had then begun to give him a place apart in men's minds, in spite of the unpopularity of his views. But from 1859 onwards, without dividing himself from Cobden, he had struck out a policy of his own on franchise reform in which Cobden, always sceptical as to the intelligence of the working-class, refused to take a share. Cobden continued to believe in the future of upper middle-class Liberalism, at a time when the upper middle-classes were becoming Conservative. And, therefore, when he died in 1865, he was no longer in the commanding position of leadership that he had occupied twenty years before.

Bright on the other hand was uniting the lower middle class and working classes in a new radical party, more formidable, because less alarming to property, than the old Chartism with its purely working-class standpoint. In the sixties Bright was the political leader of the town artisans, not on a 'class-conscious' basis, but as a part of the nation claiming their rights as such. The 'class-consciousness' seemed rather to be chargeable against the aristocracy and wealthier bourgeoisie who denied political power to the majority of their fellow-citizens. 'If a class has failed,' said Bright, 'let us try the nation.' Trade-Unionism, engaged in securing better wages and conditions, and mellowed by the general prosperity of the country, had forgotten its socialistic ambitions of the Owenite period, and encouraged its members to fall in under Bright's banner to fight for Parliamentary Reform, alongside of the radical portion of the 'collared classes'. The Protestant Christianity and Bible knowledge of the vast audiences whom Bright addressed put them in sympathy with the form and spirit of the Quaker's moral appeal, as also with a part at least of Gladstone's idealism. If Bright was a demagogue, he knew none of the baser arts of his trade, and his singleness of mind stood him in good stead with that generation of men.

The issue was greatly influenced from overseas. The Colonies had just been granted self-government without any limitation of the suffrage – a powerful argument against the restriction of the franchise at home. And now the principle of democracy as a practical form of government was undergoing ordeal by battle in the United States.

The Civil War was a question in every way suited to John Bright. He knew much more about America than did the Foreign Office or the Cabinet. The question of slavery stirred the deeps of his compassion, and put him in touch with what was best and most powerful in the England of that day. He had the sense to 'swallow his formulas' of pacifism for the occasion. For three years he lived in daily dread lest bloodshed so unexampled should induce the North to make terms with slavery and end the war before it had completed its work. He saw no less clearly that, if the great experiment of the North American Republic broke up in disaster, democracy would be discredited all the world over as having been tried and found wanting. These things he and William Edward Forster and a few others taught to the people of England.

Although there was a strong Southern party in Great Britain there were no partisans of slavery. The Southern sympathizers tried to ignore the slavery issue, but it emerged and beat them in the end. Conservatives regarded the planters of Georgia and Carolina as 'Cavaliers' and high-spirited gentlemen oppressed by a set of low-bred Yankee tradesmen and farmers. A section of Liberals, headed by Gladstone, thought they saw a brotherhood of small States rightly struggling to be free against a tyrannous empire. And many reasonable men of all parties, though disliking slavery and the slave-owners, believed after the initial Northern defeat of Bull Run that the North could never conquer the South; and that even if, contrary to all form of likelihood, it was ever able to overrun the South with its armies, it could never remake the nation by force, any more than George III could, by destroying Washington's army, have remade the Empire which he had alienated. Indeed in 1861 it needed faith to believe in any such possibility.

These views, not unnatural among people singularly ignorant of America and the Americans, were confirmed by the policy which Lincoln at first thought it necessary to pursue. For a year and a half he refused to declare the emancipation of the slaves, and represented the war as being fought on the issue not of slavery, but of union. These declarations, which were only half the truth, deceived no one in America, but deceived many in England. They were made to conciliate those border States still faithful or divided in allegiance, where slavery existed, though under different conditions from down South. But when at length in October 1862

Lincoln proclaimed the freedom of the slaves in the rebel States, he dealt a very serious blow to English sympathies with the South. From that time forward our Southern party, forced against its will into the position of a pro-slavery party, declined every month in power.

If it had not been for the avowed Southern sympathy of politicians and journalists, the official acts of the British Government need not have given very grave cause of offence to the North. The worst offender in the Ministry was Gladstone, who, unaccustomed to do anything by halves, gave vent to his enthusiasm for the new Southern 'nation' in a public speech at Newcastle in 1862. Palmerston knew better how to restrain himself in utterance, and Gladstone's indiscretions made him by antagonism more discreet. But at heart he was less friendly to Americans as such, and felt for their republic an old-world jealousy and dislike which he had inherited from his master Canning. Russell, who as Foreign Minister was the most important of the three, was the most friendly to America, and did his best to be correct, though he failed to understand the issues of the war.[1]

At the outset, Russell had angered the North by a proclamation of neutrality which accorded to the rebels the privileges of combatants; but the North itself in practice granted these privileges while denying them in theory. Russell enraged the South no less by refusing to recognize their government, and by abstaining from the intervention which was the ultimate hope of the slave-owning confederacy. If Europe never intervened, all the heroism of General Lee's armies could not ultimately hold out against superior numbers and resources, provided the North remained united and in stubborn earnest.

Christmas 1861 was the moment of greatest danger in the relations of America and Britain. Jefferson Davis had sent over two men, Mason and Slidell, to stir up England and France to interfere on the Southern side. Mason, who was coming to our country to match himself against the grave astuteness of the American Minister, Charles Francis Adams, proved so unfitted for his task that Lincoln would have done well to have given him a convoy across the Atlantic. But unfortunately an over-zealous Federal captain took Mason and Slidell off the British ship *Trent* and carried them prisoners into a Northern port. It was an outrage on

1. It is noticeable that the able contemporary essays in which Lord Robert Cecil, the future Lord Salisbury, attacked Russell's mismanagement of the Danish and Brazilian questions also attacked him for his friendliness to Lincoln's government during the Civil War.

our flag which could not rightfully be defended. But the Northerners were so sore at the British attitude, and the insolence of the Press on both sides was so great, that it required considerable moral courage for Lincoln to release the men, and it was some time before he decided to do it. Luckily Russell at the Foreign Office desired with his whole heart that peace should be preserved. Under the steadying influence of Prince Albert who, from his death-bed, painfully exerted his last energies to have the wording of our dispatches on the subject modified, our demands were so framed that America was able to give way without loss of self-respect.

Apart from this accidental crisis, the question of interference, from beginning to end of the war, arose out of the blockade. In curious reversal of the old quarrels of Napoleonic times, we stood for those troublesome rights of neutrals, and America for the detested right of search. The North blockaded the Southern ports, to starve the slave-owners out by preventing them from selling their one great export, cotton. The Lancashire mills had then no other source whence to obtain raw cotton, either in the Empire or in foreign countries. That section of the British upper class which desired for political reasons to engineer a war to destroy the Union was able to show to the unemployed men and women of Lancashire that only the breaking of the blockade could give immediate relief to their distress. But the appeal was made in vain to a population that had learnt to think for itself. Lancashire tightened its belt and suffered willingly for the cause of freedom. New sources of cotton supply were hastily organized in India and elsewhere, and before the end of the war the worst of the crisis was over, and the monopoly of American cotton had been broken.

Napoleon III had reasons of his own for desiring the victory of the South. He designed to set up a French protectorate in Mexico and Central America, and that could never be done in face of the Monroe Doctrine backed by the full force of the Union. Being therefore not unwilling to see the Union destroyed, he would have liked to draw England into a policy of joint intervention. But Palmerston, though he loved America little, loved Napoleon less, and desired no more than Canning to see a restoration of the transatlantic power of France. After the Northern success at Gettysburg in the summer of 1863, the question of interference receded into the background as the Southern prospects grew less roseate. The final surrender of Lee's army to Grant and the moving accident of Lincoln's assassination in the hour of victory converted English statesmen and journalists once and for all.

The Civil War had left over a legacy of indignation against

England in just those sections of American opinion where we were accustomed to find our best friends. The North had always been more friendly to us than the South, but we had forfeited Northern sympathy. Yet we had not made ourselves any better liked in the South, which ascribed its ruin to our half-hearted backing. Prior to 1861, the relations of Britain and America had been moving steadily towards an understanding, as Britain became more democratic and America less isolated. The animosity aroused by the Civil War, coming on the top of the great immigration from Ireland, checked this fortunate process, but could not wholly reverse it.

In particular, the Civil War left the inheritance of the *Alabama* claims. In July 1862, by a grievous and bitterly repented error of negligence on the part of Russell, a disguised privateer had been allowed to escape from Liverpool docks. Once at sea, she had hoisted the Southern colours, and began her long and destructive warfare on the commerce of the United States. Large compensation was undoubtedly due for definite losses inflicted on American property. Unfortunately, the truculence of the Northern mood after the victory was won, and resentment against the recent British attitude, took the form of grossly exaggerated demands, including hundreds of millions for 'indirect claims', on the abstract ground that the *Alabama* and her consorts had prolonged the war by two years. Bright denied that they had prolonged the war by a day. The question dragged on for a decade, causing grave ill-feeling on both sides. It was finally handled by Gladstone as Prime Minister with a moral courage in the cause of peace and justice which went far to compensate for the 'mistake of incredible grossness' that he confessed he had made in his Newcastle speech of 1862. The just settlement of the *Alabama* question in 1872 before the Geneva tribunal, which rejected the 'indirect claims' and assessed the others at fifteen million dollars, was one of the landmarks in the history of international arbitration, and put an end to a period of strained relations between the two parts of the English-speaking world.

Five years before the *Alabama* settlement, the creation of the Dominion of Canada by the statesmanship of the Canadian, Sir John Macdonald, had brought into being a 'United States' of British North America.[1] This stage in Imperial evolution had been hastened by the dangers arising from the less friendly attitude of the Republic after the war. The Federation of the Canadian

1. See p. 260, above, and maps, pp. 71 and 184.

Provinces defined and stabilized their relations with their southern neighbour, in spite of the novel difficulties of the Fenian movement on the border. There was no longer serious question of Canada joining the United States. Under the new constitution, the Dominion included all the provinces (except Newfoundland) of the Pacific and Atlantic seaboards, together with Upper and Lower Canada, once more distinct units, but now linked in the common federation. The constitution, being federal, resembled that of the United States, but it left more power to the central government.

In the following twenty years Macdonald's great project of the Canadian Pacific Railway materialized, in spite of many difficulties, including those encountered by the engineers in driving a permanent way through the Rocky Mountains. The faith of a group of men, of whom Donald Smith, Lord Strathcona, was the foremost, carried this laborious achievement through to completion in 1885. The great railway and its branches gave reality to federation, and enabled the economic life of Canada to run westward and northward on its own territory, instead of only southwards across the border. The provinces on the two oceans were thereby united in fact as well as in law, and the great resources of the centre and north were opened out.

Connexion by railway was a condition of political unity alike in Canada, South Africa, and Australia. The chief Australian railways, built by the socialistically inclined governments of the various colonies, often at a temporary loss, put an end to provincial isolation, and eventually led to the union of all the Australian Colonies in the Confederation of 1901[1]; the form of their union is indeed somewhat less close than that which has bound together the different provinces of Canada since 1867. The economic unity of South Africa had been made by the railways,[2] before the Union of 1910 became possible. This union, unlike the Australian, bound the component Colonies of South Africa even closer than the Canadian Federation. In Canada alone political union had preceded the construction of the greater railways, because of the urgency of showing a united front in relation to the neighbour Republic. But the completion of the railway system over the Rockies was essential to the reality and permanence of the new political structure.

Thus in the seventies and eighties the relationship between Britain, Canada, and the United States took on its modern features, which have since undergone development rather than change.

1. See p. 402, below.   2. See map, p. 398, below.

In 1863–4, while the American Civil War was still raging, the Danish fiasco had marked the end of Palmerstonianism in our dealings with Europe, where forces were rising too formidable to be treated by us in the cavalier fashion that had passed muster for twenty years past. The question at issue was the race problem of Schleswig and Holstein.

The status of the two provinces, partly German and partly Danish in race and feeling, was in dispute between Germany and Denmark. Germany was represented by Prussia and Austria in alliance, but in effect Bismarck directed their action. England, concerned as co-signatory of a former Danish treaty, tried to negotiate a compromise, but the Danes at first, and the Germans later on, were decidedly unreasonable. When Bismarck bullied, Palmerston rashly said that if Denmark had to fight she would not fight alone, and Lord Russell's dispatches as Foreign Minister were calculated to convey a like impression.

British sympathies were with Denmark, partly because she was the small country, partly because her Princess Alexandra had recently married the Prince of Wales. But neither the British people, the House of Commons, nor the royal family with its Germanophile head, had any real intention of going to war with the combined powers of Central Europe. And since several members of the Cabinet were opposed to the bellicose policy of the Prime Minister and the Foreign Secretary, the Queen's energetic expression of her views bore a weight which they never carried in cases where the Cabinet was of one mind and supported by public opinion.

For Britain, the prospects of war were bleak in the extreme. We had no allies. Russell and Palmerston had alienated Napoleon by repeated refusals to do what he wanted, both in America and in Europe. Russell had also alienated Russia by protesting against her infamous tyranny in Poland the year before, which Bismarck had been careful to aid and abet. If it was the object of Palmerston and Russell to oppose the rise of Bismarckian Germany, they should have prepared the ground. But they had consistently alienated France and Russia and had taught the British public to believe that the balance of power was threatened, not by Germany, but by Russia and by France. They had chosen for us a position of isolation. It followed, though they did not see it, that we must adopt a policy of non-interference. And such in fact became the Gladstonian policy in the coming era.

The forces now moving on the European field were too big for us to face without allies. We had no army that could hold its own against Prussia and Austria. In these circumstances the decision to stand down and see Denmark overwhelmed in war, though undignified, was more sensible than the threatening language we had used at first, which Bismarck had treated with a contempt justified by the event. This ignominious episode served as a useful warning, and put an end to the Palmerstonian method of dealing with European countries.

Early next year the news of Lincoln's victory gave a shattering blow to the domestic conservatism which Palmerston had so long imposed on English Liberals. But nature had not made him of the mould to be depressed by the failure of his plans or the confutation of his prophecies. His countrymen liked his pluck, and found in him a magnificent mirror of their own qualities. At the General Election of July, destined to be the last held under the old franchise, a majority was returned pledged to support him for personal rather than political reasons. In October the old man died in harness, Britain's popular Minister to the last. He had been a lover of life, and life had repaid him in full. He is less likely to be forgotten than many wiser statesmen, for he had filled great parts for many years, and when he was on the stage no one could take his eyes off the play.

CHAPTER 22

THE victory of the North and the death of Palmerston together gave the signal for another era of Reform corresponding in importance to the legislation of the Whigs during the five years after Wellington's fall. If the events connected with the second Reform Bill and its sequel were less sensational than those of the first, it was because the idea of change was no longer new and shocking, and because the supremacy of the national will had proved itself in the former battle against privilege. In 1832 the nation had been made supreme and had been so defined as to include half the middle class. In 1867 it was defined again so as to include the rest of the middle class and the working-men of the towns. The immediate consequence, between 1868 and 1875, was a long list of reforms, including, under the Liberals, Irish Church and Land Acts, popular education, army reform, the opening of the Civil Service and the Universities to free competition; under the Conservatives, sanitary and municipal legislation and new laws to assist Trade Unionism; and finally, after another interval, the inclusion of the agricultural labourer in the national franchise in 1884, leading a few years later to the establishment of local self-government in the rural districts.

In this adaptation of our institutions to the new theory that Britain was a democracy no less than her own Colonies or America, Bright and Gladstone showed the way, by inspiring public opinion and directing Parliament, while Disraeli so 'educated' the Conservative party that it offered no such resistance to these changes as it had opposed to the first Reform Bill, and even took the lead in parts of the process.

Behind the statesmen of the transition stood the philosopher, John Stuart Mill, whose writings were at the height of their influence in the sixties and seventies. He had been bred up by his father as a Benthamite of the strictest sect, but his life's work was to purify Bentham's utilitarianism of its pedantry, and to bring it up to date in an age that was gradually outgrowing *laissez faire*. It was Mill's doctrine that everyone ought to take part in the election not only of Parliament, but of responsible local bodies, so that the whole people should learn to take an interest in all that concerned them, from drains to foreign policy, from the village school to national finance.

But Mill knew that democratic machinery did not in itself secure good government. He desired to see specialist departments of State supervising the action of the elected local bodies, and making the knowledge acquired in one place available everywhere. 'Power,' he said, 'may be localized, but knowledge, to be most useful, must be centralized.' He brought together in a consistent theory the lessons of the administrative experience of the age of Chadwick, the dove-tailing of central with local government, the interplay of democratic impulse and specialist guidance, by which modern England more and more learnt to thrive.

Mill used his influence, when at its height, to popularize the idea of the equality of the sexes. It was not in his day carried out in politics, but even before he died (1873) it greatly affected social thought and custom, and about that time the laws began to be reformed as regards women's property and personal rights. The only important part of Mill's political philosophy which has not been carried into effect as law is his eager advocacy of the representation of minorities by the system known in his day as 'Mr Hare's scheme', and in ours as Proportional Representation.

Mill's treatise *On Liberty*[1] had many effects outside the political

1. The dates of the publication of his principal works were: *On Liberty*, 1859; *Representative Government*, 1861; *Subjection of Women*, 1869.

sphere. It was a plea for freedom of thought and discussion, which in the early Victorian era were much limited by social convention, though very little by law. Mill taught that what was needed in the England of that day was a change of attitude in the direction of freedom to express new ideas in word and action. The rising generation grew up with this creed. Jowett's influence was at war with old orthodoxy in Oxford, while the mid-Victorian literature – represented by Matthew Arnold, George Eliot, the Brownings, and Meredith, though the last was not yet recognized by the public – was instinct with the principle of freedom and experiment, always within the limits imposed by sound learning and the social sense. Victorian literature, essentially liberationist, was not revolutionary. As art, it had its own various traditions and standards distinct from those of journalism, which did not overshadow the world of letters till the Education Act of 1870 had had time to create a reading public co-extensive with the nation.

In the year that Mill's *Liberty* appeared, Darwin published the *Origin of Species*, and next year, in the famous arena of the British Association meeting at Oxford, Huxley vindicated at the expense of Bishop Samuel Wilberforce the right of science to investigate and teach without having first to square its results with Mosaic theology. The more obvious implications of the Darwinian theory of the descent of man were slowly working themselves into common thought during the new Reform epoch.

Science was not yet a part of the established order. In the past, most investigation had been done by individuals like Priestley or Darwin working at their own expense and on their own account, and this era of private initiative was only gradually passing into the new era of endowed and organized research. In the fifties the Natural Science Tripos had been set up at Cambridge, largely owing to the intelligent patronage of the Chancellor of the University, the Prince Consort, whose royal presence was able to charm away opposition to new-fangled learning in just those academic quarters which were usually most obscurantist. In the sixties science was making itself felt as a power in the land. And so long as it was still struggling for freedom and recognition, with the word 'evolution' inscribed on its banners militant, it could not fail to exert an influence favourable in a broad sense to liberal reform.[1]

The Whig-Liberal majority, which Palmerston's name had

1. It was remarked that in the Governor Eyre controversy, which convulsed politics and society in 1866, Darwin and Huxley were both on the side of the humanitarians and Liberals against the severity shown in repressing the negroes in Jamaica.

helped to secure at the General Election in the summer, became in the autumn the inheritance of his surviving colleagues. Russell, who had lately withdrawn to the Upper House as an earl, succeeded to the premiership, but the moving force in the Cabinet and in the Commons was Gladstone, in alliance with Bright below the gangway. 'Gladstone will soon have it all his own way,' Palmerston had prophesied; 'whenever he gets my place we shall have strange doings.' Even before Palmerston's death, Gladstone had in 1864 sent a shudder through the country houses of England by the following declaration on the franchise:

I contend that it is on those who say it is necessary to exclude forty-nine fiftieths of the working classes that the burden of proof rests. Every man who is not presumably incapacitated by some consideration of personal unfitness or political danger is morally entitled to come within the pale of the constitution.

No wonder that Disraeli said his rival had 'revived the doctrine of Tom Paine'. No wonder that at the General Election next year Gladstone lost his seat for Oxford University, and went instead to a Lancashire constituency, 'unmuzzled', as he significantly declared. The links with his past were snapping one by one.

But the ex-Palmerstonian majority which he had now to lead in the Commons contained a 'tail' of young men of fashion, the scions of great Whig houses who might just as well have been the scions of great Tory houses so far as their opinions were concerned.[1] When therefore Gladstone introduced a Reform Bill, lowering the Ten Pound voting qualifications in the boroughs to Seven Pounds, even this very moderate measure, which fell far short of the household suffrage of Bright's programme, was regarded by these elements in the party as too advanced. The revolt of this section, which Bright nicknamed 'the Cave of Adullam', because everyone who was discontented or in distress resorted there, was led with sincerity and oratorical power by Robert Lowe. But the prudence of a great leader was a gift denied to him. He turned the controversy into a class question, by contending that working-men as such ought to be excluded from the franchise on account of their moral and intellectual unfitness. Lowe's rash tactics converted a decorous discussion on a measure of 'bit-by-bit Reform' into a battle over first principles that let loose throughout the country the passions of rival classes.

1. A study of the evolution of Whig families to Conservatism, and of many other social and political phenomena of the late fifties and early sixties, will be found in one of the greatest of political novels, Meredith's *Beauchamp's Career*.

The working-men, at first indifferent to the fate of a Bill which only proposed to enfranchise a small fraction of their number, were stung to fury by the character of Lowe's opposition to it, and a great franchise agitation, led by John Bright, soon aroused feelings which could never be satisfied by so half-hearted a measure as the Bill of 1866. The Conservative party, under Disraeli's guidance, would very probably have let the Bill pass through both Houses if they had not been carried away by the example of the white-haired champion on the ministerial benches opposite. Lowe had, besides, offered them a chance of throwing out the government. A combination of the Conservatives with forty Whigs from 'the Cave' defeated the Bill in Committee, and the Russell Ministry resigned.

The cause of working-class enfranchisement gained in the end by this apparent disaster. A Bill that was at best only a half-measure was cleared out of the way. And the incoming Conservative government of Lord Derby, with Disraeli for its moving spirit, had now to deal with a situation of the utmost gravity of their own making. They were in a minority in the Commons, yet they dared not appeal to the country. They had to settle the franchise question, which was now raging like a fever in the nation's blood. The new Government was indeed in a position, if it so wished, to pass a much stronger measure than that of Russell and Gladstone, because it could ensure the acquiescence of Conservative opinion in both Houses. If the party would abandon its former convictions, stultify the vote by which it had just gained office, and throw over Robert Lowe, and if Disraeli would pass 'the doctrine of Tom Paine' into law, a signal service could be rendered to the Empire, such as Peel had rendered over Catholic Emancipation and the Corn Laws.

The Conservative party was well disciplined. The decision would be that of its chiefs, and their counsels were dominated by the transcendant abilities of a man singularly open-minded both as to the main political chance and as to the best interests of the community. Disraeli, looking with a foreigner's eyes on England, often saw things that were not the most evident to the natives. He had put together in youth a collection of political ideas, known to the public through the characteristic medium of his novels. These ideas were, like himself, a mixture of extravagance and penetration, of sentimentality and realism. He specially delighted in combinations which seemed paradoxes to that age: he believed in the Jews and in the Church of England; in the political influence of the Crown; in the 'territorial aristocracy', that is, in the Tory part

335

of it; and finally, giving the middle classes a skip, he believed in the working-men. It is true that he ended his career as the idol of the despised middle classes, but that was still in the future.

In the first half of Queen Victoria's reign, the position of a Conservative leader who believed in the working classes was bizarre, like so much else in Disraeli's outfit. But genius can afford to be odd. And now, by the defeat and resignation of the Russell Ministry, a situation had suddenly arisen in which a Conservative leader who believed in the working classes could become the man of the hour and deliver the nation from a position that might soon be one of considerable danger.

Yet even Disraeli would not have ventured to 'dish the Whigs' and to take the famous 'leap in the dark' of working-class enfranchisement but for the agitation in the country over which Bright presided in the autumn of 1866. The usual order of proceedings was that in each of the great centres of industry in the North and Midlands, the bulk of the male population of all classes, including the Trade Unionists marshalled under their banners, would march past Bright in a monster review, some two hundred thousand strong, generally on a moor near the city. In the evening he would address a mass meeting in words of classical eloquence and Radical vigour that were reported at full in the papers next day. That was all, but it was enough.[1] It was different from Chartism, because it was based on class union instead of class division. The middle and working classes, the one under-represented, the other scarcely represented at all, had come together to demand the franchise. In vain the country houses were filled that Christmas with ladies and gentlemen abusing Bright. In their hearts they were afraid, with that wise old English fear of their countrymen when thoroughly roused which has done as much to save England as many more heroic virtues.

One keen-eyed watchman was drawing his own conclusions. Disraeli, 'always an opportunist on Reform', as his biographer tells us, 'would not admit in the autumn that the success of the agitation which Bright was conducting showed that the country had determined to obtain Reform; but in January (1867) he found the evidence conclusive. As soon as Disraeli reached that point he acted with promptitude and decision.'

It was characteristic of Disraeli's determination to solve the

1. The pulling down of the Hyde Park railings by a great crowd that had been denied permission by the Government to hold a Reform meeting inside also gave people to think. It was the only violence used. More would have caused reaction.

problem in a spirit above that of party that, at the beginning of the session of 1867, he privately consulted Bright as to what measure of Reform would lay the question to rest. The counties, he said, did not matter; it was an affair of the industrial working class.

Disraeli had many years before told the world that industrialism had created a new 'nation' cut off from contact with the governing class. At length he was convinced that it could no longer with safety be left outside the Parliamentary system. In the last twenty years it had increased enormously in numbers and prosperity. It was becoming the most characteristic part of modern England. Now that the Cleveland iron deposits had been opened up, the output of British steel exceeded that of all the rest of the world together, and the yearly export of British goods, which twenty years before had been under sixty millions, was now three times as great. Such a country, Disraeli perceived, could no longer be governed by the 'territorial aristocracy' on whom he had once pinned his faith, and, since he had never shared the Whig idealization of the middle class, he was reduced to admit the political claims of the artisan.

In seeking a logical basis on which the new borough franchise could rest, Disraeli rejected the idea of another makeshift lowering of the money standard of ten pounds. He preferred to give the vote boldly to every householder who paid rates – a principle that would sound large enough to satisfy Reformers, and respectable enough to please Conservatives. But the ratepaying franchise, in the form in which he first introduced it to the House, was so hedged round with 'securities' that it was not in fact at all a large measure of enfranchisement. Reformers regarded the new Bill as worse than useless. But in the course of Committee, the position was reversed once more. There was still a Liberal majority in the House, skilfully led by Gladstone and Bright, and its pressure gradually forced the not wholly unwilling Disraeli into dropping the 'securities' one by one.[1]

When the Bill left Committee it was to all intents and purposes household franchise for the boroughs. Being sent up to the Lords

1. In Committee a 'lodger' franchise was added. But far the most important change in Committee referred to the personal payment of rates which Disraeli's Bill made the condition of enfranchisement. In many boroughs the landlord usually paid the rates and charged them in the rent. Thus most working-men would be still kept out of the vote. Disraeli, however, greatly to men's surprise, at the last moment accepted a clause promoted by Bright which made personal payment of rates compulsory for all occupiers, and so made working-class enfranchisement a reality. Two years later this expedient was repealed and compounding for rates was again permitted by law, but without disqualifying the occupier for the franchise.

by a Conservative government it passed at once into law. Lord Cranborne, formerly Lord Robert Cecil and afterwards the great Lord Salisbury, in vain denounced the betrayal. There was no one capable of playing the young Disraeli to the old Disraeli's Peel.

The upshot of these

> purposes mistook
> Fallen on the inventors' heads,

these confused Parliamentary operations of which no one of the statesmen concerned had quite foreseen the issue, was that the governing classes had recognized the needs of the new era with a wise alacrity, when once they were brought up against the facts, while the rising democracy had asserted its claims with singular dignity and good sense.

One distinct part of the nation had been left out of the reckoning – the field labourer.[1] Though agriculture was still flourishing, and the farmers' daughters were buying pianos, little of this prosperity percolated through to the labourer's cottage. The continued refusal of enfranchisement to the tiller of the soil, after it had been extended to the town worker, the continued absence of local self-government in the counties for half a century after the towns were self-governing, the suppression of Joseph Arch's attempts to form an Agricultural Labourers' Union, when other Unions were increasing in power and prosperity, strengthened the growing impression that the agricultural world was a backwater, and not a part of the forward stream of modern British life. The best of the field labourers desired more than ever to get away from social and economic helotage to the freedom and opportunity of city life, and the drift to the towns was strong among the best men. When some ten years after the second Reform Bill corn prices fell and agricultural depression set in, the rural community, socially and politically behind the times, and sullenly divided against itself, was incapable of dealing with its own distress.

The first effect of the new franchise was the return at the General Election of 1868 of a Liberal majority from which the old Whig element had disappeared. The newly enfranchised working-men chose no representatives of their own class as such, but greatly strengthened the Radical element in the Liberal party. The demand for domestic reform, made stronger by the delay which Palmerston had imposed on it in every department except finance, had behind it the mind and spirit of the new age. Since the days of Peel the load of economic misery had been lifted, and most even of

1. There were also large numbers of industrial workers, especially miners, who still had no vote, owing to residence outside a Parliamentary borough.

the poorer sections of industrial society were enjoying a prosperity which neither their fathers nor grandfathers had ever known. Partly for this reason there was a singular absence of class antagonism. The bulk of the working and middle classes and of the leaders of the professional and academic world were united in demanding religious equality, educational opportunities, and the release of the public services from aristocratic control. In 1868 Conservatism and Socialism were both temporarily in abeyance. It was a mood not likely to last for long, but the use made of it by Gladstone in his first and greatest Ministry went far to equip the country with modern services and institutions, without which it would have been ill-prepared to face the social and imperial problems of days to come.

Even before the General Election, while Disraeli as Prime Minister was still nominally holding the power which his own Reform Bill had undermined, Gladstone secured the assent of both Houses to the abolition of compulsory Church rates, and so laid to rest one constant source of sectarian bitterness.[1] In the autumn, the General Election took place; it was fought on the specific issue of Irish Church disestablishment, and more generally on the merits of the new Liberalism, which might be defined as old Radicalism made presentable. The elections were also a vote of confidence in Gladstone as the man of the hour. When the results were announced, Disraeli resigned, and his rival formed his First Ministry. The Liberal–Radical alliance was sealed by the entry of Bright into the Cabinet, though his presence there was of little more than symbolic importance, owing to the breakdown of his health and the permanent decline of his powers. Russell had already retired, full of years and honour, while the hirsute and eminently unaristocratic figure of W. E. Forster, whom Gladstone put in charge of education, made visible the fact that government by the Whig families was not to be revived.

Gladstone, now close on sixty years old, was approaching the climacteric and brief perfection of his political genius. After thirty-seven years of Parliamentary life he had reached the end of the long bridge conducting him from the old Toryism to the new Liberalism. Now, as he touched solid ground once more, he shook off the embarrassment and suspicion that had handicapped his career as a 'Liberal–Conservative'. Nor had he yet developed the aptitude

1. See p. 280, above. The question of Church rates had been fiercely agitated for forty years, but it was not till 1866 that Gladstone voted for the abolition. The change in his views on Church and State had been complete, but very gradual.

for miscalculating forces and mismanaging men which marked his more amazing but less fortunate old age. Incomparable as a legislator, he was second to none as a Parliamentarian and as an orator. He had all Bright's power of idealist appeal to the new electorate and to an age not yet disillusioned, all Peel's traditions of the honest and indefatigable public servant. His advent to power quickened the pulse of national life. Against him was set a man, his counterpart in political genius, dramatically his opposite in every point of mind and character. Since Pitt and Fox there had been no such rivals on the famous floor. Owing not a little to the personalities of Gladstone and Disraeli, the historic glamour and prestige of the British House of Commons were heightened during the first generation of real democracy, and for a while Parliamentary life had a stronger hold than ever on the imagination of every class.

The great operation of 1869 was the disestablishment and partial disendowment of the Protestant Episcopal Church in Ireland. England and Gladstone had both changed their minds on this question since the day, thirty-five years back, when Russell had broken up a Whig Government by an injudicious remark to the effect that the revenue of the Irish Church was larger than was required. It was now held no sacrilege to sever the connexion of this same Irish Church with the State, and to leave it as a self-governing corporation with very nearly three-quarters of its former revenue. The rest was to be devoted, not to religious purposes of other communions, but 'to the relief of unavoidable calamity and suffering not touched by the poor law'. This complicated measure, affecting so many interests and susceptibilities, was drawn up and handled by Gladstone with consummate care and skill.

Thus an ecclesiastical revolution, the largest since Tudor times, was proposed by one of the most devoted Churchmen in the British Islands, and met with singularly little opposition. The English bishops were the reverse of truculent. The Queen was anxious above all to prevent a constitutional deadlock. The country had just voted upon the question at the polls. The Lords, therefore, did not throw the Bill out on second reading, and their amendments were not insisted upon to the breaking-point. Indeed, throughout Gladstone's first Ministry, the House of Lords destroyed far less Liberal legislation than either before or after. The work that the country expected from Gladstone was done the more quickly, and the Conservative reaction was the less long in coming.

In the age of Palmerston, all British classes and parties had been singularly uninformed and indifferent with regard to Ireland.

Since the famine, little had been heard of the stricken island, and Englishmen vaguely hoped that the great emigration was solving her obscure problems. There was then no active Irish party at Westminster, such as later, under Parnell, laid an embargo on the time and attention of the House. The Irish representatives were still usually attached to one or other of the great English parties. This age of indifference was brought to an end by the Fenian outrages.

Fenianism was the first reaction of the new Irish America upon the British Isles. It was the return of the emigrant ships of the famine, a quicker return than that of the *Mayflower*! The end of every great war leaves a certain proportion of the combatants in an unsettled state, prepared for any project of violence. And so, when the armies were disbanded after the American Civil War, many of the late Irish conscripts devoted their military experience to attacks upon England in both hemispheres. The Americans, alienated by the recent attitude of our Press and Government during their own difficulties, looked on with mingled feelings while their new fellow-citizens, for whom indeed they had no particular love, attempted armed raids across the Canadian border. Then followed Fenian outrages in Ireland and England. Police barracks were attacked in Ireland. At Clerkenwell a gunpowder explosion killed a dozen people and injured a hundred more. But the most famous case was that of the so-called 'Manchester martyrs' in 1867. Two Fenian prisoners were rescued from a prison van in the streets of Manchester, and the policeman in charge was shot dead. The perpetrators were hanged, but some sympathy was felt for them even in England the more so as they declared that they had not intended to kill their victim. But upon the whole there was a fierce and alarming contrast between the views of the general public in the two islands. To the average Englishman the Fenians were simply rebels and assassins. To the average Irishmen they were simply idealists and martyrs.

Gradually, under the tutoring of Fenianism, the British awoke to the fact that there was still an Irish problem. Gladstone was the first of British Prime Ministers who gave it his full and sympathetic attention. When, in December 1868, a telegram from Windsor had first indicated that he was about to be called to the head of the counsels of the British Empire, the message had found him at his favourite recreation, cutting down large trees on his Hawarden estate. 'After a few minutes,' wrote an eye-witness, 'the blows ceased, and Mr Gladstone, resting on the handle of his axe, looked up and with deep earnestness in his voice and with great intensity in his face, exclaimed: ''My mission is to pacify Ireland.'' He then resumed his task, and never said another word till the tree was down.'

In the first year of his premiership, by the disestablishment of the 'alien Church', he removed one of the branches of the 'upas tree', as he himself called it, of Irish woe. That part of the national grievance which arose from unjust religious privilege became a thing of the past. But in the second of his Irish labours, the agrarian question, he met more stubborn resistance from vested interests in Ireland, and was supported by less understanding and sympathy in Great Britain. For, in our island, while the move- ment of the hour both in Nonconformist and intellectual circles was all against religious inequality, a landlord's rights of free con- tract in England and Scotland were as yet scarcely challenged. Nor were there many, except Gladstone himself, who understood the vast difference between a rural landlord in England and his counter- part in Ireland – the former putting money into the land and mak- ing improvements for the tenants; the latter merely drawing rack- rent which he often spent in England, leaving the tenants to do everything for themselves, and often evicting them wholesale without compensation for their improvements or consideration for their sufferings. In the rural England of that day the man who suffered was the labourer employed by the farmer; the tenant farmer himself was a man of substance and consideration. In Ireland, on the other hand, the tenant farmer was the helpless victim of a system, nominally of free contract, actually of grave oppression.

Gladstone grasped the essential differences between the English and Irish land systems which lay concealed under an identical nomenclature and almost identical laws. In 1870 his first Irish Land Act began the long series of measures by which the British Parliament interfered with the 'free contract' of Irish landlord and tenant. The most that could be done in the then state of opinion in England was Gladstone's Act, which gave the force of law to the custom prevalent in some parts of Ireland – known as 'Ulster tenant right' – of compensation for disturbance and for un- exhausted improvements. But it did not protect the tenant against raised rent, nor did it give him security of tenure. It did some little good in itself, but it was chiefly important because it was the first of a great series of Irish agrarian laws. This new effort on the part of England to remedy social injustice in Ireland did not cease till the landlords were bought out on a vast scale and the agrarian grievance wholly removed in the early years of our own century.

But unfortunately the change was much slower than the realization of religious equality, and the agrarian agitation had time, in the intervening years, to poison still further the sentiment of the Irish peasant towards England.

The same year, 1870, was the year of the great Education Bill. Hitherto primary education had been supplied by voluntary schools, the majority conducted on Church principles, aided by a small State grant.[1] Only about half the children of the country were educated at all, and most of these very indifferently. England, for all her wealth, lagged far behind Scotland and several foreign countries. Germany, who had conquered Austria in 1866, and was now engaged in conquering France, was in the forefront of all men's thoughts that year, and she attributed her successes to the schoolmaster as well as to the drill-sergeant. It was characteristic of the two nations that, whereas the German people already enjoyed good schools but not self-government, the rulers of England only felt compelled to 'educate their masters' when the working-men were in full possession of the franchise. It was felt that for so important a purpose as voting for Parliament, if for nothing else, it was good that a man should be able to read.

One reason why our statesmen had so long shrunk from attempting to set up a national system of education was that any proposal on the subject which the wit of man could devise must involve its authors in the fiercest sectarian controversy. Before the second Reform Bill a national system would almost certainly have been arranged on lines very favourable to the Church, though not without violent protest from her opponents. Now, however, it was expected that the opposite would be the case. The middle- and working-class Nonconformists who formed so important a part of Gladstone's electoral supporters looked to see the establishment of a system of publicly controlled schools supported from public funds. Such schools, they expected, would in the course of time replace the Church schools, to which it was assumed that no increased public grant would be given. Such a measure would no doubt have aroused the strongest opposition from the Church and the latent Conservative forces of the country, and would not improbably have been thrown out by the Lords. The actual course of events was, however, very different. Contrary to expectation the Liberal Government steered not against Scylla, but into Charybdis.

The Bill of 1870 was the work of W. E. Forster, a Churchman,

1. See pp. 169 and 246, above.

though of Quaker origin. He doubled the State grant to the existing Church schools so as to enable them to become a permanent part of the new system, while he introduced publicly controlled schools only to fill up the large gaps in the educational map of the country. These new schools were to be paid for out of the local rates and governed by popularly elected School Boards.

Gladstone welcomed Forster's Bill, glad to find that someone not himself had shouldered the responsibility of giving such generous terms to the Church.[1] Important concessions were made to the Nonconformists in Committee, particularly the famous 'Cowper–Temple' clause prohibiting denominational teaching in the publicly controlled schools. But the breach between Gladstone and many of his most ardent supporters was irreparable. It led to angry scenes in the House of Commons, and convulsed the constituencies. It was in protest against the Bill that Joseph Chamberlain, a Unitarian manufacturer, emerged into national prominence as the leader of midland Radicalism. His hold on Birmingham was already growing at the expense of that of Bright, who was too unwell to protest against the Education Act until it was too late to affect the issue.

Liberal disunion was still unhealed at the election of 1874, when Gladstone paid the penalty of having alienated the Church over the Irish and University questions, while at the same time losing the support of her enemies over education. He had performed his various tasks as national legislator without too nicely considering the electoral consequences.

England had obtained, better late than never, a system of education without which she must soon have fallen to the rear among modern nations. A school had been placed within the reach of every child, at a very low charge, and the local authority might, if it wished, make attendance compulsory. Between 1870 and 1890 the average school attendance rose from one and a quarter millions to four and a half millions, while the cost per child was doubled. In 1880 primary education was made compulsory for all, and in 1891 it was offered free of all expense.[2]

1. His biographer tells us that 'his private interest in public education did not amount to zeal, and it was at bottom the interest of a Churchman'. But the cause of University Reform was deeply indebted to Gladstone in person.
2. Mr Balfour's Bill of 1902 abolished the School Boards elected *ad hoc*, and gave power over education to the County Councils and to certain larger Borough Councils, who work through Education Committees. The same measure put the Church schools on the local rates, and in return gave the public education authorities a large measure of control over voluntary schools, including the nomination of one-third of the managers.

Meanwhile secondary and higher education were gradually emerging from the shameful state in which they had lain when the century began.[1] The Charity Commission had now been active for many years, and the Endowed Schools Bill of 1869 carried still further the work of putting ancient funds to modern uses and abolishing sectarian tests.

The higher education of women at last began to receive attention. In the course of the seventies, a group of wise enthusiasts in this cause founded women's colleges at Oxford and Cambridge. The academic authorities soon invited women to attend the lectures and compete in the examinations, though not to become members of the University. This new move greatly stimulated women's education elsewhere.

In 1873, under the inspiration of Professor Stuart of Cambridge, University Extension began; that is to say, the Universities sent out some of their best men to lecture to audiences at a distance from their walls. This movement stimulated local demands for higher education, led to the formation of some of the local University Colleges, and ultimately assisted the formation of those new Universities in great industrial centres which so strongly differentiate the higher education of our day from that with which our fathers had to be content. The Extension Lectures also led, in the twentieth century, to the further development of tutorial classes for working-men, and to the Workers' Educational Association.

Throughout the first half of the nineteenth century, with the exception of the new Universities of London[2] and Durham, Oxford and Cambridge held their old monopoly in the English academic world. Their eighteenth-century slumbers[3] had been broken, and movements of reform inside the two Universities had set up a system of vigorous competition in examinations for a number of subjects. But the advantages of Oxford and Cambridge were closed to half the nation by religious tests imposed in the interest of the Established Church, while the clerical and celibate character imposed on College Fellows, the almost complete supersession of the University by the individual Colleges, the close character of the elections to Fellowships, and the prevalence of absenteeism and sinecurism, rendered them incapable of meeting the demands of the new age, particularly in non-classical subjects, humane or scientific. Such impotence in the higher spheres of intellect and research must eventually have ruined the country in

1. See pp. 43–4 and p. 279, above.
2. See pp. 224–5, above.
3. See pp. 42–3, above.

peace and in war, when matched against foreign rivals who valued scientific and educational progress. The timely reform of Oxford and Cambridge by Act of Parliament saved the situation.

This great work was accomplished in three stages, spread over a period of thirty years (1850–82). The impulse came partly from an intelligent minority in the Universities themselves, men like Jowett at Oxford and Henry Sidgwick at Cambridge, partly from the public demand that the national Universities should be open to all the nation. Great political interest was taken in academic questions during this epoch, partly because religious and sectarian questions were involved.

The first stage, in the fifties, marked the initial victory over a strong and indignant opposition, offered in both Universities to the principle of parliamentary interference. When once the right of interference had been established in fact, the work of all subsequent inquiry and legislation was rendered more easy. The turning-point in this first crisis was the Oxford Act of 1854, passed by the Whig-Peelite Government, by the help of Gladstone's local knowledge, energy, and mastery of the art of legislation.

The second stage, the Tests Act of 1871, was the work of Gladstone's own Ministry. It did that which he would bitterly have opposed only a few years before. It opened College Fellowships and academic posts generally to men of all varieties of religious profession.[1] When once the sectarian question was laid to rest, controversy about academic reform escaped from the atmosphere of party politics in which it had previously moved. Indeed, the third stage of the movement, by which Parliament provided Oxford and Cambridge with their modern statutes, was initiated by a speech in the House of Lords by Salisbury, as the representative of a Conservative Government, dwelling on 'idle Fellowships' and other academic abuses with a radical vigour. By the ensuing legislation of 1877–82 the college system, peculiar in its full development to the two senior Universities of England, was still preserved, but was so modified and regulated as no longer to impede the progress and freedom of academic studies.

During the first half of the century, the permanent Civil Service had been jobbed. The offices at Whitehall had been the happy hunting-ground of Taper and Tadpole. Whig and Tory Ministers looked on all such patronage as the recognized means of keeping political supporters in good humour. The public services were filled with the nominees of peers and commoners who had votes in

1. See p. 280, above, on some unexpected consequences of this change.

Parliament or weight in the constituencies. Since the privileged families were specially anxious to provide maintenance at the public expense for those of their members who were least likely to make their own way in life, the reputation of Whitehall for laziness and incompetence was proverbial. Heavy swells with long whiskers lounged in late and left early. It was only possible to carry on administration with any degree of efficiency by supplying the departments with able chiefs brought in from outside.

Long after the more shameless and direct forms of parliamentary bribery prevalent under Walpole and George III had been suppressed, Civil Service jobbing was regarded as an indispensable attribute of government. Indeed, when Peel in his political purism discontinued the lavish distribution of honours and peerages on which Pitt had relied,[1] the Civil Service was the only field even of modified corruption left to Victorian statesmen. It is all the more credit to them and to their age that they were induced to give it up.

The Indian Civil Service, which had even in the days of 'old corruption' been more carefully selected than the Home Service, was in 1853 thrown open to all by the way of competitive examination.[2] But England in the days of Palmerston followed suit more slowly as regards the departments of Whitehall. Sir Charles Trevelyan, a public servant of great zeal and of long experience first in India and then as permanent head of the Treasury, made himself the protagonist of the new system. Competitive examination, derided at first as a pedantic eccentricity, proved its practical value by results, till at length it came to be generally regarded as the best means of avoiding jobbery and securing able men. From 1855 onwards it was introduced into Whitehall by slow degrees, a subject of acute controversy at every stage. At length in 1870 Gladstone's great axe fell. Patronage was abolished in almost all the public offices, and the normal entrance to a career in the Home Civil Service was made to depend upon open competition.

This change has perhaps done as much for the efficiency and good government of the country as many more renowned political measures. At last the career was open to talents. Machinery had been set up for a partial solution of the problem so often stated by Carlyle – how to find the ablest men to govern – though the sage himself had now taken to cursing and nothing would please him.

1. This custom has again, in our own day, taken on very large proportions, partly, no doubt, because the opening of the Civil Service to competition has closed the other channel by which Government used to reward its followers. If so, it is the less pernicious of two evils, because a State can afford to traffic in offices even less well than to traffic in titles.

2. See p. 312, above.

To select men for practical careers on the report of examiners showed also a belief in higher education, which was something new in England. Instead of social qualifications or wealthy friends, trained intellect was to be a young man's best passport. The Universities and the cause of higher teaching benefited greatly by the change.

In the following year a measure inspired by the same spirit, and advocated largely by the same group of men, opened promotion in the army to gentlemen of moderate means. The custom which made it necessary for an officer to purchase his commission from his predecessor at every step, forbidden by William III, had been permitted again by Queen Anne, and regulated by her successors by Royal Warrant. But the 'regulation prices' were unlawfully exceeded, and an officer, having bought his commission, had in practice the right to sell it for what he could get from some one of his subordinates. The result was that poor men were passed over. They had no chance of promotion, except occasionally in time of war, since commissions vacated by death could not be sold.[1] The army chiefs, even when they wished to make promotions by merit, had not the power to promote a man who could not purchase his step.

The Commander-in-Chief, the Duke of Cambridge, was not, perhaps, temperamentally over-zealous in the cause of promotion by merit. His influence, and that of the Queen his cousin, were strong against the abolition of Purchase, and it was argued that the regulation of the army was in some special sense a prerogative of the Crown. Against this reading of the constitution Gladstone and his able War Minister, Cardwell, tactfully but successfully contended. The Queen, who never forgot Melbourne's early lessons, gave way with a good sense which her strong opinions and personal bias rendered the more admirable. Cardwell's army reforms were carried through, but by way of compromise the Duke of Cambridge, who heartily disliked them, was left as Commander-in-Chief until 1895.

The opinion not only of the Court and the Duke of Cambridge, but of the vocal part of the army also was against the change. Public opinion, however, was aroused against Purchase during the Franco-Prussian war, when the state of our fighting forces caused

1. If an officer, therefore, was killed in action, his widow got nothing in return for the large sum which he had given for his commission, and which in many cases he had borrowed. If Purchase had not been abolished, the late war against Germany would have ruined the families of countless officers. Besides, we should have lost the war.

anxiety. As soon as the war ended the army was again forgotten, but the Government by that time stood committed. The abolition of Purchase was put through by Royal Warrant, after the House of Lords had prevented it from passing in the form of a statute. The House of Commons had voted compensation for existing holders of purchased commissions: the nation, said Gladstone, must buy back its own army from its own officers.

Edward Cardwell was one of the public men whom Peel had trained. It fell to him to transform the British Army from what Wellington had left it to what it was at the close of the century. In his reforms of 1869–71 he managed to combine increased efficiency with the economy for which Gladstone's Ministry was famous, by reducing the Colonial garrisons, a step which made for the ultimate military strength of the Empire by throwing upon Canada and Australasia the right and duty of self-defence. He abolished the system of dual control of the army, by which responsibility was divided between the Commander-in-Chief and the Secretary for War. The former was now definitely subordinated to the Minister.

Above all, Cardwell introduced the short-service system of twelve years – three or six with the colours and nine or six in the reserve. The long-service system, though loved by the Duke of Wellington, had grave defects. There were not enough young men in the ranks; there was no proper reserve to call out in time of war; and, since men left the army too late to have any chance of taking up civilian life with advantage, the prospects of a common soldier's career were so unattractive that in nine cases out of ten necessity alone drove men to enlist. Cardwell's short-service system was a lesson learnt from the Prussian victory in 1866, which had proved that two or three years' training sufficed to make good soldiers, and that large reserve classes were essential.

The change helped both directly and indirectly the better prospect opening before the British soldier. His lot was slowly but steadily improving from the time of the Napoleonic wars to the outbreak of the struggle with Germany in our own day. Before the century closed Lord Roberts could say of the men whom he commanded in South Africa, 'they bore themselves like heroes on the battlefield and like gentlemen on all other occasions'. It was not a dictum that would ever have passed the lips of the Iron Duke.[1] If a history were compiled describing the changes of one hundred years in the treatment of our soldiers and sailors, and in the regard entertained for them by their own officers and by the rest of the Community, it would be an epitome of the nation's general

1. See pp. 135–6, above.

progress in humanity, efficiency, and social solidarity. For it was the century not only of hope but of solid achievement.

CHAPTER 23

IN the summer of 1870 the irrepressible conflict broke out between the France of Napoleon III and the Germany of Bismarck. England was most afraid of France, but saw little reason to desire the success of either combatant. Both stood for a highly developed form of militarism, not likely to be improved in spirit by victory, and affording the world no prospect of future peace and goodwill.

Unlike his adversary, Bismarck knew what he wanted and how to get it. In foreign affairs the course of his *realpolitik* lay straight for the goal of Prussian power, and was never diverted by generosity, prejudice, or passion. At home, he had invented a new type of despotism. It was no longer merely negative, like the system of Metternich, the 'dead hand' stretched out to prohibit all change. Despotism under Bismarck had become an active principle in the van of progress. It was no longer timidly hostile to the mercantile class, the press, education, and science, but harnessed them all to the car of government. Like the liberalism of Cavour's régime in Piedmont ten years before, Bismarck's despotism swept along with it on its path all the activities of the nation's life. It gave the lead to the patriotic spirit, which in 1849 had fought under the Liberal flag in Germany as elsewhere. If Bismarck were to win the war with France, his system would exert an attractive power all the world over, and would become a formidable rival to those liberal ideas, mainly derived from England and France, which had for half a century been the chief motive power in the intellectual life of Europe.

The French Emperor, on the other hand, no longer knew where he was going either at home or abroad. He had failed to reconcile in practice the theoretic contradictions always involved in his 'Napoleonic ideas'. On the one hand, he stood for the general principles of nationality and plebiscitary liberalism in Europe. On the other hand, he supported the Vatican against the desire of the Italian people for Rome as capital, and he was himself the voice of France, refusing to allow the Germans to complete the edifice of their national unity. Moreover, his policy of thwarting Italian aspirations seriously damaged the best chance he had of thwarting German aspirations. All was confusion and weakness in the counsels of this man who, a dozen years before, had been the arbiter of Europe.

In 1870 he entered the lists, with prestige already lowered by a decade of failure following on a decade of success. It was but one of his disappointments that England, to gain whose friendship he had in the past made great sacrifices, would at best be coldly neutral. Sick in body and mind, he knew, before the world proclaimed it, that his grasp on men and things was failing. Wherever he looked he saw irresistible forces rising to thwart every item of his policy, beyond the Alps, beyond the Rhine, and beyond the Atlantic.

Under cover of the American Civil War to protect him from the Monroe Doctrine, Napoleon had tried to establish a Latin Empire under French patronage in Mexico. But the North had won, had shortly afterwards served him with notice to quit, and he had not risked a war on the other side of the globe against the veterans of Sherman and Grant. When the French troops were withdrawn, the Emperor Maximilian, whom Napoleon had imported from Europe, was caught by his Mexican subjects and shot. It was a bitter humiliation to the man who had sent him.

At home Napoleon now desired to have Ministers responsible to Parliament, although his Empire was a despotism founded on the plebiscite, expressly as a substitute for government by Assembly. A change of ground so fundamental was not easy of accomplishment. The French Liberals of the rising generation, whose support was essential for the success of a 'Liberal Empire', were most of them Republicans at heart, taught by Victor Hugo's example in exile, and by Gambetta's fiery eloquence, to look askance at 'the man of December'[1] and all his works.

Meanwhile his Spanish wife Eugénie, at the head of the more reactionary Imperialists, held that he was betraying his own cause by toying with Parliaments. They saw in a German war the means of reviving the glories of the French Empire, and of the Roman Church. And he, in the physical weakness and moral apathy that now disarmed his energies, had not the courage to say them nay.

Bismarck meanwhile was moving from strength to strength. He had half created the German Empire by successful war against Austria in 1866. Napoleon would neither accept the new Germany as inevitable, nor boldly oppose it while there was yet time. He protested, intrigued, demanded 'compensations', in Belgium or

1. The name given to Napoleon III on account of the *coup d'état* of December 1851. See pp. 294–5, above.

on the Rhine, for the growing power of Prussia. Bismarck nick-named such demands 'the policy of *pourboires*'. Napoleon had still a chance of bringing Austria and Italy together into the field on his side. But he would not pay Italy her price of Rome as capital. Nor had he the command over his nerves to wait even one year, till Austria should have recovered from her last defeat, and be ready to fight Prussia again. In July 1870, at the hour appointed by Bismarck, he allowed the French Imperialist party to hustle him into the war he dreaded.

The question which nominally gave rise to hostilities, the suggested Hohenzollern candidature for the throne of Spain, was so incompetently handled by Napoleon and his counsellors that, contrary to the real facts as Bismarck subsequently revealed them, France appeared to the world as the sole aggressor. Such was the impression produced in England on both Government and Opposition, although Gladstone said privately – 'On the face of the facts France is wrong, but as to personal trustworthiness the two moving spirits, Napoleon and Bismarck, are nearly on a par.' All British parties were in favour of a strict neutrality.

Indeed, when the war began it was not Germany we feared. Britons had sucked in fear of Napoleonic conquest with their mother's milk, while the idea of the dreamy Germans as a material danger to Europe was new and strange. Only a few years back their soldiers had been represented by our comic artists as funny little men strutting about under the weight of enormous helmets.[1] In 1870 these diminutive warriors shot up, in the English prints, into genial giants with bushy beards, singing Luther's hymns round Christmas-trees in the trenches before Paris. We were too ignorant of Germany to regard her as a serious rival. Only eccentric intellectuals like Matthew Arnold and George Meredith warned us that there was something in German professors and their *geist* that was at once admirable and dangerous.[2] Representative British thought of the day, whether Queen Victoria's or Thomas Carlyle's, was all for the German civilization against the French. The small but influential group of Positivists, bred up in the school of French intellectual liberalism, were almost singular in their anti-German views.

Immediately after the outbreak of war, Bismarck produced a rod that he had been keeping in pickle for France, in the shape of the

1. e.g., Dicky Doyle's *Foreign Tour of Brown, Jones and Robinson*, 1854.
2. Matthew Arnold's *Friendship's Garland* and Meredith's *Harry Richmond* (*vide* chapter xxix), both published in the year of the Franco-German war, are curiously similar in their general doctrine as regards Germany.

draft of a suggested treaty of 1866, written out in the handwriting of Benedetti, then French Ambassador at Berlin. This document had proposed the annexation of Belgium by France, as a *pourboire* in return for French consent to the union of Germany. British public opinion was deeply stirred. Gladstone wrote to Bright –

If the Belgian people desire, on their own account, to join France or any other country, I for one will be no party to taking up arms to prevent it. But that the Belgians whether they would or no, should go 'plump' down the maw of another country to satisfy dynastic greed, is another matter.

Gladstone at once proposed a treaty to France and Germany, providing that, if either combatant violated Belgian neutrality, Great Britain would cooperate with the other party in its defence, but without necessarily taking a share in the general operations of the war. By 9 August 1870 the signatures of Germany and France were obtained, and nothing more was heard of the Belgian question.

In the first week of September came the surrender of the main French army at Sedan, and the fall of the Napoleonic Empire. The next four months afforded the spectacle of the young Republic heroically attempting, under the inspiration of Gambetta, to make good the lost cause of France. Naturally British sympathies moved round not a little, but there was no question of interference. The German demand for the predominantly French provinces of Alsace-Lorraine threw a shade over the innocent beauty of the German Christmas-trees, and aroused Gladstone's intense indignation. But England had no wish to fight and there was nothing to be done.[1]

To keep England's moral indignation engaged elsewhere, and to prevent joint action by England, Austria and Russia on behalf of beaten France, Bismarck had secretly stirred up Russia to denounce the 'Black Sea' articles of the treaty of 1856. Palmerston had prolonged the Crimean War for half a year to obtain provisions which neutralized the Euxine, and prohibited Russia from keeping an arsenal on its shores or a navy in its water. Such articles, denying Russia's sovereignty in her own ports, could wisely have been struck out of the treaty by consent. But this had never been done, and Russia now on her own account declared her intention of treating them as a 'scrap of paper'. We rightly protested against a manner and method of proceeding of such evil example, while

1. Carlyle, then at the height of his fame and influence, preached the German view of the Alsace-Lorraine question in his letter to *The Times*, with great effect.

Bismarck expressed pained surprise at Russia's precipitate action! But we could not fight for an arrangement which we felt to be of doubtful justice. And so, after a due course of diplomatic conferences, we swallowed the Russian proposals and Bismarck swallowed Alsace-Lorraine.

These transactions, though the misfortune rather than the fault of the existing Ministry, left an uneasy sense that Gladstone was not vigorous enough in foreign affairs. The *Alabama* claims award[1] of the following year increased this impression at the time, although posterity feels gratitude to the statesmen who avoided war with America. There was perhaps more substance for the suspicion that Gladstone's instinct for economy in taxation inclined him to shorten supplies for army and navy; at least it caused differences with some of his own colleagues, as well as furnishing Opposition with a text. Disraeli, with his keen eye for world movements and tendencies of the age, proclaimed the Conservative party as the champion of the external honour and safety of Britain, with a special interest in the Colonies and the Empire.

It was a new departure. During the middle years of the century, Palmerston as Whig Minister had voiced the nationalist sentiments of the country, while the Conservatives, alike under Aberdeen, Peel, Derby, and Disraeli himself, had been distinctly a peace party, critical of Palmerston and his trumpetings. Neither had they shown any special interest in the Colonies, which were too democratic to arouse the enthusiasm of the territorial aristocracy. The shifting of party ground now observable in these matters was in the natural order of things, though the views and characters of Disraeli and Gladstone quickened the pace. So long as the professional and middle classes, who usually form the largest body of sensitive nationalist feeling, had been ranged under the Liberal banner, Palmerston had been their spokesman. They were now, for a variety of reasons, of which working-class enfranchisement was the chief, coming rapidly round to the new Conservatism. They brought with them their zeal for the honour and strength of Britain. And since an age of self-conscious Imperial expansion was at hand, this fact was destined to be of governing importance. Disraeli no longer spoke of the Colonies as 'a millstone round our neck'.

But the Conservative Imperialism which Disraeli adumbrated and which Salisbury and Chamberlain matured, each after his own fashion, was by none of them directed against Germany. During

1. See p. 328, above.

354

the remainder of the century British Imperialism more often came into conflict with France or Russia. Considering that Germany had become the dominant power in Europe this may seem remarkable, but the reason is clear. England was becoming less interested in Europe and more interested in colonies and in the world beyond the ocean. Now while Bismarck cared little for German colonial expansion, France after Sedan, as formerly after Waterloo, attempted to make good in Asia and Africa what she had lost on the Rhine. France, therefore, again and again appeared as our chief colonial competitor, while the huge bulk of Russia overshadowed India and the East.

But on one occasion Disraeli was compelled to interfere in Western European politics, and against the German power. In 1875 Bismarck, disappointed at the rapid recovery of France, was meditating either a fresh war to crush her to the ground for ever, or the extortion of a virtual surrender on her part of her rights to independent action. Disraeli was by that time in office. 'Bismarck,' he wrote, 'is really another old Bonaparte again, and must be bridled.' For this purpose he effected a temporary combination with Russia that gave pause to Germany, and maintained European peace without the humiliation of France.

The incident passed over, but it was ominous, and indicated the underlying forces and temper of the new age. After the annexation of Alsace-Lorraine all Europe 'breathed a harsher air'. The sense of international goodwill and the brotherhood of the human race, which had lent an ideal halo to the commercialism of the Great Exhibition of 1851, had faded into air. Abroad, the inculcation of race hatred was becoming one of the functions of modern government and of modern education. The ethical and liberal interpretation of history, which had held the field for many years, began to give way before doctrines of race war and class war as the secret of evolution. Power began to replace justice as the standard of intellectual appeal. Napoleon III had gone, and with him went the last hopes of international Free Trade, for in Europe and America high protective tariffs were the legacy of war and the expression of international rivalry. And with the departure of Napoleon went his plebiscites, a form of respect for justice to which he had adhered even when he wished to annex Savoy and Nice to France. Polish liberty, Russian reform were made far more improbable by the material and intellectual primacy of the Germany that Bismarck had created.[1] This change of atmosphere in European thought and

1. The last great change for the good that took place in Russia, the freeing of the serfs, was in 1861.

politics gradually and in milder forms had its reactions in our own island.

The years 1859–70 had seen three great revolutions accomplished – the national union of Italy on a basis of freedom, the national union of Germany on the basis of a progressive military despotism, and the closer union of the United States on a basis of Negro emancipation. The sixties were the most formative years in history between the era of Napoleon and the revolutionary convulsions following the great war of our own day. But after 1870 the period of political change came to an end. Bismarck, who had for his own purposes aided Italy in 1866, having got what he wanted, ceased to be a revolutionary, and the hour of enfranchisement passed by. The problems of liberation which were not solved before 1871 remained unsolved in 1914. The new Europe saw, indeed, an enormous increase of material prosperity, great educational progress, and a turbid intellectual activity of every kind, but it succeeded in solving no problem of the first order. Whereas in eleven years Italian unity, German unity, and American abolition and State rights were definitely settled, the next forty-six years failed to bring a solution of any one of the great problems still outstanding: Russian liberty, German liberty, the Polish question, the Turkish and Balkan questions, the race questions of Austria-Hungary, and the Irish question. And to these old problems which it failed to solve, the spirit of the new age added the universal ruin and slavery of competitive armaments.

But the gradual darkening of the world's more distant prospects, and the hardening of the international tone, did not interfere with the flood-tide of British prosperity. The bettering of conditions of life for the majority of people was the material achievement of the Victorian age, parallel to its glories in literature, intellect, and science.

In consequence of these improved conditions, Robert Owen's Socialism and all revolutionary tendencies, speculative or practical, were in abeyance in England between 1850 and 1880. It was an era of relative content. The franchise was extended. The Wholesale Co-operative movement was helping to train the character and intelligence, as well as to assist the budgets, of countless working-class families.[1] Trade Unionism grew steadily in the more highly organized industries, gradually put down the abuses of Truck payment, and secured as wages a large share of the increased profits of trade.

1. See pp. 273–4, above.

Between 1866 and 1875 this growing power of Trade Unionism, though still without a political organization or programme, was brought into the arena of national politics over its own affairs.

In some of the old-fashioned Trade Unions, especially in Sheffield, terrorism accompanied by crime was resorted to against recalcitrant workmen. Many of these stories got about and added to the general antipathy towards Trade Unions which existed among the political classes of the day. This feeling was not peculiar to one party, nor was it confined to persons out of sympathy with the working classes. Lord Shaftesbury, of Factory Act fame, wrote: 'All the single despots and all the aristocracies that ever were or ever will be, are as puffs of wind compared with those tornadoes, the Trade Unions.'

In 1866 the explosion of a can of gunpowder in a workman's house in Sheffield brought public indignation on the subject to a head. Next year, a judicial decision in the Courts seemed to deprive the Unions of the freedom which they had enjoyed for over forty years, under the laws secured for them by Place and Hume.[1] The Judges decided that the Boilermakers' Union had no legal existence and could not, therefore, sue for a debt. The Lord Chief Justice added that the objects of the Union being 'in restraint of trade' rendered it an illegal association; this decision would clearly apply to all Trade Unions, which were thus deprived by the judiciary of a position they had enjoyed since 1825.

At this stage the larger and better organized societies of the New Model[2] took the affair in hand. They detested the crimes of the badly managed Unions, which were to a large extent a legacy of the days when all combinations of workmen were illegal, when the kind of civil war described in *Shirley* was carried on by armed attacks on the houses of employers, by machine-breaking, and violence to blacklegs. The big Unions now demanded an inquiry which they were sure would exculpate the movement as a whole in its more recent developments. They also demanded legislation to give them back the liberty of which the judge-made law was threatening to deprive them. Throughout the prolonged crisis that followed they were excellently advised by Tom Hughes, their champion in Parliament, and Mr Frederic Harrison, the Positivist.

But the Trade Union world was not then organized for political action. Although in 1868 the Liberal majority had been largely returned by the votes of the newly enfranchised workmen of the

1. pp. 203–4, above.
2. p. 273, above.

towns, Gladstone was far from satisfying the Trade Unionists by his legislation of 1871. By the Trade Union Act of that year, Trade Unions became indeed legally recognized and fully protected associations. No Trade Union henceforth was to be illegal merely because it was 'in restraint of trade'. Every Union was entitled to be registered; and registration was to give it complete protection for its funds. Gladstone's Act left the Unions in such a position that it was supposed they could not be sued or proceeded against in a Court of Law except for certain very limited purposes. This was a great advantage of which they were deprived thirty years later by the next onslaught of the judiciary – the Taff Vale decision.

But what Gladstone's government gave with one hand it took away with another. For in the same year, 1871, it passed a Criminal Law Amendment Act which pronounced illegal various actions on which Trade Union power in time of strike largely rested. The Trade Unions, indeed, could not, it was then held, be sued for acts done by their members or at their orders. But the individual workman could be imprisoned for various actions customary in a strike. 'Watching and besetting', that is 'picketing' workmen continuing at work during a strike, was made illegal even when done only by a single person.

Working-class discontent with this Criminal Law Amendment Act of 1871 was one of the causes of the Liberal defeat at the polls in 1874. Disraeli had the acuteness to learn this lesson. His sympathy with the working class, which in his youth he had expressed in his novels, was now become a factor in politics. By his Bill of 1875 the Criminal Law Amendment Act was repealed; violence and intimidation were left to be dealt with as a part of the general criminal code.

But the fundamental reason of the defeat of the Liberal Ministers in 1874 was that they had done their work. When Disraeli pointed to his opponents mustered on the Treasury bench as 'a range of exhausted volcanoes', it was a jibe that contained a compliment. The Temperance arrow had gone astray, but Gladstone had shot away his quiverful mostly into the bull's-eye, and for the present had no more measures to propose, either for Great Britain or Ireland – except, indeed, the abolition of the income-tax! That he should actually have been able to prepare a Treasury plan for conducting the taxpayer into such a paradise shows what an effective guardian he had been of the national finances, but indicates how little he foresaw the future either of armaments or of social reform. Disraeli was returned at the polls,[1] and the income-tax has yet to be repealed.

Disraeli first attained power as Prime Minister in his seventieth year. But ere he reached that eminence he had already achieved a great work, curiously similar to that of the statesman whose career he had destroyed a generation before. He had taught the Conservatives to accept the new democratic conditions, but unlike Peel he had 'educated his party' without impairing its unity or cooling its devotion to himself. Alike in opposition and in office he proved himself a master in the handling of colleagues and followers and in the conduct of the party fortunes – aspects of statesmanship in which Gladstone in later life was less successful.

Disraeli did not come to Downing Street, like Gladstone six years before, pledged to a long and contentious programme of domestic legislation. His promise was to give a rest to 'harassed interests'. But he also kept his other promise, not to forget social reform.

Apart from the laws in favour of workmen's action when on strike, much useful work was done for housing, sanitation, and the ever-growing factory code. Disraeli's able Home Secretary, Richard Cross, consolidated and improved the mass of existing legislation on these subjects. The Public Health Act of 1875 marked a stage in the battle against disease to which Chadwick had committed the State a generation before. '*Sanitas sanitatum, omnia sanitas*', said Disraeli, to enliven a subject more important than entertaining. The Artisans' Dwelling Act of the same year enabled local authorities to begin to deal with the horrors of the slum areas.

In these and other ways Cross added many new functions to local government. Such Acts were part of a general process, by which the central government, by means of 'grants in aid' of local rates and otherwise, encouraged municipal activity in innumerable departments of life. Drains, water, housing, public spaces, as well as education, were now being supplied or controlled by public authorities. The modern municipal system has been called 'an application of democracy to the supply of the wants of the household'. It is also an application of scientific bureaucracy to the task of rendering life under modern conditions possible in our crowded island. Ever since the Municipal Reform Act of 1835, government

1. The election of 1874 was the first that took place under the provisions of the Ballot Act, passed by the Liberals in 1872. At the election of 1868 there were still the hustings and open voting.

after government down to our own day has helped to build up and extend the system. Gladstone in 1871 had set up a new department called the Local Government Board, on to which the business of controlling and stimulating the action of local authorities has chiefly devolved. The work of Cross was merely the work of one Minister in a long series, but it was good work, and, coming immediately after a great Conservative victory at the polls, it gave assurance of continuity in the national progress towards better conditions of life.

It was a sign of changing times that the tide had at last turned against enclosure of commons. The great enclosures which had added immensely to the area under proper cultivation had been made largely at the expense of the old-fashioned type of peasantry, now practically vanished from the land.[1] But since the middle of the century, enclosures of commons to obtain building-land and private grounds had begun seriously to affect the interests of the industrial population, who had more powerful friends than those whom the peasants had been able to muster. From 1864 onwards, a spirited agitation was conducted against the disappearance of public pleasure-grounds in the neighbourhood of great cities, and the 'lungs' within their crowded areas. Epping Forest was saved for Londoners, and many successful fights had been put up in the Law Courts against illegal enclosures that in a former generation would have passed unchallenged. The Commons Preservation Society was led by such Liberals as Shaw Lefevre and Henry Fawcett, but its supporters were not confined to one party and its influence was strongly felt in the Conservative House of Commons of the seventies.

It was also characteristic of the new age that the warm-hearted Samuel Plimsoll, the sailor's friend, by force of public opinion, and by dint of losing his temper at a lucky moment on the floor of the House, shamed honourable members into passing the first measure aimed at protecting the lives of mariners in the 'coffin ships' of the mercantile marine. But the Act of 1876 was only the beginning of such legislation, and was not in itself very effective.

Throughout the nineteenth century Russia was striving to advance towards Constantinople over the ruins of the Turkish Empire. She was drawn forward by imperialist ambition, by interest in the oppressed Christians of her own communion, many of whom were Slav by language and race, and by the instinct to seek a warm-water port – a window whence the imprisoned giantess could look

1. See pp. 152–5, above.

out upon the world. The world, however, had no great wish to see her there.

Canning[1] had planned to head off Russia's advance, not by direct opposition, but by associating her with England and France in a policy of emancipation, aimed at erecting national States out of the component parts of the Turkish Empire. Such States could be relied upon to withstand Russian encroachment on their independence, if once they were set free from the Turk. The creation of the kingdom of Greece was the immediate outcome of Canning's policy. A small Serbian State of the same national type had already begun to struggle for existence during the Napoleonic wars. The Bulgarian race was still wholly submerged. But Canning's policy gave hopes to them all.

Within a generation of the battle of Navarino, the Whig–Peelite Ministry forgot the tradition of Byron, reversed the policy of Canning, and sought to restrain Russia by the opposite method, namely, by propping up the rotten body of Turkish rule in Europe. The Crimean War succeeded in keeping Russia back for just twenty years. She was now once more on the move, in consequence of the rising of Serbs and Bulgarians against 'the unspeakable Turk'. Would England meet the new situation by reviving the policy of Canning, or the policy of the Crimea?[2] It was long since our people had been interested in the Eastern question, and much had happened in our island since the siege of Sebastopol. It was therefore by no means certain what the British would on this occasion be pleased to think. In such circumstances all may depend upon a single man. The masterful lead given by Disraeli caused official England to revive the policy not of Canning but of Palmerston.

The pro-Turkish policy was again reversed in the following generation, when Lord Salisbury declared that we had 'put our money on the wrong horse'. It was Disraeli who made the Conservatives for a few years identify the Turkish cause with the cause of our own Empire, and it was Gladstone who compelled the Liberal party to become the channel of a no less powerful anti-Turkish sentiment.

There were dissentients in both camps. Lord Derby, the son of Disraeli's old chief, now his Foreign Secretary, differed from him

1. See pp. 215–16, above.
2. Gladstone, who had sat in the Crimean Cabinet, never would allow the case had been the same in 1854 as in 1876. Between the two dates there may indeed have been a change in the general European situation and in the relation of Russia to Europe, but as regards the Christian races inside the Turkish Empire the position was the same.

and resigned, whereas Lord Hartington and Forster, the nominal chiefs of the Liberal party after Gladstone's retirement, hesitated to oppose Disraeli at critical moments, as did many of the Liberal members. But Gladstone, still in Parliament though nominally in retirement, roused one-half of the country behind their backs, and resumed the unofficial lead of the Opposition over their embarrassed heads.

The British people, when left to themselves, neither knew nor cared who massacred whom between the Danube and the Aegean. Byron's Greece had appealed to their imagination and historical sense, but the Balkans were a battlefield of kites and crows. It took the combined genius of Disraeli and Gladstone to arouse, on that obscure subject, passions as hot as any that Englishmen had felt about the doings of foreigners since the days of Burke and the French revolution.

But on this occasion the rival factions were more evenly divided. On Disraeli's side was Clubland, the Services, the majority perhaps of the middle class with its nationalist susceptibilities, and, at the critical later stages of the affair, the mass of ordinary citizens whose instinct is to support their country in a quarrel to which Government has committed her. The London music-halls were hot against Russia, and a song that asserted our preparedness with a mild oath first caused the war-party to be nicknamed 'Jingoes'.[1] On the other side was the great majority of the working class, the great majority of the religious world, and many who, like Ruskin and Carlyle, ordinarily cared little for party politics. Nonconformists and High Churchmen were for once agreed. Both were proud of Gladstone though for different reasons, and both were zealous for the martyrs of Christianity in the East.

When Gladstone said 'Five millions of Bulgarians, cowed and beaten down to the ground, hardly venturing to look upwards, even to their Father in heaven, have extended their hands to you,' there were many who could not bear that we should fight Russia in order to give them back to the Turk. Gladstone's appeal was passionate and idealist. The most famous sentence of his diatribes on the Bulgarian atrocities supplied a cant term for the policy which he advocated:

Let the Turks now carry away their abuses in the only possible manner, namely, by carrying off themselves. Their Zaptiehs and their

1. We don't want to fight
But by Jingo, if we do,
We've got the men, we've got the ships,
We've got the money too.

Mudirs, their Bimbashis and their Zusbashis, their Kaimakams and their Pashas, one and all, *bag and baggage*, shall I hope clear out from the Province they have desolated and profaned.

The successful idealism of his appeal, in an age moving fast towards materialism in politics, struck foreigners more than anything else in the incalculable conduct of our countrymen over the whole affair, and made 'Gladstone's England' popular among the Balkan Christians, in spite of the action of the British Government.

To Disraeli and to many others all this was foolishness. They saw danger in the Russian power, which they believed to threaten India already, and Europe in the long run. They feared to alienate our Mohammedan fellow-subjects by appearing to abandon the head of their religion to his Christian enemies. If Disraeli cared little about the Balkans, he cared much about India. He had proclaimed the Queen its Empress. He had, by an able stroke, bought for England an interest in the Suez Canal shares as the key to our Eastern possessions. It delighted him to bring Indian troops to Malta as a protection for the Porte and a warning to Russia.[1] If he thought the Tsardom an abomination he was not far wrong. And although his strong Jewish sympathies inclined him to look too leniently on the Turk by comparison, we now know by bitter experience that he was right in supposing the Turk to have no monopoly in Balkan atrocities.

But in one respect Gladstone, for all his idealism, was more realist than Disraeli. Gladstone believed in nationality and Disraeli did not. Disraeli believed in 'race', but he did not see why every race should demand as of right to express its genius through national freedom and self-government. His own race, of which he was so proud, throve and was famous for its own distinctive qualities, without being a nation. And so, except in the case of old-established 'nations' like England and France, Disraeli preferred cosmopolitan empires of the *ancien régime*. He had supported Austrian and papal claims against Italian aspirations. On the same principle he saw no reason why the Turk should not continue to rule over Serbs, Greeks, and Bulgars. But national feeling was the great force of the century, and had become a motive power in all human affairs. *Realpolitik* could no longer leave it out of account. It was impossible, as events have since proved, permanently to subject Serbs, Greeks, and Bulgars to the Turk.

For some ten years after the death of Palmerston, British intervention in the affairs of the Continent had been on principle reduced to a minimum. This state of things was now brought to an

1. See note, p. 110, above.

end. Disraeli was determined that England should be heard as a principal in the counsels of Europe. He would not consent that, because France was down and out, all great questions should be left to the decision of the three despotic Empires. There was much to be said for this policy in general; and much in particular for preventing the control of the Balkans and the Straits by Russia – although in 1914, under altered circumstances, we fought to place her in Constantinople itself. But Disraeli's vision, penetrating as it was, had limits in certain directions. He failed to see that England would have interfered with more powerful and lasting effect, and would have checked Russia more effectually, if she had supported instead of opposing the creation of independent Balkan States.

At the beginning of the affair, in May 1876, he declined to let England join the Concert of Europe in coercing the Porte into better government, because he feared, perhaps not unjustly, that such a course 'must end very soon in the disintegration of Turkey'. He refused to commit us to the difficult task of liquidating the Turkish problem in agreement with the other Powers. Having so refused, he could hardly be surprised that, in default of action by Europe, Russia went to war alone to save the Christian races from extirpation. After the liberation of Bulgaria in the protracted and obstinate campaign of Plevna, the Russian armies arrived under the walls of Constantinople, and there dictated the Treaty of San Stefano.

The crisis had been reached. Disraeli, now Lord Beaconsfield, threatened Russia with instant war and brought Indian troops to Malta to show that he was in earnest. By his spirited action he compelled Russia to refer the Treaty of San Stefano to a European Congress. In view of the magnitude and variety of the interests touched, such a reference was only right.

Since Derby now resigned, Beaconsfield chose Lord Salisbury to succeed him at the Foreign Office. Salisbury had little enthusiasm for the pro-Turkish part of his chief's policy. He had written in September 1876 that the 'alliance and friendship' with Turkey 'is a reproach to us, and that the Turk's teeth must be drawn, even if he be allowed to live'. Salisbury seems to have moved somewhat in the direction of Beaconsfield's views as the course of events in 1877 increased his fears of Russia. But his presence as the Premier's right-hand man during the final crisis undoubtedly helped to bring about the compromise by which war was avoided.

The essentials of this compromise were agreed to between England and Russia before the meeting of the European Congress, which took place at Berlin under the chairmanship of Bismarck, and formally substituted the Treaty of Berlin for the terms of San Stefano. Beaconsfield acted throughout with vigour, courage, and success, and, if his point of view is accepted, with ultimate moderation. But the value in terms of human welfare which these great qualities had on this particular occasion in the world's history can only be estimated by carefully contrasting the treaty he tore up with the settlement which he caused to be put in its place.

In the light of subsequent events, many students of Balkan politics think that the Treaty of San Stefano was open to grave objections, but scarcely to those objections on which Beaconsfield

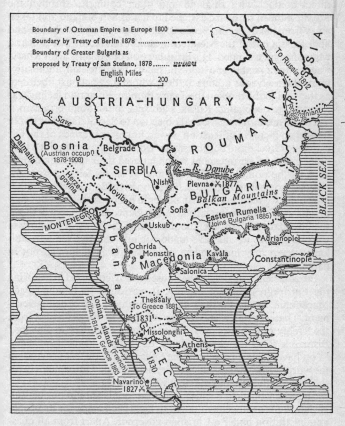

laid most stress. At San Stefano Russia had decreed the setting up of Bulgaria as a large State, adding Macedonia with its mixed races to the territories that were indisputably Bulgarian. Beaconsfield's main objection to this big Bulgaria was grounded on the belief that it would prove the catspaw of Russia. No doubt it was meant to be so, but it never could have been so, owing to Bulgarian national feeling. That factor was overlooked by Beaconsfield, who saw nothing except Panslavism. Bulgaria, as events soon proved, turned against Russia, and she would probably have done so even more effectually if she had been more powerful, and had been put in direct contact with England and other countries through the Mediterranean seaboard assigned to her at San Stefano and taken away from her at Berlin. Beaconsfield made it his boast that he had kept Russia out of the Mediterranean. But in fact it was Bulgaria whom he had excluded. His identification of Bulgaria with Russia was a fundamental and fatal mistake. The Russian authorities made themselves as odious to those whom they had just liberated, as they did to the races in the Tsar's Empire. Bulgarian feeling was a strong barrier against Russia's advance to the Mediterranean.

To our modern eyes the real objection to San Stefano lies not in its alleged increase of Russian power, but in its sacrifice of the fair claims of Greeks and Serbians, who would not have remained long quiet under an arrangement which ignored their racial rights and gave all the points to Bulgaria. Lord Salisbury felt this strongly, especially on behalf of Greece. But the merit of San Stefano was that it would have reduced Turkish power in Europe to a point not very much larger than what it is today. As a glance at the map will show, the boundaries of San Stefano, by cutting the Turkish territory in Europe in two, would have made Albania and the Western Balkans very nearly independent of Turkey in fact, though not in name.

Beaconsfield's success, as he himself saw it, consisted in restoring the European power of Turkey. It was done by handing back Macedonia to the Porte, without guarantees for better government. That was the essence of the Treaty of Berlin as distinct from the Treaty of San Stefano. 'There is again a Turkey in Europe,' Bismarck said. He congratulated the British Prime Minister – 'You have made a present to the Sultan of the richest province in the world; 4,000 square miles of the richest soil.' Unfortunately for themselves, the inhabitants went with the soil.

Since Beaconsfield decided that Macedonia should not be Bulgarian, some arrangement ought to have been made for its proper administration under a Christian governor. Apart from all question of massacres, the deadening character of the Turkish rule is well known. Lord Salisbury seems to have wished for a Christian governor, but nothing was done in that direction.

A golden opportunity was thus let slip. The Balkans had been in the hands of the Congress of Powers. The Turkish claims had been shorn away by the knife of war, and no new claims had yet been made good by Greek, Serb, or Bulgar. If, instead of deliberately restoring the plenary power of the Turk in Macedonia, they had divided up all the territory at their disposal among the appropriate races, putting 'mixed districts' under Christian governors, a great step would have been taken towards ultimate solution. But none of the parties to the Congress of Berlin could see so far. The opportunity went by, and a succession of Balkan wars in the twentieth century was rendered inevitable.

British diplomacy also secured at Berlin that the new Bulgaria should be not only reduced in size but divided into two parts, the southern part to be called 'Eastern Rumelia'. This makeshift arrangement was abolished seven years later, with the active concurrence of Lord Salisbury, who came to acquiesce in the desire of the Bulgarians for union in one State.

Another important outcome of the Treaty of Berlin was that Bosnia and Herzegovina, though freed from Turkey, were subjected, much against their will, to Austro-Hungarian rule. England promoted the arrangement, partly to win the consent of the German Powers to the general settlement, partly to prevent a chain of Slav States from extending across the Balkan peninsula. It had not yet occurred to us that we might come to fear the Teuton more than the Slav. This transaction rendered inevitable the ultimate collision between Serbia as the champion of Yugoslav nationality and the Austro-Hungarian Empire that denied it. With the connivance of England, Austria was given a great accession of unwilling subjects, and launched as a principal actor into Balkan politics. From her new basis in Bosnia and Herzegovina, she pursued her ambitions in Albania and Macedonia as representative of the Pan-German 'Drang nach Osten'.[1]

At the same time, by the separate 'Cyprus Convention' with the Porte, Beaconsfield obtained Cyprus from Turkey, and promised in return the protection of England for her Asiatic possessions, into which she once more promised to introduce reforms. But this alliance with Turkey practically went out of force on Gladstone's

1. Austro-Hungarian 'occupation' lasted till 1908, when it was converted into annexation by a high-handed act which proved one of the direct causes of the war of 1914.

return to power in 1880, and was never renewed by any government, Conservative or Liberal. The Armenians therefore lost the benefits that they might have derived from the system contemplated by Beaconsfield, by which we were to extend our protection and friendship to Turkey in a permanent form, and thereby, it was hoped, exert influence for the good on her conduct towards her Christian subjects, through the action of our Consuls in Asia Minor. The difficulty was that such friendship and alliance in fact if not in name committed us to defending the European power of Turkey in Macedonia, which was certain to be challenged by the arms of Bulgaria, Serbia, and Greece as soon as an opportunity offered. And neither Gladstone nor the Salisbury of later years would ever have asked England to fight in such a cause.

The Treaty of Berlin was received by the world with a sigh of relief, because a European war had been avoided. Even Gladstone thankfully admitted that Beaconsfield had so far failed that eleven millions of Christians had been released for ever from the Turk.

The country as a whole rejoiced to have secured peace – and 'Peace with Honour' as Beaconsfield proclaimed it to the crowds who welcomed him back to Downing Street on the night of his return from Berlin. If a dissolution had taken place in 1878 he would perhaps have obtained another lease of power.

During the prolonged crisis of the Eastern question, the Queen had been the strongest of partisans, desiring rather than fearing a war with Russia. Her enthusiasm was embarrassing to her friend the Prime Minister, whom she sometimes upbraided as too lukewarm in his own cause. Colleagues who refused to support him, and open opponents of his policy, she denounced in unmeasured terms. Disraeli had for years been flattering his royal mistress with a lavish skill of which no statesman of British race would, it is to be hoped, have been capable. His rival, indeed, never lost that reverence for the monarchy which his high Tory upbringing had installed, and felt a personal loyalty to the Queen which merited better treatment at her hands. But he alienated her not only by his views, but by his habit of industriously expounding them to her as if she were a public meeting. If the power of the Crown had still been what it was at the beginning of the century, Gladstone would never again have been in office.

Beaconsfield's loss of popularity during the year and a half that intervened between 'Peace with Honour' and the General Election of 1880 was due in part to bad times at home, including the agricultural depression which at length, in an age too late, verified his ancient prophecy that without Protection British agriculture would decline.[1] People grew tired of his spirited foreign and Imperial policy when they found themselves involved in prolonged operations against the Afghans and Zulus. Yet both these wars, after a period of reverses, ended successfully: the one in the capture of Cetewayo and the break-up of the Zulu military State after the battle of Ulundi; the other, thanks to the marches and victories of General Roberts, in the setting up of a friendly Amir in Afghanistan, pledged not to listen to the persuasions of Russia.

But people at home were no longer in a mood to be pleased. They said that the Afghan war, which was not over when Beaconsfield fell, would never have been necessary if his treatment of Russia in the Balkans had not provoked her to intrigue against us in the Middle East. It is probable that, in spite of the rejoicings in London over 'Peace with Honour', Gladstone's views on Turkey had made a more lasting impression in the provinces than many politicians knew.

The Liberals were at this time ahead of their rivals in democratic oratory and electoral organization. Gladstone's 'pilgrimage of passion', known as the Midlothian campaign, introduced new features into the methods of political propaganda. The Queen was shocked that a man who aspired to be for a second time her Prime Minister should address crowds from the window of a railway carriage on the mysteries of foreign policy. But times were changing, and Gladstone with them. The National Liberal Federation, organized, partly by Joseph Chamberlain of Birmingham, on a basis of democratic local Associations, was popularly known by the American word 'caucus'. It gave to the humbler members of the party up and down the provinces more control over the policy of the chiefs than would have been tolerated twenty years before, when the country was still ruled from Brooks's Club. The 'caucus' was undoubtedly a step away from aristocracy – whether most in the direction of real democracy or most in the direction of wire-pulling was a matter of hot dispute.

For a while the Conservatives were outdistanced in electoral machinery suited to the enlarged franchise. The 'Primrose League' was still a few years in the future; its assiduous courting of the democracy by the upper class would not have suited Conservatives of the older generation. But the world was gliding forward irresistibly into new fashions and new relationships of men and things. The Gladstonian victory at the polls in the spring of 1880, unexpected by the prophets of Pall Mall, did not lead to a period of

1. See p. 272, above.

Liberal legislation and government as successful as that of Gladstone's earlier Ministry, but it gave a great impulse to the democratizing of political thought and method in all parties. Disraeli, too, had played his own part in that process. A year later he died in retirement.

CHAPTER 24

GLADSTONE'S second Ministry was less successful than his first. In the time of the Franco-Prussian War and the *Alabama* claims, the negative and pacific treatment which he was most inclined to give to foreign and Imperial affairs had sufficed. In his second Ministry the world problems of a new age, beginning with South Africa and Egypt, dragged him unwillingly into a new set of questions which he disliked and of which therefore he was not the master. Only in Irish affairs he recognized the continuance of his old mission – 'to pacify Ireland' – and sprang at it with all his old eagerness and power. But, in spite of his new Land Act (1881), the Irish Question proved too much for him, too much for the Liberal party, and too much for the British nation; that it threatened the whole British Empire was not yet so evident as it became in the following generation.

The difference between his first and second Ministry was no less marked in domestic affairs. In 1868 he had been elected to carry out a specific and consistent programme of reform, on the general principles of which the whole party and more than half the nation were agreed. The doctrine of John Stuart Mill was to be put upon the Statute Book. In 1880, on the other hand, Gladstone came into office pledged to no extensive measures at home except county franchise, an important completion of the old programme of Mill. For the rest, no one had worked out a new set of principles to meet the needs of the new age. It had sufficed the Liberals at election time to denounce Beaconsfield's conduct of foreign affairs.

The victorious party was not a tempered weapon, but a bundle of interests and electoral forces, old and new. While Lord Hartington represented a Whig tradition already on the way to become Conservative, Joseph Chamberlain was maturing 'unauthorized programmes' of Radical taxation to hold capital to 'ransom', and a land policy for the benefit of the agricultural labourer, popularly known as 'three acres and a cow'. Chamberlain's doctrine forestalled much that has since happened in legislation and finance.

Unconsciously he heralded some of the Socialistic ideas which were just beginning, after a long interval, to re-emerge in the British Trade Union world. The leaders of the new radicalism, Chamberlain and Sir Charles Dilke, had felt the breath of the new age in regard to Imperial and Colonial questions, which they were not content to leave as assets to the new Conservatism. In this they differed from the Nonconformist old guard, still headed by John Bright, a venerable but no longer active figure.

For some years, the Liberal party was prevented from dissolving into its component sections by the authority and prestige of Gladstone. Yet the day was coming when he should accomplish the almost incredible feat of driving out from it Hartington, Chamberlain, and Bright by the same door.

The Conservative Opposition in the House of Commons was officially led by Sir Stafford Northcote, but without enough energy or vindictiveness to please four guerilla warriors below the gangway, humorously styled 'the Fourth Party'. The foremost of the group was Lord Randolph Churchill. Though a 'Tory democrat', and half a Radical in opinion, he was almost as much opposed to Gladstone in temper and attitude as Disraeli himself. A touch of genius enabled him, though new and untried, to provoke the great man with impunity, and these gladiatorial exhibitions at once raised him to the front rank in politics.

The Fourth Party made its fortune out of the Bradlaugh question: was the atheist member for Northampton, who had other claims to disapproval besides his theological views, to be allowed to take the oath of allegiance, the religious form of which could have no meaning to him, in order that he should sit in the House in accordance with the wishes of his constituents? It was sport to plague Gladstone and his Nonconformists in the name of morality and religion. This question was the first on which the Liberal party was divided. The most religious men in the House, including the Prime Minister, stood up for religious liberty, but were voted down when they proposed a Bill allowing members to affirm if they preferred not to swear. After years of controversy and scandal, including a struggle on the premises of the House between the giant Bradlaugh and a bevy of police, the question was settled by his admission to the first Parliament of 1886, and two years later by a law permitting affirmation.

If the Fourth Party brought into the new House 'the pert and nimble spirit of mirth', the 'Third Party' of sixty Home Rulers, led by the stern and humourless Parnell, brought with them the tragedy of Ireland. It was their plan to call attention to the grievances of the evicted tenantry by impeding the business of the Imperial Parliament. Their new policy of systematic 'obstruction' was ere long countered by the new rules of 'closure'. But the first sessions of the Liberal majority, so triumphantly returned in 1880, were neither dignified nor pleasant.

The Beaconsfield government, in its last three years of office, had dealt with a serious situation in South Africa. The Boer farmers who, forty years before, had moved off into the distant interior in the search for independence and isolation from the British,[1] were being hard pressed by the Zulus, and had not yet been able to consolidate their farming households into a State capable of defending them against the common enemy. In order to save this outpost of white civilization in South Africa, Beaconsfield's government crushed the Zulu military power,[2] having previously annexed the territory of the Transvaal Boers, while respecting the independence of the less distant, but more organized and wealthy, Orange Free State.

All sections of the English Opposition to Disraeli, including both Hartington and Gladstone, had denounced this 'forward policy', and their speeches against the annexation had been noted by the Boers, who unfortunately remembered them better than the speakers. When the Liberals came into office, they decided that the annexation could not be undone. All might yet have been well if they had at once given the Transvaal farmers the usual privileges of self-government within the Empire, which had been repeatedly promised even by the Conservative government. But for six months Gladstone, busy with other questions, left the Transvaal Boers to the unsympathetic rule of some very inferior men on the spot, who misled the home authorities into believing that all was well and that Transvaal self-government could be postponed till South African confederation had been arranged at Cape Town.

At length the Boers were convinced that the Liberal party, in spite of all its talk at election time, would do nothing for them. Despairing of a peaceful remedy, they rose in arms in December 1880, and two months later defeated a small British force on the boundaries of Natal by storming the steep sides of Majuba Hill.[3]

Ministers awoke with a shock to the serious nature of the situation which their neglect had created. Rather than continue the war which they now feared would extend into a race struggle all over

1. See pp. 254–5, above.
2. See p. 369, above.
3. See map, p. 398, below.

the sub-continent, they granted independence to the Transvaal under the Queen's suzerainty. Three years later this convention was renewed without an express statement of suzerainty, but subject to the condition that the Transvaal Republic would make no treaty without the consent of Britain, except with the Orange Free State.

If indeed concession following defeat in the field was the less of two evils, as the Cabinet believed, it was none the less fraught with future mischief. It embittered the feeling of the British all over South Africa, and it gave the Boers the idea they were the better men and could do what they liked. Gladstone, after Majuba, had been forced to choose between two very dangerous policies, and all because he had not been at the pains, in dealing with a few thousand farmers in a remote corner of the Empire, to establish some relation between his action in office and the expectations that he and his colleagues had raised when in Opposition.

Disraeli, in the interest of our Indian Empire and trade, had purchased for us the Khedive's very large holding in the Suez Canal shares and thus acquired an interest in its management. This was the first step towards British control of Egypt. Gladstone had disapproved of that first step, but he himself was destined to move forward to the end of the passage. He had been sincere when in his Midlothian orations he denounced Beaconsfield's ideas of Imperial expansion, and demanded a reversal of general policy. But Imperial policy, though it may be diverted into new directions, is not so easily reversed when it is borne forward on the prevailing current of the energies of an adventurous race. Maugre his Midlothian doctrine, Gladstone himself was to effect the occupation of Egypt. The spirit of the age and the exigencies of the local situation were to carry him whither he would not.

Egypt, nominally subject to the Sultan of Turkey, was actually ruled by a Khedive with but little interference from Constantinople. But the land was deeply in debt to foreign bond-holders, and was in a state of partial subjection to a number of European nations and interests. In 1881 the native army mutinied under one of its colonels, Arabi Pasha. Military grievances and ambitions were on the surface of the revolt, but underneath it was an Egyptian nationalist movement, Mahommedan in sentiment, but hostile to the Turk as a foreigner, to Christians, native or European, and to the foreign bond-holders ,officials, and financiers. In the course of the ensuing revolution, which was none too wisely handled by the Powers, the mob got out of hand and massacred fifty Europeans.

Who could deal with the situation? The Sultan of Turkey refused. And, strange to relate, France who had hitherto exerted a greater influence than any other nation in the internal development of Egypt and had, since Arabi's rising, drawn England into a joint interference drew back at the critical moment, because her Imperialist statesman, Gambetta, had fallen from office. No other Power would take up the challenge that Arabi had thrown down to Europe. Yet if Egypt were allowed to remain the prey of anarchy, the Suez Canal might be blocked and European interference would sooner or later be necessary. Would England then willingly see some rival Power established in the land which was the true meeting point of Africa, Asia, and Europe? Gladstone unwillingly agreed with the majority of his colleagues that it was England's task to save Egypt and to put her once more on her feet. If he had foreseen that the overthrow of Arabi would be the beginning, not the end of that task, he might have hesitated longer. But he hoped to come out of Egypt as easily as he went in.

The bombardment of the forts of Alexandria by the British fleet, which caused the resignation of Bright alone from the Cabinet, was followed by the landing of a British army under Sir Garnet Wolseley, who destroyed Arabi's army by storming his camp in the desert at Tel-el-Kebir.

The settlement of Egypt was a longer and more difficult work than Gladstone or his colleagues had foreseen, but they chose the right man to do it. Sir Evelyn Baring, best known by his later title of Lord Cromer, had served his apprenticeship in Egyptian finance in Disraeli's time. In September 1883 he was sent back to Egypt as British Agent and Consul-General. Working through the Khedive, he became in effect the Governor and transformer of Egypt.

Cromer's work was carried out under strange and difficult conditions, for England had no Protectorate or any defined position of authority. Nominally our troops were in Egypt as 'simple visitors', and the policy that Cromer urged upon the Khedive was, technically, mere 'advice', but it was advice to which he had to listen, for his throne depended on our support. On the other hand, his own power and ours with it were hedged round on all sides by the rights not only of the Sultan but of fourteen Christian States who possessed extraordinary privileges in Egypt under the 'Capitulations'. Many reforms of administration and justice could only be carried out with the consent of every one of these Powers.

The chief of the States concerned was France, and she was by far the most unfriendly. She remained, until the end of the century, hostile to our work and influence, often standing in the way of

Egyptian reform except in return for value received. For although France had voluntarily retired at the critical moment in 1882, she did not like to see us filling the vacancy created by her own refusal to act. Her attitude was very human and highly inconvenient.

Yet Cromer performed, even in these circumstances, the Herculean labour of restoring Egyptian finance and building up the ancient prosperity of the land of the Nile. He renovated and modernized the system of irrigation on which its welfare depends. And he gave security to the peasant from the crushing exactions and constant injustice which had been his lot for immemorial ages.

A necessary condition of Cromer's achievement was his tenure of power for twenty years or more, because Egyptian finance, the key to all other Egyptian reform, had no chance of recovery except by a long course of retrenchment in everything except productive expenditure. For this reason Baring's first object in 1883 was to withdraw the inefficient Egyptian garrisons from the Soudan, where they were isolated many hundreds of miles to the south and quite unable to hold their own against the barbarian hordes of the Upper Nile. Baring knew that the Soudan could only be conquered and held when Egyptian finances and the Egyptian army had been re-made from top to bottom. The conquest of the Soudan was necessary in the long run to the peace of Egypt, as the conquest of the Highlands had been necessary to the peace of Lowland Scotland. But there is a time for everything.

The task of the moment being to get the troops out of the Soudan, Baring was none too well pleased when the home government chose General Gordon for this delicate task. The selection had been made in a manner characteristic of the new age, as a result of a newspaper campaign conducted by Mr Stead, one of the founders of sensational journalism. If the enterprise in view had been a desperate attempt to conquer the Soudan with an inadequate force, no one could have been better chosen than the knight-errant of genius, the magnetic and mystical 'Bible Englishman' who, with his walking-stick, had turned the fate of a civil war in China and who knew the Soudan well. But to obey orders, especially orders to retreat, was beyond Charles Gordon's capacity, as Baring suspected. Unfortunately Gladstone did not.

Gordon went to Khartoum and, as might have been foreseen, stayed there attempting to reverse the policy he had been commissioned to carry out. He asked for reinforcements to 'smash the Mahdi', the new religious leader whose rule in the Soudan meant fanaticism, savagery, and the slave trade. Hartington was 'utterly bewildered' by Gordon's telegrams. Gladstone was angry with him and with himself for sending him. He was gradually cut off and besieged in Khartoum by the gathering hosts of the Mahdi. The situation in all its aspects was highly complicated and uncertain, and there was great variety of expert opinion as to the real position in the Soudan. But the upshot of it all was that the Government failed to send the relieving expedition under Lord Wolseley until just too late. As they struggled up the last stages of the difficult river journey, a thousand miles from Cairo, Khartoum was stormed and Gordon killed.

To Egypt the event made, perhaps, little difference. Even if Gordon had been rescued, the conquest of the Soudan must have been postponed; and it was all accomplished in good time. But to England the difference was immense. Gladstone's prestige never fully recovered from the blow. Coming on the top of Majuba, Khartoum created the impression that British honour and interests were not safe in his hands, and the Home Rule policy which he soon afterwards adopted was heavily handicapped in advance. The conscious Imperialism of the national sentiment in the following generation received an impulse from the fate of Gordon. An idealist, a soldier, and a Christian hero, he supplied to the popular imagination whatever was lacking in Disraeli as the patron saint of the new religion of Empire.

Only a few weeks before the tragedy at Khartoum, the Ministry had accomplished its greatest work and won its most popular triumph by passing the third Reform Bill. This measure extended to householders in the counties the franchise granted to householders in the boroughs in 1867. Since that date the need for including the inhabitants of the counties in the scheme of citizenship had been kept before Parliament and country by Mr G. O. Trevelyan. The Bill now introduced by Gladstone added more electors to the constituencies than the two earlier Reform Bills put together. It gave the vote not only to rustics but to large numbers of industrial hands, particularly miners, who had been hitherto disfranchised by the accident of living outside a parliamentary borough.

But the new fact in English life was the enfranchisement of the field labourer. For the first time since the peasants' risings against enclosures under the Tudor kings, he became a person with whom the great ones of the land must reckon. The failure of Joseph Arch's recent attempt had shown that the farm hands were in no position to organize Trade Unions. Until they obtained the vote, all that they could do, if they were sufficiently discontented with their lot, was to leave the countryside; and in fact they were leaving it fast. It might be argued that, from the point of view of the just balance of classes, they were even more in need of the vote than the better organized town workmen. But strength is added to the strong, and the agricultural labourer might never have obtained the vote but for the political action of the industrial community in the matter. So too, in the rural economic field, the liberation movement, having failed as a native product of the agricultural world, revived in the villages as an offshoot of industrial democracy, with the disadvantage that town Radicals and journalists too often knew little about the farm life and agricultural conditions which they desired to reform.

As an outcome of the new social spirit spreading from the industrial community to the village, of which Chamberlain's friend, Jesse Collings, was a missionary, and as a consequence of the county franchise, the status of the field labourer began, in the last fifteen years of the century, to receive more attention from above. A new habit of mind was engendered in many landlords who had previously, as a class, shown more consideration in dealing with their farmers than in thinking about those whom the farmers employed. The movement for providing allotments and smallholdings to the landless agricultural labourer gradually grew up, and between the third Reform Bill and our own day slowly realized most of what was practicable in the policy of 'three acres and a cow'. The movement was much helped by the fact that, owing to the increased importation from America, corn growing became relatively less profitable, while the forms of agricultural production less touched by foreign competition happened to be those more suited than corn to smaller holdings. Big farms had indeed become the permanent basis of British agriculture. But, after several generations of trial, the experiment of cultivating the big farms by labourers without land or independence had fairly broken down.

The terrible problem of rural housing also received more attention both from the landlords and the public. This change of attitude to the field labourer was partly due to the discovery that they were rapidly disappearing into the towns, and that something must be done to keep what was still left of them. But the need to consult them at election time was no less stimulating to this new sympathy, although there was also a considerable amount of intimidation at rural elections.

Another result of the parliamentary enfranchisement of the village democracy was that three years later Lord Salisbury's

Ministry established County Councils, substituting local representative institutions for the administration of rural affairs by nominated magistrates.[1] This belated change took place fifty-three years after the Municipal Reform Act had given self-government to the towns. The establishment of Urban and Rural District Councils and Parish Councils by the Liberal Government in 1894 completed the framework of representative local government.

The third Reform Bill, from which so many changes ultimately flowed, had passed the Commons with little opposition. But the Lords, while not venturing openly to oppose it on principle, held it up until a Bill to redistribute the seats should first be passed. A popular agitation against hereditary legislators arose in the country, in the course of which Bright made proposals for a limitation of the Lords' veto on which the Parliament Act of 1911 was long afterwards based. But Gladstone, who was by no means the perfect demagogue that he was sometimes represented, laboured to avoid a conflict between the Houses, and the Queen exerted her influence on the side of peace. Gladstone and Salisbury, in a series of personal conferences, arrived at a compromise by which the Franchise Bill and a scheme of Redistribution were passed as agreed measures. It is remarkable that this successful conference between party leaders did not become a precedent in constitutional custom, although the expedient was attempted on the grand scale in 1910, in vain.

The third Reform Bill and the contest with the Lords had, for the time, repaired the popularity of the Liberal government. But the fall of Khartoum immediately followed, giving the death-blow to its real power. For some months it staggered on, and at length resigned, after an unsuccessful division in the summer. Among the minor measures which stand to its credit were compulsory education for all children, a supplement to the Act of 1870; an Employers' Liability Bill; and the right conceded to tenant-farmers to kill the hares and rabbits on their farms. During his last months of office Gladstone had, at the risk of war, carried on an effectual resistance to Russian encroachment in Afghanistan.

When the Liberals resigned, Lord Salisbury took office until the General Election in the winter.[2] In order to understand that election

1. The Justices of the Peace retained, however, their judicial powers and the licensing of public-houses.
2. It was during this brief tenure of office in 1885 that Salisbury reversed an important part of the Near Eastern policy which Beaconsfield and he had formerly pursued. He supported, against Turkey, the Bulgarian national aspirations for union of the two Bulgarias. (See p. 367, above.)

378

and its consequences, it is necessary to revert to the history of Ireland.

Gladstone's disestablishment of the Irish Church and first Land Act had not, as he hoped, 'pacified Ireland'. But they had been steps in that direction. During the seventies, Fenianism was less active and a constitutional agitation grew up to demand an Irish Parliament. In 1873 the 'Home Rule League' was formed by Isaac Butt, who chose the name Home Rule in order to avoid in English minds the associations connected with O'Connell's 'Repeal', of which the new movement was a revival under changed conditions. Isaac Butt was a man of very moderate temper, more liked than feared in the British House of Commons. He hoped to persuade the English people and their leaders by a sympathetic presentation of what he regarded as a reasonable case. He failed completely, and the Fenians would soon have become impatient and again active had not the effective leadership at Westminster passed, in the last years of Beaconsfield's Parliament, into the hands of a new member, Charles Stewart Parnell.

Indignation at the hanging of the 'Manchester martyrs' had first aroused Parnell's strange and solitary mind to take an interest in his country. His powerful but almost uneducated[1] intellect had been suddenly fired by a single idea that 'filled the fine, empty sheath of a man'. But he did not go into public life for another half-dozen years, nor enter Parliament till 1875.

A Protestant and a landlord, Parnell became in a few years the leader of the Catholic tenantry, by right of his genius for tactics, his ruthless contempt for all the English held sacred in Parliament or out of it, and his silent force of character dominating an eloquent and emotional race. After Butt's death he was elected official chief of the Home Rule party in the new Parliament of 1880, in which he soon made his policy of obstruction the principal fact.

The Land League had been founded in 1879 to fight out the agrarian question against the landlords with the law and Government behind them. Parnell was in close touch with it, and worked to induce the Fenians of Ireland and America to abandon their old programme of Republicanism and promiscuous violence, in favour of the new and more practical programme of the Land

1. His residence at Magdalene College, Cambridge, had taught him little except to dislike the English more than ever. Nor was his Irish patriotism based on a study of history or literature. One day in 1889, when Mr Gladstone was talking to him about the '41' in Ireland, it was clear to the onlookers that Parnell neither knew nor cared to what century his learned ally was referring.

League and of the Home Rule party. For in Parnell's mind Home
Rule and the agrarian questions went together. Gladstone's Land
Act of 1870 had not given fair rents or security of tenure,[1] and his
Bill of 1880 for compensating evicted tenants under certain conditions was thrown out by an immense majority in the House of
Lords. That year ten thousand persons were evicted. In reply, two
thousand five hundred agrarian outrages were committed, while
the institution of the 'boycott', called after Captain Boycott, one
of its early victims, made life unendurable to agents and abettors
of unpopular acts. By the same means discipline was maintained
among the peasants themselves.

Such was the policy of the Land League. It was no longer spasmodic acts of revenge, but systematic terrorism to break the land
system from off the neck of the people. Gladstone struck both at
the terrorism and the unjust laws. On the one hand, a Coercion
Bill enabled the Government to imprison whom it liked for as long
as it liked. On the other hand, his great Land Act of 1881 aimed at
securing to the Irish tenants, in spite of all English theories of 'free
contract', the famous 'three F.s' – Fair Rents to be settled by a
Tribunal; Fixity of Tenure for all who paid their rents; and Free
Sale or the right of the tenant to part with his interest. Opinion in
England and Ireland was not yet ready for land purchase on a
great scale. But the fixing of rents by a State tribunal went a long
way towards effecting that agrarian transformation which the two
English parties were destined between them to accomplish for
Ireland. The same principles – fixity of tenure, and fair rents
adjudicated by a Commission – afterwards solved the vexed
'crofter' question in the Highlands of Scotland, where a very
similar agrarian problem was not complicated by religious and
racial feuds.[2] After the Irish Land Act of 1881, it already seemed as
if an age had passed since the Lords had thrown out the mild
Compensation for Disturbance Bill of the year before.

It was not Parnell's cue to show gratitude, and Ministers pres-
ently locked him up under their Coercion Act. He warned them
that if they removed him from the scene they would be leaving
'Captain Moonlight' in charge. And indeed, when Parnell's
relatively restraining influence was gone, agrarian outrage was
worse than ever and political assassination began to be plotted
again. But W. E. Forster, Chief Secretary for Ireland, believed that
all the trouble arose from a few 'village ruffians', whom he could
lay by the heels if he was given time. Unfortunately the statistics of

1. See p. 342, above.
2. G. O. Trevelyan's Crofters Act, 1886.

agrarian crime grew worse instead of better under coercion. Chamberlain, as the leader of Radicalism in the Cabinet, and John Morley now transferring to political journalism a reputation won as a historical and literary critic, both attacked Forster's policy. At heart Gladstone had always disliked it and experience confirmed his doubts. In 1882 he threw over his Chief Secretary and made, through the agency of Chamberlain, the famous 'Kilmainham Treaty' with Parnell, by which the Nationalist Chief was let out of prison to recover his own authority, restrain the outrages, and give the Land Act a chance. Forster and the Viceroy, Lord Cowper, resigned.

For two days after Parnell's release from prison it seemed as if the bitterness dividing the British and the Irish peoples would at last begin to be assuaged. Forster's successor, Lord Frederick Cavendish, was sent over as the harbinger of peace, the personal representative of Gladstone's good will, himself a noble warrant of England's desire for new and better things. He was murdered within a few hours of landing in Ireland. Mr Burke, the Under-Secretary, with whom he was walking in the Phoenix Park, was the object of the attack in which Lord Frederick's chivalrous defence of his companion involved him. It was an event as fatal to Ireland as the recall of Lord Fitzwilliam in 1795,[1] and this time no one could impute the fault to England or England's Ministers.

Neither did the fault lie with Parnell or with the Irish people as a whole, who were horror-struck at the news. The 'Invincibles' were a small murder club adverse to Parnell's policy, which, indeed, had never received so hard a blow as they dealt it that day. Lord Frederick, though a very different man from General Gordon, was no less calculated to arouse the affection and passionate regret of the English people. And such was his personal influence over Gladstone and his strong good sense that it is quite likely that, if he had lived, the break-up of the Liberal party in 1886 would never have taken place. The memory of his murder became one of the chief difficulties in the way of Gladstone when he tried to persuade the English to trust the Irish with self-government.

During the three difficult and dangerous years intervening between the Phoenix Park murders and the election of 1885, Lord Spencer as Viceroy governed with strength and justice, holding the scales even between Nationalist and Orangeman, and preventing any disaster from happening in Ireland, although dynamite outrages in London by Irish-Americans further incensed British opinion against the Irish cause. Parnell was not very active during

1. See p. 112, above.

this period, and did nothing to make the situation worse than it necessarily became after the Phoenix Park murders. He was biding his time.

During Salisbury's brief Ministry in the last six months of 1885 the Conservatives appeared to be seeking the Irish Alliance. They eschewed coercion, and Parnell came away from an interview with Lord Carnarvon, the Conservative Viceroy of Ireland, persuaded that he and his colleagues intended to grant some kind of self-government. Parnell had deceived himself. Lord Carnarvon was much more advanced than his colleagues or his party. But the fact that they had sent him to govern Ireland led not unnaturally to a wrong inference by Parnell, who therefore held out for higher terms from Gladstone, and threw the weight of the Irish vote on to the Conservative side at the General Election that winter.

At the polling, the Liberal party did badly in the towns but was saved by the county voters, grateful for the new franchise and hoping that attention would at last be paid to the grievances of the agricultural labourer. The net result was that the Liberals outnumbered the Conservatives by more than eighty, but the Conservatives and Home Rulers together outnumbered the Liberals by four. It would therefore be useless for anyone to form an administration without coming to terms with Parnell. This man, who a dozen years before had been a Wicklow country gentleman, moody and reserved, known outside his own family chiefly as a cricketer, had become the touchstone of the whole British Empire and the arbiter of fate to its Ministers. Such control over the Parliament at Westminster was to all appearance the summit of good fortune for the Irish cause. Actually it led to disaster. When Gladstone had asked the electors for a majority over Conservatives and Home Rulers together, so that he could settle the Irish question without Irish dictation, he had not been far wrong. But he had asked in vain.

For a week or two after the result of the elections became known, Gladstone hoped that the existing Conservative Government would take up the Carnarvon policy and pass some kind of Home Rule; in that case he was prepared to support the Ministry till the deed was done. But it soon appeared that the Conservatives had no such intention. Then the Liberal chief thought that he had no alternative but to ally himself to Parnell, turn out the Government, and prepare to deal with the Irish question himself.

Gladstone, now a third time Prime Minister, had been impressed by the great size of the majorities for Home Rule in the Irish elections under the new franchise. The eighty-five Parnellite members represented the 'self-determination', as we should now call it, of Catholic Ireland. No electoral result had ever more clearly proclaimed the will of a people. Gladstone, like various other statesmen of both parties, had for some time been turning over in his mind the pros and cons of a Home Rule policy, and now the moment for it seemed to him to have come. He would, at one stroke, secure power to govern the Empire in the only way open to any statesman without another General Election, and set up popular government in Ireland under the firm rule of Parnell, who would restrain his emotional compatriots, preserve order, and secure a good start for the great experiment.

He overlooked Protestant Ulster, for which he provided no separate status in his Bill. And he succeeded in losing not only Hartington and the more Conservative Whigs, and Bright the old Radical leader, but Chamberlain who stood for the Radicalism of the coming age. His neglect of Ulster and his handling of his party and colleagues were fatal both to Home Rule and to the Liberal cause. Old age had had upon him a strange effect. It left his gifts and energies as wonderful as ever and his mind no less open to new ideas, but it diminished his tact and prudence.

Yet the difficulties of the task he had undertaken were in any case immense. It might have passed the wit of the most prudent statesman in the world to construct a measure to which Ulster would submit, which Chamberlain would support, and yet which Parnell would accept.

The Home Rule Bill, coupled with a scheme for Land Purchase, was introduced into the Commons by Gladstone on 8 April 1886, and was thrown out two months later, on second reading, by the action of the Liberal dissentients. Then came the choice between dissolution or resignation. To resign meant postponement, a waiting on time and events, an attempt at reconciliation within the Liberal party before it was too late. To dissolve would force the Liberal Unionists to fight their old friends and to be returned by Conservative votes. Gladstone, worked up to a fervour of apostolic zeal, chose the more dangerous course. The General Election of 1886, fought on the Home Rule issue alone, made the split in the Liberal party irremediable. The Conservatives and Liberal Unionists were victorious and were in power with one brief interval for twenty years.

In that decisive election, all that energy and eloquence could do was done by Gladstone, despite his seventy-seven years. He kindled an enthusiasm for his new cause which does credit at least to the imagination and generosity of many of the Liberals, who, only seven months before, had been attacked at Parnell's orders in an embittered electoral battle by these same Irish, for whom they were now asked to postpone everything that directly interested themselves.

But the forces arrayed against Home Rule proved the stronger. Majuba, Khartoum, the Phoenix Park, the agrarian outrages, made the average Englishman distrustful of accepting Gladstone's account of the Irish and the way to deal with them. It was more natural for Protestants to sympathize with Ulster, whose determination to resist the decrees of an Irish Parliament was now beginning to make itself powerfully heard. The intellectual movement of the Victorian era, hitherto mainly on the Liberal side in politics, now for the most part broke off sharp from Gladstone and began to regard him as a demagogue. Unionism prevailed among the leaders of literature and thought, men like Robert Browning, Leslie Stephen, Lecky, and many more, as also in that part of the professional and scientific world which had not previously become Conservative. The almost complete loss of upper and middle class support forced 'Gladstonianism' to become more democratic than even the old Liberalism had been. Yet it made no special appeal to the new Labour movement, and it was helping to create by revulsion the dominant political creed of the coming era, the belief in Great Britain's Imperial destiny.

CHAPTER 25

'THE Industrial Revolution', a term invented by Arnold Toynbee in the later years of Queen Victoria, was generally adopted by economic historians to describe changes in England during the reign of George III and his immediate successors. But the Industrial Revolution never came to an end, and never can come to an end, so long as men go on making inventions, and every new form of economic life begins to be replaced by another, almost before it has itself taken shape.

In the last thirty years of the nineteenth century it was apparent that great changes were taking place in the economic structure – besides the mere increase in population, wealth, and trade, which the later Victorians in their sense of secure prosperity had come to regard almost as a law of nature. The greater industries were passing out of the hands of single 'employers' and family groups into the control of joint-stock companies, served by great industrial managers at high salaries, a class almost unknown in the first half of the century. Small businesses were being amalgamated, and the area and influence of competition were being restricted.

Incidentally this growth of joint-stock companies brought into existence a very numerous class of persons drawing part of their incomes from investments in industrial ventures in which they were not themselves employed. Such persons of all classes were unlikely to welcome the revived Socialist attack on capital, which the numerically small class of direct employers might have found it harder to resist alone. On the other hand, the big amalgamated business often attained a position and outlook leading it to come to terms with the big Unions, and to take an intelligent interest in the conditions of life of its employees.

Parallel to this amalgamation among the firms, the Trade Unions in the larger skilled trades were becoming national instead of local. Local disputes were frequently dealt with by the national organization of the trade in question, and if necessary were supported from its central funds. The Trade Union Congress had become a British institution of the utmost respectability. On the other hand, since their legislative victory of 1875,[1] the various trades had no common policy to pursue. It was an era of 'sectionalism', and the Labour movement as a whole was scarcely self-conscious. There were a few miners' representatives in Parliament, but no Labour party.

In the early eighties Trade Union policy was still very pacific. The big Unions had won most of what they had set out to win, and were more interested in the management of their sick and old age benefits than in new worlds to conquer. Trade Unionists took little account of the Labour movement, which includes unorganized labour. This attitude of mind was attacked in 1886–7 by Tom Mann and John Burns, coming forward as leaders of the 'New Unionism', and roundly accusing the 'aristocracy of labour', such as their own Amalgamated Society of Engineers, of 'selfish and snobbish desertion' of their less fortunate fellow-workmen.

The main object of the New Unionism was to assist and to organize trades where unionism was weak – unskilled labour, trades which were 'sweated', and those in which women's and children's labour competed with that of men. The new feature of the time was that these efforts received a good deal of sympathy from other classes. It was recognized by many that the immense improvement in the general lot effected since the 'hungry forties' had not brought equal benefits to all, and that housing in the slum

1. See p. 358, above.

districts was a problem which society had still to face. The old *laissez faire* doctrine that the State had hardly any function save to keep order had quite passed away. Undermined in theory by Carlyle, Ruskin, and even Mill in his later days, it had proved inadequate in practice.

The old Socialist Engels, a friend and compatriot of Karl Marx, but well acquainted with English conditions for nearly half a century, wrote in 1885, admitting that organized trades and skilled workmen were very much better off than before,

but as to the great mass of the working people, the state of misery and insecurity in which they live now is as low as ever, if not lower. The East End of London is an ever-spreading pool of stagnant misery and desolation, of starvation when out of work, and degradation physical and moral when in work. And so in all other large towns – exception made of the privileged minority of the workers.

Engels was overstating the case, but there was a big case to state. Not only Socialists but society as a whole was becoming interested in the inquiry into the state of the 'submerged'. From 1884 onwards, Commissions on Sweated Trades and on Housing, sometimes with the Prince of Wales as Chairman, examined depths hitherto unplumbed. Investigation was the watchword of the hour, and the results were not consoling. It was the era of Canon Barnett and 'Settlements', when University men of good will came to live where they could see for themselves how their fellow-citizens throve. Charles Booth's scientific study of the London poor, poured out in volume after volume over a series of years, did much to enlighten the world and to form opinion. His analysis, based on a wider and more detailed collection of facts than had ever before been made, showed in 1891 that some thirty per cent, or over a million and a quarter out of the four million three hundred thousand Londoners, fell habitually below the 'poverty line', with disastrous results to health and industrial efficiency as well as to human happiness. Charles Booth put the demand for old-age pensions on a scientific basis.

The fight against sweating, bad housing, neglect of children and aged persons, and all the problems of poverty had to wait for some of its most signal victories till the new century, but the ground was chosen and the battle was joined with success in the last decades of Victoria's reign.

The first skirmish of the New Unionism was the successful strike in 1888 of the London girls employed in making lucifer matches, one of the most dependent and helpless sections of labour, who could never have won their fight unaided or in a hostile social atmosphere. Friends pleaded their cause in the newspapers, and subscriptions from the public pulled them through. Next year there was a pitched battle between vaster forces. The unorganized mass of London dock labourers who struggled with each other for precarious jobs at the dockyard gates had the courage to strike for sixpence an hour. So widely had the spirit of the New Unionism spread that, with the help of a 'sympathetic strike' of the powerful Stevedores' Union, they held up the trade of the Port of London for ten weeks, and won the victory under the leadership of John Burns.

Neither the dockers nor the match-girls would have had a chance if public opinion had not been largely on their side, ready even to subscribe to their funds. The result of these successes, so consonant with the spirit of the new age, was the formation of many more Trade Unions among unskilled hands.

The great County Council Act of 1888 gave a whole armoury of new weapons to the 'municipal socialism' which was attempting to improve the conditions of life. Salisbury's second Ministry, though its personnel was Conservative, was dependent on Liberal Unionist support. As that was still uncertain,[1] it was all the more needful to make concessions to Liberalism in the Cabinet policy. Coercion in Ireland was yoked with democratic reform in Britain. Although the 'Tory democrat', Lord Randolph Churchill, committed political suicide by resigning office on grounds that the public considered inadequate, he had had a great effect in continuing the 'education' of the Conservative party towards broader views and more democratic methods. And the loss to Radicalism in the Cabinet occasioned by his fall was for a time balanced by the influence which Chamberlain exerted from outside on the plans of the Government. With the highly organized Birmingham democracy moving under his direction, he seemed almost to hold the balance of power between parties in the State.

Mr Ritchie's great measure of 1888 established rural self-government by County Councils,[2] and enlarged the existing machinery of urban democracy by turning the largest towns into county boroughs.

The administrative problem of London outside the old City boundaries, which had been shirked by the legislators of 1835, was dealt with in a Radical spirit by the Act of 1888. The new London

1. The 'Round Table Conference' of 1887 was a conference of Liberal chiefs, Gladstonian and Unionist, including Chamberlain, to find a basis of Liberal reunion. It failed, after a successful opening.

2. See p. 378, above.

County Council, to the chagrin of some who had had a hand in creating it, at once became the representative and agent of millions of Londoners who aspired after better conditions of daily life. The popularity and energy of John Burns of Battersea gave him success as the first apostle of a London patriotism distinct from pride in the old 'City', while the intellectual leadership of the Fabian publicists, and the organization of the 'Progressive' party formed *ad hoc*, helped London to take her place beside the foremost cities of the Empire in municipal progress, while she remained Conservative in Imperial politics.

All over the island, the last two decades of the century saw an immense extension of municipal enterprise. Baths and wash-houses, museums, public libraries, parks, gardens, open spaces, allotments, lodging-houses for the working classes were acquired, erected, or maintained out of the rates. Tramways, gas, electricity, and water were in many places municipalized. The self-governing towns of England became employers of labour and producers on a great scale. It has been largely owing to 'municipal socialism' of this kind that the death-rate and the figures of infant mortality have fallen and that some real progress has been made in the amenities of life.

Sir William Harcourt, himself a Whig and a lawyer of the old school, startled the House of Commons by saying 'we are all socialists now'. The joke had an element of real meaning which made the saying proverbial. And a few years later Harcourt himself, as Chancellor of the Exchequer for the short-lived Liberal Ministry, passed a 'socialistic' budget that laid heavy death duties on the heirs of the wealthy to pay the ever-increasing bill of social reform and Imperial defence.

Yet neither Sir William Harcourt nor any large section of the community were 'socialists' in the sense of wishing to abolish private capital and enterprise in ordinary trading concerns. Only a small but active body in the British Trade Union world was beginning to adopt the full programme of Karl Marx.[1]

Socialism may be said to have been invented in England by Robert Owen and some of his later contemporaries. But it had declined for many years in the island of its origin. The revival of

1. Karl Marx (1818–83) formulated and materialized the doctrines of Socialism. His great work, *Das Kapital*, was very different from the rather vague idealism of Robert Owen and Saint-Simon, his English and French predecessors. He aimed at pitting 'the proletariat' against 'Capital' in all countries. He pointed to the nationalization of all means of production as an inevitable historic evolution from the capitalistic era. He appealed to a 'scientific' interpretation of history.

388

British Socialism was preceded and in some sense prepared by the vogue of a different doctrine, that of the American Henry George in his *Progress and Poverty* (1879), which dealt with rent in much the same way that Marx dealt with private profit. In the year 1881 H. M. Hyndman founded the Social Democratic Federation to preach the Marxian gospel in earnest. It made headway, but not very rapidly, in the British Trade Union and Co-operative world, which had already achieved so much in a very different spirit from that of Marx. Indeed, the German leader suspected both those movements as successful rivals to his own speculative system of amelioration by class war.

Meanwhile the idealism which was abhorrent to the true Marxian materialist was upheld by the poet and artist William Morris, whose Socialism in the pleasant *News from Nowhere* was partly a continuation of Ruskin, partly an imaginary vision of what the Middle Ages might have been like without the Church. It is a rebellion hardly more against capitalism than against the ugliness of modern city life. It looks as much backwards as forwards, as much to art and beauty as to politics.

The third current of *fin de siècle* Socialism, and the most important, was the Fabian doctrine, specially connected with Mr and Mrs Sidney Webb. The Fabian Society was founded in 1883. Its name recalls a Roman general whose motto was 'slow but sure'. Eschewing revolution, and intent on the actualities of England at the end of the nineteenth century, Fabians exonerated Socialists from the heavy obligation of reading Karl Marx. Without dogmatizing as to the ultimate future of industrial organization, they preached practical possibilities, here and now – municipal Socialism and State control of conditions of labour. Equally far from Marx and Morris, they left the New Jerusalem alone, and sought to impregnate the existing forces of society with collectivist ideals.

The Fabians became experts in bringing electoral, journalistic, and personal pressure to bear on local bodies and on the Liberal or Conservative government of the hour – somewhat after the methods of action of Francis Place, but with the added power of the democratic franchise. By the end of the century it is in Fabianism that we find the nearest approach to a body of doctrine directly affecting the laws and administration of the time, like the doctrines of Bentham and Mill in the past. The Fabians were intelligence officers without an army – there was no Fabian party in Parliament – but they influenced the strategy and even the direction of the great hosts moving under other banners.

The social movement of the time had its effect upon the religious bodies. Cardinal Manning, in his old age, helped to negotiate the terms of the London dockers' victory. General William Booth's Salvation Army preached the Gospel to the 'submerged' of *Darkest England*. Like the Wesleyans of the eighteenth century, the Salvationists sought out the neglected and least promising members of society. But the modern evangelists, though by no means ashamed of 'enthusiasm', developed also an earthly paraphernalia of shelters, workshops, and emigration agencies. General Booth was of the opinion, originally formulated by the secularist Robert Owen, that environment makes character.

The activities of the National Church were more and more directed to work on similar lines, in the poorest districts of the great cities. 'Environment' gave a new character to the opinions of many of the clergy. In slum surroundings they learnt to think very differently from their predecessors of Miss Austen's time, who had lived between the rectory and the manor-house. Many of the new clergy in the towns developed socialistic sympathies.

Nevertheless, for all these new religious efforts, and the earnest attempt to evangelize the lower strata, the part played by religion in the life of the upper and middle classes, and of the better-to-do working class, was less remarkable at the end of the century than it had been when Queen Victoria began her reign. The decline of Nonconformity was not the only symptom. Everyday thought was decidedly more secular in tone. This was partly due to intellectual movements, to the Darwinian theory and Biblical criticism at work in an age when everyone was being taught to read. But it was also due to the number of other interests in life which now competed with religion. Where the Bible had been almost the only book for many households, there was now the daily paper, the cheap magazine and novelette, and, for the minority who cared for such things, the best literature and science in the world in cheap editions. Formerly entertainments and organized excitements had been rare; but now there was the football match with its democratic 'gate', the music-halls, and a thousand appeals of every kind to the popular attention.

The modern English, as soon as they had a good thing, had the means to make it common. The Gilbert and Sullivan songs might be heard in any parlour where there was a cheap piano. Football and cricket, both as games to be played and as spectacles to be watched, spread from upper-class public schools through the Universities to the democracy at large. One excellent new activity of man, mountain climbing, begun in Switzerland chiefly by some Fellows of Cambridge colleges in the middle of Victoria's reign, was by the end of the century beginning to open the rock climbs of England, Wales, and Scotland to a larger fraternity. In the nineties the 'safety' bicycle with pneumatic tyres abolished the dangers and discomforts of the high-wheeled bicycle of the former decade. Before motor-cars in the new century swept the unfortunate 'Push-bike' off the high road, it had been a principal means of popular enjoyment, had opened out country places to the city dweller, and had profoundly affected the social customs and outlook of more than one class of society, particularly of the women, to whom it gave a new freedom. The bicycle seemed the symbol of the changing *fin de siècle*. For good and for bad, the standards of Victorian 'respectability' were beginning to crumble. The balance maintained between tradition and democracy, which had been the essence of the Victorian age, was giving way. Literature was retreating before journalism, or was being absorbed in it.

The government all this while might be called Conservative, but change was never more rapid, nor the advance of the equalitarian spirit more observable. It was due, not to political propaganda, but to environment and conditions of life. A profound transmutation was in process towards a more mechanical and a more democratic world, the world of the great city instead of the country village, a world expressing itself more through science and journalism, and less through religion, poetry, and literature. In a hundred years' time it will be possible to speculate as to whether the change has been mostly for good, or mostly for evil. But in so far as men have any real knowledge and understanding of the past, it is probable that opinions on that subject will be neither unanimous nor confident.

The epoch of Lord Salisbury's two Ministries and the two Jubilees of Queen Victoria was above all else an age of prosperity at home and peace abroad. But it failed to solve the Irish question.

If our own generation, taught by much unhappy experience, had had the Ireland of Gladstone and Salisbury to deal with, it would perhaps have found the solution. But the Liberals of that day would not reckon with Ulster, nor the Unionists with the rest of Ireland. The British had had no recent experience of race hatreds and historic feuds in their own island since Henry VIII had settled the Welsh question and the statesmen of William and Anne had settled Scotland. Having no first-hand knowledge of racial strife, and very little historical knowledge or imagination, our people could not understand why the Irish tenant farmers were so unlike the British tenant farmers, who never shot landlords or houghed cattle; and why the Presbyterians of Ulster were so unlike the comfortable nonconformists of England.

The only real hope would have lain in an alliance of British statesmen to settle Ireland, as an urgent Imperial problem, objectively considered apart from our home politics. But this proved impossible. Our two-party system showed off all the defects of its qualities, and artificially excited passions which the Irish question in its nature was only too well calculated to arouse.

The Unionism that had triumphed at the election of 1886 was largely inspired by indignation against crime, from the Phoenix Park murders down to the cruel outrages on animals which Englishmen particularly dislike, and the terrorism that sought to destroy the springs of all independent action. It was barbarous work indeed, but it was the means by which Liberal and Conservative governments, from 1881 onwards, were driven step by step to abolish the evils of the old Irish land system. During their two decades of power the Unionists moved as fast in that direction as Gladstone himself, although he had begun the retreat. But the Unionists resented deeply the character of the pressure to which they yielded – the semi-warfare of the Land League and the Plan of Campaign – and this indignation affected, if it did not actually determine, the attitude of half England to Home Rule.

Parnell, though he had opposed the more murderous and futile crimes of the Irish-American societies, had in 1880 and 1881 countenanced the boycotting and terrorism of the Land League as the only possible means, in his opinion, of making the British Legislature move on behalf of the oppressed tenantry. Unionist opinion never forgave him for this and sought to bring it home to him retrospectively, now that Gladstone proposed to make him in effect the ruler of Ireland. Yet after 1886 he was less interested in the agrarian question than in Home Rule, and he knew that its electoral chances would be gravely compromised by a renewal of Irish crime. He therefore opposed the renewal of methods of sedition and terrorism and regretted, though he could not prevent, the agrarian Plan of Campaign launched in December 1886.

The Plan of Campaign was met by the Conservative Crimes Act, and a protracted battle began between the Irish peasants and Mr Arthur Balfour, who now rose to the front rank of politics as Chief Secretary. Into that conflict, fought without gloves on both sides, the Irish Parliamentary party was necessarily drawn, with the English Liberal party in its wake. Irish members spent much of their time in prison, and a good deal of the rest on Liberal platforms in Great Britain. Parnell for his part was now the cautious statesman, while Mr Gladstone was the enthusiastic protagonist in a great agitation.

At an early and critical date in this struggle *The Times* published in facsimile a letter, purporting to bear Parnell's signature, in which he was made to express partial approval of the Phoenix Park murders. The letter, if genuine, would have killed the Home Rule movement in Britain. Nearly two years later the document was proved to have been forged by a needy Irish journalist named Pigott, and to have been accepted without scrutiny as to its origin. The Royal Commission of three Judges before whom this damning revelation was made had also to inquire into and report on the general connexion of the Parnellite party with crime in Ireland, an inquiry in which it was really impossible to isolate the judicial from the political issues. But the detection of so gross a forgery, designed to ruin Parnell, overshadowed everything else in the popular mind, and the prospects of Home Rule at the next General Election began to look bright.

No one can ever tell what chance there was of a solution of the Irish question by that generation of men, nor whether Civil War or Settlement would have resulted from a decisive majority for Home Rule at the polls. The question was never put to the test, owing to the downfall of the Irish Chief.

In 1890 Parnell had been fifteen years in public life. In that short time, himself starting from nothing and with no extraneous aid, he had created a party known by his name, united the Irish nation on his policy, held up the British Parliament, made and unmade Ministries, and won the greatest British statesman of the age to devote his whole energies to carrying out his plan. The goal seemed already in sight. Suddenly the bolt fell, the prospect was eclipsed, and the structure was shattered.

For close on ten years Parnell had been living with another man's wife. At length a divorce suit was brought and no defence was possible. Mr Gladstone, for purely political reasons, decided that his ally must for a while retire from the Irish leadership, otherwise, in the then state of English feeling, he believed that a catastrophe would ensue at the approaching election which would ruin the Home Rule cause. Gladstone, now over eighty, knew that his own time was short, and that another defeat would be final. Parnell, so he decided, must make his bow to the English sense of propriety and morals, and then it was probable he would soon be able to return forgiven.

Till that moment Parnell's actions, unswayed by sentiment or passion, had been based on cold calculation of the chances and forces in the field. Neither good nor evil fortune had ever seemed to move the man set apart from his fellows. Yet all the while fires had blazed beneath, and now they burst out in wild destruction. He had always disliked and despised the English, perhaps, through some atavistic 'complex', all the more because he had English blood and a good deal of English character mixed with other elements in his mysterious being. What business had they with his private life? He would not take off his hat to their hypocrisies, and sue for their pardon, no, not if it would save the Irish cause and the work of his life from ruin.

He held to the leadership, was disowned by the majority of the party, held on, and fought, the Celtic nature or something yet more fundamental in him flashing out at last, in a berserk fight against men and gods. The Roman Church joined the fray against the 'black Protestant'. Ireland and the Nationalist party were rent from top to bottom into factions of Parnellites and anti-Parnellites. Next year he died, but his death could not at once heal the breach, could certainly not restore in England the prestige of the Irish party.

So at the General Election of 1892 the majority over the Unionists of Liberals and Irish Home Rulers combined was too small to do the work. Gladstone formed his fourth Ministry; but when his second Home Rule Bill,[1] having passed the lower House by thirty-four votes, was sent up to the Lords, it was thrown out, and the country felt relieved or indifferent.

Next year Gladstone retired from public life, which had so long centred round him. He had taught Englishmen to think nobly, and foreigners to think nobly of England. He had kept our parliamentary institutions in the forefront of all men's thoughts. He had done, perhaps, more than any one man to adapt the machinery of State to modern and democratic conditions. His achievements lay thickly scattered over many pages of our history, and, if his failures were great too, the last and greatest of them has added immensely to his fame. The comparison with the all-successful Bismarck is one from which his memory has less to fear now than in the first years after his death, when Bismarck's structure of national happiness seemed founded safely on the rock of force.

At the next General Election the Liberals were overwhelmingly defeated. The chiefs of Gladstone's succession quarrelled with each other over the defeat, and Lord Rosebery soon resigned the leadership. For the remainder of the century Salisbury ruled the country without serious challenge.

1. The Home Rule Bill of 1892 differed from that of 1886 in retaining Irish representation at Westminster.

Salisbury's third Ministry, in which the Liberal Unionists took their share as Ministers of the Crown, lasted until his retirement upon the eve of his death. It was marked in Ireland by an attempt at conciliation. Home Rule was below the horizon and the Unionists hoped to prevent its rising again by settling the agrarian question. Mr Gerald Balfour, who now held his brother's former place as Chief Secretary, aspired to 'kill Home Rule by kindness', a policy continued by Mr George Wyndham after him. Democratic local government was extended to Ireland and was worked with success. With the help of Mr Horace Plunkett and his co-operative schemes in which men of all parties lent a hand, a new era of prosperity set in. The agrarian problem was being solved. The 'kindness' was real and practical. Whether it had 'killed Home Rule', the next century would reveal.

CHAPTER 26

AFTER Gladstone's defeat, Salisbury and Chamberlain represented the forces dominant in the British Commonwealth.

Lord Salisbury was a student, a man of intellectual, religious, and scientific interests, an aristocrat by upbringing and by nature, averse from all methods of *réclame*. He stood for the old traditions of the British political nobles, bearing the load of public care with a sense of inherited responsibility. He had indeed accepted without reserve the new democratic conditions of political power, although in earlier years he had put up the last open resistance to Disraeli's Bill for household franchise. His gravity was relieved by a pungency in epigram, and a more than royal indifference to the effect of any words that fell from his lips. Though astute in his sense of what was practical, and appealing less often than Gladstone to ideal motives, he stood for character, principle, and tradition, maintained public life on a high level, and despised the sensationalism of the journalist and the tricks of the politician.

Beside him, in his third Ministry, was Chamberlain, with all the keen instincts of the modern businessman, seeing farther and less far than his grave, bearded chief. Yesterday the leader of English Radicalism and still exerting great influence in some democratic sections of the community, he was prepared for an alliance on terms with the older elements in the State.

Lord Salisbury, firm in the belief that 'Britain's greatest interest is peace', held the mere avoidance of war to be the best security against revolution as well as against other ills. He well knew that the impressive fabric of modern industrial prosperity was so artificial as to demand above all things peace. He was Foreign Minister in his own Cabinet.

Chamberlain, who had chosen for himself the office of Colonial Secretary, gave it a new importance, and undertook the propaganda of a self-conscious Imperialism. The doctrine suited the spirit of the age. A dozen years back it had received an impetus from Sir John Seeley's book of lectures on the *Expansion of England* (1883) that had since spread to circles beyond the readers of Seeley.

The two parts of the new doctrine were, first the need to attach the white democracies overseas more closely to the idea of Imperial unity; and secondly the need for the Empire to secure its share of new lands, in the scramble then going on for the rest of the world's unappropriated surface. These two aspects of Imperialism had perhaps no logical connexion, but they were connected by the men and by the events of that time. Disraeli's continental and pro-Turkish Imperialism was not revived, but the new creed might lead to complications with foreign Powers over colonial questions – though not, indeed, if Lord Salisbury could help it.

Salisbury was inclined to favour the Triple Alliance of the Central Powers, more than the Dual Alliance of France and Russia, chiefly because of the hostile attitude of France on Egyptian and Colonial questions. But he kept England free from commitments in Europe, where the balance of power could still adjust itself without the help of our weight in either scale.

Lord Salisbury's great work was the dividing up of Africa with Germany, France, and other countries without a resort to arms. This he had largely accomplished during his second Ministry (1886–92). It was a great triumph for the principles of peace and negotiation as contrasted with the endless wars of previous epochs over the sharing up of America and Southern Asia. In 1890 the boundaries of German and British possessions in South and Central Africa were defined, in connexion with the work of British pioneers in Nyasaland and the territories of Rhodes's Chartered Company. The fact that Salisbury bargained away Heligoland against Zanzibar showed how much more our statesmen were then thinking of colonial expansion than of any danger to our fundamental security in Europe or in the British seas. Such danger did not then exist.

The interior of 'Darkest Africa' opened out by Livingstone,

H. M. Stanley, and other explorers, had become ripe for white control and in places for white settlement, because railways, tinned foods, modern weapons, and tropical hygiene at length enabled Europeans to penetrate and to inhabit regions where their fathers had perished. It was fortunate that the day of the white man's unlimited power over the black had not come earlier, whilst his only idea of a relation with the aborigines had been the profits of slavery and the slave trade. That bad spirit had not indeed entirely been exorcized among all the white races in their dealings with Africa. But Britain at least made good use in Nigeria and elsewhere of the white man's new power to suppress the slave trade and inter-tribal massacres.

The new situation opened out many difficult problems for the Empire – how far and for what purposes the native might be exploited by the newcomer, what were to be his rights either of retaining or of parting with tribal land and tribal custom. In all these questions the Home Government was often in the position of umpire between missionaries and settlers, chiefs and tribesmen. As among the nations of Europe, Britain had the greatest share of Africa and the greatest responsibility in these matters. On the whole that proved very fortunate for the African.

During the last twenty years of the century, so full of romantic adventure for the commercial pioneers of the Dark Continent, an old state policy of Tudor and Stuart times was revived. Chartered Companies were formed, like those trading companies of long ago which had been the first representatives of England's political and military power in the East. Such companies, employing their own capital, were granted political authority in Nigeria, Uganda, and British South Africa. These delegations of sovereign power, useful at early stages of pioneering development, were resumable by the Crown as soon as the new district was fit to become a Colony.

It was in connexion with the most famous of these Chartered Companies that Cecil Rhodes became a figure of international importance. The child of an English parsonage, he had gone to South Africa for his health and had there become a mining magnate in the Kimberley diamond world and a leading figure in Cape politics. He valued money as a means to power, and power as a means to spread British influence and ideals. His policy, analogous to that of the Afrikander Bond, aimed at cooperation on equal terms between the Dutch and British races, and the Federation of the two Dutch Republics and the two British Colonies in a United South Africa. Chamberlain in 1889 complained that he was more of an Afrikander than an Imperialist.

But Rhodes, though friendly to the Afrikander Bond, had ideas of his own, and they sprang from an idealized belief in the British race and Empire. He had determined to extend South Africa's sphere of influence into the far northern interior, and to carry Britain's power and the progressive part of the Afrikander ideal into the lands that Livingstone had explored. Such was his dream. His nightmare was lest the Germans should be before him, and should extend their sphere of influence across Africa from the western sea to the Portuguese territory on the eastern coast. If the Germans could once make that step across the continent they would shut in South Africa from all chance of future expansion, and would incidentally get into touch with the more reactionary elements among the Transvaal Boers. These elements, represented by President Kruger, had already been much encouraged by the episode of the Majuba war.

Rhodes, ever the most practical of visionaries and the most visionary of men of business, dreamed of a Cape-to-Cairo railway through British territory. And so, in 1889, he secured from the

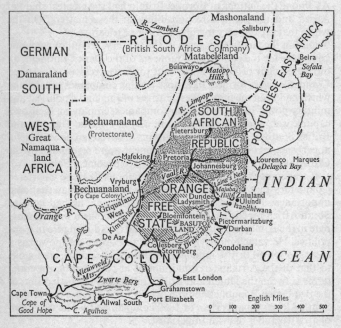

home government a Charter conferring political powers north of the Limpopo River on the British South Africa Company. Armed with the Charter, he proceeded to develop not only Matabeleland and Mashonaland, but to push the future 'Rhodesia' far north of the Zambesi, to join up with other British pioneering work in Nyasaland, along that doubtful southern border of German East Africa which Lord Salisbury was defining by negotiation.[1]

In 1890 Rhodes had become Prime Minister of the Cape. His position in South Africa and his reputation in England and the world at large was unique. He was almost as much talked about as Parnell. The two men differed from each other, but they differed still more strongly from anyone else. Some modern Plutarch should draw a parallel between them. Rhodes gave Parnell £10,000 for his Home Rule campaign, seeing its importance to Imperial Federation; he described the Irish chief as 'the most reasonable and sensible man I ever met'.

At the new year of 1895–6 came the fall of Rhodes. It was less complete than that of Parnell, but the Jameson Raid dealt to his life's work of uniting the British and Dutch on a progressive platform a blow from which the policy never recovered in his own lifetime. Up to the fatal Christmas of 1895 the Dutch of the Orange River Colony and the Cape had many of them believed in Rhodes and were not in sympathy with the reactionary party among the Transvaal Boers headed by President Kruger.

The situation in South Africa had for ten years past been complicated by a new element. The discovery of gold reefs on the long ridge of the Witwatersrand Hills north of the Vaal River led to the growth of Johannesburg as a cosmopolitan centre in the heart of the little republic of Bible-reading farmers. The seventeenth century and the late nineteenth century were brought into dangerously sudden contact, which the obstinacy of one party and the impatience of the other soon drew on to tragic issues.

Paul Kruger was a man of ability and force of character, with ideas limited to those of the farmer patriarchs whom he had accompanied on the original 'great trek' out of British territory sixty years before. He denied the Republican franchise to the newcomers, obstructed their mining developments, yet taxed them heavily. The quarrel between the 'Uitlanders' and the President waxed hot. Rhodes then held power in a double capacity, as Premier of the Cape, and as Managing Director of the British South Africa Company, whose Rhodesian developments, encircling the Transvaal to the north, added greatly to Kruger's old-

1. See p. 396, above.

world fears. In an evil hour Rhodes committed an act which seemed to justify all the President's harsh forebodings and jealousies. He secretly offered the aid of the armed forces of the British South Africa Company to a projected rising of Uitlanders. In other words, Rhodesia was to invade the Transvaal, at the orders of the Prime Minister of the Cape.

The projected rising at Johannesburg was never attempted, and Rhodes cancelled too late his orders for invasion, because the non-British section of the Uitlanders objected to the Union Jack, and aimed at an international republic. Unfortunately Dr Jameson, administrator of Rhodesia, contrary to his chief's latest instructions, began the invasion of the Transvaal with six hundred troopers, who were surrounded and captured by the Boers before ever they reached Johannesburg. They were handed over to the British Government and imprisoned.

This weak and foolish outrage united the Dutch race against the British all over South Africa. Rhodes, who was implicated to the hilt, resigned the Premiership of the Cape. He appeared before a Parliamentary committee of inquiry in London, whose proceedings did not succeed in removing from Dutch minds their suspicions of the attitude of the British government. Words used by Chamberlain in Parliament seemed to them too favourable to Rhodes, while Rhodes's public utterances gave them the impression that the English only regretted the affair because it had failed.

'I found all the busmen smiling at me when I came to London,' said Rhodes, 'and then I knew I was all right!' The excuse for the attitude of a great part of the British public towards the Raid was the telegram of the Kaiser offering his sympathy to Kruger. Three years later Rhodes met the Kaiser and said to him about these events, 'You see, I was a naughty boy, and you tried to whip me. Now my people were quite ready to whip me for being a naughty boy, but directly *you* did it, they said, "No, if this is anybody's business, it is *ours*." The result was that Your Majesty got yourself very much disliked by the English people, and I never got whipped at all!'

The reactionary party among the Transvaal Boers now had the game in their hands. They began to arm on quite a new scale for a war which they henceforth regarded as inevitable. Worst of all, Dutch sympathy in the Orange Free State and the Cape was now more with them than against them. The stage was set for the great Boer War with which the century closed.

In 1896 Sir Herbert Kitchener, Sirdar of the Egyptian army, began operations southwards against the Soudan. It seemed an answer from the far north to Rhodes's Cape-to-Cairo scheme, but in fact it was only the fulfilment of Cromer's long-cherished purpose, possible at last now that he had given Egypt sound finances and a reliable army.[1]

Long preparation and forethought, local knowledge, mechanical perfection, and withal economy of expenditure, marked Kitchener's two and a half years' campaign. It ended in the conquest of all the obstacles of the desert, and the annihilation with machine-gun and magazine-rifle of the fanatical Mahdist hordes at Omdurman outside Khartoum. The Soudan under Mahdism had been the focus of revived Mohammedan slave trade in the interior of Africa. The conquest and government of the Soudan by a civilized Power was essential to the welfare of the continent, as well as to the safety of Egypt.

Unlike Egypt, the Soudan fell unconditionally under British and Egyptian rule, free from interference by any other country. But there was first a sharp diplomatic struggle with France, at one moment threatening war. Some French explorers under Major Marchand had reached Fashoda, higher up the river even than Khartoum, at the time of Kitchener's conquest. But their claim on behalf of France was disallowed. Feeling between the two countries was further embittered by the sympathy of the British public with the wrongs of Captain Dreyfus. The victory of the 'revisionists', who had demanded his retrial, shortly afterwards made the way easier for a *rapprochement* with England.

A few years after the Fashoda incident, France realized that it was too late to renew her ambitions on the Nile, and, in return for diplomatic support of her claims in Morocco, abandoned her hostility to our presence in Egypt. The difficulties of our administration in the new century were to arise not from the Capitulations or from the hostility of European Powers, but from the spirit of nationalism, rising there as in India, and no longer to be denied, even though our administration conferred great benefits on the peasantry and the people at large.

Meanwhile the mother country had been aroused to a living interest in the Dominions and Colonies, and Australasians as well as Canadians had begun to be keenly conscious of their position in the Empire and their relation to powers outside it. Talk about secession and 'parting friends' died away as the century drew near its close. The first Imperial Conferences had been held, in connexion with the Queen's two Jubilees, the pageantry and sentiment

1. See p. 375, above.

of which took on an Imperial even more than a national aspect in appealing to the popular imagination.

There was, however, a setback to the first plans of British statesmen, who had hoped to create a formal constitution and parliament for a federated Empire. The idea was coldly received in the self-governing Dominions. Each was now a growing nation, proud of its own distinctive ideals, and more anxious to obtain security by association with kindred nations than to merge its individuality and rights of independent action in a larger whole. What great things voluntary cooperation could do for the Empire was shortly to be shown in the action of Canada and Australasia in the Boer War, as it has since been shown on a vaster scale and in a time of yet more tragic peril.

Blood-relationship, affection, and common traditions were potent, and so too was the desire for a mutual guarantee of security against outside aggression. In the eighties and nineties Australia began to be uneasily conscious of the 'Pacific problem', of the Germans in New Guinea and Samoa, and of the rising power of 'Westernized' Japan, with her critical eyes turned on the vast spaces denied to Oriental immigrants by the 'White Australia' policy. That policy, originating in the Trade Unions, has in our day become a national resolve.[1] But a national resolve of so serious a character demands a nation to enforce it. Not only a sense of the value of the Imperial connexion and of the British fleet, but the desire for internal unity was quickened among the Australian colonies in the last years of the old century. In 1900, after a decade of discussion and postponement, the terms of the Federal Union were agreed upon, the several colonies becoming States of the Australian Commonwealth.[2] Three weeks before the death of Queen Victoria, the birth of the new nation was proclaimed on the first day of the new century.

The Dominion of Canada had achieved Federal Union a generation before under the leadership of Sir John Macdonald.[3] His death in 1891 was soon followed by the end of the long supremacy of the Canadian Conservative party, to whom the Imperial connexion had owed most. But the new Liberal party, when it came to power, although it was largely dependent on the votes of the French Catholic element, learned to set a high value on

1. Australia, even more 'socialistically' inclined than the mother country, tended to care more about the distribution and less about the accumulation of wealth, more about the average quality of the citizen, and very little about the increase in population.

2. See p. 329, above. Railway construction had rendered the Union possible.

3. See pp. 260–61, 328–9, above.

the Empire during the Premiership of Sir Wilfred Laurier. His striking figure was the observed of all observers in London at the Jubilee of 1897, and his government gave to the mother country a preference of over thirty per cent in the Canadian tariff.

In the eighties and nineties the revived protectionism of Canada and the United States helped to cause friction between them. Dangerous disputes about fishing rights and the Alaskan boundary[1] at Klondyke were continually postponed and eventually settled by a series of agreements and arbitrations.

But the most serious danger of war with the United States arose on a question that did not concern Canada. Periodic disputes as to the boundary between the South American Republic of Venezuela and British Guiana had been in process for generations. It was a diplomatic 'case in Chancery', without a beginning anyone remembered or an end anyone expected. At length in the summer of 1895 the United States began seriously to put forward claims to a decisive voice in the matter, under an extended modern interpretation of the Monroe Doctrine.[2] 'Today the United States,' wrote Secretary Olney, 'is practically sovereign on this Continent, and its fiat is law upon the subjects to which it confines its interposition.' Lord Salisbury did not admit the claim. Suddenly, in December 1895, President Cleveland, hitherto noted for a generally pacific policy, sent a message to Congress asserting the claim of the United States to be a party in the dispute, at the cost, if necessary, of war.

On both sides of the Atlantic men were taken completely by surprise. But while America rose up with a shout to support the President, England gave an instinctive cry of horror at the idea of war with the United States. It was the Christmas of the 'Jameson Raid', and, when the Kaiser telegraphed his sympathies to Kruger, England was far more angry with his interference than with that of President Cleveland. Lord Salisbury, aroused to the seriousness of the situation, took the Venezuela question in hand in his best manner, and consented to submit the boundary to arbitration on certain conditions. The 'suit in Chancery' was soon settled, not unfavourably to Britain, whose claims had not been immoderate, though her objection to submit the question to an arbitrator had been carried on too long.

The outcome of President Cleveland's message was an improvement in the relations of the two countries. They now understood each other better. A new and extended interpretation of the Monroe

1. In 1867 the United States had purchased Alaska from Russia.
2. See pp. 214–15, above.

Doctrine was in essence accepted by British public opinion, even though some of Secretary Olney's phrases about 'sovereignty' are to be regarded as rhetorical. The Americans on their part discovered that England was no longer the England of Palmerston, and was very much more friendly and anxious to avoid offence than in the days of Lincoln and the Civil War. A sincere desire to prevent all danger to peace was soon dominant in both countries. An impetus was given to the movement for arbitration in general, and in particular for arbitration between Great Britain and the United States in all future cases of dispute.

In 1898 the United States went to war with Spain about Cuba. Again the instinctive friendliness of Great Britain formed a contrast to the past and a pledge for the future. While continental Europe sympathized with Spain, British public opinion was equally strongly for America. From that date a better era in British–American relations began, based on mutual goodwill, felt by practically all the British on one side, and by very large sections of the inhabitants of the United States on the other, especially among those of British origin. The Boer War of the following year would have aroused a much more formidable anti-British movement in America if it had come before instead of after the Venezuela incident and the Spanish-American War.

During the three years that bridge the old century and the new, South Africa passed through a fiery ordeal towards ultimate reconciliation and union.

In 1899 the Uitlanders of Johannesburg began to petition Queen Victoria as to their wrongs. Chamberlain took up the franchise question with President Kruger, and a conference was held in June between the British High Commissioner, Sir Alfred Milner, and the Boer President. A franchise after five years' residence was demanded, and the old claim to 'suzerainty' over the Transvaal was raised once more.[1]

Unfortunately the events of three years back had strengthened Kruger's position among the Dutch of the Transvaal. Had it not been for the Raid, the growing desire among the younger men for a settlement would probably have overborne his obstinacy. Even now it was a question for British statesmen to decide whether they should not wait for his death and for the work of time to overlay the suspicion aroused by the Jameson adventure. But they were alarmed at the military preparation in the Transvaal, and they felt that they could not permit it to go forward. In one sense,

1. See pp. 372–3, above.

indeed, they were not frightened enough by the military preparation, for they despised their enemy. They neglected all warnings, even when officially given, that in case of war the Orange Free State would join the Transvaal, and that mounted men in great numbers would be required to contend on equal terms with the Boers, all of whom were riders and marksmen, knowing the open veldt as sailors know the sea. On neither side were the negotiations carried on with a very earnest desire for peace.

In October 1899 war broke out, while our forces in South Africa were still quite inadequate. The Boers invaded our territory on three sides at once, and laid siege to Mafeking, Kimberley, and Ladysmith.[1] The gallant defence of these places saved Cape Colony from serious invasion, which political conditions would have rendered a terrible danger. In one 'black week' of December the relieving forces destined for Ladysmith and Kimberley, and the force making head against the invasion of Cape Colony, were all three defeated. The most serious of these defeats was the check to Sir Redvers Buller in Natal in his attempt to cross the Tugela River at Colenso on the way to Ladysmith.

The week of disaster roused Britain and roused the Dominions, who voluntarily came forward in the hour of need. The Imperial idea, coupled with the individual nationhood of Canada, Australia, and New Zealand, received an impetus such as no speeches or conferences could have given. France, Germany, and Europe were hostile to our side of the quarrel, but the supremacy of the British fleet was unchallenged. Vast armies of British, Canadians, and Australasians were hastily levied and poured into South Africa. The veteran Lord Roberts, of Afghan fame, was put in command, and Lord Kitchener of Khartoum was his Chief of Staff. The general direction of their march was from the neighbourhood of Kimberley through Bloemfontein to Pretoria. On the way they captured a Boer army under Cronje at Paardeberg – the turning-point of the war. Their advance relieved the pressure on the besieged garrisons, and, when the capitals of the two Republics were in his hands, Lord Roberts thought very excusably that he had brought the war to an end.

The relief of remote Mafeking, defended by Baden Powell, the destined founder of the Boy Scouts, was a welcome and romantic event, though not of great military importance. It aroused in the streets of English towns an orgy of relieved feelings and relaxed dignity. The scenes of 'Mafeking' night gave token, alarming to many, that the city dweller of the new England was very different

1. See map, p. 398, above.

from the rural John Bull who had lit his quiet bonfire after Waterloo. But it is remarkable that no such scenes of 'mafficking' were witnessed during the Great War of our own day until the news arrived of its termination.

In Lord Roberts's campaign far more men had perished of typhoid than of wounds in battle. In the relatively greater destructive power of disease, the Boer War repeated the experience of many previous wars, but affords a striking contrast to the statistics 1914–18, when typhoid and cholera inoculation reserved the greatest hecatombs of victims for Mars in person. In the Boer War artillery played only a minor part, and after the first sharp lessons in December the fighting was in very open order, a magnified and ubiquitous skirmish over the veldt. We lost 20,000 lives in the three years of the war, the greater number by illness.

Rhodes had been in Kimberley during the siege, broken in health but with energy enough left to embarrass the military authorities. After the capture of Pretoria he, like others, thought for a while that the war was over. While still under this impression he made at Cape Town a prophetic speech, which may be taken as his last political will and testament. 'You think you have beaten the Dutch!' he said to the over-eager Loyalists who had come to hear him. 'It is not so. The Dutch are not beaten. What is beaten is Krugerism, a corrupt and evil government, no more Dutch in essence than English. No! The Dutch are as vigorous and unconquered today as they have ever been; the country is still as much theirs as yours, and you will have to live and work with them hereafter as in the past.' Two years later he was dead. His errors have been repaired and his higher hopes fulfilled by other men, not least by two great leaders of those Dutchmen whom he pronounced unconquered and designated as our future friends.

But while Rhodes on that October day was prophesying over the heads of the Loyalists at Cape Town, Louis Botha and Jan Christian Smuts, no less than De Wet and De la Rey, were girding up their loins to fight to the last for their country's freedom. The astonishing resistance of the Boer farmers proved able, under great leadership, to keep the whole force of the Empire busy for two more years.

It was a guerilla war, but of a unique grandeur. The farmers were not in uniform; we accepted that irregularity and, instead of treating them as *francs-tireurs*, gave them all the rights of regular combatants. We had to employ whole armies to guard the long lines of railway which fed our troops, and the 'block-houses' with which Kitchener occupied and controlled the country. 'Drives' over whole districts brought us in prisoners and material, while the nomad Boer 'Commandos' often attacked and captured our men, and let them go again disarmed, having no means of keeping them. Finally, to catch the farmers in these vast spaces where the scattered population was on their side, it was found that no method would answer but to destroy their farms and concentrate their families in camps. Unfortunately, many of the children died there. In the end the material means of further resistance were exhausted.

A war fought under such conditions to the utmost limit of exhaustion might be expected to leave bitter memories that would prevent all hope of reconciliation. But there had been very little intentional cruelty on either side. And after the war, statesmanship and good feeling on the whole triumphed over fear and revenge, though the deaths of the Boer children in the concentration camps could not quickly be forgotten

Peace at length was made, on terms brave men could accept. If it had lain only with Milner, the war might have had no end, but Kitchener felt a wise sympathy with his foes in the field, and the Home Government was growing alarmed. By the Peace of Vereeniging the Boers became British subjects. They were promised money to rebuild their farms, self-government as soon as possible, and the Dutch and English languages in schools and law-courts. These terms were kept. The Conservative Ministry that made the Peace effected the material reconstruction, and the Liberal government of 1906, under Sir Henry Campbell-Bannerman's leadership, boldly trusted our late enemies with complete responsible self-government. Botha and Smuts rose to the head of affairs, and in 1909 the Union of South Africa was accomplished by the free act of all the Colonies concerned.

The Nineteenth Century closed with the death of Queen Victoria on 22 January 1901.

Queen Victoria had put an end to the Republican movement in Great Britain and in the Dominions, not by what she had done, but by what she had been, and by what she had refrained from doing. She had won back public respect for the monarchy in her person. And she had disarmed political hostility to the throne by effacing its occupant as a governing power. It was her habit to express to her advisers, often with unnecessary emphasis, her views on all public questions, but she had not insisted on having her way. She had been content with a purely consultative function in relation to Ministers who were in effect chosen for her by Parliament, sometimes much against her own ideas of their fitness.

She had made the monarchy welcome everywhere, as the representative of the public life of the nation in its non-political aspects. All through her reign, but most of all during its last twenty years, she had appealed to the common human heart of plain people, as a woman who was herself decidedly a 'plain person', more apt than the clever, the cultured, or the aristocratic of soul to sympathize with the elementary joys and sorrows of her subjects. When she said that she was grieved by some public or private calamity, people knew that her sorrow was sincere, and of the same nature as their own. There was nothing superfine about Queen Victoria in her widowhood. None the less, she made the world recognize in her the symbol of all that was mighty and lasting in the life of England and of the races associated with England in Empire. Because she thus combined the very human and the very high, sentiment about her person became, at the end, akin to the religious. And for an Empire which desired to hold together in brotherhood, but refused to be federated into a single parliamentary Constitution, the only possible unit, in symbolism or in law, was found at last to be the historic Crown of Britain.

The middle and later years of the nineteenth century, the most progressively prosperous and, in the sum of genius and achievement, perhaps the most solidly great in our annals, have been called the Victorian era. Victoria did not, like Elizabeth or Louis XIV, decide by her personal choice the trend and policy of the age that bears her name. And yet, when her Jubilee came to be celebrated, her people could not dissociate her from their deep gratitude for what had happened to them and to their fathers, since the day when first she had stepped from the schoolroom to take the headship of a divided and impoverished nation.

Though all was not well in 1897, yet, in those sixty years past, millions had come out of the house of bondage and misery into which the unregulated advent of the Industrial Revolution had plunged its victims. In the same years our people had spread far over the face of the globe, carrying with them, on the whole, justice, civilization, and prosperity where they went. Great men of genius in literature, science, and thought had adorned an age when civilization seemed for a while to be strong both in quantity and in quality, and had helped to make common during her reign certain standards of intellectual seriousness and freedom. As the little grey figure passed in her open carriage through the shouting streets, there was a sense that we had come into port after a long voyage. But in human affairs there is no permanent haven, and we are for ever setting out afresh across new and stormy seas.

EPILOGUE, 1902–1919
(WRITTEN IN 1937)

FIFTEEN years have passed since this book first came out, and it is by fifteen years more possible to follow the further progress of British History out of the strong even current of the Nineteenth Century, into its first plunge amid the more troubled and dangerous waters of the Twentieth. The story of a hundred years came indeed to a natural end with the deaths of Queen Victoria and Lord Salisbury, and the close of the South African War, before the age of motors, aircraft, and wireless; for that reason I stopped the book at 1901, which was not only the nominal ending of the Century, but happened to be a real point of arrival and departure in national history. I had not begun it correspondingly at 1801, because that date is in the very middle of the war with Napoleon abroad and of the anti-Jacobin régime at home. If a history were merely a work of art, it might be best to observe the limits suggested by the natural unity of periods, and to leave *British History in the Nineteenth Century* stretching from 1782 to 1901. But I am told that readers who are likely still to use this book expect a continuation approaching more nearly our own time, and, since the only use of books is to be read, I obey.

CHAPTER 1

THE prolongation of the Boer resistance in the field, for two years after the 'Khaki Election' of 1900 had been held on the ground that the war had come to a victorious end, proved a most salutary lesson to the British people. It did much to reduce self-conceit. It led to measures of Army Reform which were effected before the next and greater call was made upon our military power. And in the field of politics it put a check to the extravagant side of that Imperialism which for good and for evil had inspired British thought and practice for more than a decade past. Clearly the Anglo-Saxons were not such supermen as they had recently been led to believe, since a handful of Boers could hold them up for two years. And if we were not supermen, there were perilously few of us for purposes of Roman domination. For the 'Anglo-Saxons' were not very numerous even within the bounds of the Empire, and they were now for the most part city-dwellers, ceasing to multiply and emigrate with the rapidity of the early Victorian villagers who had peopled Canada and Australasia. Moreover foreigners were drawing together in uncomfortably large groups, all highly armed for war. Our South African campaign had been watched by a hostile world; we were exceedingly unpopular on the Continent of Europe, particularly with French and Germans, and only the British fleet had screened us from attack nearer home, while the Empire's might was being expended in a game of hide-and-seek round and round the veldt with Botha and Smuts.

Throughout the Nineteenth Century, British safety and happiness and the indulgence of all our fine whims, whether benevolent or self-regarding, had been rendered possible only because Britain really ruled the waves, not only in song, but in fact. But what if, in the century now dawning, the air became a pathway of attack? What if the submarine and rival navies put even our maritime supremacy in doubt, first in the Pacific, and finally perhaps even in the North Sea? What if long-distance guns should become capable of spanning the Channel? Such unpleasant possibilities dawned on men's minds gradually during the first decade after the South African War. But already it was a somewhat sobered John Bull who picked himself up off the pavement the morning after the Mafeking debauch.

From this new mood emerged two new policies: in the first instance a search for friends in the world, Japan, France, Russia, and always and above all, if only it were possible, the United States. This policy of seeking friends was begun by the Conservative Minister, Lord Lansdowne, and was continued by his Liberal successor, Sir Edward Grey. 'Splendid isolation' died with Lord Salisbury.

In the second place there was a movement of public opinion to substitute Social Reform at home for Imperialism overseas, and to conciliate the Boers and possibly even the Irish by the extension of self-government within the Empire to non-Anglo-Saxon peoples.

The time was ripe for change, but it was delayed until 1906, when it came with a crash. Meanwhile Arthur Balfour, as Prime Minister in succession to his uncle Salisbury, carried through a number of measures of high value and importance.

The first of these was the Education Bill of 1902.

Gladstone's and Forster's Bill of 1870 had provided the country with a system of Primary Education.[1] But Secondary Education

1. See pp. 343–4, above.

and the ladder to the Universities had hardly been provided for at all by State action. Some of the larger School Boards, like the London School Board under 'Progressive' leadership, had begun to supply 'science and art classes'. But even this was resented by many Conservative ratepayers of the old type, and in 1901 the famous Cockerton Judgement decided that the London School Board had for years been outstepping its statutory powers. By this judicial pronouncement educational progress was stopped, and Secondary Education was relegated to the private sphere.

Fortunately the new Conservative Prime Minister, like a true Scot, felt for education an enthusiasm independent of politics, and fortunately he listened to the advice of a great Civil Servant. Prompted by Sir Robert Morant, Balfour not only made good the harm done by the Cockerton Judgement, but seized the chance to put Primary and Secondary Education alike on a new and far better footing.

The town and village School Boards formed under the Act of 1870 were elected by Constituencies in most cases much too small to take a broad educational outlook. And the 'Voluntary' Schools run by the Church were, in every sense of the word, parochial. To remedy these defects, Balfour's Education Act handed over the responsibility not only for Elementary but for Higher Education to the County Councils and County Boroughs, under the aegis of the Board of Education and its rules. The County Councils were to act through County Education Committees. The improvement due to the larger area and vision of these new Education Authorities has been of great benefit to Primary Education both in the 'provided' (County) Schools and the 'voluntary' (Church) Schools. And the new system has been of still greater benefit to Secondary Education, which, instead of being held up by the Cockerton Judgement, really takes its start as a great function of State from the Act of 1902.

The reform has resulted in a wide increase of Secondary Education Schools, and the erection of a 'ladder' by which able students of small means can ascend through them to the Universities. Improved Secondary Education in schools has raised the average standard of work and intelligence at Oxford and Cambridge; and has been the making of the new Universities that sprang up apace in the new century, at Liverpool, Leeds, Sheffield, Bristol, and Reading, in addition to London, Durham, and Manchester Universities founded in the previous century, but come to full maturity in our own.

Both Gladstone in 1870 and Balfour in 1902, though they did

great services to Education, paid the political penalty for touching the sore point of denominational politics. Gladstone's doubling the State grant to the Church Schools in order to preserve them as an integral part of the new system had lost him the support of many of his Nonconformist followers at the election of 1874. Then in 1902 Balfour in his turn put these Church Schools on the local rates, thus further securing their financial position. In return, they passed under the County Education Authority, which was to 'control all secular education', and was to appoint two out of the six managers in each Church School. But as the teacher was to be appointed by the Managers and would presumably be a Churchman, the 'Church atmosphere' would be maintained. Nonconformists did not think this amount of control adequate for schools henceforth to be so largely maintained out of the public rates. They felt the more aggrieved, because most of the Church Schools were in rural villages, 'one-school areas', where no other teaching was within reach of Dissenting families. Indignation over the Nonconformist grievance reunited the ranks of the Liberal Party which the South African war had divided, and was one of the chief causes of the Conservative catastrophe at the General Election of 1906.

Although the House of Lords prevented the Education Act of 1902 from being seriously amended by later Liberal Governments, the outcry against its working has died away in the course of years. For one thing, the control exerted by the County Education Authority over the Church Schools has proved more real than Liberals expected.[1] Moreover the public attitude to religious controversy has been altering rapidly in the last generation. Church and Dissent are less hostile to one another, in presence of an increased falling away from religious observance of any kind. The growth of the new Paganism has made Christians kinder to one another. The Church clergy arouse less antagonism than of old, because they are less apt to regard themselves as the rulers of the society in which they live. They are kept in check, no longer by Nonconformist hostility, but by their own sensitiveness to the atmosphere of a new age more indifferent to ecclesiastical claims and social pretensions. Trollope's Archdeacon Grantly would think it a sad world. It is possible, however, that religion has in some respects gained in influence though it has lost in power. Church, Chapel, and Sunday School are less attended, but the

1. As a result of the storm of opposition, the Bill of 1902 finally passed in a form whereby religious instruction in Church Schools was placed under the authority of the Managers as a whole, thereby putting an end to its exclusive direction by the parson of the parish.

wireless brings religion into many homes. It is difficult to analyse the new situation. There is less aggressive anti-clericalism and more indifference than in the later Victorian era.

This diversion of the nation's interest into new channels has had its reflection in politics. The political aspect of the quarrel between Church and Dissent had been the life-blood of the Whig and Tory, the Liberal and Conservative factions in the constituencies, from Charles II to Victoria. In our own day the reassortment of parties on a basis of industrial and social questions only, with no reference to religion, was the prime reason of the disappearance of the Liberal and the advent of the Labour Party. Class-consciousness has superseded chapel-consciousness. The excitement over Balfour's Education Bill was the last party fight on the old ecclesiastical lines.

Another great reform of Balfour's Ministry was the Irish Land Purchase Act of 1903. Its three authors were the Prime Minister; the Chief Secretary for Ireland, the brilliant George Wyndham; and the great Civil Servant, Sir Anthony Macdonnell. Gladstone had been the first British statesman who sought to remove the Irish tenant's grievances by legislation, and his tentative efforts had been hampered by the resistance of the House of Peers in the interests of Irish landlords. But since those days the Irish landlords themselves were beginning to think it might be wise to sell out. If they waited till the next great Irish convulsion, they might lose all for nothing.[1]

Balfour believed in the maintenance of the Union, but he had always held that it could only survive if Irish grievances, economic as well as religious, were removed.[2] His Act of 1903 set up a machinery, oiled by a large loan on generous terms from the British Government, by which the ownership of most of the land of Ireland has passed from the Protestant landlords to the native peasant farmers. This great peaceful revolution did not, as Balfour hoped, prevent the resurgence of the demand for political self-government or quench the national aspirations of Irishmen. But it smoothed out one of the chief complications of the Irish question, which, if left unremoved, might have rendered even such settlement as we have now attained, or any agreed settlement at all, impossible in the days to come.

1. On the Irish Land System see above, pp. 342–3, 379–80.

2. Balfour used to say in private talk that he regarded George III as a great national disaster, both because he alienated America and because he vetoed Pitt's plan for granting Catholic Emancipation. He would never forgive George for giving the Union that bad start.

Next year, by his Licensing Act, Balfour dealt with an equally thorny question nearer home. It had always been a moot point whether compensation was due when a licence to sell liquor was taken away by the magisterial bench, not for misconduct in the management but in order to reduce an excessive number of public houses in the region. The Temperance party opposed compensation on principle. But the Conservative party was closely allied to the liquor trade, which had now an enormous clientele due the to holding of brewery shares by many thousands of investors. The sale of drink to the working class had become a great middle and upper class interest. But the judgement in the case of *Sharp* v. *Wakefield* had disallowed the legal claim to compensation for the non-renewal of a licence. To remedy this, Balfour's Act of 1904 arranged that compensation was to be paid, not by the public but out of funds created by the enormous profits of the trade.

The Liberal Opposition, without adopting the full temperance objection, to compensation, attacked the terms of the Bill as too generous to the Brewing Companies, since reduction in the number of licences was now to be limited by the compensation available in each particular area. But Balfour's Act passed and has since held the field, as the House of Lords prevented its alteration by Liberal Governments. Under this system the Twentieth Century has witnessed a reduction of public houses per head of population. And in the last thirty years there has been a still greater reduction in drunkenness and excessive drinking habits, at least among the working class, the clients of the public house. For this improvement there are many causes; among them are better conditions of life; better education; greater variety of amusements, interests, and distractions; and better management of houses where drink is sold. The football ground, the cinema, the wireless, are rivals to the public houses, that once was for millions the only obvious place of distraction. But while drinking has gone down, gambling has increased.

As a result of the lessons of the South African War and the disturbed state of the world there was a great outcry for Army Reform. The Conservative Cabinet failed indeed to provide a War Minister able to reform the organization of the fighting forces which Haldane afterwards achieved with success. But Balfour erected two new pieces of State machinery, the Army Council and Committee of Imperial Defence.

In 1904 the Army Council was set up to supply the Secretary for War with military advisers more useful to him as such than the

414

ever-occupied Commander-in-Chief. At the same time the office of permanent Commander-in-Chief was abolished and his functions were distributed. Next year a still more important body, the Committee of Imperial Defence, was established. It was Balfour's last great reform, and in the following years it was developed by the Asquith Government as the principal means for laying plans for the possible event of war. Its functions are consultative only; it provides the Cabinet with information and advice, and its decisions can only be carried into effect by Parliament or by Departments of State. As it is not an executive body, its composition is fluid. The Prime Minister summons whom he thinks fit – generally the Secretary for War, the First Lord of the Admiralty, the Foreign Secretary, any Dominion Prime Ministers who may be in England and the technical advisers required for the questions under discussion at each particular meeting. The Committee has, however, a Secretary of its own, whose permanence in a constantly changing body gives him great importance, especially when he is as able a man as Sir Maurice Hankey.

The importance of the Committee of Imperial Defence is twofold. It enables the problems of army, navy, air force, and home front to be considered together in their mutual relations and as parts of one general policy, of provision for possible war. And it enables the responsible statesmen of the Dominions to meet the home authorities in confidential discussion and concert plans for the defence of the Empire as a whole. On its Imperial side the Committee has political as well as military importance.

As the prime author of the Education Act, the Licensing Act, Irish Land Purchase, and the Committee of Imperial Defence, Balfour has a strong claim to be numbered among the successful Prime Ministers. Owing to the portentous character of the electoral catastrophe of 1906 that claim has not always been allowed; yet Balfour had done great things on his own initiative and by his own strength of character; like Gladstone from 1868–74 he had 'spent his majority like a gentleman'. Spent it he certainly had, but even so the completeness of the Conservative crash in 1906 was due at least as much to Chamberlain as to Balfour. Just as Gladstone broke up the Liberal Party and exiled it from power by his advocacy of Home Rule, so did Chamberlain with the Conservative party by his advocacy of Protection. Whether the adoption since the Great War of a modified system of Protection and the establishment of self-government for Ireland are to be regarded as necessary changes rendered possible in the long run by the missionary work of Gladstone and Chamberlain, as pioneers in a previous generation, is a question too difficult to answer, but sufficiently important to ask.

Chamberlain in 1902 proposed Protection, renamed 'Tariff Reform', in order to unite the Dominions to the Empire by preferential tariffs. In the second half of his great career, his foresight and enthusiasm ranged with amplest opinion oversea; and in the Conservative party to which he was now attached it was easier to promote Imperial schemes than domestic social reform, of which in his earlier days he had been the prophet. But after the South African War, the country had had enough Empire for a while, and Chamberlain's proposal for a Preferential Tariff, in the hands of his insular fellow countrymen, was soon moulded by the Conservatives into a scheme of which the prime object was the protection of British goods. This aroused the enthusiasm and opened the purse strings of many British manufacturers. But their zeal was suspect to the consumer, especially to the working-man with his family budget to consider. Free Trade doctrine was very strong in all sections of the community; it had behind it fifty years of unchallenged authority and custom; caution and tradition, usually assets to the Conservative party, supported the economic thesis of the Liberals. Moreover, the prosperity of British commerce under the Free Trade system was not yet shaken. The world's markets were not yet closed to our goods by nationalist foreign governments to the extent that they have been closed since the Great War. Chamberlain in his lifetime was beaten by the still obstinate prosperity of our staple industries. He could prophesy their ruin, but its coming was delayed.

Indeed the great interest that most clearly required protection in the first years of the new century was agriculture. Ever since 1875 foodstuffs from America and all the world had come flooding into Great Britain on a scale never foreseen in the day of Cobden and Peel, when prices had been steadied, not smashed, by free importation from Europe. But now it was no longer easy to grow food at a profit in Britain. The farm hands, who had been badly paid and treated even in good times, were deserting the land for the cities at an appalling rate. Great Britain was on the way to become an entirely urban community, unlike any other country in the world. A check ought to have been put to this catastrophe, which would be irremediable when once complete. Unfortunately the protection of British agriculture was the proposal that politicians were most afraid to advocate, though something might be done under cover of Colonial Preference. But the Free Trade system under which Britain had so long flourished had little regard for agriculture. Food was the currency in which foreign nations and our own Dominions paid for British manufactured goods. And cheap corn and meat was of great value to the wage-earning community. The absence of a democratic peasant-proprietorship like that of the European Continent made it difficult to advocate agricultural Protection. The field labourer, long ill-used by the farmer in the great arable districts, scarcely knew if he wished for Protection, as he could go off to the industrial districts and get a good wage. The most effective popular appeal of Chamberlain's opponents was the memory of the 'hungry forties', the fear of dearer foodstuffs, and the cry against the 'small loaf'. It was only after the Great War had shaken party traditions and old economic doctrines, and the German submarine had shown the use of the plough in Britain that any attempt was made by subsidies and control of imports to maintain food production within the island and so save a little of what is still left of country life, while securing by statute a minimum wage for the field labourer. The complete urbanization of life in our island would be horrible to contemplate, for a thousand reasons, together more important than any economic doctrine.

To return to the situation in 1902–05, Balfour's position as head of a party and of a government cleft in two by Chamberlain's propaganda was one of extreme difficulty. The zealots of Tariff Reform were not converting the country, but they were converting the great majority of active Conservatives. Balfour's acute and sceptical intellect already occupied the middle position between the full Protectionist and the full Free Trade doctrine which is the most usual attitude of Englishmen today, but which was regarded between 1902 and 1906 as a dishonest and laughable subterfuge. But Balfour was always singularly indifferent to public opinion, and his perfectly sincere middle position, although it then made both sides angry, admirably suited his purpose, which was to hold the Conservative Party together as long as possible. Eventually he would have to follow Chamberlain because most of the party was following him, but he would do so as slowly and for as short a distance as possible. Meanwhile he would continue in office and carry out the measures of home and foreign policy in which he believed, in spite of the fury of Free Traders and Protectionists. He would be the stillness in the midst of the tornado.

In this way Balfour held on to office till December 1905; though his party had been in disruption and the credit of the government gone for several years he passed the measures about which he cared. No doubt the refusal for so long to face the new issue at an election made the crash worse when it came.

Meanwhile, Chamberlain's propaganda had captured the rank and file of the party behind Balfour's shrugged shoulders, but had alienated many of its ablest men, not only the old guard of Salisbury's Ministers, but even his sons Hugh and Robert Cecil, and Randolph's son, young Winston Churchill. Like Gladstonianism twenty years before, Protection was not intellectually 'good form'; it helped to turn the rising generation of intellectuals towards Liberal and Labour politics. The ebbing tide of Imperialism helped to wash back Chamberlain's Protection, just as its flood tide had wrecked Gladstone's Home Rule.

Moreover Chamberlain had failed in his sincere effort to make the working classes see their interest in his new programme. His great campaign had set Englishmen thinking hard about economic questions, but many of them thought Socialism instead of Protection. Affinities govern politics: the slogan that 'Tariff Reform means work for all' was discredited not always on purely economic arguments, but because Chamberlain's allies had for so many years of power passed so little 'working class legislation'; their new zeal to cure unemployment by tariffs was therefore suspect. Disraeli, indeed, had more than dreamt of connecting the new Conservatism with the poorer and more numerous of the 'two nations' into which his youthful vision had seen England divided. He had altered the law affecting strikes in the working-class direction, and had carried out a mild programme of social reform.[1] But his lead had not been followed. Salisbury had no place for such thoughts in his capacious head. Randolph Churchill, Disraeli's spiritual successor, misplayed his hand and disappeared. Balfour, in many respects a reformer, knew very little about working-class thought and aspiration. At any rate since 1895 the Conservative-Unionist Party had remained upper and middle class in its sympathies and acts. Chamberlain indeed would have liked to run Imperialism and Social Reform together. But he had been forced to choose between the two. On the advice of his wisest supporter, the scientific philanthropist, Charles Booth, he had long advocated Old Age Pensions, but he had failed to deliver the goods. The money needed for such a policy had been swallowed in South African sands. Therefore his new Tariff Reform League was suspect to working-class opinion. It looked like a trap baited by the capitalist employers.

Moreover Labour was in these years growing 'class-conscious'

1. See pp. 359–60, above.

and determined to act politically for itself. The effective rise of the Labour Party took place at the turn of the century, and its immediate cause was the 'Taff Vale decision'.

After Disraeli's liberating legislation of 1875–86, the development of Trade Unionism went on, spreading from the skilled artisan class, the strength of mid-Victorian Trade Unionism, into the grades of unskilled labour, as in the great dockers' strike of 1889.[1] But all this time there was no demand for a change in the law, and consequently no considerable growth of political activity on the part of Labour. The 'Miners' representatives', like Burt and Fenwick, were working-men, chosen by and representing their fellows, but attached to the Liberal Party. In the last twenty years of the century the Independent Labour Party, hostile alike to Liberals and Conservatives, was founded by Keir Hardie. But at the election of 1895 all its twenty-eight candidates for Parliament were defeated, and in the 'Khaki' election of 1900 only two were elected. To the very end of Victoria's reign the great working-class constituencies, even the miners, refused to 'vote labour'. The Labour Party had little importance when the century ended, though Ramsay MacDonald as secretary was laying the foundations of its future success.

Then came the blow of the Taff Vale decision in 1901, whence much of our political history takes its origin. The Judges once more undid the work of former Parliaments, and destroyed by a legal decision the Trade Union Rights that had been held for a generation under Gladstone's Trade Union Act of 1871,[2] just as the Judges in 1867 had torn up the rights that had been held for a generation under the Act of 1825. The Taff Vale decision of 1901 gave impetus and power to the Labour Party, which became an effective Third party in the State, destined in a generation to destroy and replace the Liberal Party. The Judges have played a very great part in the development of our politics, though it was not the part they intended to play.

What then was the legal case which had such momentous political consequences? Some employees of the Taff Vale Railway Company, in South Wales, had been guilty, during a strike, of tumultuous picketing and other acts of an unlawful character. As the legislation of 1871–6 had hitherto been interpreted, the action of the railway company lay against the individuals guilty of these illegal acts, but not against the trade union – in this case the

1. See pp. 385–7, above.
2. See pp. 357–8, above.

Amalgamated Society of Railway Servants. But the railway company was persuaded by its lawyers, contrary to the usual practice, to sue the Amalgamated Society of Railway Servants, although the great union had been unsympathetic to this particular strike and had certainly not incited the illegal acts. The case was carried up to the final Court of Appeal in the House of Lords, when the Law Lords decided that the Union, though admittedly not a corporate body, could be sued in its corporate capacity for damages alleged to have been caused by the action of its officers; and that it could be sued not merely for criminal acts but for acts, not unlawful, which caused loss to others. The amalgamated Society of Railway Servants had to pay £23,000 in damages.

This entirely new and unexpected interpretation of the Act of 1871 by the Law Lords of 1901 struck at the very heart of Trade Union action. Under the Taff Vale judgement, Trade Unions durst not, under peril of losing all their funds in damages, take any strike action to raise wages or to prevent the lowering of wages. Naturally employers took advantage of this new state of things between 1901 and 1906.

The Conservative government would probably have been wise in Conservative interests if it had at once legislated to put back the law on Trade Unions' liability to the place where everyone supposed that it rested between 1871 and 1901. Disraeli would have done so. But the great industrial employers, formerly divided between the Liberal and Conservative parties, had, since the Home Rule split, most of them gone over to the Conservative Party. The Liberal Party was now in a position to take up the Trade Union cause and profit by a Labour alliance. But the Conservative Party was not. Mr Balfour's government shelved the issue by appointing a Royal Commission to report. And Mr Sidney Webb, who sat on that commission, writes:

This Commission, it is believed, was told privately not to report until after the General Election, in order that the Conservative Government might not be embarrassed by the dilemma.[1]

The General Election of January 1906 proved a catastrophe for Conservatism such as no party had undergone since the old Toryism was swept away at the election of 1833. And in the *débâcle* a great part was played by working class determination to get the Taff Vale decision reversed by legislation in order to save the Trade Union movement and recover the use of the strike weapon in bargaining. One of the posters, used in that general election,

1. *History of Trade Unionism*, ed. 1920, pp. 605–6.

represented a very fierce-looking judge putting a scourge into the hands of an employer to lay on to a working man.

Trade Union action took two forms at the General Election of January 1906. Trade Unionists voted for Liberal candidates in many constituencies, but only after exacting pledges from those candidates that they would vote for measures to secure the Trade Unions against legal liability under all circumstances. And secondly, the Labour Party ran fifty candidates of its own and secured the election of some thirty; there were also a dozen working-men members of the older sort attached to the Liberal Party, and known as 'Lib-Labs', such as John Burns and the veteran miner leaders Burt and Fenwick.

The Labour Party therefore in January 1906 came into Parliamentary existence on the floor of the House of Commons, as a Third party in the State. Moreover it had pledged the rank and file of the Liberal members to give Trade Unions complete immunity from legal proceedings.

Finally, before going to the country, the old Capitalist and Imperialist Conservatism committed a final indiscretion. At the demand of the Rand mine-owners in South Africa, advocated by Milner with his purely administrative mentality, the British Government allowed the engagement of some 50,000 Chinese coolies, imported to work the gold mines, without their families, under conditions of restriction in compounds which were decidedly unwholesome in more ways than one. It was so new and doubtful a policy, that it was scarcely wise to force it on South Africa at a time when she was not enjoying self-government. Canada, Australia, and New Zealand resented it; our countrymen overseas knew the complications of 'oriental labour'. And it was regarded by the working classes in England as the final outrage. Was it for this that 'the white man's war' had been fought in South Africa? It now seemed to many simple souls that the 'Little Englanders' had been right after all, that the mine-owners alone would benefit by all that waste of wealth and loss of blood upon the veldt. Chinese labour was a question that made everyone see red – or at least yellow. For when the Conservatives were accused of introducing 'Chinese Slavery' they too got angry, not without reason, but quite without effect until the General Election was over.

In December 1905 even Balfour felt that the sands had run out. But instead of dissolving Parliament he resigned office. He hoped that his successor, Sir Henry Campbell-Bannerman, would find such difficulty in forming a Ministry of 'Liberal Imperialists' and

'Little Englanders' together that the divisions of the party would become apparent on the eve of the polls and disgust and frighten the electors. Something of the sort nearly happened; some months before, the 'Liberal Imperialists', Asquith, Grey, and Haldane, had rashly agreed together not to take office unless the Prime Minister would consent to go to the Lords, leaving the lead of the Commons to Asquith. When this arrangement was rejected by Campbell-Bannerman, Asquith changed his mind and took office at once, and Grey and Haldane were over-persuaded at the last moment. Once in the Cabinet, they had no differences with Campbell-Bannerman either in home or foreign policy, and their personal relations with him soon became excellent.

A ministry unusually strong in old experience and young talent was formed and went to the polls in January 1906. The outcome was the defeat of Balfour at Manchester and many of his Cabinet colleagues in the country, though Birmingham stood solid by the Chamberlain family and Protection. The Conservative vote in the new House was reduced to 167; the 377 Liberals could claim a majority of 84 over all parties combined, but in fact they were allied with the Irish, and with Labour.

A new age had come in with the new century. Whatever party or doctrine would be the ultimate gainer, the old forms of militant Imperialism, and Conservative Unionism were never again to hold power. Protection, indeed, had a future. But the Conservatism that came back during and after the World War, as an alternative often preferred to Labour Governments, has been liberal in its outlook on Irish, Egyptian, South African, and Indian questions, and semi-socialist in its conception of the duties of the State to the working class. Meanwhile until the War the Liberal Party bore rule for the last time, in close though uneasy alliance with Labour, and left a deep impress on social legislation.

CHAPTER 2

FOR ten years Great Britain was ruled, for the last time, by a Liberal Government. Its leaders were men of unusual personality and power. There was Haldane, the soft-spoken lawyer-philosopher who won the confidence of the soldiers and reformed the Army; John Morley, the veteran of the Radical intellectualism of the last century, who was now on behalf of the British Government to cope with the new problem of national self-consciousness in

India; there was Edward Grey, remote, firm, and sadly serene at the Foreign Office; there was young Winston Churchill looking round for his kingdom; and there was Lloyd George, on whom time and great events should fix many diverse labels, mutually contradictory but all true. And coming on were such able administrators and legislators as Herbert Samuel, Walter Runciman, and Reginald McKenna. The working classes were represented for the first time in the Cabinet, by John Burns, a personality hewn out of old English oak. For a decade all these men most astonishingly held together, for two successive Prime Ministers knew their business: Campbell-Bannerman, an easy-tempered but shrewd Scot, who saw quite through the souls of men, started his team of colleagues in harmony; won the confidence of the raw and restive legion of Liberal recruits in the House; pacified South Africa by reversing the policy of Milner and granting responsible government before it was too late; then died in 1908, his tasks accomplished. He was succeeded by Asquith, a Yorkshireman of high integrity and unshakeable nerve, endowed with a skill in advocacy learnt in the law and applied to politics, with sound judgement to choose well between the opinions of others, and a rare skill in manipulating discordant colleagues.

The great achievement of this Ministry was the initiation of measures of social reform on a scale beyond all precedent. Old age pensions on a non-contributory basis (1908) helped to empty the workhouses, to give happiness to the old and relieve their loyal sons and daughters of some at least of the burden of their maintenance. Democratic budgets, shifting more taxations on to the wealthy – Workmen's Compensation, Miners' Eight Hours, Medical Inspection of Children and the Children's Bill, the Town-planning Act, the Sweated Industries Act, measures of Unemployment and Health Insurance, and the Small Holdings Act for rural districts – formed part of a vast programme of laws placed on the Statute Book. Such measures, implemented by municipal bodies and extended by the work of Care Committees, Play Centres, Boy Scouts, Adult Education, and other such activities outside the harsh discords of politics, together with constantly advancing medical science and practice, have in the present century, in spite of the war, raised the standard of children's health and happiness, reduced the death-rate and prolonged the average of human life by several years, and begun a more even distribution of the national income and of opportunities for happiness.

The function of Local Government has undergone immense extension under modern democracy. It is looked on now, not merely to remove public nuisances, to supply sanitation, lighting, and roads, but to act for the personal benefit of the individual citizen. It is to Local Government, controlled and aided by the State Offices at Whitehall, that the poorer citizen is beginning to look to supply the house he lives in; the electric light and gas he uses; free education for his children – including in some cases University scholarships; medical clinics and isolation hospitals; books from the Free Library; baths and swimming; cricket fields and 'green belts' of open country for his Sunday walks; trams or buses to take the family to work or school, and a hundred other benefits to make life kind.

This system of State assistance to the life of the poorer citizen is a great fact in modern English life. Its principal instrument is found in elective local bodies, empowered by successive Acts of Parliament, helped financially by Treasury 'grants in aid' of rates, and kept up to the mark by government Inspectors.

This system, of which the origins can be traced to the middle of the Nineteenth Century, has been growing faster than ever in the Twentieth. In the Rating and Valuation Act of 1925 and in the Local Government Act of 1929 we see the Central Power taking more and more control of Local Government. There is an ever-increasing tendency for the Minister and Department at Whitehall to direct the action of local authorities on a single national model. The national model is enforced on the local authorities not merely by Acts of Parliament, but also by elaborate regulations issued by Departments of State. Such regulations are called 'Delegated Legislation', because Parliament by Statute delegates to the Minister (of Health, Transport, or Education) the power to make subsidiary rules to be enforced on the local authority as if they were laws.

The elected Municipality or County Council is therefore becoming more and more the agent of the Central Government in carrying out a national policy for the benefit of the poorer citizens, largely at the expense of the richer citizens, through local rates and through national taxes that go to make up the 'grants in aid'. Under this system the local authorities have more powers but less independence than of old. They cannot refuse to carry out these multitudinous duties imposed by Act of Parliament or by the regulations issued by the Minister, and they must not invent new policies of their own. The days have long gone by since the local benches of Justices of the Peace in 1795 introduced the new national policy of rates in aid of wages without any reference either to Parliament or to any Minister or Department at Whitehall.[1]

1. See pp. 156–7, above, the 'Speenhamland Act'.

In future every government, whether called Conservative, National, or Labour, must be at least half socialist. The last Liberal Government recognized this fact, and applied great legislative and administrative ability to meet the needs of the new social and economic scene.

The Liberals, who had ceased to be in the main a middle-class party, could only maintain themselves so long as the working class would vote for their candidates. In the very first days of the new Parliament, the degree of Liberal dependence on Labour opinion was made dramatically clear. As a result of the General Election, the Taff Vale decision must be reversed – but on what terms?

The Liberal Government in 1906 introduced a Bill based on the Report of the Commission, appointed by Balfour,[1] on which Sidney Webb and others had sat. The Bill, as those Commissioners had advised, would have left Trade Unions suable for torts, but only when illegal acts had been done by their express orders, or by 'some person acting under their authority'. At once the Trade Union world was up in arms demanding complete immunity for their funds; repeated experience of the hostile ingenuity of Judges had filled Labour with a profound distrust of the law courts in cases where Trade Union rights were concerned. Those rights as held under the laws of 1825 and again of 1871 had been taken away by legal decisions after long years of secure enjoyment. And so it might be again. The Labour members in the House and a large number of Liberal Members who had pledged themselves at the election to make Trade Union Funds immune from legal actions declared that the Government's Bill was not enough. Campbell-Bannerman surrendered and accepted the demand for complete legal immunity of Trade Unions from actions for torts, though their individual members breaking the law of course remained subject to penalties. The new Bill passed both Houses, for Balfour refused to divide against it on third reading in the Commons and this agreed signal was obeyed by the Lords; they let it pass, while they threw out the new Government's Education and Licensing Bills.

It was thus already shown in 1906 that Labour was the strongest element in the progressive or left-wing side of politics, stronger than the 'old Liberal' interests, Nonconformity and Temperance. The Lords had not dared to challenge Labour, although all the Conservatives and many of the Liberals regarded complete immunity as a dangerous privilege for bodies so powerful as the

1. See p. 420, above.

amalgamated Trade Unions of the Twentieth Century; miners, railwaymen, and transport workers were becoming organized on a national instead of local basis, and bade fair to be each 'a State within the State'. And now they were rendered in large measure exempt from the control of law.

At the same time, by throwing out the distinctly Liberal measures on Education and Licensing, the Conservative leaders put the House of Lords again in the forefront of politics, a position from which the wisdom of Disraeli had preserved it. Under his wise direction, the Lords had allowed Gladstone to put on the Statute Book all his large programme between 1868 and 1874, including even the Disestablishment of the Irish Church, and the Conservatives had consequently won the next General Election. And in the eighties the Lords had restrained their natural impulse to act as a partisan body on a level of authority with the House of Commons. But in 1893 they had won popularity by the bolder course of throwing out Gladstone's Home Rule Bill; their complete success on that occasion, endorsed by the verdict of the country at the next election, misled Chamberlain, Balfour, and Lord Lansdowne into supposing that the Lords could play the same game in the more democratic Twentieth Century against a much more formidable government backed by a vast majority.

Their strategy in deserting Disraeli's caution was fundamentally at fault; but in the years 1906–8 their tactics were clever and at first successful. They passed the measures in which the working classes were most interested, but humiliated the Government by refusing to pass the measures about which its Liberal supporters specially cared. The Liberals seemed already reduced to impotence within two years of their triumphal entry into power. The bye-elections began to turn heavily against the Government. A Conservative reaction was on foot, and a little patience would have met its reward. But the Peers had no patience, and at the instigation of the party leaders proceeded to commit the greatest error in modern politics. They threw out Lloyd George's Budget of 1909.

But before dealing with the Peers' rejection of the Budget and its momentous consequences, it would be well to notice two questions, of Imperial and of Foreign policy, which illustrated the scope and the limit of the powers of the House of Lords during this period of Liberal government. In 1906 Sir Henry Campbell-Bannerman as Prime Minister persuaded his new Cabinet to adopt the bold measure of granting responsible self-government to the recently conquered colonies in South Africa. It was known that this would lead at once to the rule of the Transvaal and Orange Free State by a Parliamentary majority of our late enemies the Boers. The Conservatives, led by Milner, Balfour, and Lansdowne, declared that this would be fatal. But the Liberals regarded it as the only way to save South Africa for the Empire. In 1906 the Lords would certainly have thrown out a Bill establishing immediate and complete self-government, so the Liberal Cabinet avoided a conflict of the Houses by setting up the new constitutions for the Transvaal and Orange River Colony respectively by Letters Patent. The power of the Crown was thus used to short-circuit Parliament, as Gladstone had used it when he induced Queen Victoria to abolish Purchase in the Army by revoking the Royal Warrant that allowed it. The Lords had no say in the matter. The bold experiment in South Africa proved successful and saved South Africa for the Empire when the War came, making Botha and Smuts our fellow soldiers instead of our enemies.

On the other hand, in the year 1909 the Lords were able to exercise control over an important measure of foreign policy. The question was the ratification by Parliament of the Declaration of London. The Declaration of London was a new set of rules drawn up by the international naval experts at The Hague on the question of contraband and neutral trade in time of war. The Liberal government sponsored it. But the Lords in 1909 refused to ratify this Declaration of London, on the ground that it unduly restricted our use of sea-power against enemy trade in time of war. It was perhaps fortunate the Lords did so. For during the war we very soon found it necessary to go much further in the way of restricting neutral trade with the enemy than the principles of the Declaration of London would have allowed. Our strangle-hold on Germany would have been relaxed if we had adhered to the principles of the Declaration. And if we had in 1914 repudiated the Declaration after solemnly ratifying it in 1909, our difficulties with President Wilson as the defender of neutral rights might have been seriously increased. The Lords did a useful service in throwing it out, so that it did not bind us when the war came.

The Lords' rejection of the Budget for the year 1909, was a new interpretation of the constitutional function of the hereditary Chamber in matters of finance. It amounted to a claim on the part of the Peers to force a General Election whenever they wished; for a Government unable to raise taxes must either resign or dissolve. If the Peers could throw out a Budget, any Parliament not to their liking could be dissolved at their will. The rejection of the Budget was also a violent breach with the custom of the Constitution, of which Conservatives should above all regard themselves as the guardians. Neither Disraeli nor Salisbury would have dreamt of such a proceeding as to invite the Lords to reject the Budget of the year. Still less was the Twentieth Century a time for an hereditary chamber to claim powers it had not exercised even in the aristocratic Eighteenth. But it was in vain that King Edward VII warned the Opposition leaders of the danger of the course on which they were set.[1]

A tendency to violence and excitement had already invaded the mind of the new Century. Militant Suffragettes, Labour Unions, Irish parties, and foreign military potentates were not the only people to be subject to its influence. The Tariff Reform movement was being carried out in an atmosphere of perpetual excitement and anger; the new type of newspaper lived on sensation: Lloyd George's shrill demagogic note was new in speeches delivered by Ministers of the Crown; and the Peers caught the contagion of violence.

Lloyd George's Budget was unpopular with the upper class, justly because it proposed new Land Taxes in an ill-conceived form which proved on trial to be impracticable; and less reasonably because it made a very moderate increase of direct taxation on the well-to-do. There was to be a graduated income tax at about a quarter of what it is today (1937) and corresponding death duties, to pay for Old Age Pensions and a very necessary increase in the Navy. If the Opposition had waited, they could have won the next election and repealed the Land Taxes. But they urged on the Peers to reject the Budget, the very thing which Lloyd George most ardently desired. He made ample use of his opportunity; his harangues at Limehouse and elsewhere sharpened the edge of controversy and aroused the democratic passions. It was a good election cry for the Liberals – 'Shall Peers or People rule?' The Peers defended themselves by claiming that they had only referred the Budget to the People, and that the Land Valuation clauses were not properly financial: but the Peers were on the defensive and the

1. It had been agreed in Charles II's reign that the Lords could not amend a money Bill, but could throw it out. But since the custom had arisen of putting all the year's taxes in a single Budget Bill, the Lords had never thrown out a Budget. They had in 1860 thrown out a separate money bill, Gladstone's Repeal of the Paper Duty Bill, but passed it next year when he put it into the Budget. The Lords in 1909 claimed that the Valuation Clauses of the new Land Tax in the Budget were not proper to a Finance Bill, and that the Budget could not therefore claim the customary privilege of unchallenged passage through their House.

Opposition had given to Lloyd George the advantage of attack.

Meanwhile Asquith and his other colleagues appealed more quietly to moderate men, who had been drifting back to Conservative allegiance, but were shocked by the disregard of constitutional custom by the Lords. At the same time the Liberal Ministers were able to rally the Labour and the Irish forces to a joint effort to limit the Lords' power of veto. Another issue in the Budget controversy was Tariff Reform: it was urged by Conservatives as a method of raising money preferable to the increased direct taxation necessary under a Free Trade government.

All these issues were brought to a head together by appeal to the country. Asquith, as Prime Minister, at once gave out that he would hold a General Election which should not only decide the fate of the Budget, but should pronounce on the new principle of a Parliament Bill to abolish the Peers' right to touch money bills, and reduce their veto on ordinary legislation to a suspensory action for two years.

But at this stage, in December 1909, King Edward VII warned Asquith, that, greatly as he regretted the action of the Lords, he disliked the government's remedy as 'tantamount to the destruction of the House of Lords', and could not consent to create three hundred Peers to carry such a measure until two successive general elections had shown that the mind of the country was irrevocably fixed.

Asquith, therefore, when he went to the General Election of January 1910 knew that victory in that election would not suffice to carry the new Parliament Bill, but only the old Budget. This knowledge he kept to himself as requested by the King. Asquith's object was to keep the King out of political controversy. It should be a prime object of every statesman, as our constitutional monarchy rests on the non-partisan character of the Crown. Moreover the knowledge that two general elections would be required would have disheartened Asquith's own supporters.

It is to be observed that in 1831 a single general election on the issue of the First Reform Bill had sufficed to induce William IV to pass the Bill by threatening to create Peers. In the case of the Parliament Bill, two elections were required before the Crown would act. King Edward was justified in insisting on the two elections, because public opinion was more divided in 1909–11 than it had been in 1831–2. It was therefore not unreasonable for King Edward VII, and for George V after him, to insist that there must be particularly full proof that the will of the majority of the country was steadily set. The King must be sure that no alternative government was possible, before consenting to make three hundred Peers in order to alter the Constitution against the wish of nearly half the nation. Two General Elections held within twelve months of one another would prove that the majority of the much divided country was fixed in its determination to have the Parliament Bill passed into law.

The result of the first of the two General Elections of 1910, held in January, resulted in the Liberals losing one hundred seats, but retaining, with the Irish, a majority of well over one hundred. When the new Parliament met, the Government was in great difficulties, because the Irish now held the balance in the House of Commons, and they disliked the Budget because of the increased whiskey duty. They would only forgo their objection to this part of the budget if they were assured that the Government would pass the Parliament Bill and then have a Home Rule Bill passed through into law under the terms of the new Parliament Act.

The question of Home Rule, which had been in abeyance since 1895, now again took a front place in English politics. The crisis of the Parliament Bill was involved in the furies of the Irish as well as of the Protectionist and the Lloyd George controversies. When it became known that Asquith had not yet obtained guarantees from the King to create Peers, the Irish and the Liberals were much taken aback. However, when the Irish had received assurances that a Home Rule Bill would at once follow the Parliament Act, they did at last consent to vote for the budget, which was sent up again to the Peers and passed at once.

At this stage, King Edward VII died and was succeeded by George V. At the time of the new King's accession, the Monarchy was not pledged to make Peers, but, in view of King Edward's message to Asquith in December 1909, it might be assumed that, if a second general election should be won by the Liberals, George V would have no alternative. But no one wished to force the new King into decisions that must, whatever he chose, enrage nearly half his British subjects. The period of mourning for the late King, who had been very popular, seemed an improper time for a fierce political crisis. So the summer and autumn of the year 1910, the period between the two elections, was spent in a Conference between the chiefs of the Government and Opposition, endeavouring to find a way out by compromise. The sessions of the Conference were secret, but it is now known that the Conservative Chiefs put forward plans for dividing future legislation between ordinary legislation and constitutional changes – making it easier for the ordinary bills to pass and subjecting constitutional changes to a

Referendum. This plan, if adopted, would have carried our constitution still further in the direction of a written constitution, and would have introduced the entirely new principle of the Referendum. The Liberals could not accept this scheme, for many reasons, among others that Home Rule would be a Constitutional change and as such would have to be submitted to a Referendum, and Asquith's Irish supporters would have thrown him out sooner than consent to that.

The Conference broke up without agreement and in December 1910 the second and decisive General Election was held. Before he went to the country, Asquith had obtained in November from George V the promise to create Peers to carry the Parliament Bill if he came back with a majority not seriously diminished. He did not tell the public, or the Opposition Chiefs, of this promise, in order that the King's name should not be involved in the controversies of the election. The King hoped that after the election the Peers would submit, and that his conditional promise to coerce them need never be known at all.

The election of December 1910 rendered the same result as the election of January 1910. The Parliament Act was passed by the Commons and sent up to the Peers. Some of the Peers, led by Lord Lansdowne, tried to put forward alternative schemes of their own, reducing the hereditary element in their own body. But this, like all subsequent attempts to reform the personnel of the Lords, caused so much division of opinion among the Conservative Peers themselves that it was speedily dropped. In any case the victorious Liberals in the Commons would now accept no alternative to their measure to limit the powers of Upper House.

The Lords passed the second reading of the Parliament Bill, and then proceeded to pull it to pieces in Committee. In July 1911 the position of May 1832 was repeated. It was time to produce the King's promise to create Peers. Mr Asquith addressed to Mr Balfour and Lord Lansdowne a letter ending as follows:

Should the necessity arise, the Government will advise the King to exercise his Prerogative to secure the passing into law of the Bill in substantially the same form in which it left the House of Commons; and His Majesty has been pleased to signify that he will consider it his duty to accept, and act on, that advice.

Up till this moment the Opposition had not known that the King had given the promise. They were very angry, and their anger took the form of the famous 'die-hard' movement, to throw out the Bill regardless of consequences and leave to the weak King and his wicked Ministers the shame of creating three hundred Peers, if they dared to do so. But Balfour and Lansdowne put themselves at the head of more moderate counsels, and urged the acceptance of what was now clearly inevitable. There was no need to bring a Liberal House of Lords into existence, merely to indulge one's feelings. In the exciting division on the Third Reading of the Parliament Bill, no one knew which side would win. Prudent counsels prevailed by a small majority, many of the Conservative Peers abstaining and some even voting for the Bill in order to avoid the swamping of their house. It was a close-run thing. Asquith had got as far as drawing up provisional lists of about three hundred persons whom he would ask to accept Peerages, if the Bill were again thrown out. But the final division in the Lords carried the Parliament Bill. As in 1832, the crisis had been solved by the mere threat of creation, not as in 1712 by an actual creation of Peers to support the measures of Government. Again, as in 1832, the Prerogative of the Crown had proved the final weapon of democracy, a fact which helped to move the working classes still further away from Republican doctrine.

The Parliament Act of 1911 increases the written element in our constitution as against the unwritten. The unwritten custom of the constitution had hitherto guided the relations of the two houses. No written law had laid it down that the Peers could not amend money bills; no written law had declared that they could not throw out the budget for the year. But in practice those two customs had been observed, till in 1909 the Peers threw out the budget. It therefore became necessary to reduce the custom to a written law, because the unwritten custom had been challenged.

The other clauses of the Parliament Act, which go further than previous custom had gone, render the Lords' veto on ordinary legislation suspensive only. The Peers were rendered incapable of preventing the passage of any Bill for more than two years – if the majority in the House of Commons in favour of the measure holds together during the interval. That law of the suspensive veto had first been proposed by John Bright during the crisis over the Franchise and Redistribution Bills of 1884.

The Peers complained that the Parliament Act reduced them to impotence. It did indeed reduce their power, but it still left it considerable. The power of holding up government bills, other than money bills pure and simple, for two years, leaves a great bargaining power in the hands of the Peers. A government will accept amendments to get its bill through at once. And in case of a weak government, not likely to last two years, it enables the Peers to thwart legislation altogether, provided it is careful not to create reaction in favour of the dying government by an abuse of the suspensive power.

The Preamble of the Parliament Act foreshadowed a complete reconstitution of the Upper Chamber, 'on a popular instead of hereditary basis'. But the Preamble has never been implemented. It has often been discussed, sometimes since the War under the aegis of Conservative governments. But no party in the State can ever agree how to reform the Peers. On this question, there are almost as many opinions as politicians. Many of the Peers by no means relish the idea of being excluded from their Parliamentary privileges. Many commoners think that two elective Chambers are undesirable. At any rate, the Parliament Act holds the field, and its Preamble remains in limbo (1937).

But 1911 was not, like 1832, the end of the worst trouble. For opinion in the country was much more evenly divided than in that famous year of old, when the Lords had little save their own constitutional powers with which to maintain the fight. And the Home Rule question now came up in earnest, since under the Parliament Act the Peers could no longer defeat it, but only delay its passage. The disestablishment of the Church in Wales, the long-standing demand of Welsh Nonconformity and of the majority of the Welsh members, was also now a practicable proposition, heaping yet more fuel on the fire of men's wrath. It was passed under the Parliament Act, amid loud protests, but the settlement, financially very generous to the disestablished Church, has since the War been accepted by all parties as satisfactory. 'Few, if any,' said the Anglican Archbishop of Wales in 1923, 'now desire a return to the old order.'

But, in the last two years before the outbreak of the War, all tempers were on edge. The worst exacerbation of parties in Great Britain – a mixture of old constitutional and denominational with new social and financial antagonisms – corresponded in time with the climax of the older and more intense antagonisms of race and religion in Ireland. The prevailing spirit of the day was violence and anger: many even of the female advocates of Votes for Women – the most important of the many political crosscurrents of that distracted era – resorted to organized outrage on persons and property to advertise their cause, with the result that their cause lost ground; these women who made outrage a method of persuasion were distinguished from the law-abiding Women Suffragists by the title of 'Suffragettes'. Labour troubles, too, were acute and strikes constant; industrial strife between the vast national organizations of capital and labour in mines and railways were a new feature of life in the last years before the War. As in the Middle Ages, great corporations were threatening to become stronger than the unorganized community.

But Lloyd George, the stormy petrel, loved to ride such waves. It was in the midst of these furies, concentrated largely upon his head, that he passed the complex and unpopular Health Insurance Act, a contribution scheme to insure the whole working population against sickness, which has since proved a great blessing to the working classes, and no ill friend to the doctors, who at first looked at it with natural misgivings, sharpened by political prejudice. Two of the most valuable of the social reforms of the Twentieth Century, Balfour's Education Act of 1902 and Lloyd George's Insurance Act of 1912, were highly unpopular and injured the Governments that passed them; both were rendered possible by the work and wisdom of the great public servant Sir Robert Morant, and by the stubbornness of the two great ministers who forced them through Parliament. Though Balfour and Lloyd George were mutual opposites in politics, character, tradition, and intellect, they both liked to go out in a storm. It seemed impossible in 1912 that they should ever be friends. But strange things were lurking behind the clouds ahead.

The immediate consequence of the Parliament Act of 1911 was to render Home Rule a practical issue. The House of Lords would only be able now to hold up a Home Rule Bill for two years; after that it would become law, if the government majority survived so long. At the two elections of 1910 the Liberals had had their majority so far reduced that they could not keep in office if Redmond's Irish party voted against them, and the Irish party would certainly vote against them if Home Rule were not pushed straight through. The dependence of government on the Irish vote was a complication which rendered it very difficult for the Ministers to deal freely with the Ulster question involved in the Home Rule Bill. It was certain that the Protestant counties of Ulster would have to be excluded from the area of the Dublin Parliament, because they would fight rather than submit, and would be supported by the Unionist party in England. Already in 1912 the Liberal Government realized that some exclusion of parts of Northern Ireland would have to take place. The Cabinet discussed in February 1912 whether to insert in the first draft of their coming Home Rule Bill clauses allowing the contracting out of Northern counties by popular vote. It would have been better if they had done so straight away. But they decided to bring in the Bill as applying to all Ireland, and then to bargain by offering the contracting out clauses when the time for final agreement drew near.

The reason for taking this line was the difficulty of getting Redmond's Nationalist followers to accept the exclusion of Ulster as a principle *ab initio*. All Nationalist Ireland was fiercely against such exclusion, the more so as it would leave large Catholic minorities under Ulster rule. And the Redmondite Nationalist position was already being undermined in Ireland by the attack of the Republican or Sinn Fein extremist movement. The Liberal Government hoped that the Irish Nationalist party, though it would not accept Ulster exclusion in the first instance, would bow to the inevitable at the last moment, if it became clear that Home Rule for the whole island was impracticable. In this hope the Government did not put into the Home Rule Bill of 1912 the exclusion clauses for Ulster which they would ultimately be prepared to grant. It was a ghastly situation, whatever the English Government did, for the passions of both parties in Ireland were as fierce as the nationalist passions of the Balkans and Austro-Hungary, and the fever was spreading from Ireland to infect the tone of parties in England also. The natural desire of the Conservatives to revenge their own defeat over the Parliament Act made them all the more willing to support to the utmost limit the action of the Protestant Loyalists in Ireland.

So the Home Rule Bill was pressed through the Commons and duly thrown out by the Lords, and sent up again. It would ripen for passage under the Parliament Act in 1914. In March of that fatal year, when the Home Rule Bill was presented for the third and last time to the House of Lords under the Parliament Act, Asquith announced his intention of proposing an amendment giving each of the Ulster counties the right of voting itself out of Home Rule for six years – thus postponing the final decision. Ulster would not accept anything except final exclusion. 'Give us a clean cut or come and fight us,' was Sir Edward Carson's cry. At any rate this meant that the Ulstermen and the English Conservative leaders might submit to Home Rule for the rest of Ireland, provided a final clean cut was made of Protestant Ulster, only reversible by her own vote. The Cabinet was prepared to grant that, and probably ought to have said so sooner. Passions on all sides were now so highly wrought up that the business of delimiting the area of Ulster to be excluded had not yet been solved in July 1914. The debatable territory was the counties of Fermanagh and

Tyrone, where Protestants and Catholics were evenly divided.

The failure of English Liberal and Conservative statesmen to agree on the last details in good time had dangerous consequences in Ireland. There was the Curragh incident of unrest among the English army officers in Ireland, mishandled locally till it almost grew to mutiny. All along there was the open arming and drilling of Protestant Ulster, with which the government dared not interfere. It was countered in 1914 by the importation into Southern Ireland of arms which fell into the hands not of the Redmondite Home Rulers but of the Republican Sinn Feiners. It is impossible to say whether, if the German War had not come, civil war would have broken out in these islands.

On the outbreak of war with Germany Redmond, following Sir Edward Grey's speech, offered on the floor of the House the help of Nationalist Ireland for the Allies; Irish Catholics, he declared, were ready to fight beside their Protestant brethren of the North in the cause of Belgian and European freedom. Following on Redmond's speech there was a *détente*, which with luck or good handling might have led to a solution of the Irish question. But Ireland seldom had luck and seldom had good handling. The War Office, under the control of Lord Kitchener, 'thwarted, ignored, and snubbed' Redmond's generous offer of Irish recruiting. Meanwhile, the Home Rule Bill was put on the Statute Book accompanied by the provision that it should not come into force till a year after the end of the War.

Under these conditions, the influence of the Republican Sinn Feiners grew at the expense of the Home Rulers as the War proceeded. At Easter 1916 took place the Republican rebellion in Dublin. It had no chance of success and at the time it took place it had little support in the country, but it gave the Sinn Feiners the greatest of all assets for propaganda – a martyrology. For a dozen of the rebels were executed after capture. Their deaths made their unpopular cause popular with their countrymen in the retrospect.

When two years later the war ended in November 1918 the Redmondite Nationalist party in Ireland had lost control. The Sinn Feiners had ousted them from the affections of the people. And with their passing had passed away the chance of settling Ireland on the Home Rule basis. England had been again too late. Home Rule was on the Statute Book but it never came into force, because Ireland now rejected it with scorn. It was born dead. But the Union was also dead. A new basis of agreement must be sought, and could only be sought on the lines of Dominion self-government for Ireland. After a horrible and disgraceful civil war of ambush and murder, begun by the Irish and replied to in kind by the government Black and Tans, peace came at last. The more moderate Sinn Feiners made their famous treaty with Lloyd George's Conservative government, and the Irish Free State was established.

In the previous year Northern Ireland, consisting of the six Protestant counties of Ulster, had made its own Treaty with England, on terms very advantageous to itself, for Ulster not only obtained self-government and a Belfast Parliament of its own, but also retained representation in the Westminster Parliament. Northern Ireland, as it is officially called, is in a class by itself in the British Empire. It is not a Dominion, for it is represented at Westminster; yet it enjoys Parliamentary self-government.

Because Ulster was thus already out of the way under a settlement of its own, it had been easier for Griffith and Collins, the leaders of the moderate party in the Sinn Fein, to accept the accomplished fact of separate treatment for Ulster and negotiate their own bargain with the British Government for the rest of Ireland. By the Treaty of 1921 the Irish Free State was set up with Dominion status, on a par with Canada. The outstanding difference from the former Home Rule Bills is that Dominion status carries fiscal, military, and naval autonomy. The Statute of Westminster of 1931, defining Dominion status afresh on terms of complete equality with Great Britain, applies to the Irish Free State as well as to the other Dominions. And in 1935 the Judicial Committee of the Privy Council decided that, by the terms of the Statute of Westminster, the Irish Free State has the power to alter the terms of its constitution as set out in the Treaty of 1921. The Irish, under de Valera's leadership, have availed themselves very liberally of this right.

The story of Irish controversy in the Nineteenth and Twentieth Centuries points to an obvious moral, that when Imperial problems of great difficulty and delicacy become involved in the English party dog-fight, the result is likely to be disastrous. If the two English parties had united, at any time before 1914, to produce a solution of the Irish question agreed between themselves, they might have imposed it on Nationalist Ireland and on Ulster. But the Liberal leaders were bound to the Nationalists, and the Conservative leaders were bound to the Ulstermen. Possibly this was made inevitable by Gladstone's introduction of a full Home Rule scheme in 1886, and his insistence on remodelling the Liberal party there and then as a Home Rule party – thereby making the Conservatives, above all else, an anti-Home Rule party. It is possible also to throw the responsibility further back, and to say that when

Pitt by the Union of 1800 introduced Irish representation into Westminster, he made it certain that in course of time a hundred Irish members, caring nothing for English questions, but holding the balance of the House of Commons in their hand, would put themselves up to sale to English parties in return for the adoption of their own policies in Ireland. The Union may have been a necessary police measure at the time when it was passed, but in the course of 120 years it proved itself as intolerable to England as to Ireland herself.

CHAPTER 3

FROM Canning to Salisbury the 'splendid isolation' of Great Britain served her interests well. She avoided a whole series of continental wars – except the adventure of the Crimea, which was of her own seeking and the consequences of which were easily liquidated. In the then state of scientific invention and warlike armament, the Navy was still her sure and sufficient shield, and for a hundred years after Trafalgar no Power attempted to build a rival fleet. The Balance of Power in Europe was adequately adjusted without Britain's make-weight, and the independence of the small countries of the Rhine Delta was not seriously threatened. During the Franco-Prussian War of 1870, Gladstone had, in pursuance of the terms and the policy of the Treaty of 1839,[1] announced Britain's intention to take arms against either French or German violation of Belgium's neutrality, and on that occasion the warning was enough. In spite of Colonial difficulties with France, and Asiatic difficulties with Russia, Salisbury in the eighties and nineties saw no necessity to attach our fortunes to those of the Triple Alliance of Germany, Austria-Hungary, and Italy. We stood by ourselves alone, safe behind the shield of supreme naval power. But some, including Chamberlain, were beginning to be anxious.

With the new century, and the jealousies and hatreds let loose by the South African War, the period of 'splendid isolation' came to an end. The first steps on the new road were taken by Lord Lansdowne as Foreign Minister under Balfour. To their thinking, the number, size, and ubiquity of armed forces by land and sea all over the world rendered it necessary that we should have at least some defined friendships. An understanding with America would have

1. See pp. 234, 352–3, above.

been preferred, but her traditional policy of isolation rendered it out of the question. So the Japanese Alliance was made, originally to counterbalance the advance of Russia on to the shores of the Pacific, and to prevent the partition of China by Russia, Germany, and France, which America disliked as much as we, but would do nothing active to prevent. The Japanese Alliance also enabled us to dispense with the creation of an immense naval establishment in the Pacific. Britain's friendship served to keep the ring for the rise of the first 'coloured' Great Power, to which the other European Powers were hostile. Japan's triumph over Russia in war had many reactions upon India and on the world at large. Ten years later, the Japanese, faithful to their alliance with us, safeguarded the waters and coasts of the Far East against German designs during the Great War, besides giving effective help in the Mediterranean.

More important even than the Japanese Treaty was the simultaneous evolution in our relations with France and the German Empire respectively. The state of the Balance of Power in Europe was again giving cause for anxiety. Germany was more and more overshadowing Europe by her unparalleled military preparations, based on ever-increasing population, wealth, and trained intelligence; and moreover she was adding to her predominant army a fleet built in rivalry to our own. To Britain the sea was the primary consideration of her very existence, as it was not to Germany. It was this naval rivalry which altered Britain's attitude to the European Powers.

During the last twenty years of the Nineteenth Century we had been in constantly recurring danger of war with France or Russia, owing to the clash of our interests with theirs at various points in Asia and Africa. In the first years of the new century it was felt that the chances of such a war, with the power of Germany on the flank of the combatants, were too great to be any longer risked. If Germany had been ready to make friends with Britain and share the business of guarding the *status quo* and the peace of the world, a German Entente might have been made. But tentative suggestions of this kind by Chamberlain and others had been rejected by Germany; and her growing hostility to us and her naval rivalry were evident. There was therefore no alternative but to remove by agreement our specific causes of quarrel with the French Republic and the Russian Tsar.

In 1904 Lord Lansdowne settled the outstanding differences between Great Britain and France in Egypt, Morocco, and Newfoundland by a Treaty of Agreement on these points, and so permitted the growth of the *entente cordiale*, not yet an alliance, and not on our part hostile to Germany – unless indeed Germany would have it so. King Edward VII's popularity in France during his holiday visits helped to make an atmosphere propitious to the new friendship, but he had nothing to do with the initial choice of the policy by his Ministers.

Sir Edward Grey succeeded Lansdowne at the Foreign Office in December 1905. It was a moment of European crisis, though the English people, intent on its General Election, scarcely knew it. Germany was threatening France with regard to French claims in Morocco. A clause in Lansdowne's agreement with France of the year before pledged us to support France diplomatically in this question, in return for her recognition of our status in Egypt. Grey, in agreement with the Prime Minister Campbell-Bannerman, implemented this specific promise, and stood by France on the Moroccan issue. The other nations of Europe, except Austria-Hungary, took the same line at the Algeçiras Conference early in 1906, and so did President Theodore Roosevelt on behalf of the United States. Germany receded.

There had been more behind than the Moroccan question. Germany had resented Lansdowne's settlement of Anglo-French quarrels in 1904 and wished to show France that she could not depend on England; Grey showed her that she could. It was the testing of the Entente. If the return of the Liberals to power in December 1905 had meant, as a large part of the Liberal party wished, the return of Britain to her old isolation, France could not have resisted, and must either have fallen in war or become the vassal of Germany. Russia at that moment was crushed by her defeat in the war with Japan, and was rife for internal revolt. Germany aimed at drawing first Russia and then France into her orbit. Britain would then be at her mercy. We were no longer in a position to defy a united Europe as in Nelson's day; submarines, aircraft, and long-distance guns were depriving us of our insular safety.

The danger of such a European combination under German leadership was actual. In July 1905 the Kaiser and the Tsar had met in the Tsar's yacht off the Baltic island of Björkö, and had there signed a Treaty which put Russia on the side of Germany, by an agreement avowedly aimed against England, and as dangerous to her as Tilsit. This Treaty of Björkö had indeed been torn up immediately after signature, because some of the most important servants of the Tsar and the Kaiser disliked the new engagements so hastily made by their masters on the yacht. But the Björkö policy might be renewed at any moment, and then France would be forced to follow suit, if Britain's pledge of support to her proved valueless. Grey's action over the Moroccan crisis prevented any such development. After Algeçiras (1906) France and Russia both saw that Britain's friendship was worth having.

Grey could not, however, positively pledge England to turn the diplomatic support promised by the Lansdowne Agreement into military support, in case of war. The English people would not be pledged beforehand, until a *casus belli* arose. Grey had not the power to turn the Entente into an Alliance, any time between 1906 and 1914. Moreover, even if his colleagues, his party, and his country had consented to an obligation so definite – and that was far from being the case – Grey's own view was that a pledge to take part in the next war might encourage France and Russia to more intransigent policies and engage us in a struggle not essentially defensive. All that Grey had either the wish or the power to do was to let Germany know the great likelihood that England would stand by France in arms, if France were attacked. This he did.

On the other hand, war had come so near over the Moroccan issue that in January 1906 Grey, with the consent of Campbell-Bannerman as Prime Minister, had sanctioned 'Military Conversations' between the British and French staffs. To contemplate a contingent possibility of British intervention and yet have no war plan ready would have been madness, for while Britannia was fumbling with her sword the Germans might be in Paris in a month. The Military Conversations of January 1901 were amply justified, as events of August 1914 were to show. Campbell-Bannerman ought no doubt to have told his Cabinet about them at once, but both he and Grey regarded them as a purely departmental question. In that view they were wrong; they should have told the Cabinet. But it would have been a far more unpardonable mistake not to have any plans for a war that might break out and destroy France in a few weeks, if England had made no preparations to come at once to her help.

On the basis of the Military Conversations with France in 1906 was built up Haldane's great army reform of the next years. The Military Conversations arranged a detailed plan for the immediate dispatch of an Expeditionary Force to France in case a war should arise in which England decided to take a hand. One part of Haldane's Army Reforms of 1906–12 was the creation of such an Expeditionary Force of over 100,000 men of all arms, ready at a moment's notice to go to France by routes prearranged with the

French authorities. It was this preparation that enabled our forces to arrive just in time to save Paris from the German onrush in 1914.

Haldane also created the Territorial Force, turning the old 'Volunteers' and 'Yeomanry' into effective fighting units. Kitchener, on service abroad, did not realize that the amateurishness of the old 'Volunteers' was a thing of the past, and when called to the War Office, in 1914, refused to make use of the Territorial organization. But he used the men whom it had trained.

In the same years the Officers' Training Corps was established and a General Staff to think out military plans. The army at last had an official 'brain'.

In 1907 Grey made an Anglo-Russian agreement to remove the specific causes of quarrel with Russia, as Lansdowne three years before had removed the causes of quarrel with France. With German unfriendliness and naval power increasing every year, it would have been the height of folly to drift into war with Russia. Yet unless the Persian question were settled by agreement war would come on that issue. The Russians had Northern Persia already in their grip, and designed to push on to the Persian Gulf and the Afghan frontier; we had old and great interests on the Gulf, and the protection of the independence of Afghanistan was regarded as essential to the safety of India. The Persians could not defend themselves against Russia. We had either to leave all Persia and the Gulf to the Russians, or fight a war with them on behalf of Persian independence, or else come to an agreement as to our relative spheres of influence. Grey chose the third course, in which he was warmly supported by Campbell-Bannerman as Prime Minister and by Morley as Indian Secretary. But the Anglo-Russian agreement was attacked by the advanced half of the Liberals and by the Labour party, as showing neglect of Persian interests and friendliness with the autocracy of Russia. This section of opinion was unwilling to increase armaments, yet anxious to pursue a policy in defence of Persia which must have led to a war with Russia – with Germany and the German fleet on our flank.

Grey's Anglo-Russian agreement was the only possible course consistent with our own safety. Yet it was a bad best. It prevented a Russo-German Alliance like that of Björkö which would have overwhelmed us, but it gave to the German public the sense of being 'encircled'.

The charge that Great Britain deliberately fostered a policy of 'encirclement' of Germany, though often repeated in that country, does not stand any test of truth. Grey, in the earnest pursuit of better relations, offered Germany outlets into Asia and Africa, by the Bagdad railway agreement and the agreement that Germany should have her share in case of Portugal's sale of Colonies. That was not 'encirclement'. Moreover, in the part that Grey so often played as disinterested mediator in the Balkan troubles, he carefully discouraged the creation of a Balkan or a Slav bloc against Austria-Hungary, and he declined to oppose the dominating influence that Germany herself acquired at Constantinople.

Politically, therefore, there was no encirclement. And militarily it was precisely Germany's central position that gave her such immense and almost decisive advantage when war came. The encirclement, such as it was, was of Germany's own making. She had encircled herself by alienating France over Alsace-Lorraine, Russia by her support of Austria-Hungary's anti-Slav policy in the Balkans, England by building her rival fleet. She had created with Austria-Hungary a military bloc in the heart of Europe, so powerful and yet so restless that her neighbours on each side had no choice but either to become her vassals or to stand together for protection. The accident that the Teutons lay between the French and the Slavs put the Germans by the nature of geography in the centre of a 'circle', thereby rendering their military power all the more formidable. They used their central position to create fear on all sides, in order to gain their diplomatic ends. And then they complained that on all sides they had been encircled. When Bismarck, in evil hour, made the Alliance with Austria-Hungary, he began a system that ere long caused the Franco-Russian Alliance to follow. Germany thus began the fatal system of Alliances which prevented the 'localization' of any future quarrel between two great European powers, and in the end dragged more than half the world into a war begun on a Balkan issue.

By 1914 Grey had removed by agreement every specific cause of quarrel between England and Germany; but neither he nor any man could remove the fact of the over-great German power which in case of European war bade fair to destroy the independence of France and Belgium and face England with a Continent united under vassalage to Berlin. As the years 1906–14 went on, the increase of the German fleet in rivalry to ours and crisis after crisis of sabre-rattling on the Continent partially awakened the English people to the dangers of the situation. But at no moment was the nation willing to convert the Entente with France and Russia into Alliance. Everyone was alarmed by Germany and her fleet, but this country was unwilling to decide beforehand what her action would be until the actual occasion should arise.

Relations with Germany were largely determined by the building of the German fleet. Growing fear for our own safety at sea, on which our existence was staked, affected not only Grey's diplomacy but the public opinion that lay behind his action. During the first two years of the Liberal Ministry, Campbell-Bannerman's plan was tried out, of reducing the pace of our ship construction in the hope of tempting Germany to do the same. It appeared to have precisely the opposite effect. Germany treated the Prime Minister's friendly gesture as an opportunity to draw up into a serious rivalry of sea-power. His public proposal for an agreed mutual reduction of armaments was taken by the Kaiser as an insult and by his naval advisers as a trap, by which Germany might be persuaded to accept the existing condition of British superiority at sea.

The Kaiser had the artist's temperament that would have flourished in the *Quartier Latin*, but was warped by Byzantine pomp and power. He dashed from mood to mood and from project to project; now like Napoleon he divided the world with the Tsar in the imperial yacht at Björkö; now with 'English' humour he invited Haldane to 'be a member of my Cabinet for the evening'. Now he enjoyed like a sportsman and good companion the social life of his grandmother's pleasant realm; now he turned to vent in marginal expletives his irritation with the stubborn islanders who thought the size of his navy was any concern of theirs. Would that he had known less or more about England! His love-hate towards her and her fleet was a psychological tragedy that involved millions beside the leading actor. But in all his changes of mood and purpose he clung to two fatal misconceptions, that England's friendship could be won by frightening her, and that any agreement for mutual limitation of armaments would derogate from his dignity as the Sovereign of the most powerful State in the world.

If Holstein and Bülow and the Kaiser were fatal to Germany by raising up for her a host of enemies, Grey was correspondingly serviceable to England by preserving and increasing her friendships. Had it been otherwise we should have lost the War. Grey always kept two objects in view: one object was to preserve peace; the other was to be sure that if war came we should have a chance to win. It is difficult to see which of these two objects he could properly have neglected, though his critics often argue as if either the one or the other was of no account. The dread event proved that our margin of survival was small enough, so small indeed that we could not have won through if Grey had thrown either Russia or Italy into the arms of Germany, or terminated the Japanese Alliance, or alienated the statesmen and people of the United States. His steady, quiet pursuit of friendships for England, undeviating for years on end, so different from the giddy turns of opportunist diplomacy, achieved great results in spite of great obstacles.

In the midst of these growing dangers, England, at a certain risk to her own European policy, achieved in these years a great practical triumph for humanity and justice in bringing about the reform of the Congo. That unhappy region of Africa had long been, under an old international agreement, almost the private estate of King Leopold of Belgium. Through the agency of various companies, he had turned it into a vast slave-farm, contrary to the Treaties under which he held his powers. This state of things was exposed by the gallant and disinterested efforts of a private individual, E. D. Morel. The British public had taken fire, and the Foreign Secretary too. But the Foreign Secretary knew that fire was not enough. His plan was to encourage the Belgian State to take over the Congo from King Leopold; but he would only recognize the transfer on condition of wholesale reform, and in particular the abolition of forced labour. British rights in the Congo were in his hands the lever to secure our humanitarian demands. Neither Germany nor France nor any great Power save the distant United States cared about the matter. But thanks to Grey's firmness and tact, thanks also to the better elements in the Belgian people and Parliament, and to the high character of King Leopold's successor on the throne, Congo Reform was an accomplished fact before the war of 1914, and Belgium and England had not fallen out. Belgium might have been driven into the arms of Germany if the matter had been conducted with less skill and consideration, or by a British Minister whose character did not, like Grey's, half persuade the Europeans that this Englishman was not a hypocrite but an honest man. In the rather similar affair of the Putumayo atrocities in South America, Grey achieved a similar success. In that case humanitarian feeling in the United States was nearer to the scene and more potent as an ally.

Alike in peace and in war Grey pursued friendship with the Government and people of the United States as a primary object. Not only did he think it essential to our safety in the dangers that surrounded us, but he was idealist enough to hope that the two great sections of the English-speaking world would stand together for righteousness and peace. Both took, for instance, the same eccentric view that humanity mattered in Macedonia and the Congo. He negotiated with care and skill some very difficult passages with the United States about Mexico and about the Panama Tolls. And when the European War broke out our relations with America were excellent and Grey was on terms of personal friendship and intimacy with Ex-President Theodore Roosevelt, with Page the American Ambassador in London, and, most important of all, with Colonel House, the right-hand man and confidential messenger of President Wilson himself.

There were two storm-centres whence war might break loose over the world – the Balkans and Morocco. In 1911 a second Moroccan crisis arose out of the Algeçiras settlement of 1906. The dispute was known as 'Agadir', after the Moroccan port to which the Germans sent a warship. After several weeks of danger, during which Britain again supported France, the affair was settled by compromise: France secured the recognition of the rights she claimed in Morocco by ceding some of her Colonial territory elsewhere to the Germans.

The Agadir settlement of the Moroccan question removed the last direct cause of dispute as between France and Germany themselves. But their allies might yet fall out and drag them into war. For there remained the Balkans, and in the Balkan question was involved the fate of the Austro-Hungarian Empire: its rule was extended in Bosnia over Yugoslavs, and the free Yugoslavs in Serbia therefore desired the break-up of the Empire of the Hapsburgs, in order to unite their nationals under their flag. The hostility between Vienna and Belgrade was intense. And Germany thought herself obliged on every occasion to support her ally Austria-Hungary, and Russia to support the Slav interest in the Balkans.

Crisis after crisis arose in this region, each time nearly leading to a world war. The expulsion of the Turks from Macedonia and Thrace by the armies of Serbia, Greece, and Bulgaria was long overdue and in itself desirable, but it greatly increased the tension between Austria-Hungary and her southern neighbours. For Serbia, after her victory over the Turks, emerged as a military power of proved value, her ambitions now directed northwards to free all Yugoslavs still under Austrian rule. To maintain the threatened territories of the Empire intact the rulers of Austria-Hungary thought it incumbent on them to crush the Serbs. War on this issue was just averted in 1913 because Grey used his good offices as mediator, and Germany on that occasion helped the work of peace. Next year the outcome was different.

The atrocious murder of the Austrian Archduke Francis Ferdinand at Sarajevo was closely connected with the agitation conducted in Serbia for the redemption of Bosnian Yugoslavs. It was inevitable that Vienna would exact guarantees that this agitation should come to an end. Unfortunately the statesmen and soldiers in charge of Austro-Hungarian policy were determined not merely to get such guarantees, but to seize the opportunity of the Sarajevo murder to annihilate Serbia by war, even at the risk of the interference of Russia, whom they trusted Germany to keep off. Germany was therefore deeply concerned and her rulers ought to have insisted on their right to be consulted by their ally. Unfortunately the Kaiser and his Chancellor, Bethmann-Hollweg, though not really desiring war, gave Vienna a 'blank cheque' on 5 July to send what ultimatum she wished to Belgrade.

When the ultimatum appeared on 23 July, it surprised the Kaiser and the whole world by its extravagance: such demands had never been made of an independent State: yet Serbia did accept nine-tenths. A European Conference could easily have bridged the remaining difference. Grey urgently pressed on Germany the necessity of such mediation. But the Kaiser, though he had not approved of his ally's ultimatum, refused any Conference at all and declared that the question was a local affair between Austria-Hungary and Serbia with which neither Russia nor any other country was concerned. Such words meant war, for Russia's whole policy would be stultified by permitting the destruction of Serbia's independence; she began the slow process of her mobilization. Germany, by this time in the hands of her military men, who could think only of their timetables of war, sent ultimatums to Russia and to her ally France. At the beginning of August the huge strength of the German armies rolled, not eastward against Russia, but westward against France, through innocent Belgium.

Thus the quarrel, though it had broken out on Eastern questions which did not concern Britain, threatened at the very outset to put an end to the independence of France and Belgium, in circumstances which would have prevented those countries from ever raising their heads again otherwise than as vassals of Germany. The victory of the Central Powers would have meant the subjection of Europe to an Empire better calculated to survive and rule in perpetuity than ever Napoleon's had been. The very virtues of the German people, as the servants of their rulers' ambitions, made the danger of permanent slavery for Europe extreme.

Sir Edward Grey had made every effort to avert the war, and thereby helped to win for Britain and her Allies the moral sympathy of a large part of mankind, particularly in America. But when those efforts failed, self-preservation dictated that we should not permit the Channel Ports, the Netherlands, and indeed all Europe, to fall into vassalage to a power that was already openly our rival at sea. The violation of Belgian neutrality and the invaders' treatment of Belgian resistance was a drama that brought home, on a wave of generous emotion, the dreadful facts and necessities of the hour to the unwilling mind of the British public, which craved for nothing but peace.

Up to the moment of the invasion of Belgium, in the first days of August, British opinion had been divided as to the necessity of taking part in a European war. Neutralist feeling at the end of July was very strong, especially in the City, in the North of England, and in the Liberal and Labour parties. Half the Cabinet, headed by Lloyd George, inclined to neutrality. It would therefore have been utterly impossible for Grey, as is sometimes suggested in the retrospect, to threaten Germany with our participation in war a day earlier than he did. Any premature attempt in July to commit Great Britain to fight would have led to the break-up of the Cabinet, and the division of the country at the moment of its greatest peril. Such a disaster nearly occurred, and was only averted by the wisdom of Asquith, who held together his colleagues and his countrymen. In that week of tumult and alarm, the heated mass of opinion might have exploded into fragments flying in opposite directions. The danger of national division came to an end as a result of the actual invasion of Belgium, and on 4 August Great Britain went to war as a united country on behalf of her Treaty commitments to protect Belgian neutrality. Belgium was not the only reason why we had to fight or perish; but it was the reason why we were able to strike as a united people, in time, but only just in time, to prevent the fall of Paris and the Channel Ports into the German power.

CHAPTER 4

A BRIEF summary of the leading events of the War may be a useful prelude to remarks on its general characteristics.

The long-prepared plan of the German war lords was to hurl their main attack through neutral Belgium upon Paris, crush the French resistance at a blow, and then turn round and deal with the more slowly mobilizing forces of Russia. It came within an inch of success. The French Generals, Joffre and Foch, instead of preparing to meet the coming blow at the north of their line, began a rash offensive in Lorraine that was bloodily repulsed. Meanwhile the German armies trampled across Belgium, punishing resistance with a calculated 'frightfulness' that was meant to terrorize enemies and neutrals, and sounded the new, ruthless note of modern war. The treatment of innocent Belgium rallied England to join the fight as a united nation, and struck answering chords in America.

The British military chiefs, who had been left unacquainted with the French plans, had taken a more correct view of German intentions than their Allies. The 'Expeditionary Force' prepared by Haldane, nearly 100,000 strong, crossed the Channel without the loss of a man or of a minute, and stood in the path of the main German advance as it emerged from Belgium. The British were overwhelmed by enormous superiority in numbers, but fought delaying actions at Mons and Le Cateau which at once established the reputation of our soldiership in the new war.[1] Then followed the British 'retreat from Mons'; the French also were falling back along the whole front, and the Germans confidently expected to enter Paris in another week. All seemed lost, but then happened, for very natural causes, the 'miracle of the Marne'.

Joffre and Foch, after the great error which had cost France so dear in the first month of the war, kept their heads in apparently desperate circumstances, and brilliantly retrieved the situation by a counter-attack, taking advantage of the want of communication between the different German armies which had advanced at different speeds. The invaders were defeated by the French and British at the Battle of the Marne and forced to retreat from the neighbourhood of Paris. But they dug themselves in on enemy territory, retaining Belgium and a large slice of France, including eighty per cent of her coal and almost all her iron. But the Channel ports were left outside the German lines, so that the allied armies in France were in direct communication with England and her supplies. In that posture matters remained for the next four years. 'Trench warfare' had begun. The opposing lines from the Channel to the Swiss border, though often swaying and sagging deep, first one way then another, never actually broke until the autumn of

1. The Kaiser denied that he had ever used the phrase attributed to him at this time about 'the contemptible little British army'. But the humour of the 'Mons veterans', the original Expeditionary Force of August 1914, demanded that they should continue to call themselves 'the old contemptibles', and as such they will always be remembered by their countrymen. A. E. Housman's *Epitaph on an Army of Mercenaries* also refers to them.

1918. But to maintain that western deadlock there were poured out, in constant attack and counter-attack, millions of lives and the accumulated wealth of the past century of European progress.

Could the deadlock in the West be broken by operations in the East? The Russian masses had invaded East Prussia in the early weeks of the war and so contributed to the result of the Marne by drawing off two German army corps from the West. But even before these supports could arrive, the battle of Tannenburg had been fought: the invaders of Prussia were defeated, with a loss of 300,000 men, at the hands of Hindenburg and his Chief of Staff, Ludendorff, henceforth the Dioscuri of the German war.

After Tannenburg the war between the armies of Russia and those of Germany and Austria-Hungary was continued on a gigantic scale. There was less trench warfare in the East than in the West. For three years the struggle swayed forward and backward over great stretches of country, chiefly over the prostrate body of Poland.[1] Sometimes the Russians had success, but they were fatally handicapped by their want of arms and supplies, due to the primitive civilization of their country, and the ineptitude and corruption of the Tsarist government, staggering to its final doom. If the British could have obtained a direct and easy route to Russia her deficiencies in armament might have been better supplied. But the Baltic was closed, and the attempt failed to open a route through the Dardanelles into the Black Sea.

The year 1915, with the attack on the Dardanelles and Constantinople, was indeed the one chance that England had of achieving victory by any method save exhaustion of the combatants. Success at this strategic point might perhaps have shortened the war by two years. Turkey had joined the Central Powers, thereby involving England in an immense increase in her liabilities, for she had to defend against the Turks not only Egypt and the Suez Canal by operations in Palestine, but the Persian Gulf and its oil supplies by operations in Mesopotamia. Moreover the entry of Turkey into the war tempted Bulgaria to avenge her own griefs by an attack on Serbia. If Bulgaria marched on the enemy's side, the defence of Serbia against the overwhelming forces of Austria-Hungary would become impossible. But if, before Bulgaria threw in her lot with the enemy, England could force the Dardanelles and capture Constantinople, Bulgaria would almost certainly take our side instead, and the whole of the Balkan states would be

1. As a result of the World War, Poland in 1919 came back into existence as an independent nation, because her Russian and German oppressors, though on opposite sides, had both been defeated.

mobilized against Austria-Hungary. For these reasons the attack on the Dardanelles was attempted. But it failed, with the result that Bulgaria joined the Central Powers, Serbia was overrun, and for the next three years the French and English armies could do nothing but hold on to the Macedonian port of Salonika as a base for future advance, if and when the enemy power should begin to fail.[1]

On the other hand Italy, in May 1915, entered the war on the side of the Allies, and a trench warfare of a kind similar to that on the Western front was established in the foothills of the Alps, holding so large a part of the Austrian forces that the worst consequences of the failure in the Balkans were avoided. Austria-Hungary survived till 1918, but was unable, owing to the Italian pressure, to help Germany on the Western front, or to push the advantages gained in the Balkans and in Turkey.

The British Cabinet, led by Asquith, had ably conducted the initial crisis of the war. A financial crash had been avoided, the country had been rallied in a united Home Front, the navy had done its work well, the Expeditionary Force had been landed promptly and safely in France. The Dardanelles was the one great failure, due to divided counsels, resulting in premature and ill-supported attempts that gave the enemy warning. Soldiers, sailors, and statesmen must all share in that responsibility. If no man was the hero of the occasion, no man was solely to blame. But we lacked a Chatham or a Marlborough to give the guidance of genius to the World War.

Apart from the Dardanelles the affair at sea had been well managed. The Expeditionary Force had reached France safely and at once; enemy cruisers had been hunted down and destroyed in all the seas of the world. The Japanese Alliance secured the Far Eastern seas. Admiral Sturdee sank Spee's German squadron off the Falkland Islands in December 1914. The Grand Fleet under Jellicoe was provided with quarters at Scapa Flow, which proved safe even under modern conditions of submarine work; thence for four years it watched the enemy Grand Fleet in its harbours on the North German coast; the situation corresponded to Nelson's watch off Toulon, but owing to modern conditions the watch had to be conducted at a much greater distance. Only once the German

1. The idea, held by some, that an attack from Salonika in 1916 or 1917 would have brought down the Austro-Hungarian Empire, overlooks the fact that Germany, holding the inner line, could send troops and supplies to the Balkans far more quickly than France and England. But when the attack on the Dardanelles had been made in 1915, Germany had not then been in a position to send troops there direct across hostile and neutral territory.

Fleet emerged in force and the Battle of Jutland ensued. The result of that action, which involved severe losses on both sides, was that the German Fleet escaped, but that it never attempted to put to sea again.

The same year 1916 saw much slaughter but no real change upon the Western front. The great attempt of the Crown Prince's armies to end the war by breaking through the French defence of Verdun failed after long months of effort. The first large-scale offensive of the newly raised British armies on the Somme also gained no substantial ground.

After Jutland the Germans turned their attention to the submarine campaign, which in April 1917 had attained such success that England was in danger of starvation and the allied cause of collapse. But the situation was saved in the following months by the heroism of the merchant service, the application of new scientific instruments to the location of submarines, the convoy system, and the entry of the United States into the war as a result of the submarine campaign against her own shipping. Meanwhile the British 'blockade' was wearing down the stubborn resistance of the German peoples.

Indeed it is not improbable that Germany would have been defeated in 1917 if Russia had not that year gone out of the war as a result of her Bolshevik Revolution following on her repeated defeats in the field, due largely to governmental incompetence. The period between Russia's retirement from the struggle and the advent of the American armies in Europe in the summer of 1918 was one of great danger for the Allies. In April 1917 the French offensive at Chemin des Dames proved a disastrous failure, and there was talk of mutiny and revolution. The pressure on France was relieved by the tremendous offensive of Haig on the Ypres front in the gloomy battle of Passchendaele, fought all autumn long in rain and mud; after frightful losses it registered little positive advance. The tragic and dangerous year 1917 was cheered at Christmas-time by the capture of Jerusalem from the Turks by the British army under Allenby advancing from Egypt. In the following year Allenby conquered all Palestine, entered Damascus, and destroyed the Turkish military power. It was in these campaigns that 'Lawrence of Arabia' won his great reputation as leader of Arab irregulars.

The year 1918 would see the gradual arrival in France of the armies now being raised and drilled in America. If Germany had been wise she would have negotiated for a tolerable peace before they arrived. But her military men would not cut their losses, and were still for 'world conquest or downfall'. The destinies of Europe were in the hands of Ludendorff, who underrated the potentialities of American military power, and who hoped to conquer France beforehand by a great offensive in the spring. Owing to the falling out of Russia the Germans had for the moment a superiority in numbers in the West which tempted them to their ruin. Mismanagement, partly due to Lloyd George's distrust of Haig's tendency to attack, left the British force in France weaker than it need have been when the sudden blow fell upon it in March 1918. Perfect weather helped the Germans in their last mighty effort, which thrust back the English and the French very much as in September 1914. Paris and the Channel Ports were again in imminent danger. But the spirit of resistance in the French and British armies was not broken, and with the approach of summer they were cheered by the constant arrival of regiments of young Americans, eager for the war which had become so fearful a burden to the surviving veterans of Europe. The tide turned. A better cooperation between the allied armies was at length secured by making Foch Commander-in-Chief.

But the glory of the counter-offensive that ended the war lay chiefly with the decision of Haig and the efficiency of the British Army. The British Government did not expect the war to end till 1919 or even 1920, and to the last Lloyd George remained suspicious of Haig's love of the offensive, which this time at any rate proved right. The old continental saying that the English only win one battle in a war, and that is the last one, has a certain verisimilitude in the light of Haig's final victory over the German resistance, in August to November 1918. Ludendorff's offensive in the spring had exhausted Germany and used up her spiritual and material power of further resistance, sapped by our naval blockade. Also, on the Italian, Turkish, and Balkan fronts the allies of Germany were defeated and put out of action. Turkey and Bulgaria were conquered. Austria-Hungary dissolved, by a series of revolutions, into her component racial parts. Even Ludendorff's iron nerve was broken and he demanded an armistice. The flight of the Kaiser to Holland, the German revolution, and the Armistice of 11 November followed.

Some points of comparison with the conditions and methods of the Napoleonic Wars may be a not unfitting way to end this History.

First, there was the difference of geographical situation. Jacobin and Napoleonic France attempted to conquer Europe from the base of its North-West angle; the Germanic powers made the same attempt from the more formidable strategic centre which gave to them 'the inner line' of battle against all comers – Russian, Balkan, Italian, French, and English-speaking. Britain's communications with her allies in the East, particularly with Russia, were therefore more liable to interruption by the enemy. Also, in case the enemy won the war, it would be far more easy for the 'Central Powers' to hold Europe and Western Asia in permanent subjection than it would have been for the successors of Napoleon, who could not have kept the Germans down for ever, even if the battle of Leipzig had gone the other way.

As regards the strategy and tactics of the two struggles, Britain's part in both was to supply the money and maritime power of the Alliance, and to blockade the enemy by sea. But in the later war we also undertook another duty: we 'paid in person', sending over armies numbered in their millions, and counting our dead at a million and our wounded at over two million in the four years. In the French wars from 1793 to 1815 our military effort, though important, had been small, and our average annual loss of life not above five thousand. Against Germany our average annual loss of life was nearly two hundred and fifty thousand. We found it necessary to make the greater military effort on the later occasion, partly because of the more formidable strength and geographical position of the 'Central Powers'; if once we allowed the Germans to overrun all Europe as Napoleon had done, we should never get them out again.

But our fuller participation in the war by land was dictated also by the changes in military and naval weapons and tactics, which had already shaken the old security of our island position. The possessor of the Channel Ports could, by long-distance guns, aeroplanes, and submarines, threaten our existence much more formidably than Napoleon and his flat-bottomed boats at Boulogne. So the British people themselves, as soldiers, took a leading part in the decisive operations of the War. The modern Leipzig and Waterloo consisted of a continuous battle, fought day and night for four years along a line hundreds of miles long. Modern financial credit, and means of transporting men, food, and warlike stores, enabled the opposing nations to maintain millions of fighters continuously in the trenches, year after year, on each of the principal fronts.

The most marked difference between the two wars lay in armaments and tactics: the long Napoleonic wars began and ended with the Brown-Bess musket and close-order fighting of British line and

French column. Invention continued all the time to be applied by England to industry, but was not applied by any country to war. Wellington's weapons and tactics were much the same as Marlborough's, Nelson's ships much the same as Blake's. Napoleon recognized the relation to war of modern administration and organization, but he was fortunately blind to the military possibilities of modern science. But on the later occasion the methods of warfare, which in 1914 began with all the latest mechanical appliances and in Germany at least with the fullest national organization, were revolutionized several times over in the course of four short years. Not only did trench-warfare take the place of the war of movement, but the development of aerial and submarine warfare on a great scale, and the invention of gas-warfare by the Germans and of tank-warfare by the British, are changes without any parallel among the slow-witted and unscientific wars of Napoleon. Science was harnessed, and the whole civil population was mobilized. Our ancestors in war time had lived safe behind Nelson's shield, happily producing Scott's lays and novels, Wordsworth's poems, Constable's and Turner's pictures; but now the civil population of Great Britain was fain to devote its whole energy and brains for four years to the business of slaying and being slain.

In the days of Pitt and Castlereagh we increased our Colonial Empire at the expense of France and her allies, and we did so again at the expense of Germany a hundred years later. But the Colonies had taken no part in the earlier struggle, for in Pitt's day the First British Empire had already been lost and the Second was still in its infancy. A hundred years later it was fully grown. There was indeed no machinery of Imperial Federation to bid the Empire march into line, but by free individual choice, Canada, Australia, New Zealand, and Anglo-Dutch South Africa took each its full share in the whole long contest. Between them they raised overseas contingents of a million and a half men. When the War was over, each Dominion insisted on a full recognition of its nationhood. They claimed individual representation in the League of Nations, and the right to retain those German Colonies they had themselves taken in war. And finally, in 1931, the Statute of Westminster has given legal force to the long-established custom that the Parliament of Great Britain should legislate for the Dominions only at their own request. Laws affecting succession to the Crown can be altered only with the concurrence of each of the Dominions, and the King can take no advice about appointments or other action in the Dominions except from Dominion statesmen. In the post-war world it is no longer Parliament but the Crown that links the Empire, in symbolism, in loyalty, and in law.

India in the time of Pitt and Bonaparte had been the scene of the final struggle against French influence among the native Courts and armies. But India in 1914–15 sent over great bodies of troops, enthusiastic to take part in the European contest. Unfortunately in India, Egypt, and Ireland the protracted and deadly character of the War gave rise to unrest and political exacerbation of which the early months had shown no sign.

Since the War Egypt has become an independent State, though in close alliance with Great Britain. And India has been set on the path of self-government. For although the Empire has been governed since 1918 mainly by Conservative statesmen, their Imperial policy has been extremely liberal. The old methods of Anglo-Saxon domination were shown, during the War, to belong to a bygone age. South Africa was saved and the neighbouring German territories overrun by the Dominion force under Botha and Smuts, who only a dozen years before had been our enemies in the field.[1]

Relations with the United States during the War were subject to somewhat the same general conditions as in Napoleon's time, but, owing to wiser management and a better spirit, took an opposite turn. On both occasions, the interests of England as the great blockading Power necessarily clashed with those of the neutral merchant Power, desirous of sending her goods as usual to the European market. But whereas British Ministers in Napoleon's time had acted as though war with the United States were a matter of indifference, and had idly drifted into that catastrophe, no such mistake was made by Sir Edward Grey, who sacrificed points of real military value in permitting the passage of cotton and other articles of value to the enemy, in order to prevent an early explosion of American opinion against us. The Germans did the rest. Owing to the careful methods of British blockade-diplomacy, the pro-Ally feeling in the United States and the German submarine attack on American persons and shipping were given time to operate and draw the great neutral into the contest on our side.

Blockade conditions differed in several vital respects from those of Napoleonic times. It is true that our blockade of the enemy's principal Fleet, though conducted at long distance from Scapa Flow, was at least as effective as Nelson's close watch off Brest and Toulon in stopping all chance of invasion and in paralysing the

1. For the settlement of Ireland after the War, see pp. 436–7, above.

enemy's great ships. But the Napoleonic privateers and frigates that skirmished against British commerce in spite of Nelson were as nothing to the German submarine, which in the latter part of the War threatened to starve England into surrender. New methods of fighting the new danger were devised and carried out with a scientific efficiency wholly modern, and an old-fashioned skill and courage at sea of which the Royal Navy and the Merchant Service had not lost the secret.

England no longer fed herself, as in Napoleonic times, and the command of the sea was therefore more than ever essential to her very life. But neither, it appeared in the event, could the Central Empires feed themselves for an indefinite period. As the British blockade tightened, especially after the American entry into the War enabled the stranglehold to be increased diplomatically and navally, Germany and Austria began to starve outright. Since the Industrial Revolution, European countries had ceased to be self-supporting in proportion as they were highly civilized and modern.[1] The economic fabric by which the modern millions lived was too international and too delicate to survive for long the injuries done by acts of scientific war. When the dreadful four years came to an end, Europe was ruined, materially and morally, and has made very little recovery since. Nothing but the removal of the fear of yet another such war will enable the freedom and elasticity of higher civilized life to be resumed.

A remarkable contrast appears between the two historic wars, as regards the position of the working classes and the relations of Britons to one another. Pitt and Castlereagh fought the French as constitutional statesmen, by and through the House of Commons; but it never occurred to them or to any of their colleagues that the common people required, in time of national peril, any management or consideration beyond anti-Jacobin repression and the silencing of Parliamentary Reformers. Nor, as regards the mere winning of the War, did this reckoning prove wrong. But the dangers of the Home Front in 1914–18 had to be met by very different methods. Early in 1918, while the War was still raging, the Fourth Reform Bill was passed by general consent, giving what was practically Manhood Suffrage, and a large instalment of the new principle of Woman's Suffrage; the cessation of outrages by the Suffragettes, and the splendid war work done by women in the factories and elsewhere, had converted many objectors to their

1. It is largely this experience that has caused Nazi Germany to attempt to become self-supporting in peace time so as to be self-supporting in case of another war.

enfranchisement.[1] The element of Dictatorship was perhaps stronger than in Pitt's time, as regards the relation of the Government to the House of Commons. But the English Cabinet Ministers of 1914–18 had always to appeal deferentially to the people. For they knew that if munition workers slacked or stopped work, it was no longer in the power of 'magistrates and yeomanry' to make them go on. Since 'the lower orders' had developed into an enfranchised and partially educated democracy, only persuasion could effect what repression had accomplished in the days of the Luddites. In the struggle with Jacobin France, the war-time specific was Combination Acts to suppress Trades Unions; in the struggle with Germany it was the raising of wages to an unprecedented height, and inducing leaders of the Labour party to enter the Coalition Cabinet. The hardships of war-time did not, as a hundred years before, fall with their greatest force on the fortunes of the wage-earner. So long as the common danger of the War lasted, the spirit of brotherhood in the British people of all classes, both at home and in the field, was at any rate much deeper and more widely spread than during the wars against Napoleon.

In another respect the comparison is less favourable to modern times. In the character of the peace dictated to the conquered after victory, the wisely generous treatment of France in 1815 by the aristocratic government of Castlereagh and Wellington at the Treaties of Vienna compares most favourably with the vindictive treatment of Germany in 1919 by the democracy led by Lloyd George. In both cases the end of the war had resulted in the fall of the militaristic enemy government which had so long been the dread of Europe. Napoleon was replaced by the Bourbon Monarchy, averse from all the traditions of the fallen régime, and the France of Louis XVIII therefore found a friend in the British Government of the day. So too the Kaiser and Ludendorff were replaced in November 1918 by the German democratic Republic, to whom it was the interest of the British democracy to give a fair chance for the sake of Europe's future liberty and peace. Unfortunately this was not perceived by England until too late. The rise of the Nazi régime and the unlimited rearmament of Germany have been the direct consequence of the insults and injuries heaped on the conquered at Versailles in 1919.

How those Treaties came to be made, in a passing mood so little

1. In 1918 only women over thirty and not very many of them were enfranchised. In 1928 the Fifth Reform Bill, passed by Stanley Baldwin, enfranchised women on the same terms as men.

representative of England's usual good sense and good nature, requires some examination. When the War began in 1914 the mood of the country was that of an idealist crusade to save Belgium and liberty in Western Europe; great material advantages for ourselves were not envisaged, nor any gross revenge on the enemy. But the increasing atrocity of modern war, in which the Germans took the lead, the introduction of gas warfare, the sinking of merchantmen and hospital ships by submarines, the bombardment of open towns and bombing of cities from the air, aroused the deepest passions; and war propaganda, considered necessary to hold mass opinion on the Home Front concentrated in hate of the enemy, made the utmost of such themes. The popular press, in perpetual frenzy, painted 'the Huns' as scarcely human, and all who thought them human as traitors. The losses, sufferings, and horrors of war, strange to the experience of our happy island, hardened the courage and endurance of men and women into heroism, but also, as the terrible years went by, hardened their hearts and darkened their minds. The prolongation of such a war for four years destroyed the possibility of a reasonable peace, because the terms of peace would have to be decided before these abnormal passions would have time to cool.

If Constantinople had been taken in 1915, it is possible that victory might have been obtained in two years, by mobilizing all the Balkan States against the Central Powers and opening a free channel of supply to Russia. But Kitchener and the Cabinet failed to give proper timing and support to the spasmodic naval and military attacks on the Dardanelles, and the great opportunity of shortening the War was lost. In consequence of that failure, decision was only reached after a gradual process of exhaustion on the Western Front by the slaughter of millions, and the slow starvation of Austria-Hungary and Germany by the British blockade. When Russia fell out of the Alliance owing to the Bolshevist Revolution in 1917, her place was taken, only just in time, by the United States, unable any longer to condone the sinking of American ships by German submarines.

A Coalition War Ministry of Liberals and Conservatives had been formed under Asquith in the second year of the War. An ultimate though not an immediate consequence of the failure at the Dardanelles in 1915 was the fall of Asquith in December 1916. With him went a liberal element which would have been most useful at the peace-making, but could not survive the stresses of war. Asquith had many qualities as a Prime Minister in war-time, but he needed a great military adviser and he had not found all that was needed in his Secretary of State for War, Kitchener of Khartoum. Kitchener roused the country to an early perception of the length and magnitude of the struggle, and conjured up the voluntary enlistment of 'Kitchener's armies' in the early months, while the country was still unwilling to submit to conscription. He was indeed a great personality and had a great hold over the public imagination, but he had not the elastic mind necessary for the conduct of a world war under modern scientific conditions.

The man who rose to the height of the occasion, at least in the opinion of great masses of his countrymen, was Lloyd George. His activity as Minister of Munitions had made good the original deficiencies of the War Office. His imagination was always at work, his energy was contagious, and the state of courageous excitement in which he dealt with one war problem after another gave more confidence to the man in the street than the exasperating calm of Asquith's stoicism. There will always be widely divergent opinions as to Lloyd George's contribution to the victory, but at least his activity and courage helped to give confidence to the country, energy to its leaders and promptitude to their decisions.

The formation of the Lloyd George Ministry in December 1916, without Asquith and most of the other Liberal chiefs, led to an important constitutional change. A War Cabinet of only four or five regular members, a sort of Committee of Public Safety, took the place of the ordinary Cabinet until the end of the War. Indeed, the ordinary Cabinet was not restored until the autumn of 1919. And when the larger Cabinet came into existence again it kept the system of Secretariat and regular agenda papers which the War Cabinet had instituted. Sir Maurice Hankey, the Secretary of the War Cabinet in 1916 and of the restored Cabinet of 1919, was the first Secretary ever present at Cabinet counsels. The informality of the old Cabinet was yielding to the necessities of changed times and the increased burden and variety of ministerial work.

When at last the German line gave way before Foch's strategy and Haig's attack, and victory came with unexpected suddenness in November 1918, England and France were called upon in an instant to switch their minds from the fierce mood of war to the prudence, foresight, and generosity that peace-making requires. It was asking too much of human nature. Long years elapsed before France could think sanely, but in a year or two England had recovered her usual good nature and good sense; unfortunately the peace had to be made in the first six months, while the war passions were still aflame in every land. Nor was Lloyd George the man to risk his great popularity and spend his immense influence in a struggle against the passions of the hour, which always had an undue influence on his susceptible and mercurial mind. Moreover, the circumstances under which he had replaced Asquith as Prime Minister had led to a breach between him and the major half of the Liberal party during the last two years of war; the Armistice found him in political alliance with the proprietors of certain popular journals, then fiercely calling out for vengeance on German war crimes. And so at the General Election of December 1918 Asquith's followers, who would have stood for moderation in peace-making, were deliberately proscribed by Lloyd George and annihilated at the polls: the Liberal party was rent and destroyed, and has never recovered importance, for the Labour party in later elections step by step took its place.

In the General Election held in these circumstances between the Armistice and the peace-making at Versailles, a House of Commons was returned pledged to make Germany pay for the War. Lloyd George held a huge majority – and the huge majority held Lloyd George. After tying this millstone of a mandate round his own neck, he went to Versailles to help Clemenceau and Wilson give peace to the world. France, who had suffered more, was yet more intent on vengeance than England; and Wilson, meaning well, understood little of realities in Europe, or of opinion in America. Balfour, who was Foreign Minister and 'elder statesman', should have upheld the old traditions of moderation and foresight, but unfortunately left everything to the Prime Minister during those fatal months at the French capital.

Wilson and Lloyd George did at least prevent France from annexing the German part of the left bank of the Rhine, though the Germans were forbidden by the Treaty to occupy it militarily. This wise compromise was obtained by a promise that America and England would guarantee the frontiers of France against attack, a promise which America refused to ratify; consequently England also declined this obligation for a while, thereby losing for some years all control over the policy of France towards Germany.

Upon the whole, the drawing of European boundaries was not ill done at Versailles. The new Europe consisted of a number of States based on the real principle of nationality. Indeed Poland, and the States that became the heirs of Austria-Hungary, had been formed by the act of their own populations, as a result of the last stage of the War, before ever the statesmen met at Versailles to confirm the change. It was the War, not the Peace, that destroyed the Empire of the Hapsburgs.

The great error of the Treaty was the harsh treatment of the new

German Republic. It should have been the first object of England and France to enable it to survive as a peaceful democracy. But the German nation was humiliated by the dictation of terms on the hardships of which she was not even permitted to plead before the victors; she was forbidden to unite with Austria; she was excluded from the League of Nations; in the matter of Reparations she was treated in a manner so fantastic as to help to ruin her without benefiting her creditors. Finally all her Colonies were taken away. At the end of all previous wars the defeated enemies of England had always retained or received back some at least of their Colonies.

At the same time the League of Nations was set up and was closely associated with the terms of the Treaty. But the spirit of the League of Nations and the spirit of the Treaty of Versailles were utterly incompatible. One would sooner or later undo the other. If Germany had been treated generously, and invited into the League as an equal, the League might have flourished and given real peace to the world. Or if, after the Treaty, England, France, and America had set about to remedy what was wrong in the Treaty, and to support the League in spirit as well as letter, all might yet have been well. But England alone of the great Powers gave support to the true spirit of the League, and made some effort to remedy the grievances of Germany, particularly as regards Reparations. The mood of the unhappy General Election of December 1918, having dictated the Treaty, soon died out in the placable breasts of the English, who hastened to disarm and to put the war memories behind them, trusting with too complete a confidence in the power of the maimed League of Nations to avert the natural consequences both of the War and of the Peace. Certain that there was never to be another war, the English proceeded to scrap their air force, to let down their army, and even their navy, to a minimum, and to allow their agriculture and their mercantile marine to decay.

But France could not change or forget. She continued for years to harass the German Republic, thus preparing the way for its transformation into the Nazi régime. And America retired into herself. Having been instrumental in pledging Europe to the policy of the League of Nations, she refused at the last moment to join it. Nor would she any longer cooperate in any practical way to preserve peace. It was a vicious circle: her withdrawal made the European anarchy worse, and the European anarchy made her more determined than ever not to interfere in Europe again. She even withdrew from the Reparations Commission, where her support would have enabled England to restrain France; the French were therefore able to find a quasi-legal excuse for their rash invasion of the German territory of Ruhr in 1923, England vainly protesting. The outcome has been the Germany of Hitler that we know. The other main cause of the rise of the Fascist and Nazi forms of government has been the simultaneous imitation of and reaction against Communism, to which doctrine the success of the Bolshevist Revolution in Russia gave a great impetus throughout the Continent. The outcome of the War of 1914–18 has been to destroy liberty, democracy, and parliaments in the greater part of Europe.

While Foreign affairs have gone ill since the War, Imperial and Home affairs have passed through some violent crises, but have not done so badly, considering the general bedevilment of the world. So at least one would say at this moment of the Coronation of King George VI (May 1937).

POSTSCRIPT, 1941

I wrote these last pages in 1937. I have decided to let stand what I then wrote, for it was not untrue, though it now appears by no means the whole truth. It dealt chiefly with our failure to appease Germany before the fall of the Weimar Republic, which I still think was an opportunity missed. But since the rise of Hitler our mistakes have been of a different kind, namely the failure either to prevent German rearmament, if necessary by force, or to rearm ourselves at a speed in any degree proportionate to the mechanized power on the ground and in the air that Germany was creating.

It has always been a fault both of British statesmen and of British public opinion to treat foreign policy and armaments as two distinct aspects of national affairs. But they are in fact inseparable. A foreign policy without armaments sufficient to support it is a castle built in the air and inhabited at peril. Thus after 1933 our two rival policies of 'appeasement' of Germany and 'resistance to aggressors' were rendered alike futile by our continued military and air weakness. The political attack made on the governments of Baldwin and Chamberlain for not resisting the aggressors may have had substance, but it was conducted by parties and persons who were for the most part opposed even to conscription, and still more to the wholesale change over of industry to war production in peace-time, which alone would have rendered us a match for Germany. Neither those Conservative governments nor their Labour opponents, nor the League of Nations advocates can escape the charge of improvidence in this matter.

We were, nearly all of us, blind and foolish. We continued to hope, ill-armed, for peace; and we supposed that even if war came at last the French would again hold their frontier for a couple of years as in 1914–16, while we again made an army and completed an adequate air force. The French army was again to be our first line of defence. It was not fair either to France or to ourselves. Our statesmen said with truth that our frontier was to be on the Rhine, but in 1936 England and France allowed Germany to remilitarize the Rhineland contrary to Treaty, thereby turning the strategic flank of Belgium and northern France, and rendering it utterly impossible for the Western Powers to rescue Austria, Czechoslovakia, and Poland when they were attacked each in turn. And no attempt was made to stop the rearmament of Germany until her military power on land and in the air had been raised to its zenith.

464

The need of supporting our policies by force was overlooked. We undertook to give the law to armed Europe without adequate armaments of our own. The League of Nations would impose its decrees by economic action against aggressors. This half-and-half policy, known as 'sanctions', when applied to Italy in the Abyssinian case, lined up the Italian people behind Mussolini and threw Mussolini into the arms of Hitler whom he had before opposed. We would neither fight for Abyssinia nor leave the matter alone, and so we got the worst of all possible results.

No wonder, then, that, when Hitler's preparations for the conquest of the world were ready, he was not afraid of Britain. He knew better than we did the real weakness of the French, and he imagined that Britain and her Empire were no less decadent. Liberty and democracy seemed forms of government unable to contend, in the strong currents of the modern world, with athlete nations armed and drilled to move and wheel and strike according to secret plans formed by Dictators.

Nor was this impression of Britain's weakness and slowness entirely removed during the first six months of the war. Only after the fall of France in 1940, when friend and foe had given us up for lost, did the moral strength of Britain and the Empire appear in full. Then, when at last pleasant theories had given place to harsh facts, and delusions to grim resolve, the tough qualities of our folk were made manifest, symbolized by the leadership of Winston Churchill. The ultra-pacifist people, who had chosen to be still half-armed when the fight was forced upon them, were undismayed in 'the hour when earth's foundations fled', and put up such a fight on sea and air and land that the name of Britain became a banner to rally the forces of freedom all the world over.

APPENDIX
ENCLOSURES OF LAND

(Referring to Chapters 1 and 9)

(*a*) A fascinating field of antiquarian research and speculation is opened up by the problem of the ancient history of enclosure. In some parts, e.g. in some forest districts in the south, and in some of the disturbed borderlands to west and north, it is possible that the communal village agriculture of the 'open-field' system had never taken root, but that the original method of settlement had been the isolated farmstead with a compact holding. It is possible also that, in the west, Celtic land tenure affected early methods of farming and enclosure.

It is important to remember, in trying to visualize the England of 1760, that the 'open-field' system, described on pp. 23–4 above, was the normal type only in the big east-midland belt of fine corn-land, stretching from Yorkshire north, and from Norfolk east, to Wiltshire south and west.

(*b*) The following table gives the figures of the last great period of enclosure, about which we know far more than about the many preceding periods of enclosure:

Enclosures by Act of Parliament (*Private Bills*)

Years	Common Field and some Waste	Waste only
1700–1760	237,845 acres	74,518 acres
1761–1801	2,428,721 acres	752,150 acres
1802–1844	1,610,302 acres	939,043 acres

But the amount of land enclosed between 1700 and 1760 was greater than this table indicates, because enclosure by *Private Act of Parliament* only came in during the course of the eighteenth century, and we cannot gauge the amount of enclosure by the number of Acts with any safety before 1760. Mr Gonner has shown that enclosure was proceeding on a large scale without Act of Parliament throughout the seventeenth and early eighteenth centuries. But many of the earlier enclosures had not been accompanied by a redistribution of land so destructive to small farmers and to the old order of society as the later enclosures normally were. Thus we read in Mr Bishton's Report on Shropshire to the Board of Agriculture (1794): 'This county does not contain much common field lands, most of those having been formerly enclosed, and before Acts of Parliament for that purpose were in use. But the inconvenience of the property being detached and intermixed in small parcels is severely felt, as is also the inconvenience of having the small farm buildings in villages, the lands occupied therewith of course being distant.' He goes on to complain of the smallness of the farms.

SOME LEADING EVENTS SINCE
THE FIRST GERMAN WAR

1918 (December)	Lloyd George's General Election.
1919	Treaty of Versailles.
	League of Nations set up.
	Britain disarms, France and Italy do not.
	Montagu-Chelmsford reforms establish Dyarchy in India: disturbance and repression: Gandhi.
1920	United States Senate prevents America entering into League of Nations. America refuses to guarantee French territory and therefore Britain follows suit.
	'Ulster' obtains a separate Parliament (December).
1921	War against Sinn Fein ended by Treaty in December: Irish Free State set up as a Dominion.
1922	Turks drive Greeks out of Asia Minor: Britain stops Turks at the Straits.
	Fall of Lloyd George Ministry.
	Mussolini establishes Fascism in Italy.
1923	French occupy the Ruhr.
1924	First Labour Government, dependent on Liberal vote, lasts eight months.
1925 (December)	Locarno Treaties: temporary relaxation of European tension.
	Germany joins the League of Nations.
1926	General Strike and Miners' Strike.
1927	Disarmament Conferences fail.
1928	Local Government Act. Fifth Reform Bill: general enfranchisement of women.
1929	Second Labour Government, dependent on Liberal vote, lasts two years.
1931	World Slump and Financial Crisis.
	(August) Break-up of Labour Ministry.
	National Government formed and wins General Election against Labour.
	Statute of Westminster gives new legal status to Dominions.
1932	Unemployment question acute: gradual, partial recovery.
	World Economic Conference fails. Japan defies and leaves League of Nations about Manchuria.
1933–4.	Hitler establishes Nazi rule in Germany. Leaves League of Nations, repudiates obligations of Versailles Treaty, and rearms Germany.

European tension again becomes acute.

1935   Jubilee of King George V.

Act of Parliament gives Responsible Self-government and Federal constitution to India.

Mussolini attacks Abyssinia, a member of the League of Nations.

1936   League 'economic sanctions' fail to save Abyssinia.

Hitler re-occupies Rhineland.

Treaty with Egypt as an independent Nation.

George V dies, succeeded by Edward VIII (January–December), who abdicates. George VI succeeds.

Spanish Civil War begins.

British rearmament begins very slowly.

1938 (March) Hitler seizes Austria.

(September) 'Munich'. Hitler occupies defensive frontier of Czechoslovakia.

1939 (March) Hitler seizes Czechoslovakia.

(April) Mussolini seizes Albania.

(September) Hitler attacks Poland. Second German–British War begins.

LIST OF MINISTRIES
1770–1937

1770–82	North (Tory, King's Friends).
1782	Rockingham (Whig).
1782–3	Shelburne (King's Friends and Chathamites).
1783	Coalition of North and Fox (Whigs and Tories).
1783–1801	Pitt (Chathamites and King's Friends, gradually becoming Tory; Conservative Whigs join in 1794).
1801–4	Addington (Tory).
1804–6	Pitt's Second Ministry (Tory).
1806–7	Ministry of All-the-Talents (Whigs and Tories).
1807–9	Portland (Tory).
1809–12	Perceval (Tory).
1812–27	Liverpool (Tory), becoming more liberal in policy after 1822.
1827	Canning (Liberal Tory).
1827	Goderich (Liberal Tory).
1828–30	Wellington–Peel (Tory).
1830–34	Grey (Whig).
1834	Melbourne (Whig).
1834–5	Peel (Conservative).
1835–41	Melbourne (Whig).
1841–6	Peel (Conservative).
1846–52	Russell (Whig).
1852	Derby–Disraeli (Conservative).
1852–5	Aberdeen Coalition (Peelites and Whigs).
1855–8	Palmerston (Whig).
1858–9	Derby–Disraeli (Conservative).
1859–65	Palmerston (Whigs and Peelites, Liberals).
1865–6	Russell (Whig and Liberal).
1866–8	Derby–Disraeli (Conservative).
1868–74	Gladstone (Liberal).
1874–80	Disraeli (Conservative).
1880–85	Gladstone (Liberal).
1885–6	Salisbury (Conservative).
1886	Gladstone (Liberal).
1886–92	Salisbury (Conservative, supported by Liberal Unionists).
1892–4	Gladstone (Liberal).
1894–5	Rosebery (Liberal).
1895–1902	Salisbury (Unionist).
1902–5	Balfour (Unionist).
1905–8	Campbell-Bannerman (Liberal).
1908–15	Asquith (Liberal).
1915–16	Asquith (Coalition).
1916–22	Lloyd George (Coalition).

1922–3	Bonar Law (Conservative)
1923–4	Baldwin (Conservative).
1924	MacDonald (Labour).
1924–9	Baldwin (Conservative).
1929–31	MacDonald (Labour).
1931–5	MacDonald (National).
1935–7	Baldwin (National).
1937	Neville Chamberlain (National).
1940	Winston Churchill.

LIST OF BOOKS

Readers may find the following books useful for more detailed study of various aspects of the period 1782–1901.

1. BIOGRAPHICAL

PITT. (1) Holland Rose (2 vols.) has superseded earlier lives. (2) Lord Rosebery (short study). (3) Macaulay's *Essay in Miscellaneous Works* and *Encyclopaedia Britannica*. (4) Wilberforce's sketch of Pitt in *Private Papers of Wilberforce*, 1897.

FOX. (1) Life of, by Edward Lascelles (Oxford, 1936). (2) *Memorials and Correspondence* (4 vols.), ed. Lord J. Russell. (*The Early Life of C. J. Fox*, by Sir G. O. Trevelyan, refers to the period before the American War, but gives a picture of the political society out of which the men of the later period emerged.)

BURKE. (1) Lord Morley. (2) Sir J. Prior. (3) His own speeches and writings (many volumes).

WELLINGTON. (1) Sir H. Maxwell (2 vols., in one). (2) *Conversations of Wellington*, Stanhope. (3) Dispatches (many volumes).

NELSON. Mahan (2 vols.).

WILBERFORCE. R. Coupland.

CASTLEREAGH. C. K. Webster.

BENTHAM. A. V. Dicey's *Law and Opinion in England*, though not strictly biographical, contains the best estimate of Bentham's influence on British development.

PAINE. Moncure Conway (2 vols.).

COBBETT. (1) E. J. Carlyle. (2) G. D. H. Cole.

FRANCIS PLACE. Graham Wallas.

ROBERT OWEN. F. Podmore (2 vols.).

COKE OF NORFOLK. A. M. W. Stirling.

CANNING. H. W. Temperley.

LORD GREY OF THE REFORM BILL. G. M. Trevelyan.

BROUGHAM. (1) Atlay (Victorian Chancellors). (2) Campbell's *Lives of the Chancellors*, including Brougham, is amusing but untrustworthy.

LORD ALTHORP. Sir D. Le Marchant.

LORD GEORGE BENTINCK. Disraeli.

RUSSELL. Spencer Walpole (2 vols.).

PEEL. (1) J. R. Thursfield. (2) Parker (3 vols.), for Correspondence. (3) Lord Rosebery (short essay). (4) G. Kitson Clark.

COBDEN. Lord Morley (2 vols.).

BRIGHT. G. M. Trevelyan.

FLORENCE NIGHTINGALE. Cook (2 vols.).

DISRAELI. Monypenny and Buckle (6 vols.).
GLADSTONE. Lord Morley (2 vols.).
MILL, JOHN STUART. Autobiography.
LORD RANDOLPH CHURCHILL. Winston Churchill (2 vols.).
LORD SALISBURY. Lady Gwendolen Cecil (2 vols., others to follow).
QUEEN VICTORIA. (1) Lytton Strachey. (2) *Letters of Queen Victoria.*
BIOGRAPHICAL STUDIES. Walter Bagehot. On various statesmen of
   the century.
STUDIES IN CONTEMPORARY BIOGRAPHY. Bryce.
EMINENT VICTORIANS. Lytton Strachey.
SOME POLITICAL IDEAS AND PERSONS. John Bailey (1 vol.) On
   Queen Victoria and Disraeli.

BYRON. Thomas Moore (2 vols.).
KEATS. Sidney Colvin.
WORDSWORTH. (1) The prelude (Autobiographical).
                        (2) Life of Wordsworth, by Harper (2 vols.).
SIR WALTER SCOTT. Lockhart (6 vols.).
MACAULAY. G. O. Trevelyan. CARLYLE. Froude (4 vols.).
RUSKIN. Cook (2 vols.). WILLIAM MORRIS. J. W. Mackail (2 vols.).
CHARLES DARWIN. Francis Darwin (3 vols.).
LESLIE STEPHEN. F. W. Maitland.
A SURVEY OF ENGLISH LITERATURE (from 1780–1880). Oliver
   Elton (4 vols.).
ENGLISH THOUGHT IN THE EIGHTEENTH CENTURY. Leslie
   Stephen (2 vols.).
GENERAL GORDON. J. Buchan.
ASQUITH. Spender and C. Asquith.
J. CHAMBERLAIN. Garvin.
BALFOUR. Mrs Dugdale.
CAMPBELL-BANNERMAN. J. A. Spender.
GREY OF FALLODON. G. M. Trevelyan.

2. POLITICAL, DIPLOMATIC, AND MILITARY

HISTORY OF ENGLAND IN THE EIGHTEENTH CENTURY. Lecky
   (later vols.).
A HISTORY OF ENGLAND, 1815–75. Spencer Walpole (9 vols.).
A HISTORY OF MODERN ENGLAND. Herbert Paul (5 vols.).
CAMBRIDGE MODERN HISTORY, vols. viii–xii, *passim.*
A MODERN HISTORY OF THE ENGLISH PEOPLE, 1880–1910. R. H.
   Gretton (2 vols., first vol. to 1898).
GREAT BRITAIN, 1886–1935. J. A. Spender.
ENGLAND, 1870–1914. Ensor (Oxford History of England).
KING GEORGE V. D. C. Somervell.
THE KING'S GRACE (George V). J. Buchan.
MODERN ENGLAND, 1885–1932. J. H. Marriott.
CAMBRIDGE HISTORY OF BRITISH FOREIGN POLICY.

THE CONFEDERATION OF EUROPE. W. Alison Phillips.

MODERN EUROPE, 1815–99. W. Alison Phillips.

BRITISH DIPLOMACY, 1813–15. Select documents dealing with the Reconstruction of Europe. Ed. by C. K. Webster.

THE CONGRESS OF VIENNA. C. K. Webster; and

THE CONGRESS OF BERLIN, 1878. E. L. Woodward (small handbooks prepared by Historical Section of the Foreign Office, 1920, Nos. 153 and 154).

HISTORY OF THE BRITISH ARMY. Fortescue (8 vols.).

HISTORY OF THE PENINSULAR WAR. Oman (5 vols.).

HISTORY OF THE PENINSULAR WAR. Napier (6 vols.).

INFLUENCE OF SEA POWER UPON THE FRENCH REVOLUTION AND EMPIRE. Mahan (2 vols.).

SEA LIFE IN NELSON'S TIME. John Masefield.

THE CAMPAIGN OF TRAFALGAR. Corbett.

L'EUROPE ET LA RÉVOLUTION FRANÇAISE. Albert Sorel (8 vols.). This great and authoritative work is indispensable to a full understanding of the relation of the French Revolution and French policy to the whole Continent between 1789 and 1815. But its author had less knowledge and understanding of British than of Continental affairs. The early and middle parts of the work are the best.

THE FRENCH REVOLUTION IN ENGLISH HISTORY. P. A. Brown.

THE PASSING OF THE GREAT REFORM BILL. J. R. M. Butler.

THE UNREFORMED HOUSE OF COMMONS. E. Porritt (2 vols.).

TWENTY YEARS, 1815–1835. Cyril Alington, Head Master of Eton, 1921.

A HISTORY OF THE GREAT WAR. Cruttwell.

THE WORLD CRISIS. Winston Churchill.

Contemporary Works:

THE ROLLIAD. THE ANTI-JACOBIN. CREEVEY PAPERS (2 vols.) for early part of century. GREVILLE MEMOIRS (8 vols.) for middle part of century. CROKER'S CORRESPONDENCE (3 vols.). MEMOIRS OF THE WHIG PARTY. Lord Holland (2 vols. + 1, 'Further Memoirs' to 1821). STATE TRIALS. PARLIAMENTARY DEBATES.

3. ECONOMIC, INDUSTRIAL, AND SOCIAL

VICTORIAN ENGLAND. Portrait of an age. G. M. Young. (Oxford, 1936.)

ECONOMIC HISTORY OF MODERN BRITAIN. J. H. Clapham.

GROWTH OF ENGLISH INDUSTRY AND COMMERCE. Cunningham (2 vols.).

LE PEUPLE ANGLAIS AU XIXᴱ SIÈCLE. Élie Halévy (also in English).

THE ECONOMIC ORGANIZATION OF ENGLAND. W. J. Ashley.
OUTLINES OF ECONOMIC HISTORY OF ENGLAND. H. O. Meredith.
LIFE AND LABOUR IN THE NINETEENTH CENTURY. G. R. Fay.
TOWN LABOURER, 1760–1830, and SKILLED LABOURER, 1760–
  1830. J. L. and B. Hammond.
TRADE UNIONISM. S. and B. Webb.
CHARTIST MOVEMENT. (1) Julius West; (2) Élie Halévy in *Quarterly
  Review*, July 1921, on Chartism.
HISTORY OF CO-OPERATION. Holyoake, see also LIFE OF HOLY-
  OAKE. MacCabe.
A HISTORY OF THE ENGLISH POOR LAW, 1834–1908. Nicholls
  and Mackay (3 vols.).
ENGLISH APPRENTICESHIP AND CHILD LABOUR: A HISTORY.
  Jocelyn Dunlop.
A HISTORY OF FACTORY LEGISLATION. Hutchins and Harrison.
A HISTORY OF BRITISH SOCIALISM. M. Beer (2 vols.).
CONDITION OF THE WORKING CLASSES IN 1844. Engels.
A SOCIAL AND INDUSTRIAL HISTORY OF ENGLAND, 1815–
  1918. J. F. Rees.
ENGLISH COMMONS AND FORESTS, 1864–1894. (Commons Pre-
  servation Society.) Shaw Lefevre, Lord Eversley.

POPULATION PROBLEMS IN THE AGE OF MALTHUS. G. Griffith.
  (Cambridge, 1926.)
LONDON LIFE IN THE EIGHTEENTH CENTURY. Mrs George.
ENGLISH FARMING, PAST AND PRESENT. R. E. Prothero (Lord
  Ernle).
THE ENGLISH PEASANT AND THE ENCLOSURE OF COMMON
  FIELDS. Gilbert Slater.
COMMON LAND AND ENCLOSURE. Gonner.
THE VILLAGE LABOURER, 1760–1830. Hammond.
THE ENCLOSURE AND REDISTRIBUTION OF OUR LAND. Curlter,
  1920, and HISTORY OF AGRICULTURE, 1909.
THE FARM LABOURER. Jocelyn Dunlop.
LARGE AND SMALL HOLDINGS. Hermann Levy.

THE ENGLISH CHURCH IN THE NINETEENTH CENTURY. Warre
  Cornish (2 vols.).
THE OXFORD MOVEMENT. Dean Church.
THE CENTURY OF HOPE. Marvin.
LOCAL GOVERNMENT IN ENGLAND. Redlich and Hirst (2 vols.).
LOCAL GOVERNMENT. J. P. R. Maud (Home University Library).
SECONDARY EDUCATION IN THE NINETEENTH CENTURY. R. L.
  Archer, 1921.

HISTORY OF CRIMINAL LAW. Sir James F. Stephen (3 vols.).
LAW AND OPINION IN ENGLAND. A. V. Dicey, especially for
  Bentham.

THE CIVIL SERVICE OF GREAT BRITAIN. Robert Moses. Columbia University Studies in Political Science, vol. lvii, No. 1, 1914.
HOW BRITAIN IS GOVERNED. Ramsay Muir.

Contemporary Works:

ARTHUR YOUNG'S WORKS.
COBBETT'S RURAL RIDES (2 vols.).
INSTRUCTIONS TO YOUNG SPORTSMEN. Col. Hawker, eds. of 1824 or 1844.
Works of Jane Austen, T. Love Peacock, George Borrow, Dickens; Mrs Gaskell's MARY BARTON, Disraeli's SYBIL, Trollope's BARCHESTER TOWERS series, Meredith's BEAUCHAMP'S CAREER, and other contemporary works of fiction throw much light on social history and custom in the early and middle nineteenth century.

4. SCOTLAND

SOCIAL LIFE OF SCOTLAND IN THE EIGHTEENTH CENTURY. H. G. Graham (2 vols.).
THE AWAKENING OF SCOTLAND. 1747–1797. W. L. Mathieson.
A CENTURY OF SCOTTISH HISTORY. Sir H. Craik (2 vols.).
A HISTORY OF SCOTLAND. C. S. Terry (last chapters).

MEMORIALS OF HIS TIME. Lord Cockburn (early years of century).
Lockhart's LIFE OF SCOTT. Scott's ANTIQUARY. Galt's ANNALS OF THE PARISH, THE PROVOST, etc.

5. IRELAND

Lecky's HISTORY OF IRELAND IN THE EIGHTEENTH CENTURY (last vols.), and LEADERS OF PUBLIC OPINION IN IRELAND (for Grattan and O'Connell).
PARNELL. Barry O'Brien (2 vols.), and chapter vi of Lord Morley's RECOLLECTIONS.
THE ECONOMIC HISTORY OF IRELAND FROM THE UNION TO THE FAMINE. George O'Brien, 1921.
GLADSTONE AND IRELAND: IRISH POLICY OF PARLIAMENT, 1850–94. Lord Eversley, 1912.

6. THE EMPIRE

There are two excellent historical series of volumes on Canada, Australasia, South Africa, India, and the Tropical Colonies, respectively. The first is the HISTORICAL GEOGRAPHY OF THE BRITISH EMPIRE AND DEPENDENCIES, edited by Sir Charles Lucas, written by various hands. The other series is written by A. Wyatt

Tilby, THE BRITISH PEOPLE OVERSEAS. Sir C. Lucas's series is the more detailed of the two.

A SHORT HISTORY OF THE BRITISH COMMONWEALTH. Ramsay Muir (vol. ii).
THE BRITISH EMPIRE AND THE UNITED STATES. W. A. Dunning.
LORD DURHAM. Stuart Reid (2 vols.).

SIR GEORGE GREY. Rees.
THE LONG WHITE CLOUD (New Zealand). Pember Reeves.
    For Australian Social History see GEOFFREY HAMLYN, by Henry Kingsley, and 'Rolf Boldrewood's' works.

SOUTH AFRICA. G. Theal (5 vols.).
CECIL RHODES. Basil Williams.
IMPRESSIONS OF SOUTH AFRICA. Bryce, 1897.
'THE TIMES' HISTORY OF THE SOUTH AFRICAN WAR, edited by L. S. Amery and others (7 vols.).

WARREN HASTINGS, by Sir Alfred Lyall, and LORD LAWRENCE, by Sir R. Temple, in the ENGLISH MEN OF ACTION series.
BRITISH DOMINION IN INDIA. Sir Alfred Lyall.
THE OXFORD HISTORY OF INDIA. Vincent Smith, C.I.E.
THE LAST DAYS OF THE COMPANY, 1818–1858. A source book of Indian History by G. Anderson and M. Subedar (3 vols.).
INDIAN NATIONALITY. R. N. Gilchrist.
A SHORT HISTORY OF INDIA. W. H. Moreland and Atul Chandra Chatterjee.

ENGLAND IN EGYPT. Milner.
MODERN EGYPT. Cromer (2 vols.).

INDEX

Meeanee, battle of, 310
Meerut, 314
Melbourne, Lord (1779–1848), 227, 231, 243, 247 n., 254, 309; with Queen Victoria, 263, 348; Canadian policy, 258–9
Mendoza, Daniel (1764–1836), 175
Meredith, George (1828–1909), 268 n., 333, 334, 352 and n.
Mesopotamia, 450
Metcalfe, Sir Charles (1785–1846), 303, 309
Methodists, 30, 41, 45, 66–7, 166–7. *See also* Dissenters
Metternich, 141, 147, 350
Mexico, 183–4, 286–7, 327, 351, 446]
Middlesex, 21 n., 33, 39
Middleton, Conyers (1683–1750), 167
Midlothian 'campaign', 369, 373
Milan Decree, *see* Berlin and Milan Decrees
Military Conversations, the, 441
Mill, James (1773–1836), 187, 205
Mill, John Stuart (1806–73), 187 n., 301, 332–3, 370, 389
Milner, Sir Alfred (Lord), 404, 423, 427
Milton, John, 42, 76; study and quotation of, 37, 44, 44 n., 197 n.
Minto, Lord (1782–1859), 292
Missolonghi, 216
Moghul Emperors, 306, 311, 314
Moira, Lord, *see* Hastings, Lord
Monroe, President, 214; doctrine, 214, 327, 351, 403–4
Mons, 449
Montesquieu, 45
Moore, Sir John (1761–1809), 98, 133
Morant, Sir Robert, 411, 434
Morel, E. D., 445
Morley, John (*b.* 1838), 381, 422, 442
Morocco, 401, 439–41, 446
Morris, William (1834–96), 389
Moscow, 139
Mountains, love of, 37, 390–91
Municipalities, inefficiency of, 30, 41, 165; reform of, 243–5, 378; later developments of, 359–60, 388, 423–5

Mutiny, Indian, 312–16
Mysore, 116, 117, 315

Nana Sahib, 315
Napier, Sir Charles (1782–1853), 310–11
Napier, Lord, of Magdala (1810–90), 316
Napier, Sir William (1785–1860), 134
Naples, 105, 209–210
Napoleon Bonaparte – Captain Bonaparte, 97 n.; General Bonaparte, 95, 101, 103–105, 302; First Consul, 95, 106–107, 115–16, 120–22; Emperor Napoleon, 105 n., 118, 121–6, 127–33, 136–46; Napoleon in memory, 295, 299
Napoleon III, Louis, 294–6, 297, 317–21, 327, 330, 350–56
Nash (Beau), Richard (1674–1762), 37
Nassau Senior, *see* Senior, Nassau
National Liberal Federation, 369
Navarino, 215, 361
Navigation Laws, 206–7, 261
Nazi régime, 457 n., 462–3
Nelson, Horatio, Lord (1758–1805), 87, 95, 98, 105, 107, 135, 451; Nile campaign, 95, 103, 122; Copenhagen, 96, 107–109, 128; Trafalgar campaign, 122, 124, 136
Nepal, 306
Newcastle, Duke of (1693–1768), 51
New England, pacificism of, 1812–14, 180–81
Newfoundland, 329
New Guinea, 402
New Lanark, 188–9, 247
Newman, Cardinal (1801–90), 42, 276
New Orleans, 182
Newton, Sir Isaac (1642–1727), 42, 160
New Zealand, 69, 73, 255–6, 455
Nice and Savoy, 320, 355
Nicholas, Czar, 296–7, 310
Nicholson, John (1821–57), 314
Nigeria, 397
Nightingale, Florence (1820–1910), 300–301
Nile, battle of, 95, 103, 122

Quiberon, 99
Quincy, Josiah, 181 n.

Raffles, Sir Stamford (1781–1826), 147–8
Raglan, Lord (1788–1855), 298
Railways, 161, 223–4, 273, 329
Raja Ram Mohan Roy, 309
Ranjit Singh, 311
Rates, personal payment of, 337 n.
Redan, Fort, 301
Redistribution (1884), 378
Redmond, John, 436
Reform Bill of 1831–2, 17, 35, 234–42; of 1866–7, 240, 334–8; of 1884, 376–8
Reform movements (for franchise) – (1780–1830), 53, 55, ch. 4 passim, 125, 165, 190–95, 198, 224–32; (1833–66): 240, 249–51, 290–91, 324, 331–7; (1868–84), 376–7; 1918, 457
Retrenchment and economy, 185, 227, 235, 354, 359
Revolution of 1688–9, 31–2, 38, 41, 46, 73
Reynolds, Sir Joshua (1723–92), 36
Rhine frontier (of France), 101, 104, 121, 140–41, 143
Rhodes, Cecil (1853–1902), 396–400, 406
Ricardo, David (1772–1823), 151
Ritchie, C. T., later Lord (1838–1906), 387
Roads, state of, 26–8, 171–3
Roberts, Lord, 349, 369, 405–6
Robertson, Principal William (1721–93), 281
Robespierre, 83, 96, 99, 104, 105, 288
Rochdale Pioneers, 274. See also Co-operative movement
Rockingham, Marquis of (1730–82), 52–4
Rocky Mountains, 183, 329
Rodney, Admiral (1719–92), 56
Romilly, Sir Samuel (1757–1818), 187, 202
Roosevelt, Theodore, 440, 446
Rose, George (1744–1818), 56
Rose, Sir Hugh, Lord Strathnairn (1801–85), 315
Rosebery, Lord (b. 1847), 394

Rousseau, J. J., 37, 86, 87
Royal Society, the, 168–9 n.
Rugby School, 177
Runciman, Walter, 423
Rupert, Prince, 23
Rush, Richard, 182
Ruskin, John (1819–1900), 386, 389
Russell, Lord John (1792–1878), 247 n., 280; early years, 200–201, 218, 232; Crimea, 296; Reform Bills, 235, 291; Municipal Reform, 243–4; Corn Laws, 268–9; relations with Palmerston, 292, 294, 296, 316–18; Canada, 259; Italy, 292 n., 319–20, 323; American Civil War, 323, 326–8; Ireland, 283; Denmark, 330; Prime Minister (1865–6), 334–6
Russell, (Sir) William, of The Times (1820–1907), 300
Russia, 52, 85, 214–15; in the French wars, 92, 95, 104–5, 107–8, 137, 139–41; in the Vienna settlement, 142–3, 146, 148–9; relations to India, 107, 309–10, 313; early relations to Turkey, 58–9, 215–16; relations to Austria 1848–60, 288–9, 296, 297, 320; Crimea, 296–9, 302; from 1856 to 1876, 320, 330, 353–4, 355–6; from 1876 onwards, 359–69, 378, 396, 438–9, 442ff. See also under Holy Alliance
Rutland, 21 n., 34

Sadler, Michael (1780–1835), 246
St Arnaud, General, 298
St Lucia, 146
Saint-Simon, 388 n.
Salamanca, 139
Salisbury, Lord, Robert Cecil, Lord Cranborne (1830–1903), early years, 326 n., 338, 346; Eastern question, 361, 366–8, 378 n.; franchise negotiations (1884), 378; first Ministry (1885–6), 378, 382; second Ministry (1886–92), 387, 391–3, 396–7; third Ministry (1895–1902), 395–6, 399–407; Foreign policy, 395–6, 409–410, 438; characteristics, 395
Salonika, 451

MORE ABOUT PENGUINS
AND PELICANS

Penguinews, which appears every month, contains details of all the new books issued by Penguins as they are published. From time to time it is supplemented by *Penguins in Print*, which is a complete list of all books published by Penguins which are in print. (There are well over three thousand of these.)

A specimen copy of *Penguinews* will be sent to you free on request, and you can become a subscriber for the price of the postage – 25p for a year's issues (including the complete lists) if you live in the United Kingdom, or 50p if you live elsewhere. Just write to Dept EP, Penguin Books Ltd, Harmondsworth, Middlesex, enclosing a cheque or postal order, and your name will be added to the mailing list.

Some other books published by Penguins are described on the following pages.

Note: *Penguinews* and *Penguins in Print* are not available in the U.S.A. or Canada